Countries, Peoples & Cultures

Middle East & North Africa

Countries, Peoples & Cultures

Middle East & North Africa

First Edition

Volume 5

Editor

Michael Shally-Jensen, PhD

SALEM PRESS
A Division of EBSCO Information Services, Inc.
Ipswich, Massachusetts

Grey House
Publishing

Publisher's Cataloging-In-Publication Data
(Prepared by The Donohue Group, Inc.)

Middle East & North Africa / editor, Michael Shally-Jensen, PhD. – First
   edition.

     pages : illustrations; cm. – (Countries, peoples & cultures ; v. 5)

   Includes bibliographical references and index.
   ISBN: 978-1-61925-798-6 (v. 5)
   ISBN: 978-1-61925-800-6 (set)

   1. Middle East – History. 2. Africa, North – History. 3. Middle East – Economic conditions. 4. Africa, North – Economic conditions. 5. Middle East – Social life and customs. 6. Africa, North – Social life and customs. 7. Middle East – Religion. 8. Africa, North – Religion. I. Shally-Jensen, Michael. II. Title: Middle East and North Africa III. Series: Countries, peoples & cultures ; v. 5.

DS62 .M54 2015
956

First Printing
PRINTED IN CANADA

Contents

Publisher's Note

Countries, Peoples & Cultures: Middle East & North Africa is the fifth volume of a new 9-volume series from Salem Press. *Countries, Peoples & Cultures* offers valuable insight into the social, cultural, economic, historical and religious practices and beliefs of nearly every country around the globe.

Following the extensive introduction that summarizes this politically and physically complex part of the world, this volume provides 20-page profiles of the 21 countries that make up this region of the world. Each includes colorful maps—one highlighting the country's location in the world, and one with its major cities and natural landmarks—and a country flag, plus 10 categories of information: General Information; Environment & Geography; Customs & Courtesies; Lifestyle; Cultural History; Culture; Society; Social Development; Government; and Economy. Each profile also includes full color photographs, valuable tables of information including fun "Do You Know?" facts, and a comprehensive Bibliography.

Each country profile combines must-have statistics, such as population, language, size, climate, and currency, with the flavor and feel of the land. You'll read about favorite foods, arts & entertainment, youth culture, women's rights, health care, and tourism, for a comprehensive picture of the country, its people, and their culture.

Appendix One: World Governments, focuses on 21 types of governments found around the world today, from Commonwealth and Communism to Treaty System and Failed State. Each government profile includes its Guiding Premise, Structure, Citizen's Role, and modern-day examples.

Appendix Two: World Religions, focuses on 10 of the world's major religions from African religious traditions to Sikhism. Each religion profile includes number of adherents, basic tenets, major figures and holy sites, and major rites and celebrations

The nine volumes of *Countries, Peoples & Cultures* are: *Central & South America; Central, South & Southeast Asia; Western Europe; Eastern Europe; Middle East & North Africa; East & Southern Africa; West & Central Africa; North America & the Caribbean;* and *East Asia & the Pacific.*

Introduction

The Middle East and North Africa are often discussed together because of the profound cultural and historical importance of Islam and the Arabic language in those areas. Both the religion and the language were spread from the Arabian Peninsula beginning in the 7th century and continue to dominate much of the region. There are, however, significant exceptions. Turkey and Iran, for example, are predominantly Muslim countries, but both have languages of their own (Turkish and Farsi) and both also differ in terms of the type of Islam that is practiced: the Sunni tradition in Turkey, the Shiite tradition in Iran. Both countries also harbor significant minority communities and cannot be said to be uniform religiously, ethnically, or linguistically. Still, they and the other Middle Eastern countries are commonly thought of as belonging to a single geopolitical region and, further, are routinely joined with North Africa to form a kind of super region.

Outlines

Although there is no universal agreement as to the boundaries of the Middle East, a broad consensus holds that it is the area of southwest Asia that extends into Europe (via Asia Minor, or the Anatolian Peninsula) and northeast Africa (Egypt, Sudan). It includes the following states: Turkey, Iran, Iraq, Syria, Lebanon, Israel, Palestine (a *de jure* state), Jordan, Saudi Arabia, Kuwait, Bahrain, Qatar, United Arab Emirates, Oman, Yemen, Egypt, and Sudan. Egypt's western neighbor, Libya, is often included, but is just as often considered part of North Africa. Iran's eastern neighbor Afghanistan is sometimes also included, but is just as often treated as part of Central or South Asia. Sudan is sometimes *not* included, but, following a line of thinking common among many scholars, we do include that nation here.

As a cradle of ancient civilizations, this "middle" zone lying amid three continents has long been of great strategic importance. It also has been, beginning in the latter half of the 20th century, of fundamental economic importance because of its vast oil resources. Deep political and religious divisions, the cause of several major wars in recent decades, have kept the area in almost continuous turmoil and moreover have occasionally threatened the peace of the world.

North Africa is more easily defined. It comprises Morocco, Algeria, Tunisia, and Libya. It corresponds largely with the so-called Arab Maghreb, or the mountainous desert situated between the Mediterranean Sea and the Sahara Desert, populated primarily by Arabic speakers—persons of Arab and mixed descent. The region contains vast unpopulated or sparsely populated areas; most of its population and its economic activity are concentrated in comparatively small areas.

Lands and Peoples

Middle East

Much of the Middle East is arid and flat. The region contains some of the largest and most barren deserts on earth. At the same time, some areas near the coastal shore are mountainous and wet enough for agricultural production, and some of the river valleys and irrigated areas are fairly densely populated. The two major river systems are 1) the Tigris-Euphrates, flowing in a southeasterly direction from the Anatolian-Iranian mountains through Syria and Iraq and exiting into the Persian Gulf; and 2) the Nile, flowing north from Sudan through the length of Egypt and into the Mediterranean Sea. Both of these river valleys were home to some of the oldest civilizations on earth.

The two main bodies of water in the north are the Black Sea and the Caspian Sea, both of which are bordered at their southern edges by mountains (Pontic and Elburz ranges). On the western side of the region lies the Mediterranean and, abutting Turkey, the Aegean. The eastern edge of the Mediterranean and its inland district make up the ancient Holy Land, also known as the Levant. To the south of the Levant, separating the Arabian Peninsula from Africa, is the venerable Red Sea, which opens into the Gulf of Aden, itself an extension of the Arabian Sea. Near the center of the region stands the Persian Gulf, encircling the so-called Gulf States and dividing the Arabian Peninsula from Iran.

In terms of people, the Middle East is more of a mosaic than is commonly thought in the West. Besides the major Turk and Iranian (Persian) populations in those two countries, there are, of course, the Arabic-speaking peoples of the Arabian Peninsula, the fertile crescent (Iraq, parts of Syria), the Levant (except most of Israel), and North Africa. In addition, there is a sizeable Kurdish population in the region where eastern Turkey, northeast Iran, and northern Iraq converge, as well as a Baluchi population in Iran. (Both Kurdish and Baluchi belong to the broad Iranian language group but are distinct from Farsi.) Small groups in the Levant continue to speak Aramaic and Syriac languages, while Hebrew, of course, is the principal language of Israel (the other being Arabic). A centuries-old community of Copts (Christian orthodox) exists near Alexandria, Egypt, and adjoining areas.

These ethno-linguistic groups may be divided, further, into ethno-religious groups. Islam is generally the religion of the Arabic-speaking peoples, but within the Muslim world believers are divided into Shiite and Sunni groups. The division is based on the question of rightful succession to the leadership of the faith following the death of Mohammed in 632. The Sunni believe in the succession of a line of caliphs elected by the leaders of the community, whereas the Shia believe in the succession of the descendants of Ali, who was both the cousin and son-in-law of the Prophet. Today, the majority of Muslims in the Middle East are Sunni. But a majority of the population in Iraq and Lebanon are Shia, and Shiism is the state religion of Iran.

The Judeo-Christian tradition also originated in the Middle East. Today, that tradition is represented by small numbers of the overall population of the region—approximately 5 percent are Christian, and 1 percent Jewish. (Jews, nevertheless, are the majority population in Israel.) The Kurds are predominantly Sunni Muslim but also have communities of Shia Muslims, Sufis, and other religions. Sufism, a mystical variety of Islam, is practiced as a minority religion in various parts of the region. In Saudi Arabia and elsewhere, a conservative form of Sunni Islam, Wahhabism, is followed. The Druze, in Lebanon and Syria, have a syncretic religion and claim nearly 1.5 million adherents. Zoroastrians and Bahais form smaller religious minority communities in Iran.

Although by about 1970 a type of secular nationalism, led by the governments of Turkey and Egypt, had taken hold through much the region and relegated religious traditionalism to a secondary status, religion remained a potent factor among the populous. Indeed, by the end of the decade, beginning with the Iranian Revolution of 1979, a backlash occurred in which secularism, Western culture, and other "foreign" ways were shunned. Since then, Islamic fundamentalism has been ascendant, even as Turkey and Egypt, among others, face ongoing struggles between Islamist and secular-democratic forces.

North Africa

The Maghreb is mountainous. Its geographic backbone is formed by the Atlas Mountains, which extend 1,600 miles from Morocco to Tunisia. Along the Atlantic coast in Morocco are coastal plains, but they are relatively featureless and exposed to heavy tides. Along the rest of the Maghreb the coastal strip is narrow or virtually absent; only in Tunisia does it attain a relatively broad width. Although the climate along the coast is Mediterranean, immediately inland conditions become more extreme: very hot and dry in summer; fairly cold in winter.

The indigenous inhabitants of North Africa are the Berbers, people of mixed descent (from Roman times and before) who speak (or spoke) the Berber language. Traditionally, they practiced herding but over the centuries have diversified economically. They also adopted Islam early on, but not universally; there is a Berber Christian tradition. Some ancient Berber tribes still maintain a nomadic lifestyle in the Atlas range and the Sahara hinterlands.

The Arabs arrived in North Africa in two successive waves. The first, in the 7th century, brought the Islamic conquerors. They were relatively few in number and settled in the towns as soldiers and administrators. The second wave, in the 11th century, brought a much more significant population of Bedouins to the region. They either displaced or assimilated the Berber peoples, producing a changed ethnographic portrait.

A variety of European descendants live in the Mediterranean cities of North Africa, as do small populations of Jews. French was and remains something of a lingua franca in these areas, but today is increasingly displaced by Arabic.

Modern History

The modern history of the region begins around World War I, when the already moribund Ottoman Empire was dealt a death blow by the Western powers. (The Ottomans fought on the side of Germany and Austria-Hungary.) By the treaty of Sèvres, all former Ottoman subjects—Arabs, Kurds, Armenians, Greeks, and others—were released from their imperial obligations. The British, present in Iran and Iraq for commercial purposes (oil), continued to maintain a military presence in Iraq after the war. The French and Russians had interests in the region, as well. Indeed, the peace settlement established a mandate system (similar to a protectorate system) under which France became the overseer of Syria and Lebanon whereas Britain took responsibility for Iraq, Jordan, and Palestine, this last regarded as a prospective national homeland for the Jews. The British also maintained limited protectorates in Sudan and elsewhere, while the French did likewise in Morocco and Tunisia. Algeria remained an outright colony of France. Turkey was partitioned into Allied control zones. In Iran, the Pahlavi dynasty came to power on its own.

On the Arabian Peninsula, Ottoman rule was replaced by independent Arab governments.

With virtually the entire area under indirect foreign rule, native forces soon began to agitate for change. In Turkey, General Mustafa Kemal Pasha, who later styled his name as Kemal Atatürk (meaning "Father of the Turks"), led the Turkish nationalists. Within a few years, he triumphed over his foreign and domestic opponents and negotiated a new peace treaty (1923) with the Allies. The result was the establishment of an independent, secular republic. Other mandates and protectorates were similarly reformed as friendly, mostly conservative Arab governments were placed in power. In Iran, Reza Shah Pahlavi instituted a nationalistic and modernizing regime. Only in Palestine was a peaceful transfer of power impossible, as rival Arab and Zionist interests stood at odds with each other and with the British.

This system of independent governments cooperating with foreign powers held through World War II. It was not until the 1950s and 1960s that a new wave of more revolutionary forces, often led by the state military, took to overthrowing existing conservative parliamentary and monarchical governments. The best-known example is that of Egypt, where the nationalist Gamal Abdel Nasser led a coup against the monarchy in 1952—and remained in power until his death in 1970. In Algeria, a long and terrible war was fought between anticolonial forces and France from 1954 to 1962, producing, in the end, a free Algeria. After considerable strife, Morocco and Tunisia won their independence in 1956. Such battles, moreover, took place in a Cold War context, where rivalry between the Soviet Union and the United States (along with western European powers) influenced the course of events. In Palestine, for example, a Jewish state was created in 1948, amid a war and the partitioning of the area into Israel and two separate Arab enclaves. For decades afterward, any political solution to the situation involved the de facto approval of the United States and the Soviet Union, as each jockeyed for strategic advantage in the region.

In the wake of Iran's 1979 Islamic revolution, a fundamentalist strain of political Islam came to challenge the preeminence of secular nationalist governments in the area. Although by 1993, following the collapse of the Soviet Union, some progress had been made in reaching an accord between the Israelis and the Palestinians, by 2000 the outlook was much dimmer, thanks to challenges to secular Palestinian leadership by radical Islamist groups (Hamas, Islamic Jihad). Americans came to experience the problem of Islamic extremism firsthand with the September 11, 2001 terrorist attacks on U.S. soil, carried out by operatives of al-Qaeda. The U.S. response was war, not only in Afghanistan where al-Qaeda had found safe haven but also in Iraq, where the rationale for military action was more tenuous (particularly since the United States had fought and won the Gulf War there of 1991). The premise was that the Iraqi regime, under Saddam Hussein, was hiding weapons of mass destruction; the reality proved to be otherwise. Nevertheless, the U.S. invasion set off a series of destabilizing events and ended only in 2011, amid ongoing sectarian struggles between Sunnis and Shiites. By then, the instability had spread elsewhere, including Syria, where government opposition forces sought to bring down the regime of Bashir al-Assad. Under these conditions, a new ultra-extremist Islamist threat known as the Islamic State of Iraq and Syria (ISIS) emerged and came to control large tracts of territory. Today, ISIS remains a major force in the region and has spread its message to other areas of the globe, as well.

In North Africa, beginning in late 2010, a series of democratic revolutions took place under the name of the Arab Spring. It began in Tunisia and spread quickly to Egypt and other states, eventually encompassing, even, some of the conservative Gulf States (albeit to a lesser degree). In Egypt, the authoritarian regime of Hosni Mubarak was overturned, while in Libya, strongman Muammar Gaddafi was tossed out. And, yet, as quickly as the Arab Spring overtook the region, conservative, antidemocratic forces saw to it that they had a say, too. In some cases, these conservative forces returned as the dominant voice in the debate over the future of the state. Thus, within a few short years (2010–12) the Arab Spring had come and gone, having left an indelible mark on the region, to be sure, and yet having witnessed many of its grander visions for sociopolitical change collapse under the weight of traditionalism.

Michael Shally-Jensen, PhD

Bibliography

Bowen, Donna Lee, et al., eds. *Everyday Life in the Muslim Middle East.* Bloomington, IN: Indiana University Press, 2014.

Gasiorowski, Mark, ed. *The Government and Politics of the Middle East and North Africa.* Boulder, CO: Westview Press, 2014.

Held, Colbert C. and John Thomas Cummings. *Middle East Patterns: Places, People, and Politics.* Boulder, CO: Westview Press, 2013.

Mansfield, Peter and Nicolas Pelham. *A History of the Middle East.* New York: Penguin Books, 2013.

Naylor, Philip C. *North Africa: A History from Antiquity to the Present.* Austin, TX: University of Texas Press, 2010.

Sumait, Fahed al-, et al. *The Arab Uprisings: Catalysts, Dynamics, and Trajectories.* Lanham, MD: Rowman & Littlefield, 2015.

Willis, Michael. *Politics and Power in the Maghreb.* New York: Oxford University Press, 2014.

SER.
ROMANIA
Bucharest
UKRANIA
Krasnodar
RUSSIA
KAZAKHSTAN
Aral Sea
KAZAKHSTAN
Sofia
BULGARIA
Constansa
Sevastopol
Sochi
Aqtau
UZBEKISTAN
Nukus
MA.
GREECE
Varna
Black Sea
Sokhumi
Batumi
GEORGIA
Groznyy
Tbilisi
Caspian Sea
Dasoguz
Amu
Istanbul
Sukhumi
TURKMENISTAN
Buxoro
Marmara
Bursa
Ankara
Samsun
Trabzon
ARMENIA
AZERBAIJAN
Sumqayit
Türkmenbasy
Turkmenabat
Izmir
Erzurum
Yerevan
Baku
Balkanabat
Ashgabat
Mary
TURKEY
Van
Lake Van
Tabriz
Rasht
Mashhad
Denizli
Konya
Kayseri
Diyarbakir
Lake Urmia
Zanja
Qazvin
Herat
Antalya
Icel
Adana
Gaziantep
Mosul
Erbil
Kirkuk
Qom
Tehran
AFGHANISTAN
Aegean Sea
CYPRUS
Nicosia
Latakia
Aleppo
SYRIA
Euphrates
Kermanshah
Arak
IRAN
Mediterranean Sea
Beirut
Homs
LEBANON
Damascus
IRAQ
Baghdad
Esfahan
Kerman
PAKIS.
Tel Aviv-Yafo
West Bank
Amman
An Nasiriyah
Ahvaz
Abadan
Shiraz
Zahedan
LIBYA
Port Said
Jerusalem
Dead Sea
ISRAEL
JORDAN
Al Aqabah
Al Basrah
Bandar Bushehr
Bandar Abbas
Alexandria
Cairo
Suez
Tabuk
KUWAIT
Kuwait City
Persian Gulf
Gulf of Oman
Al Jizah
Gulf of Aqaba
Hafar al Batin
Al Jubayl
Ad Damman
BAHRAIN
Manama
OMAN
EGYPT
Asyut
Haii
Duraydah
Dhahran
QATAR
Abu Dhabi
Dubai
Luxor
Medina
Riyadh
Doha
Muscat
Ajnun
Yanbu al Bahr
SAUDI ARABIA
UNITED ARAB EMIRATES
Halaib
Jeddah
Mecca
OMAN
Red Sea
Port Sudan
Abha
SUDAN
Omdurman
Khartoum
Kassala
ERITREA
Jizan
Sanaa
YEMEN
Al Ghaydah
Salalah
Arabian Sea
Wad Medani
Asmara
Massawa
Al Hudayday
YEMEN
Al Mukalla
Taizz
Socotra (YEMEN)
Tana Hayk
Dese
Aden
Gulf of Aden
DJIBOUTI
Djibouti
Boosaaso
Berbera
Addis Ababa
Dire Dawa
Hargeysa
SOMALIA
ETHIOPIA

MIDDLE EAST & NORTH AFRICA

Sidi El Mouhoub mosque, Bejaia, Algeria

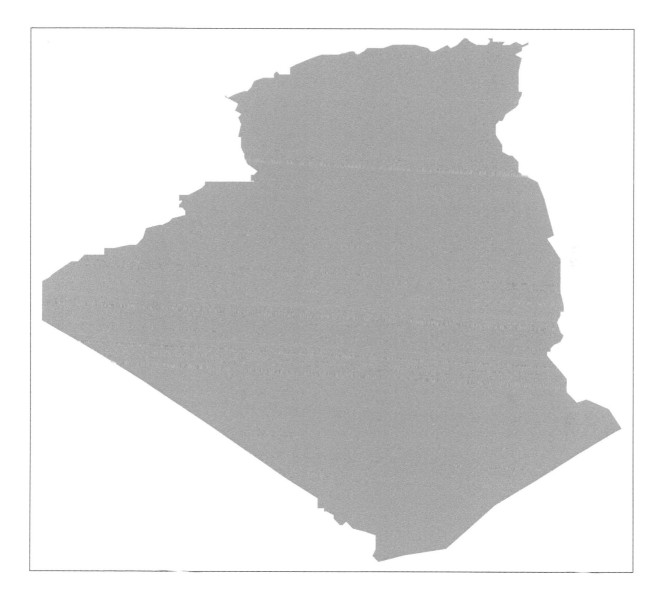

ALGERIA

Introduction

The Democratic and Popular Republic of Algeria is a Northern African nation on the Mediterranean Sea. It is bordered by Morocco, Tunisia, Libya, Niger, Mali, and Mauritania. Algeria is the second-largest country in Africa (after Sudan), almost 3.5 times larger than the state of Texas. It is also the 11th largest country in the world in terms of land area.

Beginning with the ancient Berber civilization of North Africa, Algeria has been continuously inhabited and conquered by various cultural groups from Africa, Asia, and Europe, each leaving their own cultural mark on all aspects of life. The vast majority of Algerians are a mixture of Berber and Arab ethnicity. Less than 1 percent of the population is of European descent. The Berbers first brought wheat agriculture to Algeria thousands of years ago, and it has remained a staple ever since. Algeria's national dish is couscous, served as part of an appetizer, a main dish, or a dessert.

Annexed by France in 1842, Algeria fought an eight-year war of independence, with the country achieving independence in 1954. Prolonged violence among secular and religious political forces persisted, creating instability. Small groups of militants continue to ambush government forces and attack villages in the early 21st century.

Algeria has made significant strides in health, education, and living standards since independence, but there is still much work to be done. The government-controlled economy depends heavily on oil and gas, but these resources have not solved the problems of dire poverty and high unemployment. Politically, the country is often thought to be undemocratic. In the wake of the Arab Spring of 2010-2012, however, the government did make some changes to accommodate oppositional parties and calls for more women in elected positions.

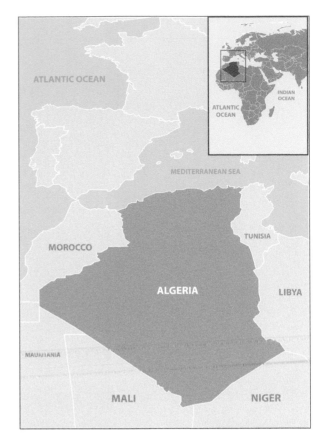

GENERAL INFORMATION

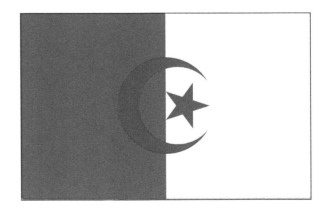

Official Language: Arabic
Population: 39,542,166 (July 2015 est.)
Currency: Algerian dinar

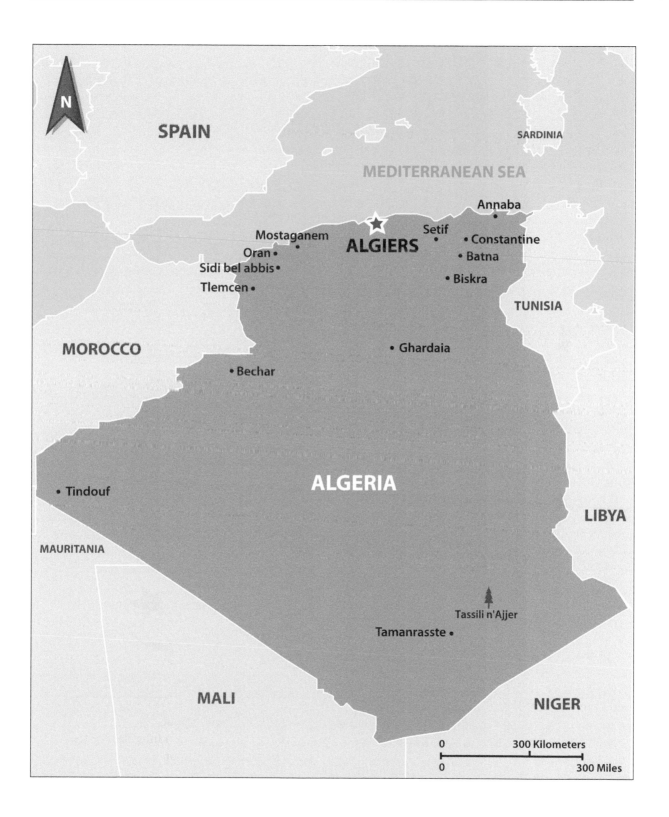

Principal Cities by Population (2012):

- Algiers/El Djazaïr (3.3 million)
- Oran/Wahran (641,240)
- Constantine/Qacentina (465,138)
- Annaba (272,807)
- Batna (324,897)
- Blida/El Boulaïda (264,598)
- Sétif/Stif (324,502)
- Ech Cheliff/El Asnam (235,062)
- El Djelfa (373,547)
- Sidi bel Abbès (233,771)
- Tiaret (229,376)

Coins: Coin denominations of the Algerian dinar include 1, 2, 5, 10, 20, 50, and 100 dinar, though the 1, 2, and 100 dinar are considered to be rarely used.

Land Area: 2,381,741 square kilometers (919,595 square miles)

National Motto: "By the people and for the people"

National Anthem: "Qassaman" (or "Kassaman") (Arabic, "We Pledge")

Capital: Algiers

Time Zone: GMT + 1

Flag Description: The flag of Algeria features two equal vertical bars of green, encompassing the hoist (left) side, and white, encompassing the fly side (furthest side from the flagpole). Centered in the flag are an embossed star and crescent, in red; the symbol universally represents Islam. The green and white colors of the flag symbolize nature and peace, respectively, while the red of the star and crescent represents the blood shed for independence.

Population

The vast majority of Algerians are a mixture of Berber and Arab. Less than 1 percent of the population is of European descent. More than 90 percent of the population lives along the narrow Mediterranean coastal strip. Another 7 percent lives in the plateau area just south of the coast, and a mere 3 percent lives on oases

in the desert. Population density is 14 persons per square kilometer (35 per square mile). The country's largest city is the capital, Algiers, with a metro population of 3.3 million (2012 estimate), located on the coast. The coastal Algiers Province, though being one of the smallest provinces, is the most populated, with a 2008 population estimated of nearly 3 million. An estimated 65 percent of the population resides in urban areas (2008 estimate). As of 2015, Algeria had a population growth rate of 1.84 percent.

Languages

While Arabic is the official language, French is widely spoken. Since independence, however, a deliberate attempt has been made to remove French influence. For this reason, Arabic is the language for legal proceedings and instruction. Tamazight, a Berber language, has been granted "national" status. Other Berber dialects are also spoken by small groups.

Native People & Ethnic Groups

Algeria's original inhabitants were the Berbers, whose occupation dates back 5,000 years. During the seventh century, Arabs began to migrate to Algeria from the Arabian Peninsula. The two groups have intermarried so much that it is impossible to distinguish the ancestry of most modern Algerians.

However, some Berber groups maintain their separate customs and languages. These groups live primarily in the mountainous Kabylie region east of Algiers. They have pressed the government for autonomy, and at times, the struggle has become violent.

Religions

The state religion is Islam, but there is some disagreement about its role in society and politics. Most of the population (99 percent) is Muslim, predominantly Sunni. Some Arab citizens, and almost all Algerians of European descent, are Christians. Christian denominations include Roman Catholic, Protestant Church of Algeria, Methodist and Evangelical. There are almost no Jews in the country.

Climate

Algeria's climate is semiarid to arid. The coast experiences mild, wet winters and hot, dry summers. The high plateaus are drier, and experience hot summers and cold winters. The Sahara is extremely hot.

Coastal temperature averages range from 11° to 25° Celsius (52° to 77° Fahrenheit). Algiers, on the coast, has a temperature range of 9° to 29° Celsius (48° to 84° Fahrenheit). Winter nights can be quite cold, with frost and snow, even after very warm days.

The Sahara has the greatest extremes of temperatures. In the summer, daytime temperatures can reach up to 50° Celsius (122° Fahrenheit). Winter temperatures can drop suddenly to as low as 10° Celsius (14° Fahrenheit). Daily temperatures vary widely when the sirocco, a hot, dry, wind full of dust and sand, blows across the desert during the summer.

The Tell receives the most rain, averaging 40 to 80 centimeters (16 to 32 inches) annually. At elevations above 900 meters (3,000 feet), precipitation is often in the form of snow. The rainy season lasts from September to May.

ENVIRONMENT & GEOGRAPHY

Topography

The second-largest country in Africa (after Sudan), Algeria is almost 3.5 times as large as the American state of Texas. Algeria is bordered on the north by the Mediterranean Sea, on the east by Tunisia and Libya, on the south by Mali and Niger, and on the west by Morocco and Mauritania. Algeria has three distinct topographical regions, the Tell, the high plateaus, and the Sahara Desert.

The Tell is the strip along the coast, ranging from 130 to 320 kilometers (80 to 200 miles) wide. The Tell is marked by gently rolling hills and the country's richest farmland in the west. Rugged mountains in the east terminate in the Tell Atlas Mountains on the southern edge of the area. South of the Tell Atlas Mountains are the

high plateaus, rising from 400 to 1,300 meters (1,300 to 4,300 feet). The area is used for grazing livestock.

Swamps and chotts (or shats), which are shallow salt lakes, form in large depressions among the plateaus during the rainy season. The largest depression, with a total area of 61,000 square kilometers (23,552 square miles), contains two salt lakes: Chott Melshir and Chott Merouane. The intermittent Lake Sebkha d'Oran, near the coast, covers 296 square kilometers (114 square miles).

About 80 percent of the country is covered by the northern Sahara Desert. This area is marked by sand dunes in some places and by bare rock, boulders and stones in others. The Saharan Atlas Mountains rise on the northern edge of the desert, and the Ahaggar Mountains rise in the southeastern desert region.

The highest elevation is Mount Tahat, rising 2,918 meters (9,573 feet) in the Ahaggar Mountains. The lowest point is Chott Melrhir, at 31 meters (102 feet) below sea level.

A few small rivers flow through the coastal region. The longest is the Chelif River, which rises in the Atlas Mountains and flows for 679 kilometers (422 miles) north and west to empty into the Mediterranean east of Oran.

Plants & Animals

The northern forests were nearly destroyed during the war for independence when the French bombed the area with napalm (jellied gasoline). Many cork oak trees have been replanted. Other trees found in Algeria include Aleppo pine and juniper in the mountains, and fig trees and olive groves in other areas. Date palms and acacias grow in the Sahara.

Indigenous grapevines are common, and the plateaus are covered with pastures of drinn and esparto grasses. Common wild animals include wild boars, fennecs (a kind of fox), African pygmy hedgehogs, Barbary macaques, gazelles, jerboas, panthers, leopards, cheetahs and jackals. Reptiles such as monitor lizards and many species of birds are also numerous.

Among Algeria's endangered animals is the serval, a large cat with markings similar to those of a leopard. Only a few are believed to survive in remote areas of the north. Mediterranean monk seals are also in danger, partly because they reproduce slowly. Also, coastal pollution and over fishing threaten their habitat. Several bat species, as well as the Algerian wild dogs, are also endangered.

CUSTOMS & COURTESIES

Greetings

A number of ethnic groups live in Algeria today. A vast majority of the population speaks Arabic as their primary language, but a large number also speak French. English is not often used, but Berber and indigenous dialects are spoken among small groups. Common greetings include "Mrahva yissouen" ("Greetings to you") and "Saha" ("Health").

When exchanging greetings in Algeria, two people generally shake hands. Members of the same sex commonly embrace and may exchange kisses on the cheek. Algerian Muslims refrain from shaking hands, embracing, or kissing the opposite sex. It should also be noted that the left hand is not traditionally used in Muslim culture when greeting or interacting, as it is used for the cleansing of the body, and is thus considered impure. Elders are customarily greeted first.

When greeting a group of people, an individual should begin with the eldest. Unfamiliar people should be addressed by an honorific title if applicable, and family name or surname. In Algeria, greetings can last for several minutes, as individuals inquire about each other's health, family, and general well-being. It is important to show interest in and care for a person's life in order to establish trust.

Gestures & Etiquette

Algerian culture is Muslim in nature—an estimated 99 percent of the population is Sunni Muslim—and cultural etiquette is mostly dictated by Muslim customs. For example, the right hand is used to pass items, since the left hand

Traditional dress in Algeria includes a headscarf and face veil.

is associated with personal hygiene, and it is considered insulting to point the bottom of one's foot toward another person. It is also considered improper to point and to maintain prolonged eye contact with members of the opposite sex. Moderate or conservative dress is the norm.

Honor is considered critical in Algerian society, and can be damaged in many ways. Turning down a request for help or a favor, insulting or criticizing a person, or putting a person in an embarrassing or uncomfortable situation all contribute to a loss of honor. Also, Algerians do not generally keep the same degree of space between themselves as westerners do. They may stand fairly close to each other or even hold each other's arms while talking.

Eating/Meals

Algerians may sit on low couches or chairs around a big table or on mats on the floor around a low table to eat meals. Men and women often sit separately to eat. Hygiene is critical and people are expected to wash before and after dining. In some households, a family member or servant will bring around water for washing before the meal.

As with passing other items, food should always be passed with the right hand. Algerians usually eat with utensils but may eat some foods with their hands. In this case, they should only use their right hand to eat. When eating with one's hand, a person should use the thumb, forefinger, and middle finger; using four or five fingers is considered impolite. Pieces of bread often serve as scoops for foods with sauces. Most meals are friendly, social events and guests are often urged to take more than one serving. A person should leave a little food on his or her plate if he or she does not want to be served more food.

Each year, Muslim Algerians celebrate the month of Ramadan. During this time, most people fast during the hours between sunrise and sunset. In the evening, after dark, family and friends gather to break their fast.

Visiting

Hospitality, like honor, is often perceived as a foundation of Algerian society, and family and friends visit one another often. It is not uncommon for such visits to be unannounced, but strangers and acquaintances are expected to contact one another or wait on an invitation. Algerians generally remove their shoes at the door when entering a home. Most also tend to dress modestly when outside of their own homes, and women are generally expected to cover most areas of skin.

Gift giving is important in Algerian society. Visitors to a home are expected to bring small gifts, such as fruit, pastries or flowers. Tulips and roses are acceptable flowers, but violets symbolize sadness and should be avoided. Muslim Algerians do not drink alcohol, so guests should not give alcohol as a gift unless they know that the host drinks alcohol. When visiting as a guest, it is considered polite for a woman to offer to help with preparing the meal or clearing away dishes and food after a meal. It is also considered impolite to refuse refreshments that are offered.

LIFESTYLE

Family

Family is the focal point of Algerian society. In the past, large extended families shared homes, a practice that continues to occur in many modern rural communities. Multiple sons and their wives and children lived together with their parents. Today, smaller nuclear families are becoming the norm, especially in urban areas with smaller living spaces. Since the 1990s, more families are having small numbers of children and distancing themselves from extended relatives. Though family ties are still important, these smaller family units are living farther from relatives and making more decisions independently.

Throughout Algeria's social history, most cultural groups have maintained a patriarchal way of life. Family roles have been clearly defined by gender, with men serving as the head of the family and working outside the home and women taking care of the household and child rearing. However, many women have always worked outside the home as well. Children are expected to help in the home and with the family business and to obey their elders. Marriage continues to function as the cornerstone of family life and symbolizes the union not only of two individuals, but also of two families. Though there is a long tradition of arranged marriages, most Algerians today are free to choose their own spouses, albeit with the approval of their families.

The Algerian Family Code, in place since 1984, provides laws to govern family life. In the past, women have married or betrothed as early as thirteen. Today, the legal age for marriage in Algeria is 18 for women, and 21 for men. Under Algerian law, men may practice polygamy and marry up to four wives; however, they must be able to justify the reasons for additional marriages to a court. They must also tell their existing wives before marrying again, and existing wives may pursue a divorce if they do not agree to the marriages. The practice of polygamy is rare in Algeria.

Housing

In recent decades, Algeria has experienced many problems with overcrowding and a shortage of housing. More than 90 percent of the population is concentrated along the Mediterranean Sea on about 12 percent of the nation's land. Just over 70 percent of the population lives in the urban areas (2015 est.), where homes vary from shacks and huts to larger, modern homes, apartment complexes and historic houses and mansions reflecting Arab, Ottoman, and French cultural styles. Building materials include stone, clay, concrete, wood, brick, glass, and metal. The capital of Algiers is known as "Alger la Blanch (Algiers the White)" for its many white-faced apartment buildings, houses, and other structures.

Many people have also settled around the cities, forming shantytowns (informal settlements) called bidonvilles. (The word "bidon" translates as "tin can.") These fringe developments are generally cluttered and impoverished, with small houses, shacks and lean-tos built from available materials such as discarded tin cans that are flattened to form sheets. The government has tried to address overcrowding by building additional low-cost housing units.

Nearly 1.5 million nomadic and semi-nomadic Bedouin live in the Sahara. Those who move from place to place carry black tents made from goat hair to erect when they stop. Those who build semi-permanent settlements construct simple, temporary homes from mud and stone. Other rural groups also use available resources to construct small huts or larger structures meant to house extended family groups. Rural peoples make their homes from stone, concrete, or adobe-like bricks made from sun-hardened mud and straw. Rural huts made from mud and tree branches, with flat tile or tin roofs, are called gourbi. Houses in eastern Algeria are subject to heavy rain and snowfall, and generally have slanted roofs to prevent moisture from seeping into the home.

Food
Algerian cuisine similar to the neighboring culinary traditions of North African and is influenced by Arabic, Turkish, Berber, and French cuisine. Generally, the Algerian diet mostly comprises grains, fruits, and vegetables, often seasoned with a variety of spices. The Berbers first brought wheat agriculture to Algeria thousands of years ago, and it has remained a staple ever since. Algeria's national dish is couscous, a crumbled

pasta dish made from a specific variety of wheat. Couscous can be served as part of an appetizer, a main dish, or a dessert. Algerians often serve couscous with lamb, chicken, or fish and mixed, cooked vegetables. As a dessert, couscous may be sweetened with honey, spices such as cinnamon and nutmeg, and fruits such as dates and figs.

Algerians also enjoy a wide variety of fruits and herbs. In the 17th century, Arabs brought numerous spices from central and eastern Asia, including nutmeg, cinnamon, cloves, garlic, coriander, cumin, saffron, mint, and ginger. In the 1500s, Spanish invaders introduced fruits such as oranges, plums, and peaches. Europeans also brought olives to the region. In the 19th century, French colonists introduced a love of bread and brought a variety of fruits and vegetables, including tomatoes and chilies, from the Americas. Today, bread accompanies most Algerian meals and is often used to scoop up food.

Mint tea is a popular drink among Algerians as is coffee, especially when served with cardamom spice. Algerian coffee is often very strong and is served with water. Apricot nectar is a popular fruit juice, and Algerians generally drink goat's milk rather than cow's milk. Most Algerians are Muslims and do not eat pork or drink alcohol.

Life's Milestones
The majority of Algerians are Sunni Muslims—an estimated 99 percent—and follow the rituals and expectations of Islam. At birth, the "Call to Prayer" is whispered into a baby's ear so that the infant may know Allah (God). A naming ceremony soon follows, often within the first week of life. Members of Christian, Jewish, and other minority groups follow the practices of their own faiths.

Under Algerian law, children ages six to 15 must attend school. The nation offers a free public education system, and more than 90 percent of youth attend elementary school. However, only a third of the youth population continues on to high school, and fewer pursue a higher education at university in Algeria or abroad. Others go on to help with family businesses, farms, herding, and other economic activity. The major milestone of Algerian society, whether urban, rural, or nomadic, is marriage. Marriage is the union of families as well as individuals, and is considered to be the true sign of maturity among most Algerians.

Although Algeria has a central government, the Berber and Bedouin still maintain their historic village and tribal ways. Both peoples have traditionally patriarchal societies, and their communities are led by councils of elders or leaders, all of who are men who have reached a certain age and status within their groups.

CULTURAL HISTORY

Art

As with Algerian architecture, the nation's fine arts reflect a blend of African, Middle Eastern, and European influences. The earliest artwork in Algeria, in the form of etched rock art, dates back more than 10,000 years and is found in the Tassili N'Ajjer mountain range. Nearly 15,000 engraved and painted images depict hunters, wild animals, horses, and cattle. Much later images depict chariots and shields as well as camels, indicating that the rocks had become a canvas for civilizations throughout the ages.

Ancient Phoenician and Roman sculptures and frescoes depict warriors, gods, goddesses, and other mythical figures. Archaeological sites and museums house these items, as well as weapons and functional items such as utensils and bowls, and silver and bronze works. Much of Algeria's national arts, whether on stone, wood, textile, paper, or another medium, bear the distinctive geometric and abstract patterning of Islamic art. Algeria's folk arts are a blend of Arabic, Moorish, and Berber influences. These include hand-woven rugs, ornate jewelry and metalwork, ceramics, woodcarvings, as well as textiles, instruments, and weapons marked with intricate patterns and detail.

French artists brought new and distinctly European styles of art such as romanticism to Algeria when they arrived in the 19th century. Primarily in painted form, French Algerian art emphasized portraiture and landscapes. In the late 1800s, the French painter Pierre Auguste Renoir (1841–1919) visited Algeria and produced nearly thirty paintings depicting Algeria and its people. In the 20th century, Algerian art continued to blend cultural styles, such as Islamic calligraphy and Western abstraction, and embraced modern artistic movements such as impressionism, realism, and fauvism.

Architecture

Because of Algeria's strategic location in relation to the Mediterranean Sea, the country and its surrounding region bear the traces of a diverse history. Beginning with the ancient Berber civilization of North Africa, which settled in the area as early as 10,000 BCE, Algeria has been continuously inhabited and conquered by various cultural groups from Africa, Asia and Europe, each leaving their own cultural mark.

The greatest examples of Algeria's architectural history are concentrated along the Mediterranean coast and include monumental Roman architecture, the ruins of which remain today. In the Aurès Mountains, the ancient ruins of the Roman colonial town of Timgad feature preserved grid planning. The ancient city features two perpendicular roads, one lined with Corinthian columns and the other defined by one of the triumphal Arches of Trajan. Another example of extant Roman urban planning is found at Djémila. The preserved ruins show how the Romans uniquely adapted their architecture to the mountainous region.

Following the decline of the Roman Empire and the invasions of the Germanic Vandals, the Byzantines spread through Algeria in the sixth century, and Byzantine churches and citadels are evident throughout the country. During the seventh century, the Arabs conquered Algeria. Al Qal'a of Beni Hammad, inscribed as Algeria's first World Heritage site in 1980, provides a glimpse of an ancient fortified Muslim city. In the capital of Algiers, the 11th-century Great Mosque built by Yusuf ibn Tashfin (c.1061–1106) bears the Moorish arches and columned aisles typical of Arabic architecture. The capital is also home to one of Algeria's best-known architectural features, the Kasbah of Algiers. The downtown area is a testament to Arab, Ottoman, Spanish, and French influences, and the site contains several Ottoman structures, including a citadel, palaces, and mosques. Narrow, winding streets and alleys reveal the Ottomans' city planning.

The Ottomans ruled Algeria from the early 1500s to the late 1800s. The mosques and ornate, arched palaces characteristic of Ottoman and Arabic architecture, are located throughout old Algiers and other cities. In Algiers, examples of Ottoman architecture include the New Mosque, the Ketchaoua Mosque, and the Ottoman Summer Palace, notable for its Moorish arches and columns. France colonized Algeria in the 1830s, introducing European architectural styles to the country. In the 19th century, the French built the monumental Notre Dame d'Afrique, a Roman Catholic church marked by domes, towers, and detailed masonry. In the newer districts of Algiers, the wider streets, cathedrals, theaters, and other buildings reveal the impact of Western European architecture.

Music & Dance

Algeria has a strong musical tradition rooted in African, Arabic, and other styles. Berber music, such as the traditional kabylian music, has been central to their rural lifestyles. It features the ajouag (flute), the ghaita (bagpipes), the t'bel (tambourine), and the bendir frame drum. The classical and instrumental hawzii, rabaab, aaroubi, malouf, and nuubaat musical styles grew from Spanish and Ottoman influences. Muslims and Jews expelled from Spain in the late 1500s brought Andalusian musical styles with them, which later merged with Ottoman styles.

Traditional Bedouin music grew around the melhoun, a form of poetry that was combined with rural folk music. It commonly featured the traditional sounds of the gasba (rosewood flute) and the guellal (drum). Raï music, one of the most popular Algerian musical styles today, grew out of a combination of Bedouin music and popular world musical styles in the early 20th century. Modern raï music, which emerged in the 1950s and 1960s, featured Western influences and instruments, and gave way to a pop style in the late 20th century.

Algerian dance traditions emerged from rural folk customs and from a blend of Arabic, Spanish, and French culture. Belly dancing traditions emerged among the Berber peoples of Algeria, particularly among the Ouled Neil Berber tribe. Other folk dance traditions, many of which were performed by women, celebrated nature, the hunt, the harvest, and other agriculture tasks such as olive collecting. They also celebrated special events such as weddings. The ruling classes of the Ottomans and the French brought courtly and aristocratic dances, which were performed during official functions and festive gatherings.

Literature & Drama

Early indigenous and nomadic peoples in Algeria passed on stories through oral traditions. Written language came to the region with the Phoenicians and Romans. These ancient Europeans passed on Greek and Roman mythology, philosophy, poetry, and drama. In the early fifth century, Augustine of Hippo (354–430), a Christian monk who spent most of his life in Algeria, began producing Christian theological works such as *City of God*. In subsequent centuries, Europeans brought other theological studies and different forms of secular European literature to Algeria. Arabic culture introduced the Koran (Islam's holy book) and other Islamic literature.

In the 19th century, the French introduced contemporary European drama, poetry, and other works. In the 20th century, Arabic and French authors began to examine their heritage and the splintering of their society. Playwright and novelist Kateb Yacine (1929–1989) and novelist and poet Mohammed Dib (1920–2003) examined the effects of the Algerian War of Independence (1954–1962). Novelist and filmmaker Assia Djebar (1936- 2015), who wrote under the pseudonym Fatima-Zohra Imalayen, wrote about women and the impact of the war and other matters on Algerian society. Perhaps the most famous Algerian-born writer is the French philosopher and journalist Albert Camus (1913–1960), who was awarded the Nobel Prize in Literature in 1957. Associated with existentialism, Camus's literary works, such as *The Stranger* (1942) and the play *Caligula* (1938), deal heavily in political, philosophical, and ethical matters.

CULTURE

Arts & Entertainment

Modern Algerian artists produce paintings, sculptures, graphic and digital artwork, and craft items. Many Algerians make the handicrafts that their ancestors have been making since antiquity. Algeria is especially known for its Berber rugs and carpets with their colorful geometric patterns, as well as for its jewelry, woodworking, musical instruments, and household items, such as teapots. Peoples of the Sahara make baskets, sandals, and rope from esparto grass.

Examples of Algerian artwork may be found in numerous museums and galleries, as well as mosques, churches, and other historic and civic buildings. The National Museum of Fine Arts features works from French painters Eugène Delacroix (1798–1863), who visited Algeria in the 1830s, and Pierre-Auguste Renoir, who traveled there in the 1880s. The gallery also showcases work from many local artists, including painters Mohammed Racim (1896–1975), known for his miniatures, Mohamed Temmam (1915–1988), and Bachir Chaouch Yelles (1921–). The National Museum of Arts and Popular Traditions, the Bardo National Museum of Prehistory and Ethnography, the National Museum of Antiquities and Islamic Art, and the National Museum of Cirta all offer remarkable examples of ancient and modern art and artifacts.

Modern Algerian music blends the sounds of traditional folk genres and global pop styles. Raï music is perhaps the most popular music in Algeria today. Born from the poetic rhythms and chants of traditional music, the genre has adapted to incorporate modern beats and a greater variety of instrumentation. Raï lyrics address the goods and ills of modern life and are sung in Arabic and French. Traditional raï musicians are known

as cheb (male) and chaba (female), while those who have a more modern pop style are known as shikh and shikha, respectively. Well-known Algerian raï musicians include Khaled (1960–) and Cheb Mami (1966–).

Many traditional dances are still performed in Algeria today, including ceremonial and festive folk dances and belly dancing. The National Institute of Dramatic and Choreographic Arts and the National Ballet each work to bring traditional and modern dance to wider audiences. The ballet troupe performs many unique Algerian dances, including many traditional rural and urban folk dances, such as the kabyle, the allaoui, the zendali, the dance of Tlemcen, and the naili marriage dance.

Modern Algerian authors and playwrights reflect many past cultural influences, but have also embraced styles and content all their own. Commonly explored themes include Algeria's war for independence and the nation's modern economic, political and social struggles. Several modern women authors have also given voice to the often unheard trials of Algeria's daughters, sisters, wives, and mothers. Leila Sebbar (1941-) and Malika Mokeddem (1949 -) are among the nation's most respected contemporary female authors. Other Algerian writers have struggled to bring together the multiple ethnicities that compose Algeria, and to preserve the traditions and words of minority peoples.

Cultural Sites & Landmarks

In addition to a wealth of archaeological sites, historical structures, and museums, Algeria is home to seven UNESCO World Heritage Sites. The oldest site protected by UNESCO is Tassili n'Ajjer, a mountain range located in southeastern Algeria. The landscape includes hundreds of natural rock arches and other remarkable landforms, and the woodlands are home to two endangered tree species, the Saharan Cypress and the Saharan Myrtle. The mountain range is also unique for its numerous Neolithic archaeological sites that reveal evidence of some of the earliest people to live in Algeria. This early culture left behind thousands of rock etchings and paintings that give clues to their hunting and herding lifestyles.

The World Heritage Site of M'Zab Valley was recognized by UNESCO as a traditional human habitat that was adapted to its environment. Founded in the tenth century by the Ibadites, an Islamic sect, the site is comprised of five ksour (traditional fortified villages): El Atteuf, Bou Noura, Beni Isguen, Melika, and Ghardaia. These ksour were designed to be family-oriented and communal, and each had a central citadel with a mosque and a tall minaret that served as a watchtower. Groups of small, modest houses were erected in concentric circles around the central citadel. These desert fortress-cities became an inspiration for modern city planners. The other World Heritage Sites represent Algeria's rich architectural heritage, and range from Roman ruins to fortified Muslim cities.

As the capital, Algiers is home to numerous cultural sites and landmarks, including the Kasbah of Algiers, a labyrinthine Islamic citadel, the Monument des Martyrs, which commemorates the country's war for independence, and the monumental Notre Dame d'Afrique, a basilica accessible by cable car. The National Library, built in 1835, has more than 1 million volumes and collections reflecting the nation's diverse cultural heritage. Other significant landmarks throughout the country include the hanging (suspension) bridges of the picturesque city of Constantine and eleven national parks and five national preserves. Seven mountains ranges and the Saharan Desert offer stunning geographic features, including the Kabylia and Chiffa Gorges.

Libraries & Museums

Algiers is home to many museums, the most notable of which include the National Museum of Antiquities, with its collections of antique mosaics, Roman glass work and sculptures, and Islamic art, and the Museum of Popular Arts and Traditions, which features indigenous arts and crafts, including carpets, jewelry, ceramics, and furniture. The History Museum showcases Ottoman-era swords and jewelry. The Bardo National Museum displays sculptures, mosaics, and bronzes excavated from Algeria's key archaeological digs. The Jihad Museum presents a historical exhibition of Algeria's struggle for independence. The Museum of Fine Arts features European paintings as well as works by contemporary Algerian artists.

The National Library of Algeria is located in the capital, and serves as the country's legal depository. It was founded in 1835, and is now ranked as one of the largest libraries in the world. Algeria's network of libraries includes over 300 small public reading rooms and eighty-three community libraries.

Holidays

Many Algerian holidays are celebrated in observance of the country's political history. National Day, celebrated on June 1, commemorates the overthrow of Ahmad Ben Bella, the country's first president, in 1965. Other official holidays include Labor Day (May 1), Independence Day (July 5), and the Anniversary of the Revolution (November 1).

Muslim holidays, including Ramadan, Islamic New Year, and others, are widely celebrated in Algeria. Many holiday dates vary because they depend on the Islamic lunar calendar.

Youth Culture

In the first part of the 21st century, more than 5 million students were enrolled in Algerian schools, which is more than double the number in earlier decades. The government has undertaken major reforms of the education system, and schooling for children ages six to fifteen is compulsory and free. More than 90 percent of students now complete the ninth grade, but fewer advance to high school. Vocational secondary schools offer students training in specific skills sets. Girls and boys generally have the same access to education, though boys are given the priority among rural families. The literacy rate has also seen marked improvement, and more than half of Algerians over the age of fourteen can read and write.

Family life has maintained its importance among the Algerian youth culture. Young

Algerians are expected to obey the authority of their parents and elders, and to help with domestic, agricultural, or family business obligations. Though the official work age is sixteen, many children in rural and urban areas continue to work on farms and in family businesses. Recreational activities are also typically family-oriented. Football (soccer) is the sport of choice, and other popular sports include volleyball, handball, and track and field activities.

Among the largely rural Berber peoples and the nomadic and semi-nomadic Bedouin, children follow the traditional ways of their families. Most Berbers are farmers and pastoralists and Berber youth are responsible for helping with their ancestral livelihood. Similarly, the Bedouin raise livestock, and Bedouin youth are expected to travel with their tribes to herd their sheep, goats, and other animals, and to find and collect resources as needed to survive.

SOCIETY

Transportation

Most of Algeria's transportation network is located along the Mediterranean coast, and includes railways, which link most of the northern cities, and paved highways. Two major routes include the Trans-African Highway network and the Trans-Sahara Highway. In the desert regions, jeeps and trucks are generally used, as are camel caravans, which have traveled the desert for hundreds of years. Between or within cities, buses and public taxis are the most common mode of transportation. Traffic moves on the right-hand side of the road.

Transportation Infrastructure

Algeria has more than 113,500 kilometers of roads, including one major north-south highway that crosses the Sahara Desert and three major east-west highways. In the south, roads and railroads connect major urban centers.

Nearly 4,000 kilometers (approximately 2,500 miles) of railroad line also connect population centers in the country and connect Algeria

to neighboring nations. The government-owned Algeria's national rail transport company (SNTF) operates the rail lines. In recent years, the Algerian government has made efforts to modernize and expand the railroads. The capital, Algiers, has also been planning to install a subway and a light rail system for passenger traffic for the past two decades, but the projects have been slow to start.

Algeria's primary international airports are located at Algiers, Annaba, Constantine, and Oran, and regional airports serve other areas of the country. As of 2010, 13 of Algeria's 64 airports (with paved runways) have international lines. The country's major ports are Annaba, Beja'a, Mostaganem, Oran, and Skikda.

Media & Communications

Algeria has an extensive media network, though the government controls most radio and television broadcasting. Algeria has seventeen radio stations that provide news, talk programs, and other radio programming. Most stations broadcast in Arabic or French, and there is also one Berber radio station in Algeria called Kabyle Radio. However, the government has cracked down on media since the late 20th century and imposes controls on content. To access uncensored material, consumers must find online radio news sources or read one of the independent newspapers. Newspapers available in print and on the Internet include *Al Fadjr, Algeria Daily, Algeria-Interface, Algérie Press Service, Djazair News, El Massa, Ennahar El Djadid, L'Actualité,* and *North Africa Journal.*

Algeria also has a satellite system and a telecommunications network that supports telephone and Internet service. As of 2014, Algeria had more than 3 million landline telephones and more than 37 million cellular phone users. Algeria's Internet usage has grown exponentially. In 2000, about 50,000 people were regular Internet users, fewer than seventeen people per 10,000. In 2010, that number had grown to 4.7 million users, representing over 13 percent of the population. The most recent estimate of Internet users was in 2014 with 6.5 million or 16.7 percent of the population.

SOCIAL DEVELOPMENT

Standard of Living

Algeria ranked 93 on the 2013 United Nations Human Development Index, which measures quality of life and standard of living indicators.

Water Consumption

According to 2012 statistics reported by the CIA World Factbook, approximately 85 percent of the Algerian population in urban areas has access to an improved source of drinking water (79.5 percent in rural areas), while an estimated 97.6 percent had access to improved sanitation (88.4 percent in rural areas). The country, however, has often been described as "water-stressed," as it lacks sufficient natural resources, and these scant water resources have been further affected by drought in the early 21st century. Rural coverage and failing infrastructure also remain concerns.

Education

Education in Algeria is free at all levels and compulsory from ages six to 16. Children attend primary school until twelve years old. Secondary education is divided into two three-year cycles.

Most instruction in primary and secondary schools is in Arabic, but since 2003, the Berber language Tamazight has also been permitted. In the universities, French is generally the language of instruction.

Algeria has 10 universities. The University of Algiers is the oldest in the country. It was established in 1909, combining schools of medicine, pharmacy, science, letters and law, which had been founded in 1879.

The government has tried to improve education, and has spent substantial amounts of money (nearly 30 percent of the national budget) for this purpose. But the population keeps growing, and the number of teachers keeps shrinking (partly because foreign teachers were removed after independence). In addition, terrorist attacks in the 1990s severely damaged the infrastructure.

The average literacy rate in Algeria is roughly 80 percent (87 percent among men and 73 percent among women). Generally, the rate of primary school enrollment for female students is lower than that of male students in Algeria; however, gender equity has been established in higher education.

Women's Rights

Women in Algeria have continued to suffer discrimination and other abuses of their rights. Like many nations, Algeria is traditionally a patriarchal society in which women are considered subordinate family members and are subject to the direction of the husbands, fathers, or other male relatives. Though the status and rights of women improved greatly following the war for independence, these gains have eroded as a result of resurgent Islamic fundamentalism.

The family code that governs family life in Algeria is strongly influenced by Muslim law and largely favors the power and position of men in the family. The marriage age for women is younger than for men (though that age was increased to eighteen recently), and Muslim women are forbidden to marry non-Muslim men. However, the family code does not restrict Muslim men from marrying non-Muslim women. Amendments to this provision have enabled women to marry foreign nationals, and to transmit nationality and citizenship to a woman's spouse and children. Women also continue to receive smaller inheritances and face discrimination in terms of retaining the property or wages that they bring into a marriage. Similarly, divorce laws are not always properly enforced.

Historically, women have been unable to pursue divorce, but the revised family code does allow women to petition for divorce for violation of pre-marriage agreements and contracts, as well as other causes. Under the new laws, women are also allowed to retain the family home until their children turn eighteen. Women also generally keep custody of their children, but must have the father's consent regarding decisions about education. Similarly, a mother cannot leave the country with her children without the father's consent. The law also permits polygamy and men may marry up to four wives. However, a man who takes multiple wives must legally notify his present wife (or wives) of additional marriages. This allows a wife to petition for divorce if she does not approve of a subsequent marriage.

Spousal abuse and rape are common and domestic violence continues to be a serious and pervasive issue. The law provides for prosecution of such offenses, but many women are reluctant to undergo this process due to social stigma and inadequate protection. For example, battery or abuse charges cannot be filed unless a woman has suffered injuries that would incapacitate her for fifteen days. Officials also require written notice from a doctor regarding these injuries in order to press charges. No laws prohibit spousal rape, and family and society generally pressure women not to pursue such charges. Non-spousal rape is prohibited and convictions carry a prison sentence of one to five years.

Women have equal access to education but lower enrollment rates than men. Many women who achieve a secondary or higher education continue to experience discriminatory hiring practices or refrain from joining the workforce. In fact, statistics in the early 21st century show that Algerian women comprised more than half of those attending universities, but made up less than a quarter of the national workforce. In addition, sexual harassment continues to be a problem, but was addressed in 2004 when the government passed the first law prohibiting sexual harassment.

Numerous women's rights groups have become increasingly active in the nation and are pressing for the enforcement of equal rights and protections for women. The Algerian government also established the Ministry Delegate for the Female Condition and for the Family to protect the rights of women and to investigate violations.

Health Care

Algeria's health care system has made great strides since independence. In the mid-1950s, there was only one doctor for every 33,000 people, and the infant mortality rate was 154 deaths per 1,000 births. Today, these ratios have improved, with one doctor for every 1,000 people, and the infant mortality rate has dropped significantly.

Medicine, medical care, and hospitalization are free for Algerian citizens. Approximately 90 percent of the population has access to medical care, and the emphasis is on preventing disease rather than just curing illnesses.

With increased access to sanitation (95 percent of the population) and clean water (nearly 84 percent), many high-risk diseases have been greatly reduced or eliminated. There is still some risk of food- or waterborne diseases such as bacterial diarrhea, typhoid fever, and hepatitis A, and the parasitic disease cutaneous leishmaniasis.

Algeria's per capita health expenditure is $169 (USD) per year. Life expectancy is 73 years overall; 72 years for men and 75 years for women (2008 estimate).

GOVERNMENT

Structure

Algeria is a republic, with universal adult suffrage at age eighteen. It is a multi-party state, but political parties must be approved by the Ministry of the Interior.

The president is the head of state. The president is elected to a five-year term, and is limited to two terms. The president presides over the Council of Ministers and the High Security Council. The president also appoints the prime minister, who is the head of government. The prime minister appoints the Council of Ministers.

The bicameral legislature consists of the National People's Assembly, whose 389 members are elected directly by all voters, and the 144-member Council of the Nation. Two-thirds of the members of the Council of the Nation are elected indirectly from among regional and municipal authorities. The remaining third are appointed by the president. Council terms are six years, and one-half of the members are replaced every three years.

Political Parties

In Algeria's multi-party system, parties must form coalition governments, as no single party can generally attain power. In the 2012 elections, the National Liberation Front (FLN) and the National Rally for Democracy (RND) won the majority of seats at 221 and 70, respectively. Other parties that won seats in the 2012 election included the Algerian Popular Movement (MPA), the Green Algeria Alliance (AAV), and the Socialist Forces Front (FFS), among others. The next elections are to be held in 2017.

Local Government

The country is organized into 48 provinces, or wilaya, each of which is overseen by a presidentially appointed provincial governor. Provinces are then subdivided into districts (daira) and municipalities (commune), the latter of which are each represented by an elected assembly, the members of which serve four-year terms, and an elected mayor. Provincial governments are responsible for education, road maintenance, agriculture, and tourism. Little autonomy is exercised among local government bodies in rural areas.

Judicial System

Algeria's legal system is based upon both Islamic legal customs and civil law. The judicial system is a three-tiered system, consisting of tribune courts, provincial courts (divided into chambers such as criminal, civil and administrative), and the Supreme Court, the highest court in Algeria. The president serves as the head of the High Judicial Council, which presides over issues such as the appointment of judges. Other councils with judicial influence include the High Islamic Council and the High Security Council.

Taxation

Algeria's tax rates are fairly moderate in sum, and include a top corporate tax rate of 19 percent and a top income tax rate of 35 percent. Other taxes levied include a value-added tax (VAT, similar to a consumption tax), property tax, and compensation tax.

Armed Forces

The armed forces of Algeria consist of several service branches, including the People's National Army, one of the largest land forces in North Africa; the Algerian National Navy, which operates out of three bases along the Mediterranean coast; and the Algerian Air Force. In the early 21st century, Algeria began a program to modernize its armed forces that included the purchase of fighter jets, tanks, and air defense systems. Russia remains one of the largest suppliers of arms to the Algerian armed forces. Compulsory military service exists for Algerians between the ages of nineteen and thirty, and consists of an 18-month term (which includes training).

Foreign Policy

Since winning its independence in 1962, Algeria has played an active role in regional politics and world events. During the 1970s, Algeria supported the independence movements of numerous other third world or developing countries. Trade and economic development are also major focal points of Algerian foreign policy. Algeria is a member of the Organization of the Petroleum Exporting Countries (OPEC), and the nation depends heavily on the export of oil as well as of fruits and minerals. Algeria also relies on economic assistance from the United States, which provided $4.4 million (USD) in aid in 2005, and is one of Algeria's chief trading partners. American companies are also heavily invested in the country.

Other significant concerns of Algerian foreign policy are the stabilization and security of northern Africa and the Middle East and the reduction of global terrorism. Algeria itself has suffered from renewed surges in terrorist violence since the 1990s. During that decade, more than 100,000 people died as a result of terrorist activity within Algeria. The violence resulted from uprising among militant and fundamentalist Islamic groups that sought to overthrow the more secular government and establish stricter Islamic controls. The fighting ebbed in the early 2000s, but Algeria has remained an important partner to the US in its global fight against terrorism. Algeria is a member of the Trans-Sahara Counter-Terrorism Partnership (TSCTP).

In Africa, Algeria has worked to mediate disputes and help negotiate peace among competing factions in neighboring countries. The nation hosted the Organization of African Unity (OAU) Conference in 2000. That same year, Algeria mediated a conflict between Ethiopia and Eritrea. Algeria has also had some conflict with neighbors, and continues to have trouble maintaining diplomatic relations with Morocco because of its support for the Polisario Front. The Polisario is a separatist group that claims to act on behalf of the Sahrawis, or the people who inhabit the Western Sahara, a territory over which Morocco claims sovereignty. The United Nations (UN) has been monitoring a ceasefire in the region since 1991. Algeria maintains that the people of Western Sahara have the right to establish an independent, sovereign nation. Borders were closed between Morocco and Algeria for a number of years, but the countries began reopening their borders in 2004 and 2005.

In the rest of the North African region, Algeria maintains friendly diplomatic relations with Tunisia, Libya, Mali, and Niger. It also has a significant interest in events in the Middle East, and has long supported the Palestinian people in their dispute with Israel. It has been an active supporter of Iraqi independence and democracy. Though Algeria opposed the US-led invasion of Iraq in 2003, it has worked to support efforts to establish and defend a new governing structure there and to maintain stability in the region.

Since Ahmed Bouteflika (1937–) assumed the presidency in 1999, he has worked to expand Algerian influence and increase its stature on the world stage. During his first term, he became the first Algerian president to visit the White House in sixteen years. Algeria is also an active member of the UN, and held a rotating seat on the UN Security Council (UNSC) in 2004 and 2005. The nation maintains diplomatic relations with more than 100 countries, and began negotiations to join the World Trade Organization (WTO).

Human Rights Profile

International human rights law insists that states respect civil and political rights, and also promote an individual's economic, social and cultural rights. The United Nations Universal Declaration on Human Rights (UDHR) is recognized as the standard for international human rights. Its authors sought the counsel of the world's great thinkers, philosophers, and religious leaders, and were careful to create a document that reflects the core values shared by every world culture. (To read this document or view the articles relating to cultural human rights, click here http://www.un.org/en/documents/udhr/.)

Algeria has a constitutional republican form of government with universal suffrage, free multiparty elections, and legal protections for basic civil liberties. The nation also has an independent judiciary for administering the laws. However, many rights are not protected to the fullest extent. The U.S. Department of State and international monitoring agencies such as Amnesty International (AI) have cited several key problem areas in regards to human rights in Algeria.

As of 2008, thousands of people still remain unaccounted for following the violence of the 1990s. These disappearances have largely been attributed to Algerian security forces, as well as terrorist organizations. In 2003, the government formed an investigative body called the Ad Hoc Mechanism on the Disappeared, but the body has little actual authority. Critics charge that the government has not fully investigated the disappearances out of a desire to protect government officials from criminal prosecution.

The Algerian constitution and its legal code both forbid torture, but Amnesty International (AI) and other such monitoring agencies have charged the government and military officials with condoning and practicing such actions. These bodies have acknowledged that the practices are becoming less common, but maintain that government and security forces need to eliminate all use of torture, particularly in military prisons. In 2003, the Algerian government stated that it would discipline officials, soldiers, and police convicted of violating human rights. However, the government continues to lack accountability and was also slow to provide security forces with an official code of conduct.

Although the Algerian constitution prohibits arbitrary arrest and detention, these practices also continue. The law allows detainees to be held in pre-trial detention for up to four months; a request and justification must be made to extend that detention an additional four months, up to a maximum of a year. In practice, officials rarely made such justifications and judges rarely refused their requests for extensions. Detainees were also deprived of the rights to communicate with family, to have visitors, and to be examined by a doctor of their choosing when their detention has ended. Similarly, the judicial system, though constitutionally independent, is interfered with by the executive branch regularly. In recent years, dozens of magistrates and officials have been investigated and fired for abuses. Also, the courts have not always upheld expectations for fair and speedy public trials. Most trials are public but defendants do not have the right to a jury. Defendants were also frequently denied due process of the laws.

The constitution protects civil liberties, including the freedoms of speech and the press, and freedom of assembly, but the government has restricted these rights. Political meetings are often monitored, and public media are censored. Individuals are threatened and intimidated for voicing anti-government opinions or criticisms. The government has also claimed emergency powers and declared that restrictions on certain liberties are necessary to maintain national security. For example, Algiers banned public demonstrations in 2000 and began requiring citizens and organizations to apply for permits for public meetings. Security forces broke up several protests, marches, and other demonstrations that occurred. Freedom of religion is also limited as Article 2 of the Algerian constitution declares Islam to be the official religion. Citizens are granted the right to hold their own religious beliefs, but laws restrict the public practice of other religions.

Corruption occurs at all levels of government, but it is difficult to identify and prosecute.

Laws restrict corrupt practices and mandate two to 10 years imprisonment for most offenses, but prosecutions and convictions have been few. Lack of government transparency is a large part of the problem. Algerian law also grants workers the right to strike, bargain collectively, form unions and pursue mediation, but workers must apply and get government permission to conduct a strike or similar action.

Under Article 29, the constitution prohibits discrimination based on a person's birth, race, sex, language or social status. However, women, Berber groups, and other minority communities continue to suffer such practices, and have accused the government of discrimination. These groups assert that they do not have full and equal rights with other citizens. Algeria also needs to address the problem of human trafficking. Algerian law does not prohibit human trafficking, and trafficking in persons, especially women, is believed to occur across and within Algerian borders.

ECONOMY

Overview of the Economy

Algeria has made great economic strides since independence; in an effort to diversify its petroleum-based economy—gas and oil account for about 97 percent of the country's exports—the Algerian government has allowed some privatization of industry to encourage more foreign investment. In particular, it has undertaken efforts to promote the Bay of Algiers as a tourist destination, on the model of the highly lucrative seaside resorts in neighboring Morocco and Tunisia. The country, however, still suffers from high unemployment, unreliable supplies of water and electricity, and a shortage of housing. In 2014, the per capita gross domestic product was estimated at $14,300 USD.

Industry

Industry is the largest sector of the Algerian economy. The government controls the development, refining and distribution of gas and petroleum, as well as the manufacture of iron and steel, textiles, and construction materials.

Chief exports include mineral fuels, lubricants, gas, and petroleum and petroleum products. Exports are worth approximately $62.1 billion USD annually (2014 estimate). Most of the gas and petroleum deposits are under the Sahara. Algeria is one of the world's largest exporters of natural gas, helping to meet the energy needs of Europe and the United States.

Labor

Out of a labor force of just over 12 million, approximately 10 percent is unemployed, and 23 percent of the population lives below the poverty line. According to recent estimates, government is the largest employer in Algeria, and accounts for approximately 32 percent of the work force. The agricultural sector employs an estimated 14 percent of Algerians, while industry accounts for just over 13 percent of employment.

In 2009, it was estimated that seven out of ten able adults under the age of thirty are unemployed. As a result, hundreds of thousands of young Algerians have immigrated, primarily to France, in search of jobs.

Energy/Power/Natural Resources

Algeria's major natural resources include huge deposits of petroleum and natural gas, plus iron ore, phosphates, uranium, lead and zinc. Algeria has the seventh-largest natural gas reserves and the 7th-largest oil reserves in the world.

Poor farming practices, such as overgrazing, have resulted in soil erosion. Rivers and coastal waters are becoming polluted by industrial and petroleum wastes and raw sewage. The sea is further polluted by oil, sil,t and fertilizer runoff. Drinkable water is scarce in Algeria.

Fishing

Algeria's fishing industry is often characterized as under-developed and artisanal fishing is widespread. The government has prioritized modernization of the fishing industry, such as the use of commercial trawlers to increase productivity and aquaculture, in recent years, while also granting foreign fishing licenses and seeking foreign investment. In 2004, Algerian fisheries produced 130,000 tons; an estimated 145,000 tons are caught annually. As of 2010, the country maintained 30 fishing ports and roughly 4,500 fishing vessels. Tuna is one of the primary species caught.

Forestry

The country does not support a significant forestry industry, but does produce pine (particularly Aleppo Pine, native to the Mediterranean) and cork. Only about 2 percent of the land is considered forested or wooded.

Mining/Metals

Outside of hydrocarbons (crude oil and natural gas), of which Algeria is a major exporter, the country produces metals such as gold, silver, iron ore, and steel, as well as industrial commodities such as barite, clays, cement, crushed stone and gravel, quartzite, helium, and marble. Overall, industrial minerals account for over 90 percent of non-fuel exports in the mineral sector, while precious metals such as gold account for approximately 8 percent. Mineral commodities showing the most increases in production in the 21st century include crushed stone and construction aggregate (such as sand and gravel), cement, steel, and iron ore.

Agriculture

Just over three percent of Algeria's land is arable. The main crops grown are wheat, oats, barley, potatoes, grapes, figs, olives, and citrus fruits. Inhabitants of the Saharan region live around oases where underground springs offer water. These springs help to irrigate date trees and grain. Desert nomads move among grazing areas to feed their camels, sheep, and other animals. As of 2014, the agricultural sector accounted for nearly 9 percent of Algeria's gross domestic product (GDP).

Animal Husbandry

Sheep, goats, and cattle are the principal livestock, many of which are maintained in the High

Plateaus region. Livestock products include cow's milk, beef and veal, poultry, sheep's milk, and mutton and lamb. As of 2010, there were 28 million heads of livestock, the majority—approximately 18 million—of which were sheep.

Tourism

More than 900,000 tourists, mostly from France and Tunisia, generate roughly $133 million USD for the Algerian economy each year. However, years of violence in the early 21st century have slowed the tourism industry. In particular, attacks by Islamist militants have had a negative effect on both tourist arrivals and investment. In 2006, the country attracted only some 1.6 million tourists, less than a third of which were foreigners. However, in 2012, Algeria saw an estimated 2,634,000 tourists, according to data from the World Bank.

Popular tourist attractions include the Mediterranean coast, the Atlas Mountains and the Sahara. Many tourists visit Algiers to view the historic casbah, the oldest part of the city.

By Christina Dendy, Ellen Bailey

DO YOU KNOW?

- Clementine oranges are said to be named for Father Clement, a French priest who reportedly began cultivating the fruit in the early 1900s, after first seeing them near Oran, Algeria.

- The term "casbah" refers to the older section of a city, featuring narrow, crowded streets crammed with houses and shops. Newer sections feature wide streets, tall buildings and open-air markets.

- Women's traditional dress, worn mostly in rural areas, is the haik, a long, white garment covering the head and lower face, and the body down to the feet. Traditional men's clothing includes a long, hooded cloak called a burnoose.

Bibliography

_____. *Algeria: A Country Study.* Washington, DC: Library of Congress, 1994.

Alan Keohane. *Bedouin.* London: Kyle Cathie Limited, 1994.

Amy L. Hubbell. *Remembering French Algeria.* Lincoln, NE: University of Nebraska Press, 2015.

Anthony Ham and Anthony Sattin. *Algeria.* Oakland, CA: Lonely Planet, 2007.

Benjamin Stora. *Algeria: A Short History.* Ithaca: Cornell University Press, 2004.

Francesca Davis Dipiazza. *Algeria in Pictures.* Breckenridge: Twenty-First Century Books, 2007.

James McDougall. *History and the Culture of Nationalism in Algeria.* Cambridge, UK: Cambridge University Press, 2008.

Martin Evans and John Phillips. *Algeria.* New Haven: Yale University Press, 2007.

Michael Brett and Elizabeth Fentress. *The Berbers.* Oxford: Blackwell Publishing, 1997.

Works Cited

"Algeria—Amnesty International Report 2008." *Amnesty International.* http://www.amnesty.org/en/region/algeria/report-2008

"Algeria.com." http://www.algeria.com

"Algeria: Country Reports on Human Rights Practices." *U.S. Department of State.* http://www.state.gov/g/drl/rls/hrrpt/2005/61685.htm

"Algeria, Democratic and Popular Republic of." *Emory Law.* http://www.law.emory.edu/ifl/legal/Algeria.htm

"Algeria." *National Geographic.* http://worldmusic.nationalgeographic.com/worldmusic/view/page.basic/country/content.country/algeria_20

"Algeria Newspapers." *Onlinenewspapers.com.* http://www.onlinenewspapers.com/algeria.htm

"Algeria." *The World Factbook.* https://www.cia.gov/library/publications/the-world-factbook/geos/al.html

"Algeria." Worldpress.org. http://www.worldpress.org/newspapers/MIDEAST/Algeria.cfm

"Algeria Internet Usage and Marketing Report." *Internet World Stats* http://www.internetworldstats.com/af/dz.htm

"Algeria—Language, Culture, Customs and Etiquette." *Kwintessential.com* http://www.kwintessential.co.uk/resources/global-etiquette/algeria.html

"Algeria to build 1 million new housing units Nairobi." *UN-Habitat.* http://www.unhabitat.org/content.asp?cid=1492&catid=5&typeid=6&subMenuId=0

"Algeria." *U.S. Department of State.* http://www.state.gov/r/pa/ei/bgn/8005.htm

"Algiers." *Subways.net.* http://www.subways.net/algeria/algiers.htm

"arts + crafts." *Oxfam.* http://www.oxfam.org.uk/coolplanet/ontheline/explore/journey/algeria/arts.htm

"Bedouin." *Tribes Travel.* http://www.tribes.co.uk/countries/jordan/indigenous/bedouin

"Country Studies." http://www.country-studies.com

"Food in Algeria." *Food in Every Country.* http://www.foodbycountry.com/Algeria-to-France/Algeria.html

Megan Romer. "Rai Music 101." About.com. http://worldmusic.about.com/od/venues/p/RaiMusic.htm

"music + dance." *Oxfam.* http://www.oxfam.org.uk/coolplanet/ontheline/explore/journey/algeria/music.htm

"Phoenician and Cypriote Sculpture." *Antiques Digest.* http://www.oldandsold.com/articles08/sculpture-7.shtml

Robert Montagne and David Seddon. *The Berbers.* 1973: Frank Cass and Company, Ltd., London.

"Roman Sculpture." *Antiques Digest.* http://www.oldandsold.com/articles08/sculpture-13.shtml

"Timeline: Algeria." *BBC News.* http://newsvote.bbc.co.uk/mpapps/pagetools/print/news.bbc.co.uk/2/hi/middle_east/country_profiles/811140.stm

Zachary Ochieng. "Algeria: Desert Dances." *The East African.* http://allafrica.com/stories/200807141386.html

"UNESCO World Heritage Centre." http://whc.unesco.org

"*World Heritage Site.*" http://www.worldheritagesite.org/

Stone arches in Qal'atal, Bahrain

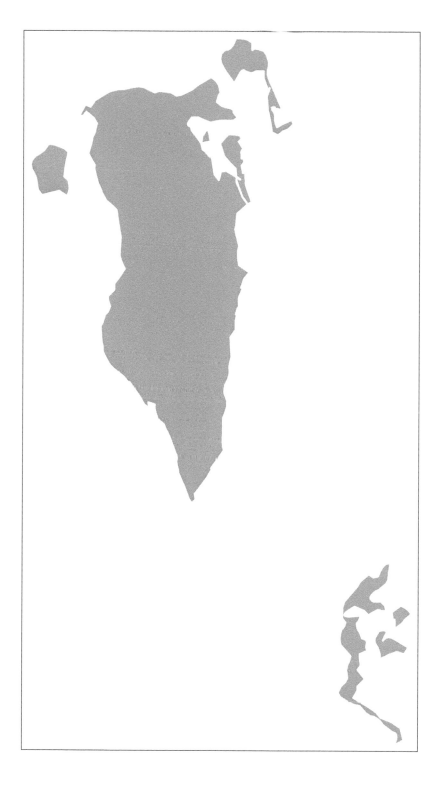

BAHRAIN

Introduction

The Kingdom of Bahrain is an island nation situated in the Persian Gulf. Though the country has been a center of trade and communications throughout recorded history, it remained relatively undeveloped until the discovery of oil in 1932. Today, the archipelago of more than thirty islands has one of the highest standards of living in the Persian Gulf region.

While it does not have a lot of its own oil, Bahrain is an important oil-refining center for other Middle Eastern nations. It is also a major financial center for the region, and many Middle Eastern companies have headquarters in the archipelagic nation. Bahrain is also considered to have a liberal or free economy for a Middle Eastern state, and Manama, the capital, is considered the wealthiest and most visited capital of the Persian Gulf region. Since 2011, the country has experienced intermittent protests and unrest stemming from the Arab Spring the affected the region.

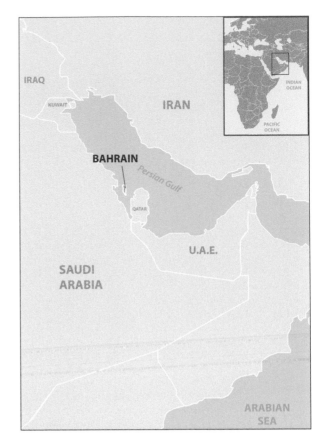

GENERAL INFORMATION

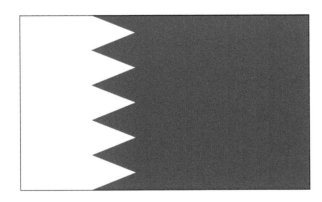

Official Language: Arabic
Population: 1,346,613 (2015 est.) note: immigrants make up almost 55% of the total population, according to UN data (2013)
Currency: Bahraini dinar
Coins: The Bahraini dinar is divided into 1,000 fils. Coins are minted in denominations of 5, 10, 25, 50, 100, and 500 fils.

Land Area: 741 square kilometers (286 square miles)
National Anthem: "Bahrainona" ("Our Bahrain")
Capital: Manama
Time Zone: GMT +3
Flag Description: The flag of Bahrain features two unequal color fields, one white (on the hoist side) and one red. The colors, of which red is a much larger proportion, are separated by a serrated line made up of five white triangles that represent the five pillars of Islam.

Population

With a population of more than 1.3 million, Bahrain is one of the most densely populated countries in the world. Just under 90 percent of the population lives in urban areas in the north of Bahrain Island, the major island in the group.

Bahrain's largest city is the capital and chief commercial center, Manama. However, the majority of the city's population is non-Bahrainis;

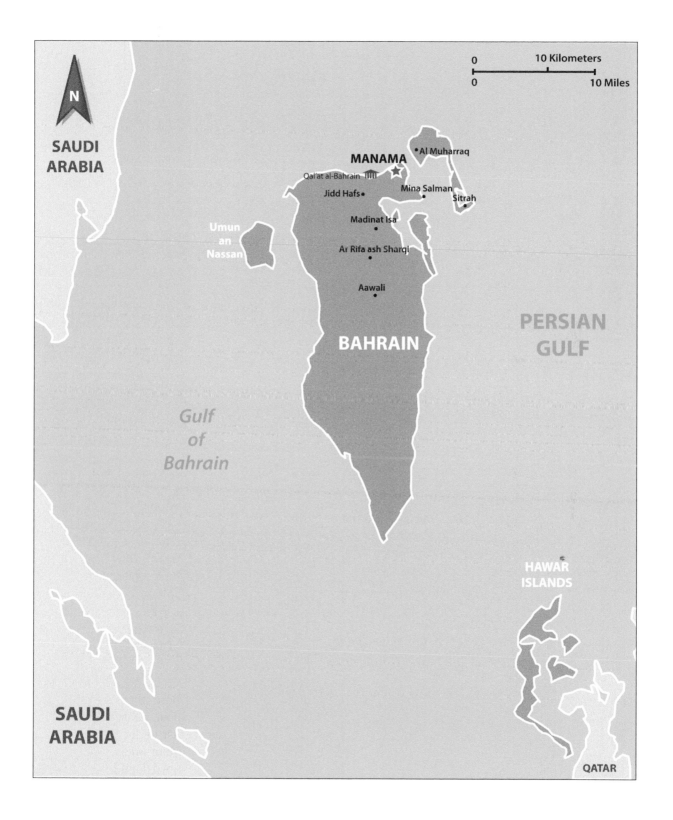

Principal Cities by Population (2012 estimate, unless noted):

- Manama (297,509)
- Muharraq (176,583)
- Rifa' (115,495)
- Madinat Hamad (133,550)
- A'ali (100,553)
- Jidd Haffs (66,588)
- Madinat 'Isa (61,293)

in fact, 2010 estimates put the entire Bahraini population at 46 percent for the entire country

Other ethnic groups include Asians, other Arabs, Africans and Europeans. As of 2013, more than half of the country's population (55 percent) is comprised of foreign worker and other non-nationals.

Languages
Although Arabic is the official language, most people in Bahrain speak English as well. Farsi and Urdu are also widely spoken.

Native People & Ethnic Groups
The main island, Bahrain, is believed to have been inhabited since prehistoric times. The island's trading empire flourished from around 3000 to 1000 BCE, when it was known as Dilmun.

About 300 BCE, the Greeks occupied the island and named it Tylos. In the seventh century, Mohammad issued a personal invitation to the islanders to convert to Islam. A series of Islamic rulers then controlled the island, followed by the Portuguese in the 16th century. Bahrain came under the control of the Persian Empire during the 17th century.

In 1782, Arabs of the Al Khalifah clan came to the islands from what is now Saudi Arabia. When they had driven out the Persians, the Al Khalifahs chose an emir from among themselves to rule. This clan continues to rule today. Saudi invaders tried to oust the clan in the early 19th century. The Bahrainis asked for British help, and in 1861, the country became a British

protectorate. Under this arrangement, Britain controlled Bahrain's foreign relations.

Religions
The state religion of Bahrain is Islam. Shias represent approximately 70 percent of the population, while Sunnis represent approximately 30 percent. Other religions are guaranteed freedom of worship. Nearly 10percent of Bahrainis are Hindu, and nearly 15 percent are Christian.

Climate
Winters (December-March) in Bahrain are mild, with a temperature range of 15° to 25° Celsius (60° to 77° Fahrenheit). January and February see some chilly, rainy days, with humidity as high as 90 percent. Spring temperatures range from 20° to 30° Celsius (68° to 86° Fahrenheit).

Summers (May-September) are hot, with temperatures as high as 48° Celsius (118° Fahrenheit). In August, the high humidity causes great discomfort. Autumn temperatures range from 25° to 35° Celsius (77° to 95° Fahrenheit).

The qaws, hot and dry winds from the southeast, often blow up sandstorms in the summer. In the winter, the shammal, another southeast wind, blows damp air over the islands.

Only about eight centimeters (three inches) of rain fall annually in Bahrain, mostly in the north during the winter. The rains come in cloudbursts that often flood the shallow wadis (depressions or dry streambeds), which are dry during the rest of the year. These flash floods can also interfere with traffic.

ENVIRONMENT & GEOGRAPHY

Topography
Bahrain is an archipelago of more than thirty islands in the Persian Gulf. The country lies in the middle of the gulf, about 24 kilometers (15 miles) off the east coast of Saudi Arabia and 28 kilometers (17 miles) off the west coast of Qatar.

The capital, Manama, is located on the main island (Bahrain), on a small peninsula on the northeastern tip. (A coastal city, Manama is bordered by the waters of the Persian Gulf on almost every side but the south.) Al Muharraq, Sitrah, and Umm Nasan are the other major islands in the group. These principal islands are connected to Bahrain Island by causeways. A causeway also connects Bahrain Island with Saudi Arabia.

Most of the country is a low desert plain, rising slightly in the center. The highest point is at Jabal ad Dukhan, 134 meters (440 feet) above sea level. Most of the land is barren desert, without rivers or lakes. Some seasonal salt marshes provide nesting for numerous species of birds. The northern coast of the island of Bahrain, however, has many freshwater springs. These provide drinking water and irrigation.

Plants & Animals

Bahrain's flora consists largely of desert-resistant and salt-tolerant species such as date palms, thorn trees, and scrub brush. The water-rich northern coast supports almond, fig, and pomegranate trees. Tubli Bay, in northeast part of the main island, supports the country's last remaining mangrove trees. Many trees have been cut down, and others have died from lack of water.

Bahrain's wildlife is more diverse than its plant life. Numerous species of birds nest or migrate to the islands, including the hoopoe lark, desert lark, graceful warbler, spotted crake, West Reef heron, black-winged stilt, sooty falcon, osprey, and greater flamingo.

Domesticated donkeys are common in Bahrain, but camels are scarce. Wild animals include reptiles such as the spiny-tailed lizard and the sand snake, Bahrain's only poisonous serpent. Hares, scorpions, hedgehogs, gazelles, and the occasional camel can also be seen. The Al-Areen Wildlife Sanctuary protects such animals as the Reem gazelle and the endangered Arabian oryx.

The shallow coastal waters are home to mackerel, shrimp, pearl oysters, green turtles, and sea snakes.

CUSTOMS & COURTESIES

Greetings

Men customarily greet each other by shaking hands. It should be noted that the right hand is always used, as in Muslim culture the left hand is associated with the cleansing of the body, and is thus considered impure. When greeting, it is also common for men to exchange kisses on the cheek, and women greet other women in a similar fashion. When men and women who are not related meet, the man should not assume it is all right to shake hands. Although women in Bahrain are more visible than in other Arab countries, there still is some cultural reticence when it comes to interacting with men outside of their families. If a woman chooses to extend her hand, however, then it is customary shake it. The common phrase when greeting is "Salaamu alcikum" ("Peace be upon you"), with "Wa'aleikum as-salamma" ("And on peace be you") the traditional response.

Honorific or professional titles are customarily used when Bahrainis address one another. For example, older men are often referred to as "sheikh," while religious figures are referred to as "hajji." It is also considered respectful to address someone by their first name only when invited to do so.

Gestures & Etiquette

Bahrainis are friendly and value personal relationships, especially when they are doing business. Patience is valued, and displays of impatience are considered extremely rude. Bahrainis tend to avoid confrontation and may prefer to talk to a person they disagree with privately rather than start an argument in public. It is customary for people of the same sex to establish contact while conversing, but non-relations of the opposite sex should avoid touching each other. Public displays of affection are also frowned upon, and foreigners should keep such displays to a minimum out of respect.

In terms of gestures, the right hand is always when taking or giving something, as the left hand is considered taboo due to its association with the cleansing of the body. Additionally, Bahrainis refrain from pointing at someone, especially with their shoes or feet. Thus when sitting, the sole of one's foot should also not face another person, as this is also considered disrespectful.

Eating/Meals

Traditionally, meals in Bahrain are eaten on the floor. People may sit on pillows or a low sofa, either kneeling or legs crossed (feet should never touch the food mat in the center where dishes of food are place). Everyone helps themselves from the shared dishes, using their right hands only—eating or passing dishes with the left hand, customarily used for personal hygiene, would be considered offensive. However, in more modern homes, especially in cities, people may eat at tables, and will use utensils. Packaged meals and Western dishes are also more common in cities than in rural areas.

Ghahwas, or coffeehouses, are an important part of the culture in Bahrain. Usually located in the souks, or marketplaces, ghahwas were traditionally gathering places for men (though women are now allowed). In a ghahwa, people can drink coffee, smoke shisha pipes, and play games. Coffee is served in very small cups and is usually drunk immediately; a person then hands it back to the server to be refilled right away. Swirling the cup tells the server that no more refills are wanted.

Shisha smokers inhale the smoke through a water pipe, which is also known as a hookah, or "hubble bubble." Each ghahwa has a shisha man who mixes the blend of tobacco used in the shishas. Ghahwas can become known for their special blends of tobacco. In some ghahwas, the fruit-flavored tobacco is accented by using fruit juices instead of water in the pipe.

Visiting

Bahrainis are known for their warmth and friendliness and enjoy having company. Upon arrival, guests should wait by the side of the door (so they cannot see inside) until the host invites them into the home. Removing one's shoes is not a requirement in every home, so guests should wait for the host to indicate what is appropriate. Visitors are then brought into the majlis, which is a public room at the front of the house where visitors are entertained; the harim or the rest of the house is for the women in the family. Men who are not part of the family should never enter the harim.

Chocolate, candy, or houseplants are appropriate gifts from visitors, but flowers and perfume are not. Also, because of Islamic law, many Arabs refrain from consuming alcohol. Gifts are usually put aside to be opened later. Traditional hospitality also requires that the host offer any possessions that a guest might admire. Food will be served in abundance and guests should try a little of everything. It is polite to leave a small amount of food on one's plate, as this indicates that the host has been generous.

LIFESTYLE

Family

Many Bahraini families are still very traditional. Thus, they are patriarchal in nature, with the father acting as head of the household and sole provider, while the mother attends to all domestic responsibilities and child rearing. In decision-making and deciding arguments, family members are supposed to defer to the wishes of the senior male.

However, women in Bahrain have experienced more empowerment in recent years. Many more women are in the workforce in Bahrain than in the past, and women have more decision-making power in the family structure. Urban families, especially those more acquainted with the many European families who are in Bahrain for work reasons, have become more Westernized.

Housing

Homes in Bahrain have traditionally been structured to deal with two issues: privacy and the heat. Tall, high walls, which created a courtyard around the house, are often erected to ensure privacy. The houses themselves had small windows to increase this sense of privacy and to prevent hot air from entering. Thick walls provided quiet and insulation from the heat, and roofs were flat so families could sleep on them to escape the stifling heat. Wind towers also worked to draw out hot air (and pull down any cool air) while also providing shade.

Although air conditioning has worked well to alleviate heat concerns in the early 21st century, many of the elements which traditionally dealt with the heat remain. Wind towers can still be seen, and houses still take advantage of as much shade as possible. However, in the urban areas of Bahrain, especially the capital of Manama, high-rise apartment buildings have taken over much of the city. Traditional homes are few and found only in historic sections. In Muharraq, the second largest city, there are more of the old-style houses, and many still have the beautiful wood carvings that once commonly decorated the walls and doors of a house's exterior.

Food

Bahraini cuisine is similar to the cuisines of neighboring Arabic countries. Fish is an important staple of the Bahraini diet, and foods such as meat and rice are prominent. Bahrain does not have a land and climate that is agriculturally friendly—it is an arid climate with inadequate rainfall and salty soil. In addition, there is not enough grazing room to support a great deal of livestock. While some fruit, such as dates, pomegranates, bananas, and mangos, grow well enough, much of the food is imported.

Falafel, shawarma, and sambousas can all be found in Bahrain, along with rice and flatbreads. Some dishes specific to Bahrain include machboos, where meat or fish are mixed with rice and flavored with a number of spices, such as cardamom, turmeric, ginger, coriander, as well as onions, garlic, and limes. Qoozi is lamb that has been grilled and filled with boiled eggs, rice, onions, and spices. Muhammar is rice sweetened with sugar, cardamom, cinnamon, and rose water that is served with fish. Khubz is a flatbread that is found throughout Bahrain. The dough is shaped into disks and thrown against the walls of an extremely hot oven to keep it flat. Halwa is a sweet that has variations throughout the Middle East. The Bahraini version is a sugar candy that is flavored with rose water, cardamom, and saffron topped with nuts.

Coffee in Bahrain is made in a very specific manner. First, water and the coffee grounds are brought to a boil. Then the mixture is flavored, usually with cardamom, saffron, and rose water, and left to steep in a coffee pot called a dalla. After about five or 10 minutes, it is served in finjans, a type of very small cup.

Life's Milestones

The official religion of Bahrain is Islam, with an estimated 70 percent of the population identifying as Muslim according to the 2010 estimate from the CIA World Factbook. Thus, most milestones are observed in accordance with the Muslim faith and Islamic law. However, one milestone that has incorporated unique and cross-cultural influences is marriage.

Weddings in Bahrain are expected to be lavish affairs. Traditionally, the wedding ceremony itself takes place during a small party at the bride's family home. A mullah, or religious leader, reviews the marriage agreement, which the bride and groom both sign in front of witnesses. Then they exchange gold rings brought by the groom. At that point the couple is married and they separate into two parties, one for the men and one for the women. Afterward, the couple is reunited, followed by another non-segregated grand reception. Wedding traditions that have been integrated into Bahrain's culture include mehndi night, an event that occurs a few days prior to the wedding, which has been imported from India. During the event, women gather and use henna, a natural deep red dye, to paint decorative designs on the bride's hands and feet. Western wedding dresses and food also are popular in urban areas.

Weddings in Bahrain have become more expensive in recent years. In fact, wedding costs, as well as the standard cost of raising a family, have increased dramatically. In 2008, several government ministers proposed that the state pay Bahraini men a sum of money to help families cover the wedding dowry, or the traditional fee that the bride's family pays to the groom.

CULTURAL HISTORY

Art

Traditional Bahraini arts and handicrafts include jewelry, embroidered and crocheted fabrics, calligraphy, basket-weaving from split palm fronds, pottery-making, goldsmithing, cloth weaving, and wood carving.

Well-known Bahraini artists include Shaikh Rashid, a painter famous for his landscapes as well as abstract works; Abdul Wahab Koheji, who paints scenes of Bahraini life; and Nasser Al Yousif, who is known for linoleum etchings. Rashid is one of the founders of the Bahrain Arts Society, a nonprofit group founded in 1983 to help support Bahraini artists. The society holds exhibitions both in Bahrain and abroad and has an art school that teaches children and adults.

Architecture

Civilization in Bahrain dates back to the third millennium (3100–2100 BCE) during the time of ancient Mesopotamia (often regarded as the cradle of civilization). Archaeologists have found architectural evidence of a city that included houses and a centrally located temple. A second temple dating back to 1900 BCE featured columns with crescents carved into them. The houses were built out of limestone, with roofs made from wood, palm leave, or mats. The houses each had a back and front door, and were clustered in small groups around a central courtyard. A temple from the same period was also found in the village of Barbar. It resembles those found in ancient Mesopotamia from that time, but is made out of stone and not the adobe used by the Sumerians. In addition to temples and houses, giant burial mounds were another form of architecture in ancient Bahrain. Built from adobe covered with limestone, these structures consisted of a lower room and an upper room, which had a slightly peaked roof. They currently cover about 5 percent of the land in Bahrain.

Sometime between 1800 and 1600 BCE, Aryan invaders destroyed the cities in Bahrain. It was later taken over by the Greeks, who renamed the island Tylos. The Greek influence can be seen in the ruins from this period. Islam came to Bahrain in the seventh century CE. The Al-Khamis Mosque, built in the late seventh to early eighth centuries, was perhaps the first mosque built in Bahrain. Columns and arches were added to the structure later, and murals were painted on the exterior. The mosque originally had only one minaret, but another was added in the 14th century, making the mosque easily visible from a distance.

In the 17th century, Bahrain was taken over by Portugal, which used it as a base for protecting other islands where it had trading posts. After a period of independence in the 18th and 19th centuries, Bahrain asked to become a protectorate of the British Empire. As Bahrain gained prominence for its pearl trade, people from other nations began to migrate to the island, bringing their own style of architecture. One noticeable import was the Iranian wind tower. The wind towers drew in breezes and directed them down to the houses, while also drawing hot air up from below. People in different parts of Bahrain added their own decorative touches to wind towers and they remain a distinctive part of the Bahrain skyline.

Bahraini architecture has been characterized by urbanization and modernism in the late twentieth and early 21st century. One of the most notable projects in recent years is the Al-Fateh Grand Mosque, built in the capital of Manama. Able to hold over 7,000 worshippers, the mosque is one of the biggest in the world, and the mosque's fiberglass dome is considered the world's largest such dome.

Drama

As in many societies, the earliest plays performed in Bahrain were didactic and religious in nature, featuring moral and instructive tales. During the Middle Ages, puppet and shadow plays became popular, with modern European drama arriving as late as the 19th century. By the early 20th century, drama and plays were being taught in school. By the 1940s, drama clubs and societies were forming in Bahraini cities. Though at first they mostly put on European classics, eventually they began to produce their own writers and plays. The Awal Theatre and Al-Jazira Theatre were established in the 1970s. Partially government-supported, they promote the works of Bahraini writers and have performed in drama festivals throughout the region. The Al-Sawari Company, founded in the 1990s, focuses on producing experimental works.

Music & Dance

Bahrain has a long tradition of folk music and dance. As in most Arabic countries, music in the past was primarily played on the oud, a stringed instrument. The oud is oval-shaped, with a short neck and usually ten to twelve strings. The rebabeh, a one-stringed instrument with a square body, is also heard in Bahraini music. Drums are also very important.

Khaleeji is a style of music popular throughout the Gulf States. Featuring multiple rhythms, khaleeji music shows an African influence derived from African slaves. The songs of pearl divers, a particularly important part of Bahrain's musical tradition, were also influenced by Africans in Bahrain. For many years, pearls were Bahrain's biggest export and slaves were brought to Bahrain to work as pearl divers. Their songs were mostly laments, which focused on mourning, such as missing their wives, or the sea's rough weather. They also had songs for the celebrations that were held before they were sent off to sea.

The pearl divers also had a traditional dance, the fidjeri, in which earthenware urns were used and the dancers were all male. Clapping provided the rhythm during the dance, and poetry was recited. Another traditional dance only performed by men is the ardha, or sword dance. Belly dancing is also found in Bahrain.

Literature

Bahrain's literary history is rooted in the oral traditions of the region's indigenous populations, with a particular focus on poetry. Tarafa, a Bahraini poet born in the sixth century, has a poem in the *Mu'Allaqat*, an anthology of pre-Islamic Arab poetry that probably first appeared in the eighth century. The poems in the *Mu'Allaqat*, also known as the "Seven Long Poems," all deal with Bedouin and nomadic life, and Tarafa's contribution is known for its lengthy description of camels. Tarafa's sister, al-Khirniq, also was a poet, and one of her surviving poems is an elegy to her husband, son, and two brothers who died in battle.

After the arrival of Islam, poetry continued to flourish until the Middle Ages, when many Arabic writers chose to focus on academic studies such as philosophy and science. Folk tales also became popular, though they were largely ignored by intellectuals. Following the Middle Ages, there was a decline in Arabic literature that lasted until the end of the 19th century, when the Arabic world experienced a major literary revival. In the 20th-century, Bahrain produced a number of renowned poets, including Ebrahim Al-Arrayedh (1908–2002), considered one of the most important poets of the Persian Gulf. In 1998, Bahrain honored him with the opening of the Ebrahim Al-Arrayedh Poetry House, a cultural center in Manama.

CULTURE

Arts & Entertainment

Bahrain has long taken pride in its arts community. Unlike other oil-rich Gulf states that have experienced an infusion of Western culture, Bahrainis have strongly maintained their own, self-generated artistic tradition. The government also generally supports the arts—the government supports handicraft centers that preserve traditional Bahraini crafts, such as basket weaving, rug weaving, and pottery—and there are many arts festivals throughout the year. More importantly, artists themselves have taken an active role in promoting each other.

The poet Qassim Haddad (1948–) is an influential figure in the contemporary Bahraini arts scene. As an adolescent, Haddad was incarcerated for five years because of his political beliefs. After his release, Haddad founded the Bahraini Writers Association and became its first president. In 1970, he was one of the founding members of the Awal Theater Group. He became famous for writing poems that address political and social issues, as well as for his willingness to try new and experimental forms of poetry. Haddad also became one of the first Arab writers to grasp the importance of the Internet; in 1994, he founded a website dedicated to promoting the work of Arab poets. He has been awarded numerous prizes, including the Prize of the Lebanese Cultural Forum (Paris) and the Sultan Owais Prize for Poetry.

In addition to its traditional music, Bahrain also has many musicians performing popular styles such as hip-hop and rock. DJ Outlaw is considered by many to be one of the pioneers of hip-hop in Bahrain. The artist is credited with forming one of the kingdom's first rap groups, as well as forming the hip-hop production label Outlaw Productions. There is also a small metal scene, although many outfits are cover bands. Many promising young musicians have used the Internet to find further exposure, and social web sites such as MySpace are increasingly being used to nurture and discover new talent.

The Bahraini film industry is small, but growing. Only three feature films have been filmed in Bahrain, all by Bassam Al Thawadi (1960-). However, there are a number of directors making short films. At the 2007 Sawary International Movie Festival in Bahrain, thirty shorts by Bahraini directors were screened. Mohammed Rashed Bu-Ali is one of many young Bahraini directors working in short, experimental film. Although the industry doesn't receive government support, a private investment group formed the Bahrain Film Production Company in 2006 to help provide financial aid for Bahraini filmmakers and to boost the nation's profile in international cinema.

Bahrain holds a number of international arts festivals each year. The Bahrain International Music Festival includes performers from all different parts of the musical world. The Bahrain Human Rights International Film Festival is dedicated to films about human rights. The Spring of Culture is a government-sponsored festival that features Bahraini artists, singers, dancers, and museum exhibits, as well as performers from around the world. Smaller organizations are also working to support Bahraini artists. The Elham Arts Group meets regularly to allow new musicians, poets, writers, and filmmakers to show their work. In 2008, they held the Live Art Festival, a three-day festival of live music, screenings of experimental films, and artists creating new works on site.

Football (soccer) is a popular sport among both Bahrainis and foreign residents. Racing of Arabian thoroughbred horses is immensely popular. Weekly races are held from October through March. Camels are also raced. Muslim beliefs forbid betting on races, however. Some Bahrainis still practice falconry, a traditional sport in which falcons (a kind of hawk) are bred and trained to catch game birds.

Cultural Sites & Landmarks

As one of the first great civilizations of the ancient Middle East, Bahrain's recorded history spans 5,000 years, from when the Sumerians first referred to the once verdant region as Dilmun. In 2005, the United Nations Educational, Scientific and Cultural Organization (UNESCO) recognized the cultural importance of this ancient civilization by including the archaeological site of Qal'at al-Bahrain, the ancient harbor and capital of Dilmun, on the World Heritage List. Six cities, dating back to 2300 BCE, were built on the site, the ruins of each layered one on top of the other. The most recent structure is a fort from the 16th century built by the Portuguese.

Bahrain is home to a wealth of historical sites, including the Arad Fort, a 15th-century fort built in the Islamic style that is located on the island of Muharraq. The square fort has been renovated using the same materials with which it was built—sea stones, lime, sand, and palm trunks. Cylinder towers anchor each corner of the fort, and the corners contain openings for marksmen to fire their weapons in defense of the fort. The eighth-century Al-Khamis Mosque, with its twin minarets, and the modern Al-Fateh mosque are both important religious landmarks in Bahrain. The ancient Barbar Temple and the ancient burial mounds found around Bahrain are also places that offer insight into Bahrain's past.

Shaikh Isa's House, in Muharraq, was built in the 19th century, and contains features of houses of that period—a wind tower, wall carvings, and lattice work. Al Jasra House, found in the village of Al Jasra, was built in 1907, and is another example of Bahraini architecture. It is a simple, rectangular building, with symmetrical arches and columns.

Libraries & Museums

The Bahrain National Museum in Manama contains artifacts from early antiquity, and covers nearly 6,000 years of history concerning the 33 islands that make up modern-day Bahrain. The capital is also home to the Beit Al Qur'an, which means "House of Qur'an," a museum dedicated to the understanding of Islam. Its Qur'an (Koran) collection includes examples that date back to the seventh century, shortly after the death of the prophet Muhammad.

The Museum of Pearl Diving was originally the first site of the Bahrain Courts. Built in 1937, it contained the kingdom's four supreme courts, as well as the directorates for Religious Endowments of the Sunnis, Religious Endowments of the Shiites, and the Minors Estate and numerous other offices. In 1984, the building was turned into a center of traditional heritage, with rooms dedicated to different aspects of Bahrain's culture.

Bahrain's Shaikh Isa National Library opened in 2008 in the city of Juffair. Considered to be the most advanced library in the Gulf region, it plans to manage a collection of over 250,000 volumes. As of that same year, the country also had 12 academic libraries and nine government-managed public libraries. In addition, the Arabian Gulf University Library contains more than 40,000 volumes.

Holidays

Bahrain celebrates its independence from British protection on December 16 which is National Day.

Most official holidays observed in the country are Muslim, and the dates are determined according to the Muslim lunar calendar. Holidays include Leilat al-Meiraj, the first day of Ramadan; Id al-Fitr, the breaking of the fast at the end of Ramadan; Eid al-Adha, which celebrates Abraham's willingness to sacrifice Isaac to God; Muharram, Muslim New Year; and Ashoura, which marks the death of Hussein, Muhammad's grandson, at the Battle of Karbala in 680.

Youth Culture

For younger Bahrainis, life generally revolves around school and family. Children attend either public or private school. There is a strong prejudice or perception of differences among schoolchildren who attend one over the other. For example, students of private schools might perceive public school students as close-minded and ill prepared for jobs in a global economy. On the other hand, public school students have a perception that children attending private schools lack values and are overly Westernized. In addition, some private schools do not separate the sexes, while gender segregation is the norm in public education. Schoolgirls are not required to wear a hijab, or headscarf, but may do so anyway due to peer pressure.

In general, Bahrain has a more open culture than many Arab countries. Bahraini youth that have access to the Internet and satellite television are further exposed to Western trends and culture, and are most likely to come from wealthy families. On weekends, it's common for young adults from other countries to come to Bahrain to enjoy the nightlife, particularly because the consumption of alcohol and inter-gender dancing is permitted in Bahraini clubs. However, while there may be a great deal of freedom for young men, young women are still held to a stricter standard. As a result, many young women limit their socialization to places that are segregated from men. Unlike other Arab nations, young women are permitted to wear fashions of their choosing, particularly cosmetics, in the privacy of homes, shops, and salons.

SOCIETY

Transportation

Within Bahrain, there is some bus service between towns, but it is generally not reliable. There is also regular bus service to Saudi Arabia. Due to the hot and arid climate, most people drive, even within cities. There are both private taxis and shared taxis, which are typically trucks that travel regular routes and carry up to five people. The fare for a shared taxi is substantially lower than that of a private taxi. Traffic moves on the right-hand side of the road.

Transportation Infrastructure

There is no rail network in Bahrain, and the nation is mostly connected by an extensive road system comprised of nearly 3,500 kilometers (nearly 2,170 miles) of highway. Many European, Middle Eastern, and Asian airlines fly into Bahrain International Airport. Bahrain can also be reached by ferry from Iran.

Media & Communications

Bahrain has a number of daily newspapers, both in Arabic and English. All television stations and radio stations are state-run; a private radio station operated from about 2005–2006, but was shut down by the government. While freedom of the press is guaranteed under the Bahraini constitution, journalists can be charged with vague crimes, such as offending the king that are not easily defined or predicted. Journalists, therefore, may be overly cautious and practice self-censorship. In 2014, CNN reported that Bahrain's king ratified a new law imposing a prison sentence of up to seven years and a fine of up to $26,500 for anyone who publicly insults him.

Mobile phones outnumber landlines in Bahrain (2.3 million compared to 280,000 in 2014). As of 2012, Bahrain had one of the highest Internet penetration rates in the Middle East, and in 2014, there were 1.3 million Internet users, representing nearly 96.5 percent of the population. However, recent reports of government shutdowns of certain websites have led to protests and questions about the issue of government-sanctioned Internet censorship. In recent years, Internet users have even been arrested for online activity.

SOCIAL DEVELOPMENT

Standard of Living

Bahrain ranked 44 out of 187 countries on the 2013 United Nations Human Development Index, which measures quality of life and standard of living indicators.

Water Consumption

Although water is available in Bahrain, mostly from desalination facilities, the country does face challenges related to increasing water demand. Over half of the water used in Bahrain comes from groundwater sources, which are not renewable. The country's growing agricultural sector and continued urbanization are expected to place huge demand on its water resources. Domestic water use and agriculture each account for approximately one-half of total water usage in Bahrain, while the industrial sector accounts for approximately six percent. The government continues to fund the development water conservation and desalination initiatives. Bahrain's water infrastructure is administered by the Bahrain High Council for Water Resources.

Education

Bahrain has made dedicated efforts to improve educational opportunities. Since 2001, school attendance has been compulsory for all children. Public school education is free, and most students learn English in school.

Slightly more females than males are enrolled at all levels, including the universities. In addition, the government provides scholarships for women graduates to pursue postgraduate work in other countries.

Bahrain has two universities: the Arabian Gulf University, founded in 1980 in Manama, and the University of Bahrain, founded in 1986. Bahrain's literacy overall literacy rate was estimated to be 95.7 percent in 2015, one of the highest literacy rates in the Persian Gulf. The government's focus on providing educational opportunities for women is increasing the literacy rate.

Women's Rights

Although the constitution grants women full rights as citizens, Bahrain has been criticized for inadequately protecting women from discrimination and abuse. As recently as 2009, a report from the UN Committee on the Elimination of Discrimination against Women (CEDAW) detailed the kingdom's continued challenges in dealing with women's rights. The report particularly noted that Sunni and Shia Muslims have different laws regarding marriage, divorce, inheritance, and child custody. According to the report, the lack of a unified family law in Bahrain has made it easy for women to be discriminated against in these matters. Furthermore, because cases are judged by religious leaders who base their rulings on the interpretation of Islamic law, the general tendency of these judges is to favor men due to a cultural bias against the equal status of women. CEDAW called upon the Bahrain government to create one set of laws, raise the minimum marriage age to eighteen from fifteen, and put an end to polygamy.

In its report, CEDAW also cited the Bahrain government for its lack of laws that criminalize all forms of violence against women. In particular, they addressed the legal protection of female migrant workers, who are frequently the targets of physical and sexual abuse by employers. The report also addressed human trafficking, citing that a significant number of women are trafficked into the country. Additionally, though women have had the right to vote in Bahrain since 2001, the CEDAW noted the low number of women holding political office—in 2008, women held only nine percent of the high-ranking government positions in Bahrain. And in the parliamentary elections conducted October 23, 2010, only one woman was elected to the State Council versus 39 men. A study conducted by the Higher Council of Women, in cooperation with the United Nations Development Program (2010), noted that the major political organizations did not nominate women candidates. Their chances of success were substantially reduced because most women ran as independents or for less popular parties. The study stated that 19 of the female candidates (95 percent) did not belong to any of the political associations, and only five percent of the women represented mainstream political associations. The CEDAW requested that the government take steps to increase the number of women participating in politics, possibly through the establishment of a quota requiring women candidates from political parties.

Another issue affecting Bahraini women is their inability to transfer citizenship to their children. Currently, if a Bahraini woman marries a non-citizen, any children from the marriage are considered foreigners; thus they do not have the rights of Bahrainis, including access to education, health care, and legal protection. Lastly, numerous organizations also have called upon Bahrain to stop its harassment of women's rights activist Ghada Jamsheer. In 2009, it was reported that Jamsheer, the head of the Women's Petition Committee, has been subject to 24-hour surveillance, threats against herself and her family, and has been banned from the media by the government. In 2006, *Time* magazine designated Jamsheer as one of the "four heroes of freedom in the Arab world" for her activism in transitioning family affairs from Islamic to civil courts.

Health Care

The government of Bahrain provides free medical care. Average annual health expenditure was nearly five percent of the GDP as of 2013. The doctor-patient ratio is approximately one doctor for every 1000 people. Average life expectancy in Bahrain is 78 years, 76 years for men and 80 years for women (2015 estimate).

Major causes of death include circulatory diseases, food poisoning, and injury, cancer, diseases of the metabolic and immune systems, respiratory diseases, digestive diseases, and congenital disorders.

GOVERNMENT

Structure

Anti-government riots in protest of British control in the 1950 and 1960s led to some political reforms in Bahrain. In 1971, Great Britain withdrew from the gulf, and Bahrain became a wholly independent state. It joined the Arab League and the United Nations in 1973. In 2002, the emir proclaimed himself king, and the country became a constitutional monarchy.

The monarch is the chief of state. The prime minister is the head of government. The bicameral legislature consists of the Chamber of Deputies, with forty members directly elected to four-year terms, and the Majlis ash-Shoura (Consultative Council), whose forty members are appointed by the king. The government operates the country's radio and television stations.

During the 1991 Gulf War, Bahrain cooperated with the United States, Great Britain, and Saudi Arabia. During the mid-1990s, the country's Shia Muslims staged demonstrations for free elections and greater employment for Shias.

Political Parties

Political parties are officially forbidden in Bahrain. Instead, political associations or "blocs" exist. Islamist blocs include the Al Asalah Islamic Society, the Al Menbar Islamic Society, and the Al Wefaq (Islamic National Accord Association). Secular political blocs include the Economists Bloc, the National Democratic Action, and the National Justice Movement.

Local Government

Bahrain is divided into twelve administrative municipalities, which are administered from Manama by the Ministry of the Interior. Since 2002, five municipal councils oversee Bahrain's administrative units. Councils are headed by a director general. The director general is appointed by the council's ten elected members. Bahrain's central government maintains tight control of budgetary decisions and development projects.

Judicial System

Bahrain's legal system is based on Islamic law and English common law. The High Civil Appeals Court is the highest court in the land. Both secular and Sharia (Islamic) courts operate in Bahrain. There are both Sunni and Shia divisions of the country's Islamic court system. The highest secular court in Bahrain is the Court of Cassation.

Taxation

Bahrain does not collect a personal income tax. Oil, gas, and petroleum companies operating in Bahrain pay a 46 percent tax of profits, but other corporate taxes are relatively low. These include municipal taxes on property and social security taxes for employees. Businesses operating in Bahrain are prevented by various treaties from being subjected to double taxation. That is, if domestic taxes are collected on profits, they are deductible in Bahrain.

Armed Forces

The Bahrain Defence Force (BDF) consists of the Royal Bahraini Air Force (RBAF), the Royal Bahraini Navy (RBN), the Royal Bahraini Army (RBA), and also the Bahrain Royal Medical Services. The armed forces have received military assistance and training from the US, as well as military training and arms transfers from the United Kingdom, and arms transfers from Oman and Turkey. As of 2009, military personnel numbered approximately 8,200 (with an additional 2,000 in the Coast Guard and National Guard).

Foreign Policy

Bahrain's foreign policy focuses on the country's strategic, economic, and political interests abroad and its continued improved relations with neighboring Arab nations and international groups. Regionally, Bahrain is a member of the Gulf Cooperation Council (GCC), established in 1981 for the purpose of improving the security and economic development among the Gulf States. It also belongs to the League of Arab States, the Organization of the Petroleum Exporting Countries (OPEC), and the Organization of the Islamic Conference (OIC). Internationally, Bahrain holds membership in the UN and its subsidiary branches such as the World Health Organization (WHO). In June 2006, Bahrain was elected as head of the United Nations General Assembly (UNGA).

Bahrain's relationship with Iran, the other big power in the region, is civil, but not close. Bahrain foiled an Iran-supported coup in 1981, and suspects that Iran also played a role in incidents of social unrest in Bahrain in the 1990s. As with all Arab nations, Bahrain is firmly on the side of the Palestinians in the Palestinian-Israeli conflict. Bahrain supports the establishment of an independent Palestinian state, including Jerusalem as its capital. It also agrees that Palestinian refugees should have the right of return and endorses the Palestinian National Authority (PNA) as the legitimate government of the Palestinian people. Bahrain supports a peaceful solution to the Palestinian question, but holds Israel responsible for not committing to the peace process, charging Israel with using aggressive and violent practices. By November 2012, when the United Nations General Assembly voted to upgrade Palestine's status to that of a nonmember observer state, 132 of the 198 members of the United Nations recognized Palestinian statehood. Several more have done so since then.

Other than their disagreement on the Palestinian-Israeli conflict, the United States maintains good relations with Bahrain. The US has had an embassy in Bahrain since 1971 and a Bahrain embassy was established in Washington, DC, in 1977. The US Navy has maintained a base in Bahrain since 1947. In 1991, Bahrain and the US signed a defense cooperation agreement (DCA), and in 2001, the US named Bahrain a major ally of the North Atlantic Treaty Organization (NATO). Furthermore, Bahraini pilots participated in the 1991 Gulf War on the side of the US, and during the 2003 US-led Iraq War, Bahrain allowed the US to use their nation as a base. Bahrain also offered humanitarian and technical support to Iraq during the rebuilding process and has aided the U.S. in terrorism investigations.

Human Rights Profile

International human rights law insists that states respect civil and political rights, and also promote an individual's economic, social and cultural rights. The United Nations (UN) Universal Declaration of Human Rights (UDHR) is recognized as the standard for international human rights. Its authors sought the counsel of the world's great thinkers, philosophers, and religious leaders, and were careful to create a document that reflects the core values shared by every world culture. (To read this document or view the articles relating to cultural human rights, visit http://www.un.org/en/documents/udhr/.)

Bahrain's constitution guarantees liberty, equality, security, education, tranquility, social solidarity, and equal opportunities to all citizens. All citizens have the right to vote, and the constitution states that all citizens have equal rights regardless of race, origin, language, religion, or belief. Furthermore, Bahrainis have freedom of speech, press, and the right to assembly, and the government opposes torture. Overall, the state of Bahrain has a strong human rights record. In 2008, the state's periodic review by the UN Human Rights Council (UNHRC) was approved, the same year Bahrain was elected to a seat on the council. However, many national and international human rights groups accused the review of ignoring numerous abuses and stated that human rights campaigners had themselves been persecuted for trying to draw attention to violations.

Human Rights Watch's 2008 report on Bahrain stated that human rights problems were on the rise. The report cited violations of the rights to expression, assembly, and association. There have been reports of abuse of migrant workers in Bahrain, with the government failing to take adequate action to protect them. Although Shia Muslims make up the majority of the population, the ruling government is Sunni, and they have been accused of suppressing Shia political activists. A 2006 report on Bahrain by the U.S. government also found violations, including various types of discrimination, restrictions on workers' rights, and infringement of privacy. They cited the judicial system for corruption and stated that the government had drawn up election districts to ensure that the reigning Sunni party remained in power.

In 2009, Amnesty International (AI) reported that 13 political activists had been arrested on terrorism charges, were tortured, and then had their "confessions" broadcast on TV. Numerous protests also broke out in early 2009 over the revelation that the government had blocked numerous websites, including those associated with human rights groups and the political opposition. In February 2011, Bahrainis joined the wave of protests sweeping across the Middle East and North Africa in order to call for greater political freedom and changes to the monarchy of King Hamad bin Isa al-Khalifa. Following the protests, however, the government intensified censorship and surveillance of the Internet.

ECONOMY

Overview of the Economy

The economy of Bahrain is mainly driven by the oil industry and finance, though it has grown more economically diverse in recent years as petroleum reserves are depleted. In addition, Bahrain is also considered to have a liberal or free economy for a Middle Eastern state; an almost non-existent taxation structure and very liberal import duties have helped Manama, the capital, to flourish. Manama, due to its strategic location in the Gulf region, is also home to numerous multinational companies, including over 200 financial corporations and banks, many of which are headquartered in the city.

The per capita gross domestic product (GDP) in 2014 was an estimated $51,700 USD. Local oil deposits are largely depleted, and the economy now depends on the refining of imported oil. Bahrain's natural gas reserves and its financial sector have become more important to the economy in recent years.

Another problem that affects the economy is the depletion of underground water. Today, 60 percent of the country's drinking water is provided by desalination plants.

Industry

Before the discovery of oil in 1932, Bahrain's most important industry was pearl diving. At its peak before World War II, the pearl industry was worth more than $1 million USD. The demand for quality Gulf pearls has dropped dramatically since the mid-20th century, however.

Today, Bahrain's major industries include oil refining, shipbuilding and repair, and natural gas. The country also produces fertilizers, smelted aluminum, ammonia, and iron pellets. Offshore banking and financial services are also important to the economy.

Exports of oil products, textiles, clothing, and aluminum generated $22 billion USD in 2014. Most exports go to the United States, Saudi Arabia, and Asia.

Major imports include crude oil, industrial machinery, and chemicals. Some of these are re-exported to other Gulf nations. Bahrain's central location and modern port facilities and warehouses, based in Manama, help the country maintain its position as a major trading center.

Labor

In 2014, Bahrain had an unemployment rate of just over four percent and the labor force totaled 705,000. In 2009 industry accounted for nearly 80 percent of the workforce, followed by the services sector (20 percent). Agriculture employed approximately one percent of the workforce.

Energy/Power/Natural Resources

Bahrain's petroleum reserves are close to depletion and are expected to anchor the country's economy for only another decade or two. Speculation regarding the country's untapped oil reserves remains. Pearls were once abundant in the surrounding waters, but today they are a minor resource, and are harvested mostly by tourists. The country has large natural gas deposits, and plenty of fish in the gulf waters.

Desertification, caused by population pressures and drought and dust storms, is an environmental concern in Bahrain. Oil spills and refinery discharge also contribute to the problem, as they damage the coastline, coral reefs, and sea vegetation.

Fishing

Although agriculture represents only one percent of Bahrain's GDP, fishing remains an important part of the country's culture. In September 2010, the Fisheries and Marine Resources Directorate began installing 15,000 artificial reefs in waters around Bahrain in the effort to rehabilitate fish stocks.

Forestry

Bahrain is a net importer of forest products and has no significant forest-based industry.

Mining/Metals

Petroleum and natural gas represent Bahrain's only economically significant natural resources. The country's oil industry represents approximately 60 percent of government revenues.

Agriculture

Agriculture practiced in Bahrain is mostly for domestic consumption. Less than three percent of the land is arable, and only 50 square kilometers (19 square miles) of farmland are irrigated. Chief agricultural products are dates, tomatoes, cows' milk, and eggs, as well livestock such as sheep, goats, and cattle. Shrimp and fish are harvested in the coastal waters.

Animal Husbandry

Common livestock include sheep, goat, and dairy cattle.

Tourism

More than nine million tourists visited Bahrain in 2013. Since 2010, the country's Culture and Information Ministry has worked to further development infrastructure to support cruise ship tourism.

Bahrain boasts numerous archaeological sites, dating back to the Dilmun culture, and forts dating to the 16th century. Other attractions include hotels, restaurants, nightclubs and the national museum. The Tree of Life is a broad, shady plant standing alone in the middle of 2 kilometers (1.2 miles) of desert. Its source of water is unknown.

The souk, or market, in Manama features many crafts, jewelry and tourist novelties for sale. Ancient tomb mounds are found near A'ali village. The village also boasts the major pottery workshop in the country.

Popular activities for tourists include pearl diving, horseback riding, scuba diving among coral reefs and old shipwrecks, night sea fishing, and golf and tennis.

Kirsten Anderson, Ellen Bailey, Ian Paul

DO YOU KNOW?

- Bahrain has been inhabited so long that some legends identify it as the site of the biblical Garden of Eden (Iraq makes a similar claim).

- Bahrain is home to the "Tree of Life," a 400-year-old mesquite tree that grows isolated in the desert, with no discernable source of water.

- The name Bahrain means "two seas" in Arabic, referring to the water springs beneath the island.

Bibliography

Andrew Hammond, *Popular Culture in the Arab World*. New York: The American University in Cairo Press, 2007.

Gordon Robison and Paul Greenway. *Lonely Planet: Bahrain, Kuwait, & Qatar*. Oakland, CA: Lonely Planet, 2000.

Harriet Crawford. *Dilmun and its Gulf Neighbors*. Cambridge: Cambridge University Press, 1998.

Harriet Crawford and Michael Rice. *Traces of Paradise: The Archaeology of Bahrain 2500 BC to 300 AD*. New York: I.B. Tauris & Co., Ltd., Palgrave Macmillan, 2005.

Harvey Tripp and Margaret Tripp. *Culture Shock! Bahrain: A Survival Guide to Customs and Etiquette*. Singapore: Marshall Cavendish International, 2009.

Miriam Joyce. *Bahrain from the Twentieth Century to the Arab Spring*. New York: Palgrave Macmillan, 2012.

Mitchell Belfer. *Small State, Dangerous Region: A Strategic Assessment of Bahrain*. Frankfurt am Main: Peter Lange, 2014.

Toby Matthiesen. *Sectarian Gulf: Bahrain, Saudi Arabia, and the Arab Spring That Wasn't*. Stanford, CA: Stanford University Press, 2013.

Works Cited

http://74.125.95.132/search?q=cache:gXYnNBVkHUUJ:confinder.richmond.edu/admin/docs/Bahrain.pdf+bahrain+constitution&hl=en&ct=clnk&cd=5&gl=us

http://bahrain.usembassy.gov/event-list2/tom.html

http://bahrainguide.org/content/view/28/84/1/4/

http://bahraini.tv/2006/05/18/qassem-haddad-the-penman-of-manama/

http://books.google.com/books?id=3f901MQK7_UC&pg=PA168&lpg=PA168&dq=Al+Khirniq&source=bl&ots=6xt24C1OFS&sig=wrBSrOARP8Kn18FR87Pddy9wvF4&hl=en&ei=BpCUSdvrL4qhtwfIreysCw&sa=X&oi=book_result&resnum=3&ct=result#PPA169,M1

http://books.google.com/books?id=7jKIOJ4qAxMC&pg=PA107&lpg=PA107&dq=tarafa+poet&source=bl&ots=6TCfGsNU4h&sig=AMkR2zO6dFDReYfkyrnvnPJceNA&hl=en&ei=mIKUSYa7KdW5twfyosmzCw&sa=X&oi=book_result&resnum=3&ct=result#PPA103,M1

http://books.google.com/books?id=W63OCzel54IC&pg=PA60&lpg=PA60&dq=awal+theatre+company&source=web&ots=ZZ-HDlVtqo&sig=V5V02l51xoHn5HxaIU5fajdf_KE&hl=en&ei=rSiXSb3_IoH8tgeboZybCw&sa=X&oi=book_result&resnum=2&ct=result#PPA58,M1

http://elhambahrain.net/category/events/

http://english.bna.bh/?ID=69327

http://globalvoicesonline.org/2008/04/07/bahrain-should-young-girls-wear-hijab/

http://mideastyouth.com/meycast/2006/12/31/podcast-student-life-in-bahrain/

http://news.bbc.co.uk/1/hi/world/middle_east/country_profiles/790690.stm

http://news.bbc.co.uk/1/hi/world/middle_east/country_profiles/790690.stm

http://news.bbc.co.uk/2/hi/middle_east/4229337.stm

http://portal.unesco.org/en/ev.php-URL_ID=38579&URL_DO=DO_TOPIC&URL_SECTION=201.html

http://whc.unesco.org/en/list/1192

http://www.afropop.org/multi/feature/ID/692

http://www.albany.edu/~joris/Tarafa.html

http://www.ameinfo.com/89977.html

http://www.amnesty.org/en/library/asset/MDE11/001/2009/en/299a4618-eef4-11dd-b1bd-6368f1b61c3f/mde110012009en.html

http://www.arabnews.com/?page=9&section=0&article=96525&d=23&m=5&y=2007

http://www.asiarooms.com/travel-guide/bahrain/bahrain-festivals-and-events/index.html

http://www.asiarooms.com/travel-guide/bahrain/bahrain-festivals-and-events/national-day-in-bahrain.html

http://www.asiarooms.com/travel-guide/bahrain/culture-of-bahrain/music-and-dance-in-bahrain.html

http://www.asiarooms.com/travel-guide/bahrain/culture-of-bahrain/music-and-dance-in-bahrain.html

http://www.asiarooms.com/travel-guide/bahrain/how-to-get-in/transportation-in-bahrain.html

http://www.asiarooms.com/travel-guide/bahrain/sightseeing-in-bahrain/index.html

http://www.asiarooms.com/travel-guide/bahrain/sightseeing-in-bahrain/tree-of-life-in-bahrain.html

http://www.asiatour.com/bahrain/e-03attr/eb-att19.htm

http://www.bahartsociety.org.bh/index.html

http://www.bahrain.alloexpat.com/bahrain_information/cuisine_bahrain.php

http://www.bahrain.alloexpat.com/bahrain_information/culture_bahrain.php

http://www.bahrainembassy.org/index.cfm?fuseaction=document.home&id=254

http://www.bahrainembassy.org/index.cfm?fuseaction=document.home&id=300

http://www.bahrainembassy.org/index.cfm?fuseaction=section.home&id=26

http://www.bahrainembassy.org/index.cfm?fuseaction=section.home&id=26

http://www.bahrainexhibitions.com/tourist_attractions.asp

http://www.bahrainguide.org/BG1/architecture.html

http://www.bahrainguide.org/BG1/architecture.html

http://www.bahrainrights.org/en/node/1630

http://www.bahrainrights.org/en/node/2173

http://www.bahrainrights.org/en/node/2215

http://www.bahrainrights.org/en/node/2539

http://www.bahrainrights.org/en/node/2685

http://www.bahrainrights.org/en/node/2685

http://www.bahrainrights.org/en/node/2757

http://www.bahraintourism.com/default.asp?action=article&ID=32

http://www.bahraintourism.com/default.
asp?action=article&id=589

http://www.bahraintourism.com/default.
asp?action=category&id=35

http://www.bbc.co.uk/dna/h2g2/A1067780

http://www.berliner-kuenstlerprogramm.de/en/gast.
php?id=1092

http://www.chroniclesofchaos.com/articles/rants/6-988_
desert_demons_-_part_i.aspx

http://www.cp-pc.ca/english/bahrain/

http://www.culturecrossing.net/basics_business_student_
details.php?Id=7&CID=17

http://www.globalsecurity.org/military/world/gulf/gcc.htm

http://www.gulfnews.com/news/gulf/bahrain/10219488.
html

http://www.gulfnews.com/news/gulf/bahrain/10219488.
html

http://www.info.gov.bh/en/CultureNationalHeritage/
ArchaeologyHeritage/ArchiologicalandHistoricalSites/
TheSiteofBahrainFort/

http://www.info.gov.bh/en/CultureNationalHeritage/
ArchaeologyHeritage/ArchiologicalandHistoricalSites/
TheDilmunianCityinSaar/

http://www.info.gov.bh/en/CultureNationalHeritage/
ArchaeologyHeritage/ArchiologicalandHistoricalSites/
SaarTemple/

http://www.info.gov.bh/en/CultureNationalHeritage/
ArchaeologyHeritage/ArchiologicalandHistoricalSites/
AradFort/

http://www.info.gov.bh/en/CultureNationalHeritage/
CultureandArts/CultureAffairs/JointPublishing/

http://www.info.gov.bh/en/KingdomofBahrain/
BahrainHistory/

http://www.infoplease.com/ipa/A0107313.html

http://www.islamonline.net/English/In_Depth/hijab_
campaign/articles/images/Hijab%20Day%20Report%20
Bahrain.pdf

http://www.kwintessential.co.uk/resources/global-etiquette/
bahrain-country-profile.html

http://www.lonelyplanet.com/bahrain/transport/getting-
around

http://www.middleeastevents.com/site/pres_dtls.
asp?pid=2658

http://www.mofa.gov.bh/mofa/en/foreignpolicy.htm

http://www.newarabia.net/Al_Jasrah_House.php

http://www.quixotiq.bravehost.com/

http://www.raqs.co.nz/me/instruments.html

http://www.state.gov/g/drl/rls/hrrpt/2005/61686.htm

http://www.state.gov/r/pa/ei/bgn/26414.htm

http://www.state.gov/r/pa/ei/bgn/26414.htm

http://www.swyaa.org/Handbook/EatingStyle/EatingStyle.
html

http://www.thehindu.com/mag/2006/07/16/
stories/2006071600260500.htm

http://www.worldtravelguide.net/country/25/entertainment/
Middle-East/Bahrain.html

https://www.cia.gov/library/publications/the-world-
factbook/geos/ba.html

The Temple of Rameses II in the village of Abu Simbel, Egypt

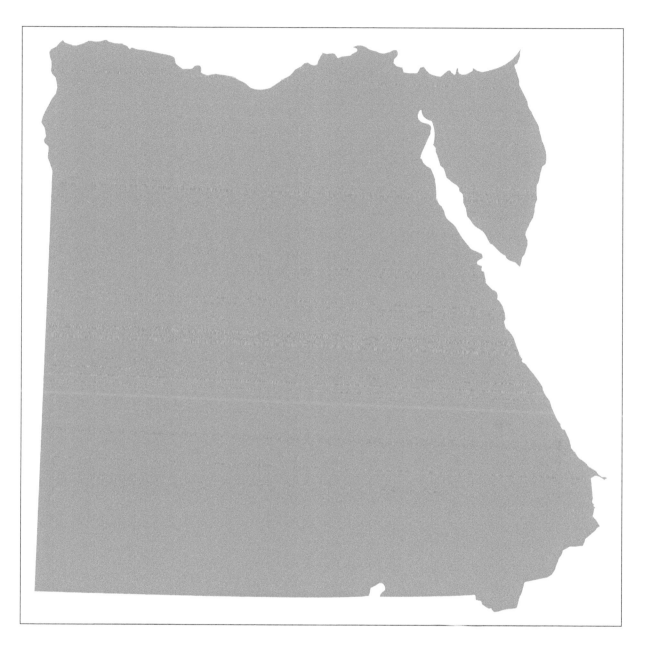

Introduction

The North African country of Egypt, formally the Arab Republic of Egypt, has played a key role in Western civilization since the beginning of recorded history. Once a pre-Christian cradle of civilization, Egypt would develop diplomatic and trade relations with the Roman Empire. The Ottoman Turks invaded in the 16th century. Following World War II, Egypt reasserted its independence, breaking away from Great Britain in 1922. During the late 20th and early 21st centuries, it has been an influential player in the complex world of Middle East politics.

Egypt is bordered by Sudan to the south, Libya to the west, the Mediterranean Sea to the north, and by Israel and the Red Sea to the east. The capital of Egypt, Cairo, or Al-Qahirah ("The Triumphant") as it is officially known, is both the most populous city in Africa and the Islamic world's largest city. Like Egypt itself, Cairo is known for incorporating elements of traditional and modern, and Western and Eastern culture.

In recent years, Egypt has been wracked by political turmoil; beginning with massive protests against the government of Hosni Mubarek in 2011—part of the region-wide Arab Spring. After Mubarek stepped down, a government sympathetic to the Islamist cause of the Muslim Brotherhood was voted in. In 2013, however, amid massive protests, that government, headed by Mohammad Morsi, was overthrown in a military coup. The leader of the coup, General Abdel Fattah el-Sisi, ruled with a strong hand, in the manner of Mubarek. Nevertheless, Sisi was elected president in 2014.

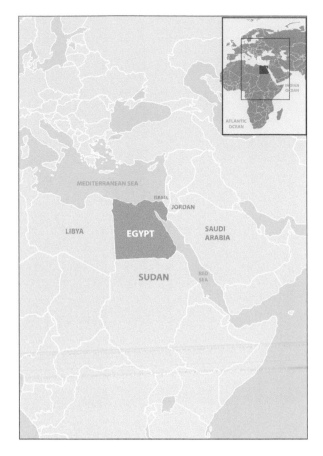

GENERAL INFORMATION

Official Language: Arabic
Population: 88,487,396 (July 2015 estimate)
Currency: Egyptian pound
Coins: The Egyptian pound is subdivided into 100 piastres. Coins come in denominations of 5, 10, 20, 25, and 50 piastres, as well as 1 pound.

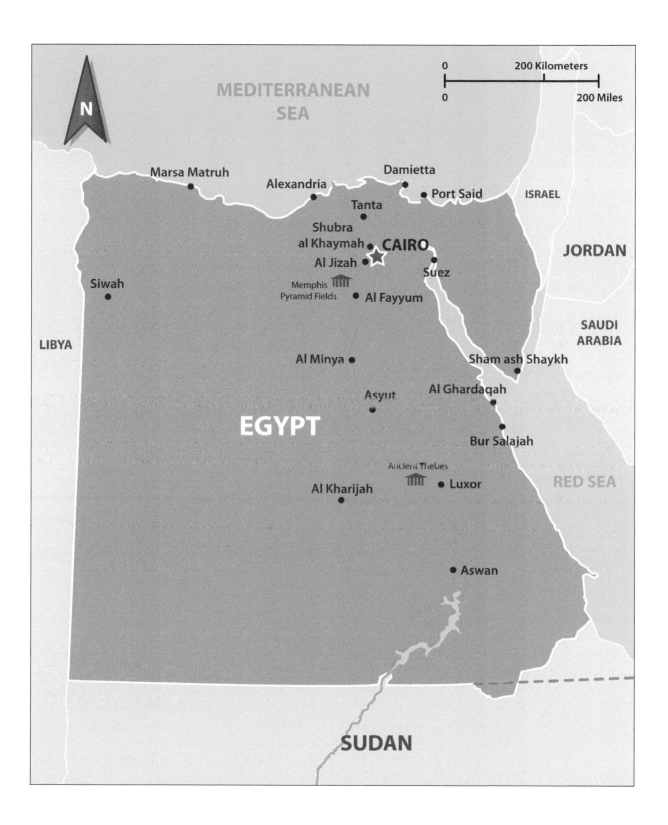

Principal Cities by Population (2012):

- Cairo (8.3 million)
- Greater Cairo (10.6 million)
- Alexandria (4.5 million)
- Giza (6.6 million)
- Shubra al-Khayma (1.1 million)
- Port Said (625,958)
- Suez (565,716)
- Luxor (506,588)
- El Mansura (495,630)
- Dakahlla (450,200)
- Al-Mahallah al-Kubra (465,278)
- Tanta (445,560)
- Asyut (389,000)

Land Area: 995,450 square kilometers (384,345 square miles)

Water Area: 6,000 square kilometers (2,316 square miles)

National Anthem: "Bilady, Bilady, Bilady" (Arabic, "My Homeland, My Homeland, My Homeland")

Time Zone: GMT +3

Flag Description: The flag of Egypt features three equally sized horizontal bands of color: red (top), white (center), and black (bottom). In the center of the white band is a gold eagle, known as the Eagle of Saladin, which holds in its talons a scroll on which the country's name appears in Arabic.

Population

Approximately 99 percent of Egypt's population lives in or near the following areas: the cities of Cairo and Alexandria, the Nile River valley, the Nile River Delta, and the Suez Canal. Roughly, 43 percent of the population lives in urban areas. The largest city is the capital, Cairo. Cairo is one of the world's most densely populated cities. The second largest city is Alexandria, which also serves as the country's main port. Another large city, Giza, is an industrial hub. The cities of Port Said and Suez lie on opposite ends of the Suez Canal.

A large part of the Egyptian population (roughly 3.4 million as of 2013) lives abroad, most often in nearby Arab countries. Saudi Arabia was home to the greatest number of Egyptian immigrants of any country in the world, at an estimated 1.3 million. There is also a small Bedouin population that lives in the desert, working as nomadic herders. Egyptians who migrate to other Arab countries tend to stay only on a temporary basis, as they are unlikely to gain citizenship in these countries.

Languages

Though the official language is Arabic, most people in the educated classes can also speak English and French.

Native People & Ethnic Groups

The majority of current Egyptian citizens are a mixture of the pre-Muslim population of ancient Egypt and the descendents of the Arabic population that took over the country in the seventh century. Because of their distinct heritage, Egyptian residents of the Nile Valley look physically different from their Mediterranean neighbors. They have darker skin and are generally stockier.

The Eastern Hamitic ethnic group, comprised of Egyptians, Bedouins, and Berbers, accounts for just over 99 percent of Egypt's population. The remaining minority includes people of Greek, Nubian, Armenian, and other European descent. In Lower Egypt, there are still remnants of the Greek, Roman, and Turkish populations that occupied Egypt throughout history. Although they are a minority in Egypt, Coptic Christians represent the largest Christian group in the Middle East. Reliable estimates are difficult to find, but as of 2015, the Egyptian government estimates about 5 million Copts – while the Coptic Orthodox Church says the number is significantly greater, somewhere between 15 and 18 million.

Egypt's Coptic Christian minority is also a target of the Islamic State of Iraq and the Levant (ISIL), an extremist militant group and self-proclaimed Islamic state and caliphate led by Sunni Arabs. In February 2015, ISIL released a propaganda video in which it showed the beheading of more than a dozen members of Egypt's Coptic Christians.

Religions

Roughly, 90 percent of the population is Muslim; the majority of Muslims in Egypt belong to the Sunni denomination. Between eight and 11 percent of the population are Coptic Christians. There are a handful of Christians from other denominations, such as Greek Orthodox and various Protestant groups. There is also a small Jewish population that continues to dwindle; only a few dozen Egyptian Jews remain today.

Climate

Egypt has a hot season and a cool season. The hot season lasts from May until September, and the cool season lasts from November to March. These can change slightly depending upon the winds blowing from the north. At the coast, temperatures tend to remain cooler but more consistent, ranging from 14° to 37° Celsius (57° to 99° Fahrenheit).

The temperatures in the desert fluctuate dramatically during the course of a day, reaching as high as 45.6° Celsius (114° Fahrenheit) and dipping as low as 5.6° Celsius (42° Fahrenheit) at night. In the winter, the desert temperature has been known to fall as low as freezing during the night.

Precipitation levels also fluctuate throughout the country. At the Mediterranean coast, the country's most humid region, there can be as much as 200 millimeters (eight inches) of rainfall per year, while in the south there can be as little as 25 millimeters (one inch). It is also possible for certain desert regions to receive no rain all year long.

ENVIRONMENT & GEOGRAPHY

Topography

Though the Nile River Valley was the cradle of ancient Egyptian civilization, approximately 90 percent of present-day Egypt is desert. Less than 10 percent of its land is cultivated or settled. Its population is concentrated in the river's valley and delta.

The Nile River flows northward through Egypt from Sudan and into the Mediterranean. Between Sudan and Cairo, the river flows through a river valley that is lined with cliffs. Above Cairo is the delta, a fertile flood plain of silt that leads to a series of lakes and the Mediterranean coast.

The Libyan Desert, which is part of the Sahara and includes the Great Sand Sea, is in the west of the country. In the east of Egypt, there is the Arabian Desert, which borders the Red Sea and the Gulf of Suez. The country's lowest point is in the Qattarah Depression, which is 18,100 square kilometers (6,990 square miles) in area and 133 meters (436 feet) below sea level.

In contrast, the Arabian Desert lies atop a plateau that gradually rises through the east from the Nile and peaks at the Red Sea, reaching 2,135 meters (7,000 feet) in height. The Nubian Desert in the south is made up of dunes and plains. Egypt's highest point is Jabal Katrinah on Mount Sinai, which is 2,642 meters (8,668 feet) high.

Plants & Animals

Like the country's population, most of the vegetation in Egypt is found in the Nile River Valley. Common trees include date palms, sycamore, carob, acacia trees, as well as mimosas, myrtles, and cypress trees. The more arid regions support alfa grass and thorn. Papyrus, which once grew on the banks of the Nile, now only grows in the extreme southern edge of the country.

There are only a few indigenous wild animals in Egypt. These include the jackal, the hyena, the desert fox, the boar, and the gazelle. However, there are many more reptiles and birds. In addition to lizards, there are asps, vipers, and crocodiles. Hippopotamus are still found in Egypt, though they aren't as prevalent as they once were. The country's birds include sunbirds, egrets, vultures, hawks, and kites. Egypt's deserts are also home to the scorpion, which is known to get into travelers' clothing or shoes at night.

CUSTOMS & COURTESIES

Greetings

Arabic, the official language of Egypt, is the most commonly used language. There are two types of Arabic spoken in Egypt. "Fusha," or classical Arabic, is used in educational and official settings. "Al Amiya," or colloquial Arabic, is most commonly spoken on the streets. There are also a number of regional dialects and colloquial, or informal, expressions that play a role in local communication.

Divisions among religious and social classes dominate Egypt's social atmosphere. Visitors are advised to follow the lead of the person they are meeting rather than initiating a social greeting. More importantly, in Egyptian culture, as in many Arab cultures, the left hand is used for personal hygiene and is therefore considered unclean. Customs of personal hygiene in Islamic culture are known as the "Qudaahul Haajah" and include strict mention of using the left hand for hygiene and the right hand for greeting and eating.

When greeting, it is common for both men and women to shake hands in Egypt, though the handshakes tend to last longer than in Western culture and are not as firm. Egyptians also tend to make direct eye contact when shaking hands, which is considered a sign of friendly intentions. Among family members and close friends, men and women may kiss members of the same sex on the cheeks while shaking hands. When a man is greeting a woman, it is also customary for the man to bow his head to the woman, and to wait for the woman to extend her hand in greeting before offering his own.

Egyptians often greet each other with the expression "Salam alekum," which means, "Upon you be peace." The traditional response to this greeting, which is common across Egypt, is "Wa alekum es salam," meaning "And peace be with you also." The related greeting "Salam," which is translated as "Peace," is often used to say "Good morning." Greetings such as "Hello" and "Goodbye" are different in Arabic, depending upon whether one is addressing a man, woman or a group of people.

Gestures & Etiquette

Egyptians use a variety of body gestures in communication, but hand gestures are often restricted to the right hand. Showing the palm of the hand is considered offensive to some Egyptians because the palm is traditionally used to ward off evil spirits. While sitting, guests should be careful not to show the soles of their feet, as this is commonly considered offensive. Closeness indicates familiarity in Egypt, though members of the same sex stand closer than in many Western cultures. Standing too close to a member of the opposite sex, however, might be considered offensive. When declining an offer, Egyptians often place their right hand over their heart and bow slightly.

The act of giving, either gratuities or gifts, is known as "baksheesh," and is common in Egypt. Compared to Westerners, Egyptians are far more insistent on receiving gratuities for any service offered. Baksheesh is expected at the end of meals, even in cases where the restaurant adds a gratuity. It is also a common practice when interacting with security guards, hairstylists, and even people who give directions on the street.

In addition, many Egyptians dress conservatively and somewhat formally by Western standards, especially in social circumstances. Despite the hot weather, Egyptians cover most of their skin in normal dress, partially due to the influence of Islam.

Eating/Meals

There are two types of group meals in Egypt; those similar to Western dining with similar utensils and customs, and those where meals are served from communal dishes and guests serve themselves. The right hand is used for eating and reaching for food, and it is considered impolite and unsanitary to reach for food with the left hand. In Arab cultures, leaving a small amount of food on the plate is a sign to the chef that no more food is needed. This differs from Western culture where "cleaning the plate" is often considered a compliment to the chef. It is generally considered complimentary, however, to accept a second helping of food when offered.

Egyptians generally eat three meals a day. Additionally, a light snack with tea in mid-afternoon is commonplace. The largest meal of the day is eaten at midday. The evening meal is generally light and may consist of the leftovers from the midday meal. Egyptians tend to mark special occasions with family feasts. In traditional communal meals, diners sit on the floor around a low wooded table and eat from communal dishes.

Meat is not as common in rural households and certain types of meat, including lamb and beef, are sometimes seen as a symbol of wealth. In addition, dietary restrictions are also maintained depending on religion. Since there are many Islamic sects in Egypt, this may affect the type of food offered and the dining customs.

Visiting

Egyptians appreciate a degree of formality in social settings. It is appropriate to dress modestly for social gatherings and to compliment the hosts. Most Egyptians do not wear shoes inside their houses for sanitary reasons. Therefore, it is generally considered polite to remove ones shoes before entering a house. Though few Egyptians adhere to every Islamic social custom, it is customary to enter a house with the right foot per Islamic tradition. In addition, the custom of offering tea in any social circumstance has a long history in Arab culture. Guests should always accept an offered beverage. However, it is acceptable to refrain from drinking the beverage once accepted.

Gifts are widely given in Egyptian culture, even in casual circumstances. Most gifts are inexpensive and simple, and may include pastries and other candies. While flowers are a common gift in Western culture, they are generally reserved for major events in Egyptian culture, typically as a gift of condolence. It is impolite to open a wrapped gift upon receiving it as this is considered an unpleasant type of social pressure. Gifts should be opened later and a note of thanks should then be sent to the individual who gave the gift.

LIFESTYLE

Family

Egyptian culture can be divided into four groups: Muslims, Coptic Christians, Nubians (a dark-skinned ethnic minority from southern Egypt), and the Bedouin (descended from nomadic tribes). Each group has slightly different traditions regarding family roles. Traditionally, Egyptians have lived in close association to their extended families, often living in the same house with uncles, aunts, cousins, and grandparents. Nepotism is common, and does not have the same negative connotations as in Western society. In addition, individual achievement is often viewed as less important than the well-being of the family. As a whole, urban families more closely resemble Western families than rural families, which tend to follow customs that are more traditional.

Egypt is a patrilineal society, meaning emphasis is placed on a person's paternal heritage. A person's name is generally a new one followed by the given names of their father and paternal grandfather. The paternal nature of Egyptian society has led to large families, as women are often expected to continue having children until at least two sons are born. In traditional Egyptian society, women who only have daughters are sometimes criticized.

Young children are encouraged at an early age to take part in family duties, including farming and herding in rural communities. In many families, uncles, aunts, and grandparents share the responsibility for childcare. Related individuals within a clan may also help each other in times of financial need. This is essential in an agricultural community, where a single poor harvest could leave a family in financial ruin. Egyptian children don't often take part-time jobs outside the home, and instead take on more responsibility in family businesses.

Overpopulation is a major problem in Egypt, and as a result, family planning has become a focus of the government. Family planning initiatives sometimes conflict with religious traditions that encourage large families and discourage birth control. Encouraged by projections indicating that the population will double by the middle of the 21st century, the government invested $80 million (USD) in 2008 to encourage family planning.

Housing

Egypt has a variety of housing alternatives. Simple mud and brick houses have been used in Egypt for centuries and are still common in rural areas due to the scarcity of wood. Modern apartments and houses, often built from concrete and brick, are common in cities.

Home ownership is rare in the low-to-middle social classes, partially because there are few opportunities for mortgage financing. According to a 2015 report from the World Bank, as many as 12 million to 20 million people in Egypt (nearly a quarter of the population) live in informal housing. As such, urban areas are largely characterized by townhouses and apartment buildings. Often, the first floor of a town house is used for a family business.

The Egyptian Parliament passed a mortgage law in 2001 to help middle-income families purchase adequate housing. However, in the four-year period following the establishment of that law, few new mortgages were completed. A lack of affordable building materials also contributes to the housing shortage. In addition, urbanization has outstripped the availability for affordable housing in certain areas. Government estimates indicate that more than 20 million Egyptians are living in inadequate housing.

In 2007, researchers at the Civil & Architectural Department Office of the National Research Centre in Cairo introduced a composite building material made of straw and sand. The material is intended to provide sustainable alternative building materials for the low-cost housing market. In the 1990s, the Egyptian government also began an ambitious plan to cultivate the desert between the major cities in an effort to expand housing and food production. By 2008, the government had "reclaimed" more than 400,000 hectares (1 million acres) of desert between Cairo and Alexandria.

In 2014, the Egyptian government launched a Social Housing Program, which aims to provide a million new housing units, including better homes for low-income families.

Food

Egyptians use a variety of ingredients that are specific to their cuisine. For example, many Egyptians cook with a unique kind of clarified butter, or ghee, called samna baladi. This is made from the milk of a water buffalo and is therefore different in texture and flavor to traditional clarified butter, which is made with domestic cow milk. A stew known as molokheya has been designated by the Ministry of Culture as one of Egypt's national dishes. Molokheya is an herb and the central ingredient in a variety of soups and stews that combine it with other vegetables, dried coriander, and various types of meat including rabbit and chicken.

Examples of Egyptian cuisine also include the shish kabob, in which vegetables and various types of meat are cooked on skewers and then served with pita bread and other side dishes. Some foods common in Egypt have become well known internationally. These include hummus, which is generally made from ground chickpeas, spices and tahini (pureed sesame seeds), and babaganoush, a dip made from blended eggplant and spices. While hummus is a popular dish that is characteristic of Middle Eastern cuisine as a whole, Egyptian hummus is unique due to its use of the spice cumin. Another popular dish in Egypt is kofta, which is a blend of minced beef, onion, milk, and spices served grilled or fried.

Bread, known as aish, and rice are staples of daily meals. Egyptians make extensive use of beans and various types of fowl. Fish and seafood are commonly eaten in the areas along the Red Sea. Egyptian food also encompasses a wide variety of international influences. Modified Greek cuisine is common, as is Lebanese, Persian, and African food.

Life's Milestones

Childbirth in Egypt is commonly accompanied by a celebration, wherein friends and family are invited to the family's house to see the new child and enjoy a feast. The birth of a male child is considered more important than the birth of a female child. Following the birth of a first son, the father will be known by the title "Abu," meaning "Father of" followed by the given name of his son, while the mother will be known by the honorific "Umm," or "Mother of." Upon the birth of a girl, it is often customary for the family to slaughter an animal for the feast, while the birth of a son sometimes warrants the slaughter of two animals. Males are usually circumcised soon after birth in Egypt, a tradition that began in ancient times.

Marriage marks the transition to adulthood in Egyptian culture. Traditionally, women have little freedom in choosing mates and the bride's father and mother, and occasionally a matchmaker, cooperate to choose a spouse. Modern Egyptian women play a more active role in choosing and courting potential spouses. A family will typically spend as much as they can afford on a wedding ceremony, which may include a banquet in addition to the legal ceremony. Marriage ceremonies differ in Muslim as opposed to Coptic Christian families. Marriage among the Bedouin is a major event, with an extended celebration characterized by decorative, draped fabric, music, and folk dancing. In Nubian culture, the marriage ceremony may last for more than ten days of feasting, music, and celebration.

Though Egypt is famous for its ancient funerary traditions, including mummification and elaborate rituals, modern traditions are similar to those practiced in other parts of the world. Funerals are often accompanied by family and community meals and the deceased may be buried or cremated depending on the wishes of the family. Cremation is prohibited, however, in Coptic Christianity and Egyptian Islam. Flowers are considered a gift of condolence in Egypt and are given at funerals or when relatives are ill.

CULTURAL HISTORY

Art & Architecture

As one of the world's oldest civilizations, Egypt has given rise to an entire field of academic study known as Egyptology. This archaeological field focuses on the development of culture in ancient Egypt. Egyptologists study the art, language, literature, history, and religion of ancient Egypt, from its foundations in the fifth millennium BCE to the emergence of foreign domination and influence in the fourth century CE. The period from 3200 to 300 BCE in ancient Egyptian history is known as the Pharaonic period. This refers to the long line of pharaohs that ruled during this time. This particular period encompasses the artistic and architectural themes that have become characteristic of Egyptian culture.

The Pharaonic period is divided into several sub-periods, each of which is known from characteristic developments in sculpture, painting, and architecture. The Predynastic period, from 4000 to 3200 BCE, and the Early Dynastic period, from 3200 to 2850 BCE, marked the emergence of Egypt's rich sculptural tradition. This includes wall reliefs and the use of gold and other metals that were considered sacred. The ancient urban settlement of Hierakonpolis, the capital of Upper Egypt during the Predynastic period, had a large community of artisans. Many artistic artifacts have been unearthed from the remains of the city. Archaeologists working at the site have also found the Narmer Palette, which is one of the oldest known historical documents in existence. It features some of the earliest Egyptian hieroglyphics ever found.

Because lumber is a rare commodity and is generally only available in the Nile Valley, stone was the most important medium for both art and architecture in ancient Egypt. Peasants in ancient Egypt often lived in huts with mud, wood and thatched palm fronds, while palaces and religious monuments were often elaborately decorated with sculpture and inscriptions. During the Middle Kingdom period, from 2040 to 1640 BCE, Egyptian architecture was evolving. This culminated in the creation of elaborate burial tombs for Egypt's rulers, and the colossal pyramids, four-sided structures built for administrative, religious, and ceremonial purposes. One notable temple was the mortuary complex, or tomb, of Mentuhotep II, the first ruler of the

Middle Kingdom. The terraced temple contained architecture unique to that period in Egyptian history.

After the fourth century CE, the Byzantine and Arab kingdoms exerted a strong influence on Egypt. The introduction of Islam in the sixth century had a profound effect on Egyptian art and architecture. In fact, Islamic influence figures prominently in modern Egyptian culture. The major Egyptian cities, Cairo and Alexandria, thrived in the Middle Ages and were among the most culturally and artistically innovative cities in the world, as well as major centers for international trade.

Egypt was part of the Ottoman Empire from the 16th to the late 17th centuries, and Cairo thrived as a commercial port. Architecture in Cairo, which was the capital of Egypt under the Ottomans, began to take on Turkish characteristics. After a short period of French control from 1798 to 1801, Egypt became a British protectorate, and a wave of modernization swept across the country. As the nation neared the 20th century, European style art and architecture was common in Egyptian cities.

During the 20th century, a nationalist movement emerged. This had a profound effect on both politics and the arts in Egypt. The School of Fine Arts, established in 1908 by Prince Yusuf Kamal, was the first Egyptian center for artistic education. Early contemporary art and architecture, known as the Neo-Pharaonic style, reflected a revival of the classical style of Egypt's golden age. Over the century, this gave way to a blend of traditional and modern art more in keeping with Western culture. The "youth generation" of the 1970s and 1980s brought Egyptian art into the mainstream. Located in urban centers like Cairo and Alexandria, artists began exploring modern artistic media, such as installation, performance art, video, and film.

Drama

Egypt's film industry has its roots in the late 19th century, with the first public film shown in 1896. The industry grew rapidly to become one of the largest in the world by the 1920s. The first film produced and directed in Egypt was director Orfi Bengo's silent film *Leila*, which premiered in 1927. The industry continued to grow in the 1930s, driven by the popularity of musical comedies. Cairo's Studio Misr became the premier film studio in Egypt.

The 1940s and 1950s are often known as the "golden age" of Egyptian cinema. During this period, Egypt produced more films than any other nation in the Arab world. Drama became popular in the 1940s as directors and writers began using film to explore social, political, and cultural issues. Actor Omar Sharif, who later became famous in American cinema, and his wife Faten Hamama were among the biggest celebrities in Egypt during the 1950s. The film industry declined in the 1970s and 1980s as fewer films were produced and funding for production decreased dramatically.

A revival of art-house film began in the 1990s. This revival was driven by several, small-scale, film studios that emerged in and around Cairo. The best known of modern Egyptian filmmakers was Youssef Chahine. He had been involved in the film industry since the 1940s, and produced a variety of films that garnered international attention. Many of his best-known works explore the daily lives of average citizens of Cairo.

Music

Music has existed in Egypt since ancient times. Archeological finds such as tomb paintings indicate that music was a part of Egyptian society as early as the fourth millennium BCE. According to hieroglyphics, the musician and singer Chufu'Ankh composed and performed music for the royal court around 2500 BCE. Early instruments, such as clappers and rattles, were more rudimentary in design. As the civilization progressed, so did its music making, with more complex instruments such as harps, flutes, and clarinets being used. Two notable instruments used in Ancient Egypt are the kithara (a type of lyre) and the sistrum (a percussion instrument used in religious ceremonies).

Literature

The history of Egyptian literature begins in the Predynastic period. During this period, writers and intellectuals began inscribing on stone tablets. Later they wrote on papyrus, an early form of paper made from the ground pith, or spongy interior, of the papyrus plant. One of the earliest and most famous Egyptian texts is the *Book of the Dead*. The book explores the concept of death and the afterlife as told in pictures and hieroglyphics on papyrus. Copies of the text were placed in coffins as part of funerary ceremonies.

After Egypt's Dynastic period, Egyptian literature passed through phases that coincided with changes in the political and religious environment. Literary historians recognize a distinct tradition of literature from the Copts, a native sect of Christianity, and a separate tradition among Egyptian Muslims. In the 19th century, European influences became more dominant in Egypt, and native literature began to resemble classics of the European tradition.

In the 20th century, Egypt became the leading center of an artistic renaissance that spread throughout the Arab world. Contemporary Egyptian writers, working in Arabic and other languages, began to produce works in every genre of literature, from poetry and realistic drama to comic books and romance novels. One of the most famous and well-respected Egyptian writers was Naguib Mahfouz who, in 1988, was the first Egyptian to win a Nobel Prize for Literature. Mahfouz's work drove and inspired the modernization of Egyptian literature in the 1950s, and his stories of life in Egypt, particularly Cairo, introduced international audiences to Egyptian culture. He died in 2006.

CULTURE

Arts & Entertainment

The arts play an important role in contemporary Egyptian society, helping to express and explore modern culture in light of the nation's rich history. Themes that have been used for centuries are preserved through sculpture, music and dancing. Cairo is the capital of mainstream arts in Egypt, with venues like the Cairo Opera House highlighting local performance art and music and art imported from around the world. However, the Egyptian government censors art in major venues. As a result, many Egyptian cities have underground art scenes where artists explore themes, such as government control and religious freedom, which would not be acceptable in mainstream circles.

The Egyptian music scene includes two major genres. The first is al jeel, or jeel, which is Egypt's premier form of pop music. Lyrics are generally written in Arabic and varieties of instruments are used from guitar and drums to synthesizers and electronic music. Jeel was the most popular music in the 1970s and has remained one of Egypt's most popular genres. In contrast, shaabi, or sha'abi, is considered the music of the modern Egyptian working class. Using a variety of instruments, from traditional Egyptian stringed instruments to electronic instruments, shaabi is known for its more "grassroots" themes, and use of comedic and social commentary.

Among the traditional arts of Egypt, belly dancing is the best known outside the Arab world. Belly dancing, or "oriental dancing" as it is sometimes known, has its roots in the Pharaonic period. After the arrival of Islam, traditional forms of belly dancing declined due to conservative social mores and government restrictions. In recent years, steps have been taken to preserve belly dancing as part of the nation's artistic heritage. Some modern dance schools have even added belly dancing to their curricula.

Cultural Sites & Landmarks

Most of Egypt's famous landmarks were built during the Pharaonic period, including more than fifty pyramids and numerous temples located on the Nile. This includes the Valley of the Kings, located on the west bank of the Nile, which is the burial site of 62 pharaohs. Images of architecture from the Pharaonic period have become so popular that in 2007, the Egyptian government initiated a program to copyright the images of the pyramids, the famous Sphinx statue, and other symbols. Royalties from the images were expected to help pay for restoration and maintenance of Egypt's historic landmarks.

In Giza, one of the epicenters for ancient archaeology, visitors can see the Sphinx, a 66-foot-high statue of a creature that is part human and part lion. Carved from soft limestone, the statue's history and purpose have remained elusive. Giza also contains the Great Pyramid of Khufu, which is the largest pyramid in existence, built from over 2.3 million stone blocks. The pyramid stands at over 147 meters (481 feet) high and contains three burial chambers. Archaeologists have uncovered artifacts in the pyramid relating to the reign of the pharaoh Khufu, from around 2550 BCE.

Though it is Egypt's most modern city, the city of Cairo itself is a historical site. The oldest portion of Cairo still contains hundreds of cultural landmarks, including Coptic churches, Turkish mosques, and a variety of other museums and historic buildings. The Cairo Opera House is another major attraction in the city. The Khan el-Khalili souk (or bazaar) has been a fixture in the city since the 14th century. Other popular street markets selling spices, perfumes, gold, silver, carpets, brass and copperware, leatherwork, glass, ceramics, fabrics, and musical instruments include Wekala al-Balaq, the Tentmakers Bazaar, Camel Market, and Mohammed Ali Street. In addition, historic Cairo is recognized as a World Heritage Site.

Egypt is also home to Lake Nasser, the largest artificial lake in the world. It occupies an area of over 5,200 square kilometers (2,000 square miles) and is located in a stretch of arid desert in the area known as Nubia. Nubia also has hundreds of ancient churches, temples, and burial sites, including the famous Temple of Rameses, which was discovered in 1817. The temple is famous for its 38-meter (124-foot) statues at the entrance, and is located in the nearby village of Abu Simbel. Though the lake serves as a tourist attraction, environmental disturbance from the creation of the lake has been a concern for native ecologists and conservationists.

Visitors to Egypt often travel to Alexandria, a city with a vast array of landmarks from ancient churches and temples to modern museums and cultural centers. Alexandria offers a more relaxed atmosphere from the metropolitan flavor of Cairo, with quiet riverfront cafes and gardens adding to the city's atmosphere.

Libraries & Museums

The Egyptian Museum in Cairo, the oldest museum in the nation, was established in 1835 under a grant from the Egyptian government. French architect Marcel Dourgnon designed the present neo-classical museum building, built in 1900. The museum contains a wealth of antiquities from the Pharaonic period, from paintings to tools of daily life. The collection of funerary artifacts is renowned in the Egyptology community. The Museum of Fine Art in Alexandria is one of the prime locations for exhibitions of modern and contemporary Egyptian art.

Dar el Kotob is the national library of Egypt and the largest in the country. The library, which is located in Cairo, also serves as the Egyptian National Archives. Its collections include historical manuscripts, some of which date back to the seventh century. The library houses several million printed works, as well as collections of ancient Arabic coins. Other major libraries in Egypt include the Bibliotheca Alexandrina and the library of al-Azhar University.

Holidays

Since Egypt is primarily Muslim, most of the holidays are related to the Islamic religion. The major exception is Revolution Day (July 23), which honors the establishment of the republic.

Major Islamic holidays include Eid-al-Fitr, which signifies the end of Ramadan and includes the giving of alms and feasting. There is also Eid-al-Adha, which is in observance of the Prophet Abraham. This celebration entails the slaughter of a goat or sheep. There is also Muharram, the Muslim New Year.

The Coptic Christian population celebrates Christmas on January 7 because it follows the Julian calendar. The country's Muslims and Christians also celebrate together in various folk festivals throughout the year.

Youth Culture

Although Egyptians are conscious of fashion trends from around the world, social customs also dictate the types of clothing worn by Egyptian youth. In some Islamic families, for instance, girls and young women are expected to wear the "hegab," a scarf used to cover the head and neck. Teenagers are often more adventurous in their choice of color for the hegab, preferring brightly colored or patterned headscarves to the traditional black and brown. Islamic tradition also requires that women cover their shoulders in public. For this reason, long sleeve tees have become popular for Egyptian girls, including a popular style of long sleeve shirts with logos or designs at the bottom of the shirt covering the hips. Clothing for boys is more casual, with jeans and tee shirts widely worn in urban areas.

Football (soccer) is the most popular sport in Egypt, and children of all ages play the sport recreationally. It is also the most important televised sport, and whole families will often gather for important matches in the Africa Cup, or other international events. Most Egyptian schools have soccer teams and both males and females play recreationally in city and rural parks and sometimes in the streets.

Much like the rest of the world, cell phones and email have changed the way Egyptian children communicate. Some Egyptian children also communicate with friends via the Internet and join social networking groups, though this is less common than in the West because fewer Egyptian families have computers. In cities, Internet cafes have emerged, where teenagers often gather and purchase time on a computer to network.

Dating among youth is less involved in Egypt than in Western societies. Mixed groups of boys and girls are less common in Egypt than in the West because of social customs restricting contact between the sexes. Despite a more conservative attitude toward male-female relationships, the average age of marriage in Egypt is around 27 for women, which is similar to that of many European nations.

Teenagers and young adults often gather at coffee shops and cafes after school or work. Though there are some Islamic sects that prohibit dancing, there are clubs and discotheques in Cairo and other cities that are frequented by adolescents and young adults. It is also common for Egyptian families to vacation at the ocean on holidays, and the seaside towns are usually filled with teenagers during school vacations.

Egyptian children are allowed to obtain a special driver's license at age 16, but are only allowed to drive under the supervision of a licensed driver and only within the town or city where the license was issued. At age eighteen, teenagers may apply for a regular driver's license, which allows them to drive on the highway system. The drinking age has been set at twenty-one, and the law is strictly enforced, because underage drinking is prohibited by both religious and legal customs.

SOCIETY

Transportation

Cairo has an extensive public transportation system that includes a network of underground trains, street trams and a public bus system. The Cairo Tram has been running since the 1890s. A similar system in Alexandria has been in continuous operation since the 1860s, making it the oldest train system in Africa. The subway and tram system in Egypt is also known for its reliability and cleanliness.

In addition to trams, buses and trains, Cairo and other cities have a variety of private taxicabs and minibuses available for travel in and around the cities. Many Egyptians own cars and foreign sports cars. Automobile traffic is heavy in Cairo and most streets are crowded, while traffic is somewhat less in Alexandria. There are also ferries that travel along the Nile River and are used for inner city and business travel. In remote rural areas, horses and camels may be the only form of transportation. Traffic moves on the right side of the road.

Transportation Infrastructure

Egypt has 88 airports, including major international hubs in both Cairo and Alexandria. Seventy-two of those airports have paved runways. A federally funded highway system connects all of the cities in the Nile Valley, and there are highways that extend into the deserts and connect the cities to regional villages. The Egyptian National Railways operates a series of trains that can be used to travel from cities to the countryside.

Media & Communications

Egypt's daily newspaper, *Al-Ahram*, is the oldest newspaper in the Arabic world. It is the largest and most-read publication in Egypt, and is read by thousands of international consumers as well. The newspaper is owned by the state, which allows the government to determine what information is suitable for distribution. Government censors also regulate imported publications before they are distributed to the public. There are a number of alternative newspapers and magazines published in Egypt, some privately owned but still subject to censorship.

Egypt's largest media company, the Egyptian Radio and Television Union (ERTU), operates the nation's largest public television and public radio station. Government officials also censor all television and radio broadcasts. Egypt began receiving broadband Internet in 2000 and access has spread from Cairo to other governates, or administrative divisions, in the Nile River Valley. As of 2014, over six million people had landlines, while just over 95 million had mobile phones. Though some Internet providers decide to censor content, Internet access has proven to be a major challenge to censorship laws; there were 42 million Internet users (roughly 48 percent of the population) in 2014.

SOCIAL DEVELOPMENT

Standard of Living

The country ranked 110 on the 2014 United Nations Human Development Index, which measures standard of life indicators. The infant mortality rate is now 21 deaths for every 1,000 live births (2015 est.), and life expectancy is 71 years for men and 76 years for women (2015 estimate). In contrast to the rest of Africa, AIDS affects less than 0.1 percent of the population of Egypt.

Water Consumption

In 2012, 100 percent of Egypt's urban population and 98 percent of its rural were using improved drinking water sources. That same year, 97 percent of its urban population and 94 percent of its rural had access to improved sanitation facilities.

Education

Education in Egypt is free and compulsory for children ages six to fourteen. After completing primary education, students may either study at a technical school, or attend a general intermediate school. This intermediate school prepares them for either university study or one of Egypt's technical/vocational schools.

There are twelve universities in Egypt, the oldest being Al-Azhar University in Cairo. Other universities include the Ayn Shams University and the University of Cairo (both in Cairo), the University of Alexandria, and the American University. In addition to the universities and technical colleges, Egypt also has several institutes for arts and music.

The literacy rate in Egypt is approximately 73.8 percent (2015 estimate). Roughly, 82 percent of the male population is literate, compared to 65 percent of the female population.

Women's Rights

In the 20th and 21st centuries, women have increased both their professional and public presence in Egyptian society. In traditional Egyptian culture, women were regarded as inferior to men. Some Egyptians believe that the roles of men and women are spiritually ordained and that women are only suited for certain types of employment. Though women professionals are now more common, they lack government support to promote equity in pay, employment, education, and legal protection. Compared to western nations, Egypt has relatively low levels of females in the workforce.

Though the Egyptian penal code prohibits spousal abuse, police often do not aggressively investigate domestic abuse. There are also substantial inequities present in the body of the penal code. For example, the sentence for murdering an adulterous spouse is set at three or more years in prison for men and lifetime imprisonment for women. Laws regarding marriage and inheritance are also heavily slanted in favor of men. Traditional Islamic law gives men the right to marry more than one spouse. Women are permitted to divorce their husbands after learning that the husband has taken a second spouse, but many have criticized the divorce process as overly complex.

Female circumcision, a procedure in which a woman's clitoris is removed, is a traditional practice in Egyptian culture. The practice is intended to "maintain female chastity" by reducing sex drive, but many international agencies believe that the process is cruel and unnecessary, and often refer to it as "female genital mutilation." The practice is generally performed around the time of puberty. Egypt passed a law prohibiting female circumcision in 1996, but it was not widely enforced, and exceptions were allowed in some cases. In 2007, the government instituted a new ban prohibiting all forms of female genital alteration. The ban came after the death of a twelve-year-old girl following a failed procedure. In 2013, a 13-year-old girl died after her doctor and father subjected her to female circumcision. Despite the ban, over 90 percent of Egyptian women under 50 have experienced the practice, according to government statistics.

Health Care

Since the 1960s, there has been a concerted effort by the Ministry of Health to improve the overall health of Egypt's population. The lack of resources in rural and the spread of communicable diseases have made this task difficult. Recently, the government has tried to coordinate health services with village councils, and has been successful in ridding the country of cholera, malaria, and smallpox. However, bilharzia, a disease caused by parasitic worms, still affects Egypt.

GOVERNMENT

Structure

Egypt is a republic with universal suffrage for citizens over 18 years of age. Suffrage is also compulsory, unlike most Western countries. The executive branch of the government consists of a president, a prime minister, and a cabinet. According to the constitution, the president is elected every six years. He is first nominated by the People's Assembly, which is one of Egypt's two legislative bodies, and is then voted in by a national referendum. The elected president then appoints a prime minister and a cabinet. Egypt's Hosni Mubarak retained the office of president for over twenty-years. In the 2014 elections, Abdel Fattah el-Sisi became president by popular vote, after Egypt's first freely elected preside–Mohamed Morsi–was removed from power in a popular military coup involving mass demonstrations against the former Muslim Brotherhood leader.

Egypt has a bicameral legislative body comprised of the People's Assembly, or Majlis al-Sha'b, and the Advisory Council, or Majlis al-Shura. The People's Assembly is the largest body, and its members are elected to five-year terms. There are 454 seats in the Assembly, 444 of which are elected by popular vote, and 10 of which are appointed by the president. The Advisory Council has 264 seats, 176 of which are selected by popular vote, and 88 of which are appointed by the president. Its members serve for six years.

Political Parties

Active political parties in Egypt include the Democratic Alliance for Egypt, the Alliance for Egypt, the New Wafd Party, and the Egyptian Bloc. The government must approve all political parties. Professional organizations and trade unions are usually approved, but religious parties are illegal. The Muslim Brotherhood, a party that espouses Islamic law, was banned in Egypt in

1954; however, the party was permitted to campaign in the 2005 elections, with its candidates running as independents. The Brotherhood party was banned again in 2013 after the Egyptian government declared it a terrorist organization. According to a CNN report in 2014, most of the group's leadership was either in jail, in hiding, or taking refuge outside Egypt.

In the 2012 elections, the Democratic Alliance for Egypt took 235 seats; the Alliance for Egypt took 123; the New Wafd Party won 38, and the Egyptian Bloc took 35. Other parties that won seats in the 2012 elections included Al-Wasat, Reform and Development Party, The Revolution Continues Alliance, the National Party of Egypt, the Egyptian Citizen Party, and the Freedom Party. Independents also took 21 seats.

Local Government

Egypt's local government comprises 28 governorates, each of which is headed by a governor and an executive council (which is appointed by the president), as well as an elected council (which has less power than the executive council). The country is further subdivided into 126 administrative districts, which are run by executive and elected councils, and further into 4,500 village municipalities and 199 town municipalities. Municipalities are governed by executive councils as well as elected councils, with the executive councils having more power.

Judicial System

The legal system is based on three factors: English common law, Muslim common law, and Napoleonic codes. The court system includes criminal courts (including primary courts, appeals courts, and the Court of Cassation), as well as administrative courts, civil courts, and a Supreme Constitutional Court. Judges are appointed by the president, under the advisement of the Higher Judicial Council.

Taxation

Taxes levied in Egypt include an income tax, corporate tax, goods and services tax (GST), capital gains tax, and export tax. As of 2013, the top corporate and personal tax rates were both 25 percent.

Armed Forces

The Egyptian Armed Forces comprise an army, navy, air force, and air defense command. The military is considered Egypt's most powerful government entity, operating like a state within a state. As of 2013, the country had approximately 460,000 active military personnel. In 2013, the BCC reported that military-owned industries accounted for around 8 to 40 percent of Egypt's gross national product.

Foreign Policy

Egypt's strategic position between the Mediterranean Sea and the Indian Ocean has historically made it a target for nations seeking a military advantage in the region. After a long series of foreign occupation, Egypt has forged functional and mutually beneficial relationships with most of its African neighbors. As a nation that blends African, Islamic, and Western influences, Egypt has maintained a position both within and outside of the conflict that existed in each of those spheres.

Relations with the Sudan have been strained due to a conflict over ownership of the Hala'ib Triangle, a small area of land on the coast of the Red Sea that became the property of Egypt in 1899. For decades, both nations maintained a permanent military presence there. In the 1990s, Sudan withdrew its troops from the triangle and Egypt has since spent a considerable amount of money to develop the area.

In the late 1970s, Egyptian President Anwar Sadat pledged that Egypt would recognize the Israeli state and work to form a lasting peace with its government. Egypt was expelled from the Arab League in 1979 for agreeing to recognize Israel's independence, but was readmitted to the league in 1989. As the Israeli-Palestine conflict continued, Egypt's leadership played an important role in peace negotiations. President Hosni Mubarak, who ascended to the presidency in 1981, hosted a series of negotiations with the United Nations (UN), Israel, and the Palestinians.

In an effort to maintain strategic access to the Middle East, the United States began supplying military aid to Egypt in 1979. Following the terrorist attacks of September 11, 2001, Egypt supported U.S. President George W. Bush and other allied nations in their "war on terror," but refused to send troops to Afghanistan or Iraq during or following the U.S.-led invasions. Egypt cited concerns that military instability would spread throughout the Middle East and that the resulting conflict would disrupt oil production. The U.S. discontinued military aid to Egypt in 2003, but began providing U.S. military support again to help in the fight against Foreign Terrorist Organizations, namely ISIS/ISIL; military support included the delivery of U.S.-made Apache helicopters.

Egypt is America's key partner on shared goals for stability throughout the Middle East. As coalition partners against ISIS, Egypt is working with the United States to provide intelligence and cut off sources of terrorist funding and recruitment. Egypt is ranked 10th among the international contributors to peacekeeping operations key to international stability The US is also Egypt's largest single trading partner, with volume reaching $6.8 billion in 2013. In 2014, US Treasury Secretary Jack Lew travelled to Egypt and announced a $200 million package to support Egypt's economy.

Egypt has maintained peaceful and economically productive relations with Europe since the end of World War II and is a major participant in the European Union's (EU) Euro-Mediterranean partnership. A majority of Egyptian trade is through the EU, with Italy, France and the United Kingdom (UK) being three of the nation's major trading partners.

Human Rights Profile

International human rights law insists that states respect civil and political rights, and promote an individual's economic, social, and cultural rights. The United Nations (UN) Universal Declaration of Human Rights (UDHR) is recognized as the standard for international human rights. Its authors sought the counsel of the world's great thinkers, philosophers, and religious leaders, and were careful to create a document that reflects the core values shared by every world culture. (To read this document or view the articles relating to cultural human rights, visit www.un.org/en/documents/udhr/.)

Egypt has not been in full compliance with Article 2 of the Universal Declaration of Human Rights. International monitoring organizations, such as Amnesty International, have alleged that the Egyptian government may persecute citizens based on sexual orientation and gender. Laws in the penal code recommend different punishments, for instance, depending on whether the offender is male or female.

Though Egypt's penal code prohibits torture as described in Article 5 of the UDHR, and prohibits detention as described in Article 9, some monitoring organizations have accused the Egyptian government of detaining and torturing political prisoners. The government has also been accused of failing to protect the legal rights of detainees, in terms of guaranteeing a fair public hearing as described in Article 10.

According to Article 18 of the UDHR, individuals will be allowed freedom of thought and religion. However, Islam is predominant in Egyptian culture, and religions that are seen as contradictory to Islam are prohibited in public, including the Baha'i faith, a sect of Islam that is not accepted by mainstream Islamic leaders. Egypt also uses the Islamic holy law, known as Sharia, as the basis for many of its laws. In addition, Egypt does not recognize the right of its citizens to convert from Islam to any other religion. Sharia also limits freedom of expression in that, according to Islamic law, individuals are not permitted to criticize openly Islam or its principles.

Monitoring agencies have also accused the Egyptian government of violating Article 21, in that the Egyptian political process has been plagued by corruption, fraud, and intimidation, depriving citizens of their right to adequate representation. Among the most serious concerns are allegations that the government has censored media from reporting on candidates associated with the leading political party. In 2008, municipal elections were postponed and, during the lead up to the elections, monitoring agencies reported that some candidates had been arrested and detained to prevent them from participating in the elections. Egypt held its first multi-party presidential election in 2005, but some monitoring agencies suspected that the process was flawed.

ECONOMY

Overview of the Economy

In 2014, the gross domestic product (GDP) of Egypt was $286.4 billion (USD), and the per capita GDP was $10,900 that same year. Egypt's economy is dominated by its services industry, which generates 46.5 percent of the country's income. Roughly, 14 percent comes from agriculture, and nearly 39 percent comes from industry, which includes the production of textiles, food, cement, and metals.

According to a 2015 report from the World Bank, construction makes up roughly five percent of Egypt's GDP, while real estate represents another three present, contributing to about 12.5 percent of economic growth and 7 percent of jobs. The report also states that construction and housing are among the largest, most labor intensive job sectors in Egypt; they made up close to 12 percent of total employment by the end of 2012 (about 2.8 million employees).

Since 1961, Egypt has become more socialized, with the government controlling trade and the banking and insurance industries. The country has chronic problems with its debt and its trade deficit. A future and potentially successful export that could help the country's economy is natural gas.

Industry

Industry employs roughly 39 percent of the country's labor force (2014). Egypt was initially held back from industrialization by Great Britain, which wanted to retain the country as a market for its own goods rather than as a producer. Eventually, upon gaining its independence after World War I, Egypt began its own industrial

revolution. After overthrowing the monarchy in 1952, industrialization grew rapidly. Significant industries include textiles, tourism, pharmaceuticals, food processing, and construction.

Labor

The labor force comprised 28.26 million workers in 2014. The unemployment rate that same year was 13.4 percent.

Energy/Power/Natural Resources

Egypt's most notable recently developed natural resource is petroleum, which the government has been trying to exploit over the past thirty years. It has been found in the coastal region of the Red Sea, as well as in Al-Alamayn on the Mediterranean, and on Mount Sinai.

The country also has supplies of gold and red granite, as well as coal, phosphates, iron, lead, titanium, and salt. To compliment its burgeoning petroleum industry, a petroleum pipeline has been built from the Gulf of Suez to the Mediterranean Sea.

Fishing

Fishing remains a relatively minor segment of the Egyptian economy; however, domestic fish production is significant in that it contributes to domestic food demand and employs over 65,000 fishermen and an additional 300,000 workers in related industries (such as food processing). Common species include tilapia, perch, catfish, snapper, mackerel, and cuttlefish.

Forestry

Egypt has virtually no naturally occurring forests. In the early 21st century, however, the country has approximately 72,000 hectares (177,915 acres) of plantation forests. Governorates with plantation forests include Ismailia, Luxor, Giza, and Menoufia, among others. Common tree species being planted include the African mahogany and eucalyptus.

Mining/Metals

Mining is a relatively minor industry in Egypt, yet the country's mineral resources are significant.

Common minerals include coal, tantalite, gold, aluminum, iron, magnesium, nitrogen, and tin. The mining industry is expected to grow in the early 21st century.

Agriculture

Approximately 29 percent of the workforce (2014 estimate) is engaged in agriculture. Egypt's agricultural products include cotton, rice, wheat, beans, corn, and vegetables. Even though the government has tried to reclaim arid land through the use of irrigation and fertilizers, Egypt's farmland is still some of the most productive in the world in terms of yield. It produced approximately 324,000 metric tons of long-staple cotton in the 1990s.

Animal Husbandry

The country's farmers produce a variety of livestock, including cattle, water buffalo, sheep, and goats.

Tourism

Because of Egypt's history and its status as a homeland for many of the world's major cultures, the country is an important destination for Christians and Muslims. In addition to its historical and religious significance, Egypt's modern cities are also attractive for entertainment that is more contemporary. Tourists can take a cruise down the Nile or scuba dive in the Red Sea. In 2006–2007, approximately 10 million tourists entered Egypt, bringing in $8 billion (USD) in revenue. Over 80 percent of those tourists hailed from Europe, more specifically Great Britain, and Russia.

However, due to extreme terrorist groups like ISIS, Egypt's tourist arrivals have been far lower than in previous years. In 2013, the World Economic Forum declared Egypt one of the most dangerous places on earth for tourists, putting the country above both Yemen and Pakistan in terms of risks for visitors. The Egyptian government is trying to lure back foreign investment, after tourists have been driven away by years of political turmoil. ISIS has also tried to attack two of Egypt's most popular tourist destinations including the pyramids and the Karnak temple in Luxor, and have bombed the Italian Consulate in Cairo.

Micah Issitt, Barrett Hathcock, Alex K. Rich

DO YOU KNOW?

- One of Egypt's universities, the Al-Azhar University in Cairo, was founded in 970 as a center for Islamic study, making it the oldest continuously running university in the world.

- The Nile River Valley, where the overwhelming majority of the population lives, is actually only about 4 percent of the actual area of Egypt's land. In total, Egypt's land area is roughly three times the size of the American state of New Mexico.

Bibliography

Afaf Lutfi al-Sayyid Marsot. *A History of Egypt: From the Arab Conquest to the Present.* New York: Cambridge University Press, 2007.

Anthony Sattin, et al. *Egypt.* Oakland, CA: Lonely Planet Press, 2015.

Arthur Goldshmidt, Jr. *Modern Egypt: The Formation of a Nation State.* New York: Westview Press, 2004.

Christine Hobson. *World of the Pharaohs.* New York: Thames & Hudson, 1990.

Claire E. Francy. *Cairo: The Practical Guide.* New York: American University in Cairo Press, 2006.

Harry Ades. *A Traveller's History of Egypt.* Northampton, MA: Interlink Books, 2006.

Ian Shaw, *The Oxford History of Ancient Egypt.* New York: Oxford University Press, 2004.

Jailan Zayan. *Egypt—Culture Smart! The Essential Guide to Customs and Culture.* London: Kuperard, 2013.

Maulana Karenga. *Maat, the Moral Idea in Ancient Egypt.* New York: Routledge University Press, 2003.

Max Rodenbeck. *Cairo: The City Victorious.* New York: Vintage Books, 2000.

Tarke Osman. *Egypt on the Brink: From Nasser to the Muslim Brotherhood.* New Haven, CT: Yale University Press, 2013.

Thanassis Cambanis. *Once Upon a Revolution: An Egyptian Story.* New York: Simon and Schuster, 2015.

Works Cited

"A Sum of Concerns." *Al-Ahram Weekly Online.* http://weekly.ahram.org.eg/2008/898/eg7.htm

"Background Note: Egypt." *U.S. Department of State Online.* http://www.state.gov/r/pa/ei/bgn/5309.htm

"Central Agency for Public Mobilisation and Statistics." *Arab Republic of Egypt Online.* http://www.capmas.gov.eg/eng_ver/nashratE.htm

"City Population: Singapore." *City Population Online.* http://www.citypopulation.de/Egypt.html

"Country Report on Human Rights Practices." *U.S. Department of State Online.* http://www.state.gov/p/nea/ci/81997.htm

"CNN report." http://www.cnn.com/2014/05/23/world/africa/egypt-presidential-election-explainer/

"Egypt Cultural Profile." *Cultural Profiles Project Online.* http://www.cp-pc.ca/english/egypt/index.html

"Egypt." *CIA World Factbook Online.* https://www.cia.gov/library/publications/the-world-factbook/geos/eg.html#Intro

"Egypt: International Religious Freedom Report." *U.S. Department of State Online.* http://www.state.gov/g/drl/rls/irf/2007/90209.htm

"Egypt: Overview." *Lonely Planet Travel Guides Online.* http://www.lonelyplanet.com/worldguide/egypt/

"Egyptian Government Services Portal." *Republic of Egypt Official Site.* http://www.egypt.gov.eg/english/

"Egyptian Center for Culture and Art Online." http://www.egyptmusic.org/

"Egyptian Museum Official Site." http://www.egyptianmuseum.gov.eg/news.asp

Ellen Knickmeyer. "Egypt"s President Urges Family Planning." *Washington Post* Online. June 11, 2008. http://www.washingtonpost.com/wp-dyn/content/story/2008/06/10/ST2008061002696.html

http://www.bbc.com/news/world-middle-east-29735574

http://www.cnn.com/2013/05/23/travel/egypt-tourism/

http://www.cnn.com/2014/05/23/world/africa/egypt-presidential-election-explainer/

http://www.cnn.com/2015/02/15/middleeast/isis-video-beheadings-christians/

http://www.egyptembassy.net/egypt-us-relations/

http://www.pkf.com/media/1954356/egypt%20pkf%20tax%20guide%202013.pdf

http://www.worldbank.org/en/news/feature/2015/05/04/opening-up-housing-to-egypt-s-poorest

"Life in Modern Cairo." *Middle East Network Information Center Online.* http://menic.utexas.edu/cairo/modern/life/life.html

"Music in Ancient Egypt." *University of Michigan Online.* http://www.umich.edu/~kelseydb/Exhibits/MIRE/Introduction/AncientEgypt/AncientEgypt.html

Samir Farid. "An Egyptian Story." *Al-Ahram Weekly Online.* http://weekly.ahram.org.eg/2006/821/cu4.htm

Sharp, Jeremy M. "Egypt: Background and U.S. Relations." *U.S. Department of State Online.* fpc.state.gov/documents/organization/84928.pdf

"The Art of Ancient Egypt A Web Resource." *The Metropolitan Museum of Art.* http://www.metmuseum.org/explore/newegypt/htm/a_index.htm

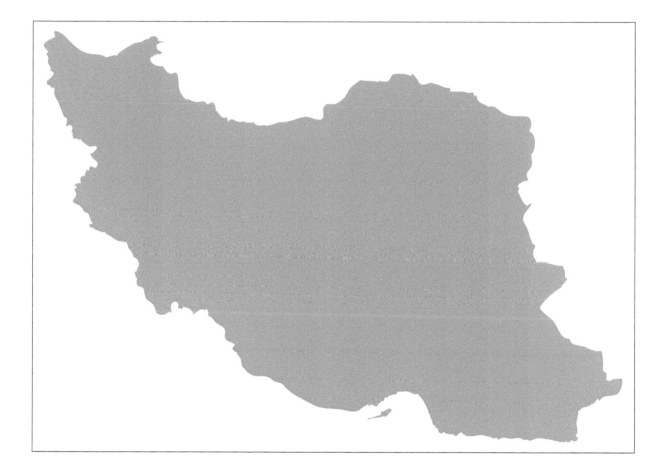

IRAN

Introduction

The proper name of Iran is the Islamic Republic of Iran. It is located in southwestern Asia, in the region known as the Middle East. Iran is bordered to the north by the Caspian Sea and Turkmenistan and to the northwest by Armenia, Azerbaijan, and Turkey. Its western border is dominated by Iraq. The Persian Gulf stretches along its southwestern border, where it meets the Strait of Hormuz, which then meets the Gulf of Oman. Iran is bordered to the east by Afghanistan and to the southeast by Pakistan.

Iran was known to the rest of the world as Persia until the mid-1930s, and Persian culture and Iranian culture remain intertwined. Traditional Persian arts still practiced in Iran today include carpet weaving, calligraphy, metal engraving, and pottery. Iranian craftsmen, as well as their fine works, are renowned throughout the world. Literature has also always been a significant part of Persian and Iranian culture, and important authors include the classical poets Ferdowsi, Omar Khayyam, and Rumi,

In the 21st century, Iran has found itself at odds with the United States and other members of the UN, who seek to limit Iran's nuclear programs. Officials in Tehran have repeatedly claimed that the nuclear programs are being used for energy, rather than weapons, but their Western counterparts have denied Iran participation in the Nuclear Non-Proliferation Treaty, which allows countries to "develop research, production, and use of nuclear energy for peaceful purposes." Hopes of some resolution have increased in recent years as relations between Iran and the West have somewhat thawed following the election of Hassan Rouhani as president.

GENERAL INFORMATION

Official Language: Farsi (Persian)
Population: 81,824,270 (2015 estimate)
Currency: Iranian rial
Coins: The Iranian rial is available in coin denominations of 50, 100, 250, 500, 1000, 2000, and 5000 rials.
Land Area: 1,531,595 square kilometers (591,352 square miles)

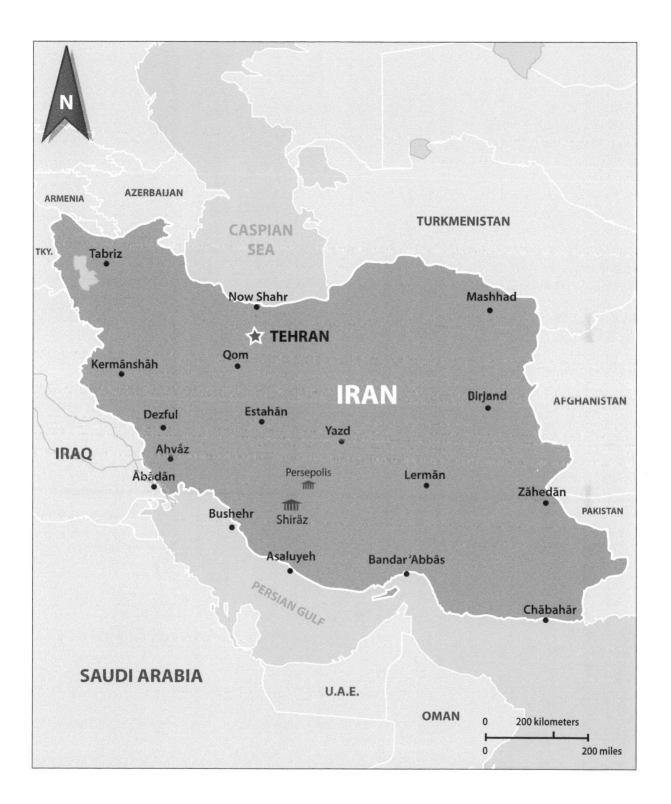

Principal Cities by Population (2015 estimate, unless otherwise noted):

- Tehran (8,432,000)
- Mashhad (3,014,000)
- Karaj (2,700,000)
- Esfahan (1,880,000)
- Shiraz (1,661,000)
- Tabriz (1,572,000) (2012 estimate)
- Ahvaz (1,100,000) (2012 estimate)
- Qom (1,100,000) (2012 estimate)

Water Area: 116,600 square kilometers (45,019 square miles)

National Motto: "Independence, Freedom, Islamic Republic." It has also been suggested that the words that appear on its national flag, "Allahu Akbar" (Arabic, "God is Greater"), may serve as its motto.

National Anthem: National Anthem of the Islamic Republic of Iran ("Sorud-e Melli-ye Jomhuri-ye Eslāmi-ye Irān")

Capital: Tehran

Time Zone: GMT +3.30

Flag Description: The flag of Iran features three horizontal bands of color: green (top), white, and red (bottom). In the center of the white band rests Iran's national emblem: a red tulip-shaped symbol meant to represent the word "Allah" in a stylized fashion. The phrase "Allahu Akbar," or "God Is Great," runs in white script along the bottom length of the green band and along the top length of the red band.

Population

The majority of Iranians (approximately 73 percent) live in urban areas. Iran's population density is 42 people per square kilometer; its highest population density areas are in the north-central and northwestern regions. The Persians, the majority ethnic group in Iran, are descendants of the Aryans of Central Asia who inhabited Iran as long ago as 1000 BCE.

Tehran province is the most densely populated province in Iran, with approximately 12 million inhabitants. The city proper is home to 8.4 million people; about 99 percent of the city's population is Muslim, and most of the population speaks Persian. Because of the massive migration that has occurred since the Iran-Iraq War, much of the character of the city has been lost, including the city's distinctive architecture. This condition is known as "Tehran Identity Disaster." More than 7 million (58 percent) of the city's inhabitants are immigrants. The large Tajik, Hazara, Pashtuns, Uzbek, and Iraqi Arab communities contribute to the blue-collar workforce in the city, and often work as day laborers for the development of Tehran.

Languages

Although Persian is the official language of Iran, there are many other languages and dialects spoken throughout the country, including Turkic, Kirmanji, Luri, and Baluchi.

Native People & Ethnic Groups

Persians make up the majority of Iranians, but there are several other ethnic populations in Iran as well, including Azeri, Gilaki, Mazandarani, Kurds, Arabs, Lur, and others.

Religions

Iran is primarily made up of Shia Muslims, but Sunni Muslims account for 10 percent of the population. Zoroastrians, Jews, Christians, and Baha'i make up about 1 percent of the population. Islam dominates Iranian social and political life.

Climate

Iran is an arid country, with subtropical regions near the coast of the Caspian Sea. Rainfall is variable throughout the country: it is most common between October and April, with an average rainfall of around 25 centimeters (about 10 inches). Precipitation varies according to the region, with the mountains receiving about 50 centimeters (20 inches) per year, and 100 centimeters (40 inches) falling each year in the Caspian region.

The climate in Iran varies by region. In Tehran, which lies at the base of the Alborz mountain range in the north-central region, temperatures can range between 5° and 30° Celsius (41° and 88° Fahrenheit). In Tabriz, in the far northwest of the country, temperatures range between 0° and 26° Celsius (32° and 78° Fahrenheit) with more annual snowfall on average than Tehran.

Tehran has a moderate climate, with warm summers and cool winters. The average temperature in July is 29° Celsius (84° Fahrenheit), while the average temperature in January is 4° Celsius (39° Fahrenheit). The city receives the majority of its 20 centimeters (eight inches) of annual rain between November and May, with occasional snowfall in December, January, and February.

ENVIRONMENT & GEOGRAPHY

Topography
Iran is a mountainous country with a central basin region. Its topography includes deserts, mountains, and valleys. The Zagros mountain range stretches 1,600 kilometers (1,000 miles) from the northwest section to the southeast, taking up most of the western part of the country. The Alborz mountain range stretches 600 kilometers (400 miles) along the northern border with the Caspian Sea. Within the Alborz range is Mount Damavand, which, at 5,671 meters (18,605 feet), is the highest point in the country.

The eastern border of Iran has some highlands. The Central Plateau is surrounded on three sides by mountains. Although there are many rivers and streams in Iran, only one is considered navigable, the Karun. Three rivers (the Aras, the Atrek, and the Shatt al Arab) form part of Iran's international borders.

Tehran is located at the foot of Mount Damavand, and among several other mountains on the southern slopes of the Elburz Mountains, at an elevation of about 1,200 meters (3,800 feet) above sea level. Most of the mountains and highlands in Tehran are in the northern end of the city, and can be seen beyond the city's skyline. The elevation declines from the northern end of the city to the lowest point in the southern desert.

Tehran's mountainous areas have a moderate climate, while the lower-lying plains have a semi-arid desert climate. There are several rivers that flow through Tehran, such as the Karaj River, the Jajroud River, and the Taleqan Roud River. Several rivers are dammed to provide the population with potable water. The city is 100 kilometers (62 miles) from the coast of the Caspian Sea. A plateau lies in the south end of the city.

Plants & Animals
Iran is home to a diverse plant and animal population. Common plants found throughout the mountainous regions include beech, oak, and conifer trees, as well as date, walnut, Siberian elm, fig, and pomegranate trees. In more arid regions, cactus and scrub plants are common. Of the nearly 8,000 species of plants in Iran, only two are considered threatened, while 100 species of plants once found in the country are now extinct.

Common animals found in Iran include species of rabbits, foxes, wolves, hyenas, and sheep. There are over fifty endangered, threatened or vulnerable species in Iran, including the Iranian Jerboa, Iranian Shrew, and Asiatic Black Bear. Iran is home to about 500 bird species, including Pleskie's Ground Jay and the Siberian Crane.

CUSTOMS & COURTESIES

Greetings
Iranians greet one another differently depending upon the circumstances. When meeting in social settings, it is customary for men to greet one another with a kiss on each cheek, or three kisses if the individuals are very close friends or relatives; women typically do the same. In more public venues, or if the individuals have not previously met or are not close, Iranians will use a simple handshake. In general, women and men only exchange kisses or handshakes with one another if they are related.

When individuals are meeting for business, the first meeting is usually focused on getting to know one another. Generally, Iranians will only participate in business with those whom they trust and respect. Tea and light snacks are often served during meetings.

Iranians cherish respect and use proper titles when greeting one another. It is only after individuals know one another well that they will use each other's first names. When addressing a man, Iranians use the word "Agha," meaning "Sir," followed by, or after, the man's first name. Iranians insert the word "Khanoom," or "Madam," either before or after a woman's first name.

The most common vocal greeting in Iran is "Salaam alaykum," which means "Peace be upon you." A simple "Salaam" ("Peace") is also often used. More formal phrases, such as "Sob bekheyr," meaning "Good morning," "Ruz bekheyr," meaning "Good day," "Asr bekheyr," which means "Good afternoon," and "Shab bekheyr," which means "Good evening," are also common. When saying goodbye, Iranians use the phrase "Khoda hafez," which means "May God be with you."

Gestures & Etiquette

One of the most interesting and unique factors of social etiquette in Iran is the concept of "taarof." This concept can be thought of as both a social ritual and a type of social game. The ritual involves, out of politeness, refusing what is offered twice before finally accepting on the third offer. Taarof's main purpose is to make oneself appear humble while heightening the status of the other individual. For example, if a person has been invited over to another's home for a meal, taarof would be applied when that guest is ready to have seconds. When offered another helping, the guest would first refuse to avoid appearing greedy, regardless of their hunger. When offered a second time, the guest would still refuse. However, on the third offering, the person would accept regardless of whether they are hungry or not, as it is considered impolite to refuse again.

Taarof can also create tricky social situations. Out of politeness, Iranians will sometimes make offers to guests that they really do not want to make. For example, if a guest compliments their

host on a beautiful or expensive item, the host might engage in taarof by offering them that item. In cases such as this, the polite course of action would be to continually refuse the item. Many Iranians derive pleasure in the old ritual of taarof, and it reflects Iranians' focus on politeness.

Since the Islamic Revolution of 1979, Iranian women have been required to follow the Islamic Republic's dress code. According to these rules, women must cover everything but their face, neck and hands in public. Some women don the chador, a cloak-like covering, while others choose to cover their heads with a scarf and wear a long jacket to fulfill the dress requirements. According to the U.S. Department of State, over two million individuals were stopped or detained in 2007 for violating the country's strict dress code.

Eating/Meals

Eating meals in Iran can be drawn-out social affairs, as the preparation of the meals often takes hours. Traditionally, meals are eaten on the floor. The many dishes—main courses, side dishes, condiments, and bread—are placed in the middle, usually on the sofreh, or tablecloth. Special dishes and decorative items are also placed on the sofreh to commemorate special events such as weddings or Nowruz, which is a traditional Iranian holiday celebrating the new year.

The family and their guests sit around the sofreh, usually on Persian carpets and with their shoes off. Meals may be eaten with the hands or with a spoon and fork. However, some Iranians commonly eat in a more Western style, which includes sitting at a table and using a knife.

A typical Iranian meal usually consists of a large variety of dishes, as it is customary for there to be an abundance of food. Generally, Iranians only eat with their right hand due to Islamic tradition, in which the left hand is primarily used for cleansing oneself.

Visiting

Gift giving also plays an important role in Iranian social etiquette. If invited over to a person's home, it is considered polite to bring a gift such as flowers or sweets. After traveling, an individual is also expected to return with gifts for close friends and relatives.

LIFESTYLE

Family

The family is a fundamental social unit in Iran. The welfare of the family, traditionally, is thought to override individual concerns and goals. The elders of the family are highly respected and are rarely sent to live in nursing homes when they reach old age. In other public venues, Iranian society is patriarchal, but in the household the authority is shared. Women who stay at home generally spend more time with the children and are responsible for domestic tasks.

Children are taught to value and obey their parents. In families that are more traditional or live in rural locations, the sons begin to work with the father at an early age, reinforcing the father as the primary male role model. The daughters of traditional or rural families generally assist their mother in housekeeping. However, challenges to parental authority, particularly by the sons of the family, are increasing in more urban areas. Generally, the father's relationship with his daughter varies; some men choose to be quite involved in their daughters' lives, while others concentrate more on their role as breadwinner.

Housing

Iranian family homes are walled in order to maintain the privacy of female family members. The walls are usually made out of wood or metal and the only ornamentation, usually indicating social status, is found on the door. Artwork and special designs are visible inside the walls. Most homes feature a hayat, or courtyard, which is often decorated with a small pool of water. This small pool is called a howz, and is usually surrounded by fruit trees, flowers, and other vegetation.

Traditional homes are built in a more communal way, with many collective spaces and rooms that open up into one another. However, Western-style homes which prioritize privacy are becoming more common. Traditionally, socioeconomic status was not reflected in Iranian homes. However, this idea has gained prominence with the increased influence of Western culture in Iran. In rural communities, the building of homes is a group activity which helps to strengthen or reinforce a sense of community. In larger cities, Western-style apartment buildings are popular, as are residential neighborhoods which tend to feature more traditional homes.

Food

Iranian cuisine is similar to other culinary traditions of neighboring Middle Eastern cultures, such as Turkish and Indian culture, while still retaining distinct features. Generally, the dishes are not overly spicy. Instead, Iranians focus on making unique dishes out of simple ingredients. The staples of a typical Iranian diet are wheat and rice. Iranian bread, called nan, is cooked in several different methods and is served with most meals. Lavash is baked in thin, smooth layers. Sangak is baked over warmed pebbles, resulting in crispy bread with an uneven surface.

Cooking rice could be considered an art form in Iran. There are a variety of methods of cooking it, many of which take much time and effort. An Iranian specialty, called tahdig, is a crunchy, buttery layer of rice from the bottom of the rice pot.

A central dish of Iran is called chelow-kebab, which is rice served with grilled meat, usually lamb. Sumac, a crushed dried berry, is often sprinkled over the top of the meat. The dish is accompanied by grilled tomatoes, red onion, butter, and egg yolk. Instead of a salad, many Iranians will have a mixture of fresh herbs. Another popular dish is called fesenjan. This dish consists of chicken or duck that is cooked in a pomegranate and walnut sauce. Since it is a difficult dish to make, being able to make good fesenjan is considered the sign of a successful chef.

Life's Milestones

Many Iranians consider marriage one of the most important milestones in life. In Iran, marriages consist of two parts. The first part, called the 'aqd, consists of the bride and groom finalizing the marriage contract in the presence of witnesses. The friends and family of the couple attend this event. As a cleric reads aloud from a specific text, two women, who are holding a light fabric over the heads of the bride and groom, symbolically sweeten the life of the couple by rubbing together two pieces of rock sugar. After the cleric is finished reading and the sugar has been crumbled, the couple feeds one another spoonfuls of either honey or fruit jam.

A special sofreh-ye 'aqd is prepared for the ceremony. All of the items of the sofreh are symbolic and include a mirror, eggs, honey, herbs, a needle and thread, sweets, the Qur'an (if the family is religious) or poems by Hafez. Following the 'aqd, although not always on the same day, is the jashn-e 'arusi. This is a party for the couple's friends and

CULTURAL HISTORY

Art

Persian culture and Iranian culture are intertwined. Traditional Persian arts still practiced in Iran today include carpet weaving, calligraphy, metal engraving, and pottery. Iranian craftsmen, as well as their fine works, are renowned throughout the world. Many examples of Persian carpets, engravings, paintings, and other graphic works are on display in such museums as the Museum of Fine Arts in Boston, Massachusetts, and the Victoria and Albert Museum in London, England.

Iran is known throughout the world for its carpets. While the exact origins of this tradition are not clear, written records place the beginning of the craft of carpet weaving in Iran as far back as approximately 330 BCE, when Greek historians mentioned the discovery of carpets during Alexander the Great's conquest of Persia. Traditionally, carpet weaving was an art encouraged by the royal courts, and creating carpets of the utmost quality and beauty was a central concern. The carpets often are decorated with

illustrations of animals, trees, flowers, and verses of popular poems.

Architecture

Traces of Iran's distinct architecture can be found in places as diverse as China, India, and Syria, largely due to the expansion of the Persian Empire. Generally, Iranian architecture is defined by its use of symbolism and symmetry, the construction of domes and vaults, and the distinctive use of minarets in the building of Islamic mosques. Often, Iranian architecture is categorized as pre-Islamic or Islamic. In addition, the varied climate of Iran has influenced the country's architecture. Iran's arid, hot weather dictates the types of materials used for building, as well as the composition of structures.

Persepolis, considered the capital of the Persian Empire in the pre-Islamic period, is thought of as a quintessential example of Iranian, or Persian, architecture. This style of classical architecture is characterized by its grandeur, use of geometry and continuity, and decorative inscriptions and motifs. Construction of the city began under the rule of Darius I (c. 549–486 BCE). Following the Arabic conquest and the establishment of Islam as the dominant religion, architects shifted their energy to the construction of mosques. Essential elements of Islamic architecture are intricate tile and mirror work, grand domes, lofty minarets, and graceful calligraphy.

Modern architecture in Iran is in a state of flux. While some discourage the use of Western styles in the creation of new structures, some architects combine elements from Western, Iranian, and Islamic traditions to create innovative designs.

Drama

While drama has not traditionally held a prominent place in Iranian culture, its importance is growing as the Iranian theatre evolves. Ta'zieh theatre, a type of religious-themed play, has been popular for centuries, while more Western-based theatre has only been in existence in Iran for a few decades.

Iranian cinema is renowned throughout the world for its originality and thoughtfulness. In the 1930s, Iran's first feature films were released. However, the introduction of cinema into Iran did not come without protest. The ulama, a class of religious scholars, disapproved of cinema, considering it an immoral vehicle to spread Western culture.

In 1947, the film studio Mitra Film was established by Esmail' Koushan, often referred to as the "father of the Iranian film industry." This was important for Iranian cinema because it allowed for the production of feature films with sound. Previously, many films shown in Iran were created in the West and then dubbed over. With the establishment of Mitra Film, Iranians could produce their own films. The films created during this period, collectively known as Film Farsi, were often melodramas with happy endings. During the 1950s and 1960s, called the "New Wave" period, Iranian cinema experienced an influx of new, young filmmakers with fresh ideas. A key feature of this style was its focus on creating films that stressed the importance of social responsibility.

Immediately following the Iranian Revolution of 1979, in which Iran transitioned from a monarchy to an Islamic republic, most films were produced by the government, and movie audiences declined. These films were concerned with spreading the message of the revolution and reinforcing moral issues. The Iran-Iraq War (1980–1988) spurred a genre of film known as "Sacred Defense" cinema that explored the sociological and psychological effects of the war. Another type of cinema that began to emerge during this time was artistic in nature, and dealt with the complex social issues in Iran. However, filmmakers had to be careful to craft films that could make it past the censoring boards. With the reform measures of President Mohammad Khatami (1997–2005), filmmakers were given more artistic freedom. Both the Film Farsi and New Wave film movements are currently enjoying a resurgence in contemporary Iranian cinema.

Music

Persians developed their own forms of classical and folk music. The classical musical style of musiqui-e assil combines such instruments as the dulcimer, drums, and flutes. Much of Iranian folk music is derived from styles that originated in the province of Mazandaran; Amiri and najma are two popular styles that are still in use. Iran has also embraced many Western forms as well, including electronic and techno music and rock music, although these may appear somewhat irreverent in the eyes of fundamentalist Muslims.

Literature

Literature, especially poetry, has a significant place in the history of Iranian culture and in contemporary society. Persian, or Farsi, is the most widely spoken language and almost all educated Iranians, regardless of their regional language or dialect, are familiar with it. Many of the best-regarded poets of Iran, including Jalalu'd-din Rumi (1207–1273), Sams-al-Din Muhammad Hafez (1315–1390), and Muslih al-Din Sa'di (1213–1292), wrote in Persian.

Rumi is perhaps the best-known Persian writer. His *Mathnavi*, which contains over 7,000 couplets, has been called the Persian version of the Qur'an (also spelled Koran), the central religious text of Islam. The literary contributions of Sa'di include poetry that focuses on providing ethical and spiritual guidance for living in a chaotic environment. Hafez is regarded as the master of the ghazal, a form best described as a lyrical ode. Some secular Iranians use his collection of poems, titled *Divan of Hafez*, in place of the Qur'an during important events. His poems are often ambiguous in their meaning, allowing readers to offer their own interpretations. His love poems can be read as devotional poems to God, romantic poems to a lover, or proof of homosexuality in Iranian history. The Persian language does not distinguish between male and female, therefore the object of Hafez's love and affections in his poems could have been of either gender.

Perhaps the most legendary piece of Persian literature is Abo'l-Qasem Ferdowsi's (935–1019) *Shahnameh*, or *Book of Kings*. This epic poem tells the story of pre-Islamic Iran. More importantly, Ferdowsi saw this task as an effort to preserve Iranian culture by writing down the myths of the past. The *Shahnameh*, a 30-year project, is made up of over 60,000 verses. Today, Iranians still entertain one another by reading the verses aloud.

In addition, classical Persian poetry has been considered the means of expression for Sufism, a mystical branch of Islam. Sufi poetry focuses on praising God and providing philosophical anecdotes. It was not until the 20th century that prose began to replace poetry among Iranian writers. At the same time, Iranian poets began to experiment with new poetic forms.

As the government of Iran changed throughout the 20th century, Persian literature helped shape the social consciousness of Iranians as it became a primary venue for writers to convey their social and political viewpoints. This type of literature, known as littérature engagée, prioritizes a writer's commitment to society. Prose writing gained legitimacy, whereas previously poetry was seen as the purest form of writing. Many writers, such as Ahmad Shamlu (1935 2000), Hooshang Golshiri (1938–2000), and Jalal Al-e Ahmed (1923–1969), actively participated in the Islamic Revolution through various leftist and nationalist groups. After the revolution, the Islamic movement persecuted many of the leftist and nationalist groups. As a result, some of the politically active writers were forced into exile or imprisoned.

Women writers have also achieved success in the Iranian literary world. One of Iran's most influential and groundbreaking poets of the 20th century was Forugh Farrokhzad (1935–1967). In her writing, Farrokhzad addressed previously taboo topics, such as her relationships and her concerns with the status of women in Iran. In addition, her free verse poems influenced the development of Iranian poetry. Other women writers, such as Simin Daneshvar and Simin Behbahani, participated in the Islamic Revolution as well.

CULTURE

Arts & Entertainment
Contemporary music in Iran has faced challenges due to strict censorship. Despite these setbacks,

the band 127 has used the Internet to promote its music. Formed in 2001, the band has also toured throughout the United States and Europe. The group plays a blend of traditional Iranian rhythms and jazz (a sound the band calls Khal Punk) and has received much international attention, most prominently as the subject of two documentaries.

Modern cinema in Iran, like literature, has been used as a vehicle to carry messages of social and political change. Filmmakers have used their medium to debate contemporary issues and question the status quo. One particular filmmaker, Abbas Kiarostami (1940-), is associated with the New Wave cinema movement. His film, *The Taste of Cherry* (1997), won the Palme d'Or, the highest prize awarded at the prestigious Cannes Film Festival in France. In 2000, *The Circle*, directed by award winning filmmaker Jafar Panahi (1960-), dealt with the issue of prostitution. Panahi created this film without following the protocol of sending his script to the censorship committee. Women filmmakers have often presented issues central to women's conditions in contemporary Iran.

The visual arts in Iran have also developed in the 20th and 21st centuries. In 2006, a milestone event for Iranian photographers took place when the first exhibition of Iranian photographs toured the U.S. The exhibit, titled "Persian Visions," was on display from 2005 through 2010. It featured 58 works of 20 photographers. Hamid Severi (1958-), professor at both Tehran University and the University of Minnesota, served as the show's curator.

Contemporary visual artists in Iran utilize traditional elements of Iranian painting such as calligraphy and Persian motifs, but approach them in a way that is heavily influenced by modern art. Artists also still have commitments to narrative as traditional Iranian paintings did, but the stories many artists tell through their paintings are distinctly contemporary.

Iranians enjoy football (or soccer, as it is called in the United States). It is a very popular sport and a source of great pride among Iranians. Iranian soccer fans typically crowd the stands of Azadi Sports Stadium on Thursdays and Fridays to watch their favorite sport. The stadium holds up to 100,000 people and also features other sports entertainment, such as wrestling and auto racing. Other popular sports in Iran include polo, wrestling, and weightlifting. Equestrian sports are also very popular.

Cultural Sites & Landmarks

Recognized as one of the cradles of civilization, Iran is rich in culture and history. In fact, Iran ranks seventh in the world in the number of historical monuments, museums, and other cultural attractions within its borders. In addition, the country is home to nine United Nations Educational, Scientific, and Cultural Organization (UNESCO) World Heritage Sites.

Shiraz, located in the province of Fars, is also known as the "city of roses" and "the city of poets." Cherished Persian poets Sa'di and Hafez were both born in Shiraz. Their well-maintained garden tombs can be found in the northern area of the city. Also in Shiraz is the popular Bagh-e Eram, a large garden populated by lofty cypress trees. Centrally located in the park is Eram Palace, which was built during the Qajar period (1795–1925).

Approximately 50 kilometers (30 miles) from Shiraz is Persepolis, the ancient capital of the Achaemenid Empire of Persia (550–330 BCE) under Darius I. Persepolis contains some of the Persian Empire's greatest ruins, including the palaces of Darius I and Xerxes I (519–465 BCE), as well as the various tombs of the great Persian kings. Just four kilometers (four miles) south of Persepolis is Pasargadae, believed to be the home of the white limestone tomb of Cyrus the Great, who established the Persian Empire during the Achaemenid dynasty.

The city of Esfahan is renowned for its exemplary Islamic architecture. The Maydan-e Emam, or Iman's Square, can also be found there. The square was built during the Safavid era (roughly 1501–1722) by 'Abass I (also called Shah Abbas the Great), an era when Persian architecture flourished. It has served as a site for polo games and parades. Two sides of the square provide entrances to mosques and another side

is the entrance to the Esfahan bazaar. Intricate mosaics composed of colorful tile adorn the domes and wall.

The Poet's Mausoleum is in the city of Tabriz in northwestern Iran. The mausoleum, a freestanding tomb, honors Mohammad Hossein Behjat-Tabrizi (1906–1988), who wrote under the pen name Shahriyar. He wrote in the Azari language, spoken by the Azerbaijanis, an ethnic group from northwestern Iran. Over 400 scholars are honored by the mausoleum due to the destruction of their tombs in the city's many earthquakes.

Iran's capital, Tehran, is home to many cultural and historic sites, most notably the Tehran bazaar. The bazaar, a permanent, open-air marketplace, offers an overview of daily life in Iran. It buzzes with hundreds of stalls and thousands of people. The bazaar contains close to a third of Iran's retail or trade sector. Often, the owners of these stalls, referred to as bazaris, wield substantial political power or influence. The Motahari (formerly Sepah-salar) Mosque and Baharistan Palace, the home of Iran's parliament, are also major attractions within the city.

Libraries & Museums

Tehran is home to nearly 70 museums, including an archaeological museum, an ethnographical museum, and at least three former palaces that have been converted into museums. The Golestan Palace, which was once the residence of Iran's royalty, houses two famous thrones: one is in the shape of a peacock, and the other is encrusted with jewels. The Sa'adabad Palace and the Marmar Palace are also now museums.

Tehran is also home to the Film Museum of Iran. The museum houses an extensive collection of equipment and memorabilia detailing the history of Iranian cinema. Inside the museum is a cinema where Iranian films, both classic and modern, are screened. The Crown Jewels Museum is a popular tourist destination in Tehran. The famous diamond, Darya-e Nur, or "Sea of Light," is displayed there. This gem is the world's largest uncut diamond and weighs around 185 carats.

The National Library and Archives of Iran are located in the capital, Tehran. The library also houses a rare book and manuscript collection, and by 2004, the library was home to more than 18,000 manuscript books. A new building to house the national library was celebrated in 2005. Another library of note in Tehran is the Malik National Museum of Iran, which also houses rare manuscripts and books.

Holidays

Iran celebrates several national holidays each year, such as Noruz (March 21-25), which is the Persian New Year, Islamic Republic Day (April 1), Death of Imam Khomeini (June 4), and a holiday celebrating the nationalization of the oil industry in 1950 (March 19).

Religious holidays include celebrations of the birth of the prophet Mohammed (April 19), the birthday of Imam Ali (August 30) and the martyrdom of several important imams.

Youth Culture

Approximately 70 percent of Iran's population is under 30 years. This unique statistic is mainly attributed to the loss of life during the Iran-Iraq War (1980–1989). Although there is no official death toll, estimates state that over 300,000 Iranians were killed and over 500,000 were injured. Also, following the Islamic Revolution of 1979, Islamic leaders encouraged large families, even providing televisions and cars as rewards for the birth of additional children. This population growth continued to be encouraged during the Iran-Iraq War.

Because the Islamic government restricts some activities of its citizens, if young people want to participate in prohibited activities, which include drinking alcohol and mingling with unrelated members of the opposite sex, they must do so in private. In cosmopolitan cites like Tehran, the state has slackened its monitoring of the youth, and young men and women are finding it easier to be seen together in public. However, in rural areas and cities such as Esfahan, which are seen as more traditional and religious, young men and women are often interrogated if they are seen together in public.

Many women find creative ways to express themselves through fashion, while still adhering to the Islamic dress code. Some will wear colorful designer silk scarves and tailored long jackets, which fulfill the dress code regulations, but are quite different from the traditional style of the chador, supported by the state as the best clothing option for women. The young men of Iran do not have as many regulations concerning the way they dress, but Western styles, including neckties, shorts, and short-sleeve shirts, are discouraged. However, some men, particularly of the younger generation, have begun to challenge these social norms.

SOCIETY

Transportation

An efficient network of rail, bus, and airlines, connects Iran's cities. Traveling via bus is the most inexpensive mode of public transportation, but rail systems are a much faster and more comfortable option for traveling between the country's major cities. Iran's airlines also offer connections between many Iranian cities, and are the quickest way for Iranians to travel. Larger cities also have bus networks. The buses are separated by gender, with women riding in the back and men in the front. Traffic moves on the right side of the road.

Transportation Infrastructure

Iran has 28 domestic airports and seven international airports. Its railroad network is run by the State Railways Company of the Islamic Republic of Iran and comprises 6,500 km (4,000 miles) of track. Rail lines also connect Tehran to the rest of Iran and to the trans-Europe rail system.

In Tehran, the streets are often overloaded with vehicles. As such, a popular and efficient way to travel in the city is its metro system, completed in 1999. The system, which is constantly growing, consisted of three lines with close to 30 stations in 2009. During workdays, the daily ridership can be close to 800,000 on certain lines. Despite this, Tehran is one of the most car-dependent cities in the world. An international airport is located just

10 kilometers (six miles) outside of the city, in Mehrabad.

Media & Communications

One of the principal achievements of President Mohammad Khatami, a noted reformist while in office (1997–2005), was granting relative freedom of the press. However, the policies of the subsequent conservative regime, under President Mahmoud Ahmadinejad, who was elected in 2005 (and reelected to a second term in 2009), resulted in increased restraint on behalf of the media. Pro-reform publications and the journalists who work for them are still targets of censorship, and many media professionals have been fired due to their pro-reform positions. In addition, several independent publications have been shut down during Ahmadinejad's administration.

In Iran, everything aired on television and radio is filtered through the office of the Islamic Republic of Iran Broadcasting. No independent broadcasters are allowed to transmit. This has led many Iranians to turn to satellite television and the Internet for news. Although satellite receivers are technically illegal, the law is not enforced and many Iranians watch Persian broadcasts coming from the US and elsewhere. These broadcasts are generally low budget, but many larger broadcasters such as the British Broadcasting Corporation (BBC), Voice of America, Radio France Internationale (RFI), and Deutsche Welle also run programs in Persian.

The introduction of the Internet has created a new forum for Iranians to express their opinions. Following the disputed 2009 presidential elections, in which the government cracked down violently on protests, Iranians used the Internet to express their frustration, even using video-sharing sites such as YouTube to post videos of protesters under attack. The blogosphere is also an extremely popular information source for Iranians. However, in recent years the state has blocked numerous blogs and websites. Popular newspapers in Iran include the *Iran Daily, Iran News*, and the *Tehran Times*, all published in both Persian and English.

SOCIAL DEVELOPMENT

Standard of Living

Iran ranked 75th out of 187 countries on the 2014 United Nations Human Development Index, which measures quality of life and standard of living indicators.

Water Consumption

Water coverage in Iran is broad, with an estimated 97 percent of the urban population having access to an improved water supply, though access to clean water remains a concern in rural areas. About 93 percent of the urban population has access to improved sanitation. As with many other areas in the country, accurate statistics and data for water and sanitation coverage and water consumption are lacking.

Education

Iranian students attend primary school for several years, then attend a middle school for three years to determine possible career paths, and then attend a four-year high school. A national college placement examination is given once yearly, and only a few thousand out of millions of applicants are placed in universities.

Iranian schools are guided by Islamic law and principles. All public school students must study Islam, and university applicants must pass an Islamic theology examination to be accepted at university. Some people both inside and outside Iran find this to be a discriminatory practice because it links religious preference to one's chances of receiving a higher education.

Iran boasts many important, prestigious universities and colleges, such as the University of Tehran, which claims to be the oldest and largest science, education, and research institution in Iran, and Sharif University of Technology.

Women's Rights

Women's rights in Iran have often been a point of contention during the many political changes of the 20th century. Women actively participated in the Constitutional Revolution (1906–1911). Reza Shah Pahlavi (1878–1944), the shah (monarch) of Iran from 1925 until 1941, issued a decree in January 1936 that forbade women from veiling in public in an effort to modernize the country. Reza Shah also increased women's access to education.

During the political unrest of 1940s and 1950s, women became members of leftist and nationalist parties. After the overthrow of nationalist party leader and former Prime Minister Mohammed Mosaddeq (1882–1967), Mohammed Reza Shah Pahlavi (1919–1980) gained power. Under his rule, some advances in women's legal and educational rights were gained. Under his "White Revolution," many rights were achieved, most notably women's suffrage. The Family Protection Law also was introduced, which limited men's power to divorce. Custody of children, which was previously automatically granted to the husband or his family upon divorce or the husband's death, was now a matter to be disputed in court.

The Islamic Revolution of 1979 furthered gender inequality in Iran. The Family Protection Law was voided, resulting in conditions that permitted polygamy, granted custody rights to the father, and made divorce inaccessible to women. For women, the legal age for marriage was lowered to nine years of age, and for men it was lowered to 14 years of age. Despite this, the average age of marriage among women had risen from 20in 1986 to 22 in 1996. Women were also required by law to cover their heads, necks, and arms. Many women were also fired from their jobs as judges or other positions that placed them in the public sphere. This resulted in women beginning to work in the private sector, seeking careers as professionals and entrepreneurs.

In response, women became active in political life, establishing publications and organizations with the aim of gaining equal rights. Some women began to offer new interpretations of the Qur'an (or Koran) that challenged the annulment of the Family Protection Law. Women also challenged laws that dismissed them from public service positions. Reforms in marriage laws were also gained during the 1990s. Women's rights to divorce were extended and women who were

divorced by their husband for reasons deemed unreasonable were given half of their former husband's property.

Despite the continued inequalities in gender status, today women make up more than half of the students entering Iranian universities. Women have also made inroads in parliamentary representation.

Women's rights in Iran were again brought to the forefront internationally in 2010 when an Iranian woman was sentenced to death by stoning due to several charges, including adultery.

Health Care

The government of Iran provides all citizens with limited health care assistance. Since the 1979 revolution in Iran, the government has had great success in expanding the national health care system and promoting medical education among residents. The number of doctors and other health care workers in Iran has grown significantly, leading to better medical care generally throughout the country.

Despite these efforts, however, there are still millions of people without any type of medical coverage at all, and the majority of them live in rural areas, a situation that is similar to that found in many Western nations.

GOVERNMENT

Structure

Because of the close ties between religion and government in Iran, the country is considered a theocratic republic. The constitution of Iran was created in 1979 when the Islamic Republic of Iran was proclaimed during the revolution.

The office of prime minister was abolished in 1989 and the powers of the president expanded. Iran is governed by the Supreme Leader, who is the highest religious and political leader; he oversees the military and the intelligence services, and is elected by the Assembly of Experts to serve for life.

Second in command is the president, who acts as the highest governmental figure in Iran;

the president is elected by national election to a four-year term, as are members of the Parliament, or Majles. The president is served by eight vice-presidents. The Council of Guardians interprets Sharia law (or law that is line with the tenets of Islam).

In Iranian politics, political parties appear to be less persuasive in advancing agendas and special issues for consideration than are the special interest and pressure groups operating across the political spectrum. These include both religious and secular groups.

The most important recent historical events in Iran include the restoration of a pro-Western ruler, a popular revolution, and a prolonged war with a neighboring country. Following the joint covert efforts of the United States and Great Britain to overthrow the government of Prime Minister Mohammed Mossadegh in 1953, Shah Mohammed Reza Pahlavi was restored to power; this led to resentment toward any Western influence in Iran. It also stirred anger toward the Shah, who was seen as decadent (or immoral) because of his relations with Western powers such as the U.S., ruthless in cracking down on religious reformers, and tyrannical. In the late 1970s, this anger boiled to the surface, particularly among students and religious fundamentalists. In 1979, the Shah was overthrown and the Islamic Republic of Iran was created.

Between 1980 and 1988, Iran was engaged in a war against Iraq, its neighbor to the west. The conflict derived from territorial disputes, the threat posed to Iraq by the establishment of an Islamic republic in Iran, and the Iraqi perception that Iran was weak.

Iran was named as part of U.S. President George W. Bush's "axis of evil" following the terrorist attacks of September 11, 2001, along with North Korea and Iraq. Following the U.S. invasion of Iraq, Iran was accused by U.S. officials of providing support to Shiite insurgent groups in Iraq, which implemented attacks against U.S. forces and Sunni Iraqi civilians.

In addition, the Iranian government has continued to defy demands by the United Nations to stop development of its nuclear technology

systems. Iran claims it has a right to develop nuclear power capabilities, but the U.S. and its supporters in the United Nations continue to accuse Iran of developing nuclear weapons technology. Despite these differences, U.S. and Iranian diplomats held low-level meetings in 2007, marking the end of a 27-year freeze of communication. These talks ultimately led to the signing of a Joint Comprehensive Plan of Action in 2015, meant to allow Iran to develop nuclear energy, while limiting its ability to develop nuclear weapons. (The plan still awaited ratification as of mid-August 2015.)

Political Parties

Conservative political parties include the Islamic Coalition Party and the Moderation and Development Party, both of which fall under the Alliance of Builders of Islamic Iran, a right-wing, conservative alliance of political organizations and political parties. Iran's former president, Mahmoud Ahmadinejad, and current president, Hassan Rouhani, are both affiliated with this group.

The Iranian Reform Movement, which is also known as the 2nd of Khordad Front, comprises political parties and organizations that support democracy and increased human rights in Iran. Some of these parties and organizations include the Islamic Iran Participation Front, the Mojahedin of the Islamic Revolution Organization, and the Association of Combatant Clerics.

Local Government

There are 25 provinces in Iran, each of which is overseen by a provincial governor. Provinces are further subdivided into 195 governorships, 5,001 divisions, 1,581 villages, and 596 cities. These aforementioned subdivisions are, according to Iran's Constitution, governed by elected councils.

Judicial System

The Iranian Constitution establishes a Supreme Court, a Court of Administrative Justice, and military courts, as well as traditional courts and Islamic Revolutionary Courts, which handle cases regarding threats to Iran's national security. Other courts include a special clerical court and a press court, which tries cases against writers and publishers.

Taxation

Taxes levied in Iran include a sales tax, value-added tax (VAT), income tax, real estate tax, corporate tax, and inheritance taxes. The highest personal income tax rate is 35 percent, while the corporate tax rate is flat, levied at 25 percent.

Armed Forces

The armed forces of Iran, officially the Armed Forces of the Islamic Republic of Iran, consist of ground forces, navy, air force, and air defense force, as well as the Army of the Guardians of the Islamic Revolution (or Iranian Revolutionary Guards), an extensive military force that also encompasses naval, ground, and air units. The country also maintains a paramilitary force, the Basij. In 2010, the budget for the armed forces was estimated at $18 billion. Conscription exists, and consists of an 18-month service obligation. The lowest age for military service is 15 years of age, for service in the Basij forces.

Foreign Policy

Iranian foreign policy is fragmented and influenced by a spectrum of political positions held by moderates, reformers, and revolutionaries. The key figure in all of Iran's foreign policy decision making, however, is Ayatollah Ali Khamenei. As supreme leader, the highest-ranking political and religious title in the nation, Khamenei has final say on all issues domestic or foreign. Khamenei is also the head of the armed and police forces, the Islamic Republic of Iran Broadcasting, and the justice branch of the government.

The Supreme National Security Council (SNSC), composed of intelligence officials, key military personnel, and leaders from the ministries of foreign affairs, advises Khamenei on key issues. The SNSC also negotiates nuclear matters. Although Khamenei is the supreme leader, decisions are often made by widespread agreement within in the SNSC. Other organizations also influence Iranian foreign policy. The Majlis, the parliament of Iran, has the authority to approve international agreements and treaties. However, a body called the Guardian Council has the ability to veto any of parliament's decisions. Six clerics and six jurists appointed by Khamenei compose the council.

When the Majlis and the Guardian Council have disagreements, a council called the Expediency Council acts as a mediating body, also working with Khamenei during this process. The Revolutionary Guard also influences foreign policy. Iran's fragmented foreign policy stems from the fact that these legislative and executive bodies often do not agree on key issues. In addition, because the Iranian economy relies on the support of foreign investment, Iran cannot lead an isolated existence.

The Iranian president's influence on Iran's foreign policy is minimal. The power he does have consists of appointing members of the SNSC. For example, President Ahmadinejad is believed to have little power in areas such as nuclear power, a hotly debated issue in the early 21st century. In addition, Ahmadinejad's anti-Israel statements have also been minimized or dismissed by Khamenei, who stated to the United Nations (UN) that a policy of non-aggression was Iran's stance toward Israel.

Iran's foreign policy concerning the U.S. is complex. Many Iranian leaders believe that the U.S. supplied Saddam Hussein with chemical weapons in the Iran-Iraq War, which has worsened ties between the two nations. Khamenei's position toward the West, particularity the U.S., has been to limit provocations, but to avoid cooperation. However, in July 2008, the two nations sent top officials to Geneva, Switzerland, in order to discuss Iran's nuclear ambitions. This marked the first semblance of serious diplomacy since both nations shut down formal diplomatic relations following the Iran hostage crisis of 1979.

Human Rights Profile

International human rights law insists that states respect civil and political rights, and promote an individual's economic, social, and cultural rights. The United Nations Universal Declaration on Human Rights (UDHR) is recognized as the standard for international human rights. Its authors sought the counsel of the world's great thinkers, philosophers, and religious leaders, and were careful to create a document that reflects the core values shared by every world culture. (To read this document or view the articles relating to cultural human rights, visit www.udhr.org/UDHR/default.htm.)

Iran has been charged with numerous human rights violations in recent years. The Islamic Republic of Iran is a theocracy, with Islam as the state-sanctioned religion. While some religious minorities find ways to practice their beliefs, others are publicly targeted. The government has been guilty of targeting ethnic minorities such as Arabs, Kurds, and religious minorities such as the Baha'i, a violation of Article 2 of the UDHR. In 2007, over 800 Baha'is were not allowed to take university entrance exams. This places the regime in violation of Article 18.

Under President Ahmadinejad, violations of Article 19 are becoming more common. The Iranian Ministry of Culture and Islamic Guidance controls publishing houses and media outlets. Individuals such as university professors and writers, as well as those working for independent presses who have been critical of the government, have been either imprisoned or fired. Many choose to leave Iran to evade the consequences of their critiques.

Freedom of assembly, as outlined in Article 20, has also been limited and violated in Iran. Approximately thirty women were arrested for peacefully assembling outside a Tehran courthouse in March 2007. The women were protesting the persecution of three Iranian women's rights activists. Hundreds of teachers were also arrested in March 2007 due to their demands for higher wages and better benefits. The government also cracked down on protests stemming from President Ahmadinejad's reelection in June 2009, a vote that the Iranian government claimed Ahmadinejad won by a huge margin. The election, which elicited record voter turnout, was decided within hours of polls being closed, and was, for that and other reasons,

perceived as fraudulent. Protests resulted in a number of sweeping arrests and post-election violence, including police beatings and numerous deaths after the Basij, the government volunteer paramilitary force, intervened. The government has also constrained cultural and political activities of the Azeri community as well as impeded the use of the Azeri language, a violation of Article 27. Azeris live in the northwestern region of Iran and speak a Turkic language.

Tehran's Evin Prison has been the focus of much international attention. It is believed that methods of torture are employed at the prison to gain confessions. General ill treatment of prisoners is also suspected. A recent event that received media attention was the detention and death of Iranian-Canadian Zahra Kazemi, who was imprisoned for taking a photo outside of the prison. Kazemi died in 2003 in a hospital due to the beatings and brutal treatment she endured during her imprisonment.

Overall, monitoring human rights violations in Iran is a difficult task, as the state has persecuted several human rights lawyers. For example, activist Emid Baghi and his wife and daughter were recently detained due to their involvement in recording and exposing human rights violations.

ECONOMY

Overview of the Economy

Iran's gross domestic product (GDP) is estimated at $404.1 billion. The per capita GDP in Iran is $17,100 (2014 estimates). Iran's most important export is oil, which accounts for around half of government revenue, and between 10 and 20 percent of the GDP. Other important exports are woven rugs (worth $600 million in 2004), chemical and petrochemical products, and fruits and nuts. Iran exports most of its goods to Japan, China, and Italy.

Industry

Most industry in Iran is state-controlled, although efforts are underway to sell off many state-owned businesses. It is considered a semi-developed nation according to international standards. The most important industries in Iran are the service sector, mining and manufacturing, and agriculture. The petroleum industry in Iran contributes the largest share of government revenue. Other important industries are petrochemicals, textiles, and food processing.

Tehran is Iran's major economic center, accounting for fully half of the country's manufactured goods. Among the goods produced or processed in Tehran are textiles, chemicals, electrical equipment, automobiles, oil, and tobacco. Pharmaceuticals, pottery, and cement are also produced in Tehran. Because of the strict Islamic government, it has been difficult for foreign companies, particularly Western companies, to operate in Tehran.

Labor
The unemployment rate in Iran was estimated at 11.2 percent in 2014, with more than 25 million Iranians employed. Iran has a deficit of skilled laborers. As of 2007, the majority of the labor force—an estimated 48 percent—worked in the services sector.

Energy/Power/Natural Resources
Iran's natural resources include petroleum, natural gas, coal, chromium, copper, iron ore, and lead. Air pollution from vehicle emissions is a major problem in high-density areas such as Tehran; factory emissions also contribute to air pollution.

Iran also experiences environmental problems from deforestation, oil spills into the Persian Gulf, and other man-made problems. Water contamination is a source of ongoing concern to environmentalists working in Iran.

Fishing
In the early 21st century, fisheries represent 1 percent of Iran's labor force. Fish products are significant exports, particularly caviar, shrimp, and sturgeon.

Forestry
The forestry industry in Iran produces paper and wood pulp, as well as sawn wood and wood

panels. Common tree species include beech, alder, maple, and hornbeam.

Mining/Metals
The mining sector is significant to Iran's economy, with minerals such as aluminum, copper, and iron ore being among the most commonly processed. Other notable minerals include zinc, barite, and manganese.

Agriculture
Iran produces a wide variety of agricultural products, including wheat, rice, caviar and various fruits (dates, figs, pomegranates); dried fruits and nuts are the country's major cash crops. Agriculture is one of Tehran's major industries; the city has been known for its pomegranates since the 10th century. Farmers also harvest sugar, which is processed in the city.

Animal Husbandry
In 2005, livestock in Iran included the following: buffalo, camels, cattle, goats, horses, and sheep. The most common livestock is cattle, of which there were an estimated 8.8 million heads.

Tourism
The tourism industry in Iran experienced a difficult period following the Iranian Revolution in 1979, and the subsequent war with Iraq. However, as of 2004, Iran considers travel and tourism vital to its economic development, and through a major travel market push, it hopes to attract 1.5 percent of the world's tourist activity by the year 2024. Tourism accounted for 6.1 percent of the GDP in 2013.

Major attractions in Iran include the ancient cities of Persepolis and Hamadan; Shiraz and Isfahan, both former Persian capitals; seaside resorts along the Caspian coast; decorative arts and cultural museums in most major cities throughout the country; and a host of beautiful mosques in all population centers, some dating as far back as the earliest days of Islam. Iran is also well known for its gardens.

Kianoosh Hashemzadeh, Craig Belanger &
Alex K. Rich

DO YOU KNOW?

- In 1974, Tehran became the first city in the Middle East to host the Asian Games.
- Iran is roughly the size of the state of Alaska.
- Persian civilization dates back to the seventh century BCE.

Bibliography

Andrew Burke, Virginia Maxwell, et al. *Iran.* Oakland, CA: Lonely Planet, 2012.

Elton L. Daniel and Ali Akbar Mahdi. *Culture and Customs of Iran.* Westport, CT: Greenwood Press, 2006.

Encyclopedia Iranica. http://www.iranicaonline.org/.

Homa Katouzian. *The Persians: Ancient, Medieval, and Modern Iran.* New Haven, CT: Yale University Press, 2010.

Marjane Satrapi. *Persepolis: The Story of a Childhood.* Trans. Mattias Ripa, Blake Ferris. New York. Pantheon Books, 2003.

Michael Axworthy. *A History of Iran.* New York: Basic Books, 2010.

Nikki R. Keddi, *Modern Iran: Roots and Results of Revolution.* New Haven, CT: Yale University Press, 2003.

Simin Davenshar. *A Persian Requiem.* Translated by Roxane Zand. New York, NY: George Braziller, 1992.

Stuart Williams. *Iran—Culture Smart! The Essential Guide to Customs and Culture.* London: Kuperard, 2008.

William R. Polk. *Understanding Iran.* New York: St. Martin's Griffin, 2011.

Works Cited

"After the Revolution: The Cinema Will Carry Us." http://findarticles.com/p/articles/mi_m1310/is_2000_Oct/ai_66495267/pg_3?tag=artBody;col1.

"An Interview with Sohrab Mohebbi." *Zirzamin.* http://www.zirzamin.se/interviews/inter_2006/127.html.

"The Art of Taarof." *The Persian Mirror.* http://www.persianmirror.com/culture/distinct/distinct.cfm#art.

"Contemporary Iranian Art Mixes Persian Symbols, Modern Approach." *Payvand.* http://www.payvand.com/news/07/may/1234.html.

"Country Profile: Iran." *BBC News.* http://news.bbc.co.uk/2/hi/middle_east/country_profiles/790877.stm#media.

Elton L. Daniel and Ali Akbar Mahdi. "Culture and Customs of Iran." Westport, CT: *Greenwood Press.* 2006.

"Essential Background: Overview of human rights issues in Iran." *Human Rights Watch.* http://hrw.org/englishwr2k8/docs/2008/01/31/iran17597.htm.

"Forugh's Life." *Forugh Farrokhzadeh.* http://www.forughfarrokhzad.org/fourughslife.htm.

"Getting Around Iran." *Irpedia.* http://www.irpedia.com/iran-trip-planner/iran-travel-facts/198/.

"Hafez." *Encyclopedia Iranica.* http://www.iranica.com/newsite/.

"Inside Iran's Most Notorious Jail." *BBC.* http://news.bbc.co.uk/2/hi/middle_east/5077180.stm.

"Iran." *The Fund for Peace.* http://www.fundforpeace.org/web/index.php?option=com_content&task=view&id=255&Itemid=345.

"Iran-Iraq War 1980-1988." *Iran Chamber Society.*

"Iran." *Kwintessential.* http://www.kwintessential.co.uk/resources/global-etiquette/iran-country-profile.html.

"Iranian Manners and Etiquette." *Iran Visitor.* http://www.iranvisitor.com/index.php?cID=416&pID=1273.

"Iranian Statistical Centre." http://www.sci.org.ir/portal/faces/public/census85/census85.natayej/census85.informationfile.

"Iran's Multifaceted Foreign Policy." *Council on Foreign Relations.* http://www.cfr.org/publication/10396/.

"Iran's Young and Restless." *Boston Globe.* http://www.boston.com/news/world/blog/2007/02/irans_young_and_1.html.

"litterature engagee." *Britannica Online Encyclopedia.* http://www.britannica.com/EBchecked/topic/343936/litterature-engagee.

Nikki Keddie. "Women in Iran since 1997." *Women Living Under Muslim Laws* (2001).

"No Clear Answer at Iran Talks." *Al Jazeera English.* http://english.aljazeera.net/news/europe/2008/07/200871915924410840.html.

"PEN." *Strange Times My Dear: The PEN Anthology of Contemporary Iranian Literature.* Eds. Nahid Mozaffari and Ahmad Karimi Hakkak. New York: Arcade Publishing, 2005.

"Tehran's 127 band on U.S. tour." *Payvand.* http://www.payvand.com/news/08/mar/1179.html.

Tehran metro. 10 July 2008 http://www.tehranmetro.com/about/facts/history.asp.

"Traveling Exhibition: Persian Visions: Contemporary Photography from Iran." *International Arts and Artists*. http://www.artsandartists.org/exh.detail.php?exhID=47.

"The Press in Iran." *BBC.* http://news.bbc.co.uk/2/hi/middle_east/4308203.stm.

Yavar Dehghani. "Farsi (Persian) Phrasebook." Victoria, Australia: *Lonely Planet Publications, 2001*.

IRAQ

Introduction

In ancient times, the region of Iraq was known as Mesopotamia, meaning "land between the rivers" (the Tigris and the Euphrates). Because of its incredibly long history, Iraq is thought by some to be the location of the mythical Garden of Eden. The ruins of Ur, Babylon, Nineveh, Assyria and other ancient cultures are still evident throughout the country. Once a thriving nation, Iraq has been devastated by wars and sanctions. In the early 21st century, the country is in the midst of experimenting with democracy.

In 2003, United States forces invaded Iraq and removed the government of Iraqi dictator Saddam Hussein from power. The fall of the Hussein regime created a power vacuum throughout Iraq that has been felt with great severity, and resulted in conflict between Shiite and Sunni militants. In addition to this conflict, various militant sects claiming allegiance with the terrorist group al Qaeda continue to operate in Iraq. The year 2007 witnessed a build-up of American troops aimed at improving the security situation throughout Iraq, and the last combat troops departed in August 2010. However, in the second decade of the 21st century, the Iraqi government remains fractious and the country's army and police forces do not appear able keep order without support from US and coalition forces. Making matters worse is the incursion by the Islamic State of Iraq and the Levant (ISIL), a self-described caliphate, which has come to control large portions of Iraq's western and northern territory and further threatens to destabilize the country and the region as a whole.

Iraq's artistic tradition dates back to the ancient cultures of Sumer, Assyria, and Babylon. As the country evolved, its culture was largely influenced by Islam. In particular, because the Qur'an (or Koran), Islam's holy book, forbids using representations of humans in artwork, Iraqi art predominantly features geometric designs and floral representations. Arabic calligraphy is so graceful, in fact, that mosques and other public buildings are often decorated with Koranic verses.

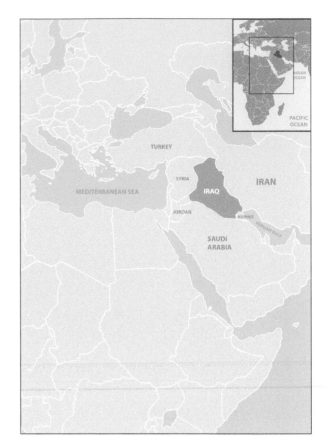

GENERAL INFORMATION

Official Language: Arabic (Kurdish in Kurdish regions)
Population: 37,056,169 (2015 estimate)
Currency: Iraqi dinar
Coins: The Iraqi dinar is available in coin denominations of 25, 50, and 100 dinar.
Land Area: 438,317 square kilometers (169,235 square miles)

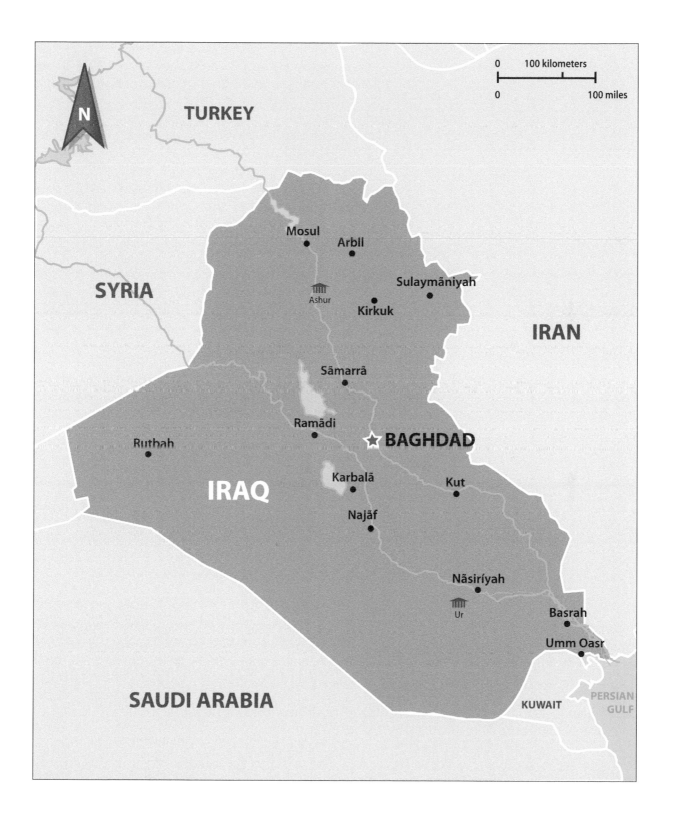

**Principal Cities by Population
(2012 estimate, unless otherwise noted):**

- Baghdad (5,500,000)
- Mosul (3,00,000)
- Basra (2,000,000)
- Arbil (1,500,000)
- Sulaymaniyah (901,028)
- Kirkuk (890,034)
- Najaf (625,000) (2009 estimate)
- Karbala (600,000) (2009 estimate)
- Hillah (524,000) (2009 estimate)
- Nasiriyah (525,000) (2009 estimate)

Water Area: 950 square kilometers (366 square miles)

National Motto: "Allahu Akbar" ("God is [the] Greatest")

National Anthem: "Mawtini" ("My Homeland")

Capital: Baghdad

Time Zone: GMT +3

Flag Description: The flag of Iraq consists of three equal horizontal bands of red (top), white (middle), and black (bottom). Centered in the white band and written in green is the phrase "Allahu Akbar," written in Kufic (calligraphic Arabic) script. As of 2010, it is considered the country's interim flag.

Population

Between 75 and 80 percent of the Iraqi population is Arab, while Kurds make up between an estimated 15–20 percent. About 75 percent of Iraq's population lives in the flat river plain between Baghdad and the Persian Gulf, and an estimated 65.9 percent of the population resides in urban areas (2015estimate). The population growth rate was roughly 2.93 percent in 2015.

Millions of Iraqis fled the country following the 2003 United States invasion and the subsequent sectarian violence that occurred in the country, and more recently following the invasion by ISIL. The organization known as Refugees International has reported that approximately 2 million people fled the country. Many Iraqis sought refuge in neighboring countries such as Syria, Jordan, and Iran.

Languages

Arabic is the official language of Iraq and is dominant in Baghdad. Other major languages spoken there include Kurdish (mostly in the north), Assyrian, and Armenian. English is the most common Western language.

Native People & Ethnic Groups

Approximately 80 percent of Iraqis are Arab. Other ethnic groups in Iraq include Kurds, who represent as much as 20 percent of the population, and Turkmen, Chaldeans and Assyrians, who together constitute less than five percent of the population (2015).

The Kurds live in the northeast, particularly in the cities of Dahuk (Dohuk), Arbil, Kirkuk, Mosul, and Sulaymaniyah. They are a non-Arab, semi-nomadic people who have long sought autonomy. During the Iran-Iraq War, both sides slaughtered them. In 1988, Saddam Hussein used poison gas on Kurdish civilians, rounded up, and executed Kurdish men. A total of 200,000 Kurds died that year. The Kurds assisted the United States invasion of Iraq in 2003. They especially hoped to regain control of Kirkuk and Mosul. As of 2015, the Kurds have been a vital component of the fight against ISIL, however, the ensuing chaos has led to increased Turkish attacks on Kurdish cities.

The Ma'dan (Marsh) Arabs lived along the lower reaches of the Tigris, at its confluence with the Euphrates. They were scattered when Saddam Hussein drained the marshes in early 1990s.

Religions

The vast majority of Iraq's population (about 97 percent) is Muslim (60–65 percent Shia, 32–37 percent Sunni). Most Kurds are Sunni. Only about three percent of Iraqis adhere to other religions, such as Christianity, Judaism, Baha'i, Mandaeism, and Yazidism.

Climate

Most of Iraq has a desert climate, with mild winters and hot, dry summers. The northern mountain regions have cold winters and occasional heavy snowfall. The melting snow sometimes causes severe flooding in the spring. Near the Persian Gulf, summers are hot and humid.

In July and August, average temperatures are often higher than 48° Celsius (120° Fahrenheit). Average rainfall is 10–18 centimeters (4–7 inches), most of it falling from December through April. Periodic dust and sand storms are common occurrences.

The temperature in Baghdad is hot and dry during summer. Spring and autumn are considered the most pleasant seasons, but are far shorter than the summer. The winter is generally cool and moist. The average summer temperature is around 41° Celsius (105° Fahrenheit), occasionally climbing to a high of 49° Celsius (120° Fahrenheit). Even with high normal temperatures, the humidity remains relatively low (10 to 50 percent). The temperature can drop dramatically from day to night.

ENVIRONMENT & GEOGRAPHY

Topography

Iraq, about twice the size of Idaho, is located in Western Asia. Nearly landlocked, it has only a narrow, 58-kilometer (36-mile) coastline on the Persian Gulf between Iran and Kuwait. Iraq is bordered on the east by Iran, on the south by Kuwait and Saudi Arabia, on the west by Syria and Jordan, and on the north by Turkey.

Iraq's highest point is an unnamed peak, 3,611 meters (11,847 feet) high. Its lowest point is on the coast of the Persian Gulf, at sea level.

Mountains mark the northern and northeastern borders with Turkey and Iran. Most of the country consists of the broad plain of the Tigris and Euphrates rivers. Along the southeastern border with Iran lie the remnants of drained reed marshes. Desert dominates most of the country's area.

The Tigris and the Euphrates are the two major rivers. The Tigris rises in Anatolia, Turkey, and flows 1,850 kilometers (1,150 miles) southeast through Iraq. At the village of al-Qurna, the Tigris joins with the Euphrates to form the Shatt al-Arab, which flows into the Persian Gulf,

around 190 kilometers (118 miles) away. The city of Baghdad lies on the banks of the Tigris.

The Euphrates, at 2,700 kilometers (1,678 miles), is the longest river in Western Asia. It rises in eastern Turkey's Armenian highlands.

Iran also has some major lakes. The largest is Buhayrat ath Tharthar, an artificial lake in the Tigris-Euphrates River basin, with a surface area of 2,119.4 square kilometers (818.3 square miles). Next in size is Bahr al-Milh (Sea of Salt), a brackish, 1,000 square kilometer (386 square mile) lake in central Iraq, south of Tharthar. Buhayrat Habbaniyah, also south of Tharthar, covers 250 square kilometers (96.5 square miles).

Baghdad, the capital, is located on a plain that lies between the desert and mountainous regions of Iraq. The Tigris River runs through the plains and divides Baghdad into two halves. The land under the city is formed largely from alluvial deposits left over from the site of an ancient sea.

Plants & Animals

Along Iraq's rivers roam wild pigs, wolves, gazelles, foxes and lions. Small animals include gerbils, jerboas, hares, hedgehogs (similar to porcupines), jackals, hyenas, and river otters. Some of the birds commonly found in Iraq include hawks, eagles, falcons, grouse, and babblers. Lizards and snakes are numerous in the desert areas.

Native trees include oak, willow, maple, tamarisk, hawthorn, pistachio, date palms, and ash. Much of the land is nutrient poor, and vegetation often consists only of shrubs and scattered ziziphus trees (jujube or jujuba fruit trees).

Iraqis use about 1,500 different medicinal plants, such as wormwood and licorice, usually taken as tea.

CUSTOMS & COURTESIES

Greetings

The traditional Arabic greeting, "Salaam aleikum" ("Peace be upon you"), is customary throughout Iraq, even among Kurds and other non-Arab ethnicities. The reply to this is "Wa aleikum salaam" ("And peace be upon you"). Iraqis typically shake hands and may kiss each other on the cheek in greeting. Sometimes Iraqis will touch their hearts after they shake hands to indicate sincerity (the gesture is typically reciprocated). However, men and women usually greet each other with a simple nod of the head. Many Iraqis are uncomfortable with physical contact between men and women for religious reasons.

In some Kurdish parts of Iraq, people may greet each other using Kurdish greetings. A common Kurdish greeting is "Rozh-bash" ("Hello"). Other common phrases are "Beyanee-bash" ("Good morning") and "Be kher bi" or "Be kher hati" ("Welcome").

Gestures & Etiquette

Iraqi etiquette has its distinctive points. Iraqis may not accept food or drink the first time it is offered, out of politeness, and a host may have to offer something twice before it is accepted. Gifts may be exchanged on any occasion. However, when a person is given a gift, he or she is expected to give another gift in return. It is considered rude in Arab countries to bring up business brusquely without first making some amount of small talk.

Islamic laws and customs are widely practiced, and the relations between the sexes are governed by strict etiquette. While friends of the same sex often hold hands in public, a man cannot hold hands with a woman in public if the two are not related. If a man speaks to, or even establishes eye contact with, a female stranger in public, it is considered a dishonor to both parties.

Additionally, there are several gestures used in Iraqi culture that might be unfamiliar to other cultures. Iraqis signal "wait" by moving their right hand up and down slightly with palm up and fingertips touching, while the head is bent slightly forward. They may signal "no" or any of its variations by clicking their tongues as they wave their heads back and forth. Lastly, eye contact is not held in the same way among Arabs as it is among Westerners.

Eating/Meals

Iraqis typically eat three meals per day, often consisting of vegetables and grains. Breakfast has become an increasingly light meal, consisting mainly of breads and fruits, with egg dishes common. Iraqis eat meat as well, though meat is expensive and is often considered a luxury. Additionally, most meals are eaten at home, as restaurants are beyond the means of many Iraqis. (However, when Iraqis eat at restaurants, the host will usually insist on paying.) The use of propane or paraffin oil stoves is a common method of cooking, and Iraqis often prepare extra food in case unexpected guests arrive.

Muslim culture has also had a profound impact on Iraq's eating customs. For example, Iraqis eat and serve themselves and others with the right hand, as the left hand is considered impure in Muslim culture since it is associated with the cleansing of the body. Additionally, during Ramadan, the ninth month of the Muslim year, most Iraqis fast from sunrise to sundown. After sundown, they eat a large meal known as iftar with their families. At the end of Ramadan, Iraqis share a festive meal known as Eid al-Fitr with friends and family.

Visiting

Hospitality is revered in Iraqi culture and in Arab culture in general. For example, it is customary to prepare an extra serving in case any unexpected guests arrive, and a host will usually give his guest the best portions of a meal. Traditionally, hosts are also expected to provide sanctuary to refugees under all circumstances.

When visitors arrive at a host's house, the women and men are usually separated, and the women are taken to the women's quarters, while the men are taken to the parlor. Guests should not complement their host's possessions, since traditional etiquette would then require the host to offer those possessions to the guest.

LIFESTYLE

Family

Most marriages in Iraq are arranged, and parents traditionally begin looking for a match for their child as soon as he or she is old enough to marry (18 is the legal age of marriage for both men and women). Though the proposals are made by the parents, either of the intended spouses may decline the marriage. Typically, a marriage in Iraq includes the traditional dowry, which, in this case, is the groom's responsibility, and is money given to the couple by the groom's family. The dowry is usually arranged between the groom, his father, and the father of the bride.

Traditionally, men in Iraq could have up to four wives, as specified in the Koran. However, a man must obtain permission from a court of law before he marries a second, third, or fourth wife. The court must decide whether he is in a position to treat his wives equally, as required by the Koran. Today, most marriages in Iraq are monogamous. Additionally, marriages were reported to have nearly doubled since the ouster of Saddam Hussein in April 2003.

Lastly, marriages between Shiites and Sunnis—the two major Muslim sects in Iraq—are not uncommon in Iraq; however, as sectarian violence has escalated since the 2003 invasion and subsequent occupation of Iraq, marital arrangements between Shiites and Sunnis have become strained. At one point, the Iraqi government offered a cash bonus to couples from different sects who married, in the hope of fostering reconciliation between the warring sects.

Housing

In much of Iraq, houses are designed to provide their inhabitants with privacy. For example, they are often hidden behind outer walls with no windows, and they commonly have a courtyard at the center. Iraqi homes also have separate living quarters for the women. In fact, some Iraqi homes have "hidden halls," which allow women to move around the house without encountering any men. In addition, most homes, including apartments, have parlors where male guests can be received without encountering the women of the household.

The villagers in the marshlands of southern Iraq live in reed houses. Typically, these include a support structure of bundled reeds and walls of woven reeds, with the roof usually rounded in the shape of a barrel. In spite of the simplicity of the building materials used, these reed houses are sometimes equipped with electricity (supplied by a cord fed through the reed wall) and feature amenities such as refrigerators and televisions.

Due to economic sanctions imposed prior to the 2003 Iraq War (which limited equipment and building materials), and due to heavy fighting and bombing during the war itself, and renewed fighting caused by ISIL, a housing shortage has remained a persistent problem in the country. Further exacerbating the situation is increasing confusion over land ownership, as well as the influx of Iraqis returning home since fleeing prior to or during the 2003 invasion.

Food

Iraqi cuisine has been strongly influenced by the culinary traditions of its neighboring countries, most notably Turkey, Iran, and Syria. Additionally, from the culinary traditions of its nomadic desert groups, Iraqi cuisine derives many meat dishes, including boiled sheep's head and leg of lamb. From the more sedentary people of the Red Sea coast, Iraq gets vegetable dishes such as tabouleh (a salad) and hummus (crushed chickpeas and tahini, or sesame paste). Like many Mediterranean cuisines, lamb and chicken are popular meats, and fruit (such as Iraqi dates) is often included in many dishes that include meat (a similarity to Iranian cuisine). However, many Iraqis today cannot regularly afford meat, so their meals usually consist of grains, vegetables, and bread. Bread is a staple food in Iraq, and is likely to accompany any meal. A popular Iraqi bread is samoons, which is a flat white bread. Meals are also likely to include soups or stews made from vegetables.

One distinctive and well-known Iraqi dish is masgouf (considered Iraq's national dish). Masgouf is fish from the Tigris River grilled over an open fire. Typically, fresh-caught fish is split down the middle, laid open over a fire, and then stuffed with vegetables and spices (such as tamarind and pepper). Due to the recent instability in Iraq, however, masgouf is now often made with farmed fish instead of fish caught in the Tigris River. Other popular dishes may include dolma, which consists of grape leaves stuffed with rice, meat, and vegetables, and kubba, or patties made of minced rice or grains and meat.

Life's Milestones

Many of Iraq's social customs are influenced by Islam, with a number of these practices, according to Islamic tradition, recommended by the Prophet Muhammad. When a child is born, it is common for the father to say adhaan—the Muslim call to prayer—into the child's ear. The parents may also put something sweet in the child's mouth. After seven days, the child's hair is shaved and weighed, and its weight in gold is given to charity. Additionally, if the child has not been named yet, he or she is named on the seventh day. Traditionally, a goat is also sacrificed, and its meat is given to friends and the poor. Muslim boys are also circumcised, which traditionally marks the boy's passage into adulthood. (The circumcision is performed by the time the boy undergoes puberty.)

Marriage also has its traditions and ceremonies. After the men on both sides of a potential marriage have informally discussed the marriage, the suitor will ask the father of the bride-to-be for her hand in marriage in front of all of the men of both families. This gathering, known as mashaya, formalizes the proposal, but it also gives the men of the two families a chance to meet formally. It is part of the process by which the father of the bride determines whether the suitor's family is suitable. Before the marriage, there is often a henna party. (Henna is a tinted dye made from the leaves of a henna plant.) At this party, friends and family of the bride paint her hands with henna designs. The wedding itself is marked with a large celebration and a feast. The best food the hosts can afford is served, often including roast lamb.

As in other Muslim countries, the bodies of the dead are washed before burial. Sometimes the bodies are washed by a professional service. The body is then wrapped in a white shroud and buried, ideally within 24 hours. Many families take the bodies of their loved ones to Najaf, a revered city that is the site of the world's largest cemetery, for burial. An important figure who was an early follower and relative of the Prophet Muhammad has his tomb in Najaf.

CULTURAL HISTORY

Art & Architecture

The region of modern-day Iraq was home to the Sumer civilization, the world's first known culture, and is often referred to as the "cradle of civilization." The Sumerian culture was particularly renowned for developing an early system of writing, called cuneiform. It remained the primary system of writing in the Middle East for two millennia. The Sumerians also made many artistic achievements. For example, they produced cylindrical seals, which could be rolled over wet clay to impress a picture into the clay in relief. As Sumerian art developed, common themes included the depiction of fantastical creatures, including animals that were half-man and half-bull, and most art was religious in nature. Other examples of excavated Sumerian art include marble statues, detailed sculptures, and ornate temple architecture.

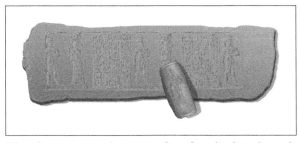

The Sumerian culture produced cylindrical seals which rolled over wet clay to impress an image.

Several other pre-Islamic cultures followed the Sumerians, including the Assyrian, Babylonian, and Akkadian cultures. Collectively, the ancient art of these cultures, along with Sumer, is often referred to as Mesopotamian art. Mesopotamia refers to an ancient region that now occupies modern-day Iraq, as well as parts of Syria, Iran, and Turkey. Art during the emergence of these cultures was largely ornate and stylized, with metal and mud brick the popular media of art and architecture, respectively. Themes of realism and mythology were prominent, and art increasingly became more secular as it evolved from its religious Sumerian origins.

The distinct artistic style of the Assyrian culture emerged around 1500 BCE. Much of their art consisted of large relief sculptures that decorated palace walls and monuments. These sculptures depicted human figures realistically, with hunting a common theme, and certain sculptures depicted figures overlapping to suggest perspective and depth. The Assyrians also placed guardian sculptures at gateways. These were often lions with human heads, or other mythical beasts.

The Babylonians built perhaps the most famous monuments and architectural feats of the ancient Middle East. The most famous of these, the Hanging Gardens of Babylon, is one of the Seven Wonders of the Ancient World. One particular ziggurat (stepped temple tower) called Etemenanki, located at a temple in Babylon, was famed for its great size (it was seven stories tall), and is thought to be the Tower of Babel described in the Old Testament. Another famous monument was the Ishtar Gate, the eighth gate of the inner city of Babylon. (It still exists, now reconstructed at a museum in Berlin, Germany, using excavated materials.) It was decorated with blue glazed tiles and relief sculptures of lions and cattle, and was originally considered one of the Seven Wonders of the Ancient World.

After the advent of Islam in what is now Iraq, Islamic art would remain predominant. Major art forms of Islamic culture include textiles, ceramics, calligraphy and painting. None of these depicts the human form, as Islam is commonly interpreted to forbid the artistic representation of humans or animals. The rise of Islam following the death of its founder, Muhammad, in 632 CE also brought new architectural techniques to Iraq, most notably the construction of mosques. One of these, the Great Mosque of Samarra, was considered the largest in the world, and featured a spiral minaret (tower) modeled on the ziggurats of ancient Mesopotamian architecture. The walls of mosques, specifically the interior, were ornately decorated, but unlike earlier art of Iraq, these decorations rarely featured representations of humans or animals. Instead, Arabic calligraphy and geometric patterns became common.

Drama

During the Ottoman Empire, a popular performance art form in what is now Iraq was pupp theater, which was known as "karagoz." European-style drama emerged in Iraq in the 20th century and is thought to have spread there from Egypt, where European theater had appeared during the 19th century. Iraqi actor Haqqi al-Shibli (1913–1985), after studying in Europe and performing with a theater troupe in Cairo, Egypt, returned to his home country and formed a theater troupe composed of Iraqi and Egyptian actors. Notable Iraqi playwrights include Yusuf al-Ani (1927–), whose play *al-Miftah* ("The Key"), dealt with the political and social tumult of the Arab world in the mid-20th century. Other well-known plays by al-Ani include *al-Kharaba* ("The Ruin," 1970) and *Kan ya ma kan* ("To Be or Not to Be," 1978).

In the late 20th and early 21st century, drama in Iraq has been hampered by wars and political instability. In late 2009, the Iraq National Theater reopened, staging the comedic play *To Enjoy the Sweetness You Must Taste the Bitterness*, which was directed, written, and performed by Iraqis.

Music

The origins of music in Iraq are obscure, but it is known that the ancient Mesopotamians played stringed and percussive instruments. Much like artwork, music played a prominent role in religion. Among the instruments they played were lutes (forms of which are still played in Iraq), harps, reed pipes and lyres. The ancient Mesopotamians also had systems of musical scales that they used to tune their instruments.

After the rise of Islam, classical music in Iraq developed alongside poetry, and the songs sung by classical Iraqi singers were often revered poems. The singing is typically accompanied by an oud (a type of lute), and may be accompanied by violins and percussion instruments. One prominent classical music tradition in Iraq is the Iraqi maqam, a song, or composition that does not have a fixed meter or musical measure, and is largely improvised. (Throughout most of the Arabic world, maqam refers to the musical mode, and not the song.) Traditional Iraqi maqam instruments include the jawzah (a four-string fiddle), the dumbak (handheld drum), and the daff (small tambourine). In 2003, the Iraqi maqam was proclaimed an Intangible Cultural Heritage (ICH) by the United Nations Educational, Scientific, and Cultural Organization (UNESCO), a specialized agency of the United Nations (UN).

During the time when Iraq was part of the Ottoman Empire, Turkish music and culture began to influence the music of the Arab world. Arab musicians in Iraq and elsewhere began using Turkish words in their songs. They also used compositional forms originating in Turkey. It was during this period that the maqamat (plural of maqat) took its present form. Additionally, maqamat performances were given a concluding song, a 19th-century Turkish innovation. Although traditional forms of Arabian music were performed throughout the 20th century, Iraq also began to absorb Western music. In the late 20th century, Iraqis embraced Western rock and pop, and many pop bands formed in Iraq.

Literature
The Sumerians developed a writing system called cuneiform—written by pressing a wedge-shaped implement into tablets of soft clay—sometime around 3000 BCE. This writing system was used to record works of literature in ancient Mesopotamia as early as 2600 BCE. The most famous work of literature in ancient

Mesopotamia is the *Epic of Gilgamesh*. The epic poem is also one of the earliest known works of fiction. Fragments of clay tablets recording this story date back to about 1700 BCE, though there were even earlier poems celebrating Gilgamesh, a legendary Sumerian king.

After the Islamic empire conquered Iraq in the seventh century CE, Iraq became an important center of Arabic and Islamic scholarship. Many literary works were translated from Greek, Persian and Akkadian into Arabic. In the ninth and 10th centuries CE, many writers produced fables and anecdotes. During this time, a draft of what would later be known as *The Arabian Nights* was created in Iraq, though many of the stories that make up the collection had been told for centuries in Arabia, Persia and even India.

The early poets of Islamic Iraq mostly adopted poetic traditions established by the Bedouin poets in central Arabia. Early in the 20th century, prominent Iraqi poets followed strict rules of meter and rhyme, and wrote poetry that resembled the classical Arabic poetry of the Arabian nomads. These poets had already left behind classical subjects, however. Where classical poets might have written of their horses or of love affairs, in the 1920s Iraqi poets wrote about social and political issues. Additionally, the first Arabic novel was written during the early 20th century—in 1913 in Egypt—and Iraqis soon adopted the new form.

By the 1950s, Iraqi poets were experimenting with other new literary forms. Many Iraqi poets wrote blank verse (verse with no rhyme) and free verse (verse with no strict meter or rhyme). The work of some Iraqi poets began to show the influence of modern Western poetry. These poets, along with Iraqi novelists, continued to write about social and political issues, and used motifs from pre-Islamic Mesopotamian mythology and history. During Saddam Hussein's rule, Iraqi poets were made to write poetry in praise of him. Like other artists, many Iraqi poets went into exile under Saddam or following the 2003 US invasion. At the same time, Iraqi poetry has adopted language that appeals to a wider audience. Today, Iraqi poetry is typically written in the Iraqi dialects spoken on the streets, instead of the literary language of traditional poetry.

CULTURE

Arts & Entertainment

The contemporary art scene of Iraq developed during a period of British mandate following World War I. The artists of this period were patronized by King Faisal I, who was installed by the British. In this early period, Iraqi artists were associated with the British occupiers, and were typically not completely embraced by Iraqi society.

During the period in which the British began to withdraw from Iraq, a group of Iraqi artists founded the Art Friends Society. The artists in the society—many of whom were trained in Europe—helped to develop a new, creative and distinctly Iraqi art scene, and often experimented with modern movements from abroad, such as cubism. They would then combine these new artistic styles with specifically Iraqi styles and themes.

Throughout the 20th century, the government of Iraq supported artists, creating the false impression that Iraq's ruling parties encouraged the discussion and dissemination of different ideas. Certain rulers also commissioned political art, such as Saddam Hussein, who commissioned monuments depicting his likeness. Because many Iraqi artists depended on state patronage, their art was subject to censorship. This led many artists to produce mostly abstract works, which were too ambiguous to be censored. Abstract art remains a dominant art form in Iraq.

The repressive measures of the Baath Party, coupled with the harsh conditions in Iraq during the UN sanctions, forced many artists to leave Iraq in the late 20th century. This flight of Iraqi talent accelerated when the US-led coalition invaded Iraq in 2003. Eventually, a large portion of Iraqi art was produced, exhibited, and sold outside of Iraq, particularly in countries such as Jordan, England, and the U.S. In the 1990s, Maysaloun Faraj (1955–), an Iraqi curator and artist whose Iraqi parents had lived in the West,

established an organization to promote the work of Iraqi artists globally. She organized an exhibit of their artwork, which was shown in the United Kingdom and the U.S., and published a definitive book on contemporary Iraqi art. Her organization became the International Network for Contemporary Iraqi Artists (INCIA), which continues to promote the work of Iraqi artists working around the world.

Nonetheless, civil society in the major cities of Iraq has largely disintegrated in the chaos of sectarian fighting following the invasion. The continuing chaos in Iraq has made it difficult for Iraqi artists to work and to support themselves. The artists who have remained in Iraq have often found it difficult to obtain supplies. Some artists have painted with tar or melted crayons instead of paint. Where artists faced government censorship before, they now face the threat of violence from Islamic fundamentalists who disapprove of their subject matter.

After the 2003 invasion, most Iraqi musicians fled Iraq. Many of these musicians continue to perform abroad. While some of them make special trips to perform in Iraq, the country remains too unstable for them to return permanently. Additionally, many musicians are being targeted by Islamic radicals. For example, traditional musicians in the southern port city of Basra, famously known for their "sea shanties," are experiencing of recent wave of violence, and have been forced to close down their shops and music halls for fear of attacks.

Football, or soccer, is popular throughout Iraq. Each neighborhood has its own team. The national team competes internationally. The team won the 2007 Asian Cup after defeating Saudi Arabia 1–0. The victory resulted in celebration and calls for unity nationwide. Recently, a women's national soccer team was formed. Other popular sports include volleyball and tennis for women; horseback riding, swimming, boxing, basketball and weightlifting for men.

Cultural Sites & Landmarks

Because Iraq is often referred to as the "cradle of civilization," it is home to numerous important archeological sites, many of which are the ancient ruins of fabled or biblical cities. One of the most famous of these ruins is Hatra, located in northern Iraq. Hatra was the capital of an Arab kingdom on the outskirts of the Parthian Empire (centered in Iran). The ancient circular city was believed to have been built sometime around the third century BCE, and features a convergence of Mesopotamian, Greek and Parthian architectural styles. It remains the best-preserved example of a Parthian city. In 1985, the ruined city of Hatra was inscribed as a World Heritage Site by UNESCO.

Another important site is the ancient ruined city of Ur, in southeastern Iraq. Ur was an important Sumerian city in the third millennium BCE, and is referenced in the Bible as the birthplace of Abraham. In its time, the city was visited by Sumerian, Assyrian, and Babylonian leaders, and is the site of a large ziggurat. There is also an ancient royal cemetery at Ur, where archeologists have recovered ancient jewelry and musical instruments. Other important ruins and remains in Iraq include the remnants of the famed city of Babylon, and the ruins of Assur (or Ashur), a capital of ancient Assyria. In 2003, UNESCO inscribed Assur, which also dates back to the third millennium BCE, as a World Heritage Site.

Samarra, near Baghdad, is another important cultural site, and the third World Heritage Site in Iraq (it is officially listed as Samarra Archaeological City). The Great Mosque of Samarra was until recently the largest mosque in the world (the al-Haram mosque of Mecca is now larger). Built in the ninth century CE, it features a large, spiral minaret reminiscent of ancient Babylonian ziggurats, and which closely resembles some depictions of the Tower of Babel. A short distance from the minaret is a large, walled courtyard where people once gathered to pray. As of 2008, an estimated 80 percent of the site had yet to be fully excavated.

Despite the cultural and archaeological importance of these sites, especially in understanding the evolution of civilization, they are mostly all endangered due to the ongoing conflict in Iraq. Most suffered some damage during or after the 2003 United States-led invasion. For example, reverberations from exploding munitions have shaken and weakened the structures at Hatra, and looters have damaged some of the decorative work. Additionally, the ziggurat at Ur was slightly damaged by gunfire from attacking aircraft, and insurgents destroyed part of the minaret at Samarra with explosives. With the invasion of ISIL things have only gotten worse, as ISIL forces have begun to systematically destroy ancient sites under their control, including bombing large parts of the Nineveh Wall in al-Tahrir, as well as the destruction of sites throughout Mosul, including hundreds of artifacts in the Mosul Museum. Both the Iraqi government and international community have vowed to do what they can to stop the destruction.

Libraries & Museums

The National Museum of Iraq once contained a wealth of art and artifacts related to the country's political and social history. However, the museum was looted heavily following the 2003 United States invasion of Iraq; little of the collection remains. The museum's collections of Mesopotamian artifacts were considered a globally important historical resource. Humanities experts worldwide criticized the lack of protection given to the artifacts by U.S. and coalition forces.

Also following the 2003 invasion of Iraq, the Iraqi Archeological Museum and the Iraqi Museum of Modern Art were also looted. In an effort to restore Iraq's museums and archeological organizations, the Iraqi government and the US government founded the Iraq Cultural Heritage Project (ICHP), announced in October 2008. Among other major initiatives, the ICHP plans to upgrade the Iraq National Museum's facilities, equipping it to better preserve and display its holdings.

The Iraq National Library and Archives (INLA), located in Baghdad, serves as the country's national library and archives, and legal depository. Burned and looted during the 2003 invasion, it is undergoing restoration.

International aid has helped to restore Iraq's war-torn libraries and to establish medical libraries in the country following the 2003 invasion.

Following ISIL's conquest of Mosul in 2015, many artifacts were destroyed, leaving the once impressive collection of Assyrian artifacts devastated.

Holidays

National secular holidays include Army Day (January 6), and Kurdish Republic Day (January 22), which marks the formation of the Kurdish Republic in 1946. Kurdish New Year (March 21) marks both the first day of spring and the anniversary of Kurdish freedom from tyrannical rule. National Holiday (April 9) commemorates the 2003 fall of the Baath regime, and Republic Day (July 14) is the anniversary of the coup by General Abdul Karim Qasim, during which King Faysal II was killed.

Islamic holidays are also celebrated throughout the year. The dates vary, as the holidays are based on the lunar calendar. The biggest religious holiday is Id al-Fitr, which marks the end of Ramadan (a month of fasting from sunup to sundown). Children wear new clothes, women use henna (red dye, also used for hair) to decorate their hands and feet, and people exchange visits and cards and give money and food to the poor.

During Id al-Adha, the Feast of the Sacrifice, people often sacrifice a lamb and donate the meat to the poor. Other holidays include the following: Islamic New Year; Ashura (or Ashoura), which commemorates the martyrdom of Imam Ali Hussein, during which Shia Muslims hold emotional processions and sometimes engage in self-flagellation (whipping); Moulo, celebrating the birth of Muhammad; and Leilat al-Meira, marking the ascension of Muhammad.

Youth Culture

The war in Iraq, and the subsequent sectarian violence, has had a profound impact on the youth culture of the country. For example, there is no place in Baghdad where young people can socialize. Additionally, universities and other institutions of learning have been targets of violence, making it difficult for these schools to maintain their operations and encourage attendance. Religious fanaticism has also become increasingly influential among youth.

Dating has also become difficult. For much of its history, Iraq has had a more open or liberal society than many of its neighbors in the Middle East (though daily life was often militant under the reign of Saddam Hussein). Since the 2003 invasion, however, religious authorities have banned dating. This religious censoring has also been applied to other facets of youth culture as well. In addition, the fear of violence has also kept young men and women from congregating, and many are effectively confined to their homes by street violence.

SOCIETY

Transportation

Networks of roads connect the cities and villages of Iraq. However, due to the instability in Iraq, many of these roads have checkpoints and roadblocks. Iraq is also connected to neighboring countries by major roads. Buses remain the popular mode of public transportation, and many people go in and out of Iraq by bus from Amman (in Jordan) or Damascus (in Syria) to Baghdad. However, security remains an issue, and public transportation costs remain high. Additionally, a metro system was scheduled for construction in Baghdad, but not completed, and traffic and blocked roads remain a persistent problem in the capital. Traffic moves on the right side of the road in Iraq.

Transportation Infrastructure

There are international flights into Baghdad and Erbil (in Iraqi Kurdistan). In Baghdad, flights arrive at Baghdad International Airport. The airport was built during Saddam Hussein's rule, with the assistance of French firms, from 1979 to 1982. International flights from the airport ceased during the UN sanctions on Iraq, but civilian international flights resumed in 2004.

Iraq has also recently agreed to a cooperative understanding with Iran to develop air, sea and rail transport between the two countries.

Iraq's railway system is in disrepair following the UN sanctions and the 2003 war. However, major routes are operational, and the United States Agency for International Development (USAID) has helped rebuild some of Iraq's infrastructure, namely railways and bridges. Additionally, in December 2008, Iraq's Ministry of Transport announced the first weekly passenger train from the capital to Samarra, which is 125 kilometers (78 miles) north of Baghdad.

Media & Communications

The media in Iraq have been subject to censorship and editorial control for much of the country's history. Under the regime of Saddam Hussein, reporters and other people working in the media could be severely punished for saying anything the Baath Party or Saddam Hussein judged to be disloyal. However, since the 2003 invasion, the media in Iraq have experienced what many consider absolute freedom, as well as fairer treatment. However, the occupying American-led coalition is sometimes accused of hampering the freedom of the press. Additionally, in a five-year period since 2003, 51 media workers—many of them support workers such as interpreters or drivers, and 50 of them Iraqi—were targeted and killed.

The primary newspaper in Iraq is *Azamman* (*The Times*). This paper was founded in exile in London in 1996. The founder, Saad al-Bazzaz (1952–), directed national TV under Saddam Hussein, but fled the country after the 1991 war. The newspaper has many correspondents in Iraq, but the editorial staff remains in London. The main TV station in Baghdad, Iraqi Media Network, is funded by the U.S., and does not have credibility with the Iraqi people. Many Iraqis have satellite dishes, which allow them to watch TV shows from abroad. However, Internet usage in Iraq remains low, with an estimated 2.8 million users—representing only 7.8 percent of the population—reported in 2015.

SOCIAL DEVELOPMENT

Standard of Living

Iraq was ranked 120th on the 2014 United Nations Human Development Index, which measures quality of life and standard of living indicators.

Water Consumption

In 2012, the United Nations estimated that, overall, 85 percent of the population was using improved drinking-water sources and 84 percent had access to improved sanitation systems. Access to water and sanitation, however, tends to be higher in urban areas.

Education

Iraq's educational system in the early 21st century is hampered by a damaged infrastructure and a loss of enrollment. It was once a model of education in the Middle East.

Under Hussein, it was difficult for academics to get permission to leave the country to study or to meet with other education professionals. Years of sanctions depleted laboratories, computers, and supplies. The bombing, burning, and looting of Iran-Iraq War, the Persian Gulf War, the 2003 US-led invasion, and the invasion by ISIL destroyed many schools and facilities.

Education is free and compulsory for both boys and girls between the ages of six and twelve. Secondary education begins at age twelve and lasts for one or two three-year terms. The country has forty-three technical institutes and colleges, twenty universities and two postgraduate commissions.

Even though all of Iraq's schools are free, enrollment has declined, especially among women and girls. Parents are keeping their daughters home because of the overcrowding, lack of sanitation, and inadequate security at most schools. Students and faculty face roadblocks, armed checkpoints, and occasional explosions. Some women who do attend bring male family members with them for protection. In 2015, the adult literacy rate in Iraq was estimated at 79 percent.

Iraq's oldest university is al-Mustansiriya in Baghdad, founded in 1233. Other universities in Baghdad include the University of Baghdad, which was established in 1957; the University of Two Rivers, formerly Saddam University; and the University of Technology. Basrah University, in the city of Basra, is the second largest in the country. Other universities throughout Iraq include the University of Salahaddin in Arbil City, Al-Anbar University in Ramadi, and Babylon University in Hilla.

Female students' access to education has been limited in the early 21st century, as violence and political instability have initiated, particularly in rural areas, a return to fundamentalist Islamic values. Female student enrollment has declined in the early 21st century, with student kidnappings (particularly of female students) and school bombings discouraging attendance.

Women's Rights

Prior to the US led invasion of Iraq in 2003, Iraqi women typically had more rights than women in most other Middle Eastern or Muslim countries. This was because the Iraqi government passed progressive measures through much of the 20th century, ensuring that women received equal education and employment opportunities. In fact, some Iraqi women were going to college as early as the 1920s, and three decades later, in the 1950s, women were given the same rights to divorce as men. The following decade, in the 1960s, Saddam Hussein's Baath Party made laws raising the status of women to encourage their participation in the workforce.

The Baath Party also established the General Federation of Iraqi Women (GFIW). The GFIW represented women's interests politically, and offered social programs for women, including job training and education. Furthermore, the Iraqi Provisional Constitution of 1970 declared Iraqi women equal to men, and gave women the right to vote. However, traditional gender roles persisted, especially in rural communities.

In the final years of Saddam Hussein's rule, some rights of Iraqi women were restricted. In this period, Saddam Hussein appealed to the traditional tribes of Iraq and the Islamic conservatives by implementing policies that are more conservative. For example, he established a law in 1990 that allowed men to kill female family members who had done something to dishonor the family (termed as honor killings). In addition, the impact of economic sanctions by the UN following the 1991 war affected women's status more than men's. Due to the economic impact, many families felt they could no longer afford to send their girls to school. Additionally, as jobs were eliminated, the government tried to open positions for men by laying off the female workforce.

Since the 2003 invasion, Iraqi women have effectively lost many of the remaining rights they previously enjoyed. In the absence of a strong government, Islamic fundamentalism, both homegrown and represented by ISIL, has imposed rules on the lives of women in some places. In these places, women may be harassed for the most mundane or simplest actions, such as driving, among other things. Professional women have also received death threats and have been forced to quit their jobs. Similarly, women activists have been forced into seclusion by death threats. Additionally, in a recent survey of Iraqi women by Women for Women International, 76.2 percent of respondents stated that the girls in their families were prevented from going to school, while many women in general have been confined to their homes.

At the same time, the new political situation has allowed international women's groups to work in Iraq, and for the formation of domestic women's groups as well. The 2005 constitution also guarantees certain rights for women, including the right to participate in public affairs and the right to vote. There remains, however, a great deal of political pressure to make Islamic law the basis of the constitutional law's treatment and perception of women.

Health Care

Little information is available about health care in Iraq since the United States invasion. Life expectancy is 74 years overall—72 for men and 77 for women (2015 estimate). Per capita expenditure on health care was approximately $97 (USD).

Decades of war and economic sanctions have severely damaged Iraq's health care system and its infrastructure. Looting and violence have damaged sanitation services and water and electricity systems. Even when services are available, fear of violence may discourage people from seeking help.

Many of Iraq's hospitals were damaged, medical equipment disappeared, and the two main public health laboratories were destroyed following the 2003 invasion. In the early 21st century, Iraq's hospitals have poor sanitation, few drugs, and insufficient personnel. Mothers and children, especially, have suffered from lack of services. The death rate for mothers, infants, and children has risen sharply since the invasion.

GOVERNMENT

Structure

The government of Iraq has been in a state of transition following the U.S.-led invasion in 2003. Various stages of intermediate governance have occurred, but in the second decade of the 21st century, the structure of the Iraqi government appears to be coalescing, due largely to the adoption of the Iraq Constitution in 2005. The Constitution establishes Iraq as an independent, democratic federation, as well as a representative, parliamentary republic. It also establishes the three branches of the federal government—executive, legislative, and judicial—as well as the structure of the country. (Regions will be established from the eighteen governorates, for example.)

The government of Iraq is divided into three branches. The chief of state, or president, and a head of government, or prime minister lead the executive branch. (Faud Masum became president of Iraq and Haydar al-Nujayfi became prime minister in 2014.)

The president's cabinet, or Council of Ministers, is composed of ministers appointed by the prime minister, deputy prime ministers, and presidency council.

Critics of the new Iraq government say it has done little to help quell the country's sectarian strife. Many have claimed that the Shiite-majority in the government has not attempted to prevent the persecution of Sunni's by Iraqi police forces. No agreement has been reached with regard to the country's oil revenues. Despite claims to the contrary made by Prime Minster Nuri Kamal al-Maliki, it is not widely believed that Iraqi forces are yet ready to take over security operations from United States forces.

Political Parties

There were over 100 political parties competing for 328 seats in the Iraqi Parliament during the 2014 elections. These parties formed six major political alliances.

The main alliances in the 2014 parliamentary elections include the State of Law Coalition (95 seats), the Sadrist Movement (34 seats), Al-Muwatin Coalition (29 seats), the Kurdistan Democratic Party (25 seats), Muttahidoon (23 seats), Al-Wataniya (21 seats), the Patriotic Union of Kurdistan (21 seats), and various other coalitions parties that each received 10 or fewer seats.

Local Government

Iraq is divided into 18 governorates and one region (the Kurdistan Regional Government). These governorates are further divided into qadhas, or districts, of which there are 111 (2011).

As the country continues to enact aspects of its 2005 Constitution, significant changes will occur in the structure of local governments. The governorates, for example, will be able to form regions, with the Constitution allowing any single governorate or group of governorates to form regions if a two-thirds majority vote of the involved governorate's councils (or one-tenth of registered voters) is won.

Judicial System

The court system of Iraq is divided into three segments: criminal courts, civil courts, and courts of personal status. These courts include Courts of First Instance, Courts of Appeal, and

Courts of Cassation, as well as a Federal Court of Cassation and a Federal Supreme Court. The highest court in the country, the Federal Supreme Court is composed of nine members, each of whom is appointed by the presidency council. A Special Tribunal for Crimes against Humanity was founded in 2003.

Taxation

As of 2010, tax rates—both individual and corporate—are capped at a rate of 15 percent. A more extensive tax system is being considered, one that would include sales taxes and, eventually, a value-add tax (VAT), which is similar to a consumption tax.

Armed Forces

Following the 2003 United States-led invasion of Iraq (a group that included twenty-one other nations in 2006), the Iraqi Armed Forces has been rebuilt, largely through assistance from American forces. The armed forces consist of three major service branches, the Iraqi Army, the Iraqi Air Force, and the Iraqi Navy. There is no conscription and the age for voluntary military service is between eighteen and forty-nine. Corruption and sectarian conflict remain concerns within the armed forces, and the army's stability and effectiveness in dealing with terrorism and sectarian violence have been called into question at the international level.

Per the U.S.-Iraq Status of Forces Agreement, all American troops were completely removed from Iraq by December 31, 2011. However, the threat of ISIL has led to a renewed American military presence in the form of increased aid and air support.

Foreign Policy

Many different kingdoms and empires have flourished in Mesopotamia, or the land that is now modern-day Iraq. Often, these kingdoms or empires have only occupied a small part of the region. The Babylonian and Assyrian kingdoms, for example, did not cover all of Mesopotamia, while at other times, Mesopotamia formed a small part of a much larger empire, such as the

Persian, Islamic, and Ottoman empires. Iraq only took its current shape when Britain defeated the Ottoman Empire in World War I and defined the boundaries of the new Iraq. This new country brought together Arabs, Kurds, Assyrians, Jew, and other ethnic groups. It also included somewhat segregated areas where most of the inhabitants followed either Sunni Islam or Shiite Islam.

The League of Nations, a forerunner to the UN, gave Britain a mandate to oversee the development of a nation in Iraq. Britain installed King Faisal I as ruler of Iraq and influenced the early form of Iraq's government. As the mandate required, Iraq eventually became an independent nation. However, the boundaries of this new country that had been chosen by Britain, and its relationship to its neighbors, were not completely settled. There were often discussions of merging Iraq with Syria to the west, or even of merging Iraq with a giant pan-Arab state, which would include Egypt, Syria, and other Arab nations.

The dictatorship of Saddam Hussein changed Iraq's relationship with the rest of the world in many ways. Saddam Hussein's political party, the Baath Party, took control of the country's oil, which had been primarily controlled by a consortium of European and American companies. Saddam Hussein also cultivated a connection with the Soviet Union, which provided Iraq assistance with processing its oil. When the price of oil was high in the 1970s, Iraqi oil helped the country to finance social reforms.

At the same time, Saddam Hussein began to persecute ethnic and religious groups that had ties to other countries or that sought independence. He exiled many Shiites, who were suspected of being sympathetic with Iraq's enemy, Iran. He also had many Shiite religious leaders executed when they criticized his policies. He fought repeatedly with the Kurds in the north of Iraq, and used chemical weapons against Kurdish soldiers and civilians.

In 1991, Iraq, under Saddam Hussein's leadership, invaded neighboring Kuwait. Saddam Hussein had been frustrated at the low price of oil, and had been unable to persuade the Kuwaitis and Saudis to decrease oil production to raise the price. A coalition of armed forces from around the world, led by the U.S., retaliated and quickly defeated Iraqi forces. Following the Gulf War, the UN imposed steep economic sanctions on Iraq. These sanctions were so harsh that ordinary Iraqis had difficulty affording or receiving food and medicine. The UN also sent weapons inspectors into Iraq. The weapons inspectors found that Iraq had produced large quantities of chemical and biological weapons, and had made progress toward developing nuclear weapons. Iraq was then forced to abandon these efforts, which nevertheless became a rationalization for the U.S. invasion in 2003.

Shortly after the invasion, the UN removed its sanctions on Iraq. It also passed a resolution giving the occupying powers—led by the U.S.—governing authority in Iraq. U.S. commanders in Iraq established new laws limiting taxes and allowing foreign businesses to invest in and operate in Iraq. Iraqi leaders, working in this provisional government, drafted a national constitution. Shortly after this, a UN resolution called for the return of sovereignty to the people of Iraq, and the U.S. gave governing authority to the newly established Iraqi interim government.

This new government continues to struggle to establish domestic security, and the US continues to maintain a large military presence in Iraq. In 2007, the US announced a surge of American troops in Iraq to quell increasing sectarian violence and insurgency. Although the surge had some success, there were frequent calls from Iraqi leaders for the US to set a timeline for withdrawing its troops. In November 2008, the Iraqi cabinet passed a pact that sets a timeline for the withdrawal of U.S. troops (which fully removed American troops by 2012). At the same time, leaders inside and outside Iraq have been discussing the possibility of dividing Iraq into a federation of three ethnically distinct regions. At the same time, the invasion of ISIL has unified many once disparate groups in the country.

Since the reestablishment of Iraq's Ministry of Foreign Affairs, as well as some degree of national sovereignty, the foreign policy of Iraq has largely been to prioritize stability and national security, reestablish diplomatic relations and bilateral agreements, and continue reconstructing the country's infrastructure and economy. Since 2003, Iraq has successfully reestablished itself in several international organizations, most notably the Arab League, the World Trade Organization (WTO), the International Monetary Fund (IMF), the Non-Aligned Movement (NAM), the Organization of Islamic Conference (OIC), and the UN. Additionally, since 2003, seventy-three countries have pledged upwards of $33 billion (USD) in support of Iraq's reconstruction.

Human Rights Profile

International human rights law insists that states respect civil and political rights, and promote an individual's economic, social, and cultural rights. The United Nations Universal Declaration on Human Rights (UDHR) is recognized as the standard for international human rights. Its authors sought the counsel of the world's great thinkers, philosophers, and religious leaders, and were careful to create a document that reflects the core values shared by every world culture. (To read this document or view the articles relating to cultural human rights, visit http://www.udhr.org/UDHR/default.htm.)

The human rights situation in post-invasion Iraq is often referred to as dire. Despite Iraq's reputation as having been one of the more liberal Muslim countries, the nation has a history of suppressing human rights among its citizens, particularly under Saddam Hussein. Mass murder, environmental destruction, and undue imprisonment and torture are just a few of the prominent human rights violations that occurred during Saddam Hussein's rule. However, in a post-Saddam Iraq, as war crimes are being documented and sectarian violence remains prevalent, many human rights abuses persist, with allegations even extending to the occupying coalition forces. Of late, most attention is focused on the crimes of ISIL, as Islamic State forces have been known to conduct mass executions including by beheading, crucifixion, and immolation.

International human rights law requires that a person be allowed freedom of thought and the freedom to hold and express his or her own opinions. The regime of Saddam Hussein suppressed this freedom in order to ensure his absolute power, largely by intimidating the population and discouraging opposition. During the reign of Hussein, political dissidents were frequently held prisoner, tortured, and often executed. Forced disappearances were common, and Iraqi citizens were subject to arbitrary arrest. Additionally, public meetings were only allowed if they were in support of the government, and only members of the Baath Party were permitted to participate in national politics. One of the most prominent example of human rights abuses involved Hussein's brutal treatment of the Kurds, an ethnic group that had long fought for an independent state in northern Iraq. Tens of thousands of Kurdish civilians were killed during Saddam Hussein's regime in mass executions and chemical attacks.

Since the toppling of Saddam Hussein's regime in 2003, a number of human rights violations have been reported. By the occupying coalition forces, the insurgent groups that have fought U.S.-occupation, and especially ISIL. All three have been accused of violating the basic human rights of Iraqi citizens. One of the most infamous instances of human rights abuses in Iraq occurred at Abu Ghraib prison, where the U.S. military held suspected insurgents. In 2004, photographs of American soldiers humiliating prisoners were released to the mass media.

(Some of the photographs featured naked prisoners in humiliating positions, and the prison was also the site of various beating deaths.) The incident sparked a worldwide protest, as many felt the treatment of the prisoners violated the UDHR, specifically Article 5. Additionally, many of the detained prisoners had been arrested on scanty evidence and held for indefinite periods, violating Article 9. The deaths of suspected insurgents and civilians—namely women and children—have also brought attention to the conduct and suspected human rights abuses of coalition forces.

Iraqi insurgents have systematically violated the human rights of Iraqi citizens and foreigners within Iraq. Among the documented abuses by Iraqi insurgents are the taking of hostages (violating Article 9 of the UDHR) and the beheading of hostages (violating Article 5 and Article 3). In June 2004, a South Korean translator named Kim Sun-Il was captured in Iraq by a group calling itself "Unity and Jihad." When South Korea refused to meet the group's demand (the group had demanded that South Korea cancel its plan to send 3,000 troops to Iraq), Kim was beheaded. Other foreign workers, most notably American executive Nick Berg, and American soldiers have also been beheaded, or have become the victims of similar atrocities, and some Iraqi civilians have been victims of decapitation. In some of the worst periods of violence in Iraq, death squads of either the Sunni or Shiite sects have kidnapped and killed large numbers of Iraqis belonging to the other sect.

Insurgents have also persecuted members of religious minorities. The Christians of Iraq (there are several hundred thousand) are often required to pay "protection money" to insurgents. Christians who refuse to pay the money are often murdered. Christians have also been targeted in suicide bombings and other violence. The Yazidis (followers of an ancient religion related to Zoroastrianism) and the Mandeans (followers of an ancient Gnostic religion) have also been targeted.

ECONOMY

Overview of the Economy

Iraq once had a strong economy, but it was significantly damaged by the war with Iran, the Gulf War, years of sanctions, and the U.S.-led invasion of 2003. The per capita gross domestic product (GDP) is $14,600 (USD), and the gross domestic product (GDP) was estimated at $522.7 billion USD (2014 estimate). The major export is oil, which is believed to have earned 10.9 billion dinars ($7.5 billion USD) in 2003. Exports of oil were sanctioned for years, but in 1996, the United Nations Oil-for-Food program allowed Iraq to export some oil in exchange for food, medicine, and other essentials.

Industry

It is estimated that Iraq has the world's third-largest oil reserve, but production was impacted by the 2003 invasion. Processing plants are outdated and deteriorating. The only way to fix them is to shut them down, but idle plants would not produce the money to pay for the repairs. Foreign companies continue to work with government to improve its oil industry infrastructure. Industry makes up an estimated 64 percent of the country's GDP (2014).

Some plants, as a result of sabotage and looting, have been able to produce no more than a third of the oil they produced before the invasion. There has been some recovery, but tens of billions of dollars are needed to replace the infrastructure and to restore operation of factories and refineries.

For a time, the situation was so bad that Iraq was forced to import 50 percent of the gasoline it used, as well as thousands of tons of other refined petroleum products such as cooking and heating fuel. As violence as been quelled in recent years, efforts to improve this situation have been restarted.

At least half of Iraq's major industries are located in the Baghdad area. Iraq's exports include petroleum and petroleum products, furniture and wood products, tobacco, bricks and stone, and leather goods. Industry manufacturing accounts for over 60 percent of the country's economy.

Labor

Official unemployment estimates in 2014 put the unemployment rate at 16 percent, but other estimates put the rate as high as 30 percent. In Baghdad, the average salary has increased by over 100 percent since 2003, but unemployment remains high. The labor force was numbered at an estimated 8.9 million in 2010.

Energy/Power/Natural Resources

Major natural resources include oil, natural gas, phosphates, and sulfur.

The draining of the marshes by Hussein destroyed much of Iraq's natural habitat, threatening many species of wildlife. Air and water pollution, soil degradation through salination, erosion, and desertification are other environmental problems threatening Iraq.

Over-fishing has depleted Iraq's lake fish, and farm vehicles damage the fragile topsoil. Timber operations and overgrazing in the Zagros Mountains have destroyed some of the country's oak forests.

Fishing

The ocean fishing industry has seen a decline in the early 21st century, due to high fuel prices, a lack of guaranteed rights for anglers, and restrictions placed on Iraq's Gulf shoreline as a result of the U.S. military presence. Another reason sea fishing has seen a decline results from the Iraq government's crackdown on its shoreline, where some individuals were smuggling oil. In response, the government instituted a system of fishing licenses; it was also reported by local fishermen that the government stopped supplying them with fuel. While the fishing industry had been a significant economic sector in the 1970s, the subsequent wars, including the Iraqi-Iranian War in the 1980s and the Persian Gulf War of the early 1990s, have damaged the fishing industry's infrastructure and destabilized its work zone: the Iraq seacoast.

Mining/Metals

The metal and mining industry in Iraq includes base metals, nonmetallic minerals, industrial rocks, and fuel minerals. In 2008, the country produces 2.4 million barrels per day of crude oil. Iraq is thought to have 10 percent of the world's petroleum reserves. Significant industrial materials include clay and gravel.

Agriculture

Only 13 percent of the land in Iraq is arable. Dates are the major cash crop. With Egypt and Iran, Iraq is one of the world's three largest producers of dates. Other crops include wheat, barley, eggs, milk, honey, rice, potatoes, tomatoes, melons, oranges, cotton, cattle, sheep, and poultry.

Agriculture employs 21 percent of the labor force, and provides three percent of the GDP.

Animal Husbandry

Domesticated animals include camels, cattle and oxen, horses, sheep, goats, and water buffalo. In the province of Kirkuk, common livestock include sheep (of which there are an estimated 750,000); goats (of which there are an estimated 55,000); and cattle (of which there are approximately 89,000), as well as buffalo (an estimated 5,000) and camels.

Tourism

Most foreigners in Iraq are active military members or journalists. Tourists are not encouraged to visit Iraq, due to risks involved with ongoing violence. In 2009, a representative of the Iraq Tourism Board stated that the country was cooperating with the World Travel Market (WTM) and the United Nations World Tourism Organization (UNWTO) to help grow tourism in the country. According to the Iraq Tourism Board, twenty-two groups of tourists from countries including Spain, Taiwan, and the United Kingdom travelled to Iraq in 2010. It is expected that, in the second decade of the 21st century, the city of Najab will become a popular tourist attraction, and the country is constructing hotels and other amenities to meet the expected demand.

Jake Gillis, Ellen Bailey, Micah L. Issitt

DO YOU KNOW?

- Iraq has the second largest proven supply of oil reserves in the country. Given this fact, Iraq's national resources are among the most valuable in the world. Some scientists believe that Iraq may contain up to 200 billion barrels of oil.

- The Tigris and Euphrates rivers are two of the most famous rivers in world history, and contributed to Baghdad's growth as a political and artistic center.

Bibliography

Charles Tripp. *A History of Iraq.* Cambridge: Cambridge University Press, 2007.

Joel Rayburn. *Iraq after America.* Stanford, CA: Hoover Institute Press, 2014.

Karen Dabrowska and Geoff Hann. *Iraq Then & Now.* Chalfront St. Peter: Bradt Travel Patrick Cockburn. *The Rise of the Islamic State.* New York: Verso, 2015. Guides, 2008.

Richard Ettinghausen, and Oleg Grabar. *The Art and Architecture of Islam 650-1250.* New Haven: Yale University Press, 1994.

William R. Polk. *Understanding Iraq.* New York: Harper Perennial, 2006.

Zaid Al-Ali. *The Struggle for Iraq's Future.* New Haven, CT: Yale University Press, 2014.

Works Cited

"Ancient Minaret Damaged in Iraq." *BBC News.* 1 April 2005. http://news.bbc.co.uk/2/hi/middle_east/4401577.stm

Antonio Castaneda. "Ancient Ruins Still Stand Among Iraqi Chaos." *Associated Press.* 15 August 2005. http://www.msnbc.msn.com/id/8962709/

"Arabic Literature." *Microsoft Encarta.* 2008. http://encarta.msn.com/encyclopedia_761561792/Arabic_Literature.html

Asharq Alawsat. "A Day in the Life of an Iraqi Youth." http://www.iraqupdates.com/p_articles.php/article/13774

"Baghdad International Airport." *Iraqi Airways.* http://www.iraqiairways.co.uk/en/bia1.htm

"Berlin: Ishtar Gate at Pergamon Museum." *National Geographic.* http://travel.nationalgeographic.com/places/enlarge/berlin-2-ishtar-gate.html

"DLI FLC: Iraqi Cultural Orientation." http://fieldsupport.lingnet.org/products/iraqi/co_ir/default.html

Glyn Williams. "Railways in Iraq." http://www.sinfin.net/railways/world/iraq.html

"iNCiA Web site." http://www.incia.co.uk/index2.html

"Iraq." *Microsoft Encarta.* 2008. http://encarta.msn.com/encyclopedia_761567303/iraq.html

Lucy Brown and David Romano. "Women in Post-Saddam Iraq: One Step Forward or Two Steps Back?" *Paper presented through the International Consortium for Arab Studies.* (Available at http://www.mcgill.ca/files/icames/iraqwomen.pdf)

"Mesopotamian Art and Architecture." *Microsoft Encarta.* 2008. http://encarta.msn.com/encyclopedia_761563062_3/Mesopotamian_Art_and_Architecture.html

Michael Spencer. "The Marsh Arabs Revisited." *Saudi Aramco World.* Volume 33, Number 2. http://www.saudiaramcoworld.com/issue/198202/the.marsh.arabs.revisited.htm

Philip K. Hitti. "History of the Arabs." London: *Macmillan,* 1970.

"The Koran Interpreted." Arberry, R. J. (translator) New York: *Simon & Shuster,* 1996.

"The Kurdish Language." *Kurdish Regional Government* 27 June 2007. http://www.krg.org/articles/detail.asp?lngnr=12&smap=03010500&rnr=142&anr=18694

"The New York Times Guide to Essential Knowledge: A Desk Reference for Curious Minds." *Macmillan.* 2004.

WorldInfo Zone. *Iraq Information.* http://www.worldinfozone.com/country.php?country=Iraq

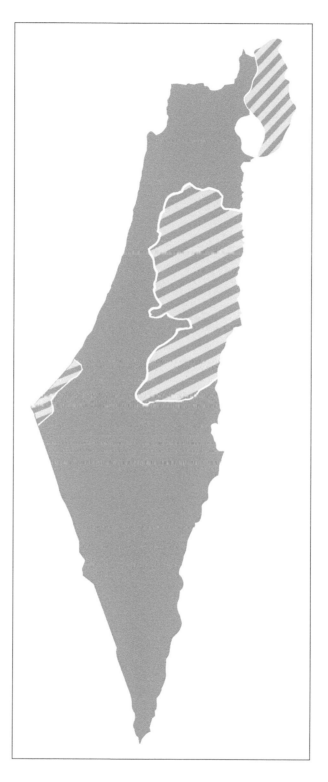

ISRAEL

Introduction

Israel is located in the Middle East, on the eastern coast of the Mediterranean Sea. The Jewish people, followers of Judaism, consider Israel their historical and spiritual homeland. Since its founding in 1948, Israel has been in a constant state of conflict with its Arab neighbors (primarily Muslims) and its Palestinian citizens, which do not recognize Israel as a legitimate state, having their own historical and spiritual claims over the land of Israel and, more particularly, on the city of Jerusalem.

Israel is bordered by Egypt to the southwest, Jordan to the east, Syria to the northeast, and Lebanon to the north. Israel, which was established after World War II, is the first Jewish state to exist in 2,000 years. As of 2013, 75 percent of Israel's population was Jewish. The country is located in one of the most politically contested regions of land in the world.

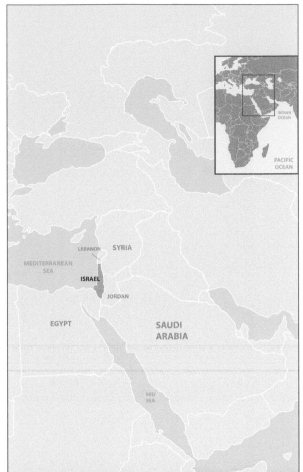

GENERAL INFORMATION

Official Language: Hebrew and Arabic
Population: 8,049,314 (includes populations of the Golan Heights of Golan Sub-District and East Jerusalem, which was annexed by Israel after 1967) (July 2014 estimate)
Currency: New Shekel
Coins: 100 agorot equal one new shekel. There is a 10 agorot coin and a half-shekel (50 agorot), 1, 2, 5, and 10-shekel coins.
Land Area: 21,642 square kilometers (8,356 square miles)
Water Area: 430 square kilometers (166 square miles)

National Anthem: "Hatikvah" ("The Hope")
Capital: Jerusalem
Time Zone: GMT +2
Flag Description: Reflecting the blue stripes on the Tallit (the Jewish prayer shawl), the Israeli flag features two horizontal bold stripes of dark blue, one on the bottom, and one on the top against a white background. In the center of the flag is a dark blue Star of David, the symbol of Judaism.

Population

The Jewish majority, accounting for approximately 75 percent of the population (2013 est.), has grown with successive waves of immigration over the past hundred years. The two major Jewish populations are the Ashkenazic Jews, who immigrated from Germany and other parts of Europe, and the Sephardic Jews, who come from the Iberian Peninsula.

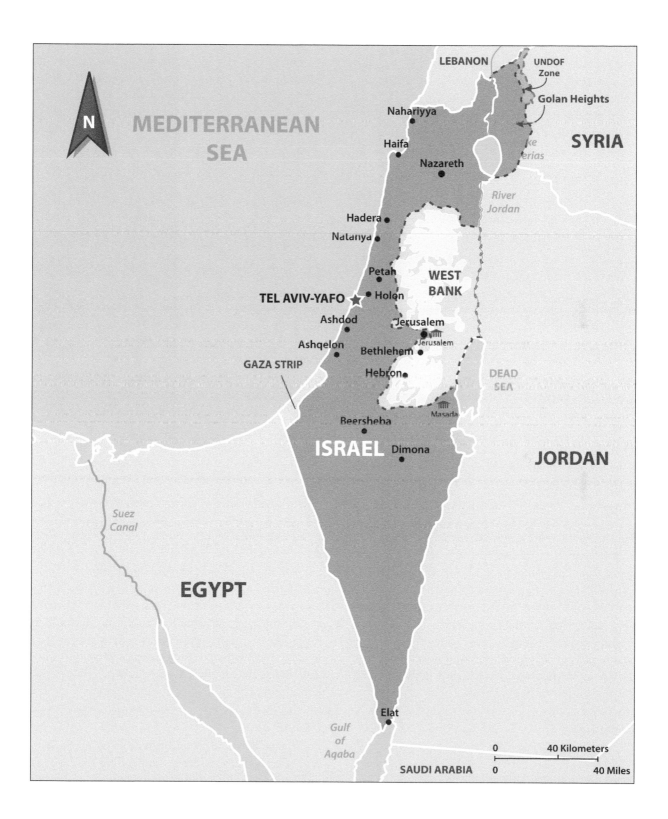

Principal Cities by Population (2012):

- Jerusalem (783,791)
- Tel Aviv (390,70)
- Haifa (269,502)
- Rishon LeZion (250,296)
- Ashdod (255,708)
- Petah Tikva (192,700)
- Beersheba (203,787)
- Netanya (188,601)
- Holon (170,500)
- Bnei Brak (152,600)

The Ashkenazim represented the first wave of Jewish immigration to Palestine in the late 1800s, followed in the mid-20th century by Jews from regions in Asia and Africa, who now constitute the majority. In addition, there was an influx of Russian Jews during the 1980s and 1990s.

Roughly, 25 percent of Israel's population is Palestinian Arab. The Arab population lived in the region known as Palestine at the time of the United Nations decree creating the state of Israel in Palestine, in 1948. Most Palestinian Arabs are Muslim, but there is also significant Christian Arab minority in Israel. Another sector of the Arab community, the Druze, lives in Galilee and Mount Carmel.

The Israeli population is growing at a rate of approximately 1.56 percent (2015 estimate). The Central Bureau of Statistics reported that in 2006, more than half of the Jewish population lived in central Israel; 20.9 percent of the population was settled in Tel Aviv. In 2013, the greater Tel Aviv area lost 7,000 residents, while the city itself lost 1,900. Jerusalem also lost 7,400 residents. Just under half of the Jewish population lived in the center of the country, while 60 percent of the Arab population lived in the north.

Languages
The traditions of European Jews came to dominate Israeli society, but there are a sizeable number of North African and Sephardi (Middle Eastern) influences as well. This is evident in the use of Yiddish words, such as kumsitz (campfire), in the Hebrew language. Yiddish is a hybrid language that developed in Eastern Europe, evolved from a combination of German and Hebrew. On the other hand, European and Sephardi Jews traditionally pronounced certain letters of the Hebrew alphabet differently; today, the Sephardi pronunciation is standard.

Native People & Ethnic Groups
Archaeologists have uncovered evidence of human activity in the region now known as Palestine that dates back 500,000 years. In addition, archaeologists and historians suggest that region was home to various Canaanite city states during the Bronze Age (2300–600 BCE) and that these settlements traded with populations in Syria and Egypt.

Although some scholars cite the Bible as evidence that the Philistine people originated in the region of modern day Israel, others have suggested that the Philistines arrived in the region from Greece and the Greek Isles. Nonetheless, the ancient history of this region of the Middle East unfurled in a continual power struggle between various Israelite kingdoms and Muslim caliphates. The debate over which group can lay historical claim to the region is one that continues to be argued among academics, historians, archaeologists and religious scholars alike.

Religions
Religion and ethnicity are primary sources of identity in Israeli culture, and perennial fault lines of conflict. Judaism is practiced by the majority of the Israeli population. Islam and Christianity are also practiced. Both faiths join Judaism in honoring many historical sites in Israel as sacred to their traditions. Jerusalem is a city that binds all three religions, each one claiming Jerusalem as a site of sacred worship and pilgrimage.

Climate
The southern section of Israel is hot and dry, with average temperatures of 46 degrees Celsius (114 degrees Fahrenheit) in the summer and 21 degrees Celsius (70 degrees Fahrenheit) in the winter. However, temperatures in the coastal

areas are much cooler, averaging 29 degrees Celsius (84 degrees Fahrenheit) in the summer and 16 degrees Celsius (61 degrees Fahrenheit) in the winter.

Israel's winter is generally cool and rainy and lasts from October until April, while the hot and dry summer season lasts from May until September. Precipitation amounts also vary with the terrain. In the south, there can be as little as 25 millimeters (1 inch) per year, while the northern part of the country could get as much as 1,120 millimeters (44 inches) of rain in a year.

ENVIRONMENT & GEOGRAPHY

Topography

Israel is bordered by Egypt to the southwest, Jordan to the east, Syria to the northeast, and Lebanon to the north. Though it is similar in size to the American state of Vermont, Israel has a varied topography. The southern part of the country opens into the Gulf of Aqaba at Elat. This southern half of Israel is the widest, and its main feature is the flat, dry Negev Desert. Sandstone hills also characterize this region.

The Great Rift Valley, through which flows the Jordan River, stretches up the eastern border of the country. Small bodies of water, such as the Dead Sea, break up this border just south of Jericho. The Dead Sea has an incredibly high salt content, and is the lowest spot on the earth, at 400 meters (1,312 feet) below sea level.

The Mediterranean coastal plain is in the center of the country. The narrowest part of Israel, the plain is only 25 miles wide at the southern edge. Farmland lies to the east, in the costal plain, which has expanded since the 1967 war. The West Bank area is currently under Israeli control, and the government funds Jewish settlements there.

To the north are the mountains of Galilee. Israel's highest mountain, Mount Meron, is 1,208 meters (3,963 feet) high. The mountain range is divided by the Plains of Esdraelon, a fertile valley that stretches from the coast to the Great Rift Valley in the east.

Plants & Animals

Despite its small area, Israel is home to a large variety of plant life. Vegetation is sparse in the southern Negev desert, and is comprised mainly of scrub bushes. However, the northern mountainous end of Israel is covered in oak tress and conifers. The ancient Cedars of Lebanon have been depleted.

Animals commonly found in Israel include jackals, hyenas and gazelles, as well as geckos and carpet vipers. There are also tiger weasels, badgers, and wildcats. The country is home to more than 380 different species of bird, some of which include cuckoos, desert larks, and sand grouse.

CUSTOMS & COURTESIES

Greetings

The population of Israel is about 80 percent Jewish and 20 percent Palestinian Arab. However, Israel is largely an immigrant nation, and even the Jewish majority represents many cultures and ethnic backgrounds. The immigrant community includes Russians, Ethiopians, Iranians, Americans and many others, and although most Palestinian-Israelis are Muslim, roughly 13 percent consider themselves Christian. As a result, greetings and common courtesies vary widely, and typically depend on age, background, and religion.

Among ultra-Orthodox Jews (Jews who follow a very strict interpretation of Judaism), women and men do not shake hands. Among secular Jews, however, it is common for men and women to greet each other with a kiss. Members of immigrant communities may speak one language with each other, but switch to Hebrew when addressing others.

Generally, Hebrew speakers usually greet each other with "Shalom" (which can mean either "Hello," "Goodbye," and "Peace"), or "Ma nishma?" (literally, "What's heard?"), which is similar to asking, "What's up?" When parting, "Shalom" or "Lehitra'ot" ("See you later") is used. Hebrew is greatly influenced by English, though, and Israelis are likely to say "Hi" and "Bye." When meeting someone for the first time, it is common to say "Naim me'od" ("Very pleased").

Among Palestinian-Israelis, the most common greeting is a series of kisses on the cheek, but rarely between members of the opposite sex. Typically, men will kiss men, and women will kiss women, three times upon meeting. If the relationship is especially close, a fourth kiss is sometimes added.

Gestures & Etiquette

Visitors are often surprised by the informal social interaction often practiced in Israeli culture. Among the Jewish majority, first names are usually used, even between children and adults. It is common for schoolchildren to call their teachers by their first name, or simply "Hamorah" ("Teacher"). It is important to note that, because of the Hebrew language's gendered nature, "Hamoreh" and "Hamorah" are the masculine and feminine forms, respectively.

It is common for near-strangers to ask for and offer personal information, such as salary or household expenses. There is a general sense among the Jewish majority that Israeli Jews are almost an extended family, and thus, such information is not entirely private. There is also a shared expectation that Israelis will help each other when in need. In addition, Israelis often pride themselves on being dugri (straightforward) in their personal and business relations. As a result, the idea of making light conversation, or small talk, is often scoffed at as insincere or meaningless. Similarly, Israelis' business attire is usually much more casual than that worn in other Western nations.

Eating/Meals

In the majority of Jewish Israeli homes, the most important meal (or meals) of the week take place on Shabbat, the Sabbath. Shabbat runs from sundown on Friday evening until after dark on Saturday. Among Orthodox Jews, it is traditional to eat three special meals with family and friends over the course of the day. In many secular families, however, this tradition is now limited to one meal. This takes place either Friday evening or mid-day on Saturday.

Typically the biggest meal of the day is lunch, which is usually eaten after noontime, typically at one or two o'clock. Lunch and dinner usually consist of one or two main dishes, which are often dairy-vegetarian, and a salad or fruits and vegetables. Breakfast often includes savory foods, such as pickled herring.

In the early 20th century, Palestinian culture was primarily agricultural. The main meal came mid-day, and was often eaten with a certain degree of ceremony. With the shift to an urban, industrialized society, many Palestinian traditions have fallen by the wayside. For many Muslim families, though, the most important meal of the week still falls on Friday, the Muslim day of communal prayer. After the family has completed their prayers, they typically return home to a large and festive afternoon meal.

Perhaps the most meaningful meals for Palestinians are those held during wedding celebrations. In small villages, automobiles will traverse the streets with speakers on the roof, calling the entire community to join a shared meal hosted by the families of the bride and groom. In larger towns, these festivities are usually limited to an extended circle of friends and loved ones, but the number of invitees is still usually quite large. In addition, wedding celebrations typically last three to four days. At the first meal, a large pot of rice and meat cooked in yogurt will be placed at the center of the crowd. Each guest is given a plate and served a generous portion.

Visiting

Israelis are quick to open their homes to friends both old and new, and food plays a central role in Israeli hospitality. Even if the guest is not invited for a meal, he or she is usually offered coffee or a cold drink, along with food, typically cake, and fruit. If invited to an Israeli's house for a meal, it is common to bring flowers, especially if it is a Shabbat or holiday.

Israeli social life tends to be casual, so making and finalizing plans is often very informal.

People also tend to be casual about the amount of time they spend together—lunch on Saturday can easily extend into afternoon coffee, too. This lack of formality also extends to parties and other social celebrations. When attending such an event, Israelis often arrive at least an hour later than invited, so hosts will adjust their invitations accordingly.

Among Palestinian-Israelis, timeliness is considered an important virtue, particularly when invited to someone's home. Guests are usually ushered into a special front room that is maintained for receiving visitors. Depending on the relationship between guest and host, a visitor may also be invited into the family's private living room. These rooms tend to be more casually decorated and located farther from the front of the house.

LIFESTYLE

Family

Israelis share a strong sense of family. Parents often remain involved in the daily lives of their children long after they have become adults. They frequently help the younger generation buy their first homes or cars, and provide childcare once grandchildren are born. This appreciation of family is even reflected in Israeli law. In 2007, the Knesset (parliament) extended maternity leave for new mothers from twelve to fourteen weeks. Furthermore, under certain conditions, fathers may take up to seven weeks of paternity leave. Fathers are often expected to play a central role in meeting the daily needs of their children, though mothers generally remain the primary caregivers.

Housing

Israeli homes tend to be small and compact, and most families live in apartment buildings. It is not unusual for all the children in a family to share the same bedroom. Among the Jewish majority, the living room often also serves as playroom, dining room, and entertainment room (where the television is located).

Because Israel has an arid climate, buildings are generally constructed from materials that serve to insulate the homeowner from the heat. In Jerusalem, almost all buildings use a pale pink limestone known as Jerusalem stone. For the same reasons, most families have plain tile floors in their homes, with occasional area rugs. In older buildings in Tel Aviv, the floors occasionally boast beautifully decorated tiles that feature recurring botanical or geometric motifs.

Palestinian-Israelis often maintain two living rooms: a formal one for guests and a much more casual one for the family. This latter room is where the family will watch television or gather in the evening. Many times, it will be furnished quite simply, with cushions and mattresses placed directly on the floor, allowing for greater relaxation.

Food

Since Israel is represented by many ethnic backgrounds, it is not home to a distinctive national cuisine. A traditional holiday dish among many Jewish families, for example, is gefilte fish, a kind of fish meatball prepared from carp. Those whose families came from Poland often eat a heavily sweetened gefilte fish. Families from other parts of Europe usually eat a salty version. Jews from North Africa and the Middle East generally don't prepare gefilte fish at all.

Some of Israel's simpler foods have become well known around the world, specifically dishes such as falafel (fried chickpea balls) and hummus (a thick dip made with chickpeas, lemon, and sesame). Both are Middle Eastern in origin, and eaten with pita bread, often with chopped or fried vegetables.

However, one universally shared food among the Jewish majority is challah, a slightly sweet white bread that is braided before rising, and served on Shabbat. Families who observe the Shabbat traditions will recite a special blessing over the challah, praising God for "'bringing forth bread from the earth.'" In addition, many Israeli Jews observe kashrut, or the laws of keeping kosher. Kashrut requires that meat and dairy never be eaten together, and forbids the eating of certain foods, including pork and shrimp. As a result, Israelis often serve dairy vegetarian meals, and have developed an industry of vegetarian versions of popular meats, such as chicken patties and meatballs. According to a 2008 Market Watch poll of Israelis, only 40 percent of secular Jews in Israel observed kashrut, while 50 percent of Israeli Jews reported that they did not observe kashrut at all times.

Falafel, hummus, and pita are also common among the Palestinian-Israeli minority. Lamb is a popular meat, and it is often dipped in a yogurt sauce. Muslims do not eat pork, or drink any form of alcohol, as per their faith.

Life's Milestones

Israel's Jewish majority follows the cultural and religious traditions of Judaism. Boys are circumcised when they are eight days old. In some families, girls are welcomed with a simhat bat (daughter celebration) within a few months of birth. Jews have traditionally considered it bad luck to give presents for a child before it is born, so baby showers are not held. Boys become bar mitzvah (son of the commandments) at thirteen, while girls become bat mitzvah (daughter of the commandments) at twelve. Couples are married under a chuppa (canopy), symbolizing the couple's future home. When a person dies, he or she is buried within 24 hours. Delaying burial is considered disrespectful of the dead, and burial customs typically involve only a simple shroud, without a casket.

An additional milestone for most Israeli families is the drafting of their children into the military, at eighteen years of age. Men serve a mandatory three years, while women are required to serve two. Because the experience is universally shared among the Jewish majority, military service is a social life-stage comparable to going to college in the United States.

In the Palestinian-Israeli community, new babies are greeted with a special celebration called the aqiqa, a reference to the goat or ram that is traditionally slaughtered in the new child's name. The meat is then cooked traditionally and served to guests. The aqiqa usually takes places roughly a week after the baby is born. Islam also requires that boys be circumcised. Though the ritual may be performed any time before puberty, it is now common among Palestinian-Israelis to perform the circumcision at the hospital within days of birth.

CULTURAL HISTORY

Art

Israel was founded in 1948 as the state of the Jewish people. Jewish culture stretches back to biblical times, and thus the Israeli arts draw on the very ancient past, as well as recent history. The Jewish people's historical dispersion across the globe meant that the modern state of Israel was formed largely by immigrants. Thus, the cultural development of the Jewish people was diasporic, and certain religious practices and social behavior developed differently in different parts of the world. This apparent contradiction is often expressed in Israeli music, literature, crafts, and even daily language.

Palestinian-Israelis also look back to ancient customs. The techniques and silk thread involved in Palestinian embroidery were originally imported from ancient China, before either had been introduced in Europe. Dyes were created from local vegetation, such as sumac or pomegranate peels. The linen on which the embroidery was done was created by local weavers. Today, women do far less embroidery than in the past, but it remains an important tradition. Some have adapted the form to other uses, such as pillowcases or tablecloths.

Much of Israeli art and culture deals directly or indirectly with issues raised by the country's on-going conflict with the Arab world. The 2007 Oscar-nominated film *Beaufort* deals with Israel's military engagement in Lebanon in the 1980s and 1990s, and the controversial "Breaking the Silence" photo exhibit was created by former Israeli soldiers to document their experiences in the Palestinian city of Hebron.

Architecture

The country's recent architecture ranges from newly constructed high-tech towers in Tel Aviv, to Jerusalem's Supreme Court Building, which combines elements of the region's distant past with aspects of modern design. From the 1930s to 1950s, architecture in Tel Aviv came to epitomize the Bauhaus Movement, a streamlined style of construction with its roots in Europe. The pale exteriors of these buildings led many to refer to Tel Aviv as "the White City," and their sheer numbers led the UN to declare Tel Aviv a World Heritage Site in 2003.

Dance

Dance in Israel has taken two forms, traditional or folk dancing and contemporary art dance. Folk dancing, which many would believe comes from a long cultural tradition, is actually a new construct, developed when Israel was established in the early 20th century. It combines elements from Middle Eastern and European traditions, and is often characterized by circle or line dances.

Ongoing tensions between the Jewish and Arab residents of Israel have meant that Palestinians occasional accuse Israelis of expropriating or depriving their culture. For example, Israeli folk dancing is occasionally claimed to be debke, a traditional Palestinian dance. While it is true that Israeli dances were influenced by the surrounding Arab culture, it may be more accurate to say that they are a fusion of many different styles and traditions, created as part of a broader effort to establish a shared culture.

Israel's first modern dance troupe, Inbal, became world-famous for its combination of both contemporary and traditional Yemenite influences. Other dance troupes within Israel include the Israel Ballet, the Kibbutz Contemporary Dance Company, the Batsheva Dance Company, and Vertigo.

Music

One of the country's most influential singers, Ehud Banai (1953–), covers topics in his music ranging from the plight of recent immigrants to biblical stories. The still-popular 1978 song "Yehiye Tov" ("Things Will Get Better") deals with the search for peace, and Israeli rapper, Subliminal, is confrontational towards Palestinian aspirations for their own state in his music. Leading singer-songwriter Yehuda Poliker (1950–) wrote an entire album based in the experiences of his parents, both of whom survived the Holocaust before moving to Israel.

Literature

The Holocaust is an important influence on Israeli art. In some cases, artists are trying to make sense of the Nazi effort to exterminate the entire Jewish people; in others, they are dealing with very personal pain and loss. The book *See Under: Love* (1986), by internationally renowned author David Grossman, deals with the traumas of the child of two such parents. Several other books by Grossman dealing with contemporary issues in Israel have been met with both widespread acclaim and controversy.

The tensions inherent in living as a Palestinian in Israeli society are expressed clearly in the works of such writers as novelist and politician Emil Habibi (1922–1996) and Mahmoud Darwish (1941–2008). Habibi wrote *The Secret Life of Saeed the Pessoptimist*, about a Palestinian-Israeli who is both pessimistic and optimistic, always struggling, but also looking toward a better future. Darwish's many books of poetry have been translated into 20 languages. Several of his poems have been set to music, and are familiar to Palestinian children the world over.

Sacred religious texts remain a strong inspiration for Israeli literary artists, and Yehuda Amichai (1924–2000), widely considered one of Israel's greatest poets, echoed the Hebrew Bible frequently.

CULTURE

Arts & Entertainment

Israelis enjoy a modern arts and entertainment culture that has seen a growing Western influence in recent years. Part of the country's cultural vibrancy comes from the international flavor of its immigrant population.

Palestinian and Jewish Israelis artists express the long Arab-Israeli conflict from different perspectives, and for Palestinians, loss, oppression and grief suffered because of the establishment of Israel are central motifs, as are the difficulties the community endures as a minority.

Modern Arab culture in Israel often focuses on poetry and literature. This is in part because the Arab community often doesn't have the resources or political freedom to produce artwork as costly as architecture or modern theater. For example, the sculptor Abed Abdi (1942–) has only recently been free to build memorials to Palestinian-Israelis who have died in the on-going violence. Applications to build such memorials were once routinely denied.

Prominent Israeli writers include Shmuel Yosef Agnon, who received the Nobel Prize for Literature in 1966. Israel's national theater company, Habima, is well regarded both at home and abroad. Commercial theatrical productions, along with more serious dramas, are extremely popular throughout Israel.

Cultural Sites & Landmarks

Israel is often referred to as "'the Holy Land.'" This is because it is home to many sacred sites mentioned in the Jewish and Christian Bibles and the Islam's holy text, the Qur'an. Many of the country's most famous sites have religious significance. The city of Jerusalem, for instance, is holy to Judaism, Christianity, and Islam. Jerusalem is often a destination for pilgrims of all three faiths.

The Old City of Jerusalem, including its ancient walls, was inscribed as a World Heritage Site by United Nations Educational, Scientific, and Cultural Organization (UNESCO) in 1981.

Within the ancient city of Jerusalem, Jews frequently pray at the Kotel (Western Wall, also known as the Wailing Wall). It is one of the few remnants of the sacred Jewish Temple that once stood at the heart of the city; it dates roughly to the year 19 BCE. Christians worship at the Church of the Holy Sepulcher. The church is built over what is believed to be sites of the crucifixion, burial, and resurrection of Jesus of Nazareth.

Muslim worship in Jerusalem centers above the Western Wall, on the Temple Mount, at al-Haram al-Sharif (the Nobel Sanctuary), a mosque complex with the Dome of the Rock, an Islamic shrine and landmark, at its center. It is believed to be the site of the Prophet Muhammad's alleged Night Journey, in which the prophet ascended into heaven.

Throughout history, the land that constitutes modern-day Israel has served as a crossroads and significant trade route for the many cultures and civilizations of the region. Trade routes to and from Europe, Asia, and Africa often passed along the Mediterranean Sea. The remains of many ancient peoples can still be found all over the country. In particular, the ancient cities of Haluza, Mamshit, Avdat, and Shivta, located in the Negev desert region of southern Israel, were destinations in the Spice and Incense Route, major trade routes of ancient times. Collectively, the desert cities were inscribed as a World Heritage Site in 2005.

Three towns of cultural significance in Israel include Caesarea, Nazareth, and Tel Aviv. The town of Caesarea is a wealthy town in modern Israel that sits next to the extensive ruins of previous cities. More than 2,000 years ago, the town was a Phoenician and Greek trading post. After the Romans conquered the area in the first century BCE, King Herod built a new city and named it for his emperor, Augustus Caesar. Among the buildings constructed during this time was a temple honoring the emperor, an extensive port, an aqueduct, and an amphitheater that remains largely intact. Today, the amphitheater is often used as a concert venue by Israeli and international artists.

Nazareth is highly revered by Christian pilgrims. It is best known from references in the New Testament as the childhood home of Jesus, and along with Galilee, a hilly region in Israel's north, it was the site of much of his adult life and activities as a religious teacher and leader. Today, Nazareth is the de facto capital of Israel's Arab citizens, or Palestinian-Israelis.

Tel Aviv was founded in 1909 and is today the center of Israel's cultural and business life.

Within Tel Aviv is the White City, a collection of roughly 4,000 houses of architectural importance built by German-Jewish architects. In 2003, it was proclaimed a World Heritage Site by UNESCO.

In addition, Israel is home to several other protected World Heritage Sites. These include the Biblical Tells (earthen mounds containing the traces of several settlements, and which are more than often important archeological sites) of Megiddo, Hazor and Beer Sheba, all inscribed in 2005; the Bahá'í World Centre buildings, used as centers of pilgrimage and administration for the Bahá'í Faith, a 19th-century Persian religion, inscribed in 2008; and Masada, the collective name for ancient palaces and fortresses overlooking the Dead Sea, inscribed in 2001.

Libraries & Museums

Israel is home to more than 120 museums. The Israel Museum, the country's national museum, is located in Jerusalem and houses important artifacts of the Judaic tradition from the region. The Shrine of the Book, a special building within the Israel Museum complex, houses the Dead Sea Scrolls and artifacts from Masada. The Second Temple model is a model of the city of Jerusalem, as it is believed to have looked prior to 66 CE.

The Yad VaShem Memorial and Holocaust Museum is located in Jerusalem and serves as a living memorial to the Holocaust. Committed to commemoration, documentation, research, and education, the organization stands as an international resource on the Holocaust. The campus houses a Holocaust museum, memorials, a museum of Holocaust art, synagogue, library, educational center, and more.

The Tel Aviv Museum of Art is a repository for many works of the 20th and early 21st centuries, including a mural by Roy Lichtenstein (American, 1923–1997), and pieces by Juan Miro (Spanish, 1893–1983), Jackson Pollack (American, 1912–1956), and Pablo Picasso (Spanish, 1881–1973).

Tel Aviv's Eretz Israel Museum serves as a natural and cultural history center, highlighting natural history, archeological finds, folklore,

and traditional arts and crafts. Other museums of note include the L. A. Mayer Memorial Museum of Islamic Art and the Sir Isaac and Lady Edith Wolfson Museum, both in Jerusalem.

Holidays

Israelis observe the major holidays of the Jewish faith, including Yom Kippur, the Hebrew day of atonement; Rosh Hashanah, the New Year celebration, also known as the Feast of Trumpets; and Passover. Since Israel does not use the Gregorian calendar, the dates of these celebrations differ from those observed by Jews in other parts of the world.

Israelis also celebrate Independence Day in April or May, and Holocaust Remembrance Day in April.

Youth Culture

In Israel's Jewish culture, it is common for young men and women to socialize freely (unless they belong to an especially religious community). Most families do not impose curfews on teenage socializing, and as a result, friends are often together until well after midnight. Both international and Israeli music, films and television programming are popular, with Israeli-produced reality shows growing in popularity. There is an increasing trend in the early 21st century of Israeli youth choosing to become more religiously observant. For example, teenagers from entirely secular homes will decide to keep kosher, or to study the religious texts.

Israel's universal draft stipulates that youth must first complete their military service before considering college studies. Many spend the last two years of high school considering their options in the service. While some youth plan to join elite units and others hope to disrupt their lives as little as possible, the majority of youth reflect on their required military service with plans or sentiments in between these two extremes. Additionally, many Israeli youth travel internationally either before, or immediately after, their military service. The Far East and South America have been popular destinations in recent years.

SOCIETY

Transportation

Until recently, car ownership in Israel was relatively low for an industrialized nation. There has been an enormous leap in the number of cars on the road since the early 1990s, however. Israel is also implemented a program designed to make electric cars cheaper and easier to use for the Israeli public, but the venture failed in 2013.

Israeli drivers drive on the right hand side of the road. Seatbelt use is required by law, as is the use of headlights for intercity driving at all times and in all weather. Cell phone use is limited to headsets and all cars are required to carry a fluorescent vest.

Transportation Infrastructure

It is relatively easy to travel around Israel on public transportation, particularly on the country's extensive bus system. The national train lines have recently been upgraded, and light rail lines are being laid in the country's biggest cities.

Today, Israel's roads are considered more than twice as crowded, per mile, than those in the U.S. are. As a result, Israel has built an unprecedented number of new roads. One of these, the 297-kilometer (185-mile) long Kvish Shesh (Highway 6), has raised a great deal of controversy. Many environmentalists believe the highway and its ongoing construction are destroying irreplaceable natural landscapes, and advocate improving public transportation as a solution to the country's crowded roadways.

Media & Communications

For many years, the government-operated Israel Broadcasting Authority (IBA) had a monopoly on television broadcasts. It maintained one television channel, which broadcast in black-and-white until the early 1980s. The Second Channel was launched in 1993 as the country's first commercial network. Today, many homes also subscribe to cable or satellite television services. Much of the programming is imported, but Israel produces many local programs as well. In 2008, several Israeli shows were adapted for American television, including *In Treatment* and *The Ex List.*

The IBA also once held a monopoly on radio broadcasts, but commercial radio was launched in 1995. Many radio stations run an hourly newscast, and talk radio is a popular format. The selection on most music stations is usually a mix of Israeli and international rock/pop. Many stations cater to very specific groups, such as the Orthodox Jewish community (which forbids the public broadcast of women's voices) or Russian immigrants (with a Russian language format).

There are several daily papers in Israel, and nearly 6 million Israelis have Internet access. (Internet access in Israel is estimated at 75.8 percent of the population in 2014.) In spite of occasional military censorship, organizations such as Reporters without Frontiers give Israel high marks for the freedom of its press. However, Palestinian reporters in the Gaza Strip and West Bank often face censorship and violence from the Israeli military (in addition to censorship by the Palestinian Authority).

SOCIAL DEVELOPMENT

Standard of Living

Israel's 2013 Human Development Index rank was 19th, on a list of 187 countries.

Water Consumption

Water, and the lack thereof, has become a political issue in the Middle East, and has become a point of contention within Israel and the occupied territories. Lake Tiberias is a major water supply for the whole of Israel. Water also comes from the Jordan River and the Yarqon River, as well as an underground water table tapped by wells. Nevertheless, the country has had to focus on drip irrigation, micro-sprinklers techniques for agricultural use. Water conservation is a way of life and the Israeli government is engaged in several efforts to increase available water, including desalinization, importing water from Turkey, rehabilitating failing wells, and sewage treatment for irrigation use. In 2012, 100 percent of the total population had access to improved drinking water.

Education
Education in Israel is mandatory until children reach sixteen years of age. Students may choose to continue their education at no cost for another two years. There is a variety of schools from which to choose, including secular, religious, and private, as well as schools that speak Arabic exclusively.

There are many universities in Israel. Three institutions formed in the early half of the 20th century are the Technion-Israel Institute of Technology, located in Haifa; the Weizmann Institute of Science, located in Rehovot; and the Hebrew University of Jerusalem. Other universities include Ben-Gurion University, the Open University of Israel in Tel Aviv (formerly Everyman's University), and the University of Tel Aviv.

According to the CIA World Factbook, Israel's literacy rate for Israel is 97.8 percent, with males at 98.7 percent and females at 96.8.

Israel's education system faces the challenge of continuing to integrate the steady stream of immigrant populations that continue to pour into Israel. The Ministry of Foreign Affairs identifies student issues of acculturation and learning the language. These concerns also have an impact on teacher populations, as they need to accommodate those students in their classrooms. At the same time, the government is working towards raising educational outcomes.

Women's Rights
Generally, the status of women in Israel often depends on their religious, ethnic, and social background. The Israeli Proclamation of Independence declares that the government is charged with upholding the social and political equality of all citizens, without discrimination based on religion, race, or sex. In certain regards, Israeli women experience a level of equality to men nonexistent in most Western societies. For example, women are drafted into the army alongside men, and enjoy up to 14 weeks of maternity leave when they become mothers. In addition, the American-born Golda Meir served as prime minister of Israel from 1969–1974, more than three decades before Hillary Clinton was considered a serious nominee for the U.S. presidency.

However, Israeli women continue to face many challenges on the road to true equality. In a country where one's military service often translates to later professional opportunities, women are not allowed to serve in combat units. Until very recently, women were not allowed to fly in the air force. On average, Israeli women earn 37 percent less than men do. Partly, the gender gap in monthly income is related to the difference in work input of men and women – men employees work an average 45 hours a week and women employees – 36 hours. In calculating hourly income, the gender gap narrows. In 2011, a woman's hourly income constituted 83 percent that of a man.

In the 1990s, the Israeli court system recognized that changes need to be made if real equality is to be achieved. The courts issued several rulings allowing for affirmative action that would advance the case of women.

Women from certain communities often face specific problems. Ultra-orthodox Jewish communities maintain a strict segregation of the sexes, and girls are not given the same educational opportunities as boys. They are raised to see motherhood as a woman's highest goal, and on average, ultra-Orthodox women have seven to eight children each. Moreover, Orthodox Jewish religious law states that any Jewish woman who wants to divorce her husband may do only do so if her husband agrees, even in situations where the husband is abusive or mentally ill. As a result, many Israeli women are forced to remain in unhealthy marriages.

Palestinian-Israeli women often face similar difficulties in their own communities, in addition to the discrimination they face as non-Jews. In some cases, they also face the threat of violence, and occasional "honor killing," if they stray from a strict sense of proper gender-based behavior.

Girls have traditionally not been as highly valued as boys, and were often not free to study or get work outside the home.

Though many problems remain, Israel has seen marked improvements in the status of Palestinian-Israeli women in the late 20th and early 21st centuries. Today it is a shared expectation that all girls will go to school, at least through high school. In fact, university enrollment is higher among Palestinian-Israeli women than among their male counterparts. In Arab societies, teaching has long been considered a male pursuit. In the late 1990s, there were 40 percent fewer female teachers than male teachers in Palestinian-Israeli schools; today, there are 10 percent more women working in schools than men.

Under the Israeli government's Advancement of the Status of Women program, the government is advancing efforts to confront, through legislation, issues related to gender inequality, domestic violence, welfare, and health concerns.

Health Care

Israel has a low infant mortality rate (3.55 deaths per every 1,000 live births in 2015) and high life expectancy rates (82.27 years). (Men are expected to live 80 years, and women 84 years.) It has a national health care system, overseen by the Ministry of Health, which also monitors private health care companies. There is national insurance as well as compulsory social insurance, welfare, and childcare programs. In 2000, the World Health organization ranked Israel's healthcare system 28th in the world.

GOVERNMENT

Structure

Immigration to a Jewish homeland began in the late 1800s, when Jews began returning to Palestine, then a part of the Turkish Ottoman Empire. The road to statehood got a significant boost in the aftermath of World War I, when these "Zionist pioneers" persuaded the British government to aid the creation of a Jewish homeland

in the Balfour Declaration of 1917. The League of Nations then placed Palestine under British control.

With the onset of World War II, Britain stopped Jewish immigration to Palestine for security purposes. By the end of the war, the Jewish population had reached over half a million. In 1947, amid international pressure and the revelation of the horrors of the Holocaust, Britain returned the Palestinian issue to the newly formed United Nations. The UN decided to divide Palestine into two states, one Arab and one Jewish. The Arab population rejected this idea.

As soon as the state of Israel was declared in 1948, it was invaded by its neighbors: Iraq, Egypt, Jordan (then Transjordan), Lebanon, and Syria. The war ended in the summer of 1949 with Israel gaining one-fifth more territory that was originally allotted by the UN. Since its creation, there has been a series of wars challenging Israel's existence and its borders.

The country itself is a democratic republic, governed by a set of "basic laws." In forming the government, Israel did not compose a constitution or a bill of rights. Instead, the composition of the Jewish state is constantly evolving creature, obedient to changes in society and politics.

The country's legislative body is called the Knesset, composed of 120 members in a single chamber. The members serve four-year terms.

The prime minister, who assembles a cabinet, heads the executive branch of the government. The members of this executive cabinet may be members of the Knesset, but it is not required. The Knesset elects a president every five years, though the office is mainly ceremonial. The president may appoint various government officials, but possesses no veto power.

Israel is subdivided into six districts, each with its own councils and elections. The minimum voting age is 18, though citizens cannot run for office until they are 21 years old. The division of the Knesset is a result of the proportion of votes each party receives. The prime minister is no longer elected by direct election—instead, the leader of the governing coalition fills the office.

Political Parties

The two main parties in the country are the conservative Likud Party and the more liberal Labor Party. Parliamentary democracies often have a large number of political parties, which have a tendency to shift in terms of political platform and their alliance with other parties sharing common interests. Often, parliamentary systems are ruled by coalitions of two or more parties that unite to form a majority coalition. These coalitions differ in nature, with some coalitions having a lasting strength and others failing to govern at all. Additionally, it is not unusual for parties to dissolve because of personality conflicts within the organization.

In 2015, 12 parties were represented in Israel, with the strongest being the Likud. Other parties that won seats included Zionist Camp, Joint List, Yesh Atid, Kukanu, Bayit Yehudi, Shas, Israel Beituneu, United Torah Judaism, Meretz, and Yachad.

Local Government

Local government in Israel is divided into cities, local councils, and regional councils based on population. Mayors and a city council that are elected for five-year terms run cities. Local councils are communities of between five and 20,000 residents. Regional councils are comprised of villages and communities of less than 2,000 residents. Local governments are charged with infrastructure, environmental protection, education, social welfare, and cultural concerns.

Judicial System

Israel's judicial system has both religious and secular courts. Secular courts concern themselves with laws and civil concerns. The Supreme Court is the highest court in the land and district (courts of first instance), magistrate, small claims, traffic, labor, and admiralty courts form the fundamental structure of its judicial system.

Religious courts, with authorities accountable to the prime minister and the chief rabbinate of Israel, are responsible for issues relative to kashrut, marriage (and divorce), religious laws, and the qualifications of local rabbis. Islamic courts address domestic concerns within that community.

Taxation

Individual income tax in Israel ranges between 10 and 45 percent of income; corporate income tax is 25 percent of undistributed profits. Capital gains and value-added taxes (VAT) are also in place.

Armed Forces

The Israeli Defense Forces (IDF) is comprised of an army (ground forces), navy, and air force. The IDF is unique in its conscription of women and in its structure, which is more cohesive between branches. Military service in Israel is compulsory; women serve for two years and men for three. Those in combat positions (men and women) tend to serve longer. Homosexuals openly serve in the IDF, and the Israeli military has even begun educating commanders and rank-and-file troops about gender identity to ensure that the handful of service members who transition each year are treated with respect.

Members of the Haredi community (ultra-orthodox Jews) may serve in a special combat unit that accommodates their dietary restrictions and limits their exposure to women. Most Haredi Jews choose not to serve in the IDF.

Israel's defense force is highly mechanized and they are recognized internationally for being on the cutting edge as far as hardware and technology. Israel has developed its own military technology to address their specific needs, namely the Merkava battle tank and Galil and Tavor assault rifles, as well as other weapons systems. In fact, the Israeli army developed the Uzi submachine gun, which was in use through the 1990s.

Foreign Policy

Israel's foreign policy is shaped by the government's perception of national security in relation to the Palestinian people and the neighboring Arab nations: after six wars, several periods of conflict and daily skirmishes, 40 years occupying the West Bank and Gaza Strip, and two

Palestinian intifadas (uprisings), much of Israeli politics centers on the question of what policies offer the most security. The ongoing conflict plays a big role in Israel's economy, the arts, and even daily conversation. Furthermore, this often-precarious situation is the reason Israel has adopted conscription, or compulsory military service.

The Arab nations refused to recognize Israel's existence for several decades after the country was established in 1948. This attitude eventually resulted in the 1967 Six Day War. Before the war, Arab leaders openly declared their intention to destroy Israel. In its aftermath, the Arab League insisted there would be "'no peace, no recognition, and no negotiation.'" The League first publicly reversed this position in 2002. It called on Israel to negotiate the establishment of an independent Palestinian state. In exchange, the conflict would be ended and normal relations established with all Arab nations. The offer was made again in 2007. In neither case, though, did Israel take decisive steps to test the sincerity of the initiative, or to open negotiations. As such, Israel still maintains no diplomatic relations with over thirty countries, most of them Muslim nations.

The single most important factor in Israel's foreign policy is its relationship with the Palestinian people. Israel was created in 1948, in the midst of fighting between the Jewish and Palestinian Arab residents of what was then called Palestine. Both peoples were fighting to establish a national home. Israel's subsequent victory in the war meant that roughly 750,000 Palestinians became refugees. Today, more than 4 million Palestinians are largely concentrated in the areas known as the West Bank and Gaza Strip. Some are refugees from what is today Israel, others are native to those areas. Israel has occupied these territories since 1967.

The two nationalities continue to battle today, with subversive activities and military actions initiated by both sides. When the Palestinian people narrowly elected the terrorist organization Hamas to lead their government in 2006, Israel coordinated a strict international blockade of the areas controlled by Hamas. The civilian population's freedom of movement has been severely limited, along with their access to necessities such as food and medical supplies.

In the early 1990s, Israel and the Palestinians attempted a less confrontational approach. Palestinian leader Yasser Arafat (1929–2004) and Israeli Prime Minister Yitzhak Rabin (1922–1995) approved a series of secret negotiations in Oslo, Norway. These led to a "Declaration of Principles" meant to guide the sides to an eventual peace treaty. However, Rabin's assassination by an Israeli extremist and several waves of violence and counter-violence led to the collapse of the peace process. Efforts have been made to get negotiations started again since the start of the second Palestinian uprising in September 2000. So far, these have met with little success. Both the Israeli and Palestinian leadership maintain that any peace treaty will involve the establishment of an independent Palestinian state alongside Israel.

The United Nations filed an investigation on Israel's Defense Forces to determine whether it violated international law during the 2014 war in the Gaza Strip. It found that both Israel and Palestinian militants were responsible for violations that could amount to war crimes. The report said, "'the scale of the devastation was unprecedented'" in Gaza, tallying more than 6,000 airstrikes, 14,500 tank shells and 45,000 artillery shells unleased between July 7 and August 26 2014. Of the death toll of 2,252 Palestinians, the report said 65 percent were civilians.

Israel's relationship with the U.S. is a vital element of its foreign policy. America's government regularly accepts Israel's policy positions, with few exceptions. Israel also receives more US aid than any other country, though 75 percent of the military aid comes back to America via Israeli weapons purchases. America has also played a key role in the efforts made to achieve peace between Israel and the Arab world. However, recent relations between Israel and the U.S. have been rocky—as the BCC reports, this is partly because of the "lack of chemistry" between the Israeli Prime Minister Benjamin

Netanyahu and U.S. President Barack Obama. Another issue is Israel/Palestine peace process, of which President Obama noted that if there were no progress toward peace, there would be an impact upon how the U.S. approaches defending Israel on the international stage around the Palestinian issue.

Human Rights Profile

International human rights law insists that states respect civil and political rights, and promote an individual's economic, social, and cultural rights. The United Nations Universal Declaration on Human Rights (UDHR), is recognized as the standard for international human rights. Its authors sought the counsel of the world's great thinkers, philosophers, and religious leaders, and were careful to create a document that reflects the core values shared by every world culture. (To read this document or view the articles relating to cultural human rights, visit www.un.org/en/documents/udhr/).

Israel is a democracy, and its legal system is designed to protect the values declared in the country's Proclamation of Independence. These include the declaration of equal rights, both socially and politically, and the freedom of religion, education and culture. However, the freedom of religious expression is one area in which rights have been curtailed. For example, only Orthodox Judaism is recognized by the state, so only Orthodox institutions receive public funding. Further, only Orthodox rabbis may conduct Jewish weddings (even if the couple being married does not want a religious wedding), and Jewish funerals must follow Orthodox rules. This can be perceived as a violation of Article 18 of the UN Declaration of Human Rights.

Most of Israel's non-Jewish citizens are Palestinian Arabs, and the rights of this group are not guaranteed on the same level as Jewish citizens, a violation of Article 2 of the declaration. For example, Jewish communities are granted larger budgets than Arab communities. This means that Arab schools, municipalities, hospitals, etc, must make do with less money than Jewish institutions. In addition, Israeli Arabs who marry non-citizens face legal problems if they try to obtain citizenship for their spouses (or even bring their spouses to the country), particularly if those spouses are non-Israeli Palestinians, a violation of Article 16.

Finally, the Palestinians living under Israeli control in the West Bank and Gaza Strip face daily violations of their human rights. Israel has occupied these two areas since the 1967 Six Day War. Since that time, Israeli policies have compromised Palestinians' right to "life, liberty and security of person" (Article 3). The Israeli military frequently takes actions that lead to death and injury among civilians. Moreover, the government imposes economic sanctions that threaten Palestinians' jobs, education, and health.

Israeli authorities also severely curtail freedom of movement in the West Bank. In recent years, the borders of the Gaza Strip have been continuously sealed, allowing no passage for persons or supplies on most days of the year. Israel defends these actions and policies, saying they are necessary to protect Israeli lives threatened by Palestinian violence. Critics say that Israel is punishing all of Palestinian society for the actions of a few, and impeding the establishment of a Palestinian state.

Migration

Aliyah, or the legal right (under the Law of Return) to assisted immigration into Israel of any eligible Jewish individual or their dependent, is an important tenet of Zionism. Aliyah has become a powerful political tool for those who want to strengthen the Jewish state and who advocate for Jewish settlements in the occupied territories.

According to the *Wall Street Journal*, in 2009, the global economic crisis spurred the migration of 4,000 North American Jews to Israel; the Palestinian population also saw an increase, as Arabs from the Persian Gulf returned to the West Bank in search of employment. In the 1990s, the Jewish population grew through immigrants from former Soviet bloc countries; Israel also experienced a large influx of Ethiopian immigrants in two waves, 1984 and 1991.

In 2009, there were about 120,000 Ethiopian Jews in Israel, called Beta Israel. In the early 21st century, land purchases through the Jewish National Fund in occupied territories have prompted conservative Israeli groups to seek Jews in other countries to increase and stabilize the population.

In 2010, the children of migrant workers face expulsion from the government, which had a goal of expelling all illegal immigrants by 2013 and reducing the number of legal migrant workers. The issue of illegal African migrants has been of growing concern in the country – according to government records, more than 59,000 illegal African immigrants have entered Israel in recent years through its southern border with Egypt. In 2012, an Israeli court approved a government plan to deport 1500 migrants from Africa. The Israeli government opposes the rights of Palestinians to return to Israel.

ECONOMY

Overview of the Economy

The Israeli economy has seen enormous growth in its technology sector and its export market is significant, totaling $44.45 billion USD in 2009. Leading exports include hardware (machinery and equipment), diamonds, software, agricultural products, chemicals, and textiles. In 2007, Israel was responsible for 10 percent of the world's exports of military equipment. In 2014, the country's GDP was estimated at $303.8 billion. Israel's labor force is dominated by the services industry at 80 percent, followed by industry (18 percent) and agriculture (less than two percent). In 2014, the unemployment rate was six percent.

Industry

Israel's manufacturing sector centers on technology, education, and research and development, helped in part by the highly educated immigrants that arrived in Israel after 1948. The country's manufacturing focuses on electronics and weapons, the market for which has grown since 1967. Other goods manufactured in Israel include fertilizers, drugs, and medical and industrial equipment.

Because of ongoing hostilities with its neighbors, Israel relies heavily on the United States and the European Union as trading partners. Israel is also part of the World Trade Organization.

Labor

Israel's unemployment rate measured six percent in 2014. Labor force participation rate in Israel has been on the rise in the 21st century. In 1990, women (aged 15 and over) made up 41 percent of the labor force, compared with 53 percent in 2011. Labor force participation of Jewish women (59 percent) was almost three times higher than that of Arab women (22 percent) in 2011.

Energy/Power/Natural Resources

Israel's most important natural resource is its water supply, which is precarious. The most fertile area of the country is around Lake Tiberias, which is a major water supply for the whole country.

Israel relies on imports of natural gas and coal. There is also some oil, mainly in the northern Negev desert and just south of Tel Aviv.

Fishing

The fishing industry in Israel has seen a decline, but aquaculture development is reviving certain sectors, and Israel is considered a major competitor to the Asian fish industry. In the European market, where Israel has seen increased market share, the quality of Israeli fish products is garnering higher prices than its competitors. Fish products from Israel include rock bass, perch, Asian sea bass, gilthead sea bream, European sea bass, trout, and salmon.

Forestry

Approximately 2.4 percent of Israel's land area is set aside as forest reserves. Israel's forest policy is to develop healthy forest stands for protective purposes (preventing soil erosion and shifting sands and for water protection) and wood production.

Mining/Metals

Though it isn't a good source for water, the Dead Sea has been an excellent source of minerals. It is rich in potash, magnesium, bromine, and salt. Israel also is a large producer of iron and steel.

Agriculture

Israel's major crops include beets, peanuts, and cotton. In addition, there are citrus groves located near the center of the country. Israel has maximized its water supply in order to support agriculture, and is working on ways to obtain more water. One agricultural advance was the conversion of the Hula Swamp into usable farmland.

Animal Husbandry

Dairy has also become increasingly important with the growth of Israel's burgeoning cheese industry.

Tourism

Given Israel's central religious significance to Jews, Christians, and Arabs, it is a popular destination for tourists, though tourist traffic slows during periods of violent conflict. Attacks by militant Palestinian groups such as Hamas make the country a dangerous place to visit.

There are many sites with biblical significance scattered throughout Israel, including the cities of Bethlehem and Nazareth, as well as the Western Wall and the Dome of the Rock. There is active archeological preservation and study underway related to the country's religious heritage. There are also popular resorts along Israel's Mediterranean coastline.

In 2009, Israel saw 2.7 million foreign tourists; it is Israel's leading industry. In 2008, tourism accounted for 4.7 percent of Israel's GDP.

After the Gaza war, tourists to Israel have dropped significantly. Figures compiled by the Israel Hotel Association for the first quarter of 2015 pointed to a 28 percent drop in tourist stays in Israel.

Emily L. Hauser, Barrett Hathcock

DO YOU KNOW?

- Tel-Aviv is the home of the largest diamond cutting and polishing operation in the world.

- At its widest point, Israel is only 85 miles wide.

Bibliography

Aaron David Miller. *The Much Too Promised Land.* New York: Bantam Dell, 2008.

Adam LeBor. *City of Oranges.* New York: W.W. Norton & Company, 2007.

Amir S. Cheshin, Bill Hutman, and Avi Melamed. *Separate and Unequal.* Cambridge, Massachusetts: Harvard University Press, 1999

Ari Shavit. *My Promised Land: The Triumph and Tragedy of Israel.* New York: Spiegel & Grau, 2015.

Blu Greenberg. *How to Run a Traditional Jewish Household.* New York: Simon & Colin Shindler. *A History of Modern Israel.* Cambridge, UK: Cambridge University Press, 2008.

Ian J. Bickerton and Carla L. Klausner. *A History of the Arab-Israeli Conflict.* Upper Saddle River, NJ: Pearson Prentice Hall, 2014. Schuster, 1983.

Joseph Telushkin. *Jewish Literacy.* New York: William Morrow and Company, 1991.

Nicholas De Lange, (ed.) *The Illustrated History of the Jewish People.* New York: Harcourt Brace and Company, 1997.

Rashid Khalidi. *Palestinian Identity.* New York: Columbia University Press, 1997.

Sachiko Murata and William C. Chittick. *The Vision of Islam.* St Paul, Minnesota: Paragon House, 1994.

Walter Laquer and Barry Rubin, eds. *The Israel-Arab Reader: A Documentary History of the Middle East Conflict.* New York: Penguin Books, 2008.

Works Cited

De Lange, Nicholas (ed). The Illustrated History of the Jewish People. New York: Harcourt Brace and Company, 1997.

Greenberg, Blu. How To Run a Traditional Jewish Household. New York: Simon & Schuster, 1983.

Murata, Sachiko and William C. Chittick. The Vision of Islam. St Paul, Minnesota: Paragon House, 1994.

Telushkin, Joseph. Jewish Literacy. New York: William Morrow and Company, 1991.

Wagschal, S. The New Practical Guide to Kashruth. Jerusalem: *Feldheim*, 1991.

http://64.233.167.104/search?q=cache:jYS7kXX4ju4J: www.jpost.com/servlet/Satellite%3Fpagename%3DJPo

st%252FJPArticle%252FShowFull%26cid%3D120526
1308165+honor+killings+israel&hl=en&ct=clnk&cd=1
2&gl=us

http://abcnews.go.com/International/story?id=4271093&
page=1

http://books.google.com/books?id=szaBAAAAIAAJ&q=
%22thinner+and+thinner%22+inauthor:AMICHAI&dq=
%22thinner+and+thinner%22+inauthor:AMICHAI&ei=
KoOfSPT6LZvOjgGswZH7BA&pgis=1

http://countrystudies.us/israel/106.htm

http://hrw.org/englishwr2k8/docs/2008/01/31/isrlpa17596.htm

http://israelidance.berkeley.edu/history.html

http://www.amazon.com/Art-Palestinian-Embroidery-Laila-
El-Khalidi/dp/0863560385

http://imeu.net/news/article003822.shtml

http://media.www.dailypennsylvanian.com/media/storage/
paper882/news/2008/02/11/News/Exhibit.Showcases.
Soldiers.Moral.Qualms-3200621.shtml

http://news.bbc.co.uk/2/hi/middle_east/3152651.stm

http://news.bbc.co.uk/2/hi/middle_east/3777385.stm

http://news.bbc.co.uk/2/hi/middle_east/4769661.stm

http://news.bbc.co.uk/2/hi/middle_east/7551918.stm

http://news.bbc.co.uk/2/hi/middle_east/country_
profiles/803257.stm

http://papers.ssrn.com/sol3/papers.cfm?abstract_id=806904

http://query.nytimes.com/gst/fullpage.html?res=990CEED
71E3BF930A2575BC0A963958260&sec=&spon=&pa
gewanted=all

http://whc.unesco.org/en/list/1096

http://witcombe.sbc.edu/sacredplaces/holysepulchre.html

http://www.noblesanctuary.com/

http://www.caesarea.landscape.cornell.edu/about.html

http://www.tel-aviv.gov.il/English/cityhall/history/
history01.htm#matay

http://www.adva.org/UserFiles/File/adva_israel_2005_
english.pdf (see page 13)

http://www.al-bab.com/arab/docs/league/peace02.htm

http://www.allthelyrics.com/song/1235052/

http://www.amazon.com/Secret-Life-Saeed-Pessoptimist-
Interlink/dp/1566564158

http://www.amazon.com/See-Under-Novel-David-
Grossman/dp/0312420692/ref=pd_sim_b_1

http://www.bankisrael.gov.il/press/eng/080617/080617k.htm

http://www.btselem.org/English/Freedom_of_Movement/
Statistics.asp

http://www.btselem.org/English/Statistics/Casualties.asp

http://www.cbs.gov.il/hodaot2007n/11_07_262e.pdf

http://www.cnn.com/2008/WORLD/meast/01/24/gaza.
egypt/index.html

http://www.cnn.com/2012/06/17/world/meast/israel-
deports-immigrants/

http://www.csmonitor.com/2007/0516/p07s02-wome.html

http://www.fas.org/sgp/crs/mideast/RL33222.pdf

http://www.forward.com/articles/12375/

http://www.guardian.co.uk/world/2008/jun/20/israel

http://www.gulf-times.com/site/topics/article.asp?cu_
no=2&item_no=213063&version=1&template_
id=36&parent_id=16

http://www.haaretz.com/hasen/spages/1008700.html

http://www.haaretz.com/hasen/spages/788940.html

http://www.haaretz.com/hasen/spages/857185.html

http://www.haaretz.com/hasen/spages/944011.html

http://www.haaretz.com/hasen/spages/947162.html

http://www.haaretz.com/hasen/spages/957101.html

http://www.iht.com/articles/2008/03/04/africa/jerus.php

http://www.israel-mfa.gov.il/MFA/Archive/
Communiques/1995/THE%20TRANS-ISRAEL%20
HIGHWAY%20-%20May-95

http://www.ithl.org.il/authors.html

http://www.jcpa.org/dje/articles2/orth-nonorth.htm

http://www.jewishsf.com/content/2-0-/module/displaystory/
story_id/12103/edition_id/233/format/html/displaystory.html

http://www.jewishvirtuallibrary.org/jsource/Society_&_
Culture/newpop.html

http://www.jiis.org.il/ (see bilingual statistic reports)

http://www.jiis.org.il/imageBank/File/shnaton_2007/
shnaton_C0206_2007.pdf)

http://www.knesset.gov.il/docs/eng/megilat_eng.htm

http://www.knesset.gov.il/mk/eng/mk_eng.asp?mk_
individual_id_t=414

http://www.knesset.gov.il/mk/eng/mkindex_current_eng.
asp?view=3

http://www.mfa.gov.il/MFA/Government/Facts+about+
Israel-+The+State/A+Free+People+in+Our+Land-+
Gender+Equality.htm

http://www.mfa.gov.il/MFA/MFAArchive/2000_2009/2001/
11/Facets%20of%20the%20Israeli%20Economy-%20
Transportation

http://www.mideastweb.org/nasser26may67.htm

http://www.newsweek.com/id/143795

http://www.nmc-music.co.il/nmc/artists/poliker/yehuda.html

http://www.nytimes.com/2005/10/06/arts/dance/06tanai.
html?scp=1&sq=sarah%20levy%20tanai&st=cse

http://www.nytimes.com/2015/06/23/world/middleeast/
israel-gaza-report.html

http://www.ochaopt.org/documents/AMA_61.pdf

http://www.pbs.org/wgbh/globalconnections/mideast/
timeline/text/links/event_634.html

http://www.rsf.org/article.php3?id_article=25434&
Valider=OK

http://www.state.gov/g/drl/rls/hrrpt/2004/41723.htm

http://www.state.gov/g/drl/rls/hrrpt/2007/100597.htm

http://www.time.com/time/world/
article/0,8599,1705518,00.html

http://www.worldarchitecturenews.com/index.
php?fuseaction=wanappln.projectview&upload_id=621

http://www.ynetnews.com/articles/0,7340,L-3362402,00.html

http://www.ynetnews.com/articles/0,7340,L-3487963,00.html

http://www1.cbs.gov.il/www/statistical/mw2013_e.pdf

S. Wagschal. "The New Practical Guide to Kashruth."
Jerusalem: *Feldheim*, 1991.

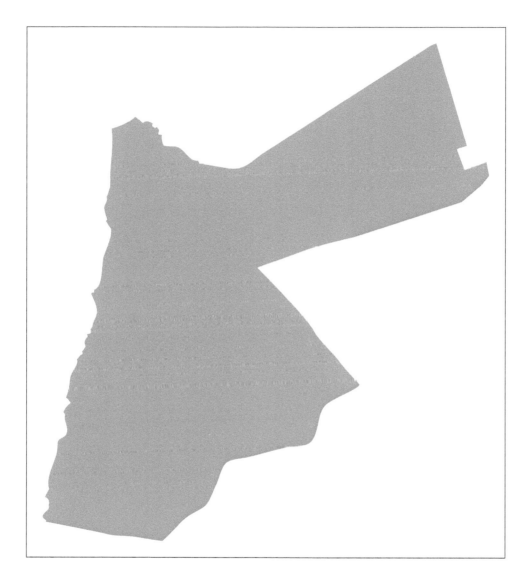

JORDAN

Introduction

Jordan is located in one of the most politically and environmentally sensitive places in the world. Bordered by Israel, Syria, Iraq, Saudi Arabia, and the Israeli-controlled West Bank, Jordan has at times played the role of peace broker in the ongoing Arab-Israeli conflict. Because of the conflict, approximately two million registered Palestinian refugees have entered Jordan, exacerbating one of the world's highest rates of population growth and putting additional pressure on a country with few natural resources. Jordan has become a model for political, social, and economic reform in the region, and continues to play a leading role in the region's efforts to protect delicate environments and conserve scarce water supplies. Yet, exacerbating its refugee problem is the ongoing civil war in Syria, which has caused tens of thousands of Syrian refugees to flood into Jordan.

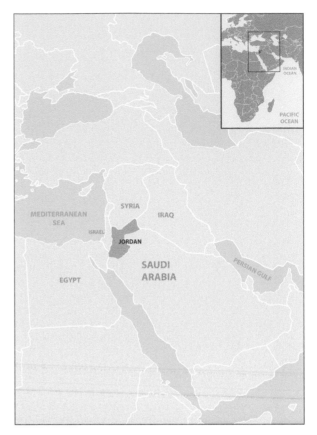

GENERAL INFORMATION

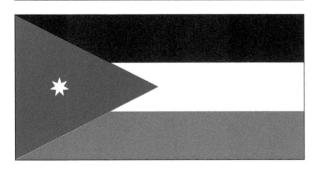

Official Language: Arabic
Population: 8,117,564 (2015 estimate)
Currency: Jordanian dinar
Coins: The dinar exists in denominations of 1, 5, 10, 20, 50, and 100 fils. However, 20-fils coins and 1-fils coins are no longer being minted. One-quarter dinar coins, half-dinar coins and 1-dinar coins were minted beginning in 1996.
Land Area: 89,341 square kilometers (45,495 square miles)
Water Area: 329 square kilometers (204 square miles)

National Anthem: "As-salam al-malaki al-urdoni" ("Long Live the King")
Capital: Amman
Time Zone: GMT +2 (GMT +3 during the summer season)
Flag Description: The flag of Jordan features three horizontal bands. The top band is black and represents the Abbassid Caliphate. The middle band of white represents the Ummayyad Caliphate and the lower band of green represents the Fatimid Caliphate. The left side of the flag has a red isosceles triangle that represents the Great Arab Revolt of 1916. In the middle of the triangle sits a white star with seven-points, each of which symbolizes a verse of the Koran.

Population

About 98 percent of Jordan's population is of Arab descent. Another 1 percent is Circassian, and 1 percent is Armenian. Roughly, 40 percent

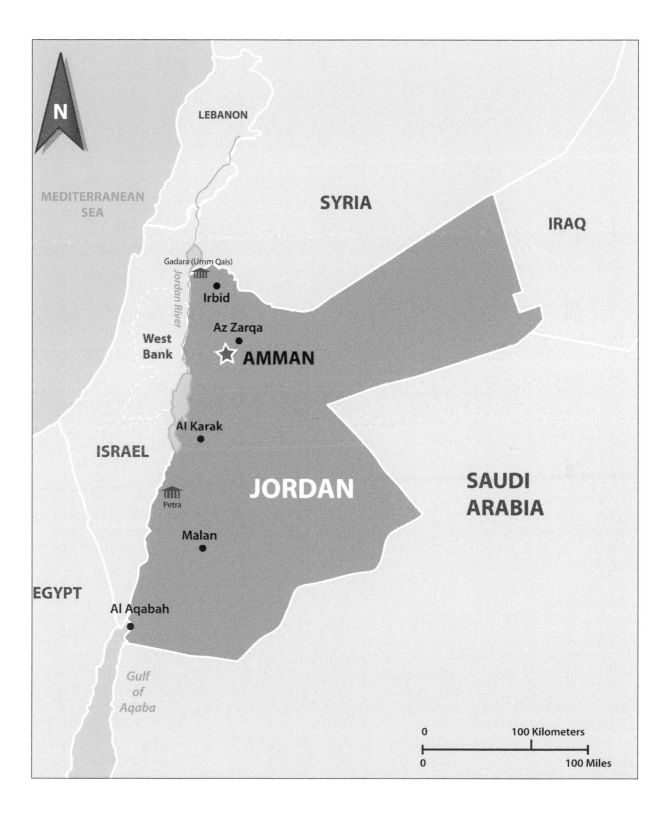

Principal Cities by Population (2012 estimate, unless otherwise noted):

- Amman (1,200,000)
- Zarqua (486,042)
- Russiefa (396,165)
- Irbid (325,996)
- Quwaysimah (248,017)
- Wadi Essier (175,133)
- Halda wa Tila-al-Ali (163,906) (2008 estimate)
- Huraybat As-Suq (122,304) (2008 estimate)
- Aquaba (108,561)
- As-Salt (87,778) (2008 estimate)

of the population is concentrated in and around Amman.

As the only Arab state to grant full citizenship to the former residents of what is now Israel, Jordan hosts about 1.7 million registered Palestinian refugees from the Arab-Israeli wars. While many Palestinians have taken Jordanian citizenship and assimilated into the general population, about 17 percent, or a little over 300,000 people, are living in refugee camps run by the United Nations Relief and Work Agency (UNRWA).

Life expectancy is 73 years for men and 75 years for women (2015 estimate). Infant mortality is an average 15 deaths per 1,000 births. The country's population continues to grow at 0.83 percent per year, with a birth rate of 25 births per 1,000 people.

Languages

Jordan's official language is Arabic, with English as the second language of education and business.

Native People & Ethnic Groups

The modern nation of Jordan was once part of the Palestine region (including Jerusalem) that is now mostly claimed by the state of Israel. The area is one of the longest-inhabited places on Earth, and has witnessed the rise and fall of Canaanite, Armorite, Sumerian, Akkadian,

Jewish, Nabataean, Roman, Christian, Egyptian, and Ottoman Empires over the past 5,000 years. The earliest known archeological finds in the area date back to about 9000 BCE.

The "Arab" designation that is given to most Jordanians only came about during the nineteenth and twentieth centuries when the various peoples, families, and tribes of the Middle East whose language derived from Bedouin Arabic were grouped under a single ethnic category. Prior to that, "Arab" referred to the nomadic Bedouin people who traveled the desert regions between the villages and cities of the Middle East, conducting trade. Modern day Jordanians include the descendents of all of these groups.

Religions

Approximately 92 percent of Jordanians are Sunni Muslim. Christians, mostly belonging to the Greek Orthodox Church, make up 6 percent of the population. The remaining 2 percent includes Shi'a Muslims and Druze (a faith derived from Shi'a Muslim teachings).

Climate

Jordan's climate is generally arid or semiarid. In the eastern deserts, the country receives less than 5 centimeters (less than 2 inches) of rainfall per year on average. Rainfall is substantially greater in the Mountain Heights Plateau region, averaging about 36 centimeters (14 inches) per year.

Temperatures vary significantly, rising above 40° Celsius (104° Fahrenheit) in the daytime during spring and summer, but ranging from only 2° to 9° Celsius (36° to 48° Fahrenheit) during the winter. However, temperatures in Amman only range from about 8° Celsius (46° Fahrenheit) during the winter to 24° Celsius (75° Fahrenheit) during the summer months. On particularly cold nights, the desert temperatures can drop below freezing.

ENVIRONMENT & GEOGRAPHY

Jordan lies at the meeting point of Southwest Asia and Arabia in the Middle East. Landlocked on all sides except where its southern tip borders the Gulf of Aqaba, the country nevertheless includes approximately 330 square kilometers (205 square miles) of water contained in the Dead Sea. Jordan's three geographical regions include the Jordan Valley, the Mountain Heights Plateau, and the Badia region (or Eastern deserts).

The Jordan Valley covers most of western Jordan, and is part of the Great Rift Valley, a 20-million-year old tectonic fissure that extends from Turkey to Africa. The Jordan Valley contains the biblical Jordan River, which irrigates much of the valley from the country's northern border to end in the Dead Sea. The northern segment of the valley, the Ghor, is Jordan's most fertile area.

Extending the entire length of western Jordan between the Jordan Valley and the eastern desert, the Mountain Heights Plateau is mountainous with rich vegetation. Because the mountains collect more rainfall than any other area of the country, this region is home to Jordan's largest towns and cities, including Amman. The mountains are cut by wadis, dry streambeds that fill with water after heavy rains. From the plateau, most of the wadis flow downward into the Jordan Valley and empty into the Jordan River or the Dead Sea.

The plateau's northern highlands have been known for millennia as the Land of Gilead. To the north and east of the region's higher elevations, the northern steppes are slowly being claimed by the eastern deserts.

Jordan's Eastern desert (or Badia region) is actually part of the Great Arab Desert and now claims about three-quarters of Jordan's national territory. Within the Badia, the Basalt Desert, Rweishid Desert, Eastern Desert, Central Desert, and Rum Desert vary in terrain, vegetation, and rainfall amounts. In Jordan's famous Rum Desert, the Wadi Rum rises into massive sandstone formations. All of the eastern desert regions include wadi oases that provide vegetation for the hardy species that live there.

Topography

The highest region in Jordan is atop Jabal Ram at 1,734 meters (5,689 feet) above sea level. South of the Dead Sea, the Jordan Valley becomes a 155-kilometer (96-mile) long basin surrounded by steep mountains.

Elevations in the basin region known as Wadi 'Araba range from 300 meters (984 feet) below sea level to 355 meters (1,165 feet) above sea level. The Wadi flows to sea level at the 40 kilometers (25 miles) of coastline in the city of Aqaba.

Jordan's lowest elevation is the Dead Sea where, at 408 meters (1,339 feet) below sea level, the land falls to its lowest point on the planet.

Plants & Animals

Once part of the biblical "land of milk and honey," modern day Jordan is striving to stop the loss of its abundant vegetation and wildlife. Nevertheless, wildflowers, including Jordan's national flower, the black iris, carpet the Mountain Heights Plateau in spring. About 220 bird species stop at the Azraq Reserve on their migratory routes. Typical Mediterranean trees like eucalyptus, pine, oak, pistachio, and cinnabar naturally thrive throughout the highlands and in areas of the Jordan Valley. Some of Jordan's olive trees date to the era of the Roman Empire.

The eastern deserts are home to hardier species like acacia trees, insects, lizards, and small mammals. Jackals, desert foxes, striped hyenas, camels, wolves, the rare white oryx, and mountain ibex also live in the desert areas.

Jordan's Gulf of Aqaba is home to one of the world's most important coral reefs. There, a wide variety of corals and other marine life find shelter in the warm, protected waters.

CUSTOMS & COURTESIES

Greetings

Greetings between Jordanians are typical Arab exchanges. They generally include wishes of peace and well-being that communicate their core values of community and brotherhood. The most common greeting is "Ahalan wa salan" ("Be at ease as if you are with family"). This is used very casually in most any context. It is customary when greeting to shake hands and give two cheek kisses;

women, though, often trade a more prolonged series of kisses among themselves. A typical farewell phrase is "Ma salamma" ("With peace").

When addressing someone, first names are typically only used by close family members. Older men and women are often called "Um" ("Mother") or "Abu" ("Father"), followed by the name of the eldest son (for example, the honorific title of "Abu Mohammed" is used to refer to Mohammed's father). Someone may also be introduced as "Haj" or "Haja," which are titles given to those who have completed the pilgrimage to Mecca. (The pilgrimage to the holy site of Mecca is considered one of the five pillars of Islam, and must be completed at least once in a Muslim's lifetime.)

Other Muslim-influenced phrases include "Bismiallah" ("In God's name"), which is usually uttered preceding everything from sharing a meal and opening a gift, to slaughtering an animal. The phrase "Insha'allah" ("If it is God's will") is also used in an array of contexts both serious and casual. If someone is receiving unwanted attention or is otherwise wishing to shame another, a stern "Haram!" reminds the recipient that their behavior is unacceptable to God.

Gestures & Etiquette

Although Jordan is quite Western in its ways, as compared to the highly orthodox behaviors of neighboring Iraq or Saudi Arabia, basic Islamic customs for male and female interaction still apply. Men typically only shake hands with men and women typically only shake hands with women. Anything outside of that should be initiated by a Jordanian man or woman, and should be received at the visitor's discretion. If nothing is offered, this is not an affront to the visitor, but rather a gesture of propriety. It is also not uncommon for Jordanians to offer an elbow to be shaken. This can indicate that the person has washed for prayer and is protecting the hands, or that the person has not washed and does not wish to extend an unclean hand.

Cleanliness of hands and feet is very meaningful in Muslim culture. The act of washing is integral to prayer and seen as a cleansing of the soul. Consequently, it is disrespectful to show dirty feet or touch a neighbor with dirty hands, as one's neighbors are perceived as incarnations of God himself. In addition, it is improper to use the left hand in most situations, as the left hand is associated with the cleansing of the body, and is thus considered impure.

Codes of dress differ widely, and it is especially important for women to read the context of the situation to determine what level of modesty is appropriate. In Amman, many women wear Western-style attire, including the queen (who routinely sports European fashions). However, in Bedouin country and when visiting rural attractions, it is expected that women will cover at least elbows and knees, even wrists and ankles if the occasion is formal (or the destination is sacred). Likewise, public displays of affection between men and women are not accepted.

Eating/Meals

In urban areas, meals more or less follow a European format. In rural areas, meals are traditionally shared in a communal dish, and men and women are segregated, with men eating first.

A typical Jordanian breakfast may consist of a hard-boiled egg and bread with jam. Traditional Muslim families might eat a breakfast of eggs and cheese following morning prayers.

For many Jordanians, lunch is the largest meal and is eaten in groups in the early afternoon while everyone catches up on the events of the day. It is generally a leisurely affair often comprised of "mezze" (small plates). The most common of these are "hummus" (pureed chickpeas and sesame paste), "baba ghanouj" (pureed eggplant), "tabouleh" (parsley, bulgur wheat, and tomato), spiced lamb kebabs, or spiced kefta meatballs.

Dinner is typically eaten late in the evening and is usually a meal of bean or vegetable soup followed by an entrée of grilled meat with olives and fresh flat bread. The exception to this occurs during the Muslim holy month of Ramadan. At that time, Jordanian Muslims fast during daylight hours. Each evening the fast is broken at sundown, with a shared and often celebratory meal, called "iftar." Preparations are basic, usually incorporating grilled meat and vegetables served with fresh flatbread, and followed by a round of strong coffee and pastries.

Restaurants typically close on Fridays, as Friday marks the Muslim holy day. Alcohol is not permitted by Muslim custom, but is available in bars, and import beer is generally served in addition to arak (anise liquor).

Visiting

Jordanians are known for their hospitality. Unity and kinship, important components of the Arabic value system, are generally extended to visitors, guests, and strangers. As such, personal questions regarding income, marital status, children, and religion are generally not considered taboo.

If invited to an upper class home, Western standards of visitation generally apply. Most Jordanian families at that status level have a family member living and working in the United States, and are typically accustomed or aware of Western customs and culture.

The southern Bedouin community, however, is more traditional. A guest should bring a modest gift that is consistent with the income level of the household and give it inconspicuously to whoever receives the door. It is best to wear slip-on shoes and offer to take them off before entering. When sitting on the floor, guests should position themselves cross-legged, as it is offensive to expose the soles of the feet.

Before the meal, a basin will be passed around for washing hands, as food is served on a communal plate and eaten without utensils. The guest usually is offered the best (or only) pieces of meat, a gesture of hospitality that should be graciously accepted. After the meal, everyone reclines for a rest and some conversation over several cups of tea or coffee. The men may retire to smoke cigarettes or drink alcohol.

After some socializing, it is appropriate to leave, though resistance from the host should be anticipated. Guests may be invited to nap or stay the night. Whether the household is urban or rural, hospitality is characteristic of the Muslim faith. Guests may refuse the invitation but should be prepared for a few rounds of insistence, as the host will want to be sure that she has exhausted all attempts to extend hospitality to her guests.

LIFESTYLE

Family

Family values form the core of Jordan's community-oriented culture and society. Respect for one's family is paramount and family honor is to be protected and defended at just about any cost. In fact, to disgrace one's family name through immodesty or unethical behavior often leads to disownment. While there are negative aspects to this philosophy, the positive side is that families are intensely committed. In addition, children traditionally live with their parents well into adulthood to help run household operations and care for their elders.

Because unemployment is so high, economic migration is typical among Jordanians, and many leave for neighboring Gulf nations, Europe, or the US. It is customary for family members who move overseas for work or study to send a percentage of their earnings home to their families.

Housing

Jordan is an arid place—80 percent of the country is desert land that is virtually uninhabitable. This means that an estimated 70 percent of the population lives in urban areas (or the remaining 20 percent of the land). In fact, 40 percent of the population lives in and around the capital of Amman. Consequently, the country is increasingly urban and modernized.

Urban housing is standard European construction, and consists of generally whitewashed townhouses or apartments with modern amenities. Houses are generally situated quite close together and very few families own land, since space is at a premium. Rural housing is vastly different and consists mainly of woven tents, as the Bedouin community is semi-nomadic.

Food

Lebanese, Egyptian and Syrian cooking, influence Jordanian cuisine. It is typically characterized by the use of cumin, olive oil, garlic, and lemon juice—four culinary components that may be found in any local dish. Other elements of its typical Arab cuisine include lamb and chicken dishes accompanied by yogurt-based sauces and marinades flavored with, mint, garlic, and tomatoes. The capital of Amman in particular offers an array of international cuisine.

A favorite meal among Jordanians is "mansaf," which is spiced lamb served with rice. Desserts are usually a sticky sweet concoction featuring phyllo dough, rose water and honey or sugar syrup. One popular treat is "kunafa," made by combining ricotta cheese, granulated sugar, and rose water.

Fish is not readily available in Jordan, and so it is rather expensive and not often prepared. Pork is not permitted in Muslim diets and is rarely offered, although the occasional foreign restaurant may serve it. Pastry shops are a popular source of desserts and other related foods.

Regarding beverages, fresh fruit juices are popular, but the favorite drink in Jordan is coffee. Jordanian coffee is bold and strong, and traditionally served in small shots sometimes spiced with cardamom.

Life's Milestones

Although Jordan is a secular state, Islam is practiced by the majority of the population—an estimated 92 to 94 percent—and influences most major traditions. When a baby is born, the first sound it traditionally hears is "Allah oo'Akbar" ("God is great,") known as the "Call to Prayer." A naming ceremony is held one week later, where the baby's head is shaved and an animal is sacrificed. Circumcision takes place when a young boy is seven years old (or older) and is celebrated with parading and feasting, as it is considered a passage into adulthood.

Marriages are arranged for the most part and it is not unusual to be paired with a cousin to keep money and dowries in the family. A marriage ceremony is generally an elaborate affair with feasting, singing, and dancing for two to three days.

CULTURAL HISTORY

Art

Jordan is a relatively young country marked by religious turmoil and territorial conflict. Once a part of ancient Egypt, the territory was later taken over by various civilizations, including the Greeks, Nabateans, Romans, and Ottomans. These ancient civilizations left a cultural impression upon the region and its art, and made the area a rich source of archaeological remains. The Nabateans founded the kingdom of Petra, which rapidly developed in the first century BCE under Hellenistic influence. They thrived on trade until occupation by the Roman Empire, which lead to a period of tumultuous changes in leadership that concluded with occupation by the Ottomans. The Ottoman Empire (1299–1923) dissolved after the conclusion of World War I when the area was taken over by the British. By World War II, the area was released from British rule and it was declared the Hashemite Kingdom of Jordan under the rule of King Abdullah I (1882–1951).

Because of cycles of instability, Jordan's art scene didn't come of age until recently. However, the region has a rich history of traditional arts due to the indigenous Bedouin, an Arab nomadic people who historically dwelled in the region's desert areas. (The Bedouin actually refer to themselves as "Bedu.") Bedouin folk art and traditional crafts included embroidery, weaving (particularly carpets) and sculpture. Other traditional arts and crafts associated with this historical region, many dating back to the Copper and Bronze ages, include decorative creations such as pottery and jewelry.

Music

Arabic music is derived from a five-note scale (as opposed to the Western seven-note scale), which makes for haunting, sometimes dissonant, arrangements. This system originated primarily in what is currently Saudi Arabia, and trickled down to other Middle Eastern musical traditions. Consequently, relatively little can be considered strictly Jordanian, save for the chants of the Bedouin. Passed down through oral tradition, these songs typically recount folkloric tales of honor and valor. They are sometimes accompanied by an oud, a lute-like instrument, but are mostly chanted in groups while holding hands and dancing around the campfire.

Literature

Because of Jordan's relative youth, the country's literary history also borrows heavily from other Arab traditions and influential manuscripts. These include the Mu'allaqat, a pre-Islamic, Arabic collection of poems often referred to as "The Hanging Poems" or "The Suspended Odes," and the Koran, Islam's central text. For literature that is unique to the region, historians usually point to the Dead Sea Scrolls, a collection of religious and historical accounts that date prior to 100 CE, and include some of the original texts of the Hebrew Bible. (Fragments of the manuscript are held at various locations around the world, one of which is the permanent collection of the Amman Archeology Museum.) As the centuries progressed and the region was filtered through various occupations, literature fell by the wayside and did not resurface until the turn of the 20th century. Notable Jordanian literature includes the poetry of Mustafa Wahbi (1897–1949), who was known for his nationalist writings.

CULTURE

Arts & Entertainment

Jordan is a relatively young nation that has struggled with internal political conflict since its inception. As a result, the work of the country's artists has been limited and the establishment of a culture industry within the kingdom has been delayed. Government funding has helped to improve the presence of the arts in Jordanian culture, including a booming craft sector. Several Jordanian writers have won prizes for their work in recent years, and the Jordan National Gallery of Fine Arts has worked to increase its collection and visitor attendance. UNESCO has designated

the city of Amman as an Arab Cultural Capital for its efforts to make art accessible to the community.

Although the government has made great strides in integrating arts into the community, it has done so by encouraging artisan trades that might support economic growth. In a society battling high unemployment, the strain of population growth, and perpetual regional turmoil, the arts are more an economic strategy than a mode of personal expression. By capitalizing on existing local handicraft production, the government has managed to stimulate small business growth and attract tourism revenue.

The primary handicraft trades are embroidery, weaving, and jewelry making, which, incidentally, are all women's trades. The traditional red roza embroidery is a skill taught to young girls so that they might embellish their future wedding garb. Jewelry making is also associated with wedding customs, as brides are traditionally given a customized silver piece (often shaped into symbols of protection or fertility) as part of their dowry. Local weaving practices originate with the Bedouin women who set up looms every summer to prepare goat hair tents and carpets that might provide for them in the colder months.

Through the joint efforts of the Jordanian government, women's advocacy groups, and international non-profit organizations, the women of Jordan (particularly rural women) have begun to organize themselves and think outside their village confines. The result is a widespread availability of one-of-a-kind artisanal products appealing to tourists. This has created a consumer market where none existed. Furthermore, this initiative has provided opportunities for rural Jordanian women to contribute to their household income, participate in their community, and work to lift themselves out of their previously marginalized status.

This push to use art for commercial growth has helped to pave the way for the emergence of other creative endeavors. Increased tourism and the growth of international trade over the years have provided more exposure to Western thought and expression. Consequently, creative literature and poetry have gained momentum. In a sector once dominated by the Egyptian and Lebanese, Jordanian writers are finding their voice. Of particular note is the use of literature by Palestinian Jordanian writers as a medium for reacting to the Israeli-Palestinian conflict. The effects of the petroleum industry and immigrant life are other popular contemporary topics.

The fine arts, once battling a reputation as the most frivolous of all of Jordan's emerging forms, are also gaining support. Under the administration of King Hussein, The Jordan Artists Association (JAA) was created in 1978 and swiftly followed two years later by the Jordan National Gallery of Fine Arts. The Darat al-Funun, also located in Amman, is a contemporary art complex complete with a gallery, art library, and workshop space. It has gained a local following for its progressive exhibitions, lectures, and forums for public dialogue. The dominant themes in Jordanian visual arts are religious persecution and political transgressions. These are expressed in an array of styles, including abstract cubism, eclectic Kufic (a form of calligraphy) script drawings, and sandstone sculptures.

Cultural Sites & Landmarks

Jordan is situated in the heart of the Middle East, an area ripe with archeological sites and dramatic landscape. The country is located between Mecca and Jerusalem and houses some of the world's most revered holy territory. The Sea of Galilee and the Jordan River Valley are the settings for countless biblical stories. The northwestern region (including the Jordan River) is also considered part of the Fertile Crescent, an area referred to as one of the "cradles of civilization."

The Al Qastal Settlement, built in the 17th century, is believed to be the oldest known settlement in the region from the Umayyad Caliphate (661–750 CE). It holds nearly all the structures of a typical settlement, including a palace, mosque, cemetery, bathhouse, several homes, and an extensive irrigation system. The classical city of Gadara dates to roughly 63 BCE, and is counted among the Decapolis (a collection of ten Greco-Roman cities that shared political, cultural, commercial, and security interests). The black basalt and lime stone ruins include a mausoleum, two theatres, a basilica, two baths, several sculptures and decorative pieces, as well as an Ottoman village that is intact.

Mukawir was the stronghold of Herod the Great, where his son Herod Antipas ordered John the Baptist to be beheaded. It was also the site of several battles against the Byzantines that helped to define the Muslim faith, including the battles at Yarmouk in 634 CE and Fahl in 635 CE.

The historical region that encompasses modern-day Jordan is best known for its contribution to architectural history. The country's long sequence of ruling empires and kingdoms has resulted in a wealth of architectural styles, ranging from Neolithic structures, to the Greek architecture of the Nabatean city of Petra, to medieval and early Islamic architecture. In addition, numerous churches and mosques featuring ornate mosaics were constructed during the Roman-Byzantine era. The early influences of Islam, which emerged in the seventh century CE, are evident in Arab castles strongholds from the medieval period. Domed mosques and elaborately decorated palaces are signs of later Islamic and Ottoman influences. Many of the materials used in these varying styles of architecture include sun-dried mud bricks, limestone, basalt, and sandstone.

Jordan's architectural heritage was recognized by the inclusion of three national sites on the World Heritage List maintained by the United Nations Educational, Scientific, and Cultural Organization (UNESCO). These include the archaeological sites of Petra and Umm ar-Rasas (Kastron Mefa'a), and the desert castle of Qasr Amra. The ancient site of Petra, often referred to as one of the new wonders of the world, is famous for its rock-cut architecture. The archaeological site of Umm ar-Rasas features architectural ruins from numerous eras. The desert castle of Qasr Amra derives from the eighth century, and is a significant example of early Islamic architecture with distinct Roman influences.

Jordan also values environmental preservation and is home to many natural treasures. The Dana Nature Reserve stretches from the Jordan Rift Valley down to the desert of Wadi Araba. Encompassing Rummana Mountain, the archeological ruins of Feinan, and the sandstone cliffs of Wadi Dana, the preserve spans 300 square kilometers (115 square miles) of woodlands, rocky cliffs and sand dunes. It also serves as a protected area for about 600 species of rare plants and over 200 species of animals.

Jordan is also home to the Aqaba Marine Park, which contains 300 different types of coral, as well as plentiful fish and sea life. Originally established to protect sea life from Jordan's bustling port and trade route, the park now accounts for 80 percent of the country's public beaches and is a popular destination for Red Sea coral dives.

Lastly, there is the Dead Sea, famous for its high salinity, which means plant and animal life cannot survive in its waters. The Dead Sea is the lowest point on Earth, at 408 meters (1,340 feet) below sea level.

Libraries & Museums

The country's primary cultural institutions include the Amman Archeological Museum, the Jordan Museum of Popular Traditions, the Amman Folklore Museum, the Jordan National Gallery, and the Martyr's Monument and Military Museum. The Amman Archeology Museum holds fragments of the original text from the Hebrew Bible in its permanent collection. The National Library of Jordan is the country's national repository.

Holidays

As in most Muslim countries, Eid al-Fitr is Jordan's largest holiday. Coming at the end of Ramadan, the three-day celebration of renewal involves donning new clothes, giving to the poor, giving presents, and feasting and festivals. Eid al-Adha, the day that marks the Old Testament story of Abraham's willingness to sacrifice his son, takes place in the Muslim month of pilgrimage.

Other public holidays include New Years Day (January 1), Islamic New Year (January or February), Eid al-Mawlid al-Nawabi (the Prophet's Birthday, in April), Labour Day (May 1), Independence Day (May 25), the Accession of HM King Abdullah on (June 9), Army Day (June 10), and King Hussein Remembrance Day on November 14.

Youth Culture

In Jordan's metropolitan areas, particularly Amman, affluent youth experience a culture similar to that of Western youth. Popular pastimes include shopping, and fashions are typically European, as are behaviors and tastes. Europe is also a popular destination for studying abroad. Despite Western influences, relations between young men and women remain traditional. Girls socialize publicly in groups and generally aren't outside of the house much after dark. Football (soccer) remains the dominant sport, and young males often congregate in coffee houses to watch sporting events. The Jordanian national football team is Nashama, and they achieved their highest international ranking—37th—in 2004.

The Bedouin community, in contrast, is often removed from this modern way of life. While many have maintained their semi-nomadic lifestyle, others have settled down to a life of cultivation, and the current population generally maintains a way of life that mixes the two. Despite a more grounded lifestyle in recent years, children are not often schooled. Instead, they contribute to the family by assuming domestic responsibilities such as cooking and cleaning, and minding younger siblings. To generate income, male youth may take up sheep herding or leading tourists on rural treks, while girls create handicrafts that they then sell.

SOCIETY

Transportation

Cars in Jordan drive on the right side of the road. Only few Jordanians own private cars, and the common modes of transportation are metered taxi or bus. Inexpensive "servees," or communal taxis, run on a pre-determined route and can be hailed at any point. The rural areas are accustomed to twenty-seat minibuses that depart when they are full and run on a fixed schedule and fixed route, although the offerings are limited—sometimes only once per week.

Transportation Infrastructure

Jordan has a well-developed network of urban roadways. Paved highways link the major cities within the country, as well as neighboring Syria, Iraq and Saudi Arabia.

Jordan's Al-Aqaba port plays a major role as the only entryway by sea. Not only is it an asset to trade but also tourism; Egypt is a mere one hour away by speedboat. There are approximately eighteen airports, and Queen Alia International Airport, outside the capital of Amman, is the largest. The Hijaz Railway is a one-track system that still employs the track installed by the Ottomans at the turn of the 20th century. However, it is primitive and rarely frequented.

Media & Communication

The Jordan Times is an English language newspaper and is the most widely read news periodical. There is also *The Star* (also in English), which prints once a week, and three nationally distributed Arabic papers. Jordan prides itself on an open media that supports freedom of speech, although criticism of the royal family is frowned upon and actively discouraged.

Radio Jordan broadcasts music and pop culture programs in English, French, and Arabic. Television channels 1 and 3 broadcast in Arabic, and Channel 3 shows edited soap operas and sitcoms from the United States, Australia, and Europe. For uncensored television, hotels and affluent households purchase satellite television to access programming from the British Broadcasting Corporation (BBC), the Cable News Network (CNN) and Al Jazeera, launched in Qatar as an Arabic news channel.

Cell phones are widely used in the urban areas, as they are inexpensive to buy and maintain. The Internet is readily available as well but mostly in the form of public Internet cafés where one can pay per use. As of March 2014, there were an estimated 3.6 million Internet users in the country.

SOCIAL DEVELOPMENT

Standard of Living

Unlike some of its neighboring countries, Jordan does not have significant oil reserves, making unemployment and poverty ongoing problems in a country with scarce natural resources. Jordan ranked 77th on the 2014 Human Development Index (HDI), which is compiled by the United Nations.

Water Consumption

Access to water is the most serious environmental challenge facing Jordan. According to the World Health Organization (WHO), Jordan has one of the lowest levels of per capita water availability in the world. A continual increase in the country's population in recent years has strained already severely limited supplies of fresh water. The government of Jordan claims that it loses some of its share of regional water to neighboring countries. Experts consider water poverty to be a major problem in Jordan and one that is growing more serious. The majority of available water in Jordan is used by agriculture and industry. Efforts continue to be aimed at optimizing water utilization. In addition, water use education programs have begun and various water-pricing policies are being considered.

Education

In spite of poverty figures, literacy rates are high in Jordan and its system of education has been used as a model by other countries in the Middle East. The average adult literacy rate is 95 percent (97 percent among men and 92 percent among women). While Arabic is the official language, English is widely spoken among middle and upper class Jordanians.

Jordan's education system includes two years of optional preschool and 10 years of compulsory education (ages six to 16). Two years of secondary school study or vocational training are required before sitting for the Tawjihi, a secondary education completion exam.

Although Jordan has one of the highest rates of female education in the region, the country's poverty has made access to both preschools and secondary schools difficult for many students. Approximately 70 percent of Jordanian students attend compulsory secondary schooling. Therefore, Jordan is currently in the midst of a radical restructuring of its educational system. With the assistance of international organizations, the Jordanian government is increasing the number of preschools, standardizing curricula, creating teacher training requirements and facilities, and aligning school curricula at all levels with new technology-based employment goals.

Federal funding of education in 2003 represented approximately six percent of total government spending. In recent years, the Jordanian Ministry of Education has required that all students in the country become computer literate.

Women's Rights

The women of Jordan enjoy more rights than most of their Middle Eastern neighbors. There is no official dress code and virtually no public segregation (except in mosques). Education statistics are strong and graduation rates are almost equal to that of males. Women have had the right to vote since 1967, and constitute 20 percent of the workforce. Many work in traditionally male-dominated fields as judges, mayors, ambassadors, and doctors. The legal age of marriage is 18 (it is 15 in most other Middle Eastern countries). In 2002, women were granted the right to file for divorce.

Much of this progress is due to King Hussein, who took an American bride (Lisa Halaby, now known as Queen Noor) in 1978. With his support, she worked fervently for women's rights, particularly through her Noor al Hussein Foundation, which has achieved international acclaim. By addressing issues such as poverty, health reform, microcredit, and even the portrayal of women in the media, the foundation has taken a holistic approach that has improved the status of women and influenced the cultural mindset as well.

Following in her footsteps is Queen Rania (1970–), whose youth and progressive attitude has invigorated Jordan's younger generations, who account for over 70 percent of the population. Queen Rania takes her role in the spotlight seriously and has put her philosophy of empowerment into action by promoting equal opportunities for education, microcredit, and small business development. Consequently, as of 2015, 92 percent of women were literate (an all-time high) and record numbers are graduating with university degrees. Small business programs are on the rise as women secure microcredit for selling handicrafts, livestock, and food products. Queen Rania's efforts also address community needs. Working on behalf of children, she has prompted improved school facilities and the formation of a national children's museum. She has also sponsored beautification projects and ecotourism initiatives. In response to international turmoil and terrorist activity, she developed the Amman Message to condemn violent extremism.

The women's movement in Jordan is not without difficulties, however. Sexual violence is rampant, especially in the form of honor crimes. It is estimated that every two weeks, a woman is killed by her brothers and father for alleged acts of indiscretion that shame her family name. This practice has strong cultural roots, though it is not encouraged by the teachings of Islam. Women also face discriminatory or biased actions because of the law. Sentences for many convicted of honor killing, if any, are lenient, and despite recent efforts to impose harsh consequences, the proposals are routinely opposed by parliament. In addition to honor crimes, sexual violence is prevalent among young women. Most assaults take place at school, leading to some international organizations such as the United Nations Development Fund for Women (UNIFEM) to integrate sex education into the national curriculum to encourage open dialogue about these atrocities.

Health Care

Although it is now under pressure from population growth and widespread poverty, Jordan's health care system has an established reputation as a model for health care in the region. The government sponsored national health insurance program subsidizes the cost of primary care, emergency care, specialist treatment, dental care, and eye care. Government-run and charitable hospitals and clinics provide access to free care for the country's poorest residents. A large network of private physicians, clinics, and hospitals are available to Jordan's wealthier residents.

Jordan's economic setbacks, most recently a result of the U.S.-led invasion of neighboring Iraq, have depleted funding for both private and public health care services. At the same time, population growth and increased unemployment have dramatically increased demand for medical care. As a result, Jordan has accepted large sums of foreign aid, including funding from the U.S. government, to renovate and build new clinics, improve health care worker training, and subsidize public health campaigns.

GOVERNMENT

Structure
Jordan is divided into twelve governorates (administrative divisions) ruled by a constitutional monarchy. The country became independent in 1946 after being ruled by Britain (as Transjordan) under a post-World War II mandate from the United Nations.

From 1948 until 1967, Jordan included Jerusalem and the West Bank territories within its national boundaries. Both areas were lost to Israel in the Six Day War between Israel and its Arab neighbors. Jordan signed a peace treaty with Israel in 1994.

Executive power rests with the king. Jordan's Majlis al-'Umma (national assembly) consists of the Majlis al-Ayan (Senate) and a Majlis al-Nuwaab (House of Deputies). The monarch from proscribed categories appoints the 55 members of the Majlis al-Ayan. Each member serves a four-year term. The 110 members of the Majlis al-Ayan are elected by popular vote based on proportional representation to serve four-year terms.

Six seats in the Majlis al-Ayan are reserved for women.

Political Parties
The most widely known and influential political party in Jordan is the Islamic Action Front (IAF). Founded in 1992, it is the political arm of the Sunni political organization known as the Muslim Brotherhood. Although the IAF basis its politics in Islam, it is less extreme than other Islamic political parties in the Middle East are. The IAF supports women's rights and pluralism. Currently the IAF hold no actual power after boycotting the 2013 elections after the king disbanded parliament halfway through its term. Several dozen other political parties exist in Jordan, including the Jordanian Democratic Popular Unity Party, the Arab Democratic Front, and the Jordanian Arab Socialist Baath Party. These parties have smaller numbers of supporters and yield far less influence than the IAF.

Local Government
Jordan is divided into 12 governorates. Each governorate is led by a governor and is divided into a collection of administrative regions. Individual administrative regions are governed by municipal councils, which are elected to four-year terms. An individual income tax is collected as well.

Judicial System
According to Jordan's constitution, the country's judicial branch is independent of the government. Judges, approved and dismissed by the king, are overseen by the Higher Judicial Council. The country's civil judicial system includes Magistrate Courts, Courts of First Instance, and the Courts of Appeal. There are also religious courts in Jordan. These courts deal with issues involving personal law; divorce, child custody, inheritance and marriage.

Taxation
The government of Jordan collects a corporate income tax of 15 percent. In addition, it collects

a social security tax, vehicle tax and fuel tax, among others.

Armed Forces

The king of Jordan oversees the country's armed forces, which includes the Royal Jordanian Land Force, the Royal Naval Force, the Royal Jordanian Air Force, and the Royal Special Forces. His Majesty's Special Security force and the General Intelligence Department are also a part of the armed forces. Jordan is considered a staunch military ally of Egypt.

Foreign Policy

Placed precariously in the midst of a region prone to unrest, the Jordanian government has managed to establish a reputation as an advocate of peace. Much of this is a credit to King Hussein (1935–1999), who ruled Jordan from 1953 until 1999. He worked diligently to build a nation that minds its Muslim faith while promoting moderate politics. As evidence of his desire to unite the country and encourage political expression, the king ended martial law in 1991. He also legalized political parties in 1992, a change which the Islamist parties actively opposed by boycotting elections in 1997. Even in the face of prolonged territory disputes (Jordan occupied the West Bank from 1949 until 1967, when the territory was lost in war to Israel), a peace treaty with Israel was signed in 1994. The two countries now collaborate on security, trade, and finance.

Since the ascension of King Abdullah II (1962–) to the throne in 1999, Jordan has undergone an effort to reform the economy and develop its political agenda. In support of Jordan's standing as a fair and impartial neighbor, King Abdullah has furthered good relationships by reaffirming the peace treaty with Israel and reinforcing ties with the US. In fact, Jordan has played a key role in restoring stability to Iraq, particularly by developing and training the Iraqi army. However, regional conflict continues to affect Jordan's economy, particularly the influx of Palestinian refugees, as Jordanian law allows any Palestinian to obtain Jordanian citizenship. They now comprise one third of Jordan's people, and as the population continues to swell, resources are thinning. King Abdullah also struggles with the consequences of opening the country's borders during such volatile times. Religious extremism is not tolerated in Jordan.

In keeping with its policy of peace and stability in the Middle East, Jordan is a member of the Non-Aligned Movement (NAM), claiming no formal alliance with or against any one international power. The country is also a member of the UN, the International Atomic Energy Agency (IAEA), the Organization of the Islamic Conference (OIC) and the Arab League, among other international organizations and governmental bodies. Jordan has also recently begun a push to develop its information technology (IT) sector to join the rapidly growing global IT force. Jordan trades primarily with the US, Iraq, Saudi Arabia and Israel. The country depends upon outside sources for oil and energy, and is working to reduce this dependence by collaborating with the Trans-Mediterranean Renewable Energy Cooperation to identify domestic solutions for solar power and pollution-free electricity.

Human Rights Profile

International human rights law insists that states respect civil and political rights, and promote an individual's economic, social, and cultural rights. The United Nations Universal Declaration on Human Rights (UDHR) is recognized as the standard for international human rights. Its authors sought the counsel of the world's great thinkers, philosophers, and religious leaders, and were careful to create a document that reflects the core values shared by every world culture. To read this document or view the articles relating to cultural human rights, visit http://www.udhr.org/UDHR/default.htm.

The Jordanian government is very involved with human rights issues in the Middle East, particularly because of its proximity to Israel and the Palestinian territories. The most pressing domestic concern is that of the Palestinian refugees. As the Israeli government proceeds with building a wall dividing its border through Palestinian territory, Jordan is receiving a flood of Palestinians.

Although the Jordanian government has stated that it will grant every Palestinian refugee Jordanian citizenship, the population growth is straining the economy. Nonetheless, in support of the UDHR, the government has agreed to also provide Palestinian refugees with free healthcare and education.

These same rights are not extended to Iraqi refugees. Whereas Iraqis were once welcomed with lenient visa policies, a 2005 bombing in Amman by Iraqi nationals soured relations. Since then, they are not recognized as refugees (who must leave their country and would be entitled under the UDHR to healthcare and education), but rather as visitors (leaving their country voluntarily) with temporary visas who, upon the visa's expiration, are deported. Iraqi "visitors" are for the most part refused visas (and, therefore entry into Jordan), and those who do enter are swiftly deported when the term of their visa is over.

Human rights watch groups have intervened to voice opposition to this policy. The international community recognizes the Iraqis as asylum seekers and insists that Jordan accept this status and make provisions accordingly. At the very least, human rights activists are petitioning the Jordanian government to loosen the visa regulations, as, in their estimation, deportation returns Iraqis to an environment of persecution and is a violation of the UDHR.

Another concern of human rights advocates are instances of arbitrary arrest, unfair trials, and repressed freedom of expression in Jordan, particularly pertaining to terrorist activity. One case involved the arrest of a man allegedly working with the terrorist organization al Qaeda, although the only evidence of this was an unlicensed weapon. Human rights groups maintain that he was arbitrarily arrested and granted an unfair trial, as the man appealed three times, and each time was sentenced to the death penalty despite the lack of evidence.

Overall, the Jordanian government routinely addresses terrorist acts with utmost severity. While this gesture shows a commitment to the well-being of Jordanian citizens, it also has human rights activists concerned about its interpretation. For example, Jordan's Prevention of Terrorism Act defines terrorism so broadly that many fear that it criminalizes even non-violent criticism and peaceful assembly. Furthermore, the law grants the state security court the power to perform secret surveillance, impound personal belongings, or prohibit a suspect from traveling. Although drafted with the intention to curb extremist behavior, the international human rights community prefers that the law be amended in a way that deters terrorists while preserving the freedoms of the country's citizens.

ECONOMY

Overview of the Economy
Unlike other Arab countries, Jordan does not have large deposits of oil; it imported most of its oil from Iraq before 2003. The country has enjoyed a Free Trade Agreement with the United States since 2001, providing for growth in Jordan's technology and service sectors. In 2014, the country's GDP was an estimated $35.77 billion (USD).

In 2014, the per capita gross domestic product (GDP) was estimated at $11,900 (USD).

Industry
Jordan's industries include textile manufacturing phosphate and potash mining, pharmaceutical manufacturing, petroleum refining, and tourism. Because Iraq is an important Jordanian trade partner, many of these industries have been affected negatively by the war in Iraq.

Labor
The United States government estimates that 30 percent of Jordanians were living below the poverty line as of 2014, and that actual unemployment rates are more than double the official 12 percent rate published by the Jordanian government.

Energy/Power/Natural Resources
Jordan is one of the world's most water-poor countries, and lacks many other natural resources, as well. However, certain areas of the country,

notably the Wadi 'Araba, have potash reserves. Jordan also has natural supplies of phosphates and shale oil.

Forestry

There is little forested land in Jordan, as much of the country's forests have already been harvested. However, there have been some reforestation efforts. As in other Middle Eastern countries, olive trees in Jordan are widely cultivated.

Mining/Metals

Jordan is not a mineral-rich country, but in recent years, it has uncovered a significant supply of uranium within its borders. A joint French and Jordanian business partnership has begun mining the uranium, which will be used to fuel nuclear power plants in France and the United States.

Agriculture

Jordan's agricultural industry is almost entirely limited to the Jordan Valley region where farms produce wheat, barley, citrus fruits, tomatoes, melons, and olives.

Animal Husbandry

Livestock raised in Jordan include sheep, goats, and poultry.

Tourism

Jordan's natural wonders and ancient ruins have made for a substantial tourist industry. Archeologists and visitors flock to Roman ruins at Jerash, Karak, Madara, and Petra, among other sites.

Scuba divers travel to Jordan to explore the coral reef in the Gulf of Aqaba, and the mineral springs and salty waters of the Dead Sea have been a health spa destination for centuries. Political instability in neighboring countries, and particularly the ongoing war in Iraq, has weakened Jordan's tourist industry in recent years.

Heidi Edsall and Amy Witherbee

DO YOU KNOW?

- The salt content in the Dead Sea is so great that the sea can sustain no forms of animal or plant life. The same salinity makes a swimmer so buoyant that it is easy for anyone to float on the surface of the water.

- Jordan's Queen Noor, widow of the late King Hussein and stepmother to the reigning King Abdullah II, was born and raised in the United States, where she received a degree in architecture and urban planning from Princeton University before meeting and marrying the late king.

Bibliography

Claudia Roden. *The New Book of Middle Eastern Food.* New York, NY: Alfred Knopf, 2000.

Donna Lee Bowen and Evelyn A. Early. *Everyday Life in the Muslim Middle East.* Bloomington, IN: Indiana University Press, 2002.

Frederick Matthewson Denny. *An Introduction to Islam.* Upper Saddle River, NJ: Pearson Prentice Hall, 2011.

James Gelvin. *The Arab Uprisings: What Everyone Needs to Know.* New York: Oxford University Press, 2015.

Karen Armstrong. *Islam: A Short History.* New York, NY: Random House, 2000.

Jennie Walker, et al. *Jordan.* Oakland, CA: Lonely Planet, 2015.

John A. Shoup, III. *Culture and Customs of Jordan.* Santa Barbara, CA: Greenwood Press, 2006.

Lawrence Rosen. *The Culture of Islam.* Chicago, IL: University of Chicago Press, 2002.

Philip Robins. *A History of Jordan.* New York: Cambridge University Press, 2004.

Pitr Bienkowski. *Treasures from an Ancient Land: The Art of Jordan.* Gloucestershire, United Kingdom: Sutton Publishing, 1996.

Works Cited

"Amnesty." *Amnesty International*. http://www.amnesty.org.

"Biography of Queen Noor." *The King Hussein Foundation*. http://www.kinghusseinfoundation.org.

"HRW." *Human Rights Watch*. http://www.hrw.org.

"Jordan Jubilee." *Jordan Jubilee: The Country and People of Jordan*. http://www.jordanjubilee.com.

"Jordan River." *Jordan River Foundation*. http://www.jordanriver.jo.

"Lonely Planet Phrasebooks. Middle East Phrasebook." Victoria, Australia: *Lonely Planet Publications*, 2007.

"Open Democracy." http://www.opendemocracy.net.

"PRB." *Population Reference Bureau*. http://www.prb.org.

"Queen Rania." *Official Website of the Queen of Jordan*. http://www.queenrania.jo.

"RSCN." *The Royal Society for the Conservation of Nature*. http://www.rscn.org.jo.

"The Office of King Hussein." *The Office of King Hussein*. http://www.kinghussein.gov.jo.

"U.S. Department of State." U.S. Government. http://www.state.gov.

"UNICEF." *UNICEF*. http://www.unicef.org.

"UNIFEM News." *UNIFEM*. http://www.unifem.org.

"UNOG." *United Nations Office at Geneva*. http://www.unog.ch.

"World Heritage." *UNESCO*. http://whc.unesco.org.

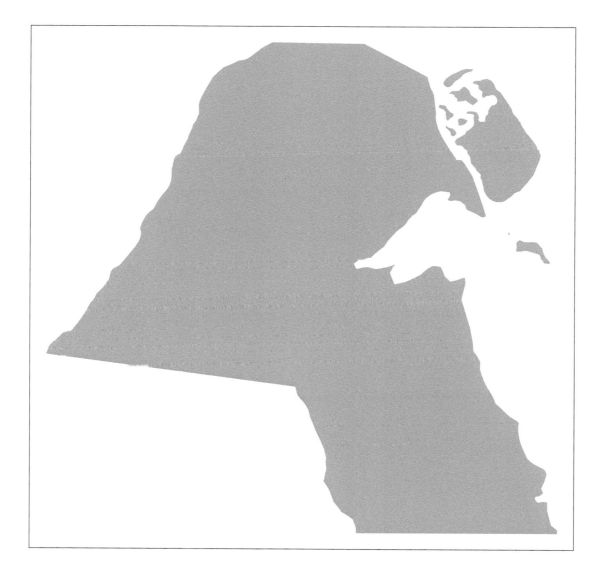

KUWAIT

Introduction

Threatened by the Turkish Ottoman Empire in the 19th century, Kuwait voluntarily became a British protectorate. Today, the small, desert nation of Kuwait, officially the State of Kuwait, is an independent nation. It is led by an emir, whose power is limited by the National Assembly. Democracy in Kuwait is arguably still limited; women did not have the right to vote until 2005. However, support of democratic ideals is stronger in Kuwait than in many neighboring countries in the Middle East.

Kuwait became prosperous and stable after extensive desert oilfields were developed following World War II. The government used the income to build excellent roads, institute free health care and social services, and support an educational system that has resulted in one of the highest literacy rates in the Arab world. In addition to receiving free education and health care, citizens pay no income tax. Modern Kuwait remains one of the world's wealthiest nations.

Due to its wealth, the country was invaded in by its neighbor, Iraq, in 1990, led at that time by the dictator Saddam Hussein. Hussein's invasion was turned back by United States forces, in what became known as Operation Desert Storm. As the Iraqis retreated from the US invasion, Hussein ordered his forces to set fire to Kuwait's oil wells. The costs of repairing oil wells severely depleted Kuwait's cash reserves. Nevertheless, Kuwait has been successfully rebuilt since the Gulf War and has remained a significant independent oil-producing presence in the Middle East.

Since Kuwait is historically situated in a trading crossroads, many cultures have influenced its art, particularly its music. For instance, some Kuwaiti music rhythms come from the Bedouins, who sang to pass the time on long journeys. Travelers on trade routes brought back other musical forms from Asia and Africa. Ceramics and jewelry are also important aspects of Kuwaiti art. The Bedouin art of sadu, another artistic heritage of the Middle Eastern country,

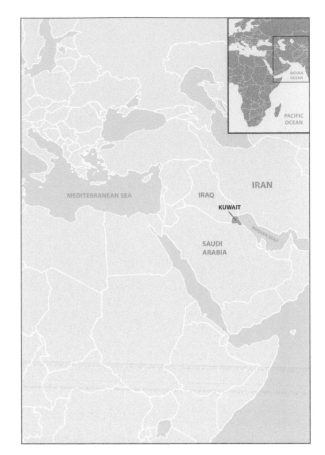

involves weaving and decorating cloth from sheep's wool.

The country witnessed, in 2009, the historic election of four women to its National Assembly. Amid the 2010–11 Arab Spring uprisings across the region, stateless Arabs, known as bidun, staged small protests in 2011 demanding citizenship, jobs, and other benefits. Demonstrators forced the prime minister to resign in late 2011.

In late 2012, Kuwait witnessed widespread protests in response to the Amir's changes to the electoral law, reducing the number of votes per person from four to one. This led to a boycott in legislative elections in 2012 and 2013. Since 2006, the Amir has dissolved the National Assembly five times and shuffled the cabinet over a dozen times, usually citing political gridlock between the legislature and the government.

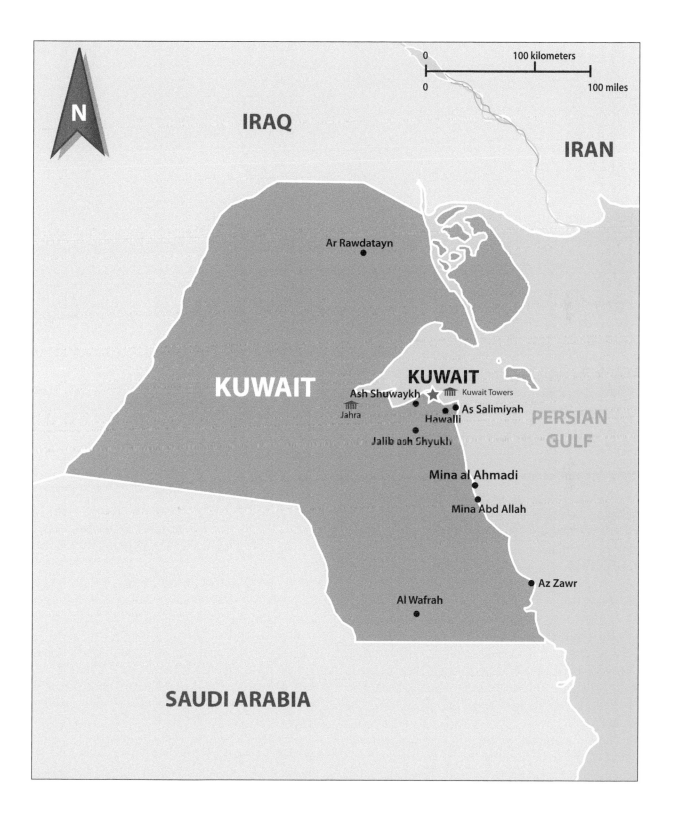

GENERAL INFORMATION

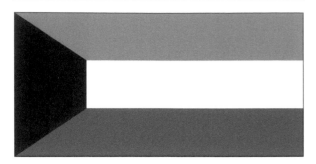

Official Language: Arabic
Population: 4,183,658 (2015 estimate)
Currency: Kuwaiti dinar
Coins: The Kuwaiti dinar is divided into 1000 fils. Coins in frequent use come in denominations of 5, 10, 20, 50, and 100 fils.
Land Area: 17,818 square kilometers (6,879 square miles)
National Anthem: Al-Nasheed Al-Watani
Capital: Kuwait City
Time Zone: GMT +3
Flag Description: The flag of Kuwait features a black trapezoid on the hoist (left) side, followed by three horizontal bands, or stripes, of green (top), white (middle), and red (bottom). In addition to representing the Pan-Arab colors, the flag's colors, also derived from a poem, stand for the defeat of the nation's enemies in war (black); the blood that covers Kuwaiti swords (red); the fertility of the country's land (green); and the purity of the country's actions (white).

Population

Kuwait is one of the most densely populated countries in the world. Nearly the entire population (96 percent) is concentrated in the country's cities, particularly around Kuwait Bay. Most of the rest of the country is empty desert. Less than 4 percent of Kuwait's population lives in rural areas.

The population is primarily divided between Kuwaiti citizens, residents with a secondary citizenship, and immigrant workers. As of 2013, the three largest groups are Kuwaiti (31.3 percent), Arabs, and Asians.

Principal Cities by Population (2015):

- Al Farwaniya (1,122,638)
- Hawalli (911,996)
- Al Ahmadi (854,366)
- Al-Kuwayt, Kuwait City (544,156)
- Al Jahra (507,793)
- Mubarak Al Kabeer (237,648)

Asians, accounting for 37.8 percent of the population, are the country's largest ethnic group. Other Arab groups account for roughly one-third (27.9 percent) of the total population. The remaining 3 percent of the country's population consists of Americans, Europeans, Africans and Canadians. The country's population boomed, mostly by immigration, after oil was discovered.

Until recently, Palestinians were the largest non-Kuwaiti group. Many left, however, after the 1990 invasion by Iraq; others were expelled after the war. Now, non-Kuwaiti groups include large numbers of Egyptians, Indians, and Iranians.

Languages

Arabic, the official language, is spoken by most Kuwaitis and by many non-Kuwaiti residents. English is also widely understood and spoken, especially by young people. Discrimination based on language is illegal in Kuwait.

Native People & Ethnic Groups

Not much is known about the inhabitants of what is now Kuwait before the 18th century. However, archaeological evidence reveals that people have lived in the area for more than 3,000 years. Failaka, the largest of Kuwait's nine islands, was evidently a trading post in the time of the ancient Sumerians. It was also known to the ancient Greeks.

Between 1710 and 1740, desert nomads from Saudi Arabia founded Kuwait; the port they built later became Kuwait City. In 1775, the British established Kuwait as the starting point of a mail and carrier service to Aleppo, Syria.

Religions

The official religion of the country is Muslim at 76.7 percent with Christian at 17.3 percent and 5.9 percent unspecified. Islam is the state religion, and religious discrimination is forbidden.

Climate

Kuwait experiences intensely hot summers and short, mild winters. During July and August, temperatures often climb higher than 49° Celsius (120° Fahrenheit) in the shade, making Kuwait one of the world's hottest countries. In August and September, the humidity is high, as well. January is the coldest month, with temperatures between 10° and 20° Celsius (50° and 68° Fahrenheit). Frosts are common during winter nights.

The average annual rainfall is 10 centimeters (4 inches). Most of this comes in the form of sudden cloudbursts from October through April. Sandstorms can occur anytime, but they are more common from March to August.

While Kuwait City is filled with skyscrapers, shops, and monuments, the capital is located amidst the desert conditions of a Saharan nation. Like the rest of the country, Kuwait City commonly experiences long, hot, and dry summers with frequent dust storms and short, warm winters, with occasional rain. Summer temperatures hover around 45° Celsius (113° Fahrenheit), while winter temperatures average around 8° Celsius (46° Fahrenheit). With this wide shift in seasonal temperatures comes an equally wide variation in annual rainfall; some years, the city receives as little as 2.2 centimeters (.86 inches), while during other years, the city gets as much as 35.2 centimeters (13.85 inches).

ENVIRONMENT & GEOGRAPHY

Topography

Slightly smaller than the American state of New Jersey, Kuwait lies at the head of the Persian Gulf, between Iraq on the northwest and Saudi Arabia on the south. A Neutral (Partitioned) Zone of 5,700 square kilometers (2,200 square miles) lies on the gulf, south of the country, and is shared by Kuwait and Saudi Arabia. The coastline is 193 kilometers (120 miles) long.

Nine islands in the gulf are also part of Kuwait. The most important (and most populous) is Falaika (or Falaykah), 19 kilometers (12 miles) off the coast. The largest island, Bubiyan, is uninhabited.

Most of the country is flat, nearly uninhabited arid desert, with some small hills. Kuwait has no rivers or lakes. Water is obtained primarily through desalination operations, which remove the salt from seawater. One large underground water source was discovered in 1960. Wells exist, but the water is brackish, or salty. The country's highest point is at 306 meters (1,003 feet) above sea level.

Kuwait City is the only major metropolitan city in the small, desert nation of Kuwait. It covers an area of approximately 200 kilometers (77 square miles) along the central Eastern coastline of Kuwait and the shores of the Persian Gulf and the Bay of Kuwait. Since there are no inland rivers or waterways, the port of Kuwait City has long served the nation as the key resource for the imports and exports of Kuwait.

Plants & Animals

Ironically, the banning of access to large areas of the desert has helped Kuwait's plant and animal species to recover, because they have not been disturbed by human activity.

Many animals found in Kuwait's desert are reptiles, such as the dhub, or spiny-tailed lizard. Non-venomous snakes include the sand boa, the leaf-nosed snake, and the rat snake. Venomous species include the Arabian rear-fanged snake, the horned viper, and the rare black desert cobra.

While only sixteen species of birds breed in Kuwait, up to 280 species migrate through the country. The lesser kestrel (falco naumanni) has been observed over Kuwait City, but it is declining in numbers.

Vegetation is sparse; scrub and grasses grow during the winter, and are sufficient to feed camel herds. Wildflowers are commonly found during rainy periods.

Sheep and goats have overgrazed the desert, damaging the plant life. Since the Gulf War, however, grazing has been banned in roughly half of the country's area, allowing plant life to begin to recover.

CUSTOMS & COURTESIES

Greetings

For most Kuwaitis, a daily greeting between men begins with a handshake and a kiss on one or both cheeks. In Muslim cultures, only the right hand is used since the left hand, associated with personal cleansing, is considered impure. Women also typically kiss one another one each cheek, especially if they are close acquaintances. Handshakes tend to be longer but may be less firm than those used in the West, and eye contact is important, particularly in business. In traditional Bedouin culture, touching the nose together three times is also a form of greeting. A Kuwaiti might also place a hand over his heart and bow slightly in a show of respect.

Kuwaiti greetings customarily require small talk, which includes questions about family, health, or common acquaintances. This light conversation is so important that business travelers are warned not to show impatience or to try to cut short conversation. Because genders are segregated, most greetings take place between members of the same sex. If a man and woman do meet one another, however, the man should not offer a handshake unless the woman does. She may reject his handshake if she feels it is inappropriate. Kissing, even on the cheek, is inappropriate between a man and woman in public, unless they are closely related.

Kuwaitis accompany their greetings with the phrase "Assalamu alaikum" ("Peace upon you"). The appropriate response is "Walaikumsalam" ("Peace upon you also"). These terms can be used regardless of whether the speaker is Muslim or a non-Arabic speaker. On departing, Kuwaitis might exchange several common phrases to wish an acquaintance well,

but the standard Arabic phrase is "Maasalamah" ("With peace").

Gestures & Etiquette

Kuwait is a cosmopolitan center, so its people are accustomed to a wide variety of cultures and etiquette. Kuwaitis are willing to overlook most matters of etiquette if they believe a visitor does not understand their customs. Conversely, Kuwaitis are highly appreciative of visitors who make an effort to understand those customs. Kuwaitis will be offended (and a visitor could be subject to arrest) for a few specific transgressions, such as the public use of alcohol or public displays of affection between genders. Sexually provocative clothing will also invite unwanted attention. Non-Muslims are not required to fast during the holy month of Ramadan, but they are prohibited from eating, drinking, and chewing gum in public during this religious holiday.

Kuwaitis commonly use gestures and other movements in their communication. A series of gestures common to Arab countries include putting the right hand on one's chest and bowing with eyes closed, used to express thanks, and clicking one's tongue while snapping upwards, used to express "No." In addition, the phrase "Ala hashmi" ("On my nose") means that the speaker is accepting a responsibility, so that someone wishing to acknowledge a responsibility will often touch his or her nose. Similarly, someone who points both forefingers toward his eyes is acknowledging a responsibility or his willingness to do a favor for his companion. Pointing the soles of one's feet toward someone while sitting indicates disrespect, and the right hand should be used for all physical contact with others.

The segregation of gender in Kuwait dictates its own form of etiquette. Males should be careful of sitting next to or approaching a woman in an abaya (a flowing garment that covers the body from head to toe), as her dress signals a more conservative approach to gender etiquette. Physical contact between genders is discouraged in public and often in private homes, as well.

Women traditionally remove to another portion of the house to socialize.

Eating/Meals

Kuwaitis traditionally gather together with family members and close friends in large numbers to celebrate family events with an abundance of food and drink. Dining in the home can be Western-style (at a central table with chairs), Bedouin-style (on floor cushions), or on cushioned benches set end to end around a central table. As in other many other parts of the world, large platters of food are often shared, and the hands are used in place of cutlery. As a result, the tradition has strict rules regarding how food is to be eaten. One uses only the right hand to eat; once touched, food belongs to the person who has touched it.

Kuwait's traditional dining culture has undergone some changes in recent decades. While large, shared dinners in the home continue to be a central part of social and family life, younger Kuwaitis in particular spend much of their time in restaurants and cafés, and American chain restaurants are now common in Kuwait. In fact, the eating habits of Kuwait youth have raised concerns in the early 21st century. Internet cafés are also important social centers in a culture that has embraced the internet with unrestrained enthusiasm.

Visiting

Arabian cultures are known for their hospitality, and the culture of Kuwait is no exception. Kuwaiti hosts are known for their generosity and take pride in welcoming visitors. When visiting a Kuwaiti, a guest should bring a simple gift. If a male offers a gift to a female, he will typically specify that it comes from his wife, daughter, or mother to avoid awkwardness. As in much of the Middle East and Asia, shoes are removed before entering a home. Visitors should accept any food or drink offered as a compliment to the efforts of the host or hostess. The host generally continues to offer food until the visitor shows he has had enough by leaving a bit on his plate.

One of the most important and oldest of Kuwait's social customs is the dewaniya (diwaniya). The dewaniya is a nightly social gathering of men, from either the family, neighborhood, or both, to discuss the events of the day. In Bedouin tradition, the dewaniya was held in a separate tent set up in front of the household complex, and this practice continues among Kuwait's dwindling nomadic population. For most Kuwaitis, however, the dewaniya now takes place in a separate room at the front of the house. Kuwaiti women do their own socializing with family and neighbors in the interior parts of the villa.

While the private nature of Kuwaiti home life discourages visits by strangers, Kuwaitis typically welcome frequent and even unscheduled visits to the workplace. Businesspeople working in Kuwait are encourage to "stop by" a Kuwaiti workplace on occasion rather than relying exclusively on written or phone communication. Face-to-face contact reinforces business and social relationships in Kuwait and is often essential to reaching a final agreement.

LIFESTYLE

Family

Family is the single most important facet of life in Kuwait. A Kuwaiti family includes not just the nuclear family, but close relatives, distant relatives, members of the same tribe, and even close friends and neighbors. This is the group with whom an individual grows up, celebrates milestones, and gathers on weekends or holidays. Because people outside this group are generally excluded from the private life of the home, the extended family serves as the center of an individual's social life and identity.

Names in Kuwait reflect familial ties. A Kuwait first name is followed by the name of her father, her grandfather, and her grandfather's tribe, all connected by "al-," roughly translated as "of." But a Kuwaiti visiting a friend's family will often refer to his friend's parents as "mother of -" or "father of -." Women do not take their husband's name upon marriage.

Housing

Affluent Kuwaiti citizens tend to live in large, detached villas that can accommodate extended families and service staff. In prior centuries, these private homes would have been constructed with mud plaster and rubble rock, but modern materials have replaced local materials in most of the country. Family villas are usually built around a central courtyard and might be clustered with other villas or extended with additional rooms in order to accommodate new generations.

State programs provide housing for all Kuwaiti citizens. However, the majority of Kuwait's population is made up of expatriates. Professionals from other Arab nations, North Americans, and Europeans who relocate to Kuwait temporarily for work are usually affluent. They tend to live in low- or high-rise apartments, or in compounds (groups of small houses clustered together with shared services). Kuwait also has a large population of service workers who are brought in from Southeast Asian as menial laborers or domestic servants. Housing for a domestic servant is likely to be a small room in the employers' home. Menial laborers often live in dormitory-style apartment buildings.

Food

The traditional cuisine of Kuwait is influenced by the country's Arab and Bedouin heritage, and has distinct Indian, Persian, and Asian influences. The national dish is machboos, which is typically made with meat or chicken accompanied by rice and spices such as saffron and cardamom. Kuwait's indigenous population still eats traditional large meals of rice and fish or grilled meat and salads. Coffee and tea are served at almost any gathering, and spiced hummus and flatbread or stuffed breads and rolls are popular afternoon snacks. Kuwaitis traditionally enjoy sweet dishes inspired from other cultures along the great trade routes of the Middle East, Asia, and North Africa. Nuts, sweetened dates, almond cookies, sponge cake, Egyptian chocolate cakes,

sweetened figs, rice pudding, baklawa, fresh fruit sweetened with rose water or orange syrup, and Turkish delight are just a few of the treats to be found in a Kuwaiti home.

With the affluence of its oil-based economy, Kuwait has adopted a modern restaurant culture as well. Kuwaiti teens, in particular, enjoy the American chains and fast food restaurants available in retail areas and malls. Rice is served with most Kuwaiti take-out meals, but hamburgers, fried chicken, and French fries have made their way into daily life in Kuwait. The widespread popularity of American-style fast food worries health advocates, who are seeing more cases of obesity in the country.

Life's Milestones

An estimated 85 percent of the population of Kuwait practices Islam, and many of life's milestones observed in Kuwaiti society derive from Muslim customs. This includes religious observances such as Ramadan, a holy month in which Muslims fast during daylight hours. Marriage is the most important event in traditional Kuwaiti life. Marriages are still often arranged by families and are often a tool to create alliances between families.

In Bedouin tradition, wedding ceremonies would last several days. The two families traveled to a meeting place, set up their tents, and began negotiations. These negotiations were a ceremony in and of themselves, called the "Al Khoutha," or proposal, which included a symbolic sharing of mint tea by the two families. Once the families reach an agreement on dowries and arrangements, the female members of the family held the "Laylat Al Henna." This was the equivalent of a wedding shower in which the bride's hands and feet were decorated with henna (a reddish-brown dye derived from the henna plant). The groom's relatives then proceeded in festive fashion to the bride's home with singing, music, and dancing. The bride's jewelry was of particular importance since it represented her personal wealth in the event of emergency. Men and women sat in separate tents while guests arrived with gifts. The groom saw his bride only after the ceremony, when she entered his home and removed her veil.

The Bedouin tradition has changed slightly in modern Kuwait. A celebration that once lasted a week now lasts one or two days, and traditional gift items have been replaced with televisions, crystal, and housewares. The groom still pays a dowry, but families have scaled down their requirements to support the efforts of young Kuwaiti men to marry. Moreover, the Kuwait government now offers a gift and loan package to any newly married Kuwaiti citizens in order to allow them to pay for their first homes.

CULTURAL HISTORY

Art

The modern nation of Kuwait is relatively young—it was founded in the 18th century but its arts and culture date back to antiquity. The ancient Greeks colonized Failaka Island, then known as Ikarus, over two millennia ago. Archaeological excavations have revealed ruins and inscriptions from the Hellenistic period (arguably 323–146 BCE). In fact, until the Iraqi invasion of 1990, the island was the longest continuously inhabited locale in Kuwait, with a pagan civilization even predating the Greek arrival. This early culture was believed to be centered on sun worship. However, the predominant founders of modern Kuwait were migrating tribes from central Arabia.

The nomadic people who settled along this part of the Arabian Gulf coastline were mostly Bedouin. They brought the Arabic language, with its rich storytelling traditions, Islamic calligraphy, and traditional musical instruments, to the region. One of the most important of the Bedouin arts was sadu weaving, a craft that involved weaving hand-dyed and spun wool into colorful geometric designs. These fabrics were used for clothing, carpets, and tent making. Today, the sadu tradition is honored at the al-Sadu House (a society which preserves Bedouin weaving), but manufactured cloth has taken the place of sadu fabrics in Kuwait life. The tribes who settled in

this area also developed their own shipbuilding and seafaring traditions. For centuries, traditional dhows (wooden boats) plied the oceans, exchanging goods such as pearls and spices with Southeast Asia. These cultures would in turn influence Kuwaiti arts and cuisine. Kuwait's maritime heritage remains an important theme in its music and literature.

As Arabic culture developed in Kuwait, Islamic art became the dominant form. This style is unique in that it forbids human depictions and is largely geometric and pattern-based. Islamic art includes calligraphy, illuminated miniature paintings, ornate ceramics, woodcarving, jewelry (pearling was an early economic endeavor), metalwork, and textile art. The architecture of Kuwait is also influenced by Islamic architecture. Early architecture was simplistic and, due to the rarity of wood, consisted of stone and mud brick and plaster. Urban architecture is often a mix of traditional Islamic elements such as the minaret (tall, crowned spires) with international and modern designs.

Architecture

Traditional Kuwaiti architecture is a blend of traditional and modern, simple structure and heavy adornment. For example, while Kuwait City is a thriving metropolis filled with modern shopping malls, fast food restaurants, and internationally known coffee shops, many Kuwaitis still frequent the more traditional souks (open-air markets) and maqahas (coffee shops). Another example is the Grand Mosque, a large, modern building with traditional Islamic designs and calligraphy. Current architecture tends toward intricate design.

The unique modern architecture of Kuwait City took on a particularly symbolic role during this period of reconstruction. Built in 1979, the Kuwait Towers have long been the most recognizable structures in the country. The towers are composed of three narrow spires that rise separately from the ground and taper to points in the sky. On two of the spires, massive balls seem to balance between earth and sky. The playful structures are actually water towers, storing one of Kuwait's most precious resources and supplying the homes and business of the city. The towers survived the invasion with extensive shell and bullet damage.

Prior to the invasion, the country's tallest building was known as the Kuwait Telecommunication Tower. In the first days after Iraqi troops were displaced, television channels around the Middle East broadcast images of the tower, with its interior ravaged by vandalism. The building was renamed Liberation Tower and became the primary symbol of Kuwait's reconstruction. Like Kuwait Towers and Liberation Tower, Kuwait's famous National Assembly Building is of European design. The building's two roofs were created by world-famous Danish architect Jørn Utzon (1918–2008) to resemble an enormous Bedouin tent. The building embodies the mix of international style and Arab tradition that characterizes Kuwait itself.

Drama

Like most Arab countries, Kuwait did not develop a theater tradition until at least the 19th century. However, the Arab artistic traditions of storytelling, puppetry, and Shiite religious plays have been part of Kuwaiti culture for far longer. While the region once entertained professional storytellers, the art of storytelling is also practiced by amateurs. Traditional themes include seafaring and desert travel, as well as riddles and proverbs. Kuwaitis once grew up hearing traditional children's stories and poetry that were also recited. The formal storytelling tradition has largely given way to new forms of entertainment in modern Kuwait. Most Kuwaiti homes include at least one television and government initiatives since the last century have improved literacy rates, particularly among indigenous Kuwaitis. However, theater has seen a slight rise in popularity in recent years, and the Kuwaiti government promotes awareness of the dramatic arts. The Gulf Theater, Popular Theater, and Kuwaiti Theater are a few of the country's theatrical companies.

Music

Kuwait enjoys an unusually rich music scene that integrates the styles and trends of music from all over the world. In particular, Kuwait's music is heavily influenced by the cultures of East Africa and India, among whom early Kuwaiti pearl divers, merchants, and shippers traded for centuries. This music uses Arab instruments such as the tanbarah and kanoon (stringed instruments), the oud (lute), the habban (bagpipes), and the mirwas (drums). Kuwaiti musicians used these instruments alongside instruments specific to Bedouin culture such as the rababa (a string instrument that might have been an early form of the violin) and the nai (a wooden flute). The kaman or kamanjah was adapted from European violins during the 19th century.

Kuwaiti musicians are usually women. They play their music for private gatherings in the home that include feasting and dancing. As a result, Kuwaitis grow up associating their traditional music with family celebrations and gatherings. Some of the best-known songs from Kuwait's Bedouin tradition include "Al-Fann," a popular wedding song, and "Mawled," the story of the Prophet Muhammad's life. Traditional Kuwaiti music is also known for its "seas songs" sung by pearl divers and sailors, ranging from work songs and celebratory songs. Many of these songs are performed in a "call and reply" arrangement and incorporate clapping and other percussive elements. Because of the seafaring traditions of Kuwait's early inhabitants, the sea is a prominent theme in the country's folk music.

Another important musical tradition in Kuwait is sawt, a genre which developed in the 19th century. It is considered the classical music of Kuwait and is based on repeated rhythms and the oud (generally, Arabic or Gulf music is based on percussions). This style of music is also known for its poetic lyrics and the use of the mirwas (hand drum).

Literature

The Arab-language cultures of the Middle East share a literary tradition that dates back centuries. Modern Kuwait still struggles to establish its own tradition, but the country has produced several world-class writers. Kuwait's most famous poet was Zaid Abdullah al-Harb (1887–1972), whose work often focused on Arab social and political life. More recently, Kuwaiti artist Naif al Mutawa (1971–) created what is referred to as Islam's first superhero comic series in 2006. Over 500 authors attended Kuwait's annual book fair in 2007, but 230 of the 560 new titles at the fair were banned by government censors.

CULTURE

Arts & Entertainment

Kuwait's appreciation of its arts and architecture in the 21st-century was shaped by the Iraqi invasion of August 2, 1990. Though United States-led forces expelled Iraqi troops from Kuwait less than a year later, the damage done to the country was considerable. Kuwaitis fled the country during the occupation and found temporary refuge in sympathetic Arab states. They returned to find museums and libraries looted, landmarks heavily damaged, and homes destroyed. The post-liberation period became a period of reconstruction. As Kuwait poured its considerable financial resources into repairing the damage done by bullets, fires, and vandalism, the country's damaged architecture and museums served as a symbol of Kuwaiti patriotism and the country's determination to rebuild.

From music to theater to film, Kuwaitis find innovative ways to blend traditions and styles. In the early 21st century, Kuwait's artists have been making themselves known throughout the Middle East and worldwide, particularly over the Internet and its associated technologies. Since the reconstruction of Kuwait City, Kuwaitis have been working to replace destroyed recordings of traditional music and to make this music widely available on the Internet. Kuwaiti artists often blend traditional forms and instruments with popular musical styles from the US, creating new traditions. In 2007, playwright Sulayman al-Bassam (1972–) brought his Arab remake of Shakespeare's *Richard III* to the Swan Theater in Stratford-upon-Avon, England (Shakespeare's birthplace). Al-Bassam received critical acclaim for his early adaptation of *Hamlet* that questioned

Kuwaiti culture in the aftermath of the Iraqi invasion.

Kuwait is a recent participant in the small but growing movement to produce Arabic-language films outside of the dominant film center in Cairo, Egypt. Inspired by both English-language films from Western culture and by their Arabic-language counterparts, Kuwaiti filmmakers have increased their presence at film festivals in Dubai and the Arab Emirates in recent years. In 2006, Kuwait hosted its first short film festival. As the country's filmmakers struggle for international recognition, Kuwait's cinemas have also flourished. Along with shopping malls, American chain restaurants, and beach resorts, movie theaters serve as public social spaces in a country with strict social conventions. However, both theaters and movie producers must contend with government censorship policies. In practice, Kuwaiti censors have been more lenient than their counterparts in neighboring Muslim states, leaving room for a strengthening tradition of political commentary in the arts.

Popular traditional sports in Kuwait include swimming, diving, rowing, navigation, hunting, shooting, horseback riding, and tracking. The Kuwait Olympic Committee was established in 1957; when Kuwait lost to South Korea in the trials for the 2006 Olympic Games, public demonstrations led to the resignation of several officials of the football (soccer) union.

Cultural Sites & Landmarks

Kuwait's national icon is perhaps the Kuwait Towers, designed by Swedish architects. It was opened to the public in 1979 and serves not only as a tourist attraction and landmark, but as an electrical source and water supply for the people of Kuwait City. The main tower reaches to a height of 187 meters (613.5 feet) and contains two spheres that include observation decks, restaurants, and conference training rooms. The middle tower is 147 meters (482 feet) above sea level. This tower serves as a water supply and contains up to 1 million gallons of water. The small tower rises 113 meters (371 feet) above sea level and controls the power that lights the other two towers, as well as many of the surrounding areas of Kuwait City. Each of the balls on the towers are covered with five thousand Chinese steel plates painted in eight different colors.

Built to represent a modern Arab nation, the structure took on a new significance following the Iraqi invasion. Pictures of its heavily damaged façade came to represent Kuwait's anger toward its former Iraqi allies.

Failaka Island, one of Kuwait's nine islands, remains a significant national cultural site. With its strategic position in the Persian Gulf, the island has been continuously inhabited by Arabic and Greek cultures for thousands of years. Older Kuwaiti structures and the ruins of a Greek settlement, including a fort, shrines, and temple, remain on the island. Iraqi troops expelled residents from the island during the invasion and planted the island's beaches with landmines. Since the liberation, the landmines have been removed and the residents compensated by the Kuwaiti government.

Completed in 1986, the Grand Mosque (Masjid Al Kabeer) is Kuwait's largest religious structure. The building is over 20,000 square meters (215,278 square feet), with a central dome that spans 26 meters (85 feet) and soars to over 43 meters (141 feet) high. One of Kuwait's newest cultural landmarks is the Green Island. Inaugurated in 1988, the island's 785 square meters (8,449 square feet) are entirely man-made with concrete stabilizers and imported sand. The island, owned and operated by Kuwait's tourism department, is richly planted with foliage sand provides restaurants and park space for family entertainment.

While most of Kuwait's cultural landmarks lay in the densely populated areas along the Persian Gulf, the town of Jahra holds an important place in the national psyche. The town lies at the intersection of three caravan routes that carried traders among the commercial centers of what are now modern-day Kuwait and Saudi Arabia. The town's "Red Fort," or "Red Palace," is an example of the early earth and brick forts used to secure towns throughout the region. This fort, built by Sheikh Mubarak Al Sabah

(1837–1915) in the early 20th century, marks the site where Kuwait forces defeated the Saudi Arabian Ikhwan military corps in 1920 to secure Kuwait's independence.

Libraries & Museums
On Arabian Gulf Street, in Kuwait City, between the palace and the parliamentary buildings, is the Kuwait National Museum, opened in 1986. The museum includes a variety of Islamic artifacts as well as diving relics, ethnographical pieces, and archaeological materials. For example, the museum houses the royal al-Sabah collection, one of the world's most significant Islamic art collections, as well as artifacts from Failaka Island that gave historians a glimpse of the pearl-trading culture that predates modern Kuwait.

The National Museum of Kuwait sustained heavy damage during the Iraq invasion. In the first days of the Iraqi occupation, the Iraqi government sent a team of archeologists to remove collections from the National Museum and the library of Kuwait University, many of which were damaged or have yet to be recovered.

For those interested in artifacts related to the petroleum industry, natural history, and flora and fauna of the region, Kuwait City also boasts the Science and Natural History Museum of Kuwait. Bedouin silver jewelry is exhibited at the Tareq Rajab Museum. Many museums exhibit Kuwaiti antiquities and art, both traditional and modern. Another popular institution in Kuwait City is the al-Sadu House. Established in 1979, the al-Sadu House exhibits a variety of Bedouin art displays, particularly handcrafted textiles made by local Kuwaiti women. Visitors to the house can purchase crafts, observe Bedouin women weaving, and even take a weaving class.

Holidays
In addition to all of the major Muslim religious celebrations, Kuwaitis observe several unique official holidays. National Day (February 25) commemorates the establishment of Kuwait as a nation in 1961. Liberation Day, observed on February 26, marks Kuwait's liberation from Iraqi occupation in 1991.

Youth Culture

Kuwaiti culture values youth and the wealthy emirate provides families with citizenship full support in raising their offspring. The Kuwaiti government provides housing subsidies, free medical care, and education through the post-secondary (university) level, and government-sponsored employment. This significantly eases the financial burdens youth face—or embody—in other countries. Since domestic servants may be commonplace in Kuwaiti households, youth are also unburdened by domestic responsibilities. As a result, the country's youth have developed a reputation around the region that is based upon their ample spending money and leisure time.

Kuwaiti youth are known for following the latest trends and fashions. This reputation is perhaps further cemented by the fact that many Kuwaiti youth choose to attend private schools for expatriates in the metropolitan areas, and thus adopt the tastes and habits of their Western counterparts. Most Kuwaiti youth also speak both Arabic and English.

Reputation aside, the youth of Kuwaiti are certainly at the forefront of change in the Islamic Middle East, both in terms of transitioning away from tradition and customs and adopting new technologies. While the Kuwaiti media reflects a concern that Western influence is too strong in Kuwait, by and large Kuwait is a metropolitan culture that actively works to integrate Western commerce, architecture, and ideas with its own Muslim traditions and beliefs. This tolerance allows Kuwait youth to blend traditions in music, art, film, and even language. Lastly, through their mass participation in emerging and revolutionary technologies such as the Internet, young Kuwaitis continue to develop a hybrid culture.

SOCIETY

Transportation

Kuwait has a substantial automobile culture. In fact, most of the country's affluent residents drive a car once they reach the driving age of eighteen. Unlike in neighboring Saudi Arabia, women in Kuwait can and do drive. In spite of the emphasis on cars, Kuwait does have an efficient modern public transportation system. Bus service is efficient and runs regularly throughout the country. Traffic in Kuwait moves on the right-hand side of the road.

Transportation Infrastructure

The country has no rail network, but an international line was proposed in 2008. There are a total of seven airports; the major air terminal for visitors is Kuwait International Airport. Kuwait's ports, marinas, and harbors sustain its international trade.

In addition to access through the Persian Gulf, Kuwait City is also accessible by the Kuwait International Airport, which is located just 16 kilometers (10 miles) south of the city. All means of modern transportation are available within the city. Kuwait has an efficient modern public transportation system, including efficient bus service throughout the small country.

Media & Communications

Kuwait's media faces less censorship than the country's Arab neighbors. The government manages all television and radio frequencies, as well as the postal system and telephone networks. However, the government stopped censoring material before its publication in the early 1990s. A clause in the Kuwaiti constitution guarantees all citizens the right to criticize their government publicly, though self-censorship is practiced in relation to the emir and other royalty, as well as in religious matters. Books and film, especially imported media, are subject to censorship on moral grounds.

There are several private dailies in Kuwait, including the English-language *Kuwait Times*, the first such daily in the Gulf region. TV Kuwait is the national broadcaster and broadcasts three different channels through thirteen television stations around the country. There are also several private broadcasters and affluent Kuwaitis also use satellite dishes to access foreign channels in a variety of languages. The state-run Radio Kuwait broadcasts in Arabic, English, Urdu, and Persian.

Kuwait's government spent a substantial amount of money repairing and improving the nation's telephone systems following the departure of Iraqi troops in 1990. There are almost half a million high quality phone lines in use in the country, and more significantly, the government estimates that there are more than 7.6 million cell phones in use (2014). According to 2014 estimates, there were about 2.4 million Internet users in Kuwait, representing nearly 86.9 percent of the population.

SOCIAL DEVELOPMENT

Standard of Living
Kuwait ranked 46 out of 187 countries and territories on the 2013 United Nations Human Development Index, which measures quality of life and standard of living indicators.

Water Consumption
According to recent studies, Kuwait has the highest water consumption ration in the world, estimated at about 100 gallons of water per individual each day. In fact, published reports in late 2010 suggest that, despite desalination efforts—the country has depleted its freshwater sources, and relies mostly on desalination plants—production barely outpaces consumption, and that Kuwait will run out of water as demand grows along with the population. According to recent statistics, the Kuwaiti population has universal access to improved sanitation and clean drinking water. Total renewable water resources are estimated at .02 cu km as of 2011.

Education
All state education in Kuwait is free. School attendance is compulsory for children between the six and 14 years of age.

The government has pushed for better education in recent decades, partly because not enough Kuwaitis are educated enough to work in the oil industry; these jobs are often filled by foreigners. Today, more than 85 percent of children attend school. Part of the result is one of the highest literacy rates in the Arab world, at 96.3 percent overall; 96.5 percent among men and 95.8 percent among women (2015 estimate).

As part of its educational reform efforts, the government opened the University of Kuwait in 1966. The country's only university, it has approximately 18,000 students. In addition, the government provides scholarships to those who want to study abroad in subjects not offered at Kuwait University. Many other students study abroad at their own expense. About 4,500 Kuwaiti students study in other countries.

Women's Rights
Women's rights are a significant topic of debate among Kuwaitis. After a long struggle, women won the right to vote in May 2005. The emir affirmed his support for women's participation in the political process by appointing women's rights activist Massouma al-Mubarak as the first female cabinet minister that same year. (Massouma would resign as health minister in 2007, but won a parliamentary seat in 2009 along with three other women.) Women were appointed to other less prominent posts soon afterward, but females are still an overwhelming minority in government. Women are also making progress in the workforce and in education. A 2009 report found that 51 percent of Kuwaiti working women were employed—up from 46 percent in 2003. By 2004, women constituted more than 70 percent of the student population at Kuwait University; of that 70 percent, nearly half were studying for a degree in medicine or engineering. However, the government enforced a segregation law in all schools in 2008, and the hours that a woman may work are restricted.

Islamic tradition dictates that a husband does not gain possession of his wife's property. Unlike in several neighboring states, Kuwaiti women choose whether they will wear the traditional abaya (robe), hajib (headscarf), and veil. Many choose instead to wear Western fashions. However, conservative interpretations of Islam and Kuwaiti laws have left women with considerably less legal power than their husbands in matters of marital status, housing, child custody, and state benefits. For example, married women are required to renew their passport through their husbands, and children born to Kuwait women who are married to foreigners are denied nationality.

Domestic violence continues to be an area of concern in Kuwaiti society. According to some estimates in the early 21st century, domestic violence occurs in 15 percent of Kuwaiti marriages. Other forms of violence, such as rape and sexual assault, are also reported to occur, particularly toward foreign domestic workers. Kuwait has also come under criticism for failing to make little progress regarding the human trafficking of women for sexual exploitation, though the government of Kuwait has defended its human trafficking record in recent years. Problems of spousal abuse are often dealt with within the family, which is the core institution of the society. There are no shelters or homes where victims of spousal abuse can seek sanctuary, and are expected to return home or make private arrangements with family/friends if they are not comfortable returning home.

Health Care

Thanks to oil revenues, health care is also completely free to Kuwaiti nationals. Average life expectancy is about 78 to 76 years for men and 79 years for women (2015 estimate). About 1.79 doctors are available for every 1000 people. The government's annual per capita health expenditure is roughly 2.9 percent of GDP.

Flies and insects present a public health problem in Kuwait. Also, the wind-borne sand and dust often aggravate infections and allergic conditions. Common health problems include respiratory infections, coughs, sore throats, colds, sinusitis, bronchitis, and ear infections.

GOVERNMENT

Structure

Kuwait became a British protectorate in 1899, as it was threatened by the Turkish Ottoman Empire. The country became independent in 1961.

In 1938, oil was discovered under Kuwait's desert. After World War II, the American-British Kuwait Oil Company developed the oilfields. In 1975, the Kuwait Oil Company was nationalized.

In 1990, Saddam Hussein, president of Iraq, invaded Kuwait, claiming that Kuwait had violated the Organization of Petroleum Exporting Countries' oil production limits. Hussein also claimed that Kuwait was really part of Iraq. A United States-Saudi-Kuwaiti coalition repelled the invasion in the 1991 Persian Gulf War.

Kuwait is a constitutional hereditary emirate. The emir is the head of state and head of government, and is chosen by the members of the ruling family from among themselves. The emir appoints the prime minister, who, in turn, appoints other ministers to the Council of Ministers, or cabinet. The unicameral Majlis al-Umma (National Assembly) exercises legislative power. The 50 members of the assembly are elected to four-year terms.

Voting rights are extended to literate, natural-born, or naturalized citizens twenty-one years or older. Women won the vote early in 2005 however, women and men must vote at separate polling places. Within a month after achieving suffrage, a woman had been appointed to the Council of Ministers and two women to the Municipal Council. Military or police members, by law, are not allowed to vote. Furthermore, all voters must have been citizens for 20 years.

Political Parties

Political parties are banned in Kuwait, but several groups act as de facto parties. These include Bedouins, merchants, Sunni and Shia activists, secular leftists, and nationalists.

Local Government

For administrative purposes, the country is divided into six governorates. These governorates are, in turn, divided into districts.

Judicial System

Kuwait's court system consists of courts of causation, appeal, first instance, and summary.

Taxation

Kuwait does not have a personal income tax, and domestic companies are not subject to a corporate income tax (corporations based in Gulf Cooperation Council-member countries are also exempt). Foreign companies, however, are subject to a flat 15 percent corporate income tax.

Armed Forces

The armed forces of Kuwait is comprised of several service branches, including an army, navy, air force, and national police, as well as a coast guard and national guard contingent. The voluntary age for service is eighteen. Conscription was suspended in the country in 2001, but a nine-month service period (for males below the age of thirty-five) is in plans to be reinstated in 2010. A large portion of the military's equipment and technical assistance is provided by the United States. Kuwait also hosts a US military camp and logistics base.

As of 2010, the total manpower available for military service was about 841,000 men and 523,000 women. That said, annually, there are roughly 17,600 men and 16,200 women reaching significant age to join.

Foreign Policy

Kuwait's foreign policy is largely defined by its regional relations and the fact that the nation holds a large percentage of the world's oil supplies and is economically dependent on the sale of oil, particularly to the U.S. For example, Kuwait often finds itself in the middle of regional conflicts between Arab states and the West and is largely dependent on U.S. military support in terms of national security. Kuwait's business sector also has close ties to the U.S. and other Western countries, but U.S. policies in the Middle East often make Kuwait's continued alliance with America difficult. Kuwait has also used its wealth to provide aid to Palestinian refugees and to other Arab nations, and continues to maintain strong international relations apart from its US relations.

The most serious criticism of Kuwait's foreign policy, particularly from its own citizens and from other Arab states, involves the ongoing US support for Israel in the Israeli-Palestinian conflict. Kuwait has repeatedly condemned Israel's policies and accuses Israel of human rights abuses against the Palestinians, but remains an important US ally in the peace negotiation process. Kuwait's policies in the region are also shaped by its own conflict with Iraq and with the Palestinian workers who lived in Kuwait before the 1990 Iraqi invasion. Suspecting that its Palestinian residents supported Iraq, the Kuwaiti government expelled all Palestinians from the country. After Kuwait was liberated, it quickly reaffirmed its support for a Palestinian state but no longer hosts a significant Palestinian population. Kuwait was also one of the few states in the region to support the US-led invasion of Iraq in 2003. It has sought to mediate between Iran and the US on the question of Iran's nuclear power program. Kuwait has shown tentative support for its neighbor in this dispute, but is struggling with Iran in attempts to negotiate a national boundary between the two countries in the Arabian Gulf.

Kuwait has maintained membership in the United Nations (UN) since 1963, and holds membership in the World Bank, the International Monetary Fund (IMF), the World Trade Organization (WTO), the Organization of Petroleum Exporting Countries (OPEC), and the Non-Aligned Movement (NAM), among others. Notable regional memberships include the Gulf Cooperation Council (GCC), the Islamic Development Bank (IDB), the African Development Bank (ADB), the Organization of the Islamic Conference (OIC), and the Arab League.

Human Rights Profile

International human rights law insists that states respect civil and political rights, and also promote an individual's economic, social and cultural rights. The United Nations Universal Declaration of Human Rights (UDHR) is recognized as the standard for international human rights. Its authors sought the counsel of the world's great thinkers, philosophers, and religious leaders, and were careful to create a document that reflects the core values shared by every world culture. (To read this document or view the articles relating to cultural human rights, visit http://www.udhr.org/UDHR/default.htm.)

The Kuwaiti government pledged its commitment to human rights reforms in 1991, after the liberation of Kuwait from Iraqi forces. Since that time, Kuwait has made measurable progress in women's rights, but continues to fall short in its treatment and protection of non-citizens. Kuwait is estimated to have over 100,000 long-term, legal residents who do not have citizenship rights. Often second or third generation Arab residents, these people are known as Bidoun, or bidoons (meaning "without"), and are unable to provide documentation of citizenship to any nation. Without documentation, the Kuwaiti government restricts their right to move freely and denies them the benefits and rights of Kuwaiti citizens. In recent years, the Kuwaiti government has moved to naturalize a limited number of long-term residents who can provide documentation and to detain or deport those who cannot.

Kuwait has also struggled to meet human rights standards in regards to the country's large population of migrant service workers. These foreign workers receive little or no protection from the government against abuses. Workers often receive substandard wages or have wages withheld and employers may withhold their employees' passports in order to restrain their movements. Female domestic workers, in particular, are vulnerable to physical and sexual abuse by employers. Charges have been made of slave labor and deceptive hiring practices. Kuwait is considered a transit and destination country for human trafficking in the Middle East, particularly for sexual exploitation and forced labor.

Censorship of the media and of individual freedom of speech is far less of a problem in Kuwait than in many neighboring countries. However, some censorship of political or moral content does occur. Lastly, Kuwait's judicial code allows for execution and the government has imposed the death penalty in cases of murder and drug trafficking.

ECONOMY

Overview of the Economy

Kuwait's economy depends heavily on oil, which provides almost half of the gross domestic product (GDP) and 95 percent of export revenues. Kuwait is a member of the Organization of Petroleum Exporting Countries (OPEC). Kuwait's per capita GDP was estimated at $51,200 USD in 2009. Most families own a car, and wealthier Kuwaitis have large homes. The government's social welfare programs guarantee a relatively high standard of living for even the poorest citizens.

Prior to the discovery of the rich oil fields of Kuwait, Kuwait City was historically known for trading in prawns and pearls, industries that persist in the early 21st century. Kuwait City has also grown in its trade, services, tourism, and banking markets, and has a thriving hospitality industry with two premier tourist agencies.

Because peak oil is predicted in the first half of the 21st century, and because Kuwait's economy is so heavily dependent on petroleum, the government is developing economic diversification plans. In 2009, it committed to a $140 billion investment over five years in an effort to move away from a petroleum-based economy, seeking outside investment, and strengthening private enterprise. In 2010, Kuwait passed its first long-term economic development plan in almost twenty-five years. While the government planned to spend up $104 billion over four years to diversify the economy away from oil, attract more investment, and boost private sector participation in the economy, many of the projects did not materialize because of the uncertain political situation.

Industry

Kuwait exports roughly 1.4 million bbl/day (2010). The government owns and operates most of the oil industry. In the wake of the Iraq invasion, Kuwait's oil industry infrastructure had to be completely overhauled, at an expense of nearly $10 billion (USD).

Other important industries include chemical production, construction materials manufacturing, and shipbuilding. Due to the country's lack of fresh water, Kuwait is home to some of the world's largest and most advanced water-desalination plants, which remove the salt from seawater.

Exports, primarily of oil and petroleum products, generate annual revenues of $16.9 billion USD. Japan, the United States, and South Korea are Kuwait's biggest export partners.

Labor

The Kuwaiti labor force was estimated at 2.4 million in 2014, and a large majority of the workforce is non-Kuwaiti (60 percent), owing to the large percentage of foreign interest in the country. Approximately 66 percent of Kuwait's workforce is employed in the services sector (2010 estimate). The unemployment rate was recorded as 2.1 percent in 2014.

Energy/Power/Natural Resources

By far, Kuwait's greatest natural resource is oil. The burning of more than 700 Kuwaiti oil wells by Iraqi forces in 1991 left large areas of the country contaminated with toxic residue. As a result, much of the desert has been posted as off-limits. Since that time, however, oil production has returned to, and surpassed, pre-invasion levels.

Other natural resources include natural gas, fish, and shrimp. Environmental issues facing Kuwait include air and water pollution, desertification, and limited fresh water.

Fishing

The Kuwaiti fishing fleet largely consists of boats owned by Kuwaiti nationals, but manned by expatriates (consisting of Bangladeshi, Indians, Egyptians, and Iranians), which can sometimes lead to conflict as these expatriates continue to seek better treatment by the Kuwaiti government.

Shrimp is a major catch (much of which is exported), followed by finfish. Kuwait's fleet is limited to its territorial waters and regulations

dictated by the Gulf Cooperation Council (GCC) caused an uproar in late 2010 when the government required that nylon nets for trawling be replaced with cotton, which the Kuwait Fisherman Association declared to be inappropriate and weak for commercial fishing. The organization also claimed that the government was enforcing regulations that other GCC countries were failing to require of their own fleets.

Given the government's interest in developing other industries, the fishing industry (which in 2010 was not a major contributor to the nation's GDP) is poised for growth.

Mining/Metals

Kuwait's exports (93 percent) and government revenues (94 percent) are highly dependent on petroleum production and refining.

Agriculture

The lack of fresh water, combined with the fact that less than 1 percent of Kuwait's land area is arable, means that few crops are grown on a large scale. Kuwaiti farmers grow dates, tomatoes, cucumbers, eggplant, lettuce, onions, cabbage, cauliflower, chilies and green peppers, pumpkins, squash, gourds, and a few other vegetables. Kuwait must import almost all of its food, except fish.

Animal Husbandry

Camels, goats, and sheep are raised on small farms. As of the early 21st century, sheep, and goats were the dominant livestock bred, followed by poultry and cattle. Livestock products include mutton and lamb, poultry, cows' milk, and eggs.

Tourism

Kuwait receives more than two million tourists a year, mostly from other Arab countries and from Asia. Tourism receipts are approximately $243 million (USD) annually, and tourism contributes approximately 3.7 percent to the country's gross domestic product. While forecasts for the Kuwait tourism industry in 2010 predict a decrease in tourism revenue and employment through 2010, the Kuwaiti government has announced plans to provide further support to the country's tourism industry.

Popular tourist attractions include the Kuwait Towers resort complex, the Kuwait Zoological Gardens in Omariya, the Kuwait Resort near the Saudi border, and the Entertainment City theme park. Kuwait City boasts many museums and cultural venues. Many visitors to Kuwait enjoy sailing and water sports. Bird watching is available in nature reserves and on the islands.

Amy Witherbee, Ellen Bailey,
Lynn-nore Chittom

DO YOU KNOW?

- Despite its desert location, Kuwait City boasts the largest ice skating rink in the Middle East. The complex includes a small rink with seats for 600 people and an Olympic rink that can seat 1,600 people. The small rink is open to the public, while the Olympic rink is used for major cultural celebrations and as a practice rink for hockey teams, including the Kuwait Falcons.

- The name Kuwait means "little fort" in Arabic.

Bibliography

Alessandra L. Gonzalez. *Islamic Feminism in Kuwait.* New York: Palgrave Macmillan, 2014.

Alī AkbarMahdī. *Teen Life in the Middle East.* Westport, CT: Greenwood, 2003. 101-116.

Ben J. Slot, ed. *Kuwait: The Growth of a Historic Identity.* London: Arabian, 2003.

Bruce Ingham and J. Fayadh. *Customs and Etiquette of Arabia and Gulf States.* 2nd ed. London: Simple Guides, Bravo Ltd, 2005.

Helen Mary Rizzo. *Islam, Democracy, and the Status of Women: The Case of Kuwait.* New York: Routledge, 2005.

Lori Plotkin Boghardt. *Kuwait Amid War, Peace and Revolution: 1979-1991 and New Challenges.* Basingstoke, Hampshire, England: Palgrave MacMillan, 2006.

Michael S. Casey. *The History of Kuwait.* Westport, CT: Greenwood, 2007.

Works Cited

"Al-Baqsami and Al-Qadiri receive international European award." *Kuwait Times* (26 January 2008): np. Online.

"Al-Diwan Al-Amiri." *Official Website: State of Kuwait.* English language edition. http://www.da.gov.kw/eng/.

Dreda Say Mitchell. "Message of rap: you are what you own." *Kuwait Times* (30 November 1999): np.

Online. http://www.kuwaittimes.net/read_news. php?newsid=MTM0NzkzMjgzNw══.

Graham Holderness. "From Summit to Tragedy: Sulayman Al-Bassam's *Richard III* and Political Theatre." *Critical Survey* 19.3: 20p. Database. EBSCO.

"Iraqi, Kuwaiti Leaders Gather on Anniversary." *USA Today* (27 February 2009):1p. Database. EBSCO.

Jamie Etheridge. "Kuwait's empowered Islamists question all things Western." *Christian Science Monitor* 100.143: 2p. Database. EBSCO.

"Kuwait." CIA. *The World Factbook.* https://www.cia.gov/library/publications/the-world-factbook/geos/ku.html.

"Kuwait Complete Residents' Guide." Dubai: *Explorer*, 2006.

"Kuwait: Criteria and procedures for granting citizenship to bidoon through DNA testing." Immigration and Refugee Board of Canada. *UNHCR Refworld.* The UN Refugee Agency. 12 February 1999. http:www.unhcr.org/refworld/docid/3ae6ad02c.html.

Sarah Alzouman. "Youth producers to shape future of Arab media." *Kuwait Times* (5 March 2009): np. Online. http://www.kuwaittimes.net/read_news. php?newsid=ODM3MzUxNTA0.

Velina Nacheva. "Kuwaiti artist captivates Oman with powerful imagery, poems." *Kuwait Times* (3 March 2007): np. Online.

Kibbah, a Lebanese delicacy, is made with ground meat, spices, and bulghur wheat.

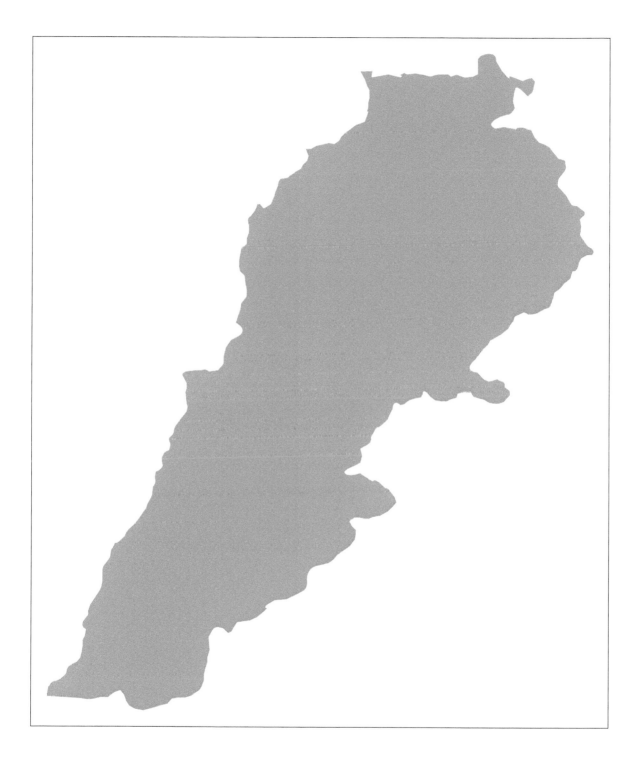

LEBANON

Introduction

Lebanon, officially the Republic of Lebanon, has been the scene of armed struggle since ancient times, as one power after another has seized control of the country. The capital, Beirut, is one of the oldest cities in the world, and has been the site of many important archeological finds. Once referred to as "the Pearl of the Middle East," Beirut is often considered the most "Westernized" city in the Arab world. Like modern-day Lebanon itself, Beirut, which has also earned the nickname of "The City That Would Not Die," is a unique blend of the ancient and the new.

In the 20th century, Lebanon consisted of a carefully constructed, but peaceful balance between Christian and Muslim populations. The arrival of Palestinian refugees sparked a fifteen-year civil war, which ended only when Syria took control of the country in 1990. There was strong opposition to Syrian rule, but Western powers favored the status quo because violence had declined. In early 2005, following widespread protests, Syria withdrew from Lebanon. Today, although the government of Lebanon is supported by Western powers, wide swaths of the country are controlled and influenced by the fundamentalist Shia Islamic group known as Hezbollah.

Hezbollah and Israel have continued attacks and counterattacks against each other following Syria's withdrawal from the country, and the two fought a brief war in 2006. Lebanon's borders with Syria and Israel remain a matter of dispute.

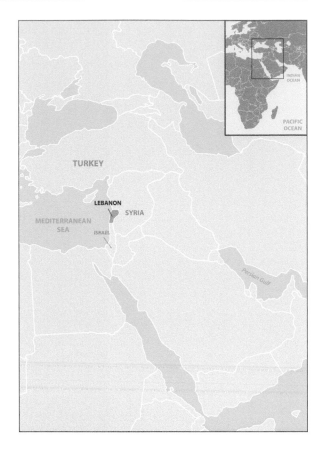

GENERAL INFORMATION

Official Language: Arabic
Population: 6,184,701 (July 2015)
Currency: Lebanese pound (or lira)
Coins: The Lebanese pound is available in bilingual (French and Arabic) coin denominations of 50, 100, 250, and 500 pounds.
Land Area: 10,230 square kilometers (3,949 square miles)
Water Area: 170 square kilometers (66 square miles)
National Anthem: "Koullouna Lilouataan Lil Oula Lil Alam" ("All of Us! For Our Country, for Our Flag and Glory")
Capital: Beirut
Time Zone: GMT +2
Flag Description: The flag of Lebanon features a bicolor design, with a central white horizontal band (called a Spanish fess, due to being twice the size of the bands beside it) between two equal, horizontal bands of red, each half the size of the white band. Centered in the white band, and just touching each red stripe, is a green

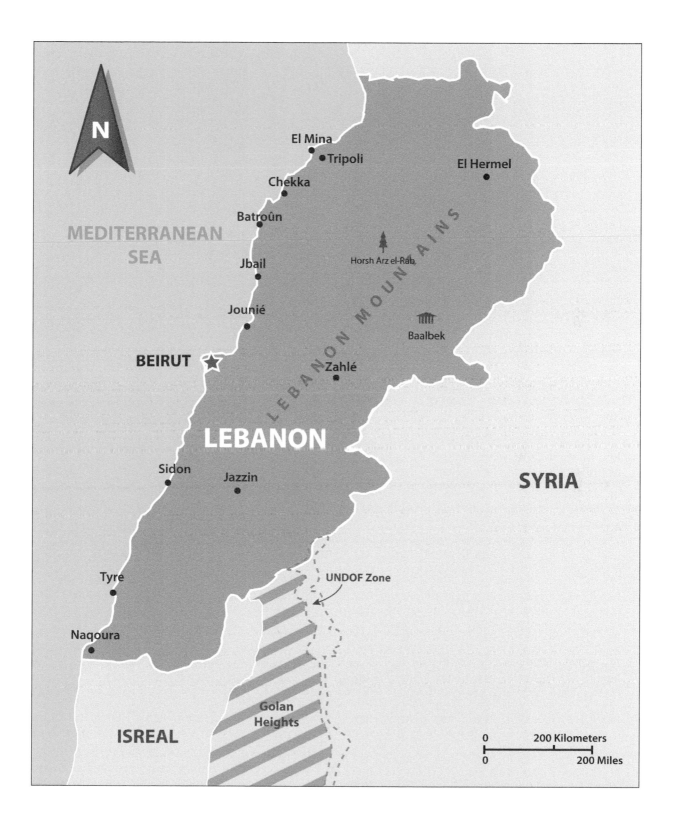

N

El Mina
Tripoli
El Hermel
Chekka
Batroûn
MEDITERRANEAN
SEA
Jbail
Horsh Arz el-Rab
LEBANON MOUNTAINS
Jounié
Baalbek
BEIRUT
Zahlé
LEBANON
SYRIA
Sidon
Jazzin
Tyre
UNDOF Zone
Naqoura
Golan
Heights
ISREAL
0   200 Kilometers
0   200 Miles

Principal Cities by Population (2012 estimate):

- Beirut (2.226 million)
- Ras Beirut (1,251,739)
- Tripoli (195,932)
- Sidon (59,948)
- Tyre (135,204)
- Habbouch (98,433)
- Jounie (96,315)
- Zahle (55,081)
- Baalbek (30,916)
- Jbail (20,784)

cedar, or Lebanon Cedar, the national emblem. Symbolically, the red represents the spilled blood of freedom, while the white, a general representation of either peace or purity, stands for the country's snow-topped mountains, themselves an extension of the concept of purity.

Population

Lebanon's population density is 417 persons per square kilometer (1,046 persons per square mile) as of 2015. Most people live in the coastal areas, and the country's major cities are all coastal. As of 2008, an estimated 87 percent of the population resides in urban areas.

Beirut is the most populous city in Lebanon, although no official census has been performed since 1932. Population estimates range roughly 2.2 million people for the city proper. Beirut's population grew from 45,000 to 90,000 between 1840 and 1860, and then later grew tenfold in the period between 1930 and 1970. The country had an estimated population growth rate of 0.6 percent in 2010.

The lack of a comprehensive census makes any kind of ethnic distinctions difficult, but groups of Arabs, Syrians, Armenians, and Kurds all make their home in Beirut—95 percent Arab, four percent Armenian and one percent other. The most easily recognizable demographic, however, is religion.

Languages

Although the official language is Arabic, most people speak Lebanese. French is a widely used second language. English and Armenian are also spoken by a few. Most Beirutis are trilingual, speaking Arabic, English, and French.

Native People & Ethnic Groups

The inhabitants of Lebanon are its native people. They are a Semitic people, a term used to apply to people of Middle Eastern origin.

However, nearly 400,000 Palestinian refugees live in camps in Lebanon, mostly in the south. The first refugees came in 1948, after the Arab-Israeli war that established the nation of Israel. Other refugees came after the Six Days' War of 1967. They and their descendants still live in the camps.

The Palestinians have no state to return to, they suffer from severe poverty, and they live in unsanitary and unsafe conditions. Numerous professions are closed to them by law, travel is restricted, and they are not allowed to own land. In many camps, there are no schools. Some of the restrictive laws were passed to preserve the delicate religious balance in Lebanon, but have created significant hardship for the Palestinians.

Violence by and against the Palestinians has been a condition of life in the camps since they were established. Israel occupied southern Lebanon for more than twenty years, finally withdrawing in 2000. A few months later, Israeli troops returned to Lebanon in retaliation for attacks launched from refugee camps by Hezbollah.

According to the CIA World Factbook, 95 percent of Lebanon's population is Arab and 4 percent are Armenian.

Religions

At least 18 religious sects are recognized in Lebanon. About 54 percent of the people are Muslim, and 40 percent are Christian. Muslim sects include Shi'a (27 percent), Sunni (27 percent), Druze (5.6 percent), Ismai'ilite, Alawite, and Nusayri. Christians are mostly Maronite Catholics (21 percent). Small groups practice Protestant religions and Judaism.

Beirut, a very religious city, is an extension of this diversity. In fact, it is one of the most religiously diverse cities in the Middle East, likely due to the number of times Beirut has changed hands in its long history. In some places, Christian churches are located across the street from Muslim mosques. Islam, Christianity, and Druze all have large populations. The city is dominated by eight primary religious denominations: Sunni Muslims, Shiite Muslims, Druze, Maronite Catholics, Greek Orthodox, Greek Catholic, Armenian Orthodox, Armenian Catholics, and Protestants.

Beirut is also believed to have a large atheist population, but the overwhelming religiosity of the city has prevented there being an accurate estimate or a significant attempt to quantify it. During the civil war, the city was split between the Sunni Muslim West and Christian East, who have since engaged in a tenuous treaty. The southern end of the city is generally the home of the Shi'a Muslims.

Climate

The weather in Lebanon depends on altitude. The coastal lowlands experience hot, humid summers with very little rain, and mild, rainy winters. The mountains receive heavy rains, and snow during winter at the highest elevations. The Bekaa Valley has an arid desert climate.

Beirut, on the coast, has an elevation of approximately 30 meters (98 feet). It experiences an average January temperature of 13° Celsius (55° Fahrenheit) and an average July temperature of 27° Celsius (81° Fahrenheit). In contrast, Ksara, at 918 meters (3,011 feet), has an average winter temperature of 7° Celsius (45° Fahrenheit) and an average summer temperature of 23° Celsius (74° Fahrenheit).

Precipitation also varies. Beirut's average precipitation is about 89 centimeters (35 inches), while Ksara receives an average of 62 centimeters (24 inches).

ENVIRONMENT & GEOGRAPHY

Topography

Lebanon is a small country on the eastern end of the Mediterranean. It is roughly wedge-shaped, with the widest part to the north. Lebanon is bounded by Syria on the north and east and by Israel on the south. It is about seven-tenths of the size of the American state of Connecticut. Its Mediterranean coastline is 220 kilometers (135 miles) long.

A narrow plain follows the coast, and the Jabal Lubnan (the Lebanon Mountains), composed largely of limestone, lie to the east. El Beqaa (the Bekaa Valley) separates western Lebanon from the northeastern Anti-Lebanon Mountains. Most of the country is mountainous. The highest peak is Qurnet as Sauda, in the Lebanon Mountains, rising to 3,088 meters (10,131 feet) in the north.

One of Lebanon's major rivers is the Nahr Al Asi (Orontes), which rises in the Bekaa Valley near Baalbek, and flows north into Syria and Turkey. About 400 kilometers (250 miles) long, the river is mostly unnavigable, but it provides irrigation.

Nahr Al-Litani (the Litani River) flows for 145 kilometers (90 miles) southwest between the mountain ranges and empties into the Mediterranean south of Sidon. The Litani waters the Bekaa Valley, Lebanon's primary agricultural area, and is the only river in the Middle East that does not cross a national boundary. The Jordan River rises in southern Lebanon and flows into Israel. Like the other rivers, it is used for irrigation rather than for navigation.

Beirut is located atop the Al-Ashrafiyah and Al-Musaytibah hills, which are home to East Beirut and West Beirut, respectively. The city sits on a peninsula in the Mediterranean Sea, at the foot of the Lebanon Mountains, and covers an area of about 67 square kilometers (26 square miles).

Plants & Animals

The mountains of Lebanon are still dotted with huge cedar trees, but not nearly in the same numbers as in ancient times. The most common mountain tree is the oak, along with the walnut, poplar, pine, carob, and locust. There are also some tamarisks, maples, sumacs, and acacias.

The sycamore, which in Lebanon is really a type of inedible fig tree, grows in the coastal lowlands. Dateless date palms are used for timber.

Juniper and barberry grow in abundance in the eastern mountains while bramble, myrtle, and clematis dominate the slopes in the west. Other common plants include lentisk, arbutus, styrax, jasmine, bay, small-leaved holly, honeysuckle, rhododendron, barberry, oleander and cypress. Prickly pear, an introduced plant, is often used for hedges.

Common herbs that grow in Lebanon include sage, rosemary, lavender, rue, and wormwood. Among the country's many flowers are varieties of hyacinth, tulip, rose, hollyhock, ranunculus, gladiolus, anemone, crocus, amaryllis, cyclamen, chrysanthemum, blue campanula, and mandrake.

There are few wild animal species left in Lebanon. Those that remain include bears, leopards, wolves, hyenas, jackals, foxes, hares, boars, mongooses, gazelles, squirrels, rats, and moles.

Numerous varieties of birds, however, are found, including eagles, hawks, kites, owls, vultures, falcons, gulls, partridges, linnets, robins, water-ouzels, thrushes, pigeons, woodcocks, and wrens.

A few varieties of freshwater fish live in Lebanon's rivers, while the ocean is home to shellfish and mullet.

CUSTOMS & COURTESIES

Greetings

Greetings in Lebanon are often lengthy, and vary considerably depending on the situation. As Arabic is the most widely spoken language in Lebanon, "Salaam" ("Peace") is often used as the common greeting. When welcoming guests into their home, Lebanese also might use the expression "Ahlan wa sahlan," meaning "You are in your family on a ground without stumbling stones." The expression "Allah ma'ak" ("Go in peace or god be with you") is the common farewell expression. If the greeting is being exchanged in an urban setting, common expressions might include the French "Bonjour" ("Good day") and "Salut" ("Hello") or the Arabic "Keef halik" ("How are you"). In rural areas, it is typical for only the Lebanese dialect of Arabic to be used.

When both greeting and saying farewell, it is common for close friends or family members to exchange kisses on each cheek. If the individuals are business associates, strangers, or simply acquaintances, they will most likely exchange a handshake. Some Muslims will also only shake hands or exchange kisses with members of the same sex.

Men and women observant of this practice will each place their right hand on their chest and nod their heads as an expression of greeting.

Gestures & Etiquette

Lebanese culture is closely connected to Muslim culture due to the predominance of Islam in the region. As a result, Lebanese etiquette is highly influenced by Islamic customs. For example, it is considered improper to give or receive an object with the left hand, as this hand is reserved for activities thought of as unsanitary (such as the cleansing of the body). It is also considered impolite to give someone items to hold, because this implies servitude. Additionally, Lebanese pay particular attention to the placement of their feet. The sole of one's foot or shoe should be directed toward the ground, and not shown to anyone. Public display of affections, even between married couples, is also frowned upon, and members of the opposite sex generally avoid direct eye contact.

The Lebanese typically accent their language with numerous physical gestures. In communicating "no" to a question, the Lebanese will raise their head upward and raise their eyebrows; this gesture can be accompanied by a clicking of the tongue. To communicate "yes" with their heads, they will tilt the head downwards. A very subtle way to say "yes" is blinking the eyes. While shaking the head back and forth is popular in

Western cultures, in Lebanese culture this gesture indicates that the person is asking a question.

Another gesture is an upward turned hand with all fingers pressed together. This gesture implies for someone to wait. If the hand does not move, this gesture indicates that one is busy and is asking for patience on the part of another. If the hand is moved up and down slowly, the gesture is comforting, as a way to tell a person "just wait, the situation will improve." The gesture can also be used in a threatening way. Some gestures are considered improper, including raising a fist into the air.

Eating/Meals

Midday is when the Lebanese generally eat their largest meal. This meal sometimes lasts more than two hours. The evening meal is typically lighter, and on special occasions, a dinner called a meza is served. This communal event includes a wide variety of dishes, and these types of meals last several hours. When eating Western food, it is common for Lebanese to use Western utensils, but when eating Lebanese foods, Lebanese will traditionally eat with their right hand and use bread or lettuce as a utensil.

Islam has greatly influenced eating customs in Lebanon. For example, devout Muslims refrain from consuming pork and alcohol. They also seek halal meat, or meat that has been prepared according to Muslim standards. During the month of Ramadan, the eleventh month of the Islamic calendar, many Muslims fast from sunrise until sunset. During this time, even those who are not fasting usually do not eat, drink, or smoke in public in order to show respect.

Visiting

Hospitality is central to Lebanese culture. For centuries the inhabitants of modern-day Lebanon have counted on one another for assistance due to the land's arid and hot climate, whether it be offerings of water, food, or shelter.

Being invited into a Lebanese home is a very high honor. The host and guest usually follow certain visitation customs. For example, when invited to a person's home it is an appropriate gesture to bring them a gift such as fresh flowers or sweets. (If the gift is wrapped, it will not be opened when received.) Shoes are usually taken off at the door, and some Lebanese will have specific slippers they wear while indoors.

When new guests arrive into the home, it is proper for everyone to stand up and greet them. Courtesy dictates that anyone also stand for a woman or elder. Visits often are quite lengthy, especially if the visit includes having a meal. It is considered rude to leave immediately after eating, and guests should stay for a while longer if the host insists.

LIFESTYLE

Family

Lebanese families are generally close-knit. It is not unusual for cousins to have very close relationships, similar to that of a brother and sister. The family unit is also considered the most important, and family businesses are common. Wealth is also shared; the more prosperous family members will often provide funds for relatives who are less fortunate. Additionally, the actions of an individual are often directly influenced by how these choices will affect the family.

Within the family structure, the father is typically the head of the household, as he is usually the primary provider. Women traditionally focus on domestic responsibilities, such as the upkeep of the home and child rearing. When women do work outside of the home, it is often due to financial necessity. Traditionally, the Lebanese family unit consists of the husband and wife, all of their unmarried children, and the families of their married sons. In the past, the members of the family would usually live together, although this is not a common practice today.

Housing

Traditional Lebanese homes are made of stone. Generally, the features of a home depend upon the wealth of the homeowner. For example, a well-off family's home typically would have a large arch framework with high ceilings, and might have more than one floor and large balconies. Tile is frequently used for the roof. This style of home, common in places like Beirut, was influenced by 19th-century Venetian architecture. Some privileged Lebanese also live in old palaces from the 18th and 19th century. Lower income families have simpler homes composed of rough stones and roofs made of wood and mud.

In larger cities, older styles of homes are being demolished to make way for high-rise apartments, office buildings, and wider streets. The war-torn country has also seen some of its older buildings destroyed during times of conflict.

Food

While Lebanese dishes are similar to the cuisine of its Middle Eastern neighbors, the country's cuisine also incorporates influences from the cooking styles of the Turkish and French. Staple ingredients in Lebanese cuisine include lamb, chickpeas, eggplant, yoghurt, lemon, tomato, cucumber garlic, mint, parsley, and olive oil. These ingredients can be mixed and prepared in a variety of ways to make truly unique, flavorful dishes.

Traditionally, a Lebanese dining experience begins with appetizers, and the types of appetizers served vary widely according to the event. For example, salad accompanied by nuts, often pistachios, is for simple occasions. Some of the other labor-intensive appetizers include a dip called baba ghanoush, which is a mixture of grilled eggplant, tahini (ground sesame seeds), olive oil, lemon juice, and garlic. This dish is usually served with bread. This is either a flat pita pocket or another type of bread called marcook, which is thin and cooked over a fire.

Main dishes in Lebanese cuisine commonly feature meat, typically lamb, chicken, or fish. A popular Lebanese main dish is kibbah (or kibbeh). While preparations vary, kibbah is traditionally made with lamb that is ground with a mortar and pestle until it attains a smooth consistency. The meat is combined with salt, pepper, onion, and burghul (cracked wheat, also called

bulghur), and then cooked. Salad and rice are also traditionally served after main dishes.

Meals usually conclude with dessert, which is commonly accompanied by tea. One type of Lebanese dessert pastry is kunafa, which is made with special pastry dough that is shaped like shoelaces. The thin pastry strings are mixed with almonds, walnuts or other nuts, as well as a rich cheese filling. The entire dish is covered with sugary syrup after baking. Traditionally, this desert is eaten during the non-fasting hours of Ramadan.

Life's Milestones

One unique Lebanese marriage custom, known as the zaffeh, occurs on the final day of the often three-day-long marriage celebration. As part of the tradition, a cheerful group of musicians and dancers escorts the groom to the bride's home, where he goes to meet his future wife. The father of the bride usually brings his daughter out to meet her future husband. As they leave, they are greeted with exuberant noises while being sprinkled with fresh flower petals and rice. Traditionally, the whole town participates in a wedding, especially during the zaffeh.

CULTURAL HISTORY

Art

Situated at the crossroads of Europe, Asia, and Africa, Lebanon has a rich and diverse cultural heritage that has been shaped by numerous civilizations—including the Phoenicians, Babylonians, Greeks, Romans, Byzantines, and Arabs. Some of the artistic heritages of these cultures include Phoenician jewelry, Roman and Byzantine mosaics (an art form featuring colored glass), and Arabic calligraphy. In addition, Lebanon is considered the birthplace of the Phoenician alphabet, the world's first alphabet. Traditional Lebanese crafts include textiles, ceramics, glass blowing (dating back to Phoenician times), metalwork, grass weaving, and wood carving (utilizing the country's famed cedars and olive trees).

Lebanon has also been at the center of the emergence and maturation of both Christianity and Islam. Religion has undoubtedly been a major influence of both ancient and modern Lebanese art, particularly the visual arts. Another significant influence was French culture, largely because of the French Mandate (1920–1943) following World War I that placed what is now Lebanon under French control. This period brought many European influences to Lebanon, but also helped usher in a distinct Lebanese identity in terms of art. One of Lebanon's most celebrated painters is Moustafa Farroukh (1901–1957). He is known for his use of color and his depiction of local culture and landscapes.

Other prominent Lebanese artists include painters such as Joseph Matar (1935–) and Hussein Madi (1938–). Matar paints landscapes, portraits, nudes, sacred art, and still life. He has stated that his landscapes attempt to preserve his view of Lebanon before war and modernization destroyed it.

Architecture

Beirut is rich with artifacts and ruins of the ancient civilizations that once ruled there. One of the more striking sites in Beirut is the group of Five Columns, which are believed to date from the first century BCE when Beirut was a Roman colony. The columns were discovered in 1963 near the St. George Maronite Cathedral. Another relic from the Roman period is a Roman Bath that once served the whole town. Portions of a wall and castle built by the Crusaders were excavated in 1995; evidence that Roman structures were incorporated into the Crusaders' buildings was also found.

During its inclusion in the Ottoman Empire, the layout of Beirut was meticulously planned, even while it expanded and grew tremendously. However, very little of the original city remains in its original form. After 1943, expansion became increasingly disorganized and confused, and after the devastating civil war, any remaining order that the city had was all but decimated. It is not unusual to see a wide range of building types on a single block, from high-rise apartment buildings to fancy villas and houses. Because much of the fighting during the civil war took place in the city center, much of the city could not be rebuilt until after the war, and as such, very few of Beirut's original streets and structures remain.

Drama

Theater emerged in Lebanon in 1847, when Arab trader Maroun Nakkash staged a production of a 17th-century French play (*The Miser* by Moliere) in the Arabic language. By the middle of the 20th century, the arts had begun to flourish. Notable Lebanese playwrights (and brothers) Assi Rahbani (1923–1986) and Mansour Rahbani (1925–2009) wrote many musicals, including *Ayyam al Hassaad* ("Days of Harvest," 1957) and *Al Mahatta* ("The Station," 1973). One of their most famous plays was *Biyya' el Khawatem* ("The Ring Seller," 1964); a political commentary, the play depicted village life in Lebanon during the Ottoman Empire.

By the early 20th century, theater in Lebanon began to express social concerns. For example, Nidal Al-Askar's *Tistifil Meryl Streep* ("To Hell with Meryl Streep," 2006) addresses topics such as sexuality and virginity in Lebanese culture, and Lina Khoury's *Haki Neswein* ("Women's Talk," 2006) is an adaptation of Eve Ensler's *The Vagina Monologues*; Khoury's play discusses gender and female sexuality in contemporary Lebanon.

Music & Dance

Traditional Lebanese musical instruments include the lute, the mijwiz, the tabla, and the rikk. The half-pear shaped lute is a stringed instrument similar to a guitar. It is often made of wood and has either a long or a short neck. The mijwiz is a reed clarinet and has several holes down its front. The tabla is a drum played with the hands, with the skin traditionally made of goat or fish skin. The drum produces a variety of pitches depending on where the player strikes the drumhead. The rikk is similar to the tambourine and has a round frame with metal discs on its edges. Traditionally, the skin stretched across the instrument's frame was either made of fish or goatskin.

While traditional music remains popular, the 20th century saw Lebanese music move in new directions. One of Lebanon's most famous singers was Fairuz (1935–); born Nouhad Haddad (Fairuz translates as "gem" or "turquoise"). When Fairuz experimented with Argentine composer Eduardo Bianco (1892–1959), a new genre of Arabic music was formed: the dancesong. Fairuz's career was launched with a song called "Itab" ("Expostulation"), and her popularity grew as she performed in musicals and began singing the lyrics of the Arab world's most famous poets.

The dabkah is the national dance of Lebanon, and is thought to have originated in Lebanon's Bekaa Valley, historically the country's most important farming region. This dance is performed throughout the Middle East, especially in Syria, Palestine, Jordan, and Iraq. Dabkah consists of dancers in line, led by the lawwih, at the head of the line. The dancers stand close to one another and sometimes hold hands. Lively footwork including jumping and stomping to the beat of the music are features of this dance, which is typically performed during community gatherings in a celebratory manner.

Literature

Lebanese literature is an important part of the culture, and there is a particularly strong tradition of Lebanese poetry. Khalil Gibran (1883–1931), a poet, essayist, novelist, and artist, is often considered Lebanon's most celebrated writer. Born and raised in Beirut, Gibran left Lebanon in 1895, immigrating to Boston, Massachusetts, with his parents. After several years, he returned to Beirut to study, devoting himself to Arabic literature. At the turn of the 20th century, Gibran began publishing his works—writing in both Arabic and English—the themes of his which include love, death, and the conditions created by a life of immigration. Gibran is perhaps best known for his romantic poetry, which paved the way for new methods of expression within Arabic literature.

CULTURE

Arts & Entertainment

The contemporary arts in Lebanon have been directly influenced and impacted by the economic and political instability in the country. In particular, the nationalist political movement has restored interest in traditional art forms such as dabkah, Lebanon's national dance, and zajal, which is Lebanese folk poetry.

A popular festival called the Baalbeck International Festival, set against a backdrop of Roman ruins, is considered the oldest cultural event in the Middle East and the surrounding eastern Mediterranean region. The festival began in 1955, and is a showcase of Lebanese talent ranging from traditional music, dance and theatre, as well as ballet, opera, and pop music. Although the festival does draw international performers, Baalbeck has served as a platform for emerging Lebanese artists, and as a way for Lebanon to promote its cultural traditions. However, from 1975 through 1996, and again in 2006, the festival shut down due to the Lebanese Civil War and instability in the region. In 2006, a musical comedy titled *Sah El Nom*, and created by the Rahbani brothers, was staged to continue the festival's tradition; it was presented in three sold-out shows.

Modern Lebanese literature has served an important purpose in cataloging the many wartorn years the country has experienced in the last century. Well-known Arab poets such as Adonis (1930–) and Nizar Qabbani (1923–1998) wrote about Beirut as a place destroyed—literally and spiritually—by the Lebanese Civil War (1975–1991). Their works are also concerned with the conditions of exile and loss that inevitably accompany war. This environment also opened space for women writers to publish their work. Women writers such as novelists Emily Nasrallah (1931–), Hanan al-Shaykh (1945–), and Ghada al-Samman (1942–) have, through their works, supplied a feminist perspective to the events of the war. Varying viewpoints, from Sunni to Shiite to Christian and Druze (a traditional offshoot of Islam predominant in Lebanon,

Syria, and Israel), have also found a platform through literature.

Visual art in contemporary Lebanon is divided into two camps: artists who focus on traditional elements of visual art by painting and sculpting such things as landscapes and figures, and artists who work with modern media, such as installations and video productions, whose work is often political in nature. One particular contemporary artist, Ayman Baalbaki (1975–), is said to be bridging this divide. Baalbaki's style borrows from traditional techniques present in religious iconography and manuscripts, and combines it with a style that is distinctly fresh and modern. His creations are often not confined to the space of the canvas, as some pieces contain sculptural elements that project off the canvas. While his work has a political conscience, the themes are approached in a poetic way that references the painting traditions of the past.

Football (soccer) is a popular sport, and Lebanon has several football leagues. Other popular sports include basketball, cricket, golf, tennis, and skiing in the winter. In past years, Lebanon has hosted the Pan-Arab Games, as well as the Asian Cup football tournament.

Cultural Sites & Landmarks

As the heart of ancient Christianity and Islam, and the root of numerous cultures and civilizations, Lebanon is home to a wealth of cultural and historic sites. While many of these sites have been destroyed and compromised due to years of civil war and strife, many ancient landmarks still stand, including five World Heritage Sites. These are sites are recognized by the United Nations Educational, Scientific and Cultural Organization (UNESCO) for their cultural and scientific significance to humanity.

One of the most famous World Heritage Sites is the archeological site of Anjar. Located 58 kilometers (36 miles) from the capital of Beirut, the ruins from this site are solely from the Umayyad period (661–750 CE), the first Islamic dynasty. The city, both in a historic and modern sense, is unique in the fact that it is the only known example of a commercial center that is not located on the coast. Another key archeological site in Lebanon that was designated as a World Heritage Site is Baalbek, an ancient Phoenician city featuring an ancient temple and imperial Roman ruins. During the Hellenistic period (roughly 323–146 BCE), it was called Heliopolis, and three deities were worshipped there.

The Ouaid Qadisha (the Holy Valley) is renowned for being the location of early Christian monasteries. The monasteries are bordered by the Horsh Arz el-Rab (the Forest of the Cedars of God), which is composed of large Lebanese cedars. These trees are thought to have been used for building materials in historically important religious buildings. Both sites were inscribed as a World Heritage Site in 1998. Tyre, which was built on an island, is believed to have been the place where purple dye was invented. In addition, the city boasts impressive Roman ruins. The remaining World Heritage Site, the city of Byblos, was inscribed for its numerous ruins of successive civilizations. It is also recognized as one of the world's oldest continuously inhabited cities.

Beirut, Lebanon's most populous city, is a bustling urban area with many attractions. Pigeon Rocks are natural arches just off the shore of Beirut, and a popular recreational site for those who seek relief from urban life. The Place des Martyrs (Martyr's Square), located downtown, is a common meeting place for public demonstrations. The main statue symbolizes the loss of Lebanese lives during World War I at the hands of the Ottoman Empire. The city is also home to several mosques, including the impressive Muhammad al-Amin Mosque. Additionally, the remains of the Maghen Abraham synagogue provide evidence of a time when religious groups lived peacefully alongside one another.

Tripoli, a city about 85 kilometers (53 miles) north of Beirut, is the country's second largest city and the location of many ruins from the medieval and Mamluk period (1250–1517). Burj Es-Sabba (the Lion Tower) is a small fortress built under the reign of the Mamluk Sultan Qaitbay (1416–1496). The fortress is believed to have served the function of protecting the coast from the neighboring Ottomans. It is considered an excellent example of military architecture of the Mamluk era. The old city of Tripoli features several traditional markets including Khan Al-Khayyatin, constructed in the 14th century; Khan as-Saboun, a soap market built in the 16th century; and Souq al-Haraj, a market for pillows, mattresses, and mats.

Libraries & Museums

The National Museum of Beirut is one of the country's principal museums, and houses an extensive archaeological collection. The museum, established in the 1940s, is particularly known for its collection of Phoenician artifacts. Also in the capital, the American University of Beirut's Archaeological Museum displays many of the tools used by archeologists. Sursock Museum, a modern art museum, is also an important landmark due to its extensive collection and the building's architecture, a combination of traditional Lebanese architecture with Italian influences.

The national library of Lebanon, damaged in the country's civil war (1975–1991), was reconstructed as the 21st century unfolded. It houses a collection of some 250,000 books. As of 2009, the country was home to approximately seventy public libraries.

Holidays

Muslim holidays, including Ramadan, Muharram (Islamic New Year), Muloud/Yum an-Nabi (marking the birth of Muhammad), and Leilat al-Meiraj (marking the ascension of Muhammad), are widely celebrated in Lebanon.

Other holidays observed in Lebanon include the Feast of St. Maron (February 9), the Arab League Anniversary (March 22), and Independence Day (November 22).

Youth Culture

Lebanon has a large youth population with 21 percent of the population representing 14 year olds and younger as of 2013. Young people feel the effects of a diversity of influences, most notably civil war, reconstruction, and increasing globalization and migration. In fact, war, for many Lebanese youth, has become a feature of daily life and has influenced the increasing number of young emigrants, as they desire to live in a more stable environment. Additionally, high levels of unemployment encourage many educated Lebanese to leave the country in search of employment. Many youth are now also now forming the base of Hezbollah's resistance movement.

Hezbollah continues to develop an active relationship with Lebanese youth, as they build schools, offer weekly lectures, and organize such events as summer camps and holiday celebrations. The Mahdi Scouts, a group composed of young Lebanese men and women, serves as a training group for Hezbollah's guerilla army or bureaucracy. Those who do not go on to official positions nonetheless help to create a firm support base for the party. Young Lebanese women who are members of the Mahdi Scouts focus on cultivating an Islamic community in Lebanon. This includes the practice of Islamic principles, which includes such things as donning the hijab (traditional Islamic dress).

SOCIETY

Transportation

Lebanon is a small country, so traveling within it is quite easy. Beirut has the only international airport in the country (there are a total of eight as of 2013), and the city features an efficient bus system. The system functions on a "hail-and-ride" system, meaning that passengers simply wave down a bus to be picked up. In larger cities and urban areas, taxis are the popular mode of transportation, and cities such as Beirut have many taxis for transport inside of the city as well to destinations outside of the city. A bus network also connects Lebanese cities. Traffic moves on the right-hand side of the road.

Transportation Infrastructure

Lebanon does not have an efficient public transportation infrastructure, and rail transportation in the country has ceased due to the ongoing political instability. Railways have not been in use since the 1980s due to damage sustained from fighting within the country. In addition, some of the infrastructure, particularly roads, bridges, and airports, remains damaged from the 2006 Lebanon War. In 2010, public works and transport minister Ghazi Aridi described the road infrastructure as being "disastrous" and stated that improving roads in the country would be an expensive endeavor, but one necessary to facilitate economic development.

Media & Communications

The Lebanese constitution provides freedom of the press, and as a result, Lebanon is known to have one of the freest presses in the Middle East region. Lebanon was the first Arab country to allow privately owned radio and television stations. As of 2007, there were six privately owned television stations (plus one state owned). All of Lebanon's many newspapers and magazines are privately owned. State censorship is not common, as many media outlets openly criticize state officials and other political figures. Additionally, in 2008, an estimated 24 percent of the population had Internet access. This figure has increase to four million users (roughly 67 percent of the population) as of 2014.

Throughout the country's many political shifts, the media has played a central role. Politics and the media share a close relationship, and many media outlets support a particular political party or ideology. In 2005, what became known as the Cedar Revolution—and which was primarily against Syrian influence in Lebanon—developed from television broadcasts of anti-Syrian media outlets. Because of the media's central role in politics, however, journalists and publishers may often work in life-threatening conditions. For example, several media professionals lost their lives as a result of their promotion of the Cedar Revolution, while others perished due to the targeting of Lebanese transmission towers by Israeli forces during the 2006 Lebanon War. As a result, many media outlets have chosen to self-censor to protect themselves.

SOCIAL DEVELOPMENT

Standard of Living

Lebanon ranked 65rd out of 182 countries on the 2014 United Nations Human Development Index, which measures quality of life and standard of living indicators.

Water Consumption

Of the countries in the Middle East, Lebanon has the largest water reserves, yet shortages occur in the 20th century because of mismanagement and inadequate infrastructure. In 2009, the World Health Organization reported that 100 percent of the population had access to improved drinking water sources and that 98 percent had access to improved sanitation systems.

The problem is that no real improvement has been made on how to preserve water resources. Current uses of water in Lebanon have cause for reduced water quantity and quality throughout the country. The quality issues will not be resolved until the practice of disposing wastewater on land and into streams and rivers stops.

Education

Lebanon has no compulsory school requirement, but primary school is free. The country has the highest literacy rate in the Arab world, at 93.9 percent overall (96 percent among men and 91.7 percent among women) as of 2015.

Primary education begins at age six and lasts for five years, followed by seven years of secondary education. Approximately 113 percent of boys and girls in Lebanon are enrolled in primary education.

Almost all secondary and higher education is private. Higher education in Lebanon includes institutions such as the American University of Beirut, the Lebanese American University, the Universite Saint-Joseph, Beirut Arab University, and the State University (LU), which is the only state university. The American University of Beirut (AUB), established in 1866, is world-renowned for its high educational standards. While AUB is secular and offers instruction in

English, most universities in the country are religiously affiliated and teach in Lebanese.

In the 2006–2007 academic year, the Educational Center for Research and Development (CRDP) estimated that there were 160,000 students enrolled in higher education in Lebanon. Around half of those students were enrolled in the State University, where female students accounted for 67 percent of the student population. The remaining half of students was enrolled at private universities, where male student enrollment was slightly higher than that of female student enrollment.

Women's Rights

Lebanese women do have the ability to participate in all aspects of society; however, they still face discrimination and unequal treatment. Women are not sufficiently protected by the law against violence within their family unit, and domestic violence remains common. Under Lebanese law, women are also not able to pass on their nationality to either their spouse or children.

Additionally, men are allowed to divorce their wife at any given moment under Shia, Sunni and Druze laws. For a woman, it is much more difficult and time consuming. Due to social pressure and customs, it is rare to happen. Often times, a mother will not go through the process of separating from even an abusive spouse, because she does not want to lose primary care of her children.

Immigrant women workers, many coming from Sri Lanka, often are the targets of discrimination. These women, who usually take on jobs as domestic workers, are forced to work lengthy hours. Oftentimes, they do not receive payment for their work and have been frequent victims of sexual abuse by their employers. It is estimated that around 200 domestic workers committed suicide between 2003 and 2007. These deaths were not investigated, and in some cases, foul play was suspected.

In 2007, Lebanon's top Shia cleric, Sheikh Muhammad Hussein Fadlallah (1935–2010),

released a fatwa, or Islamic religious ruling, banning honor killings and female circumcision. Honor killings are the sanctioned murder of a family member or close kin who has brought shame or dishonor upon their family. The fatwa described honor killings as acts that are not in accordance with Islamic Law.

As of 2014, only 3.1 percent of seats in Lebanon's government have been held by a woman.

Health Care

Lebanon once had an excellent health care system. In fact, at one time, Beirut met the health needs of the entire Middle East. After years of war, however, the system was nearly destroyed. Records were rendered missing or incomplete, facilities and staffs became inadequate, and the Ministry of Health was in chaos.

Even after a concerted effort to improve health care, average life expectancy in Lebanon is 77.4 years, 76.18 years for men and 78.69 years for women (2015 estimate). Per capita health expenditure is roughly 7.2 percent of the GDP. There are approximately 3.2 doctors for every 1,000 people.

Most hospitals are private, and even in an emergency, a patient must provide proof of insurance or other ability to pay before receiving treatment. Virtually all doctors speak either English or French. The best hospitals are in Beirut, including the American University Hospital.

GOVERNMENT

Structure

In Lebanese, the Lebanese Republic is known as Al Jumhuriyah al Lubnaniyah. Lubnan, or Lebanon, is the short form. For administrative purposes, the country is organized into six mohafazat, or governorates.

The unicameral Majlis al-Nuwab, or National Assembly, has 128 members, each of whom is elected by popular vote. Members serve four-year terms unless the assembly is dissolved following a vote of no confidence. The assembly is required to have an equal number of Christians and Muslims.

The president is chief of state and must be a Christian Maronite. The National Assembly elects (by a two-thirds majority) the president to a six-year term. The Prime Minister may not serve for a consecutive term. The prime minister, (Tamam Salam since 2013), who is the head of government, is appointed by the assembly and must be a Sunni Muslim. The Speaker of the Assembly must be a Shiite Muslim.

The prime minister, in consultation with the members of the assembly and the president, appoints his or her ministers of the cabinet. The cabinet, which must have an equal number of Christian and Muslim members, has executive power.

In July 2006, Lebanon's capital Beirut was bombed extensively by Israel forces seeking to rout the militant Islamic group Hezbollah on the Israeli-Lebanese border. Forces of the Lebanese government were not involved in the affair, and the government was critical of the United States and other Western powers for not doing more to prevent Israel's destruction of Beirut's infrastructure. A cease-fire agreement was reached in order to end the conflict, but border relations remain tense.

Political Parties

A major political alliance known as the 14 March Coalition won more than sixty seats in the National Assembly elections of 2009. Parties belonging to this alliance include the Democratic Left, which is led, as of 2010, by Ilyas Atallah; the Democratic Renewal Movement, led, as of 2010, by Nassib Lahud; the Future Movement Bloc, led, as of 2010, by Saad al-Hariri; the Kataeb Party, led, as of 2010, by Amine Gemayel; and the Lebanese Forces, led, as of 2010, by Sami Ja'ja.

Another major political alliance is the 8 March Coalition, which comprises political parties such as the Free Patriotic Movement, led, as of 2010, by Michel Awn; Hezbollah, led, as of 2010, by Hassan Nasrallah; the Nasserite Popular Movement, led, as of 2010, by Usama Saad; and the Syrian Ba'th Party, led, as of 2010, by Sayez Shukr. The 8 March Coalition won 57 seats in the 2009 National Assembly elections.

Local Government

Lebanon comprises six governorates (or mohafazah): Beqaa, Beyrouth, Liban-Nord, Liban-Sud, Mont-Liban, and Nabatiye, as well as two legislated (but, as of 2010, unofficial) mohafazah: Baalbek-Hermel and Aakar. These mohafazah, each of which is overseen by a governor, are further subdivided into districts, which are administered by district chiefs. Districts are further subdivided into municipalities, which are governed by elected councils, mayors, and vice mayors, and then into villages, each of which is run by an elected chief and council.

The power and authority of local government in Lebanon has been significantly disrupted by war, from the Lebanese Civil War (1975–1990) to the 2006 Israel-Hezbollah War.

The first round of the 2014 elections was held on April 23rd. Samir Geagea had 48 votes, Henri Helou had 16 and Amine Gemayel had one vote. In order for a candidate to win, they need to have at least 86 of the possible 128 votes. The next round for elections will be held on August 12, 2015.

Judicial System

The highest court in Lebanon is the Supreme Court, also known the Court of Cassation. Each of the country's six districts has a Court of Appeal, each of which is headed by a chief judge. Other courts include Courts of First Instance, as well as a Constitutional Court, Ecclesiastical Courts, Sharia Courts, a Labor Court, and Juvenile Courts. Within this branch, there are subordinate courts. They are the Courts of Appeal, Courts of First Instance, specialized tribunals, religious courts, and military courts.

Taxation

Lebanon's tax rates are low; the highest personal income tax rate is 20 percent, while the corporate

rate is 15 percent. Other taxes levied include a real estate transfer tax, inheritance tax (with stipulations), and a value-added tax (VAT, a kind of consumption tax).

Armed Forces

The Lebanese Armed Forces consists of several service branches, including ground, air, and naval forces. Conscription was abolished in 2007, and the military age for service is between 18 and 30 years of age. Since 2006, the Lebanese Armed Forces, which is relatively poorly equipped, have received $720 million in aid from the United States. The United Nations Interim Force in Lebanon, originally deployed in response to Israeli-Lebanese conflict in the 1970s, still maintains a force of 15,000 personnel as of 2010, including over 11,000 uniformed personnel. The military consists of Lebanese Armed Forces, Lebanese Army, Lebanese Navy, and the Lebanese Air Force.

Foreign Policy

Lebanon's foreign relations are complex and in a constant state of flux as shifts in power frequently occur. The country is divided along sectarian lines, with constant conflicts between Sunni groups, which are anti-Syrian and Shiite groups. The most prominent of the latter is the paramilitary organization known as Hezbollah. These divisions have diminished somewhat following the 2006 Lebanon War with Israel, which saw an increase in support for Hezbollah from Sunni, Druze, and Christian Lebanese.

Shiite Muslim clerics, with support from Iran and Syria, founded Hezbollah in 1982. It began primarily as a resistance movement against the Israeli invasion of Lebanon. Today, the party is still against the existence of Israel and calls for Israeli lands to be returned to the Palestinians. The party also provides social services in the form of schools, hospitals, and agricultural support to the Lebanese. Although the party is recognized as a legitimate resistance movement by most nations in the Middle East, Western countries such as the United States and Canada consider Hezbollah a terrorist organization. The United Kingdom (UK) only considers Hezbollah's military branch a terrorist organization, and Australia only considers the Hezbollah External Security Organization a terrorist organization.

Additionally, because of Lebanon's volatile political situation, many countries seek to wield influence over the nation. Both Iran and Syria are supporters of Hezbollah, and Iran is believed to provide the organization with arms and money. Syria maintains a significant influence over Lebanon's foreign relations after the two countries signed an agreement of cooperation in 1991.

Lebanon's relations with Israel are in a constant state of strain and have led to countless attacks on both sides. Israeli troops maintained a presence in Lebanon from 1982 through 2000. The tense relations between Lebanon and Israel culminated with the 2006 Lebanon War that lasted from July 12, 2006, through September 8, 2006. It is estimated that around 1,000 Lebanese civilians were killed in the conflict; approximately 120 Israeli civilians were also killed.

The influx of Palestinian refuges into Lebanon due to the rise of the state of Israel has also caused problems at times between the Lebanese and Palestinians. Close to 400,000 Palestinian refuges now call Lebanon home, and many live in refugee camps in dire conditions. Palestinians are also prevented from taking particular professions, so as not to disrupt the Lebanese job market. Refugees also are prevented from owning property and are denied access to state health care. The American backing of Israel has also strained Lebanon's relations with the U.S. However, the U.S. actively supports Lebanon with international aid. This support goes to humanitarian efforts and to foster security in southern Lebanon.

Human Rights Profile

International human rights law insists that states respect civil and political rights, and promote an individual's economic, social, and cultural rights. The United Nations Universal Declaration on Human Rights (UDHR) is recognized as the standard for international human rights. Its authors sought the counsel of the world's great thinkers, philosophers, and religious leaders, and were careful to create a document that reflects the core values shared by every world culture. To read this document or view the articles relating to cultural human rights, visit http://www.udhr.org/UDHR/default.htm.

Although human rights organizations enjoy the ability to operate free of constraint in Lebanon, the volatile political situation impedes the work of many activists. The years of civil war, frequent Israeli attacks and the Palestinian and Iraqi refugee crisis have prevented many Lebanese residents from having full access to their human rights.

Human rights remain a particular area of concern in Lebanon's handling of Palestinian refugees. For example, the 2007 Nahr al-Bared Battle between the Lebanese government and the Fatah al-Islam, which took place in a Palestinian refugee camp, led to the deaths of 166 Lebanese soldiers, 220 Fatah al-Islam militants and 40 civilians. Many of the civilians were Palestinian. This battle also led to 30,000 refugees leaving the demolished camp and increased tensions between the Lebanese and Palestinian refugees. In violation with Article 2 of the Universal Declaration of Human Rights (UDHR), the Lebanese army reportedly detained and abused refugees as they left the camp. Two refugees were also killed as they attempted to return to the camp. Those traveling on Palestinian papers also face harassment as various checkpoints. Palestinians also continue to be denied access to social services and employment opportunities.

Additionally, Lebanon is also home to approximately 50,000 Iraqi refugees, who have been recognized by the UN High Commissioner for Refugees (UNHCR) as legitimate refugees seeking asylum. Despite this, the refugees are largely treated as illegal immigrants by the Lebanese government, actions which are in violation of Article 2 of the UDHR.

The effects of the 2006 Lebanon War are still felt. It is estimated that one million cluster mines still cover the landscape of southern Lebanon. Since 2006, 34 deaths and 216 injuries have been attributed to these munitions. Exacerbating the situation is the fact that Israel refuses to provide information about the locations of the mines, which makes the process of removal lengthy and difficult. Thousands of homes and other buildings were also demolished in the Israeli attacks leading to the displacement of many civilians.

Politicians also continue to face persecution. Pro-government parliament members Walid Eido and Antoine Ghanem were killed in 2007 in separate explosions. The sectarian divide between Sunni and Shiite Muslims continues to create an instable environment. This environment prevents individuals from exercising their rights as outlined in Articles 2, 16, 18, and 19.

Although Lebanese law prevents torture, enforcing this law and holding those who violate it accountable for their transgressions has proven difficult. Punishments for those who do engage in acts of torture are also often minimal. Moreover, Lebanese prisons are extremely overcrowded. Five captives died in 2007 while in custody, and the exact cause of death is still unknown. According to the Lebanese government, an estimated 17,415 Palestinians and Lebanese remain missing due to the 1975–1990 civil war. As of 2007, little information was available regarding these individuals. Around 640 of the "disappeared" are believed to be held captive in Syrian prisons.

Migration

In 2009, it was estimated that Lebanon was home to over 400,000 Palestinian refugees. These refugees face many restrictions; for instance, they are not allowed to purchase land and are barred from practicing over 70 professions. The largest Palestinian refugee camp is Ein el-Hilweh, which is located in the southern region of the country, near the city of Sidon. In 2008, it was estimated that 50,000 Iraqi refugees, escaping war in their home country, were living in Lebanon. The overall net migration rate is -1.1 per 1000 people in 2015.

ECONOMY

Overview of the Economy

Before the civil war of 1975–1990, Lebanon acted as an entrepot (a port for receiving and reshipping cargo without paying duties) and banking hub for the Middle East. This position, along with the country's infrastructure, was seriously damaged by the war. In recent years, Lebanon has borrowed heavily in order to rebuild.

In 2014, Lebanon's gross domestic product (GDP) was estimated at nearly $81.12 billion (USD). The per capita GDP for the same period was approximately $18,000 (USD).

Like most coastal cities, Beirut has long been considered an important center for trade and business; Beirut's port is the largest in the Eastern Mediterranean. Most of Beirut's economy is based in the financial and service sectors

Industry

Industries, including manufacturing, metal fabricating, banking, oil refining, food processing, jewelry, wood and furniture products, and mineral and chemical products, account for nearly 19 percent of Lebanon's national GDP. Exports of jewelry and jewels, foodstuffs, construction minerals, machinery and mechanical appliances, textile fibers, and electric power machinery earn roughly $889 million (USD) annually.

Labor

Lebanon has a 9.2 percent unemployment rate (2007 estimate), and 28 percent of its people live below the poverty line. The labor force was recently estimated at 1.48 million (not including an estimated 1 million foreign workers as of 2007).

Energy/Power/Natural Resources

The Lebanon Mountains yield limestone and iron ore. Lebanon's other chief resources include salt, arable land and water.

Environmental concerns include erosion, desertification, and deforestation throughout the country. In addition, Beirut experiences air pollution caused by traffic and industrial waste burning. Coastal waters are polluted by raw sewage and oil spills.

Fishing

As Lebanon has a 220 kilometer-long (136 miles-long) coastline, fishing is a significant industry. According to the United Nations Food and Agriculture Organization (FAO), Lebanon's fishing industry employs an estimated 6,500 people; however, overfishing and pollution are significant threats to the industry in the early 21st century.

Forestry

Common tree species in Lebanon include maple, cedar, fir, juniper, oak, and pine. Logging generally meets domestic demand; however, paper products are an important export item, as is wood pulp.

Mining/Metals

Commonly mined materials in Lebanon include gypsum, lime, phosphate, salt, and sulfuric acid. The country also produces cement, as well as mineral commodities such as granite, marble, and sand.

Agriculture

About 17 percent of Lebanon's land is arable, and with irrigation, agriculture accounts for 10 percent of the GDP. Important agricultural products include vegetables, citrus fruit, grapes, olives, tobacco, and sheep and goats.

Lower slopes are often covered with vineyards, and extensive olive orchards flourish at higher elevations. Numerous varieties of fruit trees are grown, including pomegranate, citrus, quince, almond, and banana. Mulberry trees are cultivated primarily for the silkworm industry.

Animal Husbandry

Sheep, goats, cattle, poultry, and swine are commonly raised livestock in Lebanon. According to the United Nations FAO, there were just under half a million goats in the country around the turn of the 21st century. The most common breed of goat is Baladi, a mountainous species. Livestock products include cows' milk, pork, eggs, beef, and veal.

Tourism

Lebanon has worked hard to improve its tourist industry, with new infrastructure, shopping complexes, hotels and restaurants, roads, and telecommunications services. The effort is paying off, with more than 741,000 tourists generating more than $700 million (USD) in revenue each year. In 2010, Lebanon's economy and trade minister announced that $4 billion (USD) has been earmarked to improve the country's infrastructure, including transportation and communication infrastructure, which could, ostensibly, make the country a more attractive tourist destination. Tourism grew in 2009, with an estimated 1.8 million tourists visiting the country, contributing between $4 and $5 billion (USD) to the economy.

Multitudes of archaeological and historic sites make Lebanon a popular tourist destination.

For example, Baalbek is the first Phoenician city dedicated to the worship of Baal. The city, which was known as Heliopolis to the Romans, was named a World Heritage Site by the United Nations Educational, Scientific, and Cultural Organization (UNESCO) in 1984. Another popular tourist destination is Byblos (Jbeil), one of the oldest continuously inhabited cities in the world. Its archaeological excavations and medieval Arab and Crusader artifacts attract many visitors.

Recently, eco-tourism has become popular in Lebanon. Tourists are attracted to the magnificent natural scenery of such sites as the Horsh Ehden Nature Reserve, the Shouf Cedar Forest, the Jeita Grotto, and other protected areas. In addition, Lebanon's many vineyards and associated wineries draw tourists to the country. Some of the most famous wineries include the wine caves of Ksara and Chateau Musar.

Kianoosh Hashemzadeh,
Ellen Bailey, Alex K. Rich

DO YOU KNOW?

- When the long civil war ended in 1990, archeologists in Beirut began searching for archeological artifacts, which had to that point only been found accidentally. They hoped to find evidence of the several empires that had ruled Beirut in the past before the city's extensive reconstruction. By 1993, a partnership between archeologists and builders had uncovered evidence of Beirut's Ottoman, Mameluke, Crusader, Abbasid, Omayyad, Byzantine, Roman, Persian, Phoenician, and Canaanite incarnations. During the reconstruction, which covered 1.8 million square meters (445 acres), 250 buildings in the city center were rebuilt, and many new buildings were constructed.

Bibliography

Augustus R. Norton. *Hezbollah: A Short History*. Princeton Studies in Muslim Politics. Princeton: Princeton University Press, 2007.

David Hirst. *Beware of Small States: Lebanon, Battleground of the Middle East*. New York: Nation Books, 2011.

Elizabeth Devine and Nancy L. Braganti. *The Traveler's Guide to Middle Eastern and North African Customs and Manners*. New York: St. Martin's Press, 1991.

Fawwaz Traboulsi. *A History of Modern Lebanon*. London: Pluto Press, 2012.

Lina Khatib. *Lebanese Cinema: Imagining the Civil War and Beyond*. Tauris World Cinema Series. London; New York: I.B. Tauris, 2008.

Nubar Hovsepian. *The War on Lebanon: A Reader*. Northampton, MA: Olive Branch Press, 2008.

Salma Hage. *The Lebanese Kitchen*. London: Phaidon, 2012.

Sandra Mackey. *Lebanon: A House Divided*. London: W. W. Norton, 2006.

Works Cited

Fareed Abou-Haidar. "Traditional Lebanese Architechture-Part 1: Destruction." 1997. http://almashriq.hiof.no/lebanon/300/360/363/363.7/fareed/lebenv33.html.

"Al-Juthoor." *About Debkah.* http://www.al-juthoor.com/about.htm.

"Authentic Lebanese Recipes." http://www.habeeb.com/Vegetarian-and-Lebanese-recipes.03.html.

"Baalbeck International Festival." http://www.baalbeck.org.lb/news.asp?lng=en.

Martin Asser. "Refugee Crisis Threatens Lebanon." *BBC News.* http://news.bbc.co.uk/2/hi/middle_east/6896932.stm.

Mohamad Bazzi. "Lebanon's Bloody Summer." *The Nation.* 2007. http://www.thenation.com/doc/20070716/bazzi.

"Beirut." http://www.lonelyplanet.com/worldguide/lebanon/beirut/sights/1000716811.

"Biggest Cities in Lebanon". http://www.geonames.org/LB/largest-cities-in-lebanon.html.

Mounira Chaieb. "Young in the Arab World: Lebanon." *BBC News.* (2005). http://news.bbc.co.uk/2/hi/middle_east/4212973.stm.

"Customs of Lebanon." http://encarta.msn.com/sidebar_631522222/customs_of_lebanon.html.

Elizabeth Devine and Nancy L. Braganti. "The Traveler's Guide to Middle Eastern and North African Customs and Manners." New York: *St. Martin's Press.* 1991.

"Fairuz: A Legend." *Fairuz Online.* http://fairuzonline.com/alegend.htm.

"Foreign Relations of Lebanon." http://en.wikipedia.org/wiki/Foreign_relations_of_Lebanon.

Ayman Ghazi. "Lebanon's Culture." http://www.ghazi.de/society.html#family.

"Khalil Gibran." *Encyclopædia Britannica Online.* http://www.search.eb.com/eb/article-9036756.

"Hezbollah." *Wikipedia.* http://en.wikipedia.org/wiki/Hezbollah.

"Hezbollah (A.K.A Hizbollah, Hizbu'llah)." *Council on Foreign Relations.* http://www.cfr.org/publication/9155/hezbollah_aka_hizbollah_hizbullah.html?breadcrumb=%2Fregion%2Fpublication_list%3Fgroupby%3D2%26id%3D409%26filter%3D17.

Nubar Hovsepian. "The War on Lebanon: A Reader." Northampton, Mass.: *Olive Branch Press,* 2008.

"Lebanon." *Encyclopaedia Britannica.* http://www.search.eb.com/eb/article-23417.

"Lebanon." *World Heritage.* http://whc.unesco.org/en/statesparties/lb.

"Lebanon: Food and Drink." http://www.arab.net/lebanon/ln_food.htm.

Elise Salem Manganaro. "Bearing Witness: Recent Literature from Lebanon." *Literary Review.* Spring (1994). November 29, 2008 http://findarticles.com/p/articles/mi_m2078/is_n3_v37/ai_15373204/pg_1?tag=artBody;col1.

Joumana Medlej. "Talking with the Hands". http://www.cedarseed.com/water/handtalk.html.

"Music of Lebanon." *Wikipedia.* http://en.wikipedia.org/wiki/Music_of_Lebanon.

"Overview of Human Rights Issues in Lebanon." http://www.hrw.org/legacy/englishwr2k8/docs/2008/01/31/lebano17610.htm.

"Places in Lebanon." http://almashriq.hiof.no/lebanon/900/910/919/anjar/.

"The World Factbook: Lebanon." *Central Intelligence Agency.* https://www.cia.gov/library/publications/the-world-factbook/geos/le.html.

"Travelling to Beirut and Travelling around Beirut." *Beirut.* http://www.lonelyplanet.com/worldguide/lebanon/beirut/getting-there-and-around?a=ga.

"Tyre." *Encyclopeadia Britannica Online.* http://www.search.eb.com/eb/article-9074016.

"Under the Ummayads (661-750)". http://www.bu.edu/mzank/Jerusalem/p/period4-2.htm.

"Who Are Hezbollah." *BBC News.* (2008). http://news.bbc.co.uk/2/hi/middle_east/4314423.stm.

Kaelen Wilson-Goldie. "The Art of War." *The National.* (2008). http://www.thenational.ae/article/20081103/ART/112711944/1222.

Diana Baker Woodall. "Kunafa." http://www.dianasdesserts.com/index.cfm/fuseaction/recipes.recipeListing/filter/dianas/recipeID/3346/Recipe.cfm.

Charlene Wu. "Lebanon." *Cultural Gestures.* http://soc302.tripod.com/soc_302rocks/id6.html.

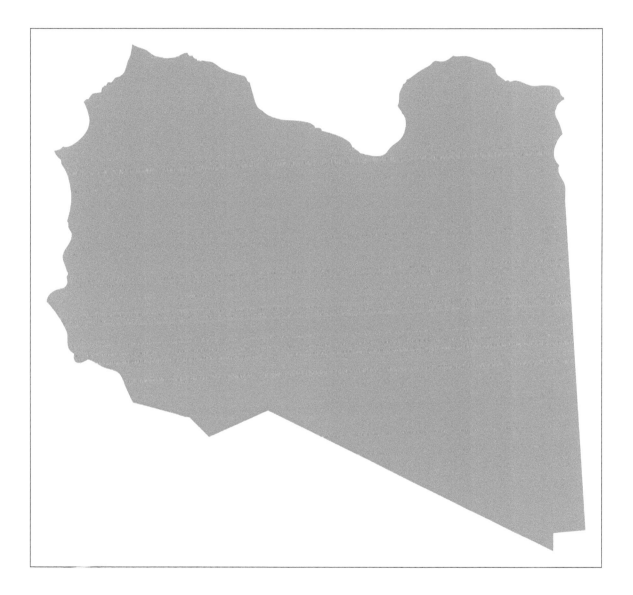

LIBYA

Introduction

Libya is a country in northern Africa. Like Egypt, Morocco, Tunisia, and Algeria, it is an African country that is considered a part of the Arab world. Located on the Mediterranean Sea between Egypt and Tunisia, Libya was long recognized on the international stage by the face of its controversial leader, Colonel Muammar al-Gaddafi, who ruled from 1969 to 2011. Libya was formerly known as the Great Socialist People's Libyan Arab Jamahiriya, reflecting the combination of Western political and economic theory and Islamic law that Libya's government espoused before the advent of the region-wide Arab Spring in 2011–12.

After months of fighting between the government and opposition forces, the Gaddafi regime was ousted in 2011. It was then replaced by a transitional government, and in 2012, formed a new parliament. A new prime minister was elected, as well.

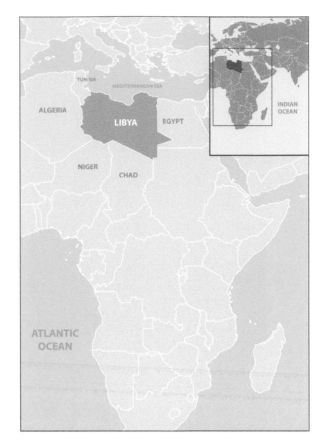

GENERAL INFORMATION

Official Language: Arabic
Population: 6,411,776 (2013 estimate)
Currency: Libyan dinar
Coins: One Libyan dinar is equal to 1,000 dirhams. Coins are available in denominations of 50 and 100 dirhams and one-quarter and one-half dinar. Although still legal tender, 1, 5, 10, and 20-dirham coins, issued in 1975, are rarely used.
Land Area: 1,759,541 square kilometers (679,359 square miles)
National Anthem: "Allahu Akbar" ("God is Greatest")

Capital: Tripoli
Time Zone: GMT +2
Flag Description: The flag of Ethiopia is one of the more plainly designed in the world, as it depicts only a color field of green, with no adornments, decoration or lettering. This plain green flag was adopted by Libya in 1977. Green is the national color of the country.

Population

Approximately 90 percent of Libya is desert and only 10 percent of the country's population lives outside the more habitable lands along its border with the Mediterranean Sea. In 2012, Libya's capital, Tripoli, had an estimated population of 1,000,000 or about 15 percent of the total population.

The birth rate is 18.03 births per 1,000 members of the population (2015), giving Libya a fairly young population (more than one-third of Libyans are under the age of fifteen). The median age in the country is approximately twenty-two

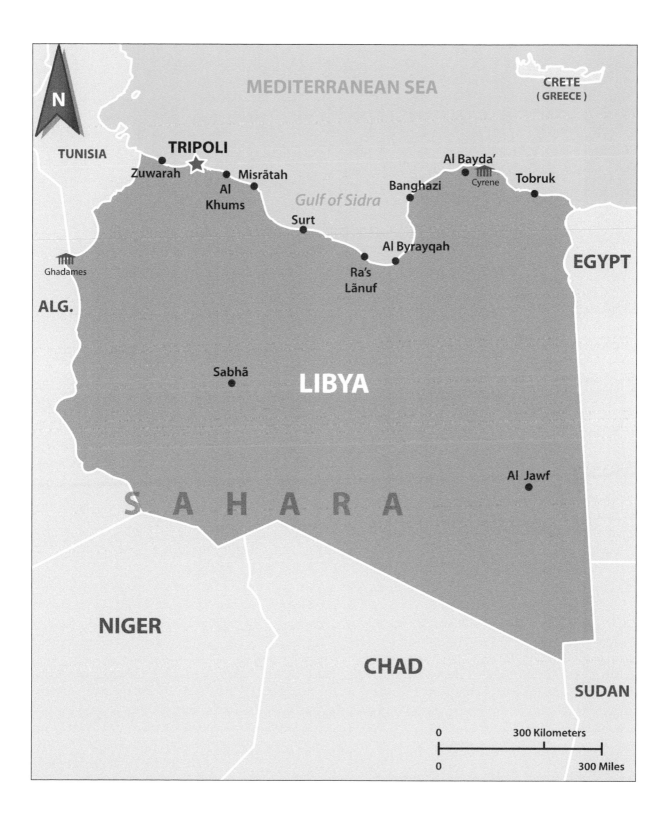

Principal Cities by Population (2012):

- Tripoli (1 million)
- Benghazi (632,937)
- Misurata (285,759)
- Tobruk (138,535)
- Zawiyah (87,316)
- Sirte (78,215)
- Al-Khoms (230,000)
- Al-Bayda' (206,180)
- Gharyan (170,000)
- Darnah (50,000)

years old. In 2015, Libya's population growth rate was estimated at 2.23 percent.

Languages

The official language of Libya is Arabic. Approximately 10 percent of the country speaks one of the related indigenous languages known as the Berber languages. The native Libyan term for a Berber language is Tamazight. English is also widely spoken. Italian may be commonly used in commerce and in urban areas.

Native People & Ethnic Groups

About 97 percent of the country's population is of Arab-Berber descent. The Berbers are a traditional nomadic people indigenous to North Africa, who have become assimilated into Arab culture. Berber tribal settlements date back to 2000 BCE on the Libyan coast and southern deserts. These tribes created trade routes across the African interior, developing complex family ties and a particular style of nomadic living, utilizing tents and camels that permitted them to spend months in otherwise uninhabitable areas between desert oases. While many descendants of Berber tribes have now settled in the towns and cities of Libya, others still earn their living with camels and trade in Libya's southern desert just as their ancestors did.

A small percentage of Libya's population is composed of members of traditional tribal groups such as the Bedouin and the Tebou (or Toubou), whose ancestors migrated from the Yemen area.

In addition, there is a small population of Tuareg, a group who were once nomads from the Sahara. Immigrants from Northern, Western, and sub-Saharan Africa also live in Libya. Urban areas include a cosmopolitan assortment of Greeks, Maltese, Italians, Egyptians, Pakistanis, Turks, Indians, Tunisians, and others.

Libya's capital, Tripoli, is home to a sizable number of expatriate workers, often from other Arab nations. Most Libyans consider the country's majority Arab population to be "native," although Arab tribes did not arrive in the region until the sixth or seventh century.

Religions

96.6 percent of Libya's population is Sunni Muslim. Islam is essentially the state religion and the practice of other faiths is restricted by the government. The government operates in a manner that adheres strictly to the faith. Approximately 5 to 10 percent of Libyans practice Ibadism, another denomination of Islam. The Vatican has sought to improve diplomatic relations with the Libyan government in order to protect the country's Christians (2.7 percent), which include Coptic Orthodox Christians, Roman Catholics, and Anglican. Along with these faiths, there are also small groups of Buddhists, Hindus and Jews.

Climate

Libya's climate is more than 90 percent desert or semi-desert. Along the coast, rainfall averages 380 millimeters (15 inches) annually; in the desert interior, rainfall levels drop to below 100 millimeters (less than four inches) annually. Rain is not consistent throughout the year, falling mainly in the winter.

Temperatures are universally warm across Libya, but the Mediterranean tends to lower temperatures near the coast, while a large desert to the south has the opposite effect. In Tripoli, on the northwest coast near Tunisia, temperatures average 30° Celsius (86° Fahrenheit) in summer and 8° Celsius (46° Fahrenheit) in winter.

In May, June, and October, Libya is prone to ghibli, sandstorms that sweep up from the southern desert for days at a time. Except during these storms, the coastal region remains fairly humid because of the winds from the Mediterranean. The same conditions have created a verdant area in the Green Mountains (Jebel Akhdar) in the coastal northeastern part of the country.

ENVIRONMENT & GEOGRAPHY

Topography

Libya has three geographic regions. Tripolitania and Cyrenaica sit on the northwestern and northeastern coastlines, respectively, separated by the Gulf of Sidra. Both areas are flat lowlands along the Mediterranean, and low plains moving inland.

Tripolitania, and to a lesser extent Cyrenaica, is dotted with fertile oases and lagoons. Moving south from the coast, Tripolitania rises into the Nafusah plateau, where elevations reach about 1,000 meters (3,280 feet). Cyrenaica contains the smaller Marj Plain and the Jabal Akhdar (Green Mountain), which rises to about 900 meters (2,950 feet).

The Fezzan, in the southern portion of the country, is part of the Sahara, a nearly barren desert with undulating sand dunes and rocky escarpments.

The capital, Tripoli, is located in the northwestern region of Libya known as Tripolitania. The city, which is set on the coastline of the Mediterranean Sea, possesses a naturally deep harbor. Tripoli's landscape is flat and covered with coarse grass, sand flats, and marshes.

Plants & Animals

With more than 90 percent of its land covered by desert or semi-desert, Libya is home to plants and animals that have adapted to the hot, dry conditions. Gazelles, wildcats, lizards, snakes, scorpion, and fennecs (small foxes) thinly populate the landscape. Libya's hardy plant species include acacia in the deserts; date palms, fig palms, and oleander in the desert oases; cypress, juniper, pine, and wild olive on the Jabal Akhdar;

and Mediterranean plants like olive trees and citrus trees along the coast.

The use of water from underground aquifers and the natural movements of the southern deserts have raised fears of desertification in Libya. Ecologists are looking closely at the region for signs that the few fertile areas in Libya are endangered by climate shifts and water depletion.

CUSTOMS & COURTESIES

Greetings

The customary greeting between two Libyan men is a handshake. Men who are close friends often greet each other with an embrace or a long, firm handshake. Men and women do not embrace in public and many Libyan women will not shake hands. A Libyan will casually place his or her hand across the chest if he or she does not want to shake hands. Kissing as a form of greeting is not as common in Libya as it is in Western cultures. Greeting a person of the opposite sex with a kiss is generally frowned upon. Women generally greet each other with a verbal greeting and in some instances it is accompanied by a light kiss on the cheek or a hug.

Common verbal greetings in Libya include "Salaamu aleikum" ("Peace be upon you"), which usually elicits the response "Wa'aleikum as-salamma" ("And peace be upon you as well"). Another casual verbal greeting is "Kayf halak?" ("How are you?"), with a common response being "Al-hamdu lilah, bahi" ("Praise to God, very well").

Gestures & Etiquette

Libyans are generally indirect communicators, especially when interacting with those with whom they are not very familiar. The concept of face, most common in Far Eastern cultures, also plays a significant role in Libyan society. Face is a combination of honor, public reputation, and dignity that is attributed to a person. In addition, Libyans value courtesy, and they very rarely display forms of public criticism. Consequently, many Libyans may not always communicate their true thoughts or feelings until a trusting relationship has been established. Most Libyans value their privacy, especially in matters relating to female family members. It is considered rude for a male non-family member to inquire about or show an interest in a female member of a household. Open criticism of Islam, the Libyan government, and politics is generally avoided.

When in conversation, Libyans customarily avoid placing their hands in clothing pockets, as this is usually seen as a lack of respect. There is also a certain amount of touching between members of the same gender during conversations. (This excludes personal contact between men and women in public places, except if they are related, which even then is usually kept to a minimum.) Libyans tend to feel comfortable standing a little less than an arm's length apart from one another, though this space is greater between men and women. To emphasize a point in a conversation, it is common for Libyans to touch the thumb with the tips of the fingers. In almost all business and social settings, it is common behavior to stand when new guests arrive at a social gathering or when a high-ranking person enters or leaves. In addition, men usually stand when a woman enters the room.

Most Libyans dress conservatively in accordance with the tenets of Sharia (Islamic law). Styles of clothing usually are dependent on generational lines, with younger Libyans and business professionals adopting more Western styles, and older Libyans keeping to traditional clothing. The custom of Purdah (secluding and veiling women) is still common, though not as prevalent as it once was. In addition, many women wear traditional gowns that cover both the head and body.

Eating/Meals

Meals are important social events and occasions for Libyan families to share quality time, and most Libyans eat their meals at home. The habits and customs of eating at home can be quite different from dining in a public establishment. Traditionally, men and women ate separately. That has changed somewhat in modern Libya,

unless guests are present. In devout households, it is customary for diners to dip their fingers into a bowl of perfumed water for ritual cleansing. In addition, a short prayer may be given. A common saying is "bismillah," which is a request for Allah to bless the meal.

Libyans typically eat on a clean tablecloth placed on a carpet on the floor or on a low table that allows diners to sit cross-legged close to the food. Large trays or platters of food are placed in the center of the eating surface for communal dining. Customarily, diners take food from the communal platters and eat with their hands. Food is always passed and eaten with the right hand, as the left hand is associated with the cleansing of the body, and considered unclean.

Ramadan is the ninth month on the Islamic calendar, during which Muslims abstain from food, drink, and other sensual pleasures from dawn to sunset. Most Muslims view Ramadan as a time of spiritual reflection and renewal. Fasting during Ramadan begins about ten minutes before the Fajr prayer at sunrise and is broken after the Maghrib prayer at sunset. Traditionally, Libyans break the daily fast by eating three dates and drinking water or milk. A traditional Libyan Ramadan meal is a soup made with meat in a tomato-based broth, with chickpeas, parsley, orzo, and mint. Umbatan is another customary Ramadan food. This contains potato slices stuffed with minced meat and spices which are then deep-fried. Libyans also eat stuffed green peppers, stuffed Swiss chard pizza, pastries, and various pasta dishes during Ramadan.

Visiting

It is common for Libyans to remove their footwear while they are at home. Guests should also remove footwear as a sign of respect. In addition, showing the soles of one's feet is considered impolite and a sign of disrespect. It is also customary for first-time guests to a Libyan home to bring a small gift. Gifts from a guest's home country are usually very well received by Libyan hosts. Libyans are generally very hospitable and generous. It is not uncommon for a Libyan host to offer a household item to a guest if the guest has complimented or commented on it. In addition, it is considered rude to refuse this offer.

Guests invited for a meal at the home of a Libyan host will usually receive the choicest pieces of food, and it is considered polite to accept and eat as much as possible. Once dinner is over, it is customary for a guest to offer to leave. If drinking tea at the home of a Tuareg family, guests are offered the first three rounds of tea. Refusing the offerings is generally considered impolite.

LIFESTYLE

Family

The family has always played a central role in Libyan society. Loyalty to family, clan, and tribe is more important than loyalty to a profession or class. Although tribal and clan allegiances within many other predominately Arab countries have weakened over time, these binds remain strong in Libya. They have also been supported by the Gaddafi regime.

The traditional Libyan household consists of a man, his wife, his single and married sons with their wives and children, his unmarried daughters, and sometimes other relatives. Families are patriarchal, and households are based on blood ties between men. Fathers are the heads of households, with wives and female children handling domestic responsibilities and child rearing. Many women, however, are now taking advantage of the educational opportunities provided by the government and are exploring jobs and careers outside of the home.

Because Libyans place such a high value on the family unit, children are well looked after. Parents generally pamper their children and both parents and close relatives are generous with gifts. Although there has been an increase in the number of daycare centers and the employment of nannies, the majority of Libyan parents prefer to take care of their children.

Women enjoy higher status in the family structures of the Tuareg and Toubou nomadic peoples of Libya. In Tuareg society, inheritance is matriarchal (through the female line), and as a general rule only women can read and write. The traditional Toubou family is made up of parents, children, and often close relatives. Husbands and fathers are the heads of households, but usually consult their wives when making decisions. For the few Toubou families that still follow the traditional nomadic life style, camp membership is always changing. Camp sizes almost never remain the same from one season to the next.

Housing

Libya underwent massive urbanization in the second half of the twentieth century. For example, urban population in the 1950s was roughly 25 percent of the population. In the early years of the 21st century, the figure is between 80 and 90 percent. This urban migration, particularly along the coast, created a housing shortage with which Libya is still dealing. Public and private funding has been used to build modern apartment complexes in Libya's urban areas, with much of the housing government-subsidized.

Before urbanization, a traditional Libyan home would have been built around a central courtyard with living quarters surrounding it. Most dwellings did not have windows on the ground floor. A reception room set apart from the living quarters served as a public space, where the head of the household would entertain friends and visitors. Contemporary Libyans are more likely to live in modern multistory apartments, complete with electricity, air conditioning, and integrated sewage systems. Wealthy Libyans often live in two-story villas with flat roofs that are used for a variety of purposes, such as a play area for children, an area for entertaining, or for hanging laundry.

Very few Tuareg families live the traditional nomadic lifestyle in the twenty-first century. The traditional Tuareg dwelling is a tent of red-dyed leather. Leather had been replaced in the 20th century with plastic or other lightweight materials. The Tuareg build and inhabit small grass huts for their semi-permanent shelters. Like most other Libyans, the Tuareg have moved or have been forced to move to urban centers.

Food

Traditional Libyan cuisine reflects Mediterranean, Turkish, and Arab flavors from the cultures that have influenced the region over centuries. More recently, the influence of the Italian occupation in the twentieth century on Libyan cuisine can be seen in the popularity of pasta dishes, particularly macaroni. Rice is an important element in many dishes, especially in eastern Libya. Couscous is popular throughout Libya, and in particular, the western regions of Tripolitania and Fezzan. Traditionally, couscous, which is steamed semolina or buckwheat, is usually served with a spicy stew made from onions, beans, chickpeas, potatoes, peppers, and meat, such as braised lamb. Couscous bil khadra is made with meats other than lamb, and couscous bil ghidded contains dried meat and green beans. Lamb, chicken, and beef are popular throughout Libya. However, pork, or haram, is forbidden by Islam.

Two traditional dishes served in many Libyan homes are bazin and matruda. Bazin is unleavened bread made from barley and flour that is cooked to a dough-like consistency. Eaten with a sauce, bazin is served from a communal tray and is often followed by a fish dish. Matruda is thick bread baked in an oven, which is then chopped into small pieces. Milk, dates, honey, and samel (homemade butter) are added while the matruda is still warm. Other popular home dishes include sharba (a soup made from either lamb, chicken, or seafood and flavored with spices, onions, vegetables, mint, and tomato paste), falafel (balls of mashed chickpeas mixed with spices that are deep-fried and often served on pita bread), and shatshouka (chopped lamb mixed with vegetables, tomato sauce, and eggs).

Coffeehouses are extremely popular throughout Libya and can be found in almost all communities, regardless of size. Arabic, or Turkish, coffee is served in small cups in which coffee grounds and water are mixed directly, producing a thick, strong brew. Libyan tea is also quite strong and is often flavored with mint, sugar, or peanuts. A staple among the Tuareg people is taajeelah. Often called sand or desert bread, taajeelah is made from flour, water, and salt and is cooked in the hot sand beneath an extinguished fire. The dough is cooked for fifteen minutes and then flipped over to cook another fifteen minutes.

Life's Milestones

For many Libyans, the first public celebration of the arrival of a baby is a feast, which also accompanies the circumcision of male babies. After the procedure, many Libyan parents have a party and guests present gifts. Among the Tuareg people, boys are circumcised between the ages of five and seven, as their initiation into manhood. In addition, Tuareg fathers present their sons a blue veil when they reach the age of fifteen or sixteen. This is usually done at an annual religious feast. Upon wearing the veil, the boy is considered a man.

Marriage is perhaps the most significant event in the lives of most Libyans. Traditionally, Libyans married within their extended families, and many marriages were arranged. Marriage is viewed not only as union between the bride and groom, but also between the two families. However, as Libyan society becomes more urbanized, and young people come into contact more often, the younger generations are choosing their partners more and more. Libyan custom demands that the groom provide his bride with a home and a significant dowry. Consequently, grooms tend to be older than their brides.

Libyan wedding celebrations once lasted an entire week. Today, most weddings are three days, lasting from Wednesday to Friday. Grooms present gifts to the brides on Wednesday, which is followed by a night of celebration with music and dancing. On Thursday, brides celebrate the wedding with her family and friends and then are taken to the groom's home. On Friday, grooms and brides celebrate separately.

Most Tuareg men marry late. The usual age for marriage is close to 30 for men and between 20 and 25 for women. Marriage is usually within clans. Similar to other Libyans, Tuareg grooms must pay a price for their bride and provide significant dowries. The price is dependent upon the beauty and social standing of the bride and the wealth of the husband. Those living the traditional lifestyle must accumulate a few camels and a flock large enough to feed the new family, as well as purchase the necessary household items. Tuareg wedding celebrations take place in the bride's camp, where the new couple will live with the bride's parents for a year before moving to the husband's camp.

CULTURAL HISTORY

Art

With a history of human settlement that spans thousands of years, Libya has a rich culture. This is due in large part to the wide range of traditional art forms developed by the ancient cultures from which Libya's people are descended. The indigenous Berbers of Ghadames (in western Libya), for example, are known for their leatherwork. These craftsmen followed the Moors to Spain, where they were called gadamaceleros (leather artists). They eventually helped develop Cordova leather, which spread throughout Europe and the Western world. Also of note are the unique shoes made by the Ghadames artisans. Known by many names, such as Telec, Tabla, Nalut, Arab, and sandals, each shoe style has distinctive color, shave and decoration. Today, Berber leather artisans also produce bags, suitcases, belts, and saddles.

Other Libyan traditional crafts include weaving, embroidery, and metal and silver engraving. Islam prohibits the depiction of people and animals, so these forms typically display bold geometric patterns, often referred to as arabesque. Many of these designs are common in older buildings found in mosques and medinas, the traditional Arab sections of North African cities. The Ahmed Pasha Karamanli Mosque and Gurgi Mosque in the medina of the capital of Tripoli, for example, have extensive examples of intricate wood and stucco carvings, as well as tiles that exemplify traditional Islamic designs.

Architecture

The ancient indigenous cultures of Libya built unique structures, some of which are still in use.

Berber and Saharan architecture was shaped by the harsh desert climate and the rugged geography of the region. The Berbers built fortified granaries called qasrs, in which they stored crops. The qasrs were built with local rock, sun-dried mud bricks, and gypsum. Underground rooms were used to store olive oil. The twelfth-century structures in Jebel and Nafusa are the best-preserved qasrs.

The Berbers are also noted for the underground homes they built to protect themselves from the cold winters and scorching summers, as well as from their enemies. The homes (dammous) consisted of a circular pit dug into the ground, often as deep as 30 feet. Rooms used as kitchens, living quarters, and storage areas were carved into the pit walls, with the open floor of the pit used as a courtyard. The Libyan towns of Gharyan, Yefren, and Zintan contain many examples of these homes.

Many of the mud-brick structures found in Saharan communities in Libya still serve as living quarters for the people of Ghadames and other desert towns during the summer months. The Saharan buildings found in the medina at Ghadames were built from gypsum and sun-dried mud bricks. Palm trunks were used to help support ceilings. The buildings are commonly three or four stories high and make maximum use of vertical space. Houses and buildings were often connected by walkways, creating narrow passageways.

The majority of Libya's mosques and madrassas (Islamic religious schools) were built during Ottoman rule (from the beginning of the sixteenth century to the early twentieth century). These structures were usually built in the Maghrebi (North African) style, incorporating intricate woodcarvings and mosaic tiles. The mosques are characterized by the Islamic style of architecture, and feature very thin minarets (towers) that are often octagonal in shape, highly decorated domes, and narrowly grouped pillars. Libya's desert regions contain the oldest examples of Islamic architecture. The Al-Kabir Mosque in Awjila, with its conical, pyramidal domes, and the mosques in Murzuq and Ghat are the best examples. Due to Italian occupation in the twentieth century, Libya also contains Italian modernist architecture that, coupled with certain aspects such as whitewashed façades (exteriors), has a native feel.

Drama

Beginning in 2005, theatrical works in Libya have become increasing political. Where works of visual art and television and newspapers are watched closely by the government, playwrights are often left alone to their work. It is considered taboo to blatantly criticize Gaddafi and his government in public, be it through political demonstration or politically-themed cultural works. Yet, Libyan playwrights such as Dawoud al-Houty have used theater to tell the story of Libya's poor and comment on social issues like health care. Nonetheless, there are generally very few plays staged in Libya.

Music

Although live commercial music performances in Libya are not that common, the country does have a rich musical tradition. Music has always played a central role in significant celebrations such as weddings and festivals. Traditional Libyan, or Arab music, differs from Western music in that it progresses in quartertones, rather than semitones. Traditional instruments include the woodwind-like gheeta, a drum called a tende, a flute called a nay, and a reed and goatskin bagpipe called a zukra. Contemporary orchestras or ensembles combine these traditional instruments with Western instruments, notably the violin and wind instruments.

One of the most unique musical forms in Libya is the mriskaawi. Mriskaawi developed in Murzuq in the south of the country, and become the basis for many Libyan songs. Mriskaawi is usually performed at wedding celebrations, usually on the Wednesday night before the ceremony. Mriskaawi music was originally played with traditional instruments. Today, however, mriskaawi is often performed on accordions.

Malouf is another style of music that is popular in Libya and North Africa. Brought to the region by Moors from Andalusia (a historically Muslim region of Spain) in the 15th century, malouf also has some elements of Berber music in the rhythms. Malouf is often played by groups of musicians using traditional instruments, and might also include singing and poetry. Malouf is commonly performed on the Thursday night of the traditional three-day Libyan wedding celebration.

Literature

The indigenous nomadic cultures of Libya have a long tradition of oral poetry and history. Centuries-old poems (as well as new ones) are still recited on important occasions, and the Libyan national radio regularly broadcasts several programs of poetry. In fact, the Jihad Oral History Centre in Tripoli, founded in 1978, was one of the first research facilities in the world to make oral history its primary research focus.

Written Libyan literature emerged during the Italian occupation in the twentieth century, with a modern tradition further developing in the years after World War II. The short story became a popular genre in the 1960s and 1970s, often called the "golden age" of Libyan literature. Following the 1969 revolution, the regime of Muammar al-Gaddafi (1942–), Libya's de facto leader, began using established writers as advocates of the revolution. Those who refused were imprisoned or exiled, or stopped writing. Censorship laws were loosened in the early 1990s, resulting in an increase in literary output. Contemporary literature contains a small amount of dissent, but books remain both censored and self-censored to a significant extent. Because of its strong local political flavor, only a portion of Libyan writings has been translated into English or other languages, although this is changing.

Novelist Ibrahim al-Koni (1948–) is perhaps Libya's most famous contemporary author. Al-Koni, who was raised in the nomadic and pastoral culture of the Tuareg people, grew up in the Saharan town of Ghadames, and much of his work evokes the Sahara desert. *The Bleeding of the Stone* (2002) and *Anubis: A Desert Novel*

(2005) are two of his most famous works. Al-Koni was awarded the 2008 Sheikh Zayed Book Award in Literature for his novel *A Call Not Too Far*, which explores the relationship between Arabs and Turkish and European invaders in the modern era. The Sheikh Zayed Book Award, established by the Abu Dhabi Authority for Culture & Heritage (in the United Arab Emirates), is given to writers who enrich Arab cultural, literary, and social life.

CULTURE

Arts & Entertainment

Soon after coming to power in 1969, the Gaddafi regime stifled free speech and artistic expression. The government has loosened its control on the arts, but Libya boasts few movie theaters or public art galleries. Public entertainment, until recently, has been almost nonexistent. Libya today is experiencing a revival of the arts, especially in the visual arts, with private galleries opening to provide a showcase for emerging artists. Aspiring artists who came of age prior to the lifting of UN sanctions often received government-funded grants to study art abroad. Now many are returning to their homeland to find inspiration for their work. In addition, new outlets for the arts, such as a collaboration between the Libyan Heritage Foundation and England's Prince's School of Traditional Arts, are helping young Libyans learn the principles of traditional Islamic art and design.

Libyan writers found their voices soon after Italy gained control in 1911. Under Italian colonial rule, half of the indigenous population was either exiled or exterminated before the end of World War II. Much of what the Libyan writers produced was censored. A large number of the most influential writers and poets lived in exile in Egypt and other countries in the Arab world and produced significant, politicized works. Literature again became a vehicle to discuss politics in the 1960s, when many in the country debated imperialism and the great social changes Libya was undergoing.

Decades of isolation kept most Libyan artists and patrons of the arts alienated from Western influences, allowing traditional Libyan folk arts to survive. Traditional folk culture thrives throughout the country, heavily influenced by traditional Berber and Tuareg folklore. The New Year Acacus Festival in Ghat is a significant cultural event in Libya. Traditional Tuareg music and dances are the highlights of the festival, which showcases singing and dancing, sword-fighting, and camel races. The annual three-day festival in Ghadames moves its venues between the ancient old city and the new. Many of the performances and ceremonies incorporate traditional Tuareg clothing. The festival is one of the best opportunities to view reenactments of traditional Tuareg dances.

In addition, Libya's visual arts are heavily influenced by Muslim prohibitions against depicting human and animal life. Instead, Muslim art uses intricate patterns, motifs, and calligraphy to express meaning and beauty, whether in jewelry or architecture. Alongside this tradition, painting in the coastal cities has become increasingly modern, with art galleries springing up in Tripoli and elsewhere to spotlight Libya's emerging artists.

Libya's most popular sport is European football (soccer), which is played by men and boys in rural villages, oases, and urban areas alike. Libyans also have a long history of horsemanship that emerges in horse races and in fantasias (demonstrations of Arab-style horsemanship skills). Libya's Muslim people do not tend to take a fundamentalist approach to the Qur'an, but conservative views have prevented the full participation of girls and women in many sporting activities.

Cultural Sites & Landmarks

Libya's capital and largest city, Tripoli, is home to many of the country's most significant landmarks and cultural sites. The medina (old town) lies within fortified walls that date to the fourth century CE. The only standing structure of the Roman occupation of Tripoli is the Arch of Marcus Aurelius within the medina. Built in

163–164 CE, the arch once stood at the crossroads of the two major Roman roads. Significant mosques within the medina include the Ahmed Pash Karamanli Mosque, which was completed in the 1730s. It is noted for its Ottoman octagonal minaret and nearly thirty domes that cover its large prayer hall.

Al-Saraya al-Hamra (Tripoli Castle) was the seat of power for Tripolitania until the 20th century. Built after the Arab invasion in 644 CE, the fortress stands atop the ruins of a Roman fortified camp that dates to the second century CE. Spaniards, Turks, Karamanlis, and Italian leaders through the centuries added to the castle, creating a citadel with alleyways, courtyards, and smaller house-like structures. Today, the Libyan Department of Antiquities occupies most of the castle's interior spaces. The castle also houses the Jamahiriya Museum, which was built in collaboration with the United Nations Educational, Scientific and Cultural Organization (UNESCO).

UNESCO has designated five locations in Libya as World Heritage Sites. Leptis Magna is located on the Mediterranean coast and is considered the most significant Roman site in Libya. Originally founded by Phoenicians in the seventh century BCE, Leptis Magna reached its height in the second century CE, during the reign of Roman emperor Septimius Severus (145–211 BCE). Preserved ruins include the town's amphitheater, old and new forums, the Hadrian baths, and the Severan Basilica (a basilica is a Roman public building).

Ghadames is located at the intersection of the Libyan, Tunisian, and Algerian borders. This oasis town is known as the "Pearl of the Desert," and its old town is a World Heritage Site. The old town represents one of the oldest pre-Saharan towns and is notable for its domestic architecture. Built from mud, lime, and palm tree trunks, the houses are characterized by a vertical division of functions. Ground floors were used for storage, then another floor for the family, and open-air rooftop terraces were used by women, who were generally kept out of public life. The houses were interconnected, creating overhanging covered alleys resembling an underground network of passageways.

Libya's three remaining World Heritage Sites include the rock-art sites of Tadrart Acacus. This mountainous desert region in southwestern Libya contains thousands of cave paintings in very different styles, dating from 12,000 BCE to 100 CE. The paintings document the various changes over time in climate, fauna, and flora of the region, as well as the different ways of life of the people who inhabited this area of the Sahara. The archaeological sites of Cyrene and Sabratha, both inscribed on the World Heritage List in 1982, are both recognized for their historical importance. Cyrene is one of the only ancient Greek cities in the region.

Libraries & Museums

The Jamahiriya Museum, located in Tripoli, takes up four floors and has forty-seven galleries. Collections include classical Mediterranean art as well as exhibits and artifacts that document Libyan history, from the Neolithic to the modern era. Notable artifacts include hand axes dated at 300,000 years old and rock art and pottery dating from 8000 to 5000 BCE. Separate galleries display artifacts from the Phoenician, Greek, Roman, Byzantine, and Islamic eras.

The National Library, with its large domed roof, is in Benghazi.

Holidays

Libyans celebrate Ras as-Sana, an Islamic New Year's celebration, and Tabaski, a feast memorializing the Old Testament story of Abraham, during the first three months of the year according to the Islamic lunar calendar. On March 2 every year, Libyans take to the streets to celebrate Declaration of the People's Authority Day. Eid al-Moulid, in the spring, recalls the Prophet Muhammad's birthday with prayers and readings during the day and fireworks, and feasts in the evening.

On June 11, Evacuation Day marks the deportation of thousands of Italians in 1970. Revolution Day is September 1, the anniversary of Gaddafi's overthrow of King Idris. On that day, groups come to Tripoli from around the country for parades, rallies, cultural events, and an address by Gaddafi. The Libyan Day of Mourning, held on October 26, remembers the thousands of Libyans killed or exiled under Italian rule.

Muslims celebrate Muhammad's reception of the Qur'an during the ninth month of the Islamic calendar with Ramadan. Fasting, prayers, and meditation between sunrise and sunset are a prelude to gatherings and feasts during the evenings. The event ends with Eid ul-Fitr, a public celebration during which Libyans dress in new clothing, give money to the poor, and decorate their homes.

The latest national holiday is Liberation Day, October 23.

Youth Culture

As of 2015, the population of Libyans under the age of fifteen is about 26.5 percent. Because of the worldwide sanctions placed on Libya, this entire generation has generally been isolated from much of the outside world. The popularity of satellite television, however, has opened windows to the Arab world. In a country with few social outlets for younger Libyans, such as cinemas or nightclubs and music venues, satellite TV can dominate leisure time. In particular, entertainment programming such as music videos and reality shows have helped draw Libyans together with the rest of the outside world.

With the Gaddafi government beginning to open up to the West, young Libyans are coming to grips with the traditional culture, Islamic values, and newly discovered Western attitudes. There are few signs that young Libyans are rebelling against the effects of the decades-long isolation. Typical forms of youth rebellion, such as graffiti and nontraditional clothing, are almost nonexistent in Libya. Enrollment at English language schools has increased dramatically and government emphasis on education has pushed the literacy rate for those between the ages of fifteen and twenty-four to 97 percent, yet the unemployment rate was 30 percent in 2004.

SOCIETY

Transportation

Automobiles are the most common means of transportation in Libya. In fact, Libya boasts the highest rate of car ownership in North Africa and the Arab world. Vehicle's travel on the right-hand side of the road in Libya. The Cairo-Dakar Highway runs through Libya, although the quality of this roadway is questionable. Especially when about 43 percent of the roads in Libya are unpaved.

Transportation Infrastructure

The national coastal highway is the main road in Libya. It stretches for 1,770 kilometers (1,100 miles) from the Tunisian border to the Egyptian border, and has sections of divided highway. Other national roads connect the major urban centers on or near the coast with only a few main roads heading south across the desert. Generally, the roads in Libya are not well maintained. Desert sand drifting across roadways is a common hazard, and domestic and wild animals often cross roads in more rural areas, making driving even more hazardous.

Libya has not had an operational railroad system since 1965. However, construction is underway on an extensive railroad network. The Libyan government eventually hopes to connect Egypt with Tunisia by rail along the coast. As of 2009, plans for rail lines to the southern city of Sabha and to the countries of Chad and Niger were also in the planning stages.

With the lifting of United Nations sanctions in 2003, several airlines now fly in and out of Tripoli International Airport at Ben Ghasir and Benina Airport in Benghazi. As of 2013, there are 146 airports in Libya, and several airlines operate daily flights and shuttles throughout the country.

Media & Communications

After nearly 40 years in power, the Gaddafi regime still maintains strict control over most of Libya's print and broadcast media. Almost all newspapers, radio and television stations are owned and operated by the Libyan government, including three of the four most prominent newspapers. The state-supported Movement of Revolutionary Committees owns the other major paper. The government censors and limits the rights of the media, and press self-censorship is widely practiced. Criticism of or threats against Islam, Libyan national security, or the government are all strictly prohibited. In 2007, the government authorized the publication and broadcasting of private news organizations. Satellite television broadcast from outside Libya is readily available, although influential Arab stations such as Al-Jazeera and Al-Arabiya do not have correspondents working inside the country.

Cellular phone usage has grown rapidly in Libya since the first system became operational in 1996. As of 2014, there were roughly 10.1 million mobile cell phones in use compared to about 710,000 fixed-lined telephones in service. Libya Telecom and Technology Company is a state-owned and operated company that has a monopoly on Internet services in the country. As of 2014, an estimated 1.4 million (21.8 percent) Libyans access the Internet on a consistent basis. Like traditional media, the Internet is closely monitored by the government. Although there is no legal framework for the government to censor Internet usage, websites viewed as threatening to the state are routinely blocked or shut down. The spread of Internet cafés throughout Libya has been a major factor in the increase in Internet usage. However, the government places strict limits on Internet users and café owners, who regularly provide the government with lists of their customers.

SOCIAL DEVELOPMENT

Standard of Living
In 2014, Libya ranked 55th out of 182 countries on the 2014 United Nations Human Development Index, which measures quality of life and standard of living indicators.

Libya has the highest Human Development Index ranking of any African nation. With its small population, its oil wealth, and the apparently effective administration of Gaddafi's socialist policies, Libyans have an extremely high quality of life. The average life span in Libya as of 2015 is 76.2 years—74.5 years for men and 78 years for women.

Water Consumption
The availability of fresh drinking water in Libya is limited and continues to decrease. Water pollution remains a significant problem in urban areas such as Tripoli, Benghazi, and Misuratha. A large amount of drinking water in Libya is supplied by coastal desalination plants and is of low quality. Efforts to further retrieve water from underground aquifers continue.

In addition, construction on Libya's Great Man-Made River Project continues. It has been estimated that the project, upon completion, will be the largest underground water pipe system in the world. Gaddafi famously dubbed the massive irrigation project as the "Eighth Wonder of the World." Construction began in 1989 and pipes now carry water to Ajdabiya, Tripoli, and Gharyan.

Education
Education has been a distinct priority for the Gaddafi government since its inception. Education is compulsory for ages six to fifteen (primary school through the preparatory section of secondary school). All education is free in Libya, and university-level students receive generous stipends.

A major redevelopment effort in the 1970s brought increased enrollment for women, thousands of new classrooms, and a program to provide on-site education for migratory desert tribes. Courses in Islamic studies and Arabic are offered at all levels of education. Since the 1980s, there have been no government grants for university attendance abroad. Military instruction is also included in the mandatory curriculum. Many boys in Libya attend Koranic schools known as madrassas.

According to the UNESCO Institute for Statistics, Libya's literacy rate was estimated at 96.7 percent in 2015. In 2015, the literacy rate of females was an estimated 85.6 percent while the literacy rate for males was an estimated 96.7 percent.

Women's Rights

Women have historically played a secondary role to men in many aspects of Libyan society, often to the extreme of isolating them from public life. Reforms passed in the 1960s helped the status of women to a degree, but Libya remains a highly patriarchal society in which many women are relegated to the private domain. Women were granted the right to vote in 1964. In addition, women were granted total equality as outlined in the 1969 Constitutional Proclamation. However, traditional views and practices continue to be used to undermine full integration into Libyan society. For example, Islamic law often overrides state law in matters of inheritance, divorce, and property ownership. In addition, men are allowed to practice polygamy, although it is uncommon in contemporary Libya.

The Gaddafi government moved quickly after coming to power to integrate women into mainstream society. The minimum age for marriage was set at sixteen for females and at eighteen for males. A 1972 law made marriage-by-proxy illegal and stated that a girl cannot be married against her will. In addition, women under the age of 21 have the right to choose their spouses and can petition a court for permission to proceed with a marriage that has been forbidden by a father. The government also granted women rights to seek divorce or separation by either customary or legal means in cases of abandonment or mistreatment.

Education has been a major factor in helping women move into more prominent roles in Libyan society. Educational differences between males and females have narrowed throughout all levels, with women making up 51 percent of university students, according to a 2006 UNESCO report. However, a significant proportion or rural women do not attend school and are likely to teach their children the traditional gender roles.

According to a 2005 International Labor Organization (ILO) report, 32 percent of Libyan women over the age of 15 were economically active. Although equal pay for equal work and qualifications has been sanctioned under the law, many women still face cultural and traditional barriers that limit and discourage them from seeking employment or careers. In addition, government policies and laws promoting gender equality in the workforce have not been too successful. Very few women are in senior positions in business or government.

Since the early 1970s, the Gaddafi government has encouraged women to seek employment or membership in traditionally male dominated positions. For example, in the early 1980s, Gaddafi began integrating women into the armed forces. He founded a special police force made up of female military academy graduates. Known to Libyans as the Revolutionary Nuns, the special force serves as Gaddafi's personal bodyguards. The Gaddafi government also established the Department of Social Affairs to oversee the integration of women into all spheres of public life. In addition, the General Union of Women's Associations is a network of NGOs that actively works on women's employment issues.

In November of 2014, a meeting was held in Cairo, Egypt on "Libyan Women's Demands for the Constitution". Over 60 Libyan women attended the meeting from all regions in the country. During this meeting, the UNDP Country Director, Selva Ramachandran, explained that women's participation in constitution-making is vital to Lybia.

Health Care

Although trade sanctions during the 1990s have depleted Libya's supply of medicines, vaccines, and medical equipment, the health care system remains strong as a result of consistent, high-level government funding. All medical care is free in Libya.

Major hospitals are located in Tripoli and Benghazi. Small villages and towns are provided with smaller hospitals or clinics. In remote areas, mobile health units bring supplies and health workers on a regular basis. The number of available specialists and of mother-and-child centers is expected to increase now that sanctions have been lifted.

Libya's government also provides life insurance, pension benefits, and disability benefits to all workers in the country. Women receive government-funded maternity leave benefits.

GOVERNMENT

Structure

Libya reached its first golden age in the second century as a Roman province that supplied the Empire with cereals, oil, and slaves. With the decline of the Roman Empire and Vandal invasions over the following three centuries, all of Libya's great cities were ruined, except Oea (Tripoli). Arab rule in the seventh century brought renewed wealth and reconstruction to the area, until the sixteenth century, when the Turkish Empire invaded and seized control. Libya was the last North African territory to be lost to the decaying Turkish Empire. Italy took control in 1911.

The period of Italian rule continues to have an impact on modern-day Libya. Half of Libya's non-European population was killed or exiled between 1911 and World War II as part of Italy's plan to reconstruct the country in its own image. During the war, the Italian government laid massive mine fields across Libya, some of which are still intact.

British and American troops established bases in the country with the defeat of Italian forces, and helped to negotiate into place the government of King Idris. The king did not have widespread support in Libya, and his inability or refusal to interfere with the foreign oil companies who owned and controlled Libya's oil fields further weakened his authority. On September 1, 1969, military Captain Muammar Gaddafi took power in a coup.

Libya is nominally ruled under a Jamahiriya ("state of the masses"), a political theory of direct rule by the people created by Gaddafi from Western Marxism, Islamic law, and tribal custom. Called (in translation) the Third Universal Theory, Gaddafi 's system of government is a de facto strict military dictatorship.

Gaddafi's support of terrorist activities during the 1970s and 1980s brought on a series of trade sanctions against Libya in 1992. Gaddafi's subsequent denunciations of terrorism and weapons of mass destruction, his payment of compensation to families affected by his policies, and his moves to lead regional peace efforts through the Organization for African Unity have reestablished friendly relations between Gaddafi's government and Western powers.

A revolution occurred in 2011, which implemented a prime minister and a more structured system. As of March 11, 2014, the Prime Minister is Abdullah al-Thini. This is also when a new cabinet was approved by the House of Representatives. Because the government is still in transition, there is currently no Judicial branch. Libya's latest constitutional change occurred in 2011. Since April 2014, a 47-member Constitutional Assembly has been meeting.

Political Parties

The Libyan government banned political parties in 1972. The government of Libya is controlled by Revolutionary Leader Gaddafi and his Revolutionary Command Council.

Currently, the parties consist of the Al-Watan (Homeland) Party, Justice and Construction Party (JCP), National Forces Alliance (NFA), the National Front (formed in 1981 as an opposition group), and the Union for the Homeland.

Local Government

Although various executive groups are represented in the General People's Congress, local government in Libya is generally undeveloped and no official municipalities exist. Even Gaddafi's son, Saif al-Islam, has been publicly critical of the countries need to better establish government representation at a local level. Although al-Islam has led efforts to reform local government in Libya, he has done so under the auspices of his father's regime.

Judicial System

Libya's court system is based on Sharia, or the sacred law of Islam. The Supreme Court is the highest court in the country. Justices are appointed by the General People's Congress. Summary courts try petty offenses. Serious criminal offenses are heard by the courts of first instance, which sits below the court of appeals.

Taxation

Tax laws in Libya have been criticized for lack of clarity and consistence. Foreign businesses in Libya are charged a corporation tax and revenue duty. Other principal taxes include salaries and wages tax and withholding taxes. In addition, Jihad tax, or religious tax, is charged. The country's tax and other revenues account for 37 percent of the GDP (2014).

Armed Forces

The armed forces of Libya consist of an army, air force, and navy. In 2009, it was reported that the military, particularly the special forces, were undergoing counterterrorism training by British special forces. As of 2012, the mandatory/voluntary service age is 18. Because of the transition in government, there is no official army. Though the government is trying to staff a new army consisting of anti-Gaddafi militia fighters and former members of the Gaddafi military.

Foreign Policy

Since 1969, when Gaddafi assumed de facto leadership of Libya, the country's foreign policy has focused on the primary goals of Arab unity, elimination of Israel, advancement of Islam, support for Palestinians, elimination of Western influence in the Middle East and Africa, and support for a range of revolutionary causes.

In 2003, Libya emerged from nearly two decades of isolation as the result of economic and political sanctions placed on the country by the UN and other countries. The sanctions were in response to Libya's support of terrorism, and in particular, the involvement of two of its agents in the 1988 bombing of Pan Am flight 103 over Lockerbie, Scotland. Libya has rid itself of weapons of mass destruction (WMD) and MTCR-class missile programs and has since cooperated with International Atomic Energy Agency (IAEA) and the Organization for the Prohibition of Chemical Weapons (OPCW). In addition, Libya is a State Party to the Chemical Weapons Convention. The United States and other countries no longer designate Libya as a state sponsor of terrorism, and have normalized relationships with the Gaddafi government.

Gaddafi's willingness to denounce terrorism, to soften many of his early foreign policy goals, and to cooperate with the U.S. and other Western countries has sparked intense interest in Libyan investments, particularly in its oil industries. With most energy-hungry countries seeking to diversify their energy sources, and emerging economies like India and China rapidly increasing their energy demands, Libya is positioning itself as a strategic energy supplier in the early years of the 21st century.

Africa has occupied a central position in Libyan foreign policy for many years, especially during the years of the UN sanctions. Libya hosted a summit of the Organization for African Unity (OAU) in September 1999 and has lobbied intensively to promote the OAU and its successor organization, the African Union (AU). Libya set up the Organization of Saharan and Sahelian States (CENSAD, formerly COMESA) in 1998 to promote regional integration and security co-operation. Gaddafi has also strengthened Libya's relationships with Egypt and Tunisia. With more than 750,000 Egyptian workers in Libya and considerable Libyan investment from Egypt, solid economic ties to Egypt are vital.

UN sanctions and the European arms embargo decimated Libya's national defense industry and left Libya's extensive military equipment in desperate need of modernization. Libya's defense industry is almost entirely state-owned. With the lifting of the UN arms embargo in September 2003, and of the EU arms embargo in 2004, foreign companies are now exploring the Libyan market. Fueled by foreign investment, Libya's defense industries are likely to expand, and consequently, strengthen the country's military capabilities.

Human Rights Profile

International human rights law insists that states respect civil and political rights, and also promote an individual's economic, social and cultural rights. The United Nations Universal Declaration of Human Rights (UDHR) is recognized as the standard for international human rights. Its authors sought the counsel of the world's great thinkers, philosophers, and religious leaders, and were careful to create a document that reflects the core values shared by every world culture. To read this document or view the articles relating to cultural human rights, visit http://www.udhr.org/UDHR/default.htm.

Although there has been some loosening in Gaddafi's authoritarian regime in the first decade of the twenty-first century, the government's human rights record remains poor. The 1969 Constitutional Proclamation and the 1977 Declaration on the Establishment of the Authority of the People detailed Gaddafi's claim that the Libyan citizens rule the country through a pyramid of congresses, communes, and committees. In reality, however, Gaddafi and his close advisors maintain a monopoly of power in all aspects of Libyan society.

Libya's constitution is generally in line with Article 2 of the UDHR. It enshrines the equality of all its citizens before the law, regardless of race, religion, or gender. Libyans of all races and religions receive benefits from the government, and the Gaddafi administration has made recent moves to further enhance these principals. For example, in 2007, the government abolished a law forbidding the use of minority Amazigh (Berber) and Tuareg names. In addition, Berber communities were allowed to display Amazigh language signs at government-sponsored events.

Article 5 of the UDHR states that no one shall be subjected to torture or to cruel, inhuman or degrading treatment or punishment. Libyan law outlaws these abuses, yet investigators from international organizations found credible evidence that government security forces routinely tortured prisoners during interrogations or as punishment. In addition, the Gaddafi government has created an extensive surveillance system that monitors and controls the activities of individuals through the use of police and military units, multiple intelligence services, local revolutionary committees, people's committees, and purification committees. The government frequently cites the 1971 and 1972 "Protection of the Revolution" laws, which criminalize activities and behavior that is counter to revolutionary ideology, as a defense for its actions. Consequently, government security services can detain individuals without formal charges and hold them indefinitely without court convictions and with impunity.

Article 19 of the UDHR protects the universal rights to freedom of opinion and expression. Freedom of expression and opinion in Libya are severely restricted. The government allows freedom of speech "within the limits of public interest and principles of the Revolution." In practice, the government has wide latitude in determining what constitutes "within the limits." There are no privatized radio or television stations, and government authorities or agencies control almost all of the country's main newspapers and traditional media outlets. In addition, all unofficial political activities have been outlawed. Because of the government's extensive security network, state-sanctioned censorship and self-censorship are widespread. Penalties for disseminating materials viewed by the government as detrimental to Gaddafi or the state include punishment and, in some cases, life imprisonment.

Libya has no independent non-governmental organizations (NGOs), and the government has outlawed independent journalist and lawyer organizations. Uncensored news is available to many Libyans, however, through satellite television and websites based abroad, but these are often blocked.

ECONOMY

Overview of the Economy

In 2014, Libya's gross domestic product (GDP) was estimated at $97.58 billion (USD). The per capita GDP for the same period was $15,700 (USD). Oil is the central focus of the Libyan economy, and the driving force behind the country's rapid growth and modernization since 1959, when oil was first discovered there. Thanks to oil revenues, Libyans enjoy a higher per capita GDP than most Africans, although most of the country's wealth is controlled by the elite classes. However, sales of oil and natural gas fell greatly during the Revolution of 2011, rose in 2012, and dramatically fell in late 2013 throughout 2014. This was due to major protest disruptions at the country's oil ports.

Foreign investment in Libya has increased since the United Nations lifted sanctions against the country in 1999, but foreign companies are not allowed to invest more than $20 million (USD) in Libya in a given year. The stock of direct investment at home accounted for $17.43 billion, while the investment abroad accounted for $24.68 billion in 2014.

Industry

Since the mid-20th century, petroleum has been Libya's most important source of revenue. Since the 1969 coup, the oil industry has been nationally owned and controlled. In addition to petroleum, Libya manufactures or processes food, textiles, handicrafts, and cement. More recently, the country has begun the processing of petrochemicals, iron, steel, and aluminum.

Labor

Libya's labor force was estimated at more than 1.7 million in 2014. The majority of the labor force—an estimated 59 percent—is employed in the services sector (2004); 23 percent are employed in industry, and 17 percent of workers are agriculturally employed. The unemployment rate was estimated at 30 percent in 2004.

Energy/Power/Natural Resources

Libya has a wealth of petroleum, natural gas, and gypsum reserves. Oil accounts for roughly 95 percent of the country's exports, and more than half of the gross domestic product (GDP).

Fishing

Despite having over 1,110 miles of coastline on the Mediterranean Sea, Libya's fishing industry represents only about 1 percent of the country's total labor force and is generally undeveloped. Annual catches of tuna and sardines are low in comparison to neighboring countries.

Forestry

The land of Libya is most desert and scrub land and the country has no forestry industry. Although the government began initiatives to plant forests beginning in the 1960s, these efforts have proved largely unsuccessful.

Mining/Metals

Libya's oil industry is the largest sector of the country's economy. Petroleum is by far the largest source of revenue for the government. Libya is a significant supplier of oil to Western Europe, producing approximately 1.5 million barrels annually. Outside of the oil sector, there is no mining or metals industry in the country.

Agriculture

Only coastal areas have sufficient rainfall to produce harvests. Fields in Tripolitania and Cyrenaica produce wheat, barley, olives, dates, citrus, vegetables, peanuts, soybeans, and cattle. Because of the limitations its climate places on farming, Libya must import approximately three-quarters of its food supply.

Animal Husbandry

Agriculture, including livestock, is the second largest sector of the Libyan economy. Sheep, cattle, poultry, and goats are bred and used for food and farm work. The country's dairy sector is operated by the government. In recent decades, the government has sponsored efforts to modernize range management and breeding practices in Libya.

Tourism

Libya has an existing tourist industry that is likely to grow larger now that trade sanctions have been lifted. The country's Mediterranean coast and trade routes boast ancient Roman ruins, some in remarkable states of preservation, and a vibrant street life of souks (marketplaces) mixed with traditional and modern architecture.

Desert safaris have become increasingly lucrative for local guides, and come complete with visits to stone-age archeological sites and geological wonders like the desert lakes of Idehan Ubari. Libya also has a stunning coastline along the Mediterranean that is popular with beachgoers, and more recently, scuba divers, who travel to Libya to explore underwater ancient ruins.

Michael Carpenter, Amy Witherbee, M. Lee

DO YOU KNOW?

- A term coined by the Egyptians, "Libya" once referred to all the lands in Africa outside of ancient Egypt.
- Because of its arid climate, Libya has no year-round rivers. During the rainy season, dry riverbed called wadis fill temporarily to bring water to fertile areas along the coast.

Bibliography

Alison Pargeter. *Libya: The Rise and Fall of Qaddafi.* New Haven, CT: Yale University Press, 2012.

Dirk Vandewalle. *A History of Modern Libya.* Cambridge, England: Cambridge University Press, 2012.

Jason Morgan and Toyin Falala. *Culture and Customs of Libya.* Santa Barbara, CA: Greenwood Press, 2012.

Roger Jones. *Libya—Culture Smart! The Essential Guide to Customs and Culture.* London: Kuperard, 2080.

Susan Raven. *Rome in Africa.* New York: Routledge, 1993.

Thomas Seligman and Kristyne Loughran, eds. *Art of Being Tuareg: Sahara Nomads in a Modern World.* Los Angeles: UCLA Fowler Museum, 2006.

Works Cited

"Chad: Toubou and Daza." *U.S. Library of Congress Country Studies* website. Online. http://countrystudies.us/chad/23.htm

"Country Profiles: Libya," released by the Bureau of Near Eastern Affairs. *U.S. Department of State.* Online. http://www.state.gov/r/pa/ei/bgn/5425.htm#political

"Doing Business in Libya: Libyan Social and Business Culture." *Communicaid* website. Online. http://www.communicaid.com/cross-cultural-training/culture-for-business-and-management/doing-business-in/Libyan-business-and-social-culture.php

"Freedom of the Press 2008: Libya." *United Nations Refugee Agency* website. http://www.unhcr.org/refworld/publisher,FREEHOU,,LBY,4871f615c,0.html

"Leptis Magna." *Encyclopedia Britannica* Online. http://www.britannica.com/EBchecked/topic/336898/Leptis-Magna

"Libya 2008 Crime and Safety Report." *Overseas Security Advisory Council* website, March 27 2008. https://www.osac.gov/Reports/report.cfm?contentID=81951

"Libya, 2005 Country Report." *Human Rights Watch* website. http://www.hrw.org/legacy/english/docs/2006/01/18/libya12227.htm

"Libya." CIA World Factbook. Online. https://www.cia.gov/library/publications/the-world-factbook/geos/ly.html

"Libya." *Encyclopedia Britannica* Online. http://www.britannica.com/EBchecked/topic/339574/Libya

"Libya." *UK Foreign & Commonwealth Office* website. http://www.fco.gov.uk/en/about-the-fco/country-profiles/middle-east-north-africa/libya/?profile=intRelations&pg=4

"Libya." *World Gazetteer* website. http://www.world-gazetteer.com/wg.php?x=&men=gcis&lng=en&des=wg&srt=npan&col=abcdefghinoq&msz=1500&geo=-133

"Libya: Country Reports on Human Rights
    Practices—2007, released by the Bureau of Democracy,
    Human Rights, and Labor." *U.S. Department of State*.
    March 11, 2008. Online. http://www.state.gov/g/drl/rls/
    hrrpt/2007/100601.htm

"Libya: Events of 2008." *Human Rights Watch* website.
    http://www.hrw.org/en/node/79302

"Libya: Food." *U.S. Library of Congress Country Studies*
    website. Online. http://countrystudies.us/libya/47.htm

"Libya: Out of the Shadows." *PBS Frontline: Rough
    Cut* website. http://www.pbs.org/frontlineworld/
    rough/2006/08/libya_out_of_thlinks.html

"Libya: The Old City of Tripoli." *The Prince's School of
    Traditional Arts* website. Online. http://www.psta.org.uk/
    index.php?n=International.Libya

"Libya: Travel.State.Gov website, released by the Bureau
    of Consular Affairs." *U.S. Department of State*. Online.
    http://travel.state.gov/travel/cis_pa_tw/cis/cis_951.html

"Libya: Tuareg." *U.S. Library of Congress Country Studies*
    website. Online. http://countrystudies.us/libya/41.htm

"Libya: Youth Literacy Rate." *Norwegian UN Association*
    website, 2004.

"Libyan Arab Jamahiriya." *UN Statistics Division*
    website. http://data.un.org/CountryProfile.
    aspx?crName=Libyan%20Arab%20Jamahiriya

"Libyan Artists Take Flight." *Power of Culture* website.
    June 2008. Online. http://www.powerofculture.nl/en/
    current/2008/june/art-libya

"Multicultural Guide." *Manitoba Office of Rural and
    Northern Health* website. Online. http://cartwrightmb.ca/
    immigration/multicultural_guide_web.pdf

"Music of Tunisia" Nationmaster Encyclopedia. Online.
    http://www.nationmaster.com/encyclopedia/Music-of-
    Tunisia

"Old Town of Ghadames." *UNESCO World Heritage*
    website. Online. http://whc.unesco.org/en/list/362;

"Ramadan and Eid in Libya." *Libyaonline* website. 2009.
    http://www.libyaonline.com/news/details.php?id=525

"Rock-Art Sites of Tadrart Acacus." *UNESCO World
    Heritage* website. Online. http://whc.unesco.org/
    en/list/287. http://www.britannica.com/EBchecked/
    topic/471439/Portugal

"The Tuareg." *Bethany World Prayer Center* website.
    Online. http://kcm.co.kr/bethany_eng/clusters/tuareg.
    html

"Tripoli." *Encyclopedia Britannica* Online. http://www.
    britannica.com/EBchecked/topic/605829/Tripoli

"Tuareg." *Encyclopedia Britannica* Online. http://www.
    britannica.com/EBchecked/topic/608089/Tuareg

Anthony Ham. Libya. London: Lonely Planet, 2007.

Briginshaw, David. "Libya's First Two Railway Lines Start
    to Take Shape." *BNet* website. http://findarticles.com/p/
    articles/mi_m0BQQ/is_1_41/ai_69709357

Culture Crossing website. Online. http://www.
    culturecrossing.net/basics_business_student_details.
    php?Id=7&CID=238 http://www.state.gov/g/drl/rls/
    hrrpt/2007/100579.htm

Ian Black. "Great Grooves and Good Grammar."
    The Guardian website, April 10, 2007. http://
    www.guardian.co.uk/education/2007/apr/10/
    internationaleducationnews.tefl

John Alterman, "Libya's Generation Gap." *Center for
    Strategic and International Studies*. February 2006.
    www.csis.org/media/csis/pubs/060224_menc.pdf

Khaled Mattawa. "Preface to the Libya Issue of Words
    without Borders. *Words without Borders Online
    Magazine*, July 2006. http://www.wordswithoutborders.
    org/article.php?lab=PrefaceLibyaJuly06

Lee Hudson Teslik. "Libya's Odd Bargain." *Council
    on Foreign Relations* website. http://www.cfr.org/
    publication/13916/libyas_odd_bargain.html?breadcrumb
    =%2Fregion%2F146%2Flibya

Libya Defence & Security Report." *Business Monitor
    International* website. http://www.businessmonitor.com/
    libya_defence.html

Libyan General People's Committee of Tourism website.
    http://www.libyan-tourism.org/Standard.aspx?ID=23;

Old and Sold Antiques Auction & Marketplace website.
    Online. http://www.oldandsold.com/articles01/
    article799.shtml

OpenArab website. http://www.openarab.net/en/node/362

Richard Bangs. "Fleeing the Hot Breath of the Desert."
    Slate Magazine. June 11, 2004. Online. http://www.
    slate.com/id/2101814/

Roger Jones. Culture Smart! Libya. London: *Kuperard*.
    2008.

Shiekh Zayed Book Award website. Online.
    http://zayedaward.com/en/BranchDetails.
    aspx?branchID=52&cycleID=20

UK Trade & Investment website. Online. https://www.
    uktradeinvest.gov.uk/ukti/appmanager/ukti/countries?_
    nfpb=true&portlet_3_5_actionOverride=%2Fpub
    %2Fportlets%2FgenericViewer%2FshowContentIt
    em&_windowLabel=portlet_3_5&portlet_3_5naviga
    tionPageId=%2Flibya&portlet_3_5navigationConten
    tPath=%2FBEA+Repository%2F326%2F227028&_
    pageLabel=CountryType1

UNEP/UNESCO. *YouthXChange* website. http://www.
    youthxchange.net/main/b273_using_cars-b3.asp

Water peddler in Marrakech, Morocco

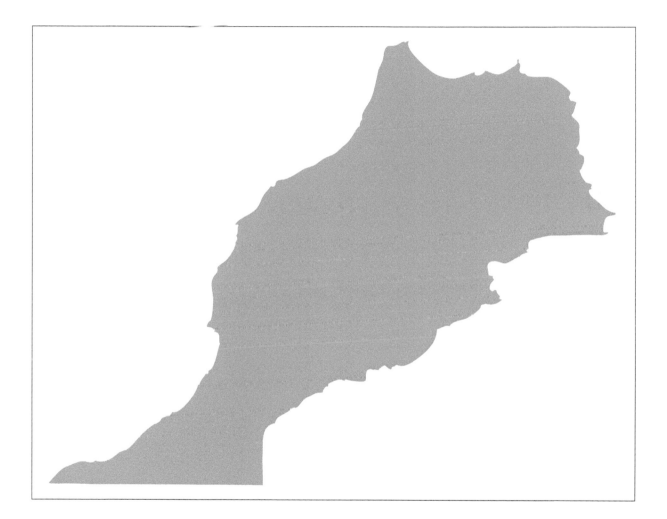

MOROCCO

Introduction

Morocco is located on the northwest coast of Africa. It is a three-hour ferry ride from the south of Spain and a favorite European tourist destination. Throughout history, the country's native Berber population has been subject to conquest by Muslim Arabs, Christian Europeans, and others. While the Islamic influence is dominant, the culture remains a rich melting pot of African, European, and Middle Eastern influences.

In early 2011, King Mohammed VI responded to pro-democratic "Arab Spring" protests by creating a new constitution. It was passed by popular referendum in July 2011, granting more power to the parliament and prime minister while keeping the monarchy intact. Later in November, the Justice and Development Party (a moderate Islamic party) won the largest number of seats in elections, and they became the first Islamist party to lead the Moroccan government.

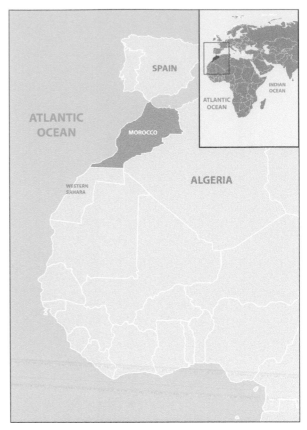

GENERAL INFORMATION

Official Language: Arabic
Population: 33.3 million (2015 estimate)
Currency: Dirham
Coins: The Dirham exists in denominations of 1, 5, 10, 20, and 50. A 1, 2, and 5 Dirham coin also exists.
Land Area: 446,550 square kilometers (172,414 square miles)
Water Area: 250 square kilometers (97 square miles)

National Motto: "God, Country, King"
National Anthem: "Hymne Chérifien" (Sharifian Hymn)
Capital: Rabat
Time Zone: Western European Time (WET) (equivalent of GMT); in the Summer: Western European Summer Time (WEST) (GMT +1)
Flag Description: The flag of Morocco is red. In the center is a green pentacle or five pointed star. The star is known as the Seal of Solomon.

Population

Northwest Africa's native population is generally described as Berber. However, this native Muslim population merged with Islamic Arab immigrants beginning in the eighth century. There are a small percentage of people of sub-Saharan African heritage living in Morocco. France and Spain colonized the nation in the early 1900s.

While Morocco has been independent since 1956, European ancestry (particularly French) is

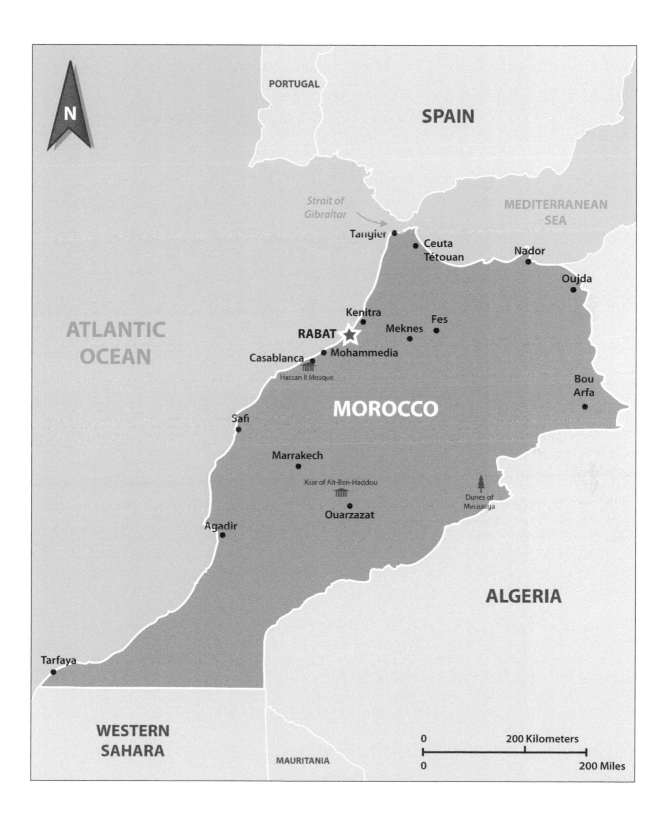

Principal Cities by Population (2012 estimate):

- Casablanca (3.4 million)
- Fez (1.1 million)
- Rabat (1.9 million)
- Agadir (600,177)
- Meknes (616,110)
- Tangier (793,776)
- Oujda (435,378)
- Kenitra (418,22)
- Tetouan (359,142, 2004)
- Marrakech (953,305)

also common among the Berber-Arabs that make up 99 percent of the population. Arabic descent is predominant, with typical estimates that the population is 60 percent or more predominately Arab and 35 percent predominately Berber. Approximately 75 percent of the population has some Berber ancestry.

More than 60 percent (2015) of Morocco's population lives in urban areas with an annual rate of 2.26 percent (2010–2015). The country's largest cities are along the Atlantic coastline; Casablanca is the largest, with a population of almost 3.5 million. It is the country's business center and primary seaport. Rabat, the capital, is the country's seat of government and a principal cultural center. Other large cities include Fez (Fès), an important religious and education center, and Tangier, a port city with close ties to Spain.

Languages

Arab/Islamic control led to Morocco's acceptance of Arabic as its official language, but there are still numerous pockets of traditional Berber tribal languages left throughout the country. Tamazight is the most commonly spoken. Other Berber dialects include Tarifit (Rifi) and Tachelhit. French is the most common European language, but is largely confined to urban areas. Spanish is spoken along the northern coast to accommodate tourists from nearby Spain and Portugal.

Native People & Ethnic Groups

The area that is now Morocco has been inhabited since approximately 8000 BCE. The Berbers were already living there when the Phoenicians settled the area in 1100 BCE. The region was controlled by the Romans until the end of the 17th century, when the Arab conquest began.

After years of Arabic domination of Moroccan culture, efforts were formalized in 2001 to promote and protect Berber (also known as Amazigh) heritage and language. King Mohammed created the Royal Institute for Amazigh Culture, calling the country's Berber heritage a "national treasure." He added that Morocco should "strengthen the pillars of our ancestral identity."

The vast majority of Morocco's population, by some estimates over 99 percent, is Arab-Berbers. The country does have a small population of foreign nationals from France, Spain, and Italy.

Religions

Modern Morocco is an Islamic nation, and almost all citizens are Sunni Muslims (99 percent). There is a tiny Christian minority, accounting for roughly one percent of the population. At one time, there was a significant Jewish minority, but as Arab-Israeli tensions mounted after World War II, this population left the country.

Islamic extremism has been largely absent from Morocco as compared to neighboring Algeria. However, this has been a growing concern following crimes attributed to a group called Salafia Jihadia surrounding the 2002 elections, and the March 2004 terrorist attack in Spain.

Climate

In Rabat and Casablanca, the average January temperature is about 12° Celsius (54° Fahrenheit), and the average July temperature is 22° Celsius (72° Fahrenheit). Morocco receives little rain: almost none in the summer months, and less than one week per month during the rainy season, between November and March.

Away from the moderate, subtropical coastal climate, the temperatures are more extreme.

Mountain ranges are routinely capped in snow for most of the year. Marrakech features a more typical desert climate, with an average winter temperature of 21° Celsius (70° Fahrenheit), and blistering summer average of 38° Celsius (100° Fahrenheit).

ENVIRONMENT & GEOGRAPHY

Topography

Morocco lies 13 kilometers (eight miles) south of Spain, across the Strait of Gibraltar. It is bordered by Algeria on the east and southeast, the Atlantic Ocean on the west, and the Mediterranean Sea on the north. A large area called Western Sahara runs along the southern border. Although a group of native Sahrawis tribespeople have sought independence for this region (under the banner of the Polisario Front) it remains under Moroccan control.

Morocco is easily divided into four regions: the highlands, the mountain ranges, a wide plains region, and lowlands that run into the Sahara Desert.

The Atlas Mountain's Grand Atlas range includes Jebel Toubkal, the highest peak in North Africa at 4,165 meters (13,665 feet) above sea level. The mountains run across the country from southwest to northeast. The highlands region, Er Rif, runs along the northern coastline with the Mediterranean. This area reaches an elevation of 2,440 meters (8,000 feet). Between the two elevated regions is the Taza Depression, a natural transportation corridor.

The remainder of the coastline to the west marks the beginning of the plains region. This area is the most hospitable to human development and is home to most of Morocco's large cities. To the southeast of the Atlas Mountains, a lower plains region eventually merges with the Sahara Desert.

Morocco's rivers flow into both the Mediterranean and the Atlantic. The two largest rivers are the Moulouya and the Sebou. They are mostly used for irrigation and hydroelectric power. As with most deserts, low-lying areas are susceptible to flash floods as water rushes over the sandy soil. In Morocco, these areas are called wadi.

Plants & Animals

Forests cover about seven percent of Morocco's area; the most common trees are oak, found in mountainous areas. The southern plains are home to a large (28,000 hectares) forest of the native argan tree, Morocco's second most common tree species.

Morocco's mountainous areas are home to rabbits, squirrels, and otters. Larger animals include the mouflon (a wild sheep) and fennec (a type of fox). The southern plains regions are home to more typically African animals such as gazelles, wild boars, panthers, baboons, and macacos (a type of monkey). Common birds include swifts, swallows, martins, and storks.

CUSTOMS & COURTESIES

Greetings

Greetings are an important sign of respect in Moroccan culture. It is believed that to acknowledge a neighbor with kindness is to acknowledge Allah himself with that kindness. As such, to pass over this phase of conversation can cause great offense. When visiting someone's home, for example, it is expected that one will enter the room and individually greet each family member and guest present there. Even routine tasks, such as purchasing a loaf of bread, should always begin with a proper greeting before any business is conducted.

The traditional Moroccan greeting is, fundamentally, a wish of peace. The first person begins with "Salem" ("Peace be with you") and his neighbor responds with the same. This is followed by each person asking "La bas?" ("How are you?"), to which a typical reply would be "La bas, hamdullah" ("Fine, praise God"). When greeting someone unfamiliar or for the first time, this exchange is performed with a handshake followed by placing one's right hand over one's heart. In more familiar circles, and usually between women, the hand-shake is replaced by a hug. In turn, the "Salem, la bas?" exchange is rapidly repeated multiple times with a round of kisses on each cheek. The phrase "Shu'kran" ("Thank you") may be graciously added to this interaction, and "Buh salamma" ("With peace") is considered a standard farewell.

Exchanges between men and woman can be delicate. While interactions among family members are often quite physical and exuberant, full of hugs, handholding and kisses to the cheek, the opposite is true among strangers or acquaintances. Greetings and conversations among men and women are very reserved, and physicality is kept to a minimum. Often only a brief handshake is exchanged and sometimes just dialogue alone with one's hand over one's heart. In conservative circles, it is typically customary for a woman to avert her eyes when greeting a man to maintain particular modesty.

Gestures & Etiquette

A deep sense of community is at the heart of Moroccan culture, and interactions are very physical. For example, it is common for men to hold hands while walking together and for women to sit closely against each other. Generally, Moroccan hospitality can be very insistent and the concept of "personal space" is not observed. For example, children and young men are notorious for trailing alongside travelers and strangers asking questions and attempting to lead them to a place of interest.

Body language is a major component of Moroccan social etiquette with cleanliness being particularly important. In fact, the act of cleansing oneself is even incorporated into the ritual of Muslim prayer. One of the most critical points of etiquette involves the left hand. The left hand is used for personal hygiene, and is considered unclean. It is considered impolite for the left hand to be exposed to others and to be used for eating or drinking. Similarly, feet are regarded as unclean and it is insulting to for the bottoms of one's feet to be shown; when Moroccans sit barefoot, they typically cross their legs and tuck their feet under their bodies.

Other essential important aspects of social etiquette involve relations between men and women. In Moroccan culture, it is common to socialize only with hosts of the same gender. For men especially, it is crucial that attention is not given to a young woman unless it is sanctioned by her parents. Reckless interactions could cause irreparable damage to her reputation. Additionally, conservative clothing that conceals elbows and ankles is the norm, and typically expected of travelers and tourists.

Eating/Meals

Moroccans typically eat three main meals per day. Moroccan breakfast generally includes coffee, a hard-boiled egg, yogurt, and harsha, a dense, fried bread made from semolina, a type of wheat flour. Lunch is commonly the largest meal of the day. It is a family affair—children leave school to eat at home—and can take up to two hours, as it generally concludes with a nap. The focus of the meal is tagine, a spiced meat and vegetable stew often flavored with fruit and spices. It is a staple of Moroccan cuisine. Tagine is eaten by tearing pieces of fresh flat bread to pinch the meat and vegetables.

Dinner is usually eaten late, around nine or ten o'clock at night. This consists of a main course (for example, chicken with olives or lamb with prunes) eaten with fresh bread. Mint tea follows every meal and is enjoyed between meals: once mid-morning and once midday. It is traditionally prepared in a pot of green tea that is stuffed with sprigs of fresh mint and heavily sweetened with sugar.

In villages and rural Morocco, meals are typically modest. Meat is difficult to come by, as livestock is needed to produce milk, eggs, and wool. On the other hand, potatoes, carrots, and tomatoes are inexpensive and readily available. During lean harvests, these common ingredients are often the only components of a family's tagine.

Friday is the Muslim holy day and is celebrated with a couscous (steamed semolina) lunch prepared with either a savory mix of meat and vegetables or a sweet mix of meat with cinnamon raisins and candied onions. Couscous is typically served communally in a broad, round dish centered on the table. It is eaten with the right hand by scooping the mixture and forming it into a ball to pop in your mouth. This is sometimes washed down with l'bin, a creamy milk drink, and rounded off with fruit and mint tea.

Visiting

As a guest in a Moroccan home, one can expect to share in a large meal. As such, a gift of food to add to the table is appreciated. A cone of sugar is inexpensive and always acceptable. Items such as fruit, nuts, olives, and honey are more luxurious and are gladly received. A visitor is typically expected to dress appropriately, with particular attention to modesty in smaller towns and villages.

Shoes are usually removed upon entering and guests are guided to the living room, likely to watch television. It is unlikely that guests would be shown the kitchen, which is almost exclusively the women's domain, or the bathroom, which is rarely spoken about. Should the bathroom be needed, it is best to ask subtly a host of the same gender.

Just before mealtime, it is common for a woman of the household to bring around a kettle of water and a basin so that each person might rinse his or her hands. One probably does not wash with soap, as the fragrance spoils the flavor of the meal, which is commonly eaten with the hands. The meal is typically presented in common dishes and everyone gathers around a low, round table. Food is taken only with the right hand and it is impolite to eat outside the boundaries of what is situated in front of each person. Any meat in the dish is portioned out and traditionally served to guests first. The meal might be followed with a round of mint tea and a brief nap. It is customary for guests to stay, as it is a time to take pleasure in the meal that has been shared and hosts are commonly honored to provide this opportunity for rest.

LIFESTYLE

Family

The Moroccan family unit is traditionally very close-knit. Family obligation is often regarded almost as highly as religious practice. Children live at home until they marry, at which time brides move in with their husband's family. Elders are revered and cared for by their families in their old age; nursing homes are generally only utilized in the city by individuals who have no surviving kin. A typical household might include an extended family of grandparents, aunts, and cousins. In urban areas, the men of the house often leave to find opportunity overseas and opt to send money home. This situation is mirrored in rural areas, where men leave to find work in the city and visit their bled (village of origin) only for holidays and special occasions.

This emigration of men in turn affects the family left behind, particularly with regard to education. In urban areas, fathers who are fortunate enough to do business abroad generally school their children in Europe and prepare them for a life overseas as well. By contrast, when village families lose their men to the city, children, particularly girls, must forgo schooling to help with farming and other household duties.

Housing

Urban housing is typically the dar, a townhouse made of plaster and concrete, often sporting a whitewashed façade (front exterior) and a tall-gated entrance. Dars typically have few exterior windows and often feature an interior, multi-storied courtyard that disperses both light and air. The courtyard serves to regulate temperature and offers protection from the natural elements, such as wind, sand, and sun. Instead of a backyard, many Moroccan households have an expansive roof deck that serves as a space to air-dry laundry. These spaces might also serve as sleeping quarters should the interior be too uncomfortable on a hot night.

Rural housing is normally a one-story square formed with mud and straw and topped with a flat bamboo roof. The space is multi-functional, used for both eating and sleeping. If a family owns animals, they are kept in a separate pen attached to the house, also fashioned out of mud and straw. Some larger households also add a small room for cooking, which houses the fire pit, clay bread oven, and any provisions or cooking utensils. Many rural houses incorporate a courtyard. This, coupled with the mud construction, helps to regulate temperature, particularly in the harsh desert climate.

Food

Moroccan food is characterized by a variety of rich spices. Saffron and cumin are present in nearly every dish, and coriander, cinnamon, and paprika are widely used. Ras el hanoot ("From the head of the shop owner") is a custom blend created by the local spice merchant and may incorporate up to 100 different herbs and spices. Its complexity complements meat and poultry and is a frequent additive in tagine.

Tagine, is a stew named for the conical clay dish in which it is prepared. The tagine has a rounded base which is heated over a fire and in which all the ingredients are placed Typically this includes a generous pour of olive oil, followed by a large cut of chicken or lamb and several potatoes, cut into wedges. Chunks of carrot, onion, and tomato are added and briefly sautéed. Lastly, spices are liberally added, followed by water, and the conical top is secured to steam the mixture. The completed stew is removed from the fire and eaten from the dish by scooping it with pulls of flatbread. Variations include sweet lamb tagine with prunes and roasted almonds, and chicken tagine with olives and pickled lemon.

Couscous is usually reserved for special occasions. The grain is created by taking wheat semolina, wetting it with handfuls of water, and rolling it between the palms to break it down into tiny granules. The standard couscous pot has a tall bottom, which houses the meat and vegetables, and a steamer with tiny holes that fits above. Often, marinated meat, root vegetables, onion, and tomatoes are added, along with chickpeas, several cups of water and spices to taste. Dry couscous is placed in the top and covered

for steaming. Everything is left to cook down, adding water as needed to keep the mixture soup-like. When cooking is done, the couscous is fluffed with a fork and spread in a large dish with the meat in the center and vegetables spooned around it. The broth is poured over all to moisten and the remainder is usually reserved to add as desired.

Life's Milestones

When a Moroccan baby is born, the first words spoken to it are "Allah oo'akbar" ("God is great"), also known as the Call to Prayer. Seven days later the baby is named, its head is shaved and a sheep is slaughtered, all accompanied by Qur'anic verses and prayer. Community members offer sugar, tea and other food items. A child's name usually has some family significance, with the exception of the first-born son, who is named after the Prophet Mohammed or some derivative thereof. Circumcision normally occurs between seven and 12 years of age.

Marriage ceremonies are the most extravagant of Moroccan celebrations and can last up to three days. The men normally lounge and drink tea in a separate room from the women, who dance and feast dressed in embroidered silk kaftan dresses. Before the ceremony, the bride's hands and feet are traditionally decorated with intricate henna (dye from a henna plant) designs that symbolize fertility and a fortunate life. Later, throughout the celebration, the bride is ushered through several changes of ornate, custom-made kaftans, headdresses, and gold jewelry.

Funerals are simple and mournful. Traditionally, the body is shrouded and paraded through town before being laid in a tomb above ground, facing Mecca.

CULTURAL HISTORY

Art & Architecture

Morocco is a Muslim country and its culture is best explored in the context of Islam, a religion that has influenced the country's evolution over thousands of years. Prior to the establishment of Islam during the seventh century, art and culture in Morocco dated back to the Neolithic period, a prehistoric period of the Stone Age that began around 10,000 BCE in the Middle East. Rock engravings from Neolithic cultures dating between 4000 and 2000 BCE can be found between the Anti-Atlas Mountains and the Draa Valley. Following this period, the Berber people were largely the first inhabitants of what is now Morocco and Northern Africa, with their settlement in the area dating beyond the pre-Roman era. Ceramics offer some of the only lasting evidence of their art and culture.

However, Berber culture became largely integrated with Islam and other invading cultures and peoples. As such, other developments in art, particularly painting, are minimal, as Islam objects to artistic representation of living things. Furthermore, religious architecture has always been the greater focus, as evidenced in the grandeur of Morocco's Islamic mosques, the oldest of which dates back to the ninth century.

Painting in Morocco began to flourish in the early-to mid-20th century, largely due to the influence of European painters. The prevalent style of this period was pictorial and landscape painting, most notably Moroccan social scenes and life. Famous painters from this era include Mohamed Ben Ali R'Bati (1861–1939), Moulay Ahmed Drissi (1924–1973) and Mohamed Ben Allal (1924–1995). In addition, many Moroccan painters during the 20th century were self-taught.

Zellij, the intricate had-cut mosaics that often decorate the walls and floors of mosques and palaces throughout Morocco, is one of the most lasting of Morocco's art forms. It was influenced by the mosaics of the Byzantines and Moorish Spain and flourished in Morocco between the 10th and 14th centuries. Brilliant palettes and complex geometrical patterns typically distinguish Zellij. In fact, there are more than 360 shapes in the portfolio of a standard zellij artist. Other traditional arts from Morocco include carpet weaving and calligraphy.

Historically, Moroccan architecture has been largely influenced by Islamic architecture, which is characterized by decorative calligraphy, elaborate domes, arches, minarets and courtyards, and complex geometrical patterns. Moroccan architecture was also heavily influenced by Spanish architecture and traditions, particularly during the Middle Ages.

Morocco's numerous mosques are perhaps the best examples of the nation's rich architectural history. The oldest mosque in Morocco dates back to the ninth century. Mosques all share similar construction: tall minarets and courtyards with a central pool. Decorations are typically abstract to avoid imitating God's creations, and the most notable are elaborately tiled with gilt, a golden finishing.

Music & Dance

Morocco is home to a rich musical tradition. One of the country's distinctive styles is Arab-Andalucian music, a blend of Arab and Spanish influences largely developed in ninth century Muslim Spain by a Persian composer named Ziryeb. He is credited with creating the nawha, a system of alternating rhythm and vocals and instruments that is highly orchestral. Its formality lends itself to ceremonial celebrations and religious observation. Another musical tradition is Gnaoua, or Gnawa, which dates back to the 16th century. This type of music combines drums, reed pipes and metal castanets, a percussion instrument, to create intensely rhythmic songs. Often, these songs recount the journeys of slaves from sub-Saharan Africa.

In addition, Moroccan music is usually accompanied by dancing, a favorite mode of expression at holidays and celebrations. The most notable dance is haidous, where alternating circles of men and women sing and undulate shoulder to shoulder around a group of traditional drummers. A'houaj is a derivative of haidous that is performed by women alone, typically in a circle of performing musicians.

Literature

Because of hundreds of years of social and political change and development—most notably colonialism, government censorship and illiteracy—Moroccan literature saw little development outside of the Qur'an and other supporting religious texts. Nonetheless, the founding of the University of Al-Karaouine in the city of Fez in 859 was largely influential in the development of Moroccan literature. Early significant Moroccan writers include Ibn Battuta, a 13th century explorer and scholar who recorded his exotic travels; the poet Malik ibn al-Murahhal (1207–1300); and Ahmad al-Mansur, the "poet-king" who reigned as a sultan from 1578–1603.

Generally, mainstream literature did not gain a foothold until the late 19th century, and even then, it was mainly bland, traditional poetry that could escape government scrutiny. During the 20th century, Mohammed Khaïr-Eddine (1914–1995) was considered one of Morocco's greatest and most influential writers, renowned for his poetic and distinctly Moroccan voice. Several other contemporary writers have emerged in the last century to voice perspectives on the colonial independence movement and other sensitive social issues. Among them is Ahmed Sefrioui (1915–2004), a Berber writer who is celebrated for illuminating ordinary Moroccan life through colorful characters. His works include *La Boite á Merveilles* ("The Box of Wonders"), an autobiographical novel written in 1952. Another influential contemporary writer is Tahar ben Jelloun (b. 1944–), noted as one of the most outspoken critics of his time for his portrayal of the Moroccan emigration experience.

CULTURE

Arts & Entertainment

Moroccan architecture often shows European and Moorish influences. Western-style entertainment is sparse in this conservative Islamic nation. Movie theaters are common in large cities, but films are usually dubbed in French.

Cultural festivals, such as the Festival of Popular Art in Marrakech, are commonly held in the spring. Traditional Berber storytelling and music shows are commonplace. Traditional music is played with the rabab, ud, qanun and percussion. Modern urban music is called rai, featuring both modern and traditional instrumentation.

Despite difficult odds surrounding trade and standards, Moroccan artisans create some of the most exquisite and most enduring works in the world. Trades such as weaving textiles, leatherwork, sewing and embellishing traditional jelleba and kaftan garments, hammering and etching jewelry and brassware are time-honored traditions that have been passed down through generations of political repression and turmoil.

Artisan cooperatives are gaining ground in modern-day Morocco. Members of these cooperatives have been responding favorably to rules and practices. As a result, their collaboration is consistently profitable and is encouraging sound business practices.

Largely, however, Moroccan artisans don't have the luxury of artistic expression; art is a livelihood, and a family's well-being may depend upon its success. Artisans learn their trade at an early age, usually by attending an apprenticeship program. Unfortunately, these programs do not discriminate between applicants and the market is sometimes flooded with large volumes of inventory. In addition, artisans are commonly taught craft but not business skills.

The thuya artists of Essaouira are one example. Made from the thuya tree, a sweetly fragrant conifer that is indigenous to Morocco, their intricately carved woodwork is found in wealthy homes and religious monuments and is highly regarded for its exceptional workmanship. The thuya artisans, however, cannot depend upon the occasional commissioned work, and turn instead to the tourist market. The result, predictably, is that too many artisans saturate the market with hundreds of mass-produced wooden trinkets. Prices are driven down until the artisans are no longer profitable. Additionally, the thuya forests are being depleted rapidly because they cannot keep up with production demands.

This lack of business understanding or regulation also manifests itself in the rural carpet trade as well. Carpet weaving is typically considered women's work, and is often delegated to woman and children whose husbands and fathers have left to seek work in the cities. Because they are not allowed to travel outside their village, the women must pass their carpets to an intermediary who transports them to town and brokers their sale at a carpet house. In the end, the money is absorbed by the carpet merchant and the broker, with barely five percent trickling down to the woman who made it. More and more, various international aid organizations are intervening to assemble the village women and form cooperatives that regulate processes and protect profitability.

In addition to issues of fair trade, another consequence of a deregulated arts sector is health and safety risks, as evidenced by the pottery industry. These poor standards for dyes and glazes have hurt domestic sales as well as any prospect of exportation. Leatherworkers in Fes traditionally dye hides using antiquated methods of stomping the leather in giant vats of dye and pigeon dung. So-called "advances" in production, have replaced some natural dyes with chemical compounds, and prolonged exposure causes artisans to develop respiratory disease and infection.

Cultural Sites & Landmarks

Morocco is home to many cultural treasures, both historical and contemporary. The Palais de la Bahia, or Bahia Palace, is a private palace built in the late 19th century in Marrakesh. The royal palace's architecture combines elements of Spanish and Islamic architecture. In contrast, a visit to a Berber ksar (fortified village), typically fashioned out of mud and clay, offers a look at simple, ancient construction that has stood the test of time. One such site, Aït Benhaddou in Ouarzazate, is a United Nations Educational, Scientific and Cultural Organization (UNESCO) World Heritage Site. The site has also been featured in a number of Hollywood films, including *Lawrence of Arabia* (1962) and *Gladiator* (2000).

Morocco is home to seven other UNESCO World Heritage sites. The Roman ruins of Volubilis date back to the third century BCE and are found outside Meknes, a city in northern

Morocco. Another is the ancient Medina of Fez, founded in the ninth century. Medinas are older, walled, maze-like sections of ancient Northern African cities. The medina in Fez houses a wealth of architecture from the thirteenth and fourteenth centuries and is home to what is considered the oldest operating university in the world, University Al-Kairaouine. The medinas of the cities of Essaouira, Marrakesh, and Tétouan are also designated as World Heritage Sites. Others include the historic city of Meknes and the fortified Portuguese city of Mazagan, which was designated in 2004 for its blend of Moroccan and European culture.

Two of Morocco's most renowned mosques are the Kairaouine Mosque in Fez and the Hassan II Mosque in Casablanca. The Kairaouine is the oldest mosque in Morocco, having been built in the ninth century. The Hassan II Mosque is considered the second largest in the world, topped only by Masjid al-Haram in the holy city of Mecca. Other religious sites include the Mausoleum of Moulay Ismail in Meknes and the modern Mausoleum of Mohammed V and Hassan II in Rabat.

The old section of Rabat, known as the medina is a popular shopping destination. Lined with busy stalls, it offers everything from a leatherwork bazaar to embroidery, carpets, brass bowls, and fresh mint leaves for tea.

Morocco is also gaining popularity as an ecotourism destination due to the country's abundance of natural treasures. The Middle Atlas, the heartland of Morocco, features the Cascade d'Ouzoud waterfall amid a surprising oasis of lush forests. In the High Atlas Mountains, Toubkal National Park is home to Northern Africa's highest peak. Toubkal Mountain stands at 4,167 meters, or 2.6 miles. The park was created in 1942 and offers visitors opportunities to hike and camp while overlooking the Marrakesh countryside. To the east are the deep and snaking Gorges of Boulmane Dades and Tinghrir, which draw hikers and climbers to their sheer, steep faces.

Further southwest outside of Agadir, in cooperation with the United Nations, the Souss-Massa

National Park, and Biological Reserve was formed as a preservation and conservation effort. Visitors can observe over a dozen species of plants and animals that have eluded extinction. Preserved species include the bald ibis, Barbary macaque, African marsh owl, Spanish festoon butterfly, fir tree, and cork oak.

The Sahara Desert is considered Morocco's most majestic natural wonder. The vast desert is best accessed from the Errachidia province, where visitors trek on camelback to the immense Dunes of Merzouga, a spectacular dune field containing numerous oases.

Libraries & Museums

Besides archaeological monuments, Rabat is also home to several museums, including the Archaeology Museum and the Museum of Science and Nature. The prize exhibit in the former is a collection of ancient Roman artifacts. The science museum contains an impressive reconstructed Atlasaurus skeleton. Another museum in Rabat is the Currency Museum, located at the Bank Al-Maghrib.

Holidays

Public holidays in Morocco are a combination of national holidays and religious observances. National holidays include the Feast of the Throne (March 3), Islamic New Year (April 8), National Feast (May 23), Anniversary of the King's and People Revolution (August 20), Anniversary of the Green March (November 6), and Independence Day (November 18). The birthday of the current monarch is also celebrated as a national holiday.

Moroccans also observe all of the major Muslim holidays, including Ramadan, Eid al-Fitr, and Eid al-Adha.

Youth Culture

American pop culture continues to be an overriding fascination for urban Moroccan youth in the early 21st century. For example, popular television programming includes edited versions of *Baywatch* and *Beverly Hills 90210*. In addition, movie theatres show American releases dubbed in French, and the discotheques, or dance clubs and venues, play the latest in American and European pop music. Despite conservative dress codes, denim jeans have become a fashion staple and American products such as Coca-Cola have become household names. Moreover, McDonald's restaurants are as popular for their environment—modern décor and televisions broadcasting the Music Television (MTV) network—as for their food.

For the rural demographic, where running water and electricity can be considered luxuries, the culture remains traditional. Teens are segregated, and boys play soccer while girls gather at home. Whereas urban teens are discouraged from working until their studies are completed, rural youth contribute to their household income by apprenticing with artisans in town (boys) or weaving rugs and making traditional handicrafts (girls).

As in other cultures in the early 21st century, advanced technology greatly influences socialization among young people. Cell phones are inexpensive and most popular among young men. Internet cafés are numerous and popular, and an hour of usage costs little more than a typical soft drink. Both of these media make it easy to build friendships and to engage in communication, often across gender, which is otherwise prohibited in Muslim culture.

SOCIETY

Transportation

Moroccans drive on the right hand side of the road. The United States Department of state warns visitors to the country of dangers related to road travel, given the lack of driver education and traffic laws. Additionally, many roads are poorly lit and many traffic lights do not function properly. Roads in rural regions of Morocco are often unpaved. Only about 29.5 percent of roads are paved. As for international travel, there are 55 airports (31 paved) in the country (2013).

Throughout Morocco, walking is the most common mode of transportation. The towns and cities are laid out practically, with all major activity being centrally located, and are very walkable. Cars are a luxury and rather unnecessary as taxis, buses or trains are inexpensive and easy to access. Inter-city taxis are typically cheap and numerous. Bikes and mopeds are popular alternatives for urban young men. Many towns also offer a taxi stand of old Mercedes-Benz cars that provide a faster and more comfortable intracity travel option. Passengers can buy one seat or an entire taxi, understanding that drivers sell four seats in the back of the car and three in the front.

Transportation Infrastructure

There are 55 airports in Morocco. Of the total airports, 31 of them have paved runways as of 2013. Trains run frequently between the larger cities and buses are plentiful, connecting between most cities and towns. Despite the advantage of availability, public transportation can be slow and unpredictable. Buses are old and frequently break down, and navigating the mountainous terrain throughout the country can cause accidents and slow traffic. As a result, the culture has adapted a slower pace, particularly in rural regions, where transport to town may come only once a day or once a week.

Media & Communications

Morocco is a sovereign state, which owns and operates its media. The government supports freedom of expression and freedom of the press, though these rights are rarely protected. This is especially evident in reporting on Islam and affairs of the monarchy, as journalists are frequently prosecuted and jailed for criticism. Cell phones and computers are very popular among young men and women wanting to communicate covertly with 44 million users. Internet usage in 2014 was estimated at 60.3 percent of the population (19.9 million users).

Morocco's primary television network is the state operated Radiodiffusion Télévision Marocaine (RTM). The network broadcasts programming in languages such as Arabic, French, Berber, Spanish, and English. RTM also operates a radio network and some private networks.

Most other radio stations are broadcast out of Tangier or Casablanca, with Radio Casablance, 2M Radio and Radio Sawa Morocco among the more popular stations. The official Moroccan news agency is the state-owned Maghreb Arab Press, which publishes in Arabic, French, Spanish, and English. There are roughly twenty-six daily newspapers in Morocco. As of 2009, the broadcast stations include AM NA, FM 15, and shortwave NA.

The Berber community accounts for 50 percent of the population but is rarely represented in the media, largely because Berbers live almost exclusively in Morocco's rural south and west. The Berber language is divided into three primary dialects (Tamazight, Tashelheit, and Tarifit). The language has been fighting for survival, as schoolchildren conduct their studies in Dirija (Moroccan Arabic) and, later, French. Additionally, the Qur'an and all religious communications are conveyed in Classical Arabic, which further alienates the illiterate and unschooled. This splintering of language inhibits access to higher education, resulting in dramatic class divisions. Upon taking the throne in 1999, King Mohamed VI launched an initiative to integrate Berber dialects into the school curriculum in an effort to unify communication among the general population.

SOCIAL DEVELOPMENT

A moderately developed nation, Morocco relies on tourism, textiles, agriculture and mining, although at the turn of the 21st century, the monarchy is gradually allowing foreign investment in energy, and manufacturing and striving to improve education.

Standard of Living

Despite the fact that Morocco is a wealthy country, much of its population is poor, particularly those living in rural areas. The country ranked 129th out of 182 countries on the 2014 Human Development Index. Moroccans living in rural areas continue to live off subsistence farming and remain malnourished and without access to education. Major cities in the country, such as Casablanca, are home to Morocco's elite, wealthy class, but they are in the minority.

Water Consumption

Although tap water and bottled water is available in major cities in Morocco, in rural areas, the availability of clean water remains a cause for concern. In recent years, the government has introduced the Rural Water and Sanitation Project. The World Bank has provided a $60 million loan to support the project. In addition to demographic pressures, Morocco has contended with recurring drought in the past two decades, which have further exacerbated its water problems. As of 2011, the renewable water resources consist of about 29 cu km.

Education

Education reform is a major challenge for Morocco. The country's literacy rate is just over 50 percent. However, significant progress is being made among young people between 15 and 24 years of age. Among this group, literacy improved from 55 percent in 1990 to an estimated 68 percent in 2001.

Primary school is mandatory for nine years, although there is a significant discrepancy between attendance among boys and girls, with girls falling about ten percent below the full attendance of boys. There is also a large discrepancy between children of Arabic and Berber descent. Berber children are more likely to leave school at a young age due to the use of the Arabic language in almost all primary schools.

Less than half of young people in Morocco receive secondary education. Alternatives for higher education have expanded greatly since 1970, moving beyond the traditional religious institutions Al Qarawiyin University in Fez and Mohammed V University in Rabat to include new universities in Fez, Rabat, Marrakech, Casablanca, Agadir, Ifrane, and Oujda.

Morocco's national literacy rate was an estimated 68.5 percent in 2015—78.6 percent among males and 58.8 percent among females.

Women's Rights

The status of Moroccan women is complicated and seemingly contradictory. As mothers and caretakers they are regarded as the nucleus of the family, and are typically and traditionally shown considerable respect by their children and community. In fact, to shame a young man who is acting disgracefully one says "Seer al muk" ("Go to your mother"), which serves to remind him that his poor behavior dishonors her reputation. However, outside of the home, women are consistently dismissed from the legal realm and have a weak voice in the political process.

In recent years, particularly under the reign of King Mohammed VI, steps have been taken to elevate the position of women. Learning from the success of other forward-thinking Muslim administrations, such as Jordan, the king and his advisors recognize that women represent a sizeable segment of the population. They have realized that to improve women's standing stimulates the country's growth overall. This is an attractive prospect when the government is grappling with an average 40 percent illiteracy rate and eight percent unemployment rate in the early 21st century.

A top priority for the women's movement is the push for greater legal rights, particularly for married women. In 2003, the king announced a revolutionary new Family Law. In a historic triumph for gender-equity, the law highlighted the following: the legal marrying age for women was raised from 15 to 18 (the same as men); women were given the right to divorce and the right to divorce by mutual consent with a court-ordered ruling (whereas men previously had the right to a unilateral divorce with no financial obligations); and the practice of polygamy was made conditional upon the consent of the current wife. Recognized internationally for its expert blending of women's rights and Muslim heritage, this law is proving to be a significant step toward integrating women into the political process.

Equally as important is access to higher education and professional development. Female-centric literacy programs are on the rise, reaching far into even the most rural areas. International grass-roots organizations, often in cooperation with the Moroccan government, are finding success in providing resources for women to learn to read and write. Furthermore, participants in these programs consistently highlight improved senses of self-worth and initiative. Many go on to take part in micro-credit programs and small business enterprises. In urban settings, international corporations are demonstrating their solidarity by offering trainings in business, administration, and information technology. Many of these programs also lend career counseling or job placement assistance and are showing exceptional participation and retention rates.

As of 2014, there have been major issues with the laws. In 2004, Morocco rewrote the code of family laws that placed limits on polygamy and raised the minimum marriage age for women from 15 to 18 years old. Despite the changes, judges continue to grant permission in most cases.

One law, set down in the Quran, states that male relatives receive two times the amount of inheritance. The problem is that, as of 2014, more women have become the ones who support, or providing significant contributions to, their families. This has caused much of uproar among feminists in Morocco.

Lastly, international organizations such as the UN Development Fund for Women (UNIFEM) continue to expose inequalities and encourage development. In addition, the Democratic Association of Moroccan Women (ADFM) advocates for further reform. Overall, awareness is mounting and the cultural mindset is evolving. For Moroccan women, the next generation promises to be one of increased socio-political maturity.

Health Care

There are both state-sponsored and private health care systems in Morocco. For-profit clinics are common in cities. There are more than 2,000 basic care units across the country and more than 100 hospitals. Good health care is far more prevalent in urban areas than among the rural population.

GOVERNMENT

Structure

Although occupied by British and American forces during World War II, Morocco formally gained independence from France in 1956. The government became a constitutional monarchy in 1962, with its first elections held in 1963. However, the monarch retains ultimate power. The king appoints a prime minister to head the legislature and a cabinet called the Council of Ministers, currently Abdelilah Benkirane (appointed 11/29/2011). Moroccan law specifies that the monarch must be male.

The constitution was revised three times between 1972 and 1996. The last revision created a popularly elected bicameral legislature. The 325 members of the House of Representatives are popularly elected to five-year terms. The 270 members of the Chamber of Advisers (Councilors) are elected to six-year terms either by vote of local political councils, or as representatives of business interests or labor unions.

The judiciary includes the Supreme Court in Rabat (with justices appointed by the king), courts of appeal, regional and local tribunals and 14 labor tribunals. Eighteen months of military service is required for all Moroccan men.

Political Parties

Political parties in Morocco encompass a wide spectrum of ideologies and philosophies. On the left, there are such parties as the Socialist Union of People's Forces, the People's Movement, and the National Popular Movement. The right is comprised of the Independence Party, the Justice and Development Party, the National Rally of Independents, and the Constitutional Union. There are also centrist parties, including the Authenticity and Modernity Party and the Amazigh Moroccan Democratic Party, among others. The king appoints the prime minister of Morocco.

Local Government

There are about 1,500 local councils, called communes, which are grouped into 39 provinces and eight prefectures. These are further grouped into sixteen administrative regions, known as cercles, which are headed by individuals known as superqaids or caidats. Superqaids govern with the help of a council of nine to 51 members (depending on the land area of the region) who are elected to six-year terms. The Ministry of the Interior, which is overseen by the king, oversees divisions of local government.

Judicial System

The Moroccan judicial system is comprised of both secular and judicial courts. The most power secular court in the country is the Supreme Court, which is divided into five separate chambers. These chambers are named after the types of cases they hear; the constitutional, administrative, criminal, civil appeals, and social. The secular judicial system also consists of lower courts, including appellate courts, district courts, and communal courts. A military court oversees cases involving the country's armed forces.

Additionally, criminal and civil cases are heard in Morocco by a system of twenty-seven Sadad courts, which operate under Islamic law and, in some cases, Jewish law.

Taxation

Morocco's taxation system has undergone significant and rapid change in the past two decades, as the country has begun to do more business with the European Union and become a full member of the World Trade Organization. As of 2014, taxes and other revenues have consisted of 26.1 percent of the GDP. Moroccan corporations operate under a unitary tax system, which means their taxes are based on worldwide taxable income. This prevents companies from taken advantage of what might be more favorable tax conditions in other parts of the world.

Citizens of Morocco and those who make their residence in the country pay a personal income tax. This tax is based on individual revenue and can range from 13 percent to over 40 percent. Property taxes are paid, though mostly in urban areas.

Armed Forces

The Royal Moroccan Armed force has three main branches: the Royal Moroccan Air Force, Army, and Navy. The Royal Moroccan Gendarmerie, Auxiliary Forces, and the Moroccan Royal Guard make up the smaller branches of the kingdom's armed forces. The total number of enlisted members is just over 225,000. As of 2012, 20 is the voluntary military age.

Foreign Policy

Morocco had been under Arab rule for roughly seven centuries before European interest began to take shape in the 15th century. By the mid-19th century, France had established a "sphere of influence" over Morocco and received government approval to police the country jointly with Spain. By 1912, the Treaty of Fes declared Morocco a protectorate of France and allocated the northern and southern zones to Spain. This continued through World War II, which brought forth the Atlantic Charter in 1941. This agreement between the United States (US) and Britain stated that people have a right to choose their own government. This incited talk of independence and nationalist movements took root, eventually earning Morocco independence from France in 1956.

Since then Morocco has proven itself as a moderate Islamic state. The government maintains close relationships with Europe, particularly the European Union (UN), and the U.S. It is a member of the UN and actively contributes to peacekeeping agreements in Africa and abroad. Morocco is also a member of the Arab League, the Organization of the Islamic Conference (OIC) and the Non-Aligned Movement. Furthermore, the Moroccan government consistently supports peace in the Middle East and has maintained international relations with Israel. In addition, Morocco has assisted in stabilizing Iraq after the U.S.-led invasion in 2003, and has repeatedly denounced terrorist activity domestically and abroad.

However, despite a rather sterling record of international diplomacy, Morocco has been involved in the disputed Western Saharan territory. The Western Sahara is inhabited by the Saharawi tribe. The territory was first administered by Spain, as declared by the Treaty of Fes. On November 12, 1975, Morocco (claiming religious sovereignty over the Saharawi tribe) invaded the Western Sahara via King Hassan II's famed "Green March" of 350,000 unarmed civilians. Subsequently, Spain, Mauritania, and Morocco established a partnership to share administration of the territory, with Spain eventually relinquishing its responsibilities. However, in 1976 the Polisario Front, a rebel Saharawi organization or movement for the independence of Western Sahara established the Sahrawi Arab Democratic Republic (SADR). This partially recognized state claimed sovereignty over Western Sahara. Three years later, in 1979, Mauritania also surrendered claims on the territory. The Polisario continues to oppose Moroccan occupation, and relations remain fragile.

A one-time member of the African Union (AU), Morocco withdrew from the organization in 1981 when the AU granted delegation to the Polisario. Although the Moroccan government and the Polisario entertain negotiations, no agreement has ever been achieved. Continued efforts by the UN to broker cease-fires and other peacekeeping terms have met with little success. The Moroccan government remains unwavering in its position as sovereign of the Saharawi people and administrator of the Western Sahara. This stance has also resulted in a tenuous relationship with neighboring Algeria, whose leaders support the independence of the Saharawi tribe and its right to choose its government. The Moroccan government recently proposed an autonomy plan for a certain degree of self-government of Western Sahara, which was rejected by the Polisario Front.

The dispute over the Western Sahara is a delicate subject for any Moroccan. Tribes of the far south are continuously embroiled in the pressure to support their government unconditionally in the face of repeated atrocities. The conflict in the Western Sahara remains urgent not only in the foreign policy domain, but on the international human rights front as well.

Human Rights Profile

International human rights law insists that states respect civil and political rights, and promote an individual's economic, social, and cultural rights. The United Nations Universal Declaration on Human Rights (UDHR) is recognized as the standard for international human rights. Its authors sought the counsel of the world's great thinkers, philosophers, and religious leaders, and were careful to create a document that reflects the core values shared by every world culture. To read this document or view the articles relating to cultural human rights, visit http://www.udhr.org/UDHR/default.htm.

Morocco's stance on the UN Universal Declaration on Human Rights would seem rather neutral. Domestic matters rarely make the international news and the government is not prone to sensational acts of violence or oppression. Nevertheless, Morocco is on the radar of top human rights advocates for its repeated violations of UDHR articles. These include Article 10 (the right to fair trial), Article 18 (the right to freedom of thought) and Article 19 (the right to freedom of opinion and expression), particularly in reference to the continued dispute over occupation of the Western Sahara.

The Western Sahara and its inhabitants, the Saharawi tribe, have been caught in the crossfire between the Polisario and the Moroccan army, which has occupied the territory since 1975. Morocco administers 80 percent of the territory and fights to maintain this presence based on its disputed claim that the majority of the Saharawi people favor Moroccan occupation. Human rights groups have reported instances of intimidation and silencing of advocates of independence by Morocco.

Indeed, Morocco's interior ministry officially supports the allocation of space for public assembly and protest. However, peaceful activists and members of non-governmental human rights organizations are consistently arrested and harassed, beaten, even tortured, because they are attacking Morocco's "territorial integrity." Moreover, in a blatant violation of Article 10, legal trials meant to expose the corruption are often dismissed. In one such case, two representatives of a human rights organization were arrested, beaten, and forced to sign one-page statements that they were not allowed to read. They were then told that the statements would be used against them if they continued their activities. Later, when granted an impartial trial, only the Moroccan police were permitted to testify and the investigation was closed.

This treatment is not exclusive to human rights groups and protesters. In fact, the victims are most frequently Moroccan journalists who choose to practice their freedom of expression by investigating injustices in the Western Sahara. Often, these journalists are arrested and convicted of "publishing false information that disturbs public order." Similar convictions result when a journalist publically questions the king's policies or Islamic law. In addition, advocacy efforts by organizations such as the Human Rights Watch and Amnesty International are regularly ignored by the Moroccan authorities.

ECONOMY

Overview of the Economy

Morocco's economic growth has been hampered by its shortcomings in higher education. However, inflation has remained low and the economy has remained stable. In 2000, the government initiated a new program to fight poverty, improve education, and strengthen industry, including privatization and incentives for oil and gas exploration.

In 2014, the per capita gross domestic product (GDP) was estimated at $7,600 (USD). By comparison, per capita GDP in highly industrialized nations is usually more than $30,000 (USD).

Industry

Industry accounts for about 20.3 percent of employment and 24.9 percent of GDP. The European Union consumes the great majority of Moroccan exports.

Phosphate production is Morocco's principal industry. Petroleum and steel processing have increased since 1980. Traditional crafts industries, especially textiles and leatherwork, are also important to the economy.

Labor

The total labor force consists of 12 million people. Urban unemployment remained around 9.1 percent in 2014, although it was as high as 30 percent in some areas. In 1999, approximately 19 percent of the population was living below the poverty line.

Energy/Power/Natural Resources

Morocco has limited energy resources and imports more energy than any other North African country. In 2007, nearly 70 percent of its energy came from oil, and over 20 percent came from coal. In 2010, oil imports estimated at 122,900 bbl/day. Crude oil imported by the country is domestically refined. Morocco also generates energy from thermal power plants and hydroelectric plants. Government officials, with the assistance of the United States, have taken preliminary steps to establish a nuclear power plant, which Morocco intends to use for desalination and electricity. About 22 percent of electricity comes from hydroelectric plants and only 4.9 percent of comes from renewable sources.

Natural resources exported by Morocco include phosphates, fish, and manganese, lead, silver, and copper.

Fishing

Morocco's coastal location has made fishing a major industry for generations. In 2000, the country harvested more fish than any other African country. The country's canning industry processes a large annual harvest of sardines, and deep-sea octopus, squid, and shrimp. Morocco exported $950 million worth of fish products to Europe and the United States in 2000.

Forestry

Since the 1980s, Morocco has initiated a reforestation initiative that has increased the amount of woodlands in the country. Forestry itself is not a major industry in Morocco, and accounts for approximately $120 million in exports annually. The country's principal forest product is cork.

Mining/Metals

Morocco is the world's third largest producer of phosphate for use in fertilizers, and phosphate accounts for about 87 percent of mineral exports. Total mining output accounts for 35 percent of total exports. Most of the mining industry is state-owned, although efforts toward privatization are underway.

Agriculture

Agricultural products are Morocco's principal export to the European Union. These include fish and fruits (citrus, grapes, dates); produce (tomatoes) and flowers. Crops grown for domestic consumption include wheat, barley, beets, olives, and potatoes.

Agricultural accounts for 40 percent of employment in Morocco. As a whole, agriculture accounts for about 15 percent of GDP.

Animal Husbandry

Moroccan farmers raise sheep and goats. Periods of drought and overgrazed land have had detrimental effect on livestock as a source of agriculture. Nonetheless, Morocco produced approximately 150,000 tones of beef and mutton in 2001 and some 255,000 tons of poultry.

Tourism

Services, led by tourism, account for 35 percent of jobs in Morocco. More than two million tourists visit annually, most from Europe. In addition to resorts in the large cities, smaller resort communities cater primarily to tourists. For example, Agadir is a favorite of German tourists.

Heidi Edsall, John Pearson, M. Lee

DO YOU KNOW?

- Morocco was the first nation to recognize the independence of the United States in 1777.

- Morocco claims the world's oldest university (the University of Fez, founded in 859).

- The famous film *Casablanca* (1942), set in the Moroccan city, was largely shot in Florida. However, more recent productions such as *Black Hawk Down* (2001), *The Mummy* (1999), and *Alexander* (2004) have all been filmed on location in Morocco.

- Rabat is one of four cities in Morocco, the others being Fez, Meknes, and Marrakesh, which have served as the country's capital at one point or another. For that reason, Rabat is known as one of the country's "imperial cities."

Bibliography

Daniel Jacobs and Keith Drew. *Rough Guide to Morocco.* London: Rough Guides, 2013.

David Crawford, et al. *Encountering Morocco: Fieldwork and Cultural Understanding.* Bloomington, IN: Indiana University Press, 2013.

Donna Lee Bowen and Evelyn A. Early. *Everyday Life in the Muslim Middle East.* Bloomington, IN: Indiana University Press, 2002.

Frederick Matthewson Denny. *An Introduction to Islam.* Upper Saddle River, NJ: Pearson Prentice Hall, 2011.

Lawrence Rosen. *The Culture of Islam.* Chicago, IL: University of Chicago Press, 2002.

Orin Hargraves. *Culture Shock—Morocco! The Essential Guide to Customs and Culture.* London: Kuperard, 2012.

Paul Clammer, et al. "Morocco." Oakland, CA: Lonely Planet, 2014.

Raphael C. Njoku. *Culture and Customs of Morocco.* Santa Barbara, CA: Greenwood Press, 2005.

Susan Gilson Miller. *A History of Modern Morocco.* New York: Cambridge University Press, 2013.

Works Cited

"Amazigh World." http://www.amazighworld.org.

"Amnesty." Amnesty International. http://www.amnesty.org.

"Arabic News.com." *Arabic News.* http://www.arabicnews.com.

"HRW." *Human Rights Watch.* http://www.hrw.org.

"Open Democracy." http://www.opendemocracy.net.

"PRB." *Population Reference Bureau.* http://www.prb.org.

"UNICEF." *UNICEF.* http://www.unicef.org.

"UNIFEM News." UNIFEM. http://www.unifem.org.

"UNOG." *United Nations Office at Geneva.* http://www.unog.ch.

"U.S. Department of State." U.S. Government. http://www.state.gov.

"World Heritage." *UNESCO.* http://whc.unesco.org. http://www.morocco.com/culture/

"WSRW." *Western Sahara Resource Watch.* http://www.state.gov.

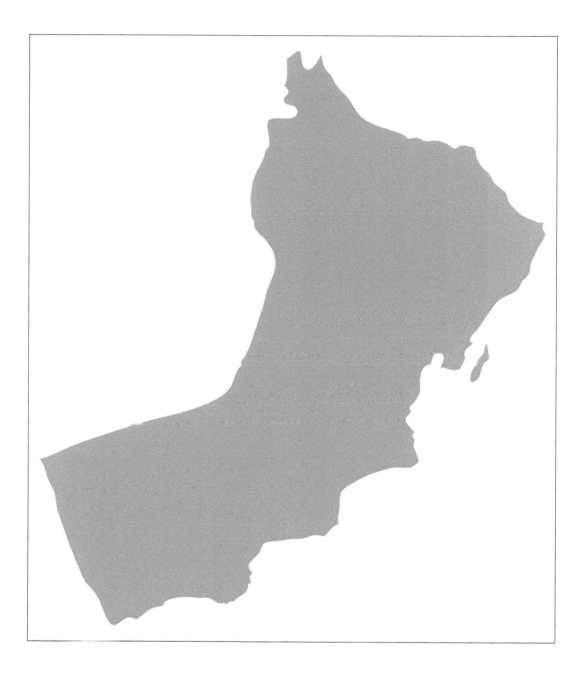

OMAN

Introduction

Oman is an independent nation in the Middle East, located on the easternmost point of the Arabian Peninsula. Known for its petroleum-rich land, ornate silver work, and incense, Oman was once famous for its frankincense trade. Its people are known as Omanis.

Prior to the 20th century, Oman was known as the Sultanate of Muscat and Oman. A sultan ruled Oman, and an imam, or religious leader, governed Muscat. This status changed in 1970, when the British government named a single sultan to govern the region, making Muscat the capital of the Sultanate of Oman.

Between January 17, 2011 and April 8, 2011, Oman experienced a wave of protests that were part of what has become known as "Arab Spring." Protestors demanded higher wages, lower costs of living, job creation, and an end to political corruption. As a result, one-third of Sultan Qaboos bin Said Al Said's consultative cabinet was dismissed and the minimum wage for private sector workers was increased by over $150 per month. The sultan also promised to create 50,000 more government positions in response to protestors' demands. The Gulf Cooperation Council (GCC), of which Oman is a member, agreed to allocate an aid plan of $10 billion USD to assist Oman in upgrading housing and infrastructure over the next decade.

GENERAL INFORMATION

Official Language: Arabic
Population: 3,219,775 (2014 estimate)

Currency: Omani rial
Coins: One hundred baisa equal one rial. Coins are issued in denominations of 5, 10, 25, and 50 baisa.
Land Area: 309,500 square kilometers (119,498 square miles)
National Anthem: "Nashid as-Salām as-Sultānī" (Arabic: "The Sultan's Anthem")
Capital: Muscat
Time Zone: GMT +4
Flag Description: The flag of Oman has a bold vertical red stripe on the hoist side, with three horizontal stripes of white (top), red (middle), and green (bottom) to the right. The country's emblem, the badge of the Al-Busaidi Dynasty, is depicted in white on the upper hoist side of the flag. The white in the flag stands for peace and prosperity, the red for former battles, and the green for fertility. A solid red flag used to serve as the former flag of the Sultanate of Muscat and Oman.

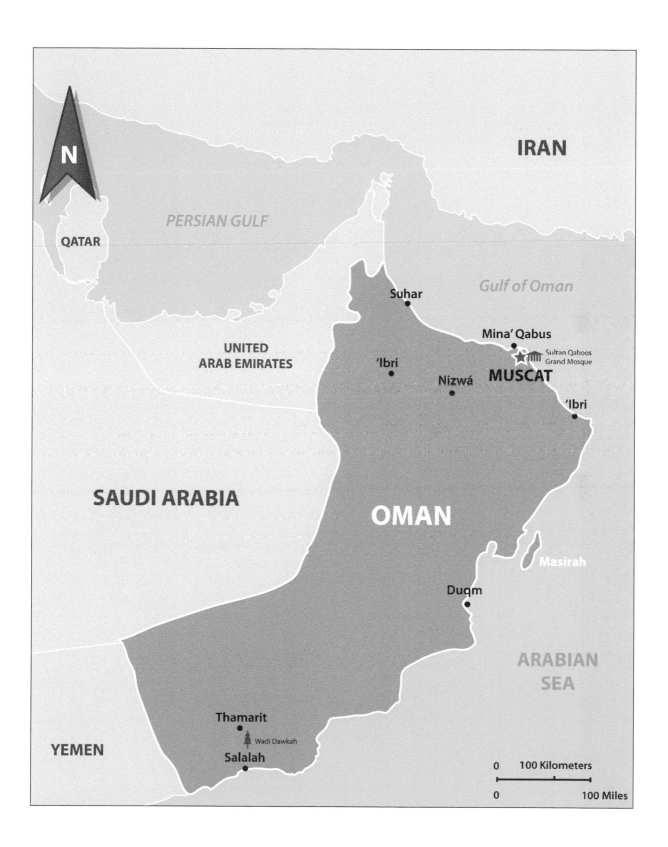

Principal Cities by Population (2014):

- Muscat (1,288,330)
- As Sib (237,816)
- Muttrah (216,578)
- Salālah (163,140)
- Bawshar (159,487)
- Suhar (also Al Sohar) (108,274)
- Al-Buraymī (96,613)
- Nizwa (72,076)
- Al-'Āmarāt (70,000)

Population

The majority of Omanis are of Arab ethnicity. Minority groups include people of Baluchi, East African, Indian, Pakistani, Sri Lankan, Bangladeshi, Persian, and African descent. The ethnic Baluchi people—also known as Baloch or Balochi—are seminomadic and hail from the Arabian Sea coast in Iran and Pakistan. Roughly, five percent of Omanis are nomadic herders, while the majority of Omanis live around the major cities.

Muscat, the capital and largest city, contains the sultan's palace and several large ancient forts. The metropolitan area of Muscat constitutes nearly 41 percent of Oman's total population and estimated to be almost 1.3 million (2015 estimate). Unlike other oil-producing nations in the region, the majority of residents in Muscat are native born, although, according to 2013 United Nations data, 30 percent of the total Omani population are immigrants and non-nationals coming primarily from India, Pakistan, Sudan, and Egypt. These expatriates, many of whom are non-skilled laborers, have filled jobs that were created in the wake of Oman's rapid growth. Still, the sustained majority of Omani-born residents can be attributed to a national program known as "Omanization," the goal of which is to replace foreign-born workers with Omanis.

Matrah (or Muttrah), in the Muscat province, is the third-largest city in terms of population and is the site of Port Sultan Qaboos (formerly Mina Qaboos), one of the Middle East's busiest ports.

Matrah remains the center of Oman's commercial activity. Other major cities in Oman include Salālah, the capital of the Dhofar region in the south, and Nizwa, which was the Omani capital during the sixth and seventh centuries. Most cities include a souk (or souq), which is a central marketplace.

Omanis who live in rural areas primarily inhabit the coastal region, which is the nation's agricultural center. In this area, known as al-Batinah (also al-Bāṭinah), most residents live in villages and work on date palm plantations. Homes along Oman's coast are typically built from palm leaves, which allow maximum ventilation. Mudbrick huts are common in the country's interior.

Omani women wear an abaya (or 'abāyah), which is a full-length cloak that is traditionally black. It covers all but the hands, feet, and face, which is usually concealed by a veil called a niqab (or niqāb) that covers all but the woman's eyes. Sometimes a full-face veil, known as a burqa (or burkha) is worn; it features a semi-transparent fabric grill that entirely conceals the features, but can be lifted if the woman wishes to reveal her eyes. The typical clothing of Omani men is the dishdasha. Formalwear for men includes a turban and a ceremonial dagger called the khanjar, which is tucked into an ornate sash. The khanjar is also at the center of Oman's official symbol, which appears on the flag.

Ethnic groups generally live in harmony in Oman, though discrimination against women is common. Women are expected to care primarily for families and are not encouraged to seek education or employment.

Languages

Although Arabic is the official language, English is also widely spoken. Other languages used in Oman include Baluchi, Urdu, Swahili, and several Indian dialects. One Arabic colloquialism, commonly used as a greeting, is "As-salamu alaykum," which means "Peace be unto you."

Native People & Ethnic Groups

The earliest inhabitants of what is now Oman were hunters and were probably members of the

Al-Āriba ethnic group (also known as Qahtani or "pure Arab," believed to be direct descendants of Noah).

The first known civilization in Oman was that of the Persians, who built an irrigation system of canals called aflaj and tunnels called qanat (or qanāt). As early as 5000 BCE, the Dhofari tribes in the far south of Oman established a trade in frankincense, an aromatic tree resin, which made the region wealthy and renowned.

Descendants of the area's native population now inhabit the Ras Musandam region, which is the northernmost tip of the peninsula formed by Oman. Ras Musandam is a small piece of Omani-owned land separated from Oman by the United Arab Emirates. The people in this region, known as the Shihuh, were driven from mainland Oman and have lived in Ras Musandam for centuries. The Shihuh, descended from native Southern Arabians, speak their own native dialect, and have their own capital, Kumzar.

In 1507, Portuguese explorers established a military presence in Oman and seized control of the frankincense trade. In addition to Portugal, Great Britain, the Netherlands, and Iran attempted to seize Oman by force. The Portuguese were finally expelled from Oman in 1650 and the Iranians in 1741.

Religions

There are several sects of Islam practiced in Oman. Three-quarters of Omani nationals are Ibadhi Muslims, though the Sunni and Shia sects are practiced as well. Overall, 85.9 percent of the population is Muslim. Christians (6.5 percent) and Hindus (5.5 percent) constitute the majority of the non-Muslim population. However, there is a small population of Buddhists (0.8 percent) and Jews (0.1 percent).

Climate

Oman's climate varies across its regions, but is generally hot and humid throughout the year. Muscat often experiences summer temperatures as high as 45° Celsius (113° Fahrenheit) and received about 10 centimeters of rain annually, while the desert plains can reach temperatures of

54° Celsius (130° Fahrenheit) and get little to no rain at all.

The Dhofar region experiences its own climate, characterized by the khareef (colloquial Arabic term for the southeastern monsoon) season during summer months. During the khareef season, the average temperature of 30° Celsius (86° Fahrenheit) drops to around 20° Celsius (68° Fahrenheit). The khareef brings light rain on a daily basis, yielding an average of 64 centimeters (25 inches). The rest of Oman receives an average annual rainfall of only 10 centimeters (four inches).

Natural hazards in Oman include flash floods, droughts, sand storms, and dust storms.

ENVIRONMENT & GEOGRAPHY

Topography

Oman borders Saudi Arabia on the west, Yemen on the southwest, the United Arab Emirates on the northwest, the Strait of Hormuz on the north, and the Arabian Sea on the south. The country's capital, Muscat, is situated along the coast of the Gulf of Oman, on the edge of the Arabian Peninsula in the northeastern part of the country. The city is surrounded by volcanic mountains on three sides. Considered an aesthetically pleasing blend of modern and ancient architecture, Muscat is comprised of a metropolitan area—approximately 3,500 square kilometers (1,400 square miles)—and an old port area.

The sultanate is comprised mostly of desert plains. The coastal plain, which includes the al-Batinah region, is the lowest in elevation and the most fertile. The inland plateau contains the Sharqiya Sands (formerly known as the Wahiba Sands), where the dunes rise as high as 61 meters (200 feet). The Al-Hajar Mountain range separates the coastal plain from the central plateau. The Al-Hajar range contains Jebel Shams, which is the nation's highest point at 3,027 meters (9,934 feet) above sea level. Another significant mountain in the Hajar range is Jebel Akhdar (meaning "The Green Mountain").

In the southern Dhofar region are the Jabal al Qara Mountains. The Rub' al-Khali, or Empty Quarter region of Saudi Arabia, is the desert that makes up eastern Oman. The northern Ras Musandam is made up of fjords and mountains.

Two sets of islands lie off the eastern shore. These are the Kuria Muria (also Khuriya Muriya) group and the larger Masirah (also Mazeira) Island. Between Ras Musandam and the northern point of mainland Oman is a small Omani-owned enclave known as Madha (or Wadi Madha).

There are no major rivers or lakes in Oman, but there are several large wadis, which are dry riverbeds, that only contain water during periods of rain. The largest of these are the Wadi Aswad and Wadi Qitbit. In addition to wadis, there are smaller streams formed by hot springs. Oman's water area is negligible.

Plants & Animals

Oman is home to several species that are endangered due to excessive hunting. These species include the oryx, which is a kind of antelope, and the tahr, a stocky, longhaired mountain goat.

Muscat gazelles and Omani wild sheep are just two mammals distinctive to the country. However, Oman's habitats also shelter fox, leopards, wild cats, panthers, wolves, hyenas, porcupines, hyrax (an herbivore resembling the North American groundhog), hedgehogs, hares, jerboa (a large-eared desert rodent), bats, toads, and lizards. There are several species of large, poisonous spiders and dangerous snakes, such as the horned viper and boa constrictor.

Oman boasts 494 bird species, which include three varieties of grebe, four varieties of petrel, and three varieties of pelican, along with kingfishers, Indian rollers, lanner falcons, sooty falcons, houbaras, Ibises, and flamingoes. The Al Hajar Mountains are also home to the Omani Owl. The ostrich, once found in Oman, have experienced localized extinction. Inland fish include the blind cavefish. Dolphins live offshore, and dolphin watching is a popular tourist activity. The Nature Reserve in Qurm Park protects many of Oman's animal species.

Plant life in Oman reflects the region's lack of precipitation, although—according to the Kew Royal Botanical Gardens taxonomic research projects—there are still 1212 vascular species within the country's borders, 79 of which are specific to Oman. Acacias are the most common trees, followed by date and coconut palms. Other trees include the golden shower tree and the royal poinciana, also known as the "flame tree" or "flamboyant tree." Especially important to Oman's trade are frankincense trees (Boswellia sacra), which grow throughout the country. Their resinous sap continues to be highly prized and, in ancient times, was more valuable than gold.

Oleander, peach, apricot, date, and almond trees grow in the Dhofar region, as do wild pansies, cowslips, and dandelions. Other indigenous varities of plant are the fruit-bearing nabag and the camelthorn, which likes dry, rocky soil, and is considered a noxious weed harmful to animals.

CUSTOMS & COURTESIES

Greetings

Omani people greet each other with a ritual of formal words and gestures. One person will begin the greeting by saying, "As-salamu alaykum" ("Peace be upon you"). It is considered polite for the other person to respond by saying "Wa-Alaikum-Salaam" ("And upon you, peace"). In addition, it is common for men to shake hands. Often, men will kiss each other three times on the cheek, alternating between cheeks. Kissing, however, is a sign of affection and is usually reserved for close friends or family.

Women will also lightly shake hands and kiss each other. However, men will not kiss women, and some Omani men may not shake hands with a woman either, especially if she is not Muslim. It is common for Bedouin men to touch nose to nose instead of kissing on the cheek.

Gestures & Etiquette

While Oman is often described as the bridge between the West and the Arab world, it remains very much a conservative, Islamic culture. As such, modest dress is expected at all times. Although there is no dress code formally enforced by the government, dressing modestly is ingrained in the Omani culture as a sign of respect and purity. Women who wear tight clothing, skirts or shorts that end above the knee, or beachwear (often forbidden by non-Western resorts not on or near the beach) are perceived as disrespectful. Indeed, such clothing is offensive to the Omani people.

Omani men must wear a white dishdasha (or dishdāshah) when conducting business. Men in all Arab nations traditionally wear this robe-like garment, although the length of the robe and sleeves can vary by country. For example, in Oman and Morocco, the sleeves tend to be shorter to allow for greater comfort in the hot climate. Business in Oman is conducted casually and informally. The culture in Oman is non-confrontational; any business tactics that use stress or pressure to persuade or make a sale are frowned upon. An Omani's career is not considered to be separate from his personal life. For this reason, honor in business dealings and saving face (that is, avoiding embarrassment) are important to all Omani citizens.

In Oman, making others feel comfortable is also important. Therefore, public displays of affection, even between spouses, are avoided. Conversations are kept low-key when out in public, and loud or boisterous behavior is rare. Privacy is highly regarded and protected, and for this reason, Omanis rarely carry or use cameras in public places.

Ramadan is the most important month of the year for Muslims. This holy month is a time of intense fasting and prayer, followed by a time of feasting and celebrating with family and friends. Muslims do not smoke, eat, or even drink during each day's hours of fasting, which last from sunrise to sunset. During this time, non-Muslims visiting or living in the sultanate are also expected to refrain from such behaviors while they are in public.

Eating/Meals

In Oman, the largest meal is eaten at midday, with a lighter meal later in the evening. Breakfast is also typically a small meal consisting of light fare, usually fruit, bread, or teas (which, along with leftovers from the midday meal, are also commonly consumed for dinner).

In traditional Omani households, family members eat separately rather than all together. The men eat first in their quarters, followed by the women and children. Food is often served on shared plates placed upon the floor, which may have a protective covering. It is considered impolite to stand while eating. Instead, Omanis kneel or sit cross-legged to eat. Meals are also eaten with the hands, particularly the right hand, which is used to serve food from the shared plates. In Muslim cultures, the left hand is used for personal cleaning, and thus considered impure.

Visiting

Omanis are known for being a gentle and hospitable people. It is not uncommon for guests to be served kahwa (strong coffee) and light fare, such as fruit or dates, upon entering the home of a host. Usually, this offering follows an invitation for the guest or guests to wash their hands. It is also customary to take off one's shoes before entering the home of another. It is also customary, but not required, to bring a simple gift.

At mealtimes, the host will typically refrain from eating until the guests have eaten. In the event of a full meal, the males will be served first in their quarters, followed by the women and children. Homes in Oman may have separate designated areas or rooms for men, for women, and for family. Children often eat and spend most of their time in the women's quarters.

LIFESTYLE

Family

Families in Oman have great influence over each other. It is considered the duty of each family member to make sure that the other family members adhere to the culture and customs of the Arab world. Any family member that does not dress or carry him or herself in the proper manner brings great shame to the entire extended family.

Men are the head of the household in Oman, and women are expected to do the bulk of the work in terms of raising the children and caring for the home. Men usually try to obtain a home of their own before they marry, while girls live in their father's house until they marry or attend university. However, sons are expected to take care of their elderly parents and will often move their wives and families to their elderly parent's home when the time comes to care for them. Although men and women have the freedom to choose their own spouses, the traditional custom of presenting the bride with a dowry is still followed by many families.

Housing

Omani families usually live in large, attached or detached villas with their entire extended family, with one family living in each villa or wing. In the center of the villas is usually a courtyard surrounded by a garden. Carports and garages are almost always provided for every residence due to the very hot summer temperatures. More traditional-style housing includes those of the Bedouins (desert-living, nomadic Arabs), who reside in tents made from the hair of their herd animals, usually camels or goats.

In urban areas, blocks of apartment buildings, mostly inhabited by expatriate workers, are common. These apartments, though rather plain on the outside, are roomier than their European or Western counterparts, as indoor space and airiness are important aspects of architecture in Oman. Many of these apartment buildings are contained in gated compounds, which also include pools and other amenities.

Food

Oman sits along the coast of the Arabian Peninsula in Southeast Asia and at the crossroads of the Far East, Middle East, and Africa. Due to its unique location, its cuisine has been influenced by many different cultures. Some of the more distinct influences include Turkish and Indian cuisine. Thus, the Omani cuisine is often considered quite different from the Arabic cuisines of neighboring Gulf States. Additionally, as with many countries, the cuisine also varies regionally.

Generally, Omani cuisine is based around rice, usually served with meats, such as chicken or fish. (Meats that are more traditional include goat, lamb, and mutton.) Due to Oman's coastal location, fish is an integral ingredient in many soups, sauces, and curries. Although traditional Omani cuisine is often regarded as rather simple, herbs and spices feature prominently, including lime and garlic and the more exotic cardamom and saffron. A staple at almost every meal in Oman is rukhal bread, which is flat and round.

Examples of traditional Omani dishes include shuwa, which is whole, cooked goat. Oftentimes, families will keep a goat in their yard, fattening it up to be used for the shuwa meal. Traditionally, the goat was prepared in an elaborate way, involving a day's worth of preparations using many spices and palm leaves, and another 24 hours of cooking in a clay oven. Today, however, the goat can be cooked in any number of ways. Killing and cooking a goat is usually reserved for special holidays and events only. Many Omani people also favor Turkish meals of shawarma (donair, or döner)—a combination of tomatoes, cucumbers, onions, hummus, and shredded meat, often goat meat, wrapped in pita bread. Falafel, a deep-fried ball of fava beans or chickpeas, is another popular dish.

Yogurt drinks are popular and so is a drink called laban, which is made from salted buttermilk. Qahwa, the strong Arabic coffee, is also extremely popular and is always served to guests.

Life's Milestones

Common rites and customs in Oman, such as birth, marriage, and the observation of death, are largely rooted in the Islamic faith. As such, Islamic observances and rituals, such as the daily call to prayer (heard five times daily) and Ramadan, the Islamic month of fasting, are held in high importance. The dominant faith in Oman is Ibadhism (also referred to as Ibadi Islam or Ibāḍiyya), a distinct form of Islam that has similar rituals to the Sunni faith of Islam (though there are distinct differences in the teachings of each).

Omanis, as practicing Muslims, typically celebrate the arrival of a new baby with great joy and worship. On the seventh day following the child's birth, a ritual is held to shave the baby's head. For baby boys, the head is completely shaved, which is believed to remove impurities, and for baby girls, the hair is usually either snipped or trimmed, but this is also done over the entirety of the scalp. The hair is weighed, and its weight in gold is donated to the poor. This seventh-day ritual also traditionally includes the slaughtering of a goat—two for a male child. The goat is then cooked and shared with family, friends, and the poor. According to the tradition, the goat must be slaughtered before the family shaves the baby's head.

CULTURAL HISTORY

Art

The culture of Oman dates back to pre-Islamic times, when prehistoric cultures carved extensive drawings into rock. Rock art, or rock calligraphy, has become an important part of Oman's cultural heritage, and over 500 such examples are found in the Oman territory of Madha alone. (Madha is a sparsely populated exclave of Oman, with only 3,000 residents; it is completely surrounded by the United Arab Emirates.) Though the dating of rock art remains inexact, many of these inscriptions feature extinct animals and traditions of prehistoric cultures that predate the arrival of Islam.

In addition, archaeologists in Oman have discovered artifacts dating back to the Stone Age, including shells and stone tools. Archaeologists have also unearthed evidence of ancient Sumerian settlements, copper mines, and artifacts dating back to 3000 BCE, establishing metalwork as one of the earliest art forms in Oman. Other early crafts that have been unearthed include incense burners, indicating the importance of the frankincense trade in Oman (frankincense is an extracted aromatic tree resin). Frankincense trees (*Boswellia sacra*) grow over wide areas of the sultanate and have always been an important part of the region's trade economy. In fact, in 2000, the United Nations Educational, Scientific and Cultural Organization (UNESCO), designated Oman's Frankincense Trail (which was part of the much larger Incense Road—an ancient trading route) as a World Heritage Site.

Another important aspect of Oman's cultural heritage is the country's seafaring past. Oman's close proximity to the trade routes of the Indian Ocean helped the country to spread Islam and, in turn, introduced the art and artifacts of other cultures, such as drums, textiles, and even types of dances. The Omani people are also historically known for their prowess in sailing and seamanship. The traditional fishing village of Sohar, for example, is often referred to as the birthplace of the legendary Sinbad (also Sindbad) the sailor. Shipbuilding thus became an important craft in ancient Oman, as evidenced by the skillful artistry of their wooden dhows—a traditional sailing vessel with lateen rigging and one or two masts—still prevalent throughout ancient Arabia.

With the arrival of the Prophet Muhammad and the advent of Islam in the seventh century CE, Oman began to adopt a unique culture in which Islamic art was predominant. (The country would create its own form of Islam, a faith called Ibadhism, which is more moderate than other forms of Islam and allows leaders to be chosen by the people.) Art forms that began to flourish during this period include calligraphy; pottery; jewelry; weaving, most notably of palm leaves; and metalworking. Silversmithing, in particular, became popular, and many consider it to be the oldest craft practiced in Oman. One outstanding example of this type of metalwork is Oman's traditional weaponry, particularly daggers and swords. The Omani khanjar, an elaborately carved, silver dagger, is now the national symbol of the country.

Architecture

Oman's Islamic history is apparent in its architecture. This influence can be seen not only in the Oman's numerous mosques, ornate palaces, and the fortified designs of preserved forts, but in ordinary buildings as well. Oman is also known for its traditional architecture, which includes the use of sun-baked bricks, palm fronds, mud, and other such materials.

Mosques are a superb example of Islamic architecture at its most beautiful. There are three common characteristics of a mosque besides its distinctive, dome-shaped roof: the minaret, the minbar (also mimbar), and the mihrab. The minaret is the most obvious feature and was traditionally used for the call to prayer. They usually appear as very distinctive, tall spires topped with spherical crowns. A minbar is a pulpit, or lectern, from which the imam, or prayer leader, speaks to the congregation. They are small, tower-like platforms, with steps leading up to the seat at the top. A mihrab is niche that is built into the wall of the mosque. The niche indicates the direction of Mecca and may be lavishly decorated. Additionally, the bulk of a mosque's adornment typically appears in the building's interior. This reflects the fact that Islamic architecture most often focuses on decorating the interior of a space, as opposed to the exterior. This focus on enclosed space can also been seen in the design of Muslim houses.

Traditional Omani architecture most commonly uses palm fronds, stones, or mud bricks. These houses are made up of simple, rectangular shapes, usually surrounding a courtyard. Each wing of the house is reserved for a different use (such as the women's quarters), and more wings can easily be added as necessary. Larger houses, such as mansions belonging to the very wealthy (historically, the mercantile class), also typically adhere to the basic rectangular design, although they can be three or more stories high. Mansions often have more ornate decoration, such as carved doorways, painted tiles, pillars and archways, and rooms singularly reserved for devotional activities.

Drama

Theater in Oman is largely viewed as a Western construct and is largely enjoyed by only a small segment of society. It was not until the 1950s that literary theater came to the country, and eventually small clubs, such as Muscat's Domestic Club, began to stage open-air plays to segregated audiences (separate performances for men and women). In the 1970s, the government tried to develop a dramatic arts culture by sponsoring festivals, which helped spur development of a theater community. The Omani Youth Theatre began staging plays in the 1980s and, in an effort to foster unique Arab works, enlisted the help of Egyptian playwright Mansour Makawi, who came to regularly write and produce plays for Omani audiences. His work, *Al-Mahar (The Dowry)*, was the first play that came to be produced outside of Muscat.

Since the 1980s, several dramatic troupes have developed in Oman. In the early 21st century, travelling troupes from India perform in Muscat, and the Salalah Tourism Festival features some dramatic works. In 2010, the Salalah Tourism Festival featured a nine-part tableau chronicling the events of Oman's past forty years. The theatrical community in Oman suffers from a lack of appropriate performance spaces and a lack of dramatic arts training.

Music & Dance

The traditional music of Oman is similar to the ancient musical traditions of Arabia and was passed down orally. Rhythm and melody are emphasized over harmony, and music consists of chords from the Arabic musical scale, or double harmonic scale, which is different from the Western scale. (The Arabic music scale features notes called quartertones—often called "halfway notes"—which are not present in Western music). Traditional Omani music has also been influenced by the country's history as a seafaring nation and its contact with neighboring cultures (such as the Bedouins, a nomadic people typically of Arab descent) and regions (such as East Africa). This wide range of influences gave rise to over one hundred different known types of Omani folk dances and music.

Folk songs and dances vary widely according to the different regions in Oman. For example, the songs of the fishing tribes feature praises to the sea gods. Omani dance also borrows from the traditional dances of East African tribes. Fann

At-Tanbura (also Fann aṭ-Ṭanbūra) is one such dance, performed with Swahili lyrics and the tanbūra, a bowl-shaped lyre (a type of stringed instrument). In addition, because of the emphasis on rhythm in traditional Omani music (and traditional Arabic music as a whole), percussive and rhythmic instruments, such as drums, are an important part of Omani's musical heritage.

One musical performance that transcends all regions of the country and incorporates song, swords, and poetry, is the razha. Performed by men, this dance features sword throwing and acrobatic dancing, along with periods of music and poetry. Used in the past during wartime as a form of communication, it is now primarily performed for His Majesty Sultan Qaboos, Qābūs bin Saʿīd ʾĀl Saʿīd, during special occasions.

CULTURE

Arts & Entertainment

The Omani people are very proud of their Islamic heritage. To the Omani, there is often little separation between the arts, Islam, and the folk traditions of the country's indigenous peoples. For example, in September 2008, Oman's minister of heritage and culture presided over a ceremony in the capital of Muscat in which the Oman Arabic Calligraphy Institute (OACI) presented a new Omani version of the Quran (Islam's holy book). The decorative and leather-bound version was accompanied by the launch of an electronic version, or e-copy, the "E-Quran." The release of the book coincided with the inaugural three-day exhibition "Islamic Art in Oman," which focused on the achievements of Omani culture through Islamic art.

The Ministry of Heritage and Culture is responsible for preserving the history and culture of the sultanate. One of its projects includes recruiting and training men in the lost art of handcrafting khanjars, as well as collecting and restoring valuable historical documents. The ministry also supports the work of the Omani artisans who create the beautiful silver and gold handicrafts for which the country is known. The Ministry of National Heritage and Culture is also responsible for preserving the folk dances and music of the country as it modernizes and is responsible for the three-day Omani Song Festival. After the turn of the 20th century, Oman also launched its own film festival, the Muscat International Film Festival, also known as MIFF. In 2014, the festival played host to 110 celebrity actors and directors from more than 30 countries.

Shipbuilding is one of Oman's most famous art forms. The Sohar, a ship built in 1980 as a replica of a traditional Omani ship, was built without using nails and was sailed to China.

Visual arts in Oman are primarily ethnic in theme, both to appeal to tourists and to preserve and embrace the country's heritage. Modern artists, however, are slowly gaining in popularity, and more galleries are hosting artwork by modern and contemporary Omani painters, like the Muscat-based, self-taught painter Ibrahim Gailani. Other important Omani artists include Muscat-based photographer, painter, and installation artist Hassan Meer (1972–), who studied at the Savannah College of Art & Design in the US and who recently curated of an exhibition of contemporary art forms in Oman. Co-founder of the Omani Art Movement, Anwar Sonya (1948–) has staged exhibitions for the Ministry of Heritage and Culture and has received several awards from the sultan for his contributions to Omani art. He is represented by and shows frequently at the popular Bait Muzna Gallery in Muscat.

Music is discouraged by Ibadhi Muslims, but is used in some ceremonies and celebrations. Omani festivals often incorporate music played on drums, flutes, and a stringed instrument called the rebab. The sword dance is the most common form of ceremonial dance in Oman.

Soccer is the most popular sport in Oman. Other popular sports in Oman include camel racing and bull butting, a sport in which two Brahma bulls, raised by local farmers, are pitted against each other in a test of strength. Unlike traditional bullfighting, no bulls are ever killed in this event.

Life's Milestones

Common rites and customs in Oman, such as birth, marriage, and the observation of death, are largely rooted in the Islamic faith. As such, Islamic observances and rituals, such as the call to prayer (heard five times daily) and Ramadan, the Islamic month of fasting, are held in high importance. The dominant faith in Oman is Ibadhism (also referred to as Ibadi Islam or Ibāḍiyya), a distinct form of Islam that has similar rituals to the Sunni faith of Islam (though there are distinct differences in the teachings of each).

Omanis, as practicing Muslims, typically celebrate the arrival of a new baby with great joy and worship. Often, family members place gifts of money in the newborn's swaddling clothes. Immediately following the child's birth, chewed dates are rubbed onto the baby's gums and the call to prayer is whispered in his or her right ear. A prayer to protect the child against evil is whispered in the left ear. On the seventh day following the child's birth, a ritual is held to shave the baby's head. For baby boys, the head is completely shaved, which is believed to remove impurities, and for baby girls, the hair is usually either snipped or trimmed, but this is also done over the entirety of the scalp. The hair is then traditionally weighed, and its weight in silver is donated to the poor. This seventh day ritual also traditionally includes the slaughtering of a goat—two for a male child. The goat is then cooked and shared with family, friends, and the poor in a meal called the nasika. On the day of nasika, boys are circumcised and children receive their names. On the birth of each son, a date tree is planted and, according to tradition, is intended to keep the male child from starvation, should he fall on hard times.

Cultural Sites & Landmarks

One of Oman's most striking features is its collection of forts, citadels, and ancient fortifications. In fact, there are over 500 forts, castles, and citadels throughout Oman. Some of the more famous and imposing fortifications sit along Oman's coastline. Two of the most prominent forts, Al Jalali and Al Mirani, are important landmarks in the capital of Muscat. Built during the 16th century by the Portuguese to guard Muscat Bay, the forts have since been used as watchtowers, prisons and, most recently, museums. Additionally, one of the oldest fortifications is Rustaq Fort, built in the 13th century. The fort features four striking towers and has been restored to its original condition.

The Bahla fort, built between the 13th and 14th centuries and a UNESCO World Heritage site since 1987, is located in the village of Bahla, in the Oasis of Bahla, which was the home of the Banu Nebhan tribe. This tribe ruled the area for four centuries, until the end of the 15th century. It left behind the remains of a large, ancient, and unique fort, a village, and the remnants of its culture, including the pottery for which the town is known. The fort itself was falling into disrepair due to the yearly monsoons, which were serving to destroy the outer earthen brick walls. However, beginning in 1993, it underwent significant renovation and was subsequently removed from UNESCO's "List of World Heritage in Danger" sites in 2004.

The Sultan Qaboos Grand Mosque is one of the few mosques in the Middle East open to non-Muslims, although there are strict visiting hours and dress codes. The mosque was a gift from the Sultan Qaboos and was completed in 2001, after more than six years of construction. Made from over 300,000 tons of sandstone, the mosque is immense, covering an area of 416,000 square meters (4,477,786 square feet). It can hold as many as 20,000 worshippers. Some of the most beautiful features of the mosque are the prayer carpet—one of the largest in the world, with 1,700 million knots—and a Swarovski crystal chandelier that is considered the second largest in the world.

In addition to the Frankincense Trail and the Bahla Fort, Oman is home to two other World Heritage Sites. These are the archaeological sites of Bat, Al-Khutm, and Al-Ayn, and the Aflaj Irrigation Systems, an ancient watering system that archaeologists believe may date back to 500 CE. The sites are believed to form the world's most complete collection of settlements dating from the third millennium BCE. However, Oman also has the distinction of having lost a World Heritage Site. This occurred in 2007, when the Arabian Oryx Sanctuary, inhabited by a rare species of antelope, had its protected area reduced in size by 90 percent, with only four mating pairs of Oryx remaining. The site thus became the first World Heritage Site deleted from the list.

Oman is also famous for its souqs (or souks), or traditional Arabic marketplaces. One of the most famous is Souq Al Dhalam in Muttrah, a popular bazaar whose name translates as "darkness." During certain hours, it is not penetrated by the sun, and shoppers use lanterns to navigate the various stores and stalls. Some of the more popular items found at a souq are the famous silver khanjar daggers and the traditional incense burners. In recent years, some of the more popular souqs have undergone modern renovations, such as adding walkways, to appeal to tourists.

Libraries & Museums

The Main Library of Sultan Qaboos University serves as Oman's primary library and is often designated as the national library. Other important cultural libraries include the Oman National Museum's Islamic Library in Muscat and the Ministry of Heritage and Culture's Library of Manuscripts and Documents. The library contains more than 4,300 manuscripts, with the oldest dating back to 617 CE.

The Natural History Museum is one of Oman's leading cultural institutions. Other museums include the Sultan's Armed Forces Museum; the National Museum, located above the Islamic Library; the Muscat National Museum; the Natural History Museum; the Bait Al Zubair Museum, a private institution featuring one family's collection of Omani artifacts; the Bait Al Baranda Museum of history and prehistory; the Muscat Gate Museum; the Marine Museum; the Omani Museum; the planetarium; and the Omani-French Museum, a palace that was once home to the former French consul and has honored Omani-French relations since its establishment in 1992.

Holidays

Oman's still celebrates the birthday of its former leader, HM Sultan Qaboos, on November 18 and consider this its "National Day." The celebrations of National Day last two days and include a military parade and public decorations. Most holidays observed in Oman are Muslim celebrations, such as May's Lailat al-Mi'raj, which commemorates the ascension of the Prophet Mohammed, and October's Al Hijra, which marks the Islamic New Year.

Youth Culture

Youth are typically highly valued in Omani society, and as of 2015, it was estimated that just over 30 percent of Oman's population was below the age of fourteen, while nearly 20 percent were between 15 and 24 years of age. Beginning with the expansion of the national educational system in the 1970s and 1980s—in which education up to the secondary level was provided free of charge to both sexes—the government has continuously emphasized the importance of its youth culture.

This effort continued with the 2004 creation of the Ministry of Youth Affairs and Sports, which replaced the General Organization for Youth, Sports, and Cultural Affairs. The government-sponsored organization helped create more opportunities for youth participation in sports. In addition, the sultanate's extensive educational curriculum includes a required physical education element at all grade levels.

Water activities and other sports are also extremely popular with young Omanis, and many youth belong to yacht clubs, diving clubs, and field hockey and soccer teams. In addition, theater in Oman is performed almost entirely by Omani youth and was started in the early 1980s as a way to educate Omani children in their religion and heritage. Theater is now under the leadership of the Ministry of Youth Affairs and Sports and is considered an extracurricular activity, secondary to sports.

Shopping is also a popular activity among Omani youth. However, due to Islamic law, the sexes do not intermingle very often in Oman and almost never in public. Therefore, most Omani youth have a close circle of friends of the same sex, and they spend most of their free time with that group. Due to the protective and close-knit nature of Omani families, it is uncommon for Omani youth to be involved in drugs or other illegal activities, though a drug culture has developed in recent years.

Omani youth are also generally well informed about electronics and technology. While certain aspects of Western culture, such as video games and films, are censored or modified to remove offensive content, it is not uncommon for Omani youth in more urban areas to own an iPod, cell phone, or a gaming system. Additionally, the capital of Muscat also boasts an interactive children's museum, and there are continued plans to build a state-of-the-art children's library.

SOCIETY

Transportation

Bus service in Oman is widespread and inexpensive and operates through the Oman National Transport Company (ONTC), based in Muscat since 1972. Minibuses and taxi service—including metered cabs and hired cars—are also common, although more expensive. Many Omanis own roads link automobiles and all major areas of the country. In fact, Oman has two expressways—the Muscat Expressway and the Al Batinah Expressway—and 29,685 kilometers (18,445 miles) of paved roads.

Rail transportation has been non-existent in Oman, though the construction of a joint railway has been proposed among six Gulf States—Saudi Arabia, Bahrain, Kuwait, Oman, Qatar and the United Arab Emirates—at a cost of $14 billion USD. In preparation, the government set up Oman Rail in 2014. While this rail line was set for completion by 2016, efforts to complete the Omani portion have been temporarily suspended because of the drop in crude oil prices, which has, in turn, effected a hiring freeze and deferment of the railway project. Concerning

the transportation of goods, the Omani port of Salālah is considered the premier off-loading site in the Persian Gulf. In fact, water transportation plays a large part in the movement of goods in and out of the country, especially in light of the absence of railways.

Cars in Oman travel on the right-hand side of the road.

Transportation Infrastructure

In 2015, Oman has two expressways—the Muscat Expressway and the Al Batinah Expressway—and 29,685 kilometers (18,445 miles) of paved roads. In 2012, Oman still had 30,545 kilometers (18,979 miles) of unpaved roadways. In general, the road conditions in Oman are considered excellent. Additionally, as of 2015, Oman had seven airports with paved runways, including two international airports, Muscat International (formerly called Seeb International) and Salālah, and approximately 142 smaller airports with unpaved runways.

Media & Communications

The government regulates media in Oman and restricts or confiscates any media that might be offensive to the values of the Omani people (including Western films and any materials brought into the country by tourists). This includes vulgar language, overt sexuality, and anything that criticizes or stereotypes the culture or government of Oman. Additionally, Oman has a state-run news agency that evaluates news and other information before it releases such information to its media outlets, including six daily newspapers. Four of the papers are privately owned, but subsidized by the government. The *Muscat Daily*, launched in 2009 and—for the first time—covering political and crime stories, recently eclipsed the *Times of Oman* as the leading daily. It has been lauded for its unbiased coverage of the 2011 uprisings. The government's subjective dissemination of information has also extends to radio and television stations, all of which are state-controlled.

The Internet is also censored and monitored by the government. The Oman

Telecommunications Company (Omantel) will block any website that may include profanity, lewd material, or anything critical of the Omani way of life. The government owns 70 percent of the company. In fact, once an Internet user enters a new site address (not previously evaluated by Omantel) into a search engine, the site will be reviewed for 24 to 48 hours before being allowed or disallowed as part of the Omani network. In 2014, 39.44 percent of Omani households had an internet connection, up from 31.7 percent in 2013. In addition, 67.44 percent of the population is Internet users. Omnatel also provides most telecommunication in the country, although it does not have a monopoly on mobile phones. Oman's Telecommunications Regulatory Authority (TRA) regulates mobile telephone access.

SOCIAL DEVELOPMENT

Standard of Living

In 2014, Oman again ranked 56th out of 187 nations on the United Nations Human Development Index, which measures quality of life and standard of living indicators.

Water Consumption

Oman depends on both rainfall and groundwater for about 65 percent of its water; 35 percent of its potable water is produced through desalinization. According to the World Health Organization in 2012, 86.1 percent of Oman's rural population had access to improved drinking water; 95.5 percent of the urban population had the same access. Further, 94.7 percent of the rural population had access to improved sanitation and 97.3 percent of the urban population had the same.

Education

Under the sultanate that has reigned since 1970, many facets of Omani society have been improved by socio-economic reforms. Before 1970, Oman had only two primary schools and no secondary schools or universities. There are now over 500 schools and several universities, including Sultan Qaboos University outside of Muscat.

Education in Oman is free, but is not compulsory. Students attend primary school between the ages of six and 12 and secondary school until 18 years of age. Attendance levels are high. In addition to state universities, there are a number of Islamic colleges.

In 2015, Oman's average literacy rate is 91.1 percent (almost 93.6 percent among men and 85.6 percent among women). Between 1990 and 2006, the literacy rate for adults went from 54 percent to 81 percent; even more remarkable, the youth literacy rate rose from 85 percent to 97 percent between 1990 and 2006 due to the government's investment in education and literacy.

Women's Rights

In 1997, the sultanate passed the Personal Status Law, which granted women equality with men in regard to education and employment opportunities. The law also protects Omani women (as well as men) under the age of 18 from being forced to marry and allows freedom of choice to marry after that age. Families, however, still play a large role in deciding whom a woman might marry, and arranged or approved marriages, and their related pressures, are still common.

Omani women have the right to vote, own property, and attend higher education programs. In recent years, more Omani women are working outside the home and in 2011 made up 28.3 percent of the nation's workforce. According to the Oman Ministry of State, as of 2012, there were women holding positions in all levels of the government. In fact, women comprise 9.6 percent of parliament. However, while women are allowed to become lawyers, they are not allowed to serve as judges.

Women who work also typically earn the same salaries as their male counterparts. Nonetheless, Islamic law still has a profound effect on women in Omani society. For example, Omani women are expected to dress in a conservative manner (as are all Omani citizens). Additionally, while the majority of Omani girls under the age of 12 typically do not wear the hijab (traditional headscarf) unless it is Ramadan, most Omani women wear the hijab and the abaya (traditional, long-sleeved over garment) when out in public. However, it is common for Omani women to choose to wear their abayas close-fitted, and they often wear jeans rather than the traditional skirt or dress underneath.

Domestic violence against women is not specifically addressed in the Omani constitution, nor is it often, if at all, mentioned in the media. In addition, there are no laws protecting women from sexual harassment in the workplace, and spousal rape is not considered a criminal act. (Rape is criminalized, but convictions are criticized as being few.) Women are also not allowed to travel abroad without male companions and do not have equal inheritance rights as their male counterparts. Certain legal matters, particularly inheritance disputes, are usually automatically settled in favor of the male client. The government has promoted many family planning programs since 1994, which have lowered the mortality rates of women and newborns. Healthcare, including birth control and counseling programs, is free at all hospitals for women and children. Abortion, however, is illegal in the sultanate.

Health Care

Like the education system, Oman's health care system has benefited greatly from improvements made by the sultan. Before the 1970s, Omani life expectancy was under 50 years. Today, the average life expectancy is 75 years—73 for men and 77 for women (2015 estimate). In 2013, Oman spent 2.6 percent of its GDP on health care for citizens. Currently, there are 2.4 physicians and 1.7 hospital beds for every 1,000 people.

Potable tap water is now available throughout the country, and major diseases such as malaria have been wiped out. In addition to these changes, more than 100 hospitals and health centers, along with a free health care system, have been established. The system, available to all Omanis, includes social security and welfare.

GOVERNMENT

Structure

Oman is an independent sultanate that functions as an absolute monarchy. The sultan has the highest authority in the nation, and is the chief of state, head of government, and prime minister. His duties include appointing the executive cabinet and the 83 members comprising the Majlis al-Dawla (Council of State).

In 2002, universal suffrage was granted to all Omanis 21 and older. However, voters may only elect legislative officials, as the monarchy is hereditary. The bicameral Majlis Oman is the government's legislative branch. The upper chamber, the Majlis al-Dawla, consists of 83 sultan-appointed seats. The lower chamber, elected by popular vote, is the 84-seat Majlis al-Shura.

The highest authority in Oman's judicial branch is the Supreme Judicial Council, which oversees all judicial activity. Oman's courts support both Islamic law (Sharia) and secular law.

Oman's monarchy underwent numerous coups d'état in the 20th century. The Imam, a religious leader elected by Muslims, attempted to overthrow the sultan in 1913. The nation was divided in civil war until 1920. In 1954, another Imam rebelled, prompting Egypt and Saudi Arabia to support the overthrow.

Coups continued until 1970, when the Sultan was overthrown by his son. The new sultan rose to the throne, ended rebellions in the Dhofar region, and initiated numerous beneficial reforms.

Oman has had defense agreements with the United States since 1980 and agreements with bordering Arab states since 1981, at which point Oman joined the Gulf Cooperation Council (GCC). Oman assisted Kuwait's liberation from Iraq in 1990, but did not take part in the 2003 invasion of Iraq.

Political Parties

As an absolute monarchy, where the hereditary sultan is head of both state and government,

Oman has no political parties, and its legislature is consultative in nature.

Local Government

Oman is divided into 59 districts, each led by a governor (wilayats). Governors collect taxes, ensure public safety, and are under the purview of the Ministry of the Interior, with the exception of the governor of Dhofar, who holds cabinet rank. The central government handles regional planning.

Judicial System

Oman follows Sharia, or Islamic law. A Supreme Judicial Council oversees the judiciary in accordance with article 66 of the Omani Constitution. Under the Supreme Judicial Council, civil, criminal, and commercial cases are heard by the Courts of First Instance. One of six appeals courts then hears appeals of these decisions. Sharia courts hear personal or family cases, while article 67 of the constitution outlines how administrative courts handle government-related cases. Military courts adjudicate martial law cases. All decisions are rendered in the name of the sultan, and delay in administering punishments is against the law. According to article 71 of the Omani constitution, winning parties may pursue criminal action against the court that delays or fails to fulfil judgements.

Taxation

Because the government receives revenues from oil resources, taxation in Oman has been characterized as moderate. There is no personal income, estate, or gift tax. Corporations pay profit, interest, royalties, and capital gains taxes, and taxes on the sale of petroleum products has stood at 55 percent since 1970. In addition, a labor levy, social security levy, and customs duties are applied to companies as appropriate. Some areas of the private sector enjoy tax exemptions, including those businesses involved in mining, tourism, hospitalization, education, fishing, fish processing, livestock breeding, and dairy production.

Armed Forces

The Sultan of Oman's Armed Forces are made up of an army, navy, air force, a royal guard, and the Royal Oman police. Headquartered in Muscat, the armed forces have more than 70,000 active personnel and 20,000 reserves. In 2013, military expenditures constituted 11.5 percent of the GDP and came in at $9.3 billion (USD).

Foreign Policy

The foreign policy of Oman is largely influenced by the country's Ibadhi interpretation of Islam and the emphasis on forward thinking and tolerance. Generally, the sultan's approach to foreign relations is based on national security and prosperity and the building of mutual beneficial and cooperative relations with as many nations as possible, without an extreme emphasis on ideology. As such, Oman is one of the more pro-Western Arab nations and has established excellent relations with the U.S. and the European Union (EU). Overall, Oman has official diplomatic relations with over 135 countries. Moreover, of all the GCC states, Oman has enjoyed the most harmonious relations with its northern neighbor, Iran. Consequently, Iran has begun small initiatives to increase bilateral trade and investment.

Overall, Oman's relationship with other Arab nations, particularly neighboring Middle Eastern countries, is excellent. The sultanate strives to work with other Arab nations, both through organizations such as the Arab League, the Organization of the Islamic Conference (OIC), and the six-member Cooperation Council for the Arab States of the Gulf (CCASG), and independently as well. This backing varies in breadth, from supporting the Middle East peace process and the Palestinian situation in Israel. The sultan is also vocal in his dislike of terrorist organizations and tactics, especially those groups that identify themselves as Muslim.

In addition, Oman has an easy relationship with its closest neighbor, Yemen. In 1997, the sultanate settled a long running border dispute, with both countries drawing up new maps to illustrate the new border. In fact, Oman is proud of the fact that it has demarked almost all of its land and sea boundaries, something that is very difficult to do without cooperation from the adjoining countries. The northern boundary with United Arab Emirates, however, has not yet been bilaterally defined.

Oman is an active player on the world stage as well. As a member of the UN, it has assisted in numerous UN-led initiatives and coalitions, most notably the Gulf War in the early 1990s. Oman also maintains membership in the World Trade Organization (WTO), the World Health Organization (WHO), the Non-Aligned Movement (NAM), the International Monetary Fund (IMF), the World Bank, and various other regional and worldwide organizations. In particular, Oman's ties with Asia and East Africa stretch back centuries, dating to the country's early oceanic trading routes. Those ties can be seen in the sultanate's efforts to establish the Indian Ocean Rim Association for Regional Co-operation (IORARC) in 1997, which opened up new economic opportunities for all participating countries. Lastly, Oman further cemented a mutually beneficial relationship with the US after the September 2006 signing of the United States-Oman Free Trade Agreement (OFTA). Implemented on January 1, 2009, OFTA has established the free trading of goods and services between the US and the Omani sultanate.

Human Rights Profile

International human rights law insists that states respect civil and political rights and promote an individual's economic, social, and cultural rights. The United Nations Universal Declaration on Human Rights (UDHR) is recognized as the standard for international human rights. Its authors sought the counsel of the world's great thinkers, philosophers, and religious leaders and were careful to create a document that reflects the core values shared by every world culture. (To read this document or view the articles relating to cultural human rights, visit http://www.ohchr.org/EN/UDHR/Pages/Introduction.aspx.)

The Sultanate of Oman, for the most part, follows the decrees in the UDHR. Article 17 of its constitution declares that all Omani citizens are equal before the law, regardless of gender, ethnic heritage, religion, or socioeconomic status. (The text of the constitution is also called the Basic Law, and usually shortened to Law.) However, one notable exception is that the country's labor laws do not yet apply to domestic workers, who are predominantly foreign. Human rights watch groups claim that these workers are often abused by their employers. While Oman has been one of the most highly regarded Arab nations in terms of the establishment and protection of human and citizens' rights and was the first Arab country to fund and create a government commission on human rights, manipulations of the law have been reported, particularly in relation to the freedoms of expression and assembly. Political demonstrators are regularly jailed for the crime of "insulting the sultan" and "illegal gathering." Legal defense is frequently delayed or withheld, although pardons can be issued following extended detention. According to Human Rights Watch, on July 29, 2013, pro-reform activist Sultan al-Saadi was arrested by Omani authorities at a gas station while traveling with his family. Omani Intelligence detained al-Saadi until August 20, when he was released. However, they confiscated his laptop and other personal items.

Articles 6 through 11 of the UDHR outline rights related to arrest, trail, and presumption of innocence. In comparison to the Omani constitution, articles 22, 23, 24 and 25 guarantee Omanis the right to trial, a state-provided lawyer, and the presumption of innocence until proven guilty. As of 2008, there were no reports of any political prisoners or detainees. In regards to freedom of religion, it is guaranteed in Article 28 of the Basic Law. However, this freedom must be practiced "in accordance with recognized customs" and "accepted standards of behavior." The government also monitors non-Islamic groups, particularly the content of sermons, and allows non-Islamic worship only at government-sponsored sites.

The rights to freedom of speech and expression, as outlined in Article 19 of the UDHR, are allowed for by Articles 29 and 31 in Oman's constitution. However, it includes the exception that these freedoms are only guaranteed "within the limits of the Law." This written exception allows the state to effectively negate some freedoms of speech and expression. For example, the 1984 Press and Publication Law restricts freedom of press by prohibiting any published works that may lead to unrest among the citizens of Oman. These published works may include those, which might offend the dignity of an Omani, or works that could threaten state security. Fines for offending parties can be as high as $5,000 (USD) and, often, imprisonment. In addition, freelance journalists are not allowed to practice in the country, and journalists who do not wish to work for state-run media outlets must apply for a license with the government.

The right to assemble, outlined in Article 20, is again protected "within the limits of the Law" by Articles 32 and 33 of the Omani constitution. According to the sultanate's constitution, national associations can only be formed for "legitimate objectives," the definition of which is left up to the state. For this reason, the arrest of political or environmental demonstrators on the charge "illegal gathering" often occurs.

ECONOMY

Overview of the Economy

Oman has a relatively stable economy, although inflation has been on the rise. In 2014, its estimated per capita GDP was $39,700 (USD). The nation has continued to experience strong growth since petroleum deposits were discovered in 1964, and the economy is, therefore, largely focused on the industrial sector. Unlike many other nations in the region, Oman is not a member of the Organization of the Petroleum Exporting Countries (OPEC), a group of oil-producing nations that work together to set global oil prices.

In addition to plans to diversify the economy, the sultanate has instigated a plan for "Omanization," an economic program to create more jobs for Omani citizens and reduce the amount of dependence on foreign workers.

Muscat is a port city and, much like Oman as a whole, has a trade-based economy. Muscat's main trading port is Mina Sultan Qaboos ("mina" means port in Arabic), which was the most important port in the region until the Jebel Ali Free Zone was created in nearby Dubai.

In August 2015, the falling price of crude oil to below $50 USD precipitated a hiring freeze in private sectors. In the public service sector, both hiring and the execution of government projects were put on hold in January and are expected to continue suspension until 2016.

Industry

Service jobs coupled with oil production make up the largest sector of Oman's economy. Industrial activity is focused mainly on crude oil production and refinery. Other industrial products include natural gas, cement, copper, steel, chemicals, and optic fiber.

Oman's major exports include petroleum, fish, metals, and textiles. The country's major trading partners in 2013 included, in order of magnitude: China (38.2 percent), Japan (10.3 percent), United Arab Emirates (10 percent), South Korea (8.7 percent), and India (5.6 percent).

Petroleum Development Oman is a major trade company in the country. This oil export company manages 70 percent of the country's petroleum production and all of its natural gas reserves, and has its central offices in Muscat. It is 60 percent government-owned, while 34 percent is owned by the Shell Group. Other important trade companies include the multifaceted Suhail Bahwan Group, which includes telecom, chemical, and engineering, logistics, construction, furnishings, and energy divisions; the Saud Bahwan Group, which has construction, equipment, automotive, oil, and travel departments; and Zubair Automotive Group, which deals exclusively in car and truck imports.

The government of Oman continues to work toward privatization of industry. According to Oman's Ministry of Manpower, 215,056 Omani nationals were registered to work in private sector jobs. However, by 2014, this number dropped to 192,873. To correct this imbalance, the Omani government has been undergoing a process to encourage most businesses to cease dependence on foreign labor and imports. However, corporations operating within the Sultanate usually pay Omani workers minimum wage and provide few if any incentives. With the rise of inflation, this has made sustaining a family's lifestyle difficult and caused Omani nationals to drop out of the private sector and return to government-sponsored work.

Labor
Oman's unemployment rate continued at 15 percent in 2015.

Energy/Power/Natural Resources
Petroleum is Oman's most significant natural resource and is the basis for most of the nation's economic activity. Other natural resources include copper, asbestos, marble, limestone, chromium, gypsum, and natural gas.

Fishing
Fishing is also a significant aspect of Omani agriculture; catches include sardines, anchovies, bluefish, mackerel, sharks, tuna, lobsters, oysters, and abalone. This struggling economic sector has an emerging, if still anemic, commercial segment. However, the government, through the Oman Fisheries Development and Management Project, is attempting to aid its growth through subsidies, including grants to purchase fiberglass boats and outboard engines and funds to build jetties and cold storage facilities along the coast.

Mining/Metals
Oman's mining potential is currently being explored, and the country's abundant ophiolite rock—igneous rock that once served as oceanic plate and constitutes the country's various mountain ranges—are the perfect environment for the development of copper, gold, silver, chromite,

lead, nickel, manganese, and zinc veins. A five-year plan has been laid out by the Directorate General of Minerals and Ministry of Commerce and Industry, and in 2014, thirty-four companies, including Northern Minerals and Gulf Mining Materials, confirmed their participation in exploratory mining and quarrying activities in Oman.

Agriculture
Most of Oman's agricultural activity is subsistence farming along the fertile al-Batinah region of the coastal plain, although there are five larger agricultural regions: the Musandam Peninsula, the aforementioned al-Batinah coast, the valleys and high plateau of the east, interior oases, and the Dhofar region. Dates, limes, bananas, alfalfa, onions, pomegranates, tobacco, tomatoes, and wheat are commonly farmed. Locust plagues are a significant threat to Omani crops. Efforts to boost the country's agricultural sector have been stalled by the reluctance of Omani farmers to move toward commercial production.

Animal Husbandry
The most common forms of livestock are cattle and camels, although goats, sheep, and donkeys are also widely raised. Dhofar is home to a high-volume and profitable cattle-raising industry.

Tourism
Tourism is a growing sector of Oman's economy. In 2014 alone, 1,490,879 international visitors crossed Omani borders (an increase of 156,484 from the previous year), and 85,002 Omani-nationals traveled as tourists inside the country's borders (an increase of 10,547 from 2013). According to the Oxford Business Group, in 2013, Oman's tourist industry exceeded $1 billion (USD).

There are a number of natural and cultural tourist attractions in Oman. The sultan's palace in Muscat, also known as Al Alam Palace, along with castles such as Sunaysilah Fort and Bilad Sur, are among the country's architectural attractions.

The Oman Dive Centre, a scuba resort in the Muscat Governorate, is a popular tourist spot, as is the Bimmah Sinkhole, located in the Hawiyat Najm Park in northern Oman. Off-road vehicles can be driven on guided tours through the dunes of the Sharqiya Sands, once known as the Wahiba Sands. Tourists also visit the Nakhal Hot Springs, near the recently restored Fort Nakhal, which is just 10 minutes away. Wadi Shab and Wadi Tiwi, both of which include lush vegetation, caves, and turquoise-colored pools, are among the most frequented wadis.

Many visitors to Oman stay in Muscat's Al-Bustan Palace Hotel, part of the high-end Ritz-Carlton chain. It offers access to a well-kept, private stretch of Quron (also Qurum) Beach and is considered one of the world's finest hotels. Cultural attractions in Muscat include the Sultan's Armed Forces Museum; the National Museum, located above the Islamic Library; the Muscat National Museum; the Natural History Museum; the Bait Al Zubair Museum, a private institution featuring one family's collection of Omani artifacts; the Bait Al Baranda Museum of history and prehistory; the Muscat Gate Museum; the Marine Museum; the Omani Museum; the planetarium; and the Omani-French Museum, a palace that was once home to the former French consul and has honored Omani-French relations since its establishment in 1992.

April Sanders, Richard Means,
Ian Paul, & Savannah Schroll Guz

DO YOU KNOW?

- Ubar, an ancient lost city popularly known as "Atlantis of the Sands," was once located in the Rub' al-Khali, but is now thought to be buried under large sand dunes. Thousands of artifacts dating as far back as 5000 BCE have been discovered in the region.

- A sheathed khanjar, the traditional ceremonial dagger of Oman, and two crossed swords appear on the country's flag. In the national emblem, the two swords and khanjar are bound together at the center by a horse bit.

- Muscat's National Museum is home to an important holy relic: a letter dating back to the eighth century, allegedly sent by the Prophet Mohammed to the rulers of Oman, inviting the people of Oman to convert to Islam.

- On June 6, 2007, Cyclone Gonu (Super Cyclonic Storm Gonu) struck Muscat and the surrounding region, causing extensive damage. It was the strongest tropical cyclone to hit the Arabian Sea and the most powerful named cyclone in the Indian Ocean. It is considered Oman's worst natural disaster.

Bibliography

"Destination Oman Home Page." *Sultanate of Oman Ministry of Tourism.* 27 Jul. 2015. http://www.destinationoman.com/.

"Insight Guide to Oman and the UAE." Insight Guides. Duncan, SC: *Langenscheidt Publishers.,* 2012.

"Official Website for the Sultanate of Oman." *Ministry of Information.* 27 Jul. 2015. http://www.omaninfo.om/.

Abdulrahman Bin Ali Alhinai. "Ceremonies and Celebrations of Oman." Berkshire, UK: *Garne Publishing Ltd.*, 2000.

Alan Keohane. "Bedouin: Nomads of the Desert." London, UK: *Kyle Books.*, 2012.

Gavin Thomas. "The Rough Guide to Oman." New York: *Rough Guides/Penguin,* 2011.

Jeremy Jones & and Nicholas Ridout. "Oman, Culture, and Diplomacy." 2nd ed. Edinburgh, Scotland: *Edinburgh UP,* 2013.

John Beasant, Christopher Ling, and Ian Cummins. "Oman: The True-Life Drama and Intrigue of an Arab State." London: *Mainstream Publishing/Random House,* 2014.

Marc Valeri. "Oman: Politics and Society in the Qaboos State." London, UK: *Oxford UP*, 2014.

Salma S. Damluji. "Salma S. The Architecture of Oman." Berkshire, UK: *Garnet Publishing Ltd.*, 1999.

Simone Nowell. "Oman—Culture Smart! A Quick Guide to Customs and Etiquette." London, UK: *Kuperard*. 2009.

Works Cited

"Birth Rights and Rituals." *Religious Tolerance: Islam in the Sultinate of Oman.* ARABIA FELIX Synform, GmbH & the Oman Ministry of Endowments and Religious Affairs, 2015. http://www.islam-in-oman.com/en/exhibits/modern-day-oman/birth-rites-and-rituals/.

"Diplomatic Doings: Omani Ambassador" Washington Report. American Educational Trust, Jul. 2008. http://www.washington-report.org/archives/July_2008/0807069.html.

"Flora of Oman." *Kew Royal Botanic Gardens.* Kew, 2015. Web. http://www.kew.org/science-conservation/research-data/science-directory/projects/flora-oman.

"Oman News Feed." *Reporters without Borders.* 2015. http://en.rsf.org/oman.html.

"Oman." Amnesty International Report 2014/15. *Amnesty International.* 2015. https://www.amnesty.org/en/countries/middle-east-and-north-africa/oman/.

"Oman: A Unique Foreign Policy Produces a Key Player in Middle Eastern and Global Diplomacy." *Rand Corporation Research Briefs.* Rand Corporation, 2015. http://www.rand.org/pubs/research_briefs/RB2501/index1.html.

"Oman's annual international tourism revenue exceeds $1bn mark." *Economic News Update.* Oxford Business Group, 28 Aug. 2013. http://www.oxfordbusinessgroup. com/news/oman%E2%80%99s-annual-international-tourism-revenue-exceeds-1bn-mark.

"Oman's Constitution." *Verfassungsgeschichte* (*Constitutional History*). Prof. Dr. Axel Tschentscher/ Universität Bern, 2 Dec. 2014. http://www.servat.unibe.ch/icl/mu00000_.html.

"Oman: Events of 2013." World Report 2014. *Human Rights Watch.* 2015. https://www.hrw.org/world-report/2014/country-chapters/oman.

"Population of Oman." *CityPopulation.de.* Thomas Brinkhoff, 15 Mar. 2015. http://www.citypopulation.de/Oman.html.

"Welcome to Destination Oman." *Destination Oman.* Destination Oman, 2015. http://www.destinationoman.com/socialcustoms.html.

Anne Marie Ruff. "Araby's Most Fabulous Destination" *Time.com* Time Inc., 27 May 2002. http://www.time.com/time/magazine/article/0,9171,501020603-250063,00.html.

Brett Nelson. "Emirates Crush Dissent at Home, Tarnishing Image Abroad." *Freedom House.* 21 Mar. 2013. http://www.freedomhouse.org/template.cfm?page=179.

Neil Halligan. "Oil price slide said to force hiring freeze in Oman." *Arabian Business.* Arabian Business Publishing Ltd., 4 Aug. 2015. http://www.arabianbusiness.com/oil-price-slide-said-force-hiring-freeze-in-oman-601444.html.

Saleh Shaibany. "Sunday Beat: Why thousands of Omanis quit jobs in private sector?" *Times of Oman.* Muscat Media Group, 15 Nov. 2014. http://timesofoman.com/article/43246/Oman/Sunday-Beat-Why-thousands-of-Omanis-quit-jobs-in-private-sector?.

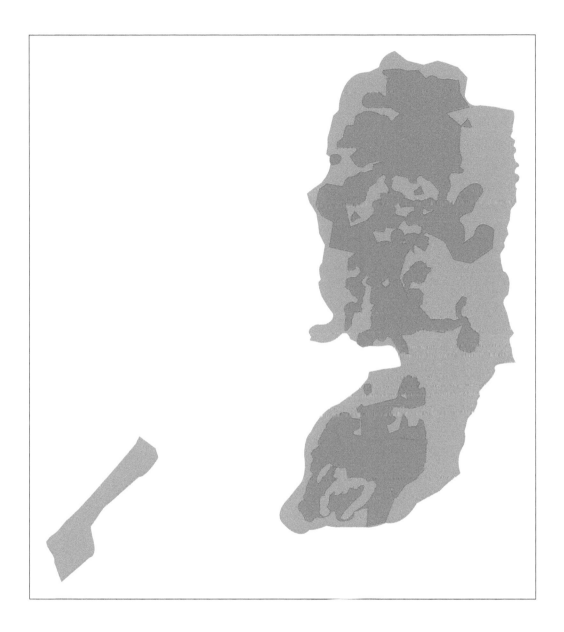

PALESTINIAN TERRITORIES/
STATE OF PALESTINE

Introduction

Palestine was, and to some extent remains, a region in the Middle East along the Mediterranean Sea. It is in an area of the world known to Jews, Christians, and Muslims as the Holy Land.

The cultural legacy of the people who live there is rich, but complex, and marred by social, cultural, and political unrest. It unites Palestinian Arab people in a way that geography cannot, and poetry is one of its most important art forms.

Historically, the land is well acquainted with occupation. It was ruled by the Ottoman Empire and later the British Empire. In 1948, world politics forever changed the face of Palestine and ushered in an era of significant turmoil, which Palestinians refer to as Nakba, or "the catastrophe." In the aftermath of World War II, the United Nations decreed the creation of Israel, a sovereign state and homeland for the Jewish people. Its borders were set in Palestine. The Arab population living in Palestine at the time violently opposed the creation of a new state and the new borders in the region.

The Palestinian territories, known as the West Bank and the Gaza Strip, border Israel, Egypt, and Jordan and are governed by Arab leaders. The majority of Palestinian Arabs live in these territories, but many Palestinians also live in Israel, particularly East Jerusalem, as well as in exile in other countries, such as Lebanon, Jordan, and Syria, where multigenerational Palestinian camps have developed to accommodate them.

Although Palestine does not yet exist as a universally recognized state, Palestinian Arab leaders have been working in the last decades towards a goal of establishing self-rule in an independent Palestinian state that is separate from Israel. Conflicts between Palestinian leaders and the Israeli government over land, travel, security, and settlement rights have previously prevented a resolution to the cause of a

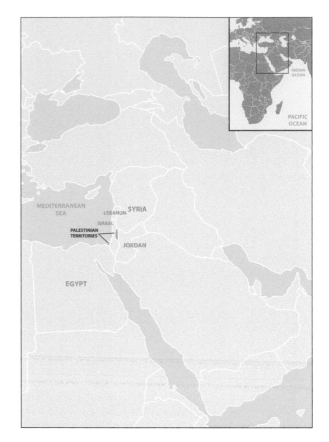

self-governing Palestinian state. The movement toward a unified identity has been further complicated by serious infighting between Hamas, an Islamic resistance movement that controls the Gaza Strip, and Fatah, which controls the West Bank. However, in November 2012, the United Nations General Assembly resolution 67/19 elevated the Palestinian territories to the status of "non-member observer state," which reflects significant progress toward the territories' international goal of independent nationhood. With this UN nod, what had previously been referred to as the "Palestinian National Authority" and "Palestinian Territories, Occupied" has been known since 2013 as the State of Palestine.

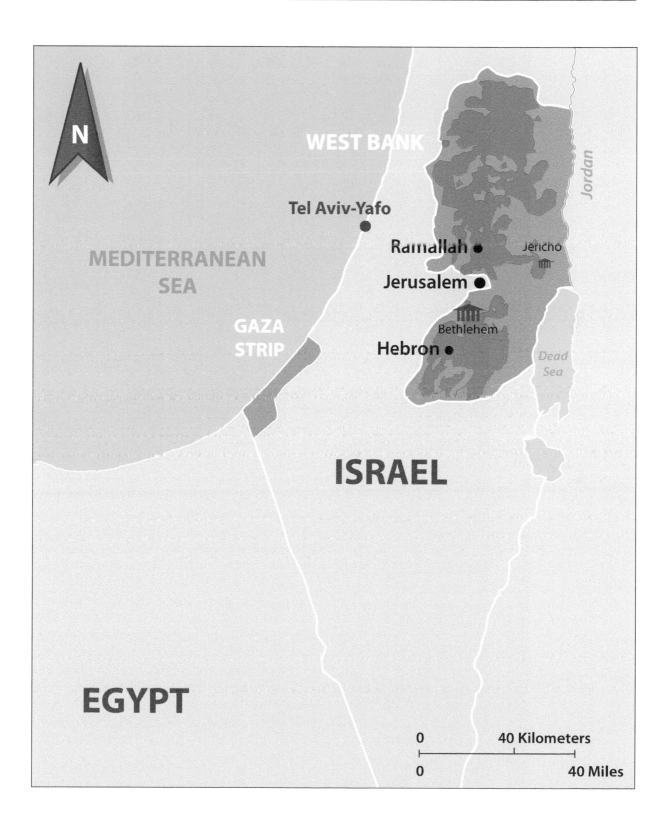

GENERAL INFORMATION

Official Language: Arabic

Population: 4,654,421 (2015 estimate)

Currency: The Israeli new shekel is the official currency, but the Jordanian dinar (West Bank) and Egyptian pound (Gaza) are also used.

Coins: One hundred http://en.wikipedia.org/wiki/Israeli_agoraagorot equal one shekel. Coins are issued in 10 agorot and 1/2, 1, 2, 5, and 10 Israeli new shekalim (shekalim is the plural of shekel).

Land Area: 6,020 square kilometers (2,324 square miles); West Bank 5,655 square kilometers (2,183 square miles) and Gaza Strip 365 square kilometers (141 square miles)

National Anthem: "Fida'i" ("Fedayeen Warrior," also "My Redemption")

Capital: Ramallah is currently the de facto administrative center; the state, however, has sought and continues to seek to make East Jerusalem the capital. Israel, however, does not permit Palestinian government offices within city limits.

Time Zone: GMT +2

Flag Description: The Palestinian flag is a tricolor with three equal stripes of black (top), white (middle), and green (bottom). A red equilateral triangle overlaps the stripes on the hoist (left) side. The colors are traditional and represent different Arab dynasties: the black refers to the 'Abbāsid Dynasty, the white symbolizes the Umayyad Dynasty, the green represents the Fāṭimid Dynasty, and the red triangle represents the Hashemites.

Principal Cities by Population (2014):

- Gaza (including Ash-Shati' camp) (591,400)
- Jerusalem (255,700)
- Khan Yunis (including camp) (220,300)
- Jabālyah/Jabalia (including camp) (212,900)
- Hebron (202,200)
- Rafah (including Tall as-Sultan refugee camp) (196,400)
- Nablus (146,493)
- Bayt Lāhīyā, Beit Lahia (83,200)
- An-Nusayrat/Nuseirat (including camp) (80,600)
- Ṭūlkarm/Tulkarem (including camp) (70,100)

Population

The Palestinian population includes a significant number of Palestinians living in refugee camps within the Palestinian territories, but does not account for the approximately 5 million refugees under the care of the United Nations Relief and Works Agency (UNRWA) in fifty-eight registered camps in the neighboring Arab countries of Jordan, Syria, and Lebanon. The plight of those in refugee camps spans generations, with many occupants born in camps and raising their own families there—without the basic rights of citizenship granted to the citizens of the host country. The whole of the Palestinian diaspora, which is spread worldwide, numbers around 6.5 million, with large populations of Palestinians in the territories (Gaza and the West Bank), Jordan, Israel, Chile, Syria, Lebanon, and Saudi Arabia. Americans United for Palestinian Human Rights (AUPHR) estimates that one in three refugees is Palestinian.

Within Israel, the United States Central Intelligence Agency estimates that the 2014 Palestinian population is 2,785,366 million in the West Bank, 117,400 in East Jerusalem, and about 1,869,055 million in Gaza.

Languages

Arabic is the most dominant language of the Palestinian territories, but most Palestinians can speak Hebrew as well. English is also commonly understood.

Native People & Ethnic Groups

Archaeologists have uncovered evidence of human activity in the region now known as Palestine that dates back 500,000 years. In addition, archaeologists and historians suggest the region was home to various Canaanite city-states during the Bronze Age (3200–600 BCE) and that these settlements traded with populations in Syria and Egypt. Although some scholars cite the Bible as evidence of the Philistine people originating in the region, others have suggested that the Philistines emigrated from Greece and the Greek Isles. Nonetheless, the ancient history of this region of the Middle East unfurled in a continual power struggle between various Israelite kingdoms and Muslim caliphates. The dispute over which group can lay historical claim to the region is one that continues to be debated among academics, historians, archaeologists, and religious scholars alike.

Another sector of the Arab community, the Druze, lives in Galilee and Mount Carmel. There is also a significant minority of Christian Arabs, mostly Greek Orthodox, or Greek Catholic, living in Israel.

Religions

Most Palestinian Arabs—around 80 to 85 percent in the West Bank and between 98 and 99 percent in the Gaza Strip—follow the Muslim tradition and are predominantly Sunni. In the West Bank, a small portion of the population is Druze Arabs (less than 1 percent) and Christian (one to 2.5 percent), and principally Greek Orthodox. Between 12 and 14 percent of the West Bank population is estimated to be Jewish. In the Gaza Strip, in addition to the Muslim population noted above, there is tiny Christian population of less than 1 percent. Following the withdrawal of settlements in 2005, Jews no longer live in the Gaza Strip.

Climate

The Palestinian territories are located between a subtropical wet region in the south and a subtropical arid region in the north. Because of this situation, the south sees little rainfall, while northern areas can experience heavy rainfall during the rainy season. The Mediterranean Sea also influences the weather in the region, causing depressions that affect barometric pressure and precipitation.

The region is sunny, particularly in desert areas, although periods of rainfall typically occur from November to May. The Palestinian territories experience a summer monsoon season that creates humid, windy conditions. From May to November, the weather tends to be dry. The mountain regions in Hebron and Upper Galilee generally see some annual snowfall at elevations over 800 meters (2,500 feet).

The temperature in the Palestinian territories varies with the elevation, with lower areas reporting the highest temperatures. The hottest weather occurs in the Rift Valley, and the coldest in Upper Galilee. Depending on elevation, coastal areas see more moderate temperatures of around 20° to 21° Celsius (68° to 70° Fahrenheit). Temperatures range from 5° to 10° Celsius (41° to 50° Fahrenheit) in January and 26° to 38° Celsius (79° to 100° Fahrenheit) in July and August.

ENVIRONMENT & GEOGRAPHY

Topography

The Palestinian territories have a varied landscape, extending from the heights of Upper Galilee (Mount Meron, the area's highest point, is 1,200 meters/4,000 feet) to the lowest land depth on the planet (400 meters/1,310 feet) in the Jordan Valley. The region is bounded on the east by the Jordan River and on the south by the desert region of the Negev and the Gulf of Aqaba. To the north lie Israel and Lebanon, with the coastal lowlands of the Mediterranean Sea to the west. Among its various physical features are plateaus, hills, mountains, plains, rivers, lakes, and valleys.

There are a few important rivers that bring valuable water to the land, including the Qishon

River (also, Kishon River) and the Harod River. The water that feeds these rivers comes in part from rainfall and snowmelt in the wooded highlands and limestone plateau of Upper Galilee. The Jordan River is perhaps the most famous river in the region, with historical, religious, and political significance. It winds through the land, connecting Lake Kinneret with the Dead Sea. The Jordan River is also a boundary between the West Bank and Israel.

The Jordan Valley is a rift valley. It varies in width from 2.5 to 22 kilometers (1.5 to 13 miles). It is hot and dry; water can be found in oases, and any crops must be irrigated. Lake Tiberias, or the Sea of Galilee, is located in the valley, and is an important part of the rich religious history of the region. The Dead Sea is an inland sea that has a very high mineral content, situated about 423 meters (1,388 feet) lower than the Mediterranean Sea. At 200 meters (660 feet) below sea level, Lake Kinneret (another name for the Sea of Galilee) is the world's lowest freshwater lake.

Plants & Animals

Most ecological diversity in Palestine occurs near water; however, many species have adapted to dry conditions and habitats throughout the region.

Around the Jordan River, there are over 2,000 plant species. In areas that have a Mediterranean climate, plants can be grown without irrigation. Common species of tree include the Aleppo pine, the common oak, and the Palestine terebinth. Lower-growing plants include the calycotome thorn bush, the rockrose, and the salvia. The bushy bean-caper, a desert plant, can survive with very little water. Other vascular species include the dark-purple Iris, the sedge, bedstraw, Danin fennel, stork's bill, and an orchid species specific to the area (*Anacamptis israelitica*).

A number of animal species live in the region, including four species of blind mole rat (backhuys) and the Negev shrew. In addition, common to the territories are marsh lynx, Acacia gazelles, the ibex, and jackals. Animals adapted to tropical habitats live in the Jordan Valley, including the cheetah, the honey badger, the tropical cuckoo, and the carpet viper. The griffon vulture is a rare bird that almost became extinct in the 1930s, and the Hula Painted Frog, previous thought extinct, has been rediscovered and represents the lone surviving species of its genus.

CUSTOMS & COURTESIES

Greetings

When Palestinians greet each other, they are often also expressing something about their relationship. For example, youth are expected to show respect when they greet elders, and often refer to seniors or other parental figures as "ammy" (my uncle) or "khalati" (my aunt). Even as adults, children who have not seen their parents or grandparents for some time are expected to greet them with a kiss on the hand. The back of the hand will then be brought to the kisser's forehead as a sign of further respect.

Moreover, greetings often follow a kind of script. The most common initial greeting in the Palestinian territories is "Marhaba" ("Welcome"), similarly used as the American greeting of "Hello." However, the recipient usually responds with a slightly different phrase, usually "Marhabtayn" ("Two welcomes"). An enthusiastic acquaintance might offer a variation such as "one hundred welcomes" or "one thousand welcomes." Other greetings include the traditional Arabic expression, "As-salam alaykum" ("Peace be unto you"), the common response to which is "'alaykum as salam" (and unto you, peace). Among elders or more traditional villagers, the opening part of a conversation can be prolonged for several minutes before any actual information is exchanged. In this way, greetings are typically followed by a variety of purely courteous phrases, such as "You honor us by coming" and "No, it is you who honor me," or "You bring light to our village" and "No, the village gives me light."

During the 1990s, when it seemed that relative peace was at hand during the Israeli-Palestinian conflict, more than 100,000 Palestinian-Americans moved back to the territories. Their arrival added odd elements to daily conversation. Many of the older returnees still used older forms of address, and thus sounded old-fashioned. Their children, on the other hand, carried over the informal English that they had adapted to, occasionally offending elders who expected greetings that are more respectful.

Gestures & Etiquette

One of the biggest differences between Palestinian and Western manners and mannerisms concerns the issue of physical affection. Among Palestinians, it is very common to see grown women walking down the street arm-in-arm, and it is equally common to see men doing the same. While sitting next to each other, male friends may hold hands or drape their arms over each other's shoulders. It is common, and even expected, for men to greet each other with kisses. On the other hand, men and women who are not married or blood relatives will rarely touch each other. In fact, devout women often place their hands on their chests if men try to shake their hands. This is a polite way of clarifying that handshakes are improper, but that they still wish to greet graciously.

A common hand-gesture involves pinching the thumb and first two fingers together, while the fourth and fifth fingers lie against the palm and the arm is bent at the elbow. The meaning is either "wait a minute" or "slow down." The gesture might be used, for instance, if the person they are speaking with is drawing an incorrect conclusion.

Palestinians are known for their hospitality, and this usually includes a meal. The sheer quantity of food served often comes as a surprise to Westerners. It should be remembered that the cook (usually a woman) has purposely prepared too much. A Palestinian host would likely be embarrassed if little or no food were left over at the end of a meal—this would be indication that she had not prepared enough. Similarly, if a guest did not take seconds, it would be assumed that the food was not acceptable. Unsurprisingly, a Palestinian family is likely to reserve their best offerings for guests, which would include the best cut of meat if dining. (It should be noted that vegetarianism is still rare among Palestinians.)

Eating/Meals

In the past, Palestinian kitchens were located outside of the main house, and virtually every family had its own taboon, or bread oven, in their yard. Large extended families lived under one roof, and the time-consuming work of traditional cooking was shared by many hands, usually female. Regional specialties varied widely, often because of geographic factors that led to varying agricultural produce. While Palestinian women remain responsible for food preparation, the move from rural to urban living and from village to suburban life has brought the kitchen into the house. Moreover, many women now work outside the home and fewer extended families live together. Thus, cooking has grown more standardized and is often far simpler than in the past.

The midday meal is typically the largest meal of the day and often based around the traditional mahashi (stuffed vegetables) or yakhani (mutton stew, sometimes with a yogurt gravy). Ma'alube (literally, "upside down") is a casserole of chicken, almonds, and rice, presented upside down on a serving tray, while the similarly popular musakhan involves chicken roasted with sumac (a dark red, pungent spice), onions, allspice, saffron, and pine nuts, served on rounds of taboon bread. Special meals, such as wedding feasts or graduation parties, will often feature lamb and rice dishes, served from a communal plate and generally accompanied by or cooked in yogurt. The entire village, neighborhood, or large, extended circle of friends and family most often shares these.

Visiting

Palestinians have a strong tradition of hospitality. In fact, the first Arabic word or phrase a non-native might learn is "kool, kool" ("eat, eat!"). Palestinians often maintain a separation between the private and public spaces in their homes. A visitor is likely to be welcomed into a formal living room area, while the family's private quarters will be more modest and private. Sometimes this separation is expressed by either the presence or absence of the family's female members. For example, in many traditional homes, only male family members are permitted to greet and sit with a male visitor. In such cases, refreshments will be provided by a woman with her gaze averted, and she will quickly remove herself from the room. A non-Arab female visitor will often be treated as something of an honorary male and will be free to converse with both the men and women of a family.

The serving of coffee (qahweh arabiyya) is a ceremonial act of hospitality. Arabic coffee is brewed in a small copper or stainless steel pot and boiled several times, with care that it does not scald or boil over. The coffee grounds may be spiced with green cardamom (coffee beans and cardamom pods are roasted separately, ground, and then mixed together for traditional use), and the drink is served in small cups, typically about the size of an espresso cup. The coffee is general more bitter if the occasion calls for it, such as for funeral repasts, when it is prepared the night before. Stopping by some's house for coffee in the late afternoon—considered the most appropriate time for visiting—will usually involve first being given a cold drink, then fruits (often slightly unripe, in keeping with the Palestinian fondness for sour flavors), then tea and pastries, and finally coffee. The coffee is traditionally sipped slowly, the cup put down between sips, to allow for conversation.

Upon leaving, particularly when the last sip of coffee is finished, it is considered customary for the guest to say "Daymi" ("Always"), meaning "May you always be able to serve such coffee." Certain events call for a very different leave-taking, however. After drinking coffee at a funeral, for instance, one might say "La arakum allah makruh" ("May God not make you see further hardships") or "Vislam raskum" ("May you stay in good health.)

LIFESTYLE

Family
The Israeli occupation has put a significant strain on the Palestinian family. Palestinian communities were once part of a traditional, agrarian society in which family roles were clearly defined. These were based on generational hierarchy and a gender-based division of labor. The family's patriarch, or father, tended to the land and provided for the family, while the matriarch, or mother, was responsible for all domestic tasks and child rearing. Traditionally, children lived at home until they were married and were expected to obey their parents until they moved out (and often afterward).

The loss of land, constant violence, and socioeconomic factors such as unemployment has disrupted this traditional structure. Extended families have been separated, sometimes into different refugee camps. While temporary in nature, these camps have developed into somewhat permanent fixtures. For those Palestinians living in camps within the Palestinian territories, continual violence and unrest, the lack of fundamental rights, and the inability to ensure a safe future for their families is a constant concern. For those families displaced from their homeland, noncitizenship in the host country, employment limitations, and an inability to care for their families are also concerns. In some camps, radical fundamentalists have established strongholds, drawing fire from host nation troops and endangering the lives of those confined within the camps. Such was the case in the Nahr al-Bared camp in Lebanon in 2007, when the Lebanese shelled the camp, essentially destroying it. In 2014, many camps, like the traditionally Palestinian Yarmouk camp, near Damascus, Syria, has now become home to both Syrian and Palestinian refugees, all fleeing violence. Conflict between armed groups has made life in the camps dangerous. The UN estimates that, in Yarmouk alone, some 18,000 civilians, of which an estimated 3,500 are children, are currently forced to live in life-threatening conditions.

In the Palestinian territories, women often hold jobs outside of the home. However, many do so not out of choice, but because their husbands need help in providing for the family. In such cases, their job can be perceived as a mark of shame rather than social advancement. Furthermore, there has been an increasing trend in which young Palestinian males have rejected the authority of their fathers (and the older generation in general) because they have failed to provide for their families or end the Israeli occupation.

Housing

In the past, the typical Palestinian dwelling consisted of a cave or single-room house, divided into two stories. Animals were kept on the bottom floor and the top floor served as storage and housed the family. Living quarters tended to be very small and usually not more than the average hotel room. Mattresses would be laid out at night and collected in the morning, and eating was done on the floor from communal dishes on a shared cloth.

Today, people are more likely to live in stone homes with several rooms, and fewer families own farm animals or work their own land. Frequently, when a son gets married, the father will add an addition to the family home, allowing the young couple to move in. The Israeli occupation has made it difficult to maintain this tradition, however, as the authorities often make it very difficult for Palestinians to obtain building permits, especially in the Palestinian parts of Jerusalem.

Within camps, housing can range from tents to cinder block or concrete homes. As camps have become more entrenched, housing has improved, and the tradition of adding an additional floor above the family home for a new generation is not uncommon. Still, many of those in refugee camps acknowledge that life in the camps is temporary until the return to their homeland.

According to Amnesty International, in 2014, Israeli forces conducted forced evictions of Palestinians living in the West Bank and, as punitive measures, demolished homes of those who fought back are otherwise refused to comply. Houses built without official Israeli permits were likewise destroyed.

Food

Palestinian cuisine is similar to other Arab cuisines such as those from Lebanon, Jordan, and Syria (often referred to as Levantine cuisine, the traditional cuisine of the eastern Mediterranean), and it has distinct Turkish and Mediterranean influences. Westerners are likely to associate falafel, hummus, and pita bread with the Middle East, but for most Palestinians, these are fast foods, eaten on a street corner or in a casual restaurant when one cannot get home for a real meal.

Rice plays an essential role in Palestinian cuisine—from the stuffing of vegetables to the delicacies at a wedding—in spite of the fact that it grows nowhere near the Palestinian territories. This is because the historical region of Palestine stood at the crossroads of civilization, with trade routes from the Far East, Africa, and Europe running the length of the Mediterranean shores. It is likely that rice was introduced to the regional diet as a result of this cross-cultural experience.

In addition to rice, Palestinian cooking is heavily dependent on olive oil, sesame oil, sumac, and vegetables such as eggplant, zucchini, tomatoes, and okra. Many foods are cooked in lemon juice, yogurt, or tamarind (a fruit somewhat similar to carob), giving them a slightly sour taste. Palestinians are also known for their love of sour fruit and nuts, from green almonds to oranges that are not fully ripened.

Life's Milestones

In Palestinian society, religious rituals are semi-private events, but the celebration after is shared with the entire community. For example, a wedding ceremony will be attended only by a small family group, but the reception may include hundreds of people. This might mean an entire village, but in an urban society such as today, families often simply invite a wide circle of friends and acquaintances. Nonetheless, weddings remain the biggest social event, though the ongoing Israeli occupation has meant drastic changes in what was once an extended and festive milestone. Due to escalating violence or the simple presence of roadblocks, many invitees cannot attend, and fewer are invited. Additionally, many weddings now end before sundown and feature quiet and subdued celebrations.

The birth of a child is celebrated with the Aqīq, a special ritual in which a goat or ram is traditionally slaughtered in the new child's name; the child's head is shaved, a ritual considered to eliminate impurities; and boys are circumcised. Often the weight of the baby's shorn hair is measured, and a commensurate amount of silver is given to the poor as alms. The Aqīq is generally held seven days after the baby's birth. Another important milestone is graduation from high school or college. Relatives and friends gather to congratulate the graduates, usually at a party thrown for all of that year's class.

CULTURAL HISTORY

Art

Palestinian embroidery is an entirely local and female art form. The techniques and silk thread were imported from China long before either arrived in Europe. The linens used were produced by local weavers, and natural vegetation, such as sumac or pomegranate peels, were used to create dyes. In an agricultural society that often knew poverty and struggle, rich, colorful needlework made a powerful statement. Traditionally, girls began to learn embroidery when they were about six years old and would wear their most beautiful garments for the first time at their wedding. While modern Palestinian women practice less embroidery than in the past, it remains an important tradition and serves as one of the main symbols of Palestinian identity. Some women have even adapted the form to other uses, such as decorative pillowcases or tablecloths.

Jewelry was also an important Palestinian handicraft, and a significant part of a Palestinian bride's wedding trousseau (traditional attire). Local silversmiths produced bracelets, necklaces, ankle bracelets, chains (such as those hung from a woman's headdress), chokers, and rings and nose-rings. These often incorporated beads, well-known shapes and patterns, or verses from the Koran (or Qur'an, Islam's holy book). The jewelry served a triple purpose: providing beauty and ornamentation, functioning as a statement of the woman's wealth and status, and, perhaps most importantly, as protection from evil forces. In particular, blue beads secured the wearer against the classical evil eye (which is present in Islamic doctrine); amber was associated with healing and was believed to have curative powers; and a silver hamsa symbol, or Hand of Fatima (symbolized as a "protecting hand"), represented abundance and protection. In addition, odd numbers are considered lucky, so Palestinian jewelry traditionally features odd-numbered embellishment, such as a triangle (three sides) or seven chains.

Music

Palestinians, particularly older generations, are fond of traditional Arab music, often sung by artists such as Umm Kulthum (1898/1904–1975), an Egyptian singer who sang both traditional and modern Arab music in the 20th century and was dubbed "Al-Sitt" (the Lady) by her admirers. Kulthum's recordings reveal a musical style that closely resembles narrative or storytelling accompanied by music, with rhythm and intonation (chanting) conveying the emotional nature of the music. Accompanying instruments often include the oud (lute), daf (or dap, a frame drum), and ney (flute). Palestinian folk musicians have reinvented traditional tunes with more modern lyrics, often singing of the loss of homeland and suffering.

In the 21st century, new styles of music have taken root in the Palestinian territories—rap and hip-hop. DAM is considered the first Palestinian hip-hop group. Founded in 1999, the group produces songs primarily in Arabic, but in Hebrew and English as well. The band's members claim that the reason they rap in Hebrew as well as Arab is because they want their Jewish neighbors to know who they are and what they face. Their music is distributed over the Internet, and they have gained worldwide recognition as pioneers within Israel and the Palestinian territories. The hip-hop and rap genre in the territories has adopted Arab tunes and Western beats to produce a unique Palestinian sound. Other Palestinian rappers include Palestinian Rapperz, the Philistines, and Arapeyat (a female rap group, whose name is loosely translated as "Arab Women Who Rap").

Dance

Dance is an art form shared by both genders in Palestinian society—though not always together. Women and men have long danced to the sounds of the tabla (a goblet-shaped hand drum), and perhaps the best-known dance is the dabke, a line dance characterized by high kicks and spins. Communal festivities traditionally feature dancing, and today many young people take classes to improve their skill and learn more about their heritage.

Dances are generally segregated by gender, though in the past, men and women often danced under the same roof if the village was small. As communities grew larger, adults became uncomfortable with the mixing of unmarried young men and women. Today, the genders are often more fully segregated. However, professional Palestinian dance troupes often feature men and women dancing side by side.

Literature

One of the most important Palestinian art forms is poetry, which has its roots in the ancient Arabic-language ode, or qasidah (also kasida). The qasidah is a long, intricate poem written for the purpose of recitation, traditionally by men. The piece typically begins with a personal tale (nasib) and ultimately serves to praise a ruler or mourn a death. Early poetry was also a form of satire directed against foes (hija'). The structure of the qasidah is very formal and includes a single rhyme structure throughout and between 60 and 100 lines. Qasidahs written before the advent of Islam in the seventh century are considered the cultural bedrock of Arabic-language literature, with many still recited today.

The Palestinian territories are also home to the Palestinian hikaye, a narrative form of oral expression traditionally practiced by women. These narrations are usually attended only by women and children during winter evenings, and any female over the age of seventy is considered a hikaye teller. This oral tradition has evolved

to include current political and social concerns, but is in rapid decline. In 2005, this tradition was proclaimed one of the Masterpieces of the Oral and Intangible Heritage of Humanity by the United Nations Educational, Scientific, and Cultural Organization (UNESCO).

Since 1948, poetic artistic expression has dealt mostly with politics. The most famous Palestinian poet is Mahmoud Darwish (1941–2008). He was born in an area of Palestine that became part of Israel, and though he never made his home in the Palestinian territories, he is widely considered the Palestinian national poet. His poems detail the Palestinian refugee experience and their loss of a motherland. Writing in the classical Arabic style and using traditional metrics, he has won numerous awards, and his work has been published in over 20 languages.

The character of Hanthala, a 10-year-old cartoon boy with his back forever turned to the viewer, is also an important Palestinian symbol. Drawn for many years by the Palestinian cartoonist Naji el-Ali (c. 1938–1987), Hanthala was a witness to the suffering of his people, his hands always clasped behind his back, his feet bare. El-Ali's cartoons were very political, criticizing any abuse of power, and he was eventually assassinated in 1987. To this day, however, the image of Hanthala can be seen in many public places in the Palestinian territories, and many Palestinians wear Hanthala necklaces, the image of the character often hanging next to a charm in the shape of historical Palestine.

CULTURE

Arts & Entertainment

The arts flourish with the support of a number of institutions, including the Bethlehem Peace Center; the Khalil Sakakini Cultural Center; and the non-governmental organization, the Palestine Popular Art Centre. One of the earliest arts organizations in the territories is the Palestinian National Theater, a non-profit institution in Jerusalem. Cinema and theater productions take place at the Al-Kasaba Theatre and

Cinematheque, which hosted an international film festival from 2006 to 2010.

Contemporary Palestinian art is overwhelmingly influenced by the Nakba ("the catastrophe"), which refers to the 1948 anniversary of the creation of the state of Israel and the division of Palestine. Palestinian art, as a result, is also heavily influenced by the refugee experience and the ongoing occupation. This influence was further intensified by the fact that, until the Oslo Accords of 1993, Israel forbade the flying of the Palestinian flag. In response, many artists chose to use the flag's colors (red, black, white, and green) in their art, and traditional folk arts, such as dancing and embroidery, often served as national symbols.

Literature has also become an important contemporary artistic pursuit for the Palestinian people, who often have neither the freedom nor the resources to pursue other artistic expressions. Author Sahar Khalifeh (1941–), one of the most important voices of Palestinian literature, was born in the West Bank city of Nablus and is a leading Palestinian feminist. She founded the Women's Affairs Center in Nablus in 1988, and the center now has branches in Gaza and Amman, Jordan. The novels *Wild Thorns* (1975) and *The Inheritance* (1997) are considered her most notable works, and both have been translated into English. Her 2002 novel, *The Image, the Icon, and the Covenant*, won the 2006 Naguib Mahfouz Medal for Literature.

Yahya Yakhlif (1944–) is another leading author who also served as a deputy minister in the Palestinian National Authority's Ministry of Culture. He is known for the novel *A Lake Beyond the Wind* (1991), which deals with the Nakba and its long-term effects on the Palestinian people.

Hip-hop has also become a popular form of poetic expression in recent years. Some artists have been known to create backing tracks for their work by recording street sounds and remixing these with their vocals. Like their poetic literary brethren, many Palestinian hip-hop artists detail the discrimination they experience as Palestinians or Palestinian-Israelis.

Well-known Palestinian visual artists include Abed Abdi (1942–), a graphic designer, sculptor, and mural artist as well as painter and art historian Samia Halaby (1936–), who taught at the Yale School of Art between 1972 and 1982. Asim Abu Shaqra (1960–1990) frequently used the image of the cactus in his oil paintings. Rana Bishara (1971–) specializes in performance works and installations that make statements about Nakba and employ unconventional media, such as tear gas canisters, barbed wire, cacti, even flatbread.

Sports organizations in Palestine include the Palestinian Football Federation and the Palestinian Tennis Association. In both Gaza and the West Bank, there are soccer teams that travel outside the territories to participate in matches.

Cultural Sites & Landmarks

Many sites in the West Bank are mentioned in the Muslim holy book, the Koran, and also the Jewish and Christian sacred texts. Among these are the ancient city of Jericho, thought to be the oldest continuously-inhabited city in the world; Bethlehem, considered to be the birthplace of Jesus of Nazareth and a site of Christian pilgrimage (particularly the Church of the Nativity); Rachel's Tomb, a biblical gravesite located outside of Bethlehem that is considered one of Judaism's holiest sites; and the city of Hebron, considered the second holiest city in Judaism after Jerusalem. Within Hebron lies the Cave of the Patriarchs (or Cave of Machpelah), a complex featuring a series of subterranean caves that have biblical importance.

The West Bank is home to several historical landmarks, including a site holy to both Christians and Muslims: the 16th-century Monastery of St. George, located in Wadi Qelt. Legend has it that Saint George slew a dragon on the site in the third century, an act of bravery that, along with St. George's public declaration of his faith, won many new Christian converts. Ultimately, he was martyred by the Romans and became a powerful symbol as a protector of the defenseless. The entrance to the village of el-Khader, where the monastery is located, is marked by a stone archway, on which the figure of St. George, astride a horse, is slaying a dragon; many Palestinian homes feature a similar adornment above their front door. Another famous church is Burqin Church, or St. George's Church, a Byzantine-era Greek Orthodox church in the Palestinian town of Burqin. It is considered the third oldest church in existence.

The Palestinian territories are located within the larger area of Israel, often referred to as the "Holy Land." The city of Jerusalem, governed by Israel, is the center of Jewish faith and Israeli national identity. It is also referred to as the third holiest city in Islam. As a result, it has long been the one of the most sensitive issues in the Israeli-Palestinian conflict. Muslim access to al-Haram al-Sharif (the Nobel Sanctuary), a mosque complex in Jerusalem's Old City, is sometimes restricted in times of unrest, for reasons of security.

Libraries & Museums

Established by the Arab Women's Union in 1979, Baituna al-Talhami Museum, or the Bethlehem Folklore Museum, stands as a repository for Palestinian cultural artifacts, as well as a refuge for Palestinians seeking assistance. It was initially a center for refugees seeking a meal or employment (such as doing embroidery for sale). It has grown to house a collection of Palestinian artifacts from typical homes, and the structures themselves are traditional in nature. One building is said to be very typical of the homes that would have been in existence around the birth of Christ. The center also serves as the host for Palestinian cultural festivals.

The privately owned Gaza Museum of Archeology boasts a collection of artifacts discovered in Gaza. Among the collection of 350 relics are coins, tools, pottery, and statues, with some articles dating back to the Bronze Age. Hamas has censored some of the works in the collection, and, as a result, these cannot be displayed. One of the censored pieces is a statue of Aphrodite, whose garments are deemed too revealing. The museum sustained some damage in 2009 due to bombing.

In Jerusalem, there is also the L. A. Mayer Institute for Islamic Art, which features a collection of art, watches, and clocks. The museum has a unique collection of clocks and watches created by Abraham-Louis Breguet (1747–1823), a Swiss-born French horologist. The Islamic art on display dates as far back as the seventh century.

Holidays

Land Day is celebrated on March 30. On this holiday, Palestinians protest what they see as illegal Israeli settlement on their lands. Each year, they participate in labor strikes, protests, parades, and memorial services. While the holiday activities are often peaceful, they have, at times, been accompanied by violence.

Youth Culture

Palestinian society is sharply divided along gender lines, starting at a very early age. Teenage boys and girls are not allowed to socialize without adult supervision. When they do interact, there are limitations on what they can do. For example, youth are generally allowed to meet friends of the opposite sex at a café on weekends, but social dancing is typically forbidden. Due to Israeli occupation, Palestinian youth are generally more politicized early on. They are often involved with political movements throughout adolescence and focus their admiration on political heroes.

One particularly popular form of entertainment among Palestinian youth is to watch music videos, typically broadcast via satellite TV. Unlike American music networks, such as MTV, whose programming largely revolves around reality television shows, Palestine's satellite networks specifically broadcast music videos. This exposure to music is significant because the borders of the territories are closed to almost all Arabic singers, and travel restrictions make it difficult to attend the performances of local bands. Thus, satellite TV is often the only medium outside of radio and the Internet for musicians to reach effectively their audience.

SOCIETY

Transportation

The issue of transportation is among the largest difficulties faced by the Palestinian people on a daily basis. Israel controls the borders and the airspace of both Gaza and the West Bank, meaning it controls movement into and out of these territories. Hundreds of roadblocks and a series of Israeli-only roads on the West Bank severely limit travel for Palestinians, affecting employment, schooling, and the use of health services. Israel's construction of an extensive security barrier along the West Bank's edge further complicates matters. At many spots, the wall slices villages in half, separating people from their fields, or cutting off villagers from the towns on which they depend for services.

In Gaza, the wide-scale destruction of roads and bridges resulting from Israeli attacks critically hampers driving. Near-constant border closures mean that access to gasoline and car parts is severely limited. In both parts of the Palestinian territories, people often resort to walking or donkey use, or they try to move closer to their job or children's school in order to avoid the problem altogether.

Cars travel on the right-hand side of the road in Israel and the Palestinian territories.

Transportation Infrastructure

The transportation infrastructure in the Palestinian territories suffers from a lack of investment. While the Palestinian National Authority has an infrastructure plan, it hinges on ending the conflict, developing the infrastructure in marginalized areas, and improving the infrastructure. Water, sanitation, and electricity are of primary importance.

Media & Communications

Almost every Palestinian home has at least one television, and an estimated 94 percent have a satellite dish that receives international broadcasting. The Al Jazeera news network, based in the country of Qatar, is a very popular source of information, along with other international media organizations and networks, such as the British Broadcasting Corporation (BBC), Cable News Network (CNN), Palestine TV (owned by the Fatah government in the West Bank), and Al-Aqsa TV (run by Hamas in the Gaza Strip).

The Internet is an important source of information, though only 47 percent of Palestinian homes have computers, and only 15.1 percent have Internet access as of 2014. Internet cafés are very popular; university libraries allow free Internet access, and most coffee shops and hotel lobbies offer free wireless access. When Israeli travel restrictions made it difficult to access these sources, handheld devices became an important information source. Texting has also become an important method of conveying information for Palestinians. Non-governmental organizations (NGOs) or concerned individuals often send out mass text messages as events unfold. The reports, though often incomplete, frequently serve as the first source of news.

The Israeli and Palestinian governments exert little censorship over the Palestinian media. However, reporters and editors, knowing that they may be harassed or threatened for covering certain events or expressing certain opinions, typically practice self-censorship. Since the 2007 civil war that resulted in Fatah governing in the West Bank and Hamas governing in Gaza, journalists have been arrested or threatened for being associated with or writing positive stories about the party not in power in either place.

SOCIAL DEVELOPMENT

Standard of Living

The Palestinian territories ranked 107th out of 187 countries on the 2014 United Nations Human Development Index, which measures quality of life and standard of living indicators.

Water Consumption

An estimated 81.8 percent of the Palestinian population has access to clean water and 94.3 percent of the population has access to improved sanitation (2012). Because of military incursions that occur in occupied territories, these statistics are in a state of flux, as military actions often take out basic infrastructure. In 2010, UNICEF and the Palestinian Authority were working with NGOs and the United Nations to address humanitarian needs of more than 4 million Palestinian people.

According to a May 2014 UNICEF (United Nations Children's Fund) report, Gaza's aquifer will become unsuitable by 2016, with irreparable damage possible by 2020. In fact, an estimated 95 percent of the water is unpotable.

Education

Education is highly valued by the Palestinian people. However, because of the lack of stability and the economic problems in the region, education is challenging for Palestinians. Nevertheless, the CIA reported that, in 2013, the number of years a Palestinian student expected to stay in school was an average of thirteen years, with twelve for men and fourteen for women. According to UNICEF, net attendance to the last primary school grade in 2012 was 96.3 percent overall, with 91.9 percent for girls and 91.3 percent for boys. In the same year, net enrollment for females in secondary school was 85.3, and for males, net enrollment was 77.5.

Many students and teachers have been killed, injured, or arrested in the ongoing violence. Because of checkpoints and curfews, some students and teachers have a difficult time getting to school. In addition to these difficulties, a number of Palestinian schools have been closed by the Israeli government. The Ministry of Education and Higher Education of the Palestinian National Authority is attempting to improve education in the region, updating the curriculum and by moving schools away from areas of intense conflict. The Ministry of Education has received support from a number of countries and organizations, including the United Nations.

In 2010, the Palestinian minister of education and higher education, UNICEF, and the United Nations Relief and Works Agency for Palestine Refugees in the Near East (UNRWA)

declared their concern that Palestinian educational standards were on the decline despite their best efforts. Among their concerns were the lack of safe access to schools, a lack of facilities in East Jerusalem, schools sustaining damage that had yet to be repaired, and a lack of materials. Such issues continue to be a concern as of 2015.

There are many universities and colleges in the region, including Al-Quds University, with campuses in Jerusalem, Abu Dis, and al-Bireh; Birzeit University, which—having been founded in 1924—is the oldest university in the state of Palestine; and Bethlehem University, which was the first university in the West Bank in 1973.

The adult literacy rate in 2015 stands at 96.5 percent, with women at 94.5 percent and men at 98.4 percent.

Women's Rights

Palestinian society tends to be traditional and patriarchal. The life of the individual is closely bound with the family and broader community, and individuals are often expected to make personal decisions based on communal or familial needs. As such, younger women and men are obliged to defer to their older counterparts, including older siblings, and women are further bound to patriarchal and traditional values and rules. In fact, a family's social value is often shaped and reflected by the behavior of its female members. Thus, Palestinian women frequently are not allowed to make their own decisions regarding their educational or career choices, without first gaining approval from their father, husband, or older brother. While these attitudes and conventions do not hold true for every Palestinian family, they contribute to a general tone in which Palestinian women are treated as less-than-equal.

Violence against women is a prevalent issue and is often accepted and sometimes encouraged. Existing laws offer inadequate protection, and in the rare case that a woman reports abuse, she may be returned to the "care" of her attacker due to an indoctrinated cultural belief that certain victims deserve to be mistreated. This is further exemplified by the fact that prison sentences are reduced if the victim was attacked for committing adultery, and a rapist will be absolved of his crime if he agrees to marry his victim. Further complicating the issue of violence against women is the fact that medical personnel often lack the training they need to help female victims. Women have also been subject to honor killings, in which a woman suspected of inappropriate behavior is murdered by someone in her own family. In 2011, the Palestinian Central Bureau of Statistics reported that 35 percent of married women had been subjected to some form of physical violence during the preceding twelve months, while 40 percent of unmarried women had been abused by someone in their household during the same period.

Women's struggles are often compounded by the Israeli occupation. Men who are mistreated at roadblocks or in Israeli prisons often carry that anger into their home life, and women who must work to support their families may be treated with jealousy and contempt by men who cannot support their families on their own. Women are also passed over in terms of education; when only one child can be sent to school, a son is more likely to be chosen than a daughter is. Additionally, Israeli restrictions often prevent, postpone, and limit weddings, education, and health care, all of which in turn limit opportunities for Palestinian women to advance.

In terms of political representation, Palestinian law requires that women fill a certain minimum of seats in parliament. As of 2005, that number was thirteen of the 132-seat Palestinian Legislative Council. For the most part, however, men control decision-making.

Health Care

Like teachers and students, health care workers face the dangers and difficulties of doing their jobs amid violence. Israeli curfews and roadblocks make it difficult for emergency medical services to reach Palestinian patients and for patients to reach hospitals and doctors. Delays in reaching medical services affect all who live in the Palestinian territories, especially pregnant women and the very sick.

Efforts have been made to improve health care services, such as mobile health clinics, local clinics in villages, hospitals, and training for health care workers. The Palestinian government has been trying to implement a national health care system. The Palestine Red Crescent Society, which is similar to the American Red Cross, works to supply emergency medicine and ambulance transportation. As of 2013, there are two physicians and 1.3 hospital beds to every 1,000 people in Gaza. In the West Bank, there are 1.3 physicians and 1.2 hospital beds for every 1,000 people.

GOVERNMENT

Structure

Until 2013, when the UN voted to recognize the Palestinian territories as an independent state by upgrading their observer status, the Palestinian National Authority was recognized as the governing body in the West Bank. Fatah was the political party that led the Palestinian National Authority (PNA) and has headquarters in the West Bank. The militant Islamic group Hamas has traditionally controlled Gaza. Hamas is considered a terrorist organization by many countries because a key element of its political doctrine calls for the destruction of Israel.

The Palestinian National Authority has traditionally had the power to manage security and civilian control and consists of three branches: a legislative branch, the Palestinian Legislative Council (PLC); the executive (the cabinet); and an independent judiciary. The president is elected directly by those Palestinians living in the territories; the president appoints the prime minister, who, in turn, appoints a cabinet of ministers.

The PLC is an elected body with 132 members that approves of the prime minister and his cabinet. This unicameral body has been reputed to hold significant authority in the Palestinian territories.

In 1994, following the Oslo Agreement between Israel and the Palestinian Liberation Organization (PLO), the Palestinian National

Authority was recognized as the governing body in the West Bank and Gaza. Government control changed when Palestinian voters gave Hamas a narrow victory in legislative elections. Voters used the election to express anger over political corruption and the failure of Fatah to create a Palestinian state.

Efforts to create a unified and shared government failed, and in 2007, the political rivalry between Fatah's Palestinian National Authority and Hamas led to outright civil war. Hamas took over Gaza, and Fatah's leadership fled to the West Bank. The political situation in the region remained fractured, tense, and violent. However, with support from the international community, the peace process prevailed, and, in April 2014, Hamas and Fatah agreed to hold elections that would create a unity government before the end of the year. Although as of 2015, this election has not yet taken place, on June 2, 2014, the interim unity government was formalized and functioning with Fatah leader Mahmoud Abbas as president.

Political Parties

Two major parties dominate Palestinian politics: the Fatah party (secular, left of center), which makes up a large faction of the Palestinian Liberation Organization (PLO), and Hamas, or the Islamic Resistance Movement, a more conservative, fundamentalist party that has been designated a terrorist organization and has a military branch known as the Izz ad-Din al-Qassam Brigades. In the 2006 PLC elections, Hamas, working within the Change and Reform alliance, received 44 percent of the vote, and gained 74 seats. Fatah achieved 41 percent of the vote and 45 seats. The 13 remaining seats were shared among a series of minor political parties and independents.

In 2007, following the Battle of Gaza (a June battle between Hamas and Fatah forces), Hamas gained control of Gaza and removed Fatah officials from local administration. In response, President Mahmoud Abbas expelled Hamas officials from the Palestinian National Authority in the West Bank. As of September 2010, Fatah and Hamas were in peace talks at the same time that the Palestinian National Authority was sitting

down with representatives from the Israeli government. A unity government was achieved in April 2014 and formalized by June, with Fatah leader Mahmoud Abbas as president.

Following the establishment of the national unity government in 2014, a general election in Palestine was slated for sometime within six months of the original April 2014 election date. However, as of October 2014, elections have been delayed indefinitely. The president must announce elections three months before they are held, in order to give time for the Central Elections Commission (CEC) to prepare for them.

Local Government

Theoretically, local government in the Palestinian territories consists of municipal councils, village councils, and local development committees depending on the size of the city or town.

Judicial System

Palestinian laws are under the purview of the Palestinian National Authority as dictated by the 1993 Oslo Accords, legal agreements between Israel and the Palestinian Liberation Organization (PLO) in which each mutually recognized the other; the PLO recognized Israel as a state, and Israel acknowledged the PLO as the representative of the Palestinian people. The Oslo Accords actually created the Palestinian National Authority, which formed in 1994.

Yet, the legal system in the Palestinian territories is, as of 2014, still in a state of confusion. Laws enacted over the years, instead of replacing others, remain in effect, so that many layers of laws exist from the region's history, including vestiges of Islamic law, English common law, and Jordanian, Egyptian, and Israeli law. The establishment of Palestine's sovereignty, the indivisibility of its lands, and its republican system are outlined in Article 4 of the proposed constitution. Articles 5, 6, and 7 respectively establish Islam as the nation's official religion, Arab as the national language, and Sharia (Islamic law) as the foundation for legislation. Other basic tenets are outlined in the draft constitution, which has yet to be adopted.

As of June 2015, the High Judicial Council is the highest authority in the Palestinian judicial system and oversees Palestine's court system. This system is comprised of a Supreme Court, subdivided into a High Court of Justice and a Cassation Court; Courts of Appeal, which are located in Jerusalem, Ramallah, and Gaza; Courts of First Instance, eight of which are in the West Bank and three of which are in Gaza; and Magistrate Courts, thirteen of which are in the West Bank and six of which are in Gaza. In addition to these courts, there is Corruption Crimes Court; two income tax appeals courts, one in each territory; and a first instance and appeals court for customs-related issues.

Taxation

Tax revenues in the Palestinian territories go to the Palestinian National Authority as well as to the Israeli government. Income taxes, tariffs, and value-added taxes (VAT) are levied in the territories.

Armed Forces

The Palestinian National Security Forces are a paramilitary group accountable to the Palestinian National Authority and are comprised of the Public Security Force, the Civil Police Force, the Preventive Security Force, the General Intelligence Force, the Military Intelligence Force, the Presidential Security Force, the Navy Police, Air Force, Coastal Police, and Civil Defense. Also part of the national security forces is Force 17, a commando and special ops division originally part of the Fatah movement. The Oslo Accords, signed in 1993, paved the way for the establishment of armed forces in Palestine, and since 2007, the Palestinian soldiers have received some level of training from U.S. Special Forces troops, as well as from Jordanian troops and international military personnel.

Foreign Policy

Technically, the Palestinian National Authority is not responsible for the foreign relations of the Palestinian territories. That role is exercised by Israeli authorities. For example, the PNA is not free to negotiate a trade agreement with Jordan, or establish border-crossing regulations with Egypt. However, the Palestinian leadership clearly maintains relationships with other nations. In 1988, the Palestinian National Council, the legislative arm of the PLO, issued a declaration of independence and declared the State of Palestine. At that time, ninety-four nations recognized the state, in spite of the fact that it did not geographically exist.

Furthermore, the United Nations acknowledged the proclamation of Palestine and affirmed the sovereignty of the Palestinian people. In November 2012, the United Nations General Assembly resolution 67/19 elevated the Palestinian territories and the PNA to a "non-member observer state," paving the way for international recognition of their political autonomy. Since the signing of the Oslo Accords in 1993, a framework for future Palestinian and Israeli relations, the international community has treated the PNA as a quasi-government, often providing aid and assistance. Additionally, most of the Arab world does not maintain relations with Israel and frequently champions the right of the Palestinian people. For example, in 2002 and 2007, the Arab League and all its member states (led by Saudi Arabia) offered a peace proposal, which would normalize all Arab-Israeli relations in exchange for a two-state resolution of the conflict. Israel did not respond to the proposals. Egypt and Jordan, both of which have long-standing treaties with Israel, have often mediated between Israel and the PNA.

The United States and European countries are often heavily involved in efforts to resolve the conflict, and serve as go-betweens when dealing with smaller issues. The US government brokered a transportation agreement between Israel and the PNA in 2005, for example, while many Western nations provide the PNA with aid. Since the rise of Hamas, however, much of this aid has been largely cut off or channeled to the Fatah-led government in the West Bank.

Human Rights Profile

International human rights law insists that states respect civil and political rights and also promote an individual's economic, social, and cultural rights. The United Nations Universal Declaration on Human Rights (UDHR) is recognized as the standard for international human rights. Its authors sought the counsel of the world's great thinkers, philosophers, and religious leaders and were careful to create a document that reflects the core values shared by every world culture. (To read this document or view the articles relating to cultural human rights, visit www.ohchr.org/EN/UDHR/Pages/Introduction.aspx.)

A major human rights problem facing the Palestinian territories is related to their complex relationship with Israeli authorities. In brief terms, Israel captured the West Bank and Gaza Strip in 1967 during the Six-Day War. Since that time, the Israeli military has occupied the West Bank. So, too, Gaza, until Israel removed its forces from that territory in 2005. In its role as both an occupying force in Gaza, and as a neighboring sovereign state, Israel has introduced government policies that compromise the human rights of Palestinians. These include violent military operations in the region, kidnapping suspects from their homes, spontaneous forced evictions, and regular border closings. The Israeli government also imposes economic sanctions that hinder access to jobs, education, and health care in the territories.

The situation is further complicated by the rivalry between Palestinian leaders in Gaza and the West Bank. Palestinian authorities on the West Bank often cooperate with Israeli security in an effort to eliminate or weaken Hamas in Gaza. This effort includes arbitrary detention by both Palestinian and Israeli forces. In many cases, the detainee is held twice without benefit of trial or access to lawyers and often faces abuse or torture from both security services.

In the West Bank, freedom of movement is severely limited by hundreds of roadblocks and roads built exclusively for Israeli use. Moreover, since January 2006, the borders of the Gaza Strip have been nearly permanently closed in response to the victory of the Hamas party in democratic elections. No people or supplies are allowed in or out on most days of the year, including food

and medical supplies, although in June 2015, Egypt has begun to allow both supplies, like cement needed for rebuilding, and Palestinians citizens across their border. The Israeli government claims the closure of Gaza's borders and other similar policies serve to protect Israelis threatened by Palestinian violence. However, critics believe the Israeli government is punishing all Palestinians for the behavior of a few, and impeding the establishment of a Palestinian state. All of these measures violate a number of articles in the UDHR.

The Palestinian governments and security services are themselves guilty of gross human rights violations. Both Hamas and Fatah conduct arbitrary arrests of political opponents, in violation of Article 2 of the UDHR. Detainees are regularly tortured and opposition organizations or media outlets are closed. Both sides claim that arrests only apply to those who have been involved in, or are planning, violence, but the evidence shows that arrests also involve non-violent political activists and supporters. Detainees are often tortured and forced to sign statements promising to cut ties to a given opposition organization.

Exacerbating matters is the breakdown of the judicial systems in both the West Bank and Gaza. Palestinian law requires that detainees be brought before a prosecutor within 24 hours, but this often does not occur. Lawyers are often kept from seeing their clients or getting information necessary for their defense. Security force members are rarely held accountable for serious abuses, and prosecutors and judges often lack experience.

The political leadership also regularly interferes with the legal process. In some circumstances, it replaces judges unsympathetic to its cause. In other cases, leaders continue to detain prisoners who are under order to be released.

Those Palestinians in refugee camps in other Arab nations, such as Lebanon, Syria, and Jordan, find themselves in a state of limbo. They have no property, political, and economic rights; often lack the freedom to earn a living in their chosen profession; and face the possibility that they will be expelled from that nation through no fault of their own, as has happened in both Kuwait and Iraq. The original group of over 700,000 refugees expelled from their homeland to refugee camps in Arab nations has grown to 5 million, and these people are still officially designated as "persons whose normal place of residence was Palestine between June 1946 and May 1948." Only Jordan has begun to naturalize these refugees—the remaining nations have failed to assimilate Palestinian populations.

Migration

Emigration from and immigration into the Palestinian territories are both difficult to quantify and highly politicized. For these reasons, migration rate data is unavailable.

ECONOMY

Overview of the Economy

The Palestinian economy has undergone many changes throughout the 20th century, often as the result of the region's political status. When it was divided in 1948, the region experienced a number of economic difficulties. Many Palestinian Arab farmers lost their farms and grazing land to Israel, and refugees crowded into the West Bank and Gaza.

The large influx of refugees glutted the employment market, lowered wages, and made local resources scarce. With assistance from countries like Egypt, Palestinians were able to develop an agricultural industry that depended largely on citrus crops. Smuggling also became a way to earn a living.

The 1987 Palestinian uprising known as the "intifada" (literally, "shake" in Arabic) (December 1987–September 1993) saw a decline in the economy, with more barriers to employment and fewer jobs in the manufacturing industries, although about 40 percent of Palestinians still worked in Israel each day. As of July 2014, there were an estimated 762,288 refugees in nineteen camps in the West Bank alone. In Gaza, held by Hamas, there were 1.26 million

Palestinian refugees in eight camps, making it one of the most densely populated areas in the world.

The economic picture in the two territories is very much a tale of two cities, with some progress made in the West Bank under the control of the Palestinian National Authority. Some semblance of stability has allowed the economy to grow, but much of the economy still relies on international aid. It is estimated that for the Palestinians to undergo significant economic growth, they must regain access to land and resources, secure freedom of movement, gain the ability to negotiate trade agreements, and facilitate private sector growth.

Industry

There are no major industries in the Palestinian territories. Most industry comprises cottage and family businesses that produce textiles, soap, woodcarvings, and souvenirs made from mother-of-pearl.

Labor

The estimated 2014 unemployment rate in the Palestinian territories was 45.1 percent in Gaza and 16 percent in the West Bank; the labor force in 2014 in both Gaza and the West Bank numbered 1.066 million. Of those employed, most people work in the service industry—79.3 percent in Gaza and 54.1 percent in the West Bank. Moreover, in Gaza, only 12.3 percent of the workforce is employed in manufacturing and industry, while the West Bank measures about 34.4 percent employment in that area. Approximately 11.5 percent of the workforce in the West Bank and 8.4 percent in Gaza find employment in the agricultural sector.

Energy/Power/Natural Resources

The Palestinian territories are not rich in natural resources. Potash, an ingredient in fertilizer, is found throughout the region. The mineral barite can also be found, but has not been widely extracted. Other resources include limestone, which is a major export commodity; marble; sand; and gravel.

While the Dead Sea contains many potentially valuable minerals, the Palestinian territories have not been able to develop an industry to extract them. The water supply in the region is not abundant; however, there are reliable sources of water available for use.

Until 2014, it was believed the region had no known fossil fuel deposits. However, with the discovery of the expansive Meged 5 oil field, located under both Israeli and Palestinian land, new tensions have developed over who owns the resources and attendant revenue. The Palestinian Authority, which faced a $2 billion (USD) deficit in 2014 alone, would benefit significantly such an economic boost.

In May 2014, UNICEF indicated that Gaza is experiencing a power crisis, as megawatts purchased from Israel and Egypt, along with that produced by the Gaza Power Plant, provide only 46 percent of the region's demands.

Agriculture

Because water is not plentiful in the region, little of the land in the Palestinian territories is arable, or suitable for growing crops. Much of the land is too arid or steep for agriculture. The areas that can be used to grow crops require investment, particularly in areas such as irrigation, to be successful.

Traditional crops grown by Palestinian farmers include cotton, olives, citrus, wheat, corn, barley, and sesame. Olives and citrus crops, such as oranges, remain important to the economy. The Plain of Esdraelon (also known as the Jezreel Valley) is a fertile area where many crops are grown.

Tourism

Continued political violence makes tourism difficult. However, the region is of interest to many because of its historical and religious sites. There are numerous antiquities in the city of Hebron, which is 6,000 years old. The most recent tourism numbers available indicate that, in 2010, 4.6 million people traveled within the Palestinian Territories. Of this number, 2.2 million were foreign visitors, while the remainders were resident tourists.

Emily L. Hauser, Christina Healey, & Savannah Schroll Guz

DO YOU KNOW?

- Although not previously recognized as a sovereign nation, Palestine has been represented by a team of athletes at the Olympic Games since 1996.

Bibliography

Amir S. Chesin, Bill Hutman and Avi Melamed. *"Separate and Unequal: The Inside Story of Israeli Rule in East Jerusalem."* 2nd ed. Cambridge, MA: *Harvard University Press.* 2001.

Baruch Kimmerling and Joel S. Migdal. "The Palestinian People: A History." Cambridge, MA: *Harvard University Press.* 2003.

Bronwyn Winter. "Hijab & the Republic: Uncovering the French Headscarf Debate." Syracuse, NY: *Syracuse University Press*, 2009. Gender and Globalization Ser.

George P. Monger. "Marriage Customs of the World: An Encyclopedia of Dating Customs and Wedding Traditions." 2 vols. Santa Barbara, CA: *ABC-CLIO.* 2013.

Ian J. Bickerton and Carla L. Klausner. "A Concise History of the Arab-Israeli Conflict." New York: *Pearson.* 2009.

Iman Saca and Maha Saca. "Embroidering Identities: A Century of Palestinian Clothing." Chicago: *The Oriental Institute of the University of Chicago.* 2006.

Jennifer Harris, (ed). "Textiles: 5,000 Years." Reprint. Washington, DC: *Smithsonian Institution Press.* 2011.

Laetitia Bucaille. "Growing up Palestinian." 2nd ed. Princeton Studies in Muslim Politics Ser. Princeton: *Princeton University Press*, 2006.

Laila El-Khalidi. "Art of Palestinian Embroidery." London, UK: *Saqi Books*, 2001.

Mariam Shahin. "Palestine: A Guide." Northampton, MA: *Internlink Publishing.* 2005.

Noam Chomsky and Ilan Pappé. "On Palestine." Ed. Frank Barat. New York: *Haymarket Books*.s 2015.

Nur Masalha and Lisa Isherwood, eds. "Theologies of Liberation in Palestine-Israel: Indigenous, Contextual, and Postcolonial Perspectives." Milton, Ontario, Canada: *Pickwick Publications*. 2014. Postmodern Ethics Ser.

Rashid Khalidi. "Palestinian Identity: The Construction of Modern National Consciousness." 2nd ed. New York: *Columbia University Press*, 2009.

Sachiko Murata and William C. Chittick. "The Vision of Islam." St. Paul, MN: *Paragon House*. 1998.

Samih K. Farsoun. "Culture and Customs of the Palestinians." Westport, CT: *Greenwood Publishing Group*. 2004. Cultures and Customs of the World Ser.

Shelagh Weir. "Embroidery from Palestine." Eastbourne, UK: *Gardners Books*. 2006.

Works Cited

_____. "Palestine Refugees." *UNRWA. United Nations Relief and Works Agency for Palestine Refugees in the Near East*. 2015.

_____. "State of Palestine: Water and Sanitation reports 2014." *UNICEF*. 2014. http://www.uniccf.org/oPt/wes_9230.html.

_____. "Where We Work: Gaza Strip." *UNRWA. United Nations Relief and Works Agency for Palestine Refugees in the Near East*. 2015. http://www.unrwa.org/where-we-work/gaza-strip.

_____. "Where We Work: West Bank." *UNRWA. United Nations Relief and Works Agency for Palestine Refugees in the Near East*. 2015. http://www.unrwa.org/where-we-work/west-bank.

"Art Center." *Popular Art Centre Official Website*. 2015. http://www.popularartcentre.org/.

"Census." *Palestinian Central Bureau of Statistics*. State of Palestine, 2015. http://www.pcbs.gov.ps/site/lang__en/881/default.aspx#Census.

"How to Make Arabic Coffee, or Boiled Coffee with Cardamom." *Bint Rhoda's Kitchen*. Blogger.com, 3 Feb. 2014.
http://bintrhodaskitchen.blogspot.com/2014/02/how-to-make-arabic-coffee-or-boiled.html.

"More women for Palestinian parliament." Al Jazeera. *Al Jazeera Media Network, 2015*. http://www.aljazeera.com/archive/2005/12/200849132147950310.html.

"Syria: UN agency warns violence near refugee camp endangering thousands of Palestinians." *UN News Centre*. 1 Apr. 2015. http://www.un.org/apps/news/story.asp?NewsID=50483#.Vc4jxWBRHIU.

"The Palestinian Hikaye." *Third Proclamation of Masterpieces of the Oral and Intangible Heritage of Humanity*. UNESCO, 2005. http://www.unesco.org/culture/intangible-heritage/30arb_uk.htm. http://www.unrwa.org/palestine-refugees.

Ahmad Melham. "Palestine Pulse: Palestinian elections on hold until further notice." *Al-Monitor: Pulse of the Middle East*. Al-Monitor, 28 Oct. 2014. http://www.al-monitor.com/pulse/originals/2014/10/palestine-presidential-parliamentary-elections-on-hold.html#.

Al-Kasaba Theatre and Cinematheque, 2015. *Al-Kasaba Theatre and Cinematheque Official Website*. 2015. http://www.alkasaba.org/english.php.

Amnesty International. "Annual Report: Israel and Occupied Palestinian Territories." *Amnesty International Report 2014/15*. 2015. https://www.amnesty.org/en/countries/middle-east-and-north-africa/israel-and-occupied-palestinian-territories/report-israel-and-occupied-palestinian-territories/.

At a Glance: State of Palestine Statistics. UNICEF. 31 Dec. 2013. http://www.unicef.org/infobycountry/oPt_statistics.html.

Diaa Hadid. "Gaza Welcomes Break From Strife and Reopening of Border With Egypt." *New York Times*. The New York Times Company, 20 Jun. 2015. http://www.nytimes.com/2015/06/21/world/gaza-welcomes-break-from-strife-and-reopening-of-border-with-egypt.html?_r=0.

High Judicial Council. "Numbers and Statistics." *State of Palestine Judicial Authority*. Palestinian High Judicial Council, 6 Feb. 2015. http://www.courts.gov.ps/details.aspx?id=HYYnoMa62815698aHYYnoM.

Jonathan Cook. "The Nakba Continues: Israel Continues Its Theft of Palestinian Natural Resources." *Washington Report on Middle East Affairs*. American Educational Trust, Jan/Feb. 2014. http://www.wrmea.org/2014-january-february/the-nakba-continues-israel-continues-its-theft-of-palestinian-natural-resources.html.

Naji Al-Ali. "Handala: Through the Eyes of a Palestinian Refugee." *Handala.org*. Handala.org, n.d. http://www.handala.org/.

Palestinian Constitution Committee. "Text of the Palestinian Draft Constitution." *Palestinian Center for Policy and Survey Research*. 14 Feb. 2001. http://www.pcpsr.org/en/node/487.

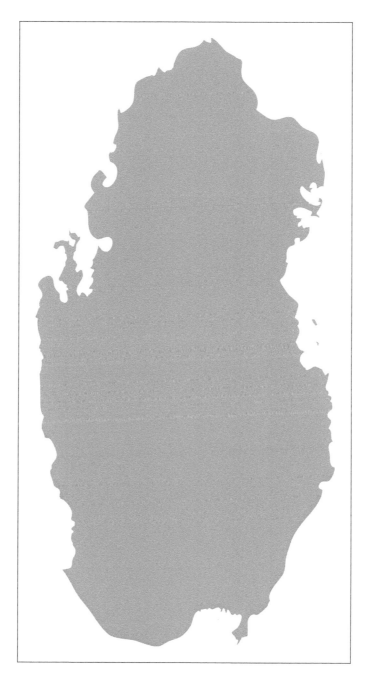

Introduction

The State of Qatar is an emirate in southwestern Asia. The country gained independence from Great Britain in 1971. It is situated on a peninsula that juts into the Persian Gulf, east of Saudi Arabia and northwest of the United Arab Emirates. A desert country with little water and very hot temperatures, particularly in the summer months, Qatar has extensive oil and gas resources, was an original member of Organization of the Petroleum Exporting Countries (OPEC), and belongs to the Gulf Cooperation Council (GCC). Once considered a regional diplomat, it has, since the outset of the Arab Spring, begun to encourage civil unrest and regime changes throughout the Middle East, both through pointed Al Jazeera coverage and direct monetary support of rebel forces, particularly in Syria. Although working with British and US forces to facilitate Western efforts in the wars against Iraq and Afghanistan, Qatar is, however, a noted Taliban backer, having allowed the group to set up a political office within Qatari borders. The country is also a supporter of the Muslim Brotherhood and several Syria-based rebel groups. For this reason, in March 2014, Bahrain, Saudi Arabia, and the United Arab Emirates withdrew their ambassadors from Qatar, and tensions—although mitigated by GCC diplomatic efforts—persist. Qatar has a relatively friendly relationship with Iran, with which it shares a natural gas reservoir—the largest in the world.

Islam shapes Qatar's culture, laws, and social infrastructure, and the majority of the population is Sunni Muslim. However, of the nearly 76 percent of Muslims in Qatar, 10 percent are Shi'a. Moreover, a blend of Asian and Middle Eastern influences is very much a part of life in the capital of Doha, and globalization has brought elements of Western and European culture to the city.

Qatar showcases its Bedouin past in museums and art collections, but only a very small number of Bedouin continue a nomadic life in the region. The vast majority of Qataris today live in an urban setting.

GENERAL INFORMATION

Official Language: Arabic
Population: 2,194,817 (2015 estimate)
Currency: Qatari riyal
Coins: Each riyal is subdivided into 100 dirham, which come in denominations of 1, 5, 10, 25, and 50.
Land Area: 11,586 square kilometers (4,473 square miles)
National Anthem: " as-Salām al-Amīrī" ("Peace to the Amir")

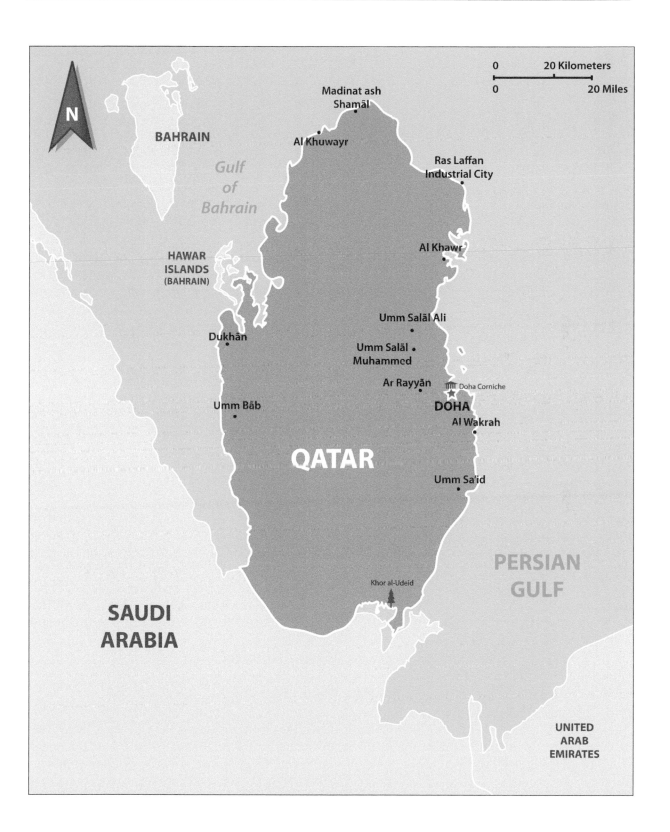

Principal Cities by Population (2010):

- Doha (796,947)
- al-Rayyan (455,623)
- al-Khor (193,983)
- al-Wakra (141,222)
- Umm Salal (60,509)
- Mesaieed (35,150)

Capital: Doha
Time Zone: GMT +3
Flag Description: The flag of Qatar is maroon with a vertical white strip on its hoist (left) side, the edge of which is serrated; this serrated edge yields nine white points that extend into the maroon.

Population

According to the CIA World Factbook, the population of Qatar was 2,194,817 in 2015. According to the US Department of State, in 2014, foreign workers are estimated to make up as much as 90 percent of the country's population. Countries of origin for foreign workers include Nepal, India, Pakistan, Sri Lanka, and the Philippines. The vast majority of the population lives in or near the capital of Doha.

Around 40 percent of the Qatari population is of Arab descent and, in Doha, a majority of the population is of Indian, Iranian, Pakistani, or Bangladeshi descent. Pakistanis and Indians are the two second-largest minorities in the nation, each representing approximately 18 percent of the population. Iranian's represent 10 percent of the population. There is also a small community of American citizens in the country.

Language

With a diverse population of foreign residents, there are many languages spoken in Doha, though Arabic is the nation's official language and is used in educational and administrative settings. English is commonly used as a second language, and a majority of residents are bilingual. Farsi and various Indian languages are also commonly spoken.

Native People & Ethnic Groups

Qatar has been inhabited since prehistoric times. The original inhabitants were Arab tribes that migrated from surrounding areas on the Arabian Peninsula. They made their living through fishing and pearling and settled near coastal areas. It is believed that migration to Qatar grew from the need for grazing land, water, fishing ports, and for religious reasons.

Three major migrations of mostly Bedouin peoples occurred from the mid-18th through the early 19th centuries. The first took place in the 1760s and consisted of tribes that moved in from Kuwait. Later, the growth of Wahhabi Islam prompted more people to migrate from the Saudi province of al-Hasa and from other nearby countries. Today, descendents of these early tribes, including the Awamir, Manasir, and Bani Hajir, still live in Qatar. Members of these tribes are referred to as native Qataris, and they comprise around 10 percent of the population in 2015. The remaining population is made up of foreign workers, many of whom hail from countries in the Middle East or Southeast Asia.

Religions

Islam is the state religion of Qatar and the practice of other religions, while not prohibited, is curtailed. State laws prohibit displaying Christian or other non-Islamic religious symbols in public and also place restrictions on proselytizing, or religious recruiting. Roughly 77 percent of the nation is Muslim, and there are small Christian populations (8.5 percent), as well as groups following other faiths, including Hinduism and Judaism, which together account for 14 percent of the population.

Climate

Qatar has a subtropical desert climate and a desert environment. There is very little precipitation, and most rain falls during December. Precipitation averages around 76.2 millimeters (3 inches) annually. Winter in Qatar lasts from December through March, and is characterized by colder weather, high humidity, and increased rainfall. Summer tends to be very hot and lasts from June through September.

Summer temperatures average 41° Celsius (106° Fahrenheit), but can reach 46° Celsius (114° Fahrenheit). In the winter, the temperature remains around 26° Celsius (78° Fahrenheit) but can drop to 7° Celsius (44° Fahrenheit). The spring and fall often have the most comfortable temperatures and weather.

The major winds that affect the country are the shamal, a northwest wind that often induces sand storms between March and August, and the sharqui, also a dry, summer wind that similarly accompanies hot weather.

ENVIRONMENT & GEOGRAPHY

Topography
The peninsula of Qatar is around 160 kilometers (99 miles) long and varies in width from 55 to 90 kilometers (34 to 56 miles). The terrain is predominantly flat, desert country, although there is some variation in the landscape. The country also includes some offshore islands in the Persian Gulf, such as Halul.

Doha, the capital, is located midway down the eastern coast. The city stretches east to west for approximately five kilometers (three miles). The city has one main port, Doha Port, located in the oldest part of the city. The center city is laid out in three rings, known as A ring, B ring, and C ring, that form semicircles around Doha Port and contain a majority of the city's financial and administrative buildings.

The West Bay area is the newest area of Doha and is most of the upscale development to date, with skyscrapers and contemporary, urban architecture. The area also boasts luxury accommodations, hotels, and an entertainment district. The center city is crowded with small streets and little open space; in the surrounding districts, such as Nuaija, streets are wider with more open space. A majority of the newer buildings in the peripheral parts of Doha are of modern, European design, while Islamic architecture and early British buildings are still present in some parts of the old city and surrounding suburbs.

In the western region of Qatar, the land rises slightly up to a central plateau. There are also some cliffs on the eastern coast that rise above sea level. Large sand dunes can be found in the southeastern part of the country, created from sand that blows from the desert. Qatar's western hills, or jebels (the equivalent of North American mesas), are located above its major oilfields and reach up to 99 meters (325 feet) in altitude. The country has an irregular coastline. Salt flats, or sabkha, are located toward the western end of the peninsula.

Plants & Animals
Few animals live in Qatar's desert interior. Some of the larger mammals that can be found there are the jerboa, or desert rat with long, rabbit-like ears, and the Arabian gazelle (referred to in Qatar as "rheem"), which are becoming rare. Qatar's dugong is the country's largest mammal, and the world's second-largest population of this marine creature—a relative of the manatee—can be found in the Persian Gulf, off Qatar's coast. The International Union for Conservation of Nature lists its status as vulnerable.

Qatar is also home to many species of reptiles and amphibians, such as toads, monitor lizards, sand boas, common house geckos, and tortoises. Large animals such as sheep, goats, cattle, and camels inhabit grazing areas. Cattle are mostly maintained in the north, while camel herds are

Typical small rodent found in Qatar.

found primarily in the south. The majority of these herds are domesticated rather than wild.

There is a diverse bird population in Qatar, particularly along the coast. Some common birds include flamingos, cormorants, osprey, hoopoes, kestrels, and plovers. Hunting with falcons is a traditional pastime in the country. There is an increasing awareness of the need for wildlife conservation in Qatar. For example, the ostrich went extinct in Qatar around 1945, but was reintroduced to the country in the latter part of the 20th century. As of 2015, they largely populate the Ras Abrouq area.

Over 130 desert plants can be found in Qatar, including the desert apple, desert hyacinth, shrubby horsetail, and yellow trumpetbush. Lycium shawii, a low-growing shrub, produces red flowers and berries. Zizyphus nummularia is a favorite plant of the Bedouin people; it produces flowers that are shaped like stars. Many of the plants native to Qatar produce fragrant flowers and fruit.

CUSTOMS & COURTESIES

Greetings
Native Qataris make up only about 10 percent of the country's population. In 2014, the majority of the remaining population came from countries such as India (545,000); Pakistan (90,000); Nepal (400,000); the Philippines (200,000); Egypt (180,000); Bangladesh (150,000); Sri Lanka (100,000); and several other Arab nations, including Iran. Most are in Qatar for work—as much of 90 percent of Qatar's labor force is made up of foreigners—and it is estimated that there are nearly four times more males than females in the population. In 2015, these numbers stood at 1,695,234 men and boys and 499,583 women and girls. Most non-Qatari Arabs and Pakistanis are also Muslim, with practicing Muslims standing at over 77 percent. However, each national group brings its own culture and customs.

The official language in Qatar is Arabic, and the customary Muslim greeting is "As-salaamu alaikum" ("Peace be upon you"), to which the appropriate response is "Wa-alaikum-salaam" ("And also upon you, peace"). Other common greetings include "Sabah al-khair" ("Good morning"), "Masah al-khair" ("Good evening"), and "Masaa an-nuur" (the common reply to "good evening"). The greetings "Marhaba" ("Hello") and "Maasalama" ("Good-bye") are used on a more informal basis.

One phrase that is heard frequently is "Il-hamdu li-lah" ("By the grace of God"). This is used in a variety of circumstances as a simple way to indicate that one can never be certain of one's plans. Similarly, when one speaks of the Prophet Muhammad, the speaker may follow the Prophet's name with the phrase "'Alayhi as-salām" ("Peace be upon him), or the longer version, "Salla llāhu 'alay-hi wa-alehe-wasallam" ("may Allah honour him and grant him peace").

Gestures & Etiquette
The official state religion of Qatar is Islam, specifically the Sunni branch of the faith.

Traditional dress for Qatari women.

The Qataris, like their neighbors the Saudis, follow a strict interpretation of Sunni Islam known in the West as Wahhabism. However, Muslims who follow the creed call themselves Muwahhidun (Unitarians) from the Arabic meaning "one who proclaims the unity of God." This was also the original name of the North African Almohad Dynasty. The prominence of Islam and the strict interpretation followed by most Qataris plays an important role in Qatari etiquette.

Men and women refrain from physical contact and a strict segregation of the sexes is maintained. In some offices, a series of doors are constructed so that if a man needs to go to the woman's side, he need never actually see the women working there. On the other hand, men are likely to kiss on the cheeks and embrace when greeting and may also hold hands. However, Qatari society is more liberal than other Arab societies. For example, women may own their own businesses and can attend one of the non-segregated American university branches in Doha's Education City.

A simple matter of etiquette that is important in Qatar and other Muslim cultures is the exclusive use of the right hand. This is because the left hand is associated with the cleansing of the body and personal hygiene and, therefore, is considered unclean. Thus, the right hand is solely used for shaking hands, passing objects, and eating. It is also disrespectful to point or show the soles of one's feet to another.

Eating/Meals

Qataris generally rise early and eat a light breakfast, which often includes cheeses and fresh fruit. The midday meal is traditionally the most important meal of the day, and many Qataris may leave work or school in order to eat with their family. (Qatar is also a very hot country—from May through October, temperatures can reach as high as 54° Celsius, or 120° Fahrenheit—and people often prefer to maintain a daily rhythm that allows them to rest at home during the hottest part of the afternoon.) The meal is typically begun with a selection of small appetizers, followed by a meat and rice

dish that may be served with fruits and vegetables. Flat bread generally accompanies meals and is used to scoop the food. The evening meal is served late and is also typically light. Coffee is served at both the start and end of a meal. At home, meals are generally eaten on a carpeted floor.

One change in traditional eating habits can be seen in the growing frequency with which Qataris dine out, as a wide variety of cuisines are now available in urban areas. During the fasting month of Ramadan, Qataris' daily rhythm changes considerably. Rising well before dawn, they will eat a pre-fast meal and then spend the day without food or drink of any kind. When daylight passes, large, festive meals are held, and friends and relatives host each other throughout the month.

Visiting

Hospitality plays an important role in Qatari culture, and it is not unusual for newly-met friends to be invited to join family celebrations, such as weddings or holiday meals. However, a fairly strict system of gender segregation means that women are generally hosted in one part of the house and men in another. The room reserved for men is known as the majlis, a word that now refers to a place where men gather to talk, but originally indicated a council charged with community decision-making.

When visiting, it is generally considered disrespectful to refuse an offer of refreshments, even in the middle of the business day, and most offices regularly have tea available. Shared meals are traditionally lavish, and dinner begins and ends with Arabic coffee. At the end of the meal, it is polite to accept at least two cups of coffee, but not more than three.

Most Qataris follow the Persian Gulf custom of burning incense in the home, using a clay mijmar, or incense burner. Frankincense is commonly used, and some families create their own personal scent. It is common to pass the mijmar around among guests before they leave, so that they will carry the scent of their hosts' home with them at the end of a visit.

LIFESTYLE

Family

In Qatar, the notion of family extends out from the nuclear and extended family groups to include the clan, a group of closely related families, and then the tribe. The members of a tribe trace their ancestry back to a common ancestor, and most people prefer to marry within their tribe. In most families, at least one son will raise his family in the home of his parents, so as to care for them in their old age. However, most Qataris now hire servants to handle the mundane tasks of running a home. Men are the head of their household, but it has become increasingly common for wives to hold jobs outside of the home.

Housing

Though Qatar showcases its Bedouin past in museums and art collections, the Qatari lifestyle has changed dramatically (and some Qataris question the official emphasis on Bedouin culture). Only a very small number of Bedouin continue a nomadic life, living in tents and regularly moving across the desert. The vast majority of Qataris today live in an urban setting, most of them clustered in the cities of Doha and al-Rayyan.

With one of the world's highest per capita incomes (the CIA, World Bank, and International Monetary Fund all ranked Qatar first in the world in 2014), Qataris tend to prefer large homes. These often feature a courtyard and several sitting rooms on the ground floor. These sitting rooms are segregated by gender and used for welcoming visitors. Private life is conducted elsewhere, with bathrooms and bedrooms located above the ground floor. Decorative accents tend to be ornate, and are influenced by traditional Islamic architecture.

Food

Qatari cuisine is very similar to neighboring Middle Eastern cuisines. For example, popular Qatari dishes, such as stuffed vegetables and hummus, which is mashed chickpeas made with sesame paste (tehina, or tahini), are shared throughout the Arab world. Qatar's coastal position and the abundance of foreigners have also left a distinct influence on the national cuisine. Seafood is widely available, including shrimp, lobster, kingfish, red snapper, and tuna, and South Asian spices, such as curry, are often used. American food is becoming increasingly popular, while biryani—a traditional Indian dish of rice, spices, yogurt, and either a vegetable or a protein (either boiled eggs or meat)—is a favorite.

Qataris also enjoy various lamb dishes, particularly on the occasion of religious holidays. One dish, ghuzi, can include an entire roast lamb, or lamb pieces, presented on a bed of rice that has been prepared with pine-nuts. Muslims fast during the daylight hours of the holy month of Ramadan, and special foods are prepared to break the fast at day's end. In Qatar, hareis is often served, which is a combination of ground lamb and wheat that requires almost a full day to cook. Islam also forbids the eating of pork or drinking of any alcoholic beverage (or even its use in cooking). All pork and pork products are thus illegal in Qatar, but alcohol can be found in internationally-owned hotels.

Qatari culture emphasizes the correct preparation and serving of qahwa, or Arabic coffee. This coffee is much stronger than American coffee, and is generally unsweetened (though it might be flavored with cardamom). Qataris traditionally serve their coffee with dates, which provide a sweet counterpoint to the bitter drink. Tea is also a popular beverage and is often an important part of Qatari hospitality.

Life's Milestones

Weddings in Qatar are lavish events to which large groups are typically invited. Marriages are often arranged by the families of the bride and groom, and the groom's family is expected to pay a mahr, or bride price, when the match is made. The religious customs in Qatar demand a fairly strict separation of men from women, and weddings are no exception; segregated celebrations are held, with feasting and dancing for each gender. Young women are considered of marriageable age when they complete their compulsory education—at 15 or 16 years of age—but they typically marry men who are slightly older. On special occasions such as these, a woman's clothing will likely be stitched with gold thread.

CULTURAL HISTORY

Art

The Koran stands at the center of Islamic culture and has played a significant part in the development of calligraphy as an important Islamic art form in Qatar. Beautifully inscribed copies of the Koran continue to be produced. In fact, Arabic calligraphy has maintained its relevance as a form of creative expression in Islamic culture. Two important contemporary Qatari calligraphers include Yousef Ahmed (1955–) and mixed-media artist Ali Hassan (1956–). Ahmed—who helped Sheikh Hassan assemble the pieces that would become the foundation for both Doha's Orientalist Museum and Mathaf: Arab Museum of Modern Art—is credited with adding a new element to calligraphy with his bold treatment of color, while Hassan is known for his use of the Arabic alphabet in his works. Munira al-Meer, a pioneering ceramic artist, is also influenced by Arabic calligraphy and strives to express a divine creative force in her sculptures.

Qatar is also renowned for its traditional arts and crafts. These include shipbuilding, goldsmithing, and embroidery. Early shipbuilders were known as "al-Gallaf," and they traditionally used moisture-resistant woods, such as teak, or a hard pinewood, like cypress. Today, only one traditional shipbuilding workshop, the Emiri Shipbuilding Workshop, remains. Goldsmithing, which was traditionally passed down from one generation to the next, was influential in the crafting and trading of Qatari jewelry and weaponry. The art of embroidery, one of the oldest Arabic arts in the region, also includes gold- and silver-lined clothing, and Qatar was once renowned for its woven fabrics. It is believed that the Prophet Muhammad (c. 570–632 CE) and his family had their clothes made from fabric woven in the region that is today Qatar.

During the early 18th century, Bedu (or Bedouin) tribes moved into the region, and the roots of this Bedouin past are still present in contemporary culture. Bedouin weaving and textiles (created mostly by women) were an important Bedouin art and can still be found across Qatar. Carpets, tents, rugs, and pillow covers are traditionally woven from camel or goat hair, and baskets are woven from palm and cane fronds that are sometimes dyed to create a pattern. These art forms are a reflection of the nomadic Bedouin culture in which even objects of beauty have to be functional to justify carrying them across the desert.

Architecture

The arrival of Islam has served as an important architectural influence in Qatar. This Islamic heritage is reflected in civic architecture, including palaces and castles, military architecture, and religious architecture. Qatar is home to more than 1,227 mosques, the majority of which are designed in the traditional Islamic style. Other examples of prominent Islamic architecture include the Moab Fort in western Qatar, which reflects the Abbasid Dynasty's (758–1258 CE) architectural tradition, and the National Museum, which is considered an outstanding example of eastern Arabian architecture. Traditional building materials included clay and unpolished stones, with gypsum and wooden frames used in modern times. Gypsum was also popularly used for housing ornamentation.

Qatar, particularly the capital of Doha, is also known for its modern architecture. In the decades since achieving independence in 1971, Qataris have substantially expanded their cities, most notably Doha. In fact, it is estimated that between 80 and 90 percent of the population lives in Doha or al-Rayyan, just northwest of the capital. There, traditional Islamic influences can be seen juxtaposed with sleek Western-style architecture and striking, postmodern designs. A prominent example includes the Qatar National Convention Centre, located in Education City. The building is anchored by enormous, highly sculptural, steel replicas of two sidra trees (a Qatari icon), which together support an overhanging roof and are part of the building's façade. Another example is Doha's Sheraton Resort and Convention Hotel, which resembles a step pyramid, or ziggurat. Some critics have argued that the use of steel, glass, and concrete in these new structures is not suitable for the local climate.

Drama

Traditional Qatari drama features dancing and singing, and actors generally wear colorful costumes. Plotlines usually involve love, loyalty, and betrayal. Traditional Qatari drama is still performed in the country, at venues such as the Qatar National Theatre in Doha.

Music

The traditional music of Qatar was heavily influenced by Bedouin culture. Common instruments in Qatari music include the Arabian flute and the tambura, a long-necked mandolin, as well as the oud, which is much like a lute, and rebaba, a long-necked stringed instrument that is played with a bow. Percussion instruments include the al-ras, a large drum; the takhamir, a smaller drum; and the al-mirwa, a small hand drum. These instruments are often used to accompany traditional dances.

Dance

The roots of Qatar's Bedouin past are still present in contemporary culture. For example, traditional Bedouin dances, such as the ayyalah, are widely performed at weddings and other celebrations. When performing the ayyalah, two lines of male dancers, from young boys to older men, reenact a battle scene, using sticks and ornamental swords in stylized combat. They keep time with cymbals, tambourines, and drums.

Literature

Traditional literary forms of Qatar can be traced back to the country's Bedouin past. Qatari literature finds its roots in the oral traditions of the Bedouin culture, particularly in Bedouin song, poetry, and storytelling.

CULTURE

Arts & Entertainment

Qatar, a relatively young nation, is still developing a sense of its modern artistic expression, which is most often a meeting between traditional Bedouin elements and modern forms. The arts in Qatar are largely based on Bedouin culture, especially traditional Bedouin poetry. The Bedouin were nomadic people whose cultural trademarks are dance and oral literature, including poetry. One form of traditional dance, the al-Ardha, is performed on Friday afternoons in the capital, and is specially performed during the Independence Day holiday. The Lewa dance has been influenced by East African culture and involves both male and female dancers. There are also a number of dances only performed by women, such as the al-Khimar.

Many dances are accompanied by percussion instruments such as the al-ras drum. Music is also performed using tambourines, cymbals, and the Arabian flute. Traditional stringed instruments include the oud (a lute-like instrument) and the rebaba (a long-necked, stringed instrument that must be played with a bow).

The annual Doha Cultural Festival showcases local folklore, poetry, and theater alongside international dance and musical performances. The Qatar National Theatre hosts performances from around the world, with occasional events in English. In 2008, Qatar's first privately-owned art gallery, the Souq Waqif Art Center, opened in Doha and features works from numerous pioneering women artists.

Sports are popular in the country, which has facilities for soccer, tennis, golf, swimming, scuba-diving, and horse racing. The Aspire Academy for Sports Excellence in Doha is highly regarded and has served as the training camp for several foreign soccer clubs, including one of Munich's two home football teams, FC Bayern. Moreover, Qatar built the complex as part of its bid to host the FIFA World Cup tournament in 2022. Arabian horses are similarly prized in Qatar, and equestrian events and competitions are frequently held there. Sailing and scuba diving are favorite activities in coastal waters. "Dune bashing," a relatively new leisure activity, involving SUVs and the country's many sand dunes is advertised by Qatari tourist organizations as a popular activity from March through October. Training and hunting with falcons is a traditional Qatari sport; it originated with Bedouin tribes that used the birds to hunt for food.

Cultural Sites & Landmarks

The capital of Doha is the heart of Qatar and home to many of the peninsula's best-known landmarks. The National Museum was established in 1975 in an early 20th-century palace. The museum's collection includes archeological artifacts, weapons and armor, clothing and textiles, numismatics, dhows (traditional boats), pearls, and modern Arab art and photography. In March 2010, French architect Jean Nouvel unveiled a new museum design comprised of interlocking disks that mimic the shape of the desert rose—that is, crystal clusters of gypsum or barite that form in Qatari desserts from compressed and heated sand. Nouvel's design was built around the original palace and now features, in addition to the aforementioned exhibition galleries, an auditorium, a park with native Qatari plants, research labs, scholarly study centers, restaurants, and retail areas.

The Doha Corniche, or boardwalk, runs along the coast and is one of the city's most well-known sites. Landmarks and cultural sites along the corniche include a large fountain in the shape of an oyster holding a pearl, reflecting the city's pearl-diving past, and Al Bidda Park, or Rumeila Family Park, a large expanse of land with a skate park, irrigated lawns, restaurants, amusement park rides, and a swimming pool. The Doha Corniche is also home to a monument in the shape of a traditional Arab coffee pot (dallah) that features elements of Islamic architecture. The monument is a symbol of traditional Islamic hospitality—Arab Muslims were the first to bring coffee to the rest of the world, and

coffee drinking is an important ritual in Arab culture.

Off the coast of Doha is Palm Tree Island. Like Al Bidda Park, Palm Tree Island caters to families seeking entertainment. However, there is also a pier for dhows, traditional sailboats once used in Doha's pearl trade. Dhows are still used in al-Wakrah, a fishing town south of Doha known for its beautiful mosques and traditional homes. A museum has been established in the city to display Bedouin arts.

The Waqif Souq is the city's traditional shopping district, located in downtown Doha. It consists of a system of alleys and narrow streets lined with small merchant shops and vendors selling a variety of goods, from traditional crafts and clothing to modern amenities. Designated by the Qatari government as one of the nation's national heritage sites, the souq, or "standing market," is one of the best existing examples of a traditional Middle Eastern bazaar, which also serves as a social center.

Located near the Waqif Souq is the Al Koot Fort, which was built in 1927 to protect the souq from thieves. The fort has also been designated as a national heritage site and provides an example of Islamic military architecture. In the fort's central courtyard is a small open-air mosque that was built to serve prisoners of the fort.

Approximately 20 kilometers (12.4 miles) from the city center is the Doha Zoo, which occupies more than 42 acres and contains more than 1500 animals. While many of the zoo's animals represent foreign ecosystems, there are some native animals included in the displays, including the endangered Arabian Oryx. The zoo also features a small amusement park. As of 2015, the Doha Zoo has been undergoing ambitious renovations and has been closed. It is expected to reopen in 2017.

Qatar is also home to impressive natural sites as well. On Qatar's southern border with Saudi Arabia is Khor Al Udeid, or the Inland Sea. A large inlet into the peninsula, it can only be reached by off-road vehicles. Qatari families as well as tourists camp on the shore, and the sea is home to the dugong, a marine mammal in the same family as the manatee. Another area with impressive sand dunes is Mesaieed, once known as Umm Said. The town is today largely an industrial center, but its beaches are surrounded by high dunes with fine sand.

Libraries & Museums

Another significant contribution to the Qatari art scene, including the structure itself and the collection housed within, is the Museum of Islamic Art, which opened in December 2008. The building, designed by award-winning modernist architect I.M. Pei (1917–), is meant to reflect the culture of Islam. The museum's clean lines and imposing tower surrounded by stacks of square and octagonal blocks recalls Arab forts and palaces. Qatar's ruling family agreed to build an island just off Doha to house the museum and prevent the building from becoming surrounded by future projects.

The works inside the museum were gathered over two decades, and the Islamic art collection is considered one of the most comprehensive. It includes textiles, ceramics, metalwork, coins, pearls, and manuscripts. For example, the museum houses the earliest known copy of Islam's holy book, the Koran, or Quran, dating to the seventh or early eighth century.

The Qatar National Museum is the largest museum in Doha and serves as the country's historical, political, natural history, and maritime museum. Exhibits at the museum focus on traditional Bedouin culture, Islamic and Arabian ocean exploration, and Islamic art. The museum was established in 1975 in the former residence of Sheikh Abdullah bin Jassim al-Thani, which was built in 1901. While the building serves as a prime example of early 20th-century Islamic architecture, it is now entirely surrounded by French architect Jean Nouvel's 2010 building design, whose innovative shape is based on the 'desert rose' crystals that form as a result of heat- and compression-fused sand. The new space has many more visitor and scholarly amenities, including restaurants and shops, an auditorium and horticultural area, as well as an extensive research lab and study center.

The National Library of Qatar (QNL) is located in Doha's Education City. Founded in 1962, it houses 173,800 volumes. Since 1982, the library has also served as Qatar's legal deposit. In 2011, the QNL integrated Sheikh Hassan bin Mohamed bin Ali Al Thani's personal collection of rare Arab and Islamic books and manuscripts, which he began accumulating in 1979. This segment of the library is known as the "Heritage Collection." A new building, designed by renowned Dutch architect Rem Koolhaas, will open to the public in autumn 2015.

Holidays

Qatar celebrates its independence on Independence Day, which is observed annually on September 3. However, the celebrations are typically spread over a three-day period. Streets and public buildings are decorated, and the al-Ardha dance is performed. There are also military parades and other festivities. All other public holidays revolve primarily around the Islamic faith, including the celebration of Ramadan.

Youth Culture

Education in Qatar, including postsecondary education, is free to all citizens and compulsory only through the elementary level. The literacy rate, as of 2015, is close to 100 percent, and many young Qataris go on to study at a university, either in Qatar or abroad. Schools are segregated by gender, as is Qatar University, but the six American universities that maintain branches at Education City in Doha—Virginia Commonwealth, Weill Cornell Medical College, Texas A&M, Carnegie Mellon, Georgetown, and Northwestern—hold desegregated classes. In recent years, Qatar has focused on the US model in organizing its educational system, and student life at the six American universities is similar to campus life in the US.

Due to Qatar's status as an oil-rich nation, Qatari society is an affluent one. Many youth are, therefore, not accustomed to part-time employment or sharing in domestic responsibilities, duties that are often expected of youth in other cultures. Also, youth have developed a social stigma concerning certain occupations. They particularly feel that certain jobs are "beneath" the native population. Socially, youth activities are segregated and girls might go out as part of a group if they are accompanied by an older escort. Boys typically congregate at coffee shops and the cinema. Qatari youth are increasingly technologically savvy, and texting and the use of Bluetooth technology allow youth an opportunity to avoid social restrictions on communicating with the opposite sex. Many youth still marry in their teens, with marriages usually arranged by the families of the bride and groom.

SOCIETY

Transportation

Private transportation is perhaps the most popular method of transport in Qatar. The private ownership of automobiles is strengthened by the fact that gas in Qatar is inexpensive, and the per capita income is among the highest in the world. Public buses and taxis, now both government-owned, are common modes of public transportation. In 2009, Qatar also announced plans to become the first Gulf Cooperation Council (GCC) country to implement cycling lanes and circuits. An underground subway system is planned for Doha and is expected to be completed by 2019.

Traffic in Qatar moves on the right-hand side of the road.

Transportation Infrastructure

In preparation for the 2022 FIFA World Cup, which will bring the country a tremendous influx of tourists, Qatar is attempting to modify and enhance its transportation infrastructure. Currently, the country is working on construction of a 12 kilometer (7 mile), sub-sea tunnel that will connect the financial center of Doha to the nearby Hamad International Airport, which is the only international airport in Qatar.

A cost-effective option for getting around Doha are public buses, which now offer 35 routes throughout the city and require only very small fares.

The government-owned company Mowasalat supplanted some 3,000 privately-owned cabs with their own sedans and airport taxi vans.

There are currently no major rail lines in Qatar. However, Qatar Railways Development Company (QRDC), created in 2011, has begun to plan a railway network that will include 750 kilometers of track and 100 stations. In June 2013, QRDC secured $8.2 billion (USD) for phase one of a three-line subway system in Doha. These efforts will be especially important for the upcoming World Cup games, as subway stations will link various stadiums. Completion is slated for 2019.

Media & Communications

The Al Jazeera news channel is perhaps the most recognized feature of the Qatari media. In addition to being the largest Arab news network in the Middle East, the news channel is also the first independent, Arabic-language television channel. Founded in 1996, Al Jazeera is funded—but not operated—by the government and has been critical of the Qatari government, as well as other regional rulers and cultures, which has created diplomatic strains. Seen in twenty-two countries, it has an estimated audience of 40 million. However, the network has come under fire from Western countries for granting a forum to Osama bin Laden and for showing graphic footage of the 2003 Iraq War. Similarly, Arab countries have asserted that the network has distinct foreign influences and have criticized the station for interviewing Israeli officials. Nonetheless, in a region where freedom of expression is often compromised, Al Jazeera maintains an important influence.

Qatar's domestic press is much tamer than Al Jazeera. Official censorship was lifted in 1995, but the broadcast media are controlled by the government. Newspapers are linked to the royal family and their supporters, and self-censorship is routine. Popular dailies include the *Al-Watan* (*The Homeland*), *Al-Rayah* (*The Banner*), and *Al-Sharq* (*The East*).

The state-run television broadcaster is Qatar TV, and the state-run radio broadcaster is Qatar

Broadcasting Service (QBS). International radio broadcasts such as Radio France Internationale (RFI) and the British Broadcasting Corporation (BBC) World Service (in Arabic) are also available. As of 2015, there were an estimated 1,297,500 daily Internet users, representing almost 60 percent of the population.

SOCIAL DEVELOPMENT

Standard of Living
Qatar ranked 31st out of 187 countries on the 2013 United Nations Human Development Index.

Water Consumption
According to the World Health Organization, 100 percent of Qatar's population (both rural and urban) has sustainable access to improved drinking water sources and sanitation (2015).

Education
Qatar's policies toward education reflect its desire for a skilled working class that can effectively manage its natural resources and industry. All education is funded by the government and under the purview of the Supreme Education Council and the Ministry of Education, which also pays for books, clothing, and transportation. The government encourages students to travel abroad for higher education and will fund students who do so with scholarships and awards. English and Arabic languages, science, and religious instruction are considered some of the most important areas of study.

The educational system is divided into primary, preparatory, secondary, and higher education. Children generally begin attending school at the age of six and must stay in school until age sixteen. The University of Qatar is one of the country's major educational institutions. It was founded in 1973 and focuses primarily on the sciences. As of 2015, Qatar has an overall literacy rate of 97.3 percent, with 97.4 percent for men and 96.8 percent for women.

The gender gap in education has largely closed in Qatar; in fact, more women than men are enrolled in secondary education in the early 21st century. For example, between 2005 and 2006, for every 100 male students in higher education, there were 194 female students. In 2007, for every 100 male students, there were 108 female students in higher education. In 2014, Qatar's Ministry of Development, Planning, and Statistics reported that there were twice as many females as males enrolled in Qatari universities. Moreover, two-thirds of graduates were women.

Women's Rights
Women's rights in Qatar are closely bound with Sharia (or Sharī'ah, Muslim law) and significantly limited by social and cultural customs. They are particularly limited in their employment opportunities; for example, women are legally forbidden from taking jobs considered dangerous to either their health or morals, and they are believed to be unsuited for positions such as judges due to the cultural perception that they are overemotional or mentally inconsistent. Women are also not equal before the law. For instance, in certain legal circumstances, the testimony of women is either not admissible, or does not carry the weight of a man's testimony.

Qatari women are taught from an early age to engage males with gentle persuasion rather than direct confrontation, a behavior that tends to perpetuate existing inequality. Women are actively involved in every aspect of family life, but men are expected to have the final word in decisions. They can be kept from leaving the country by their male "guardians" (closest male kin). Though women have the legal right to bring discrimination complaints to the police or the National Council for Human Rights, they very rarely do so, for fear of shaming their families.

Domestic violence is a particularly difficult issue and the penal code lacks penalties that address domestic violence and family crimes. Though prohibited by Sharia, violence against women is often condoned. If a woman is judged to have been immodest, or has, in some other way, damaged her family's honor, she may be beaten or, in some cases, murdered in what are known as "honor killings." In one notable 2007 case, the Qatar Appeal Court commuted the three-year sentencing of a teenager who murdered his sister in an alleged honor killing. The government has begun to recognize that domestic violence is a serious issue in Qatari society, but there are still no laws that specifically forbid it. Foreign women are also subject to violence and sexual assault, often at the hands of their employers, and many have been forced into what amounts to slavery. These women are not protected constitutionally and face a lengthy, sometimes perilous deportation process if they speak out. Some domestic workers who report sexual assaults end up serving one-year prison sentences for engaging in illicit relations. In Sumail Central Prison, women who have borne children resulting from such forced sexual relationships, serve their sentence with their babies.

The government has taken steps to begin to address Qatari women's fundamental inequality. Certain professional areas have been opened up to Qatari women (in part to help lessen the country's dependence on foreign professionals) and a variety of organizations have been founded to encourage women's involvement in business. The Supreme Council for Family Affairs was established by the government to protect and support families, and it has launched a public dialogue on the question of domestic violence. Women can obtain legal aid at the Qatar Foundation, headquartered in Doha. But while the foundation provides support to women and generally works to raise awareness of women's issues, various factors also limit these efforts; perhaps most notable is that both the foundation and the Supreme Council for Family Affairs are entirely dependent on the government. Ultimately, too, many social limitations keep women ignorant of their options.

Health Care

The Qatari government provides free health care services for its citizens. Public health care includes medical exams, hospitalization, and pharmaceutical costs. Other important public services include immunization and school health services. In 2013, healthcare expenditures represented 2.2 percent of the GDP. Between 2010 and 2012, there were 7.7 physicians and 1.2 hospital beds for every 1,000 people. The average life expectancy is just over 78 years (2015 estimate).

The Rumaillah General Hospital in Doha is one of the country's most sophisticated medical institutions and provides services such as radiography, physiotherapy, and pathology. The World Health Organization (WHO) has played an important role in modernizing the Qatari health care system and in training medical personnel.

GOVERNMENT

Structure

Before the formation of the State of Qatar in 1971, powerful Arab families headed by sheikhs traditionally ruled the country as absolute monarchs. In 1872, the region fell under the control of the Ottoman Empire. Later, in a 1916 treaty, Qatar became a protectorate of Great Britain until it became independent on September 3, 1971. In this agreement, Britain was given a number of administrative powers in Qatar as well as control over the administration of the country's finances.

The discovery of oil and the transformation of the working class from fishermen to skilled industrial workers shifted the political atmosphere of the country. By 1956, oil workers began striking for better wages and working conditions, and anti-British, anti-government sentiment began to rise. The country's leaders perceived the strikes as a threat to national security, and a new police force was instituted as a result.

Today, in its movement from an absolute, repressive government toward democracy and modernization, Qatar guarantees certain civil rights, such as freedom of the press. The people were allowed to vote in a referendum on the country's constitution in 2003; after receiving public approval, the constitution was ratified in 2004. The country's first legislative elections were expected in 2010, but were delayed until June 2013, at which point Emir Sheikh Hamad bin Khalifa al-Thani stepped down, transferring the government to his son, Crown Prince Sheik Tamim bin Hamad al-Thani. As of mid-2015, the promised elections have not been rescheduled.

Traditionally, the most powerful family in Qatar has been the al-Thani family. Sheikh Hamad bin Khalifa al-Thani became emir, or head of state, in 1995, a post he held through June 2013, after deposing his father. The emir is granted absolute power; however, he is subject to Islamic law, or Sharia. For much of the 20th century, the Qatari government was a constitutional emirate set up along patriarchal family lines; however, its constitution, which was passed in a 2003 popular referendum, refers to the country as both a democratic state and a hereditary emirate and affirms its basis in Sharia law.

Political Parties

The Qatar Constitution, approved in April 2003 by popular referendum and ratified in 2004, does not permit political parties, but does establish the unicameral Consultative Assembly (Majlis al Shura), to which thirty of the 45 members will be elected and the remaining fifteen appointed by the emir. While legislative elections to determine the assembly were slated to take place in June 2013, Sheikh Hamad bin Khalifa al-Thani abdicated his throne and turned power over to him son, Crown Prince Tamim—an act that further delayed elections. They have not been rescheduled. Despite its democratic tone, the constitution does little to limit the executive authority of the emir, who has the power to dissolve the Consultative Assembly, block legislation, and pass his own laws.

Local Government

As of 2015, Qatar is divided into seven municipalities (or baladiyah), each of which has an appointed official to oversee it. Every four years, beginning in 1999, elections are held for the Central Municipal Council (CMC), the consultative body that oversees the municipalities and advises their appointed officials.

Judicial System

The 2003 Qatar Constitution established the High Judicial Council, which is a body of judicial authority composed of senior judges and presidents of the country's courts. The High Judicial Council can offer judicial opinions and also recommend legislation to aid the development of Qatar's judicial system. Courts in Qatar include a Court of Cassation, a Court of Appeal, and a Court of First Instance.

Taxation

There are no individual income taxes in Qatar, and no corporate tax is levied on businesses owned by Qatari citizens. However, foreign-owned businesses do pay a corporate tax. As of 2015, this once graduated tax rate, which previously ranged from 10 to 35 percent, has been changed to a flat 10 percent rate. There are also import and services taxes, such as those imposed by hotels. In 2011, however, a movement to lift service tariffs was begun.

Armed Forces

The Qatar Armed Forces includes an army, air force, and navy. With an annual budget of $1.9 billion (USD), military expenditures generally represent 1.5 percent of the country's GDP. In 2014, there were 11,800 active personnel.

Foreign Policy

Qatar's ruling family has long had to balance the demands of many different forces in its foreign policy. As a Muslim state, Qatar has much in common with the surrounding nations, but as a Sunni-dominated state, it has occasionally felt threatened by the Shiite Muslim government in Iran, although it maintains friendly relations over the natural gas field reserves the two countries share. As an Arab state, it supports the rights of the Palestinian people to an independent country, but it has also worked to normalize relations with Israel. Its oil and gas reserves have provided Qatar with tremendous wealth, and the country has used this wealth to open itself up through initiatives, such as the Al Jazeera news channel and

Doha's Education City. Qatar is also emerging as an important mediating force in the region, particularly between Western-allied nations such as Saudi Arabia and nations such as Iraq and Syria, a role strengthened by Qatar's financial standing.

The Iran-Iraq War (1980–1988) was a particularly stressful time for Qatar. As a small, oil-rich state, Qatar was a potential target for both the imperialist ambitions of Iraq and the Shiite revolutionaries in Iran. In 1981, Qatar and the other Persian Gulf emirates (small countries governed by an emir, or prince) formed a mutual defense pact, the Gulf Cooperation Council (GCC). The GCC tried, but failed, to mediate between the two warring countries. In the end, the GCC largely supported Iraq, as the threat from Iran was considered worse. The members of the GCC also work on joint economic development projects.

Relations with Saudi Arabia are complex, despite the fact that the two countries have much in common. In 1982, both countries signed a bilateral defense agreement, but Saudi forces allegedly attacked a Qatari border post in 1992, killing two people. Arguments have also arisen over the reporting of Al Jazeera, headquartered in the capital of Doha. Saudi Arabia has accused the network of serving foreign interests, resulting in the withdrawal of Saudi Arabia's ambassador in 2002. In 2008, the Saudi ambassador returned to Doha and the two countries signed a new border agreement and announced plans to cooperate on various industrial and commercial issues. However, in March 2014, Saudi Arabia again withdrew its ambassadors in response to both Qatar's support of the Muslim Brotherhood and their interference in Syria's civil war; such intervention in other governments' domestic affairs is expressly prohibited by the GCC compact.

Qatar has traditionally had strained relations with the neighboring island nation of Bahrain. The al-Khalifa family that rules Bahrain also once ruled the peninsula that is today Qatar, and the two nations engaged in a territorial dispute over the Hawar Islands. Eventually the disagreement was referred to the International Court of Justice (ICJ). In 2001, the ICJ ruled that Bahrain would keep the main Hawar Island, but that a handful of smaller islands, important to Qatar's natural gas industry, would remain in Qatari hands. In March 2014, Bahrain joined Saudi Arabia and the United Arab Emirates in withdrawing their ambassadors from Qatar to protest both Qatar's involvement in the Syrian Civil War and their support of the Muslim Brotherhood.

Qatar's relationship with the United States is excellent, but also complicated. The US government has often been very angry over the actions of Doha-based Al Jazeera, particularly its outspoken opposition to the Iraq War and refusal to censor Osama bin Laden. (Important to note is that Al Jazeera was founded by Emir Sheikh Hamad bin Khalifa Al Thani soon after he came to power in 1995, and the news outlet has often been seen as a government messenger service.) On the other hand, the establishment of several leading American universities at Education City in Doha is seen as a clear indication that Qatar looks to the US as a model for the future of its higher education. Qatar allowed America to use its airbases in the 2003 invasion of Iraq, and the US military has a base outside of Doha. However, soldiers must generally remain on base and dress in civilian clothing when they leave. Further complicating US relations is the fact that Qatar discreetly backs Taliban activities, and Doha is home to a Taliban satellite headquarters. The country similarly supports several Syrian extremist groups as well as the Muslim Brotherhood, another point of contention for the US. Notable is that Qatar has supplied the greatest amount of capital to government opposition forces during Syria's civil war, and Doha is where the Syrian National Coalition (or National Coalition for Syrian Revolution and Opposition Forces) was founded in November 2012.

Human Rights Profile

International human rights law insists that states respect civil and political rights and also promote an individual's economic, social, and cultural rights. The United Nations Universal Declaration on Human Rights (UDHR) is recognized as the standard for international human rights. Its authors sought the counsel of the world's great thinkers, philosophers, and religious leaders and were careful to create a document that reflects the core values shared by every world culture. (To read this document or view the articles relating to cultural human rights, visit: www.ohchr.org/EN/UDHR/Pages/Introduction.aspx.)

Qatar's human rights record is problematic for a variety of reasons, and Qatari citizens face a range of limitations that are not in keeping with the UDHR. For example, there are no elections beyond the municipal level and political parties are illegal. Censorship exists on various levels; self-censorship is commonplace, and the government monitors Internet communications (including chat rooms and email) and blocks certain websites. Furthermore, there are strict regulations on forming non-governmental associations, and the only demonstrations that have been allowed were rallies in support of government opinion. Qataris also occasionally have their citizenship revoked or passports rescinded for political reasons.

The most frequent offenses occur in the area of labor rights. The non-citizen population—some 90 percent of those living in Qatar—suffers the most from these types of human rights violations. Qatari law requires that foreign workers be sponsored by an employer, a process called the kafala (sponsorship) system. Once they are in the country, required exit visas trap foreign labor inside the country, where they are unable to change jobs without their sponsor's consent. Between January and June of 2013, The Philippine Overseas Labor Office took in over 600 maids, who reported having been subjected to physical and sexual abuse, insufficient food, passport seizure, and denial of wages and leisure time. The following year, several hundred more Filipino domestic workers sought help from their embassy. Without passports, repatriation can take months, and this time is often spent in overcrowded deportation camps. Similarly, foreign workers who serve in low- or unskilled positions often live in labor camps, and these camps are frequently cramped, unsanitary, and dangerous.

Worse yet, Qatar is a destination for human trafficking for the purposes of involuntary servitude and sexual exploitation. Royal Decree No. 126/2008, issued by the Qatari government in 2008 and otherwise known as the Law Combating Human Trafficking, cites a punishment of fifteen year's imprisonment and monetary fines for human trafficking violations, either for forced labor or sexual exploitation.

In this way, some effort is being made to address human rights issues in Qatar. The government has formed several organizations that are meant to advocate for equality and human rights, most notably the National Council for Human Rights (NCHR). The NCHR has issued honest accounts that criticized Qatar's human rights record, especially with regard to human trafficking. Ultimately, however, such organizations are dependent on the government they criticize, limiting their effectiveness.

ECONOMY

Overview of the Economy

Oil was discovered in Qatar in the 1930s; however, it was not until the 1970s that the country was able to transform its most important natural resource into a successful industry. Today, Qatar is a member of the Organization of Petroleum Exporting Countries (OPEC). In the 1990s, the country experienced a recession and recovery due to fluctuations in oil prices. While its oil supplies are beginning to decline, it has made up for any economic decline with its substantial natural gas reserves.

Qatar's major export partners are Japan, South Korea, India, China, and Singapore. Import partners include the US, Britain, United Arab Emirates, China, Germany, Italy, and Saudi Arabia. In 2014, the gross domestic product (GDP) was approximately $323.2 billion USD. The per capita GDP that same year was $144,400 (USD).

Industry

Although it has been in decline since 1990, the oil industry is still the most important sector in

Qatar, bringing in 92 percent of export earnings and representing 62 percent of government revenue. It helped to transform Qatar from an impoverished country into a wealthy one. Natural gas is another crucial industrial sector and has helped to stabilize the economy after oil prices faced a downturn in the 1990s. Qatar is said to sit on more than 25 trillion cubic meters of natural gas, which represents 13 percent of the world's total estimated gas resources.

In addition to petroleum refineries and natural gas pipelines, Qatar's industrial infrastructure includes a fertilizer plant, a steel plant, and a petrochemical factory. The pearl industry, while historically an important economic sector in Qatar, fell into decline when cultured pearls were introduced in Japan in the 1930s.

Labor

In 2014, the labor force of Qatar was estimated to be around 1.553 million. Most Qataris work in either the government or industrial sectors, with a small fraction of the population employed in agriculture.

Energy/Power/Natural Resources

Qatar has rich petroleum reserves; however, it is estimated that these will be depleted by 2023. Therefore, Qatar is investigating other natural resources. Gas fields, like the South Pars/North Dome—which Qatar shares with Iran and which is the world's largest gas reservoir—are vital to the country's economic future.

Fishing

Qatar's fishing industry, which was once the largest among the Persian Gulf countries, has declined in recent years. However, it still remains an important source of employment and keeps the country 96 percent self-sufficient in supplying its citizens with the per capita 12 kilograms of fish the country consumes annually.

Mining/Metals

Metals and minerals produced in Qatar include aluminum, gypsum, magnesium, cement, nitrogen, and sand. The country also has significant reserves of petroleum and natural gas.

Agriculture

Although it is a privatized industry, agriculture in Qatar is heavily supported by The Qatar National Food Security Programme (QNFSP), a taskforce that is part of the Ministry of Industry and Agriculture, which began to modernize and develop farming and husbandry in the early 1970s. The government provides services such as plowing and pesticide treatment, and also donates free seeds and saplings to well over 2,000 private farmers.

Before the 1960s, nearly all of Qatar's agricultural produce had to be imported. One of the country's goals after gaining independence was to become agriculturally self-sufficient; however, most food still must be imported. Growing plants and animals in Qatar is difficult and costly because of the lack of water and arable land. Land often must be reclaimed from the desert through irrigation before it is useful for farming. However, QNFSP is working on enhancing Qatar's own food production by way of hydroponic technology in a long-range plan that extends to 2040.

Some common crops grown in Qatar include fruit such as melons, dates, guavas, pomegranates, figs, bananas, and grapes. Citrus fruits and vegetables are also successfully grown there. In 2014, agriculture accounts for roughly 0.1 percent of the country's GDP.

Animal Husbandry

The majority of Qatar's livestock are sheep and goats, although chickens, cattle, and camels are also raised. Qatar is not yet self-sufficient in this sector, and The Qatar National Food Security Programme, a government taskforce, has created a plan by which the country can develop greater efficiency in animal feed production, including investment in hydroponic technology, which will reduce the need to import animal forage and, ultimately, meat and dairy products. The plan involves long-term implementation and extends to 2040.

Tourism

In order to promote tourism, the Qatari government has established the Qatar Tourism Authority (QTA). The goals of this organization are to create policy relating to tourism and to develop the tourist trade. The country has an exhibition center, hotels, beach resorts, museums. The Souq Waqif, an open-air bazaar, and Katara Cultural Village, which features art galleries, restaurants, and an amphitheater for opera, theater, and concerts, are areas the QTA actively markets. Qatar hosted the Asian Games in 2006 and will host the FIFA World Cup soccer tournament in 2022. QTA advertises that the country has spent $2.8 billion USD on the creation of infrastructure to support a greater number and variety of athletic competitions.

Emily L. Hauser, Christina Healey,
Micah Issitt, & Savannah Schroll Guz

DO YOU KNOW?

- The myth of the unicorn is thought to be based on the Arabian white oryx, which has become part of wildlife conservation efforts in Qatar. The oryx is also the country's national animal, just as it is for Jordan and the United Arab Emirates.

- Qatar has the world's largest natural gas field, known as the South Pars/North Dome field, which it shares with Iran.

- According to some sources, the term "Bedouin," which is used by non-Arabic speakers, is actually a double plural. Translated from Arabic, the correct term is Bedu.

- The Aspire Tower, also known as The Torch Doha, is one of the tallest buildings in Qatar at 318 meters (1,000 feet) and is located in the part of town called Sports City. The building is covered in lights that can broadcast light shows over the city's skyline.

- Pearling, also known as pearl hunting, was once the primary industry of Doha. In the 19th century, pearl hunters retrieved pearls by free diving and were sometimes required to dive more than 50 feet on a single breath. A dangerous occupation, many divers died after blacking out and drowning.

Bibliography

Allen J. Fromherz. "Qatar: A Modern History." Washington, DC: *Georgetown UP*, 2012.

Diana Untermeyer and Henry Dallal. "Qatar: Sand, Sea, and Sky." Houston, TX: *Bright Sky Press,* 2012.

John L. Esposito. "Islam: The Straight Path." 4th ed. Oxford: *Oxford University Press*, 2010.

Kristian Coates Ulrichsen. "Qatar and the Arab Spring." London, UK: *Oxford UP*, 2014.

Lisa McCoy. "Major Muslim Nations: Qatar." Rev. ed. Philadelphia: *Mason Crest Publishers*. 2014.

Marshall G. S. Hodgson. "The Venture of Islam: Conscience and History in a World Civilization." 3 vols. Chicago: *University of Chicago Press*, 1974.

Mehran Kamrava. "Qatar: Small Plate, Big Politics." Ithaca, NY: *Cornell UP*, 2015.

Neil MacFarquhar. "The Media Relations Department of Hizbollah Wishes You a Happy Birthday: Unexpected Encounters in the Changing Middle East." *New York: PublicAffairs*. 2009.

Ray Takeyh. *"Guardian of the Revolution: Iran and the World in the Age of the Ayatollahs."* 2nd ed. Oxford: *Oxford University Press*. 2011.

Terri Willis. "Qatar: Enchantment of the World." New York: *Children's Press*, 2004.

Works Cited

"Al Jazeera: Chronology of Coverage." *New York Times*. The New York Times Company, 2015. http://topics. nytimes.com/top/reference/timestopics/organizations/a/ al_jazeera/index.html?scp=4&sq=al-Jazeera&st=cse.

"Bedu." Countries and Their Cultures. *Advameg, Inc.* 2015. Web. http://www.everyculture.com/wc/Rwanda-to-Syria/Bedu.html.

"Collections at MIA" *Museum of Islamic Art.* 2015. http://www.mia.org.qa/en/collections.

"Middle East: Qatar." *The World Factbook.* Central Intelligence Agency, 2015. https://www.cia.gov/library/publications/the-world-factbook/geos/qa.html.

"Museums & Galleries." *Qatar Museums.* 2014. http://www.qm.org.qa/en/museums-galleries.

"National Museum of Qatar by Jean Nouvel." *Dezeen.* Dezeen Limited, 24 Mar. 2010. http://www.dezeen.com/2010/03/24/national-museum-of-qatar-by-jean-nouvel/.

"Our Collection." *Mathaf: Arab Museum of Modern Art.* http://www.mathaf.org.qa/en/collection.

"Qatar Country Profile—Overview" *BBC News.* 21 May 2015. http://news.bbc.co.uk/2/hi/middle_east/country_profiles/791921.stm.

"Qatar National Museum Website." Qatar National Museum. 2015. http://www.qnm.8m.com/.

"Qatar Tourism Authority Website." *Qatar Tourism Authority,* 2015.

"Qatar." *World Report 2014.* Human Rights Watch. 2015. https://www.hrw.org/world-report/2014/country-chapters/qatar.

"Qatar: Chronology of Coverage." *New York Times.* The New York Times Company, 16 Jul. 2015. http://topics.nytimes.com/top/news/international/countriesandterritories/qatar/index.html?scp=1-spot&sq=qatar&st=cse.

"Statistics Sector." *Ministry of Development Planning & Statistics.* Ministry of Development Planning & Statistics, 2014. http://www.qsa.gov.qa/Eng/.

"U.S. Relations with Qatar." *Bureau of Near Eastern Affairs Fact Sheet. U.S. Department of State.* 26 Aug. 2014. http://www.qatarvisitor.com/index.php?cID=415&pID=1003. http://www.state.gov/r/pa/ei/bgn/5437.htm.

Kristian Coates Ulrichsen. Qatar & the Arab Spring: Policy Drivers and Regional Implications. *Carnegie Endowment for International Peace.* Carnegie Endowment for International Peace, 24 Sept. 2014. http://carnegieendowment.org/2014/09/24/qatar-and-arab-spring-policy-drivers-and-regional-implications.

Lawrence Pollard. "Doha museum stakes cultural claim." *BBC News.* BBC, 23 Nov. 2008. http://news.bbc.co.uk/2/hi/middle_east/7744586.stm

Leslie Walker. "Female university students in Qatar outnumber men 2:1." *Doha News.* 12 Jun. 2014. http://dohanews.co/female-university-students-outnumber-males-nearly.

Rebecca Falconer. "Qatar's foreign domestic workers subjected to slave-like conditions." *The Guardian.* Guardian News and Media Limited, 26 Feb. 2014. http://www.theguardian.com/global-development/2014/feb/26/qatar-foreign-workers-slave-conditions.

Roula Khalaf. "Abdication of Qatar's ruler avoids risky elections." *Financial Times.* The Financial Times Limited, 25 Jun. 2013. http://www.ft.com/cms/s/0/595fa8a8-dd9d-11e2-892b-00144feab7de.html#axzz3h31Ui4Q7.

The Kaaba Shrine in Mecca, Saudi Arabia

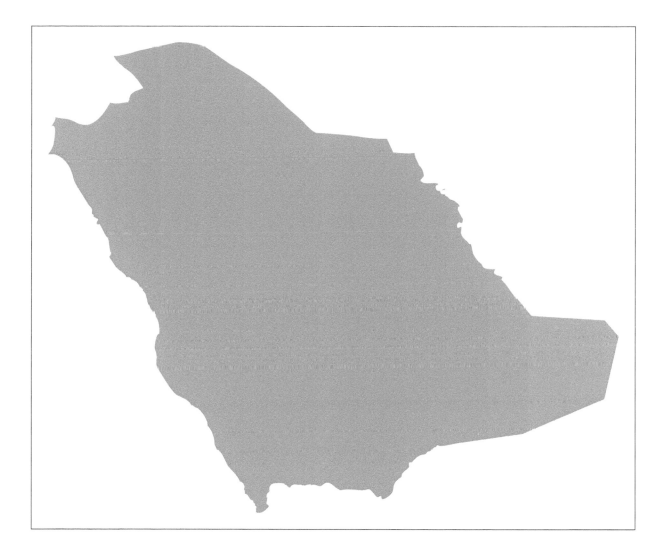

SAUDI ARABIA

Introduction

The Kingdom of Saudi Arabia is the largest nation on the Arabian Peninsula. It is bordered on the north by Jordan, Iraq, and Kuwait; on the east by Qatar, with the island nation of Bahrain lying off its eastern shore in the Persian Gulf; on the southeast by the United Arab Emirates and Oman; and on the south by Yemen. The Red Sea and Gulf of Aqaba lie to the west.

Saudi Arabia is a Muslim nation ruled by members of the Saudi royal family, known as the House of Saud. The country derives its global economic influence over much of the Middle East and the world at large from its vast deposits of oil. Riyadh is the capital of Saudi Arabia, and the country's oil revenues have made it one of the richest capitals in the world.

The country has come under scrutiny in recent years for its connection to radical Islamic fundamentalism, human rights abuses, and allegations of state-sponsored terrorism. Nonetheless, it has remained a politically moderate voice in the region, and is an ally of the United States and other Western nations.

In 2011, Arab Spring arrived in Saudi Arabia. Protests in the country directly followed unrest that began in Tunisia. Demonstrations were organized to protest the makeup of the government and the detention of political prisoners. Women protested for suffrage (in a campaign called "Baladi," or "My Country"), and in April 2011 women in Riyadh, Jeddah, and Dammam attempted to register for municipal elections. After similar protests and violence, King Abdullah declared women could participate in the 2015 municipal elections and could be considered for the Consultative Assembly, the King's advisory board.

Ultimately, although the Arab Spring effected some positive change within the country, the protests also revealed the extent of the monarchy's censorship and repression. Some foreign journalists' visas were revoked, while others were summarily imprisoned. Citizens were wounded or even killed for participation in peaceful demonstrations. Ten human rights activists were imprisoned until they repudiated their earlier demands for political reform. The full import of Saudi's

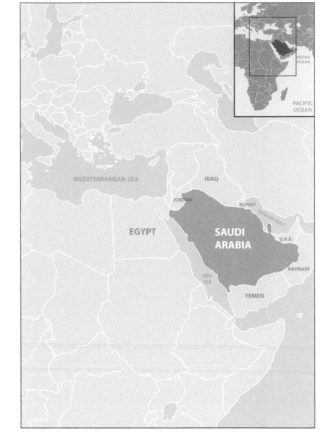

Arab Spring continues to develop. Certainly, however, a new chapter began for Saudi women with the August 2015 municipal elections.

GENERAL INFORMATION

Official Language: Arabic
Population: 30,770,375 (2014 estimate)

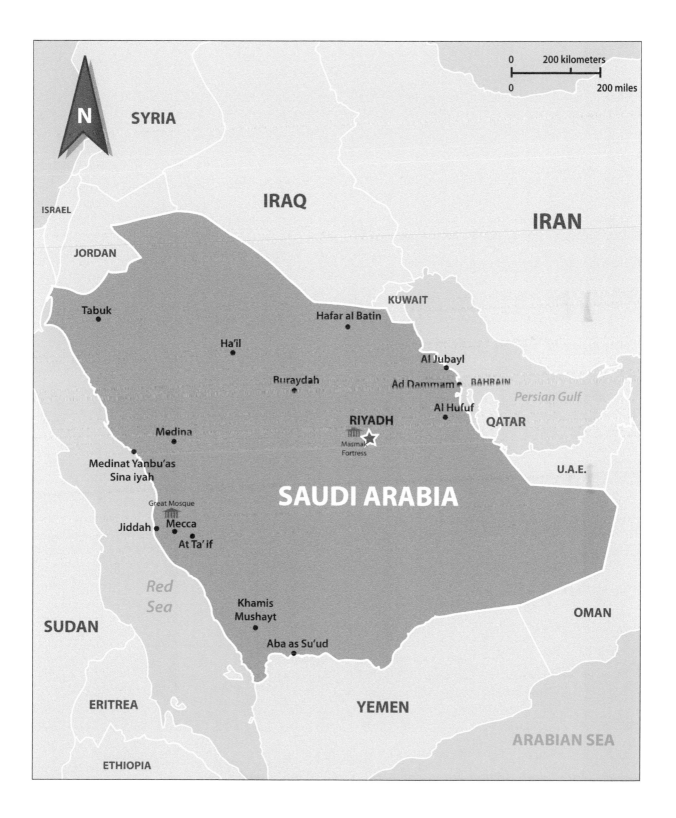

Principal Cities by Population (2014):

- Riyadh (5,451,000)
- Jeddah (3,578,000)
- Mecca (1,591,000)
- al-Hofuf & al-Mubarraz (1,500,000)
- Medina (1,142,000)
- Dammam (941,000)
- Khamis Mushayt, also Ḥamīs Mušayṭ (713,000)
- Buraydah (614,093)
- Tabuk, also Tabūk (534,893)
- Ta'if (521,273)

Currency: Saudi Riyal

Coins: One hundred halala equal one riyal. Coins are issued in denominations of 5, 10, 25, 50, and 100 halala.

Land Area: 2,149,690 square kilometers (1,071,000 square miles)

National Anthem: "an-Našīd al-Waṭaniyy" ("Hasten to glory and supremacy!")

Capital: Riyadh

Time Zone: GMT +3

Flag Description: The flag of Saudi Arabia is solid green, with the Muslim declaration of faith, the *shahada* (or *aš-šahādah*, "the testimony"), written in white. The declaration reads, "There is no God but Allah and Muhammad is the messenger of Allah." Beneath this inscription is a white sword, symbolizing justice.

Population

Approximately 90 percent of Saudi Arabia's population is Arab, while the remainder is comprised of Afro Asians and foreign nationals. The foreign national population is largely composed of Arabs from other Middle Eastern regions, as well as a large population of Muslims from India, Pakistan, and elsewhere. In addition, more than 100,000 people from Western nations live in Saudi Arabia.

The largest city in Saudi Arabia is Riyadh (population 5.45 million), the capital, in the central part of the country. The city also had the highest standard of living in Saudi Arabia and

was once ranked 55th worldwide, above both Los Angeles and Houston. However, in 2011 and 2012, this international ranking fell to 157, just below Dakar, Moscow, and Sarajevo. Other large cities include Jeddah (population 3.6 million), Mecca (population 1.6 million), Medina (population 1.14 million), and Dammam (population approximately 941,000). Until the 1970s, much of Saudi Arabia's population lived in rural areas, but by the turn of the 21st century, most of the semi-nomadic or nomadic population had migrated to cities throughout the country. The country's city-dwellers constitute 83.1 percent of the population in 2015, and this number continues to grow at an annual rate of 2.1 percent.

Languages

The official language is Arabic, and English is a common second language among the business and political classes.

Native People & Ethnic Groups

The Bedouin peoples of Saudi Arabia have traditionally made up the majority of the nomadic or seminomadic population in the desert region. Prior to the mid-20th century, most Bedouins formed migratory herding communities linked to each other through loose tribal affiliations. However, many joined the population migration to large urban centers after the oil boom brought rapid industrialization and economic change to the peninsula. As of 2013, around 1,532,000 Bedouins live with Saudi Arabian borders. Overall, 90 percent of the population is Arab, while 10 percent is Afro Asian.

Religions

Saudi Arabia is a Muslim nation and recognizes no other religions within its borders. Freedom of religion is not offered or guaranteed. According to Saudi law, all residents of Saudi Arabia are Muslim. Most Saudis are Sunni Muslims (between 85 and 90 percent), and there is a small population of Shia Muslims (approximately 10 to 15 percent). Salafism (a term that Saudis prefer over "Wahhabism") is the primary Islamic code of Saudi Arabia, and it dictates how Islam is to be followed and taught throughout the kingdom.

Climate

In general, Saudi Arabia lives up to its reputation as a dry, hot desert nation. Overall, Saudi Arabia's climate is characterized by cold temperatures at night, hot temperatures during the day, and slight annual rainfall. The coastal regions are hot and humid, while the southwestern Asir ('Asīr) highland region, which shares a border with Yemen, experiences occasional, heavy rainfall, usually between 30 and 50 centimeters (12 and 20 inches) each year. The average annual rainfall is less than 120 millimeters (5 inches) per year, but some areas can go years without receiving any rain at all.

The peninsula also experiences a strong, northwesterly wind called a shamal, which causes extreme dust and sand storms and can last for months at a time. The average annual temperature in Jeddah is 28° Celsius (82° Fahrenheit) and, in the summer, can sometimes reach more than 43° C (109° F). In Riyadh, the average is 36° Celsius (96° Fahrenheit). The average annual temperature for the country as a whole is 32.3° Celsius (90.4° Fahrenheit).

ENVIRONMENT & GEOGRAPHY

Topography

Saudi Arabia borders large bodies of water, but has no significant lakes or rivers within its borders. The country has been described as a large, flat rock covered in sand.

In general, the country is desert, with some mountains and highlands in the west, a central arid plateau, and fertile eastern oases. The country's vast desert area contains parts of the Arabian Desert and the Rub'al Khali Desert (also known as the "Empty Quarter"). There is a coastal plain, called the Tihamah, along the western Red Sea coast. Taken together, Saudi Arabia's east and west coastlines measure approximately 2,320 kilometers (1,450 miles). The country's highest point is at Jabal Sawda

3,133 meters (10,278 feet) above sea level in the southwest corner of the country, near the border with Yemen.

Riyadh is located on the Najd plateau in the central part of Saudi Arabia. The city covers an area of approximately 1,554 square kilometers (600 square miles).

Plants & Animals

Animals common found in Saudi Arabia include mountain baboons, gazelles, foxes, and several species of large cats, including the Arabian leopard and the Asiatic cheetah. Other animals typically seen in the country are hyraxes (herbivores that resemble groundhogs), Indian porcupines, jerboas (rodents with rabbit-like ears), gray wolves, oryxes, mountain goats, Ibex, hyenas, lizards, flamingoes, ostriches and pelicans, a variety of sand-dwelling rats and snakes, and oryxes. Arabian Horses and Arabian Camels are also common.

Although not associated in the popular imagination with lush greenery, Saudi Arabia does feature a wide variety of wildflowers and other exotic plants. In fact, within Saudi Arabia, there are 2,282 known species of flora, 600 of which are considered endangered. Common throughout the country are date palms and wheat, which are important food staples.

Endangered species include the green turtle, the Arabian Oryx, and the Nubian Ibex. Beginning in the late 20th century, the Saudi government began a program of captive breeding combined with other conservation measures, in an effort to preserve the country's dwindling wildlife population.

CUSTOMS & COURTESIES

Greeting

A very common greeting throughout Arabia is "As-salamu alaykum" ("Peace unto you"). The common reply to this is "Wa-Alaikum-as-Salaam" ("And peace be upon you"). A less formal greeting is "Marhaba" ("Welcome" or "Hello") or "Ahlan wa sahlan" (also "Welcome,"

"Hello"). Some other common greetings are "Sabah al-khair" ("Good morning") and "Masaa al-Khair" ("Good evening"). The proper reply to "Sabah al-khair" is "Sabah al-noor," and the proper reply to "Masaa al-Khair" is "Masa al-noor."

Saudi men typically shake hands when they greet each other. Friends and family may also customarily greet by kissing each other on the cheek. Often, this is done three times: once on one cheek, once on the opposite cheek, and then a third time on the first cheek. Sometimes a Saudi man will put a hand over his heart after shaking hands. This gesture is expected to be reciprocated.

However, shaking hands or kissing with the opposite gender is generally not practiced. In addition, physical contact between men and women in public is forbidden. A man should also refrain from verbally addressing a woman he doesn't know, as speaking with a stranger of the opposite sex risks shaming and offending the person.

Gestures & Etiquette

Saudi Arabian etiquette is shaped by Islam and the practical necessities and social structure of tribal life in the desert. Hospitality, in particular, is one of the most highly praised virtues among Saudis. This is often attributed to the traditional Bedouin nomads. As they traveled the desert with only the water their camels could carry, and perhaps a sack of dates (fruit of the date palm tree) as food, they often had to rely on the hospitality of strangers. As such, Saudis treat their guests with great generosity.

One of the most notable aspects of etiquette in Saudi culture, and in Islamic culture in general, is the avoidance of eating with the left hand. This is because the left hand is used for hygiene and is, therefore, considered unclean. Additionally, the soles of the feet, which touch the ground, are also considered unclean. As such, Saudis avoid pointing the soles of their feet at people, particularly within their social circle.

It is common for a man to hold hands with other men in public as a sign of friendship.

However, an unmarried man and woman cannot hold hands in public. Generally, men are expected to keep a distance from women and are not to speak to them. However, an exception is made for close relations. For example, a man may speak freely to his sister, but not necessarily to his female cousin (whom he could marry).

In Bedouin tribes, close relations include people who were nursed by the same woman, as a mother's milk is considered an important line of inheritance. Two cousins who have been breast-fed by the same woman are as closely related as siblings are. Therefore, a man is free to speak to a female cousin—or any other woman—who was nursed by the same woman as he was, though he may not marry her.

Saudis typically stand in the presence of their superiors. The usual way to address a superior is to use the honorific "Ustād" ("Master"). The king is addressed as "Your Majesty," while other rulers are addressed as "Your Highness" or "Your Royal Highness." In addition, the honorific title of sheikh is commonly used for senior members of ruling families.

Eating/Meals

Meals in Saudi Arabia are usually eaten at leisure, with plenty of conversation. Traditionally, a main meal is eaten in the evening and often consists of spreads of meats and other foods. It is traditional to eat meals while seated cross-legged on the floor, typically on rugs. In addition, the Saudis drink a lot of coffee (qahwah), and coffee is often served with meals. Alcohol is forbidden to Muslims and is illegal in Saudi Arabia, so meals are accompanied with only non-alcoholic drinks. Saudis usually eat without utensils, using only their right hand. However, many homes have utensils and will present them to guests. Generally, entertaining and cooking for guests are considered important social customs, and Saudis will put a great deal of work into preparing a lavish meal.

When dining out, the host usually pays for the entire meal and, generally, tips. Women are often required to eat in special "family sections," where single men are not allowed. Many Saudis say that this restricts the single men more than it restricts women. In places where restaurants do not yet have family sections, it is not uncommon for a family to request partitions to avoid the stares of single men. Furthermore, the muṭawwi' (agents of the Commission for Promotion of Virtue and Prevention of Vice), who are famed for making sure women wear veils—which are required by Sharia law—are legally not allowed to enter the family sections of restaurants. Thus, women may enjoy slightly more freedom in family sections than in other public places.

The influence of Islam is also apparent in certain dining customs, especially during the holy month of Ramadan, which honors the period during which the Koran was revealed to the prophet Muhammad. After sundown during Ramadan, Muslims eat an evening meal called iftar, traditionally beginning with a date. For some Saudis, iftar can consist of nothing more than a few dates and water, although others enjoy soups or stews, like Shorba (a grain-based soup with vegetables and chicken or mutton), when breaking their fast.

Visiting

A Saudi host is expected to treat his guests with great generosity, and a guest is expected to accept the host's generosity. Guests will most likely be offered coffee or tea, and it is polite to accept. After one or two cups, a guest may signal that he or she has had enough by gently shaking the cup back and forth. Traditionally, if a guest praises any of a host's possessions, the host is expected to offer it to the guest. (The guest is then expected to reciprocate with a gift of equal or greater value.)

In addition, when guests arrive at a host's house, the women among them are often separated from the men and join the women of the household. Guests are typically expected to remove their shoes in the reception room. Although alcohol is illegal in Saudi Arabia, a full bar is a status symbol in certain circles, even if the hosts never drink. A Saudi host entertaining a foreign visitor may offer him or her alcohol, even while abstaining himself.

Overall, Saudis generally tend to be private, and visitors should not drop in uninvited. In addition, if a male visitor arrives at a house and encounters the women of the house alone, it could cause great embarrassment. It can even cause embarrassment if a man calls a house on the telephone and a woman answers the call, though this taboo is generally observed to a much lesser extent.

LIFESTYLE

Family

Saudis tend to be private people and spend much of their time with their families. In restaurants, families usually eat in special "family sections," or request partitions to keep other diners from watching them. Additionally, the windows of family cars are usually darkened to prevent people from seeing in. While extended families (consisting of grandparents, aunts, uncles and cousins) living in one household were traditionally the norm in Saudi culture, this is changing in contemporary society.

Islamic law dictates the rules of marriage in Saudi Arabia. Men may have up to four wives, as specified in the Koran. However, many men have only one wife, and monogamy seems to be emerging as the dominant family structure in recent years. Traditionally, the women of the two families arrange marriages, and the potential groom's grandmother traditionally approaches the mother of the potential bride with a proposal. The girl's father or guardian must then give consent. Once this is obtained, the couple is typically allowed to meet without the use of a veil. Finally, the father of the bride and the groom decide upon a nuptial agreement specifying a dowry.

Saudis may also choose their own spouses, though it is difficult in Saudi society for single men to meet single women. While there are Internet dating sites that cater to Muslims and where some Saudis advertise, some of the ads on these sites are posted by parents looking for matches for their children. Others are posted by foreign workers or divorced women (divorced women cannot legally remarry in Saudi Arabia and so must remarry abroad).

Housing

Until recently, Central Saudi Arabia was sparsely populated. Most of the country became urbanized only after the discovery of oil reserves. Saudi Arabian territory sits atop an estimated 25 percent of the world's known oil reserves. Prior to the middle of the 20th century, the only Saudi cities that had apartment buildings were near the coast of the Red Sea: Mecca, Medina, and the port city Jeddah.

In Jeddah, known for its beautiful buildings and called "the Paris of Arabia," the old apartment buildings were up to five stories tall and often-featured balconies or bay windows encased in an intricate wooden façade with wooden grating. They were typically made of coral limestone (that is, a stone comprised of the compressed skeletal fragments of marine life). Many of Jeddah's builders, for example, used Red Sea coral, while others used stone or, more rarely, red brick. However, many of these old apartment buildings have since been demolished in favor of more contemporary structures, which feature clean, spare lines and light colors.

In the capital of Riyadh, apartment buildings were first built in the 1950s. At about the same time, houses with yards, particularly courtyards, became increasingly popular in the city. Courtyard housing remains a prominent tradition in rural areas. Houses are the preferred type of residence for Saudis and have been built rapidly throughout the country. Apartment buildings have also been built rapidly, fueled largely by an influx of migrant workers.

Within a traditional Saudi household, men and women usually live in separate areas. Most homes have a reception room, where guests are entertained with coffee and tea.

Food

Saudi Arabia's cuisine has been shaped by religion, climate, the culinary traditions of the nomadic Bedouins, and other neighboring Arab cuisines. For religious reasons, Saudis abstain from pork and alcoholic beverages. Traditional meals might include coffee—specially prepared with cardamom and sometimes even saffron—or tea, and meat (lamb, chicken, beef, camel, or fish), prepared with rice, spices, and oats or wheat.

Favorite Saudi dishes include muttabaq, a meat and onion-filled pastry; saliq, a rice and meat mixture similar to pudding that is spiced with cardamom, cinnamon, and cloves; harisah, a wheat-based meal made with meat, tomatoes, and green chilies; and a wealth of spiced seafood dishes. A list of spices that are included in traditional Saudi cuisine includes cinnamon, cardamom, cloves, tamarind, sumac, cilantro, and saffron. In addition, dates, yogurt, mint, curry, and other ingredients are typically included in Saudi cooking.

Unleavened bread or fatir (flat bread) are common accompaniments to most meals. For the Bedouin of Saudi Arabia, dates and flour or bread, supplemented by camel or goat milk are typical foods. Millet is a staple food in rural areas, and it is not uncommon for meat to only be consumed on special occasions. While sheep, goat, and camel may be consumed, Islam forbids pork.

Saudi Arabia has long been known for maintaining a traditional national cuisine and diet. However, contemporary Saudi cuisine also has distinct Lebanese influences, and many of the foods common in Saudi Arabia are of Lebanese origin, such as hummus and stuffed grape leaves (mahshy warqenab). Lebanese cuisine is also become standard fare at restaurants in recent years.

Additionally, a large number of restaurants are offering a wide variety of ethnic foods, such as Indian or Afghan, to serve the country's growing expatriate community. The preparation of a variety of nontraditional foods is also becoming more common in contemporary households, and includes spiced rice, dips for bread and for dates, tabbouleh (a salad of wheat and vegetables), chicken, and lamb.

Saudi cultural tradition holds that women prepare the food, while men are in charge of making coffee, but even that tradition has begun to change, leaving women in charge of most food-related tasks.

Life's Milestones

Saudi families have a number of customs that they observe when a child is born. Family members, friends, and neighbors customarily bring gifts to the mother upon a child's birth. Traditionally, the newborn child's family then sacrifices a sheep and gives the meat to the poor. On the seventh day, the child is named. If it is a boy, he is also circumcised on the seventh day. The day after the child is circumcised, the lights in the house are turned off, and any children of the family and friends of the family take candles through the house and sing prayers asking that the child to be blessed.

Saudis also have many traditional customs pertaining to marriage. Before a woman is married, either the bride's family or a hired professional paints her with henna (dye from the henna plant). The painting of the bride has become a prenuptial party for the women of the bride's family. On the day of the wedding, there are typically two events: a large dinner party for male friends and family, and a more intimate party for immediate family members—both men and women. The groom attends the first dinner party, and after dinner, he and his immediate family join the bride's family for the more intimate party. At the second party, both the men and women from both families may sing and dance.

When a person dies, the body is buried as soon as possible, typically within 24 hours. Traditionally, the deceased is washed and shaved (including the body, to simulate the state in which they appeared on earth as infants), but never embalmed. Once shrouded, the body is transported to a site where funeral prayers are said (often by men only) and then buried facing Mecca. The family subsequently observes a three-day mourning period.

CULTURAL HISTORY

Art

Saudi Arabia has a wealth of prehistoric rock art, much of it in the desert of the north (An Nafud) or the high plain of central Arabia (Najd, also Nejd). The rock art is comprised of pictures of animals and human figures carved into rock. The animals depicted include many species that probably once thrived in the Arabian Peninsula, such as cheetahs and ostriches. The climate of the Arabian Peninsula was once wet and could support many animals no longer found there. It is uncertain when these depictions were created, as some of them are probably 4,000 years old, while others may be more than 8,000 years old.

With the abundant coral of the Red Sea, the turquoise of Mecca, and other precious stones found in Saudi Arabia, the Saudis have been able to create beautiful, colorful jewelry. In addition to precious stones, Saudi jewelry often features filigree (fine wirework), chains, and bells. Jewelry has often been thought to possess supernatural powers. Bells on trinkets, for instance, are said to be able to ward off evil, while turquoise protects the wearer from the evil eye (a cultural belief linking unlucky events and envy). The people the Bedouins traded with, such as the peoples of South Arabia and the Far East historically influenced the jewelry of the Bedouins of Saudi Arabia. Typically, Saudi men do not wear jewelry, but traditionally, they have decorated their swords, horses, and camels.

It has often been observed that the Bedouins of pre-Islamic Arabia placed little importance on any of the arts besides poetry. The popular interpretation of Islam perhaps reinforced the lowly position of the arts. Many scholars interpret passages from the Qur'an, or Koran (Islam's holy text), as forbidding depictions of animals and human figures. At the same time, Islam inspired the art of calligraphy. Artisans began painting verses from the Koran on the walls of mosques and inscribing them on ceramics, manuscripts and other objects. The art of calligraphy eventually became very important and respected in the

Islamic world. Islam also brought central Arabia into contact with new cultures, so that it incorporated some of their artistic influences. For instance, the new religious buildings featured mosaics similar to the Christian mosaics of Syria and Palestine.

Contemporary Saudi art is now enjoying global attention. In 2003, Edge of Arabia, a collaboration between British artist Stephen Stapleton and Saudi artists Ahmed Mater (1979–) and Abdulnasser Gharem (1973–), was founded and, as if 2015, has presented the work of emerging Saudi artists, like Omanah Alsadiq (1991–), Mohammed Al Ghamdi (1959–), and Dana Awartani (1987–), to more than 300,000 visitors through traveling exhibitions. Especially notable is the activity of the many female artists, like Manal Al-Dowayan, who create works that serve not only aesthetic purposes, but also serve as a form of cultural critique, ultimately intended to reframe perceptions.

Architecture

Perhaps the earliest permanent structures in central Arabia are the rock carvings of the Thamud. The Thamud were a people who probably migrated out of south Arabia sometime in the first millennium BCE. Into rocky monoliths, they carved large rooms. On the outside of these rocks, they carved columns and other architectural features in relief, so that on one side, the rocks resemble buildings assembled from blocks. These architectural features are very exact, with straight, even lines and planes that reveal a high degree of artistry. The structures were probably tombs, though they are often misidentified as dwellings.

The predominant architectural style of Saudi Arabia was largely influenced by Islam. As the cultural and political influence of Islam spread over ancient cosmopolitan cities such as Alexandria (Egypt) and Constantinople (Turkey), the Islamic empire absorbed the older architectural styles of the Byzantine Empire (330–1453 CE) and further developed them. This Islamic style of architecture, incorporating influences from all over the Mediterranean and Persian

Gulf areas, was Saudi Arabia's most expressive style. It long coexisted with simple structures of earthen material that are uniquely suited to Saudi Arabia's climate and resources, such as coral, limestone, and adobe (mud or clay bricks).

Two prominent examples of Islamic architecture in Saudi Arabia are the Great Mosque of al-Haram (also Al-Masjid al-Haram, meaning "the sacred mosque") in Mecca and the Prophet's Mosque (also Al-Masjid an-Nabawi) in Medina, considered the holiest mosques in the world. When the Great Mosque of al-Haram was first built, it was a simple wall surrounding a large prayer area. The Saudi rulers have expanded the mosque several times since they came to power, adding nine minarets (towers) and other features of Islamic architecture. The Prophet's Mosque in Medina evolved from a simple square enclosure with a roof of palm branches to a larger mosque built around the original, which included the tomb of the Prophet Muhammad (c. 570–632 CE), Islam's central and founding figure. Beginning in the 13th century, the mosque was expanded, including the construction of a larger dome over the prophet's tomb and new, smaller domes. Notable examples of Islamic calligraphy adorn the interior of these smaller domes.

Music

Traditional music in Saudi Arabia is rooted in the sung poetic verses of the Bedouin and the area's importance as a center of trade and culture. For example, in addition to being an important commercial and religious center in ancient times, the city of Medina was also a source of converging musical styles. Because of a thriving slave trade, Medina was a central place to buy and sell slaves. Among these slaves were singing girls, who were required to be musically talented and have a wide knowledge of Arabic poetry (which was usually sung), as they were often used as entertainers in wealthy homes or accompanied tribes to battle. In addition, the sailors or laborers aboard the pearl-diving ships that sailed the Gulf region had their own repertoire of work-related ballads.

The slaves of Medina were musically important in another respect: some historians credit slaves from other parts of the world—laborers as well as singing girls—with introducing important musical styles and techniques to the Arabs. The most famous of the early singers was perhaps Tuwais ("Little Peacock"), a 17th-century musician who imitated the style of the Persian slaves he heard in Medina. Traditionally, songs were often accompanied by such instruments as the oud, a wood-bellied lute, or its skin-bellied predecessor; the mizmar, a double-reed wind instrument; and some form of percussion.

Dance

Numerous regional folk dances originated in Saudi Arabia. Most notable is the Al Ardha, or men's sword dance, which is considered the national dance. The folk dance was traditionally performed by male members of the Bedouin tribes before heading into battle, but has since become associated with cultural events and festivals. Many other folk dances are associated with a distinct style of music and, thus, share the same name. Samri, for example, involves sung poetry and percussion, generally using a daf (also dap) drum. Many traditional dances in Saudi Arabia incorporate African and European influences in their technique and musical accompaniment.

Literature

The earliest records of the cultural achievements of the nomadic people of central Arabia are poems that were probably composed between 500 and 622 CE. However, these poems were not written down until a hundred years later, when Arabic writing became widespread. (Scholars widely credit the Bedouins, as the nomads of Arabia are known, with developing this poetic art centuries before these poems were composed.) The popularity and influence of poetry is attributed to the traditional belief that poets were often thought to have an almost magic power. Poets were seen as inspired by the jinn (invisible, malevolent spirits) of the desert and were thought to be able to harm their enemies by composing satires (hijd) against them.

The poems that survive from the sixth century are qasidas (also qasidahs), which involve an intricate, closed meter of between 50 and 100 lines. They typically have a strict and difficult rhyme scheme. A notable qasida is "Qasida Burda" ("Poem of the Mantle") by Imam al-Busiri (1211–1294). Many scholars believe that the qasida may have evolved from hida, the songs of camel drivers, which typically have a loose meter (known as rajaz) that resembles the rhythm of a camel's gait. The qasida remains the only standard form of Arabic poem. In addition, with the spread of Islam, the Qur'an (Koran) became the predominant literary model and text in Saudi Arabian culture.

CULTURE

Arts & Entertainment

Modern Arabic culture in general is reliant on Qu'ranic ideas and customs for its substance, in much the same way that some Christian cultures have drawn artistic inspiration from biblical scripture and ideology. Examples of this may be found in the literature and decorative arts of Saudi Arabia. However, because of the restrictive nature of fundamental Islam, such modern arts as the cinema and even older ones, such as dance and theatre, are frowned upon.

Movie theaters and stage theatres are both banned in public places, although some do exist in the cities. For example, there is one IMAX theater in Khobar. Additionally, some city cafes show movies on televisions within their establishments. The official attitude towards cinema appears to be lightening, however, since the country's first government-funded film festival was held in 2008. And in February 2015, the government again sponsored the five-day Saudi Film Festival, during which Golden Palm Trees were awarded like American Oscars. The sixty competing works by filmmakers from Saudi Arabia and around the Persian Gulf were screened at the arts center in Dammam, on the country's Gulf coast. In addition to Golden Palm Trees, winners received grants to fund future projects.

The Saudi sound recording industry is thriving, even though music is still somewhat culturally restricted for religious reasons. More traditional-minded Saudis might disapprove of many forms of popular and even folk music, but the mass-media awareness brought about by the telecommunications revolution of the last few decades has guaranteed a place for Western and Arabic music and arts in the modern Arab world.

Traditional arts have clearly been preserved in Saudi Arabia. The qasidas (odes) that were composed in the century before Islam spread across the Arabian Peninsula are still learned and sung by Bedouin musicians. There are more recent qasidas, but those of the early period are widely considered the best. A singer may perform alone, often playing an oud (lute) as he sings. Or he may be accompanied by several other men playing the oud, the tabl (a double-headed drum), and the jalayit (a rattle). A section of stringed instruments, such as violins or violas, is also common.

Many conservative Muslims have interpreted passages in the Koran as prohibiting the representation of humans and animals, and this interpretation prevails in Saudi Arabia. While there are very few paintings and fewer painters in the kingdom, calligraphy is still a revered art form and is still practiced. Inscriptions are used to decorate everything from kitchenware to office walls. More importantly, the walls and ceilings of mosques are often decorated with passages from the Koran in elegant calligraphy.

Saudi Arabia has grown quickly since the 1970s, and Riyadh is the site of several notable examples of contemporary, international styles of architecture. The tallest building in Riyadh, the Kingdom Centre tower (992 feet), is a striking example. This building has an elliptical base. Near the top, an opening in the shape of an inverted parabola divides the building into two tapering prongs, which are joined by a crossbar that is actually a functioning sky bridge. The building was designed by a Saudi firm in collaboration with an American firm. Many contemporary buildings in Saudi Arabia were designed by international firms.

Cultural Sites & Landmarks

Saudi Arabia is home to the two holiest cities in Islam, Mecca and Medina. They are both considered haram (forbidden to nonbelievers), and a nonbeliever caught within either city is at risk. Saudi Arabia is also home to two of the greatest mosques in the Arab world, the Great Mosque of al-Haram (also Masjid al-Haram, or "Sacred Mosque") and the Prophet's Mosque (also Al-Masjid an-Nabawi). The Saudi kingdom is considered to be the caretaker or custodian of these supremely important mosques. This is a source of great national pride, and through the attention of the Saudi rulers and earlier caretakers, the mosques have become perhaps the most spectacular buildings in Saudi Arabia.

Mecca is Islam's holiest city (one of the Five Pillars of Islam states that a follower of Islam must make a pilgrimage to Mecca at least once in their lifetime). It is the site of the Kaaba (also Ka'bah) shrine, a cubic building that is considered Islam's holiest place, and the Great Mosque of al-Haram. The Kaaba contains a sacred black stone which many Muslims believe dates back to early biblical times. All Muslims direct their prayers toward the Kaaba. As such, mosques around the world usually have a mihrab, a niche in one wall that indicates the direction of Mecca and, more specifically, the Kaaba. The Kaaba is contained within the Great Mosque of al-Haram, which sprawls over 3,840,600 square feet and can accommodate 900,000 people. Some of the entryways are flanked by tall minarets, nine in total. These are towers from which Muslims are called to prayer. Within the mosque are large prayer halls and, roughly at the center of the mosque, a large courtyard containing the Kaaba.

The city of Medina is considered the second holiest city in Islam and was also an important historic and cultural center during the rise of the Islamic empire. Medina contains the Prophet's Mosque, which is the burial location of Muhammad, the prophet of Islam. The Prophet's Mosque is a large rectangular structure in Medina with tall minarets rising from the corners and entrances. Like the Great Mosque of al-Haram, the Prophet's Mosque has undergone many changes over the centuries. The Saudi rulers had two of the existing minarets replaced with minarets in the architectural style prevalent during the reign of the Mamluk Sultanate (1250–1517) to match the dome and other renovations. They also added a library and new minarets, so that there are now 10 in total. The current structure can hold nearly one million people during the Hajj period.

In addition to cultural sites within the influential sphere of Islam, there are numerous other historic locations and landmarks within Saudi Arabia. These include Old Riyadh, the historic section of the city of Riyadh, which features traditional architecture and the Masmak Fortress, a clay, and mud-brick fort of vital historical importance to both the city and the kingdom. The fortress dates to 1865 and is one of the few historical buildings still standing in Riyadh. It is a major tourist attraction and is especially well-known for its Diwan, which is the king's sitting room.

The Kingdom Centre is the largest skyscraper in Saudi Arabia and home to the world's highest mosque, a hotel, shopping mall, and an observation bridge suspended 300 meters (984 feet) above the city. Other sites include King Fahd's Fountain in the city of Jeddah, listed as the world's tallest fountain; and the al-Hijr Archaeological Site, which contains traces of civilizations dating back to the second millennium BCE. In 2008, this archaeological site became Saudi Arabia's first World Heritage Site, as recognized by the United Nations Educational, Scientific and Cultural Organization (UNESCO).

Libraries & Museums

The King Abdul Aziz Military Museum in Riyadh displays military artifacts. Other museums in the city include the National Museum, and the Museum of Antiquities and Folklore, both of which display various items of historical significance.

Holidays

Much of the Muslim world uses an Islamic calendar, which is based on lunar cycles and so differs considerably from the Gregorian calendar used by most other nations. Saudis celebrate Ramadan, which is the ninth month of the Islamic calendar; Ramadan has no fixed date and, so, can occur anytime during a particular lunar cycle. In 2005, for instance, Ramadan occurred between October 4 and November 2. In 2015, it occurred between June 17 and July 17.

Eid al-Fitr marks the end of Ramadan and the first day of the month of Shawwal, the tenth lunar month. Eid al-Adha, another feast, is celebrated on the tenth day of Dhul Hijjah, which, in 2005, corresponded with January 21 and, in 2015, corresponded with September 23. In addition, Saudis celebrate national unification, also on September 23.

Throughout the Arab world, the month of Dhul al-Hijjah—the 12th and final month of the Islamic calendar—is the month when millions of travelers visit Mecca for the annual pilgrimage, or Hajj. Every Muslim is expected to go to Mecca at least once in his lifetime (women are to be accompanied by a male relative or spouse).

Youth Culture

Men and women are strictly segregated in Saudi society. Young women attend girls-only schools, typically ride in cars with deeply tinted windows, and are accompanied by a male chaperone in public. Consequently, there are few, if any, places where young men and women can socialize together.

With limited opportunities for public interaction, many young Saudis have begun using cell phone and Bluetooth technology to circumvent cultural obstacles to dating. Young men have also developed certain social practices to meet young women. One such practice is "numbering," in which young men advertise their phone numbers to young women, typically while driving. There are even belts that use Bluetooth technology to automatically broadcast the wearer's telephone number to passersby.

Dating is essentially forbidden; youths are expected to wait for marriage to develop relationships. As such, young people typically develop close ties with friends of their own gender, but usually have no involvement in romantic relationships.

A young woman typically does not meet her groom until she is engaged. At this time, a showfa, or viewing, takes place, and the young man is permitted to view his fiancé without her abaya or hijab (traditional Islamic over garments). However, it is becoming more socially acceptable for engaged women to converse with their fiancés using the phone or Internet.

In spite of tradition, young people do sometimes date illicitly. But because they are expected to marry the person of their parents' choosing, these relationships often end when one of the couple gets married.

SOCIETY

Transportation

Although reputed to be reckless drivers, most Saudis own cars and rely on them for daily transportation. (Saudis drive on the right side of the road.) In fact, Saudi Arabia has one of the world's highest highway fatality rates. Jobs that involve commutes are hazardous for this reason. For example, so many teachers (who often have long commutes to get to villages) have been killed on the road that the Saudi government recently released a study of the issue, naming auto accidents an occupational hazard for teachers.

Because women are forbidden to drive in Saudi Arabia, many of them are driven by family members or drivers.

Transportation Infrastructure

Saudi Arabia generally has a well-maintained network of highways, some of them eight lanes wide, and is well served by airlines. Major highways connect the capital, Riyadh, with Dammam on the Persian Gulf, the holy cities Mecca and Medina, and the ancient port city of Jeddah. There are six international airports in Saudi Arabia: one each in Jeddah, Riyadh, Dammam, Medina, Yanbu, and Hofuf. There are also twenty domestic and regional airports in Saudi Arabia. In addition, the Saudi Public Transport Company (SAPTCO) runs buses between major cities. It also provides transportation during the Hajj, the annual pilgrimage to Mecca.

Rail lines connect Riyadh to Dammam and Hofuf. A rail line is planned to connect Jeddah, an important port city on the Red Sea coast, with the Riyadh and with Jabail, a port city on the Persian Gulf coast.

Media & Communications

The Saudi government aggressively censors the media. Local television stations are state-controlled by the Broadcasting Service of the Kingdom of Saudi Arabia (BSKSA), and most Saudis use satellite TV to receive fast and uncensored reporting from foreign news stations. Al Jazeera ("al jazeera" means "the peninsula"), which broadcasts out of neighboring Qatar, is one of the most popular stations available to Saudis. Al Jazeera's coverage, which is often controversial, has included criticisms of Saudi rulers and videotapes of Osama bin Laden, who, before his death in May 2011, had long worked to overthrow the Saudi government. The Saudi government has frequently complained about the coverage and has not allowed the station to operate in Saudi Arabia. However, in 2007, the government of Qatar assured Saudi Arabia that Al Jazeera's coverage would improve. Since then, the station's coverage of Saudi Arabia has been relatively positive.

Saudi newspapers are privately owned but must get permission from the government to operate, and they must have their editors approved by the government. In some cases, editors may be government-appointed. Despite the strict government control, under King Abdullah, Saudi newspapers have begun reporting on previously forbidden topics, such as women's rights and political reform. There are ten major dailies operating in Saudi Arabia, with two of the most popular being *Al Riyadh*, published in the capital of Riyadh, and *Al Jazirah*, published in Jeddah.

Beginning in 2000, Internet usage in Saudi Arabia increased from under 1 percent of the population to more than 9.8 million users, or 38 percent of the population, in 2010. In 2014, that number nearly doubled, climbing to 17.4 million users. In general, the Saudi government has enacted strict rules pertaining to the use of the

Internet, and access to many websites is blocked. The government has also tried to restrict blogging, though blogs are becoming increasingly popular, especially among women.

SOCIAL DEVELOPMENT

Standard of Living

In 2014, Saudi Arabia ranked 34th out of 187 countries on the United Nations Human Development Index, which measures quality of life and standard of living indicators.

Water Consumption

According to UNICEF (United Nations International Children's Emergency Fund), 97 percent of Saudis continue to have access to improved drinking water in 2015—whether located in rural or urban areas—and 100 percent have access to improved sanitation. As one of the driest places in the world, Saudi Arabia depends on non-renewable groundwater, desalinated water, surface water, and some renewable groundwater. Conservation efforts are being implemented and are showing results. More desalinization plants have come on line in the early 21st century—Saudi Arabia is now the largest producer of desalinized water in the world.

Education

Education from pre-school through college is free for most Saudis, but not compulsory. The Saudi government spends a considerable amount of money on extending its education system; as a result, literacy and school attendance have increased considerably in recent decades.

In 1960, Saudi women were granted the limited right to an education. Despite this, there is still some gender segregation in the education system; for instance, women may study medicine, but not engineering. In addition, Saudi schools serve as religious institutions and follow strict educational codes based on Islamic law. Among the most important colleges and universities in Saudi Arabia are King Saud University, originally known as Riyadh University; Islamic

University in Medina; and King Abdul Aziz University in Jeddah. The average literacy rate is 94.7 percent (97 percent among men and 91.1 percent among women).

Princess Noura Bint Abdulrahman University (originally the Riyadh University for Women) was established in 1970 and renamed in 2008. It is a university designed exclusively for women and offers courses in science, medicine, pharmacy, business administration, computer sciences, education, and languages. It is considered the largest women's university in the world, with a total enrollment of 52,308.

Women's Rights

Human rights advocates have been concerned about women's rights in Saudi Arabia for decades. Court cases involving women in Saudi Arabia typically shock outsiders, highlighting the disparity between women's rights in Saudi Arabia and in the rest of the world. This is illustrated by several high-profile cases, including the case of the young woman who was sentenced to 90 lashes after she brought the men who raped her to court. Another case in 1990 involved seventy women who congregated in a parking lot in Riyadh so that they could drive (women are forbidden to drive a vehicle in Saudi Arabia), many of whom had the support of their husbands. Nevertheless, the women were arrested, and many were dismissed from their jobs. In addition, a group of Saudi businesswomen who removed their veils during a conference in Jeddah in 2004 were harshly condemned by the legal authorities. These cases all demonstrate the conservatism of the Saudi legal system and the status of women in a strict Islamic society.

The judges of Saudi Arabia are ulema (also ulama), or Islamic scholars, whose religious decrees amount to law. They are versed in the conservative interpretation of Islam as embraced by the Saudi kingdom and followed by most ordinary Saudis. It is known in the West as Wahhabism, after an 18th-century Islamic reformer who greatly influenced Saudi religion. Under this interpretation of Islam, women are generally required to cover their faces and hair, and they have significantly fewer freedoms than men do. In fact, according to the rules of Saudi society, a woman needs written permission to carry out what amounts to the most routine of social practices, such as finding employment, furthering education, or even purchasing such items as an airline ticket. Additionally, the tenets of Wahhabi Islam limit social contact between men and women who are not married or otherwise related.

Further, any time a woman makes an important decision, she must get the permission of her husband, father, or guardian. For example, a woman cannot marry without her father's permission. While recent reforms have allowed a woman to travel without her husband or guardian, she still must obtain the permission of her husband or guardian before traveling. However, a campaign against the ban on women drivers has recently begun, with some describing it as the suffragette movement of the Arab world.

Women also have unequal rights in marriage. A man may divorce a woman fairly easily, but a woman cannot divorce a man. In addition, once divorced, a man may remarry, but a divorced woman cannot. Thus, it is widely argued and criticized that these laws make women dependent on men.

The muttawa—the vice-prevention agents of the kingdom, also called the Islamic religious police—are notorious for scolding women if their veils do not completely cover their faces. Women are required to wear the veil in public and whenever they are in the presence of men who are not immediate family. This is part of an effort to segregate men from women. However, as foreign as these traditional dress requirements may be to outsiders, some Saudi women support the requirements for religious reasons, while others state that the veil has practical advantages.

King Abdullah (1924–), has made some gestures towards reform of women's rights. Nonetheless, a strong opposition against reform remains prevalent among religious leaders in Saudi Arabia. In some instances, the division between men and women has grown even wider in recent decades. For example, in 1994,

Saudi Arabia's highest religious authority—Grand Mufti Sheikh Abdulaziz bin Abdullah al-Sheikh—issued an edict against women without a veil mingling with men. During the 2008 Summer Olympics in Beijing, China, Saudi Arabia remained one of the few countries without female representation. However, after pressure from the International Olympic Committee, Saudi Arabia agreed to allow women athletes to participate, and in London's 2012 Summer Olympics, Wojdan Shaherkani competed in judo and Saudi-American Sarah Attar represented Saudi Arabia in the 800-meter track event.

Health Care

According to its constitution, Saudi Arabia provides health care for all citizens of the kingdom. The Saudi government allocates a considerable portion of its budget to maintaining the health care system and encourages medical education among its students. In this, as in most other modernization efforts, Saudi Arabia has been very successful. There are 2.5 doctors and 2.1 beds to every 1,000 people. The infant mortality rate stands at a little over 14 deaths per 1,000 live births. Average life expectancy is almost 75 years: 73 years for men and 77 years for women (2015 estimate).

GOVERNMENT

Structure

Saudi Arabia is divided into thirteen provinces. It is a hereditary monarchy ruled by the House of Saud, the founding family of the nation and descendants of Saud ibn Muhammad ibn Muqrin (d. 1725). As an absolute monarch, the king is head of state, head of government, and prime minister. He appoints his cabinet, mostly comprised of other members of the royal family. There are approximately 25,000 members of the House of Saud.

The king also appoints a consultative council, which serves as the legislative branch of government. Currently, the highest court is the Supreme Judicial Council, which oversees the nation's Sharia legal code. Sharia law dictates all levels of social and religious law in Saudi Arabia. The Saudi constitution is based on the Qu'ran (Koran), the holy book of Islam.

During municipal elections in 2005, Saudi men were allowed to vote for the first time since the early 1960s. Traditionally, Saudi women were not granted the right to vote. However, in the 2015 municipal elections, King Abdullah has indicated that women will be permitted to participate, as both voters and municipal candidates.

Political Parties

No political parties are permitted in Saudi Arabia.

Local Government

Saudi Arabia is divided into thirteen provinces (or emirates), which are then divided into governorates and then sub-governorates. The next municipal elections are scheduled for August 2015.

Judicial System

The Saudi judiciary has been in a state of reform since 2007, when King Abdullah issued a decree to create a new court system and effect other related reforms, which have yet to be fully implemented. Abdullah's plan will see the creation of a supreme court and a modernized, first-instance court system that will hear general, criminal, personal interest, commercial, and labor cases, thus transferring the extensive authority once held by Sharia courts and administrative tribunals. Sharia law, however, still defines the system. Additionally, appeals courts will be established for all provinces.

Taxation

The Saudi government levies taxes on corporate income, along with a 20 percent capital gains tax on disposable company shares. And while there is a 2.5 percent zakat (religious tax) on capital assets, there is no sales, property, or local taxation.

Armed Forces

The Ministry of Defense and Aviation Forces is composed of land, naval, air, air defense, and strategic rocket forces, as well as a national guard. In 2013, military expenditures accounted for $52.9 billion (USD) and 11.4 percent of the GDP. There are currently 200,000 active personnel, 1,000 of which have been deployed to Bahrain. There is currently no conscription.

Foreign Policy

Saudi Arabia's foreign policy has developed in the face of complicated local challenges and even more complicated global challenges. Generally, the foreign policy of Saudi Arabia is defined by several significant aspects: its relations with Western nations, its status as a prominent Islamic and Arabic country, and its economic relations with other oil-producing nations. Regional security is also a key concern in the defining of foreign policy.

The United States and Saudi Arabia maintain strategic and bilateral relations, stemming from the exploration and discovery of oil by an American company, Standard Oil, in the 1930s. During this early period, Saudi Arabia was eager to keep Britain and other former colonial powers out, and it worked closely with American companies to advance its developing business interests. Saudi Arabia also played a pivotal role in the US-led Gulf War of 1990–91. However, following the terrorists attacks of September 11, 2001, relations between the two countries became strained. This largely stemmed from the fact that 15 of the 19 terrorists were Saudi nationals, and Saudi Arabia refused to cooperate when the U.S. requested background information on the terrorists and sought interviews with the hijackers' families. However, relations have improved since the 2001 U.S.-led "War on Terror" began.

Saudi Arabia generally maintains close relations with other Middle Eastern countries, largely due to concerns about regional security and Arab nationalism. For example, Saudi Arabia is credited with historically cultivating conservative Islam throughout the Arabian Peninsula, encouraging solidarity between strongly Muslim nations and funding religious institutions and schools. (It was thought that Islam would dissuade people from following atheistic communism.) In addition, Saudi Arabia was largely influential in the formation of the Organization of Petroleum Exporting Countries (OPEC). Members of OPEC work together to control oil price fluctuations and to protect themselves from substantial price declines. Saudi Arabia was one of the founding members of OPEC, along with four other countries.

Saudi Arabia is also a member of the Gulf Cooperation Council (GCC), to which Bahrain, Kuwait, Oman, Qatar, and the United Arab Emirates belong. This coalition of countries assists one another with security issues through a unified military, known as the Peninsula Shield Force, a force in which 40,000 troops are currently active. The GCC was also founded to facilitate the creation of scientific research centers; to share technology that can be implemented in mining and other industrial sectors; to increase member trade and private sector cooperation; and, ultimately, to establish a common currency. In the 2013, the GCC has begun to work even more closely with U.S., purchasing large amounts of arms and other military equipment from the U.S. for the purpose of regional defense.

Saudi Arabia's relations with Israel are also important to note, particularly in light of Saudi Arabia's prominent role in furthering Islamic causes. Saudi Arabia originally opposed the creation of the nation of Israel, warning that increased immigration of Jews to the region would lead to tension and conflict. However, with the U.S. as a close ally, Saudi Arabia became a strong supporter of the partition of Palestine and the creation of the Israeli state. Saudi Arabia's opponents in the Middle East have long criticized the country for its association with the US for this reason. Saudi Arabia has also indicated a willingness to recognize Israel's right to exist under three conditions: if a separate nation were created for the Palestinians, if Israel gave up its 1967 territorial gains, and if Israel ceased hostilities with its neighbors. A resolution has so far not been attainable.

In addition to its prominent membership in OPEC, Saudi Arabia is a founding member of the UN and plays influential roles in both the World Bank and the International Monetary Fund (IMF). Saudi Arabia also serves as the headquarters for the Organization of the Islamic Conference (OIC), as well as the Islamic Development Bank (IDB).

Human Rights Profile
International human rights law insists that states respect civil and political rights and also promote an individual's economic, social and cultural rights. The United Nations Universal Declaration on Human Rights (UDHR) is recognized as the standard for international human rights. Its authors sought the counsel of the world's great thinkers, philosophers, and religious leaders and were careful to create a document that reflects the core values shared by every world culture. (To read this document or view the articles relating to cultural human rights, visit www.ohchr.org/EN/UDHR/Pages/Introduction.aspx.)

When the UN Assembly adopted the UDHR, Saudi Arabia was one of three UN members to abstain from voting on the issue. (The other two to abstain were the Soviet Union and South Africa; every other member voted in favor.) Instead of following the articles of the UDHR, Saudi Arabia adheres closely to Islamic law (Sharia), which is often at variance with the UN Declaration. The Saudi constitution (adopted in 1992) makes this explicit, saying "the state protects human rights in accordance with the Islamic Sharia." As a result, many laws enforced in Saudi Arabia violate the human rights enshrined in the UDHR.

While non-Muslims are tolerated in Saudi Arabia, Muslims are forbidden to change their religion, and apostasy (renouncing Islam) is punishable by death. Witchcraft is also punished by death, and many people say that the "witches" executed in Saudi Arabia are actually just members of other religions or disfavored sects of Islam. These policies violate Article 18 of the UDHR, which guarantees the freedom of religion and the freedom to change religions. Article 18 also guarantees the freedom to cultivate or spread religion through teaching, which is forbidden to non-Muslims in Saudi Arabia.

Many people in Saudi Arabia are punished for various crimes by torture, flogging, and amputation of the hands or feet. In addition, there are reports of prisoners being beaten, subjected to electrical shock, having their nails pulled, and being burned. A person may be sentenced to flogging for a variety of crimes. In one highly publicized case, a young woman who pressed charges against seven men who had sexually assaulted her was sentenced to 90 lashes for being alone with a man before the incident. (The king later pardoned her.) The punishment for theft is sometimes the amputation of a hand or a foot. Capital punishment is also prevalent and often carried out in traditional means and without proper representation. Amnesty International reported that, in 2013 alone, Saudi Arabia carried out seventy-nine such executions, nearly half of which involved foreign nationals. Executions are usually public and can be carried out through the act of stoning, firing on, or beheading the convict. Of the 345 executions that took place between 2007 and 2010, all involved beheadings. These practices violate Article 5 of the UDHR. This article guarantees that no one will be tortured or subjected to cruel or inhuman punishment.

The government of Saudi Arabia broadly censors the media. Many websites are blocked, the press is subjected to government oversight, and television and radio broadcasts are state-controlled. This censorship violates Article 19, which guarantees freedom of speech. Finally, it has often been observed that the women are denied many of the basic rights enjoyed by men, violating Article 2.

Despite the widespread assertions by international organizations such as Amnesty International and Human Rights Watch that human rights abuses occur frequently within Saudi Arabia, the government of Saudi Arabia has passed recent legislation in regard to human rights. In 1997, Saudi Arabia enacted the UN International Convention against Torture and established the independent National Society for Human Rights (NSHR) seven years later. Saudi Arabia also participated in the adoption of the Arab Charter on Human Rights in 2008, which formally adopts the articles of the UDHR. However, the Saudi government continues to be criticized for political, religious and sexual discrimination.

Migration

Saudi Arabia's net migration rate in 2015 was estimated at −.55 migrants per 1,000 people.

ECONOMY

Overview of the Economy

Prior to the discovery of oil in 1938, Saudi Arabia was a poor nation of mostly nomadic and semi-nomadic peoples. Since then, as the oil dependency of most of the world has grown, so have the fortunes of Saudi Arabia. At the beginning of the 21st century, it is one of the wealthiest countries in the world. In 2014, the country's gross domestic product (GDP) exceeded $1.6 trillion USD, with a per capita GDP of $52,200 USD.

The government is the major source of employment in Riyadh, followed by the financial, petroleum, and manufacturing industries, which includes the production of chemicals and plastics.

Industry

The major industry in Saudi Arabia is its petroleum industry. It is estimated that Saudi Arabia contains one-quarter of the world's oil reserves, much of which is located in the eastern part of the country and in the Persian Gulf. This amounts to approximately 268 billion barrels, a reserve second only to Venezuela's, which was discovered, in 2011, to be larger than previously thought. Saudi Arabia produces over 9,735,200 million barrels per day, and as the world's second largest exporter of oil products—just behind Russia—the country exports about 7 million barrels daily.

With so much power behind its petroleum industry, Saudi Arabia is a major political and diplomatic power in the Middle East, as well as a key ally to Western nations. The major beneficiaries of the country's oil wealth are the House of Saud and other oil industry figures.

Other exported goods and major industries in Saudi Arabia include the production of natural gas and petrochemicals, petroleum refining, ammonia, industrial gases, sodium hydroxide, cement, fertilizer, plastics, commercial ship and aircraft repair, limestone, gold, silver, and other metals. The Saudi Arabian government has also prompted privatization in the electric and telecommunications industries. The kingdom's major export partners are China (13.9 percent), the United States (13.6 percent), Japan (13 percent), South Korea (9.8 percent) and India (9.5 percent).

Labor

Saudi Arabia's labor force numbers 11.2 million people, with about 80 percent of this workforce being non-nationals in 2014. The unemployment rate in Saudi Arabia in 2014 was 11.7 percent, which accounts for Saudi males only. (According to the US Central Intelligence Agency, the true unemployment rate may be as high as 25 percent.)

Energy/Power/Natural Resources

The list of Saudi Arabia's natural resources includes iron ore, gold and copper, but by far the most important natural resources are petroleum and natural gas, which are among the largest deposits in the world and the key to the nation's economic influence throughout the world.

Conservation issues arising from the oil industry include water pollution from spillage and manufacturing. Others areas of concern include desertification and a lack of water resources and waste disposal areas.

Fishing

Saudi Arabia enjoys coastlines on the Persian Gulf and the Red Sea—which facilitate shipping of petroleum, but also provide for a vibrant and developing fishing industry. Production from the Red Sea accounted for about 50 percent of the country's supply, with the remainder coming from the Gulf. Shrimp dominate the Gulf catch while the Red Sea catch includes grouper, emperors, Spanish mackerels, mullets, snappers, scads, and jacks. With aquaculture on the rise,

it is thought that its development will account for about one-third of the country's needs. Corporations like the Saudi Fisheries Company, operating under the brand name Al Asmak, work within Saudi Arabia's territorial waters and international waters to either raise or catch a diverse selection of fresh and frozen fish products.

Mining/Metals

In the government's efforts to diversify its economy and develop the mining industry, more resources have been devoted to its development. Large deposits of phosphate and bauxite, as well as copper, gold, iron, tungsten, zinc, potassium ore, lead, silver, and tin have been identified in the Arabian-Nubian Shield, which is an area of exposed Precambrian-era crystalline rock, located on the country's western coast. In 2010, the Saudi government announced that it would expand its gold mining operation, with a goal of doubling its gold resources. And as of 2015, the country's Ministry of Petroleum and Mineral Resources has begun to explore the sediment of the Red Sea floor for naturally-occurring commodity materials, which they will process at the Yanbu petrochemical complex. Recently, the ministry has located over 1,200 sites where precious stones can be now mined, and it continues to seek new domestic mineral sources.

Agriculture

Over the last three decades, the Saudi government has worked to enhance the country's agricultural production and farming technology, so that it might expand beyond its basic production of dates, fruits, and grains. Tapping deep wells, the use of desalinization plants, and trapping rain water via dam complexes now ensure that adequate irrigation is available. And to assist in securing these resources, the Saudi Arabian Agricultural Bank (SAAB) offers interest-free loans and even grants to help small commercial enterprise. The Grain Silos and Flourmills Organization (GSFO) similarly assists farmers by purchasing and storing both wheat and animal feed. It also constructs flour mills to assist in grain processing. For this reason, the meagre

400,000 acres once cultivated in the mid-1970s has expanded to include millions of acres in the early 21st century. The country is now self-sustaining in its supply of milk, eggs, and meat.

Animal Husbandry

Sheep, goats, fish, cattle, and camels are raised in Saudi Arabia. Commercial poultry farming, often in climate-controlled conditions, has grown exponentially, thanks to government incentives that began in the 1980s.

Tourism

In 2012, 14.3 million people crossed Saudia Arabia's borders, many of whom arrived as part of their Hajj, or annual pilgrimage to the sacred Islamic city of Mecca. Medina, another holy city, is revered as the birthplace of the first Islamic state. Like most other developing areas in Saudi Arabia, the tourism industry receives a generous amount of support from the government. In 2003, plans were announced for a major increase in the number of hotel rooms and tourist facilities, with a goal of attracting 44 million tourists per year by the 2020s. Most visitors to Saudi Arabia are Arabs or Muslims from neighboring regions. In 2013, Saudi Commission for Tourism and Antiquities (SCTA) began issuing tourist visas intended to encourage foreign nationals to visit historical sites. An associated law, issued by the Ministry of the Interior, declares all tourist areas to be publically owned; they can no longer be privately held and, consequently, closed to tourists at the owner's discretion.

Aside from the holy cities of Mecca and Medina (neither of which are accessible to non-Muslims), travelers come to Saudi Arabia to see such sights as the festivities related to the holidays of Ramadan, Eid al-Fitr (Feast of Breaking the Fast), and Eid al-Adha (Feast of the Sacrifice). There is also a festival held each year to celebrate Arab folklore and culture. Major attractions include the city of Jeddah, the oasis city of Najran, Asir National Park, and the Farasan Islands in the Red Sea.

Jake Gillis, Craig Belanger,
Alex K. Rich, & Savannah Schroll Guz

DO YOU KNOW?

- The British explorer, author, and scholar Sir Richard Francis Burton took advantage of his Arab language skills to secretly visit Mecca in 1853 to witness the Hajj. The trip was a dangerous one, and in order to prevent his detection as an outsider, he underwent the Muslim practice of circumcision in preparation for the journey.

- Islam originated in the area now known as Saudi Arabia in the seventh century.

- The Rub'al Khali (or "Empty Quarter") in southern Saudi Arabia is the largest single body of sand in the world, measuring approximately 647,000 square kilometers (250,000 miles).

- Riyadh's name is derived from the Arabic word "rawdah," which means "garden" or "meadow" and recalls the city's historic status as dessert oasis.

Bibliography

_____ and Sebastian Maisel. "The Kingdom of Saudi Arabia." 2nd ed. *U Florida P*, 2010.

"The Lure and Legend of Arabian Jewelry." 1997. *Royal Embassy of Saudi Arabia*. Office of the Royal Embassy of Saudi Arabia in Washington, DC, 2015. http://www.saudiembassy.net/files/PDF/Publications/Magazine/1997-Winter/jewelry.htm.

Albert Hourani. "A History of the Arab Peoples." 1992. Cambridge, MA: *Belknap Press*, 2010.

Arthur J. Arberry, ed. "The Koran Interpreted." New York: *Simon & Shuster/Touchstone*. 1996.

David E. Long. "Culture and Customs of Saudi Arabia." Cultures & Customs of the Middle East Ser. *Greenwood Publishing Group*, 2005.

G. E. Von Grunebaum. "Classical Islam: A History 600–1258." 1997. Chicago: *Aldine Transaction.* 2005.

Hassan Habib Touma. "The Music of the Arabs." Portland, OR: *Amadeus Press.* 1996.

Karen Elliott House. "On Saudi Arabia: Its People, Past, Religion, Fault Lines--and Future." Reprint. New York: *Vintage.* 2013.

Lisa Urkevich. "Music and Traditions of the Arabian Peninsula: Saudi Arabia, Kuwait, Bahrain, and Qatar." New York: *Routledge.* 2014.

Martin Lings. "Muhammad: His Life Based on the Earliest Sources." Rev. ed. 2003. Rochester: *Inner Traditions International.* 2006.

Nicholas Buchele. "Culture Smart! Saudi Arabia." London: *Kuperard.* 2008.

P. K. Abdul Ghafour. "Tourist Visas to be Introduced." *Arab News.* 14 Jan. 2014. http://www.arabnews.com/news/488301.

Peter North and Harvey Trip. "Culture Shock! Saudi Arabia: A Survival Guide to Customs and Etiquette." Culture Shock! Guides Ser. Tarrytown, NY: *Marshall Cavendish*, 2012.

Philip K. Hitti and Walid Khalidi. "History of the Arabs." 1970. Rev. 10th ed. London: *Macmillan.* 2002.

"Thicker than Oil—America's Partnership with Saudi Arabia." New York: *Oxford University Press.* 2008.

Robert Irwin. "Night & Horses & the Desert: An Anthology of Classical Arabic Literature." 1999. Norwell, MA: *Anchor.* 2002.

Roger Allen. "An Introduction to Arabic Literature." Cambridge, UK: *Cambridge UP.* 2000.

Richard Ettinghausen. Oleg Grabar and Marilyn Jenkins-Madina. "Islamic Art and Architecture 650–1250." 2nd ed. New Haven: *Yale University Press.* 2003.

Sheila S. Blair and Jonathan M. Bloom. "The Art and Architecture of Islam 1250–1800." New Haven, CT: *Yale University Press*, 1994.

Sir Richard Burton. "A Personal Narrative of a Pilgrimage to al-Madinah and Meccah." 1906. 2 vols. Mineola, NY: *Dover.* 2011.

Tom Lippman. "Saudia Arabia on the Edge." 2012. Washington, DC: *Council on Foreign Relations Books.* 2012.

Works Cited

_____. "Saudi King Pardons Rape Victim Sentenced to Be Lashed, Saudi Paper Reports." *New York Times.* The New York Times Company, 18 December 2007. http://www.nytimes.com/2007/12/18/world/middleeast/18saudi.html?scp=27&sq=saudi%20arabia%20women&st=cse.

"Agriculture & Water." *About Saudi Arabia.* Royal Embassy of Saudi Arabia, Washington DC, 2015. Web. http://www.saudiembassy.net/about/country-information/agriculture_water/.

"Cinemaless Saudi Arabia's second film festival opens." *The Guardian.* Guardian News & Media Limited, 19 Feb. 2015. Web. http://www.theguardian.com/world/2015/feb/19/second-saudi-arabia-film-festival-opens.

"First Film Festival in Saudi Arabia." *New York Times.* The New York Times Company, 20 Feb 2008. http://www.nytimes.com/2008/02/20/arts/20arts-FIRSTFILMFES_BRF.html.

"Saudi Arabia Constitution." *Verfassungsgeschichte (Constitutional History).* Prof. Dr. Axel Tschentscher/Universität Bern, 2 Dec. 2014. http://www.servat.unibe.ch/icl/sa00000_.html.

"Saudi Arabia Guide: Social Customs." *JustLanded.com.* Just Landed, 2015. http://www.justlanded.com/english/Saudi-Arabia/Tools/Just-Landed-Guide/Culture/Social-Customs.

"Saudi Arabia." *The World Factbook.* Central Intelligence Agency, 2015. https://www.cia.gov/library/publications/the-world-factbook/geos/sa.html.

Reuters. "Saudi Arabia's Top Cleric Condemns Calls for Women's Rights." *New York Times.* The New York Times Company, 22 Jan. 2004. http://www.nytimes.com/2004/01/22/international/middleeast/22SAUD.html?ex=1223006400&en=4ed5876aa92adea0&ei=5070.

"Thamud." *Encyclopædia Britannica.* Encyclopædia Britannica Online, 02 Oct. 2008 http://www.britannica.com/EBchecked/topic/589948/Thamud.

"The Press in Saudi Arabia." *BBC News.* BBC, 13 Dec. 2006. http://news.bbc.co.uk/2/hi/middle_east/6176791.stm.

_____. "Out with the Boys for a Night of Numbering." *New York Times.* The New York Times Company, 13 May 2008. http://thelede.blogs.nytimes.com/2008/05/13/out-with-the-boys-for-a-night-of-numbering/?_r=0.

Ambah, Faiza Saleh. "Saudi Women Rise in Defense of the Veil." *WashingtonPost.com.* The Washington Post, 1 Jun. 2006. http://www.washingtonpost.com/wp-dyn/content/article/2006/05/31/AR2006053101994_pf.html.

Carol Fleming, Carol. "Saudi Arabia and Burying their Dead." *American Bedu.* WordPress.com, 24 Apr. 2009. http://americanbedu.com/2009/04/24/saudi-arabia-and-burying-their-dead/.

Central Department of Statistics & Information. "Latest Statistical Information." *Official Website of Central Department of Statistics & Information.* Central Department of Statistics & Information, 2010. http://www.cdsi.gov.sa/english/.

Donna Abu-Nasr, Donna. "Female Teachers Dying on the Roads in Saudi Arabia." *USA Today.* Gannett Co., 29 Apr. 2008. http://www.usatoday.com/news/world/2008-04-29-1515814314_x.htm.

Edge of Arabia Official Website. Edge of Arabia, 2015. Web. http://edgeofarabia.com/

Frances Harrison, Frances. "UN Call for Saudi Women's Rights." *BBC News.* BBC, 1 Feb. 2008. http://news.bbc.co.uk/2/hi/middle_east/7222869.stm.

Hassan M. Fattah, Hassan M. "Saudi Arabia Debates Women's Right to Drive." *New York Times.* The New York Times Company, 28 Sept. 2007. http://www. nytimes.com/2007/09/28/world/middleeast/27cnd-drive. html?scp=2&sq=hassan%20fattah%20right%20to%20 drive&st=cse.

Heba Saleh, Heba. "Pleas for Condemned Saudi 'Witch.'" *BBC News*. BBC. 14 Feb. 2008. http://news.bbc.co.uk/2/ hi/middle_east/7244579.stm.

John Kenton, John. "Human Rights Declaration Adopted by U.N. Assembly." *International New York Times.* The New York Times Co., 11 Dec. 1948. http://select. nytimes.com/gst/abstract.html?res=F60E17F7385A 157B93C3A81789D95F4C8485F9&scp=1&sq=sau di%20arabia%20u.n.%20declaration%20human%20 rights&st=cse.

Katherine Zoepf, Katherine. "Love on Girls' Side of the Divide." *New York Times*. The New York Times Company, 12 May 2008. http://www. nytimes.com/2008/05/13/world/middleeast/13girls. html?pagewanted=2&sq=love%20on%20girls'%20 side%20of%20the%20divide&st=cse&scp=1.

Michael Slackman. "Young Saudis, Vexed and Entranced by Love's Rules." *New York Times.* The New York Times Company, 12 May 2008. http://www. nytimes.com/2008/05/12/world/middleeast/12saudi. html?pagewanted=1&_r=1&sq=saudi%20 arabia&st=cse&scp=29.

Najah Alosaimi. "Restaurant Partitions—Part of Culinary Experience." *Arab News*. 4 July 2007. http://www. arabnews.com/?page=1&section=0&article=98151&d=4 &m=7&y=2007.

Rima Maktabi, Jon Jensen, & Catriona Davies. "Saudi's New Breed of Artists Push the Limits." CNN.com. *Cable News Network*. 7 Mar. 2012. http://www.cnn. com/2012/03/07/world/meast/saudi-artists-push-limits/.

Robert. F. Worth. "Al Jazeera No Longer Nips at Saudis." *New York Times*. The New York Times Company, 4 Jan. 2008. http://www.nytimes.com/2008/01/04/world/ middleeast/04jazeera.html?pagewanted=1.

Sandra L. Olsen. Sandra L. "Najd behind Qaryat al Asba" Arabian Rock Art Heritage. *Layan Cultural Foundation Project.,* 2015. http://saudi-archaeology.com/ background/geography-arabian peninsula/attachment/ najd-behind-qaryat-al-asba/.

Scott MacLeod, Scott. "The Al Jazeera Invasion." *Time*. Time Inc. 14 Nov. 2006. http://www.time.com/time/ world/article/0,8599,1559468,00.html.

Youssef M. Ibrahim, . Youssef M. "Mideast Tensions; Saudi Women Take Driver's Seat in a Rare Protest for the Right to Travel." *New York Times*. The New York Times Company, 7 Nov. 1990. http://query.nytimes.com/gst/ fullpage.html?res=9C0CE2DE1739F934A35752C1A96 6958260&sec=&spon=&pagewanted=1.

Men and women in colorful tradition dress leaving a mosque after prayer in Kassala, Sudan

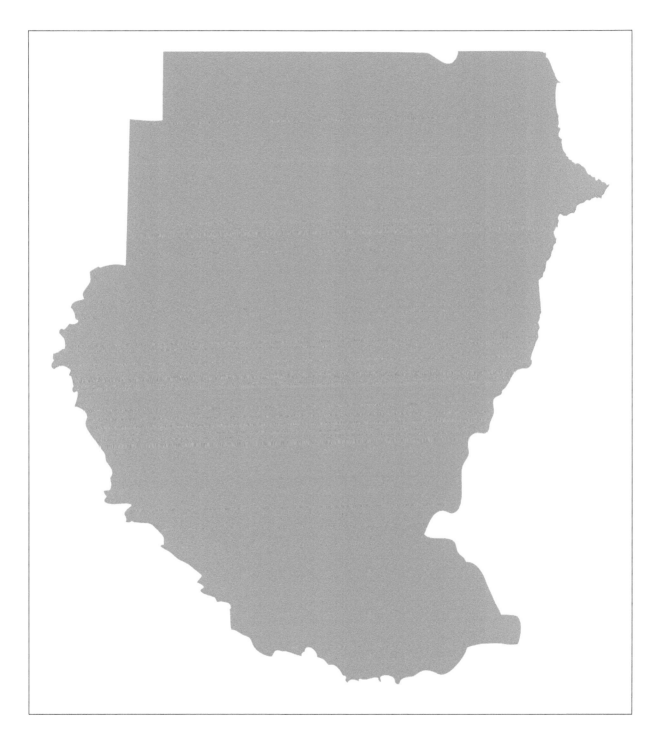

SUDAN

Introduction

The Republic of the Sudan was once the largest country on the African continent, with a diverse mix of climates and cultures. However, in July 2011, the largely Christian and Animist south voted to split from the Republic, ending decades of civil war, during which an estimated 1.5 million people were killed. Still, the countries' shared border and the division of joint oil revenues continue to be contested issues, exposing the presence of lingering tensions.

Sudan's culture has ancient roots, dating to the Kingdom of Kush (1070 BCE–350 CE). The country lies immediately south of Egypt and is the starting point of the Nile River. Fed by the Blue Nile and the White Nile, which converge at Sudan's capital, Khartoum, the greater Nile River flows north through Sudan and into Egypt.

During its colonial period, Sudan was administered by the United Kingdom and Egypt, from which it gained its independence in 1956. The decades after that were marked by civil conflict between the Arab-dominated north and African rebel factions in the south, who sought independence in one of the longest and bloodiest wars in Africa. The First Sudanese Civil War, also known as Anyanya Rebellion, lasted over sixteen years, from August 1955 to March 1972, and involved administrators Egypt and Britain, who attempted to combine the previously distinct northern and southern regions of Sudan before granting independence. Fearing a loss of promised sovereignty, the Southern Sudan Liberation Movement took action. In the years that followed, 500,000 people, the majority of whom were non-combatants, were killed in the violence, while hundreds of thousands more were displaced from their homes. The Addis Ababa Agreement, which established the Southern Sudan Autonomous Region, brought a nearly decade-long break from fighting, although tensions lingered.

Conflict between the Muslim north and the Christian and Animist South again erupted in 1983, when Sudan's president Gaafar Nimeiry declared all of Sudan a Muslim country and subject to Sharia law, effectively abolishing the

Southern Sudan Autonomous Region, where significant oil reserves had been discovered in 1978. The ensuing Second Sudanese Civil War lasted for 22 years. In the 1990s, Sudan aligned itself with Saddam Hussein during the Gulf War and was subsequently classified as a "rogue state" by the Clinton administration, which barred American trade with and investment in the country. Ultimately, the January 2005 Comprehensive Peace Agreement brought an end to the infighting and six years of autonomy for the south, followed by a referendum on independence. This referendum resulted in Sudan's 2011 division.

Sudan also came to international attention in 2004, when reports of government-backed genocide in the western province of Darfur first surfaced. Despite an international outcry against blatant human rights violations at almost every level, the violence and refugee crisis continued until 2010, when a cease-fire agreement took hold. The conflict continues to simmer, however, and has strained relations with neighboring Chad.

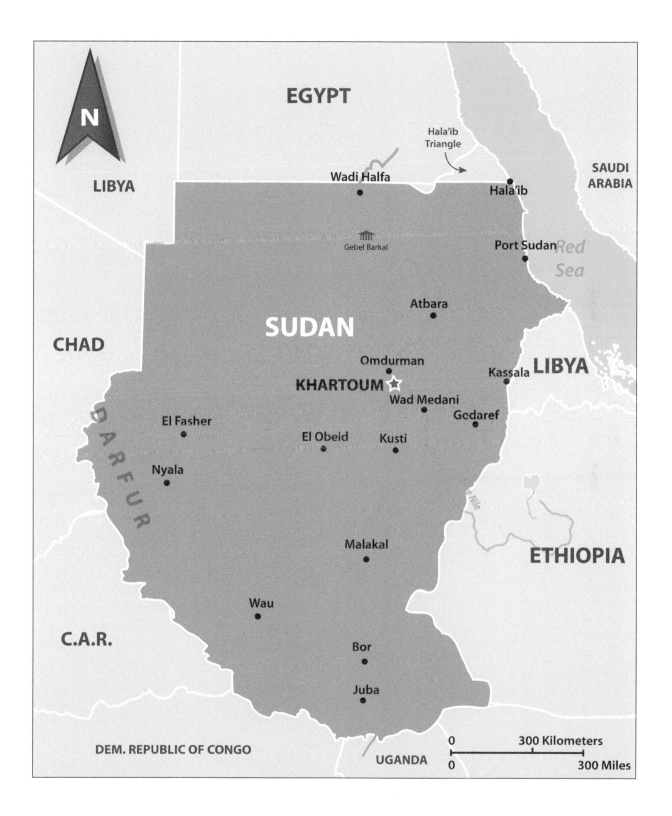

GENERAL INFORMATION

Official Language: Arabic
Population: 36,108,853 (2015 estimate)
Currency: Sudanese pound
Coins: The Sudanese pound is divided into 100 piasters. Coins come in denominations of 1, 5, 10, 20, 50 piasters, and 1 pound.
Land Area: 1,861,484 million square kilometers (718,722 square miles)
Coastline: 853 kilometers (530 miles)
National Motto: "An-Naṣr lanā" (Arabic, "Victory is Ours")
National Anthem: "Naḥnu Jund Allah, Jund Al-waṭa" ("We Are the Soldiers of God, the Soldiers of the Motherland")
Capital: Khartoum
Time Zone: GMT +3
Flag Description: The flag of Sudan consists of three horizontal bands of red, white, and black, and a green equilateral triangle. The base of the triangle rests against the hoist (left) side of the flag, and its tip reaches one quarter of the way across the flag's width, its apex in the white band. The flag's colors symbolize sacrifice and freedom (red), peace (white), the people of Sudan (black; Sudan means 'black' in Arabic), and Islam (green).

Population

In July 2015, the population of Sudan was estimated to be 36,108,853. Sudan's population is young and growing, yet still impeded by a high infant mortality rate (nearly fifty-two deaths per 1,000 births in 2015) and low life expectancy (just under sixty-four years in 2015), although these statistics have been improving. The median age is nineteen years old for both men and women.

Principal Cities by Population (2014):

- Khartoum (7,221,323)
- Omdurman (also Umm Durmān) (2,395,159)
- Khartoum North (also Bahri) (900,000)
- Nyala (also Nyālā) (561,879)*
- Port Sudan (also Bōr Sūdān) (499,279)
- Kassala (455,669)
- Al-Ubayyid (El Obeid) (420,929)
- Kūstī (415,593)
- Wad Madanī (356,978)
- Al Qaḍārif (353,686)

Average population density is twenty-one persons per square kilometer, and just under 34 percent of the population lives in or near urban areas. The region along the Nile and its tributaries, particularly where the White and Blue Nile Rivers meet, is the most densely populated region. Khartoum, with over seven million people, is the largest city and the nation's capital. Other large urban centers include Omdurman, the country's commerce center; Khartoum North, also known as Bahri; and Nyala. An estimated 33.8 percent of the country's total population lives in urban areas.

Approximately 39 percent of the Sudanese are of Arab lineage and 30 percent are of African origin. The remainder of the population is of mixed African-Arabic descent. Those with African origins usually comprise native tribal groups, such as the Fur, Beja, Nuba (Nubian), and Fallata. Each of these ethnic groups includes tribal sub factions, each of which speaks a distinctly separate language and observes disparate customs. For example, the Fallata can be subdivided into Zaghawa, Masalit, Haussa, Fulani, and Berti.

* Indicates statistics may be imprecise, as refugees fleeing tribal militia cause significant population fluctuations. According to the UN Office for the Coordination of Humanitarian Affairs, as of January 2014, there were an estimated 321,929 displaced persons settling in temporary camps around cities like Zamzam and Nyālā. Moreover, it is estimated that Nyālā's population has doubled since 2014 because of this refugee influx.

Overall, tribes are geographically concentrated. Nubians are in the far north as well as southern Kordufan; the Beja are in the east; the Mapan and Angassana are located in the southern Blue Nile region; and the Nilotic, an ethnic group that includes Dinka cattle herders, are in the country's southern areas, extending into South Sudan.

Languages

Arabic is the dominant language of northern and central Sudan, and the government has attempted to expand this dominance to all Sudanese people in a process called "Arabization." However, the task will be daunting, as all sub-Saharan Sudanese tribes speak one of the sub-groups of the Eastern Sudanic language family. There are more than 100 languages and around 570 ethnic dialects spoken in Sudan. Minority languages include Beja and Nubian, whose origins are among the most ancient of the eastern Sudanic languages.

Native People & Ethnic Groups

Traditionally, tensions between Arabs and black Africans have been strong in Sudan. Years before South Sudan's secession in 2011, the Christian- and Animist-dominated south feared Arabic and Islamic influence from the north and, therefore, formed the Sudanese People's Liberation Army (SPLA) in 1983 with the intention of achieving independence. The independence of South Sudan was ultimately achieved, although tribal violence has made the new country highly unstable. Similar tensions between Arabs and black Africans have contributed to the human calamity in the western province of Darfur.

Slavery has long been a traditional practice in Sudan, though precise figures for its modern manifestation are unavailable. Nevertheless, it is known that, even after the 2011 secession of South Sudan, people from the southern tribes are still kidnapped and enslaved by northerners in the country of Sudan.

Religions

Islam exerts the most influence in Sudan, with 70 percent of the population identifying itself as Sunni Muslim; it dominates at the government level. Christians, who make up approximately 5 percent of the population, are concentrated in and around in Khartoum. The very small minority also practice diverse traditional African religions, sometimes incorporated into a Christian framework.

Climate

The northern desert, the central plains, and the equatorial far southwest have distinct climatic conditions. In the arid desert areas, rainfall is extremely low, winters are cool, and summers are hot, reaching over 40 degrees Celsius (104 degrees Fahrenheit) each day and can sometimes peak at 45 degrees Celsius (113 degrees Fahrenheit). When rainfall does occur in the north, it is because winds have brought precipitation from the Mediterranean. However, in areas near the Egyptian border, like Wadi Halfa, it is not uncommon for years to pass without any rainfall at all. There, skies are unfailingly cloudless.

In the central plains, it is also hot and annual rainfall on average measures between 30 and 60 millimeters (one and 2.36 inches). Nearly all of the precipitation occurs during the rainy season, generally between April and August, and this is brought by moist, southwesterly winds originating in the Congo River Basin.

Dust storms, known as haboob, are common on the central plains and in the north before the onset of the rainy season. Should the winds fail or come late, severe droughts can occur. Drought can destroy the agricultural season of the central plains, causing famine. During the rainy season, the Nile and its tributaries can also flood, destroying property, and displacing people who live nearby.

ENVIRONMENT & GEOGRAPHY

Topography

Sudan currently borders Egypt, Eritrea, Ethiopia, South Sudan, the Central African Republic, Chad, and Libya. The Red Sea forms part of its eastern border.

Low mountains ring the Nile basin, which accounts for most of Sudan's area. These mountains include the southern Nuba Mountains in the state of Southern Kordofan and the Red Sea Hills along the coast; Deriba Caldera in the Marrah Mountains is the highest point of the country and measures 3,042 m (9,980 feet). The north is otherwise dominated by desert: the Nubian Desert to the east of the Nile, and the Libyan Desert to its west. Savannah begins on the fertile central plains and continues into swampland known as the As Sudd (or al-Sudd) region, which is now part of the country of South Sudan.

The Nile River, whose confluence lies in Khartoum, where the White Nile and Blue Nile meet, extends through Sudan for 3,000 kilometers (1,864 miles) before traveling into Egypt, Sudan's northern neighbor. Feeding the main Nile River is the Blue Nile, the source of which is Lake Tana in Ethiopia, and the White Nile, the source of which is the world's largest tropical lake, Lake Victoria, shared by Uganda, Kenya, and Tanzania. These rivers then meet in Khartoum to form the Nile, which flows northward into Egypt. The Atbarah, which is 805 kilometers long (500 miles), is the Nile's most important tributary.

Plants & Animals

Most of Sudan's plant and animal life is found on the savannah-like central plains, where it is comprised largely of sparce shrubbery and grasses. Despite the dearth of precipitation, the Kew Royal Botanic Gardens still estimates that Sudan has over 4,000 plant species. Rivers support trees such as the acacia, ebony, baobab, and mahogany. Animal life also flourishes thanks to the region's lifeblood, the Nile. Crocodiles and hippopotamuses inhabit the rivers, while lions; rhinoceroses, which are close to extinction within the country; zebras; and a species of six-foot, two-ton antelopes—called giant eland—inhabit the savannah. Equatorial forests are home to leopards and monkeys as well as reptiles, birds, and insects.

Besides the rhino, other endangered or vulnerable species include the African wild ass (or wild donkey), the chimpanzee, several types of gazelle, Grevy's zebra, the African elephant, and the cheetah.

CUSTOMS & COURTESIES

Greetings

Sudanese greetings generally involve questions about each other's well-being, including home life, work, and health. It is considered a great offense to disregard this protocol. Most Sudanese speak Arabic, though the Arabic spoken in Sudan has developed a very distinct dialect over centuries of mixing with indigenous languages. Both the north and the south have their own variations. Nonetheless, greetings in either region begin with the customary "As-salammu alaykum" ("Peace be unto you"), followed by "Wa-Alaikum-Salaam" ("And unto you, peace").

Sometimes friends will greet each other with smiles and gentle shoves on the shoulder before shaking hands. Thereafter, they will enquire about the other's well-being and if everything is "tamam" ("well").

"Kayf haaluk" ("How are you?") is a customary and informal greeting. "Al hamdillou Allah" ("Praise be to Allah") is a sort of all-purpose response used for any comment. For example, a man may say that his family is doing well. It is customary for both people then to say "Al hamdillou Allah" or "Insha Allah" ("Allah willing") in response. Verbal greetings are often given quickly and may include repetitive cycles of inquiry with the other person asserting the will of Allah.

Gestures & Etiquette

Handshakes and a pat on the shoulder are common gestures of greeting. The latter is generally reserved for close friends, as it involves a sort of embrace. It is not unusual to see men embrace in public as well. Sudanese women commonly embrace and kiss each other on the cheek. Sudanese tend to stand very close to one another during any conversation, although this is not customary between men and women. In fact, men and women, in accord with Islamic custom, refrain from touching publicly. Sudanese are direct and friendly and eye contact is both crucial and expected in conversation.

Pointing directly at another person is considered rude and even carries with it some superstitious undertones. It is more appropriate to motion to another person with the arm extended out, palm down, motioning towards one's body in a scooping fashion.

Eating/Meals

Most Sudanese eat one large meal per day, at dinner. This is usually cooked and served by the women of the household. Many dishes take several hours to prepare as they involve going to the market, peeling and preparing produce, and stewing spices and ingredients long enough to tenderize meat and increase flavor. Once dinner is ready, it is traditionally served on several dishes on a shared tray that is then situated on a low table or on a mat on the floor. In each case, kissra (flat bread made of durra, or corn) or a stiffened millet porridge (asida) is served with the meal and used as an edible utensil to scoop and eat stews and sauces. Sudanese rarely drink with a meal, but they will often have a spicy coffee brewed from the jebena pot after dinner. The coffee is sweet, spiced with ginger or cinnamon, and served in small cups. Fruit or herbal teas are also enjoyed following dinner. A popular tea is kakaday (hibiscus). Fruit or a crème caramel usually accompanies this for special occasions. Peanuts, which are extremely popular, can also be made into macaroons, and these are occasionally served as an accompaniment to coffee.

During the day, many Sudanese refresh themselves at one of the numerous water stations. Large, clay pots are porous and allow steam, caused by the hot afternoon sun, to escape, acting as a natural cooling mechanism for the water. Generally, the women selling the water have reusable cups that they dip into the water and then serve to their patrons. Sudanese also snack throughout the day. Snacks include grilled meats and roasted, salted peanuts or groundnuts.

Visiting

Visiting is a common practice throughout Sudan. Generally, visits are unannounced, though advance notice is appreciated. Once a guest arrives, he or she is customarily invited to take a seat in the area normally reserved for visiting. This may be a mat outside, usually under a tree, or in a specified room designated for entertaining. Some families have televisions or radios, and these often act as a backdrop or the reason for the visit. Soccer and national and international news programs are the most frequently watched or listened to programs.

Once a guest has been offered a seat, he or she is invariably offered something to drink. Tea, helamour (a dark, sweet-and-sour drink made of toasted herbs and spices, sweetened with sugar), abre (a yogurt or milk-based drink in which kisra, or flatbread, is moistened), or tabrihana (a lightly sweetened, non-alcoholic fruit drink), are all commonly offered. Guests socialize with their hosts and may even stay to eat a meal. It is a general custom that the hospitality of a visit is reciprocated. This often takes the place of bringing gifts when visiting.

LIFESTYLE

Family

Sudanese families traditionally extend beyond the nuclear family unit (husband, wife, and their children) to include cousins, uncles, aunts, and grandparents. The extended family in Sudan is the clan and includes neighbors and distant relatives, leading to the wider community functioning as an overarching family unit. Under Sharia (Islamic law), a man may have up to four wives legally, though in a few tribes men take more. Often, however, it is sometimes difficult for men to sustain more than two wives, particularly among nomadic groups. With the Beja peoples, for example, polygamy exists but is relatively rare.

Important to note is that, although marriage between Muslims and non-Muslims is extremely rare in Sudan, it does occasionally occur. For this reason, there are laws placing certain restrictions on such unions. Specifically, a Muslim man may marry a non-Muslim woman, but a non-Muslim man cannot marry a Muslim woman unless he converts to Islam.

The housing in Sudan is mostly uniform in both urban and rural areas. Sudanese have two designs for their homes, circular and rectangular, and two materials: mud bricks or dried mud. In rural Sudan, where the majority of the population lives, the traditional circular building, with mud walls and a conical, thatched roof, are called *gottias* and are generally made from straw. Homes typically have a reddish hue because of the color of the mud. In urban Sudan, the vast majority of the people live in rectangular homes built from mud bricks. The bricks are mortared together with a different mud mixture and are sometimes painted. Most urban homes have a walled courtyard area. Several buildings may all be part of one household.

Food

The cuisine of Sudan, like its inhabitants, is diverse. Depending on the region, it includes rich spices, thick stews, hearty cornmeal, and wheat-based flatbreads. Moreover, some of its dishes reveal the influence of British rule, and incorporate spice palettes brought by both Syrian traders and settlers from the Mediterranean region.

Generally, the main dish put out at mealtime is often a large platter filled with a sauce, or a thick stew. These stews range in spice and flavor, but can contain any of the following: goat, lamb, beef, or fish, as well as beans, okra, onion, peanuts, and hot peppers, and spices such as cumin, curry, and pepper. Sauce is stewed, possibly for a few hours, and then served alongside a boiled or fried starch. However, the most common way to eat stew is with kissra, or flatbread. This staple of the Sudanese diet is made from rye and wheat batter that is dropped onto an oiled griddle and cooked much like a crepe. It is commonly torn and used like a utensil to scoop up stew.

Various porridges (Asseeda, or asida) are made from wheat flour, corn, millet, or even stewed sorghum. These serve as a meal's main starch and can either be served in its original porridge form or fried into patties. All regions of the country have porridge-based dishes into which other sauces are mixed and eaten as one dish. For example, Kajaik, a sauce made from dried fish, vegetable fat, and spices, is mixed with aseeda. Sharmout abiyad is a similar dish, made

with dried meat and mixed with aseeda. Eastern regions are influenced by their culinary neighbors the Ethiopians and have integrated banana paste and many plant roots into their sauces.

Throughout Sudan, many fruits and fruit juices are eaten as both appetizers and desserts. Tabrihana is a homemade fruit juice served to guests before a meal. The tabaldi, aradaib, karkadai, and guddaim are all fruits that are also consumed before and after dinner.

Life's Milestones

In Sudan, birth, transition into adulthood, marriage, and death are commemorated as life's major milestones. Birth among all Sudanese is celebrated as a joyous renewal of life. In some clans in southern Sudan, births are celebrated differently depending on the child's gender. The birth of a boy is seen as a guarantee of carrying on the family line, and is thus celebrated as an accomplishment. Baby girls are traditionally celebrated for their potential to secure a future bride price.

Transition into adulthood in Sudan involves varying tribal customs. An estimated 90 percent of girls undergo the controversial practice of female circumcision, when the external genitalia are excised and the vaginal opening is stitched to create only a very small opening. This usually occurs sometime between the ages of five and fourteen, but usually before puberty. Nuba girls also receive scars from their breasts to their navel, and after menstruation commences or following the birth of their first child, they receive additional marks on their legs, back, arms, and neck. Among the Nuba and Beja, rites of passage for young men include combinations of body painting, dancing, physical challenges, and scarification of their torsos and forearms.

Most marriages in Sudan are still arranged in some way by family members. Once a marriage has been decided upon, the bridegroom's family will present the bride's family with "bride wealth" (sadag), also known as a "bride price," or a gift in return for the loss of a daughter. Often first cousins, usually the children of brothers, are wed.

Death is celebrated throughout most of Sudan and traditionally viewed as a natural transition to the spirit world. The Nuba paint their bodies entirely with white paint and dance the dead into the spirit world.

CULTURAL HISTORY

Art

Sudan is Africa's largest country in terms of geographic area, resulting in a diverse mix of climates and cultures. The nation's dominant Sunni Muslims, who in 2015 numbered approximately 70 percent of the population, inhabit the northern desert region. Sudan's art is similarly influenced by the culture of South Sudan, which only recently became a separate state. This area, along with the western sub-Saharan regions, are densely covered with tropical forest and populated by the minority animist and Christian tribes, as well as tribes that blend animism and Christianity. Animism is characterized by the belief that spirits also inhabit animals and inanimate objects. Ultimately, Sudan is under Sharia, or Islamic law, and their artwork generally abides by its tenets.

Among the Sunni Muslim population, which is a subgroup of Muslims, an estimated 70 percent are African Sudanese and the remaining population is a combination of Arab, Fur, Beja, Nuba, and Fallata. The Muslim population in Sudan generally speaks a branch of Arabic called Sudanese Arabic. Devotion to Islam is not limited to urban Africans and Arabs, but rather extends to many former animist tribes in the northern region. Though their conversion to Islam dates back centuries, many have fused their belief systems into a hybrid version of Islam. The artistic practices of the Muslim population include calligraphy, woodwork, and leatherwork. Islamic art features the predominate use of geometric shapes and patterns, and forbids human representation.

Architecture

The first obvious architecture style in Sudan emerged during the Kingdom of Kush (1070 BCE–350 CE) and was influenced by Egyptian culture. This is reflected in the use of pyramid architecture. However, Kushite architecture is noted for steeply sloping pyramids with plateau tops instead of the classical peaks associated with Egyptian pyramids. This newer style of pyramid can be seen outside of Kuraymah and at Meroë, the largest archeological site in Sudan. As Christianity spread from the Middle East, the Byzantine Empire (330–1453 CE) developed a style of architecture noted for its use of vast space and the domed ceilings. Curved arches, large interior spaces, and domes all characterized the churches of Sudan during the Christian-influenced Makuria Kingdom (750–1312 CE).

A distinct Ottoman influence in Sudanese architecture is evident in the Turkish graves and the ruins of Mahdi's Tomb in the city of Khartoum. The two buildings exemplify the Islamic style perfected by the Ottoman Empire (1299–1922 CE). The Ottoman contribution was significant in that it added the open spaces and vaulted ceilings associated with mosques, as well as the characteristic cupola dome. Mahdi's Tomb is famous for its bright silver cupola that contrasts starkly with its rust-colored mud walls. Other evidence of Ottoman Islamic architecture exists on Suakin Island, where three-story buildings bear the intricate arabesque designs of Islamic architecture. One significant architectural feature of the Suakin buildings is that they are covered in coral, which was excavated from the surrounding shores.

Drama

The British introduced western drama to Sudan in the early 20th century, particularly following the 1902 opening of Gordon Memorial College, which introduced the work of playwrights such as William Shakespeare. Another theatrical ritual common in pre-colonial Sudan (and popular into the 21st century) is known as Zaar. During Zaar, a performance ritual in which only women participate, one woman dances to a rhythmic drumbeat, called ayoub. Ayoub, a 2/4 beat, is intended to induce a trance-like state and is sometimes used by dervishes of the Mevlei Order as an accompaniment to their whirling meditations. With Zaar, the women dancing to the Ayoub then behaves as though a spirit or ghost has inhabited her. During these performances, the entranced woman often strays from societal and religious expectations by drinking alcohol, which is normally prohibited.

Music & Dance
The music of the north has long been characterized by its Muslim influences. The first performances were Koranic (relating to the Koran, Islam's holy book) recitations interpreted dramatically. This style, also known as madeeh, fostered the development of Sudan's unique style of haqibah music and dance. Haqibah, which originates in the 1920s, involves the harmonic a cappella performance of Koranic verses accompanied by the percussive beat of a riq, a tambourine-like instrument. The ritual also involves dance. Sufism, or mystic Islam, has strong roots in Sudan in and around Khartoum. Sufis are widely known for their dervishes, or wild, spinning dances, aimed at putting the dancer in an altered state.

When Sharia was established as national law in 1989, most music was outlawed. Many artists were either imprisoned or silenced by the new government.

Literature
The Christian Nubian kingdoms of ancient Sudan were remarkable not only for their great acquisition of wealth, but also for their absence of written language. When the Byzantines extended their influence into Northern Africa, they ignited a love of literature in the Makuria Kingdom, what is now southern Egypt and Sudan. However, much of that writing was linked to the churches and has been lost to time. In the centuries that followed, a new empire, the Songhai Empire under the rule of Askia the Great (c. 1442–1538), expanded to encompass Western Sudan. Askia was a supporter of literature and devoted many of his efforts to developing universities—the largest and most famous in Timbuktu—and developing a great literary tradition in Western Sudan.

Today, nearly all Sudanese literature is written in Arabic, though some Beja poetry (written in the Beja language of northeastern Sudan) is still transcribed. Contemporary authors generally

deal more in politics, Islam, and fiction based on social issues. Perhaps the most famous work to come out of contemporary Sudan is *Season of Migration to the North* (1966) by Al-Tayyib Salih (1929–2009). The story captures the coming of age of a young Sudanese man as he returns from his British life to live in Sudan. It is often described as the most significant Arabic novel of the past century.

CULTURE

Arts & Entertainment
Sudan is a historic cultural crossroads that defines the African continent. Among Arab Muslims, the Koran is the single most important work of literature. It has influenced the classical language, the legal system, social interactions, and artistic expression, which generally entails geometric decorations and calligraphy. The country's contemporary art, on the other hand, reflects the influence of European colonial rule.

In Sudan, this began at the Gordon Memorial College in Khartoum, a university established in the early 20th century by the British for Africans and Europeans. The university's art department taught European styles and techniques, but incorporated the culture and creativity of Sudanese styles. It included courses on traditional Sudanese leatherwork, woodwork, calligraphy, and pottery. The head of the department, Jean-Pierre Greenlaw, is often referred to as the founder of modern Sudanese art. UK-educated, Greenlaw also wrote and provided illustrations for his 1976 book, *The Coral Buildings of Suakin*.

Following World War II, the school had a large enough following to form the independent School of Design, or Khartoum School. With Greenlaw still in charge, the school easily became affiliated with the School of Applied and Fine Arts and began offering a three-year diploma in art. The graduates of this era—the self-proclaimed "Khartoum School" of painters and sculptures—went on to study in London and America. While abroad, these artists refined their skills and began to develop a body of art reflective of Sudan's African and Muslim roots. Images in the works from this era often included Sudanese Arabic calligraphy superimposed on a more traditional African scene.

Ibrahim El Salahi (1930–), who is also a former Sudanese diplomat, is famous for his strong linearity, dynamic abstractions, and Picasso-inspired painting and drawings. Rashid Diab (1955–) uses broad, impressionistic brushwork and bold color combinations that evoke the color field work of Mark Rothko. Diab's stunning horizons behind abstractions of the human form can both jar and hypnotize the viewer. The mixed-media artist Hassan Musa (1951–), one of Sudan's most famous creative figures, is perhaps best known for his elegantly wrought figurative drawings, which artfully employ calligraphy as their compositional foundation. These works have appeared on album covers and in magazines and other publications. He is also a painter and performance artist famous for his "Graphic Ceremonies." In these street performances, Musa paints on a large canvas in front of an audience, eventually inviting onlookers to participate in the creative process in order to demonstrate the universality of creating art.

While Sudan does not have a particularly robust cinema culture, many filmmakers have worked to bring the story of the Darfur crisis to those outside the country. Since 2003, the subject of several documentaries has been the ethnic conflict and its living victims, who are often forced into exile and struggle with both the loss of identity and loved ones. *Lost Boys of Sudan* (2003), for example, traces the lives of two young men forced to make the pilgrimage to a Kenyan refugee camp following a governmental edict to kill all Christian youth. The film then follows the young men to America, where they struggle to acclimate themselves to the culture and learn the fate of their family members. Other films about the Darfur conflict include *A Great Wonder: The Lost Children of Sudan* (2003), *God Grew Tired of Us: The Lost Boys of Sudan* (2006), and *Life Stories: The Lost Boys of Sudan* (2008).

Football (soccer) is the most widely played sport in Sudan. Other popular sports include volleyball, basketball, and wrestling.

Cultural Sites & Landmarks

Human habitation in the region of modern-day Sudan dates back to the Paleolithic era, or the Old Stone Age. As such, many cultural sites and landmarks in Sudan are prehistoric in nature. The archaeological site of Cemetery 117, including the graves of roughly fifty men, women, and children, predates all other organized societies in the region. The skeletons were radiocarbon dated and found to be between 13,140 to 14,340 years old. Nearly half of the remains show evidence of a violent death, with sharpened stones lodged in the trunks of their bodies and in their skulls. Other artifacts found at the site include pottery and stone projectiles suggestive of the use of a spear or arrow. The site is renowned for its glimpse into prehistoric warfare.

The ruins of the second kingdom of Kush, scattered over five distinct archaeological sites, were included as a World Heritage Site by the United Nations Educational, Scientific, and Cultural Organization (UNESCO). Collectively known as Gebel Barkal and the Sites of the Napatan Region, they contain tombs, pyramids, temples, and palace complexes. The remains at Gebel Barkal (or Jebel Barkal), a small mountain, consist of thirteen temples and three palaces, and were once under Egyptian control. The mountain was believed to be the home of the god Amun, an Egyptian deity. The Temple of Amun extended in a T-shape from the foot of the mountain and some of these original foundations still stand today. With the fall of Egypt, the Kush came into their own and built numerous pyramids and lavish burial grounds for their fallen Nubian kings. While improving upon their monuments, the Temple of Amun fell into great disrepair until it was refurbished and expanded in the eighth century BCE. The result was the second longest temple in the world.

The capital, Khartoum, is a relatively young city divided naturally by land and river into three sections: Khartoum, Khartoum North, and Omdurman. It was founded in the early 1800s by the Egyptian army, where the two branches of the Nile River converge. The name Khartoum, thought to derive from the word "khartum," meaning "elephant's trunk," refers to the shape of the natural land formation. The newness of the city is evident in its colonial-dominated architecture and its relative polish compared to some of the older sites in the country. An especially unusual sight is the architecture of the Corinthia Hotel Khartoum, which opened in August 2008. The Libyan government owns the building, which houses the five-star hotel, but it's unusual shape—intended to resemble a ship's sail—along with its curving white façade, blue rows of windows, and unconventional postmodern presence punctuates the Khartoum skyline.

Perhaps the most significant site in Khartoum is the National Museum, which houses the Byzantine frescoes safely removed from the Nubian Christian churches before Lake Nasser flooded the entire region.

Libraries & Museums

The library of the University of Khartoum is Sudan's de facto national library and features a comprehensive collection of Sudanese authors and literature, along with maps, preserved documents, and dissertations, among many other records of interest to researchers of Sudanese culture and politics. It also has branches specializing in medicine, law, science, education, and agriculture. The National Museum, founded in 1971, is also located in Khartoum. Its collection includes regional artifacts from the Stone Age, as well as relics from the ancient kingdoms of Egypt, Nubia, and Kush. In 1999, the Republican Palace Museum was founded in Khartoum. Housed in a cathedral built in 1912, the museum's collections include musical instruments, presidential cars, and gifts given to Sudanese heads of state. Other museums include the Natural History Museum, which features collections of Sudanese wild game and birds, and the National Museum of Ethnography, which displays practical handcrafts representing Sudan's various regions.

Holidays

The most important holidays in Sudan are religious. The significant Islamic holidays are Ramadan, the month of dawn-to-dusk fasting; Eid-al-Fitr, or Sugar Feast, at the end of Ramadan; and Eid-al-Adha, the Feast of the Sacrifice, which commemorates Abraham's willingness to sacrifice his son to God. Muslims also celebrate Mawlid, the birthday of the Prophet Mohammed. These holidays entail feasts, gatherings of family and friends, and the distribution of both food and alms to the poor.

The following holidays pertaining to Sudanese nationhood are observed: Independence Day (January 1); Uprising Day, marking the anniversary of the 1985 public rebellion against Gaafar Muhammad an-Nimeiry's military rule (April 6); and Revolution Day (June 30), which commemorates the bloodless coup that brought the current president of Sudan, Omar al-Bashir, to power in 1989.

Youth Culture

Sudanese youth are exposed to different cultures and lifestyles depending on the region. For example, in the northern and northeastern regions where there is relative peace, nearly 70 percent of youth attend school. In addition, youth in these regions mostly derive from a stable home environment and eventually attend college. In contrast, youth culture is harsher in the western regions. Roughly 50 percent of youth in the Darfur region attend school, although this a robust estimate and actual attendance numbers may be much lower. Youth in these regions are consistently subjected to violence and sexual abuse at the hands of the various soldiers or militia members living there. Child kidnapping, trafficking, prostitution and child soldiers are all rampant in conflict zones. Orphaned boys have often turned to fighters for a path out of homelessness, while orphaned girls are often forced into prostitution as a means of survival.

SOCIETY

Transportation

When the French left Sudan in the late 1950s, they left behind Africa's best rail system. Today, the trains do not run as frequently, but are still considered an upscale manner of travel. Prices reflect this and discourage many locals from using rail transport.

Most Sudanese prefer to walk or to ride in minibuses, known as bokasi, and pick-up trucks. Both vehicles are often overcrowded and may be include animals and cargo. Often, it may take half a day for a bus to fill up, depending on the destination. In the meantime, men and women sell all manner of goods in the bus parking lots.

Roadways tend to be poorly maintained. Only major highways and certain main streets are paved. In the north and west regions of the country, year-round sandstorms known as "haboobs" can eliminate visibility on roadways. Traffic moves on the right-hand side of the road in Sudan.

Transportation Infrastructure

There are approximately 11,900 kilometers (7,394 miles) of roads in Sudan, approximately 4,320 km (2,684 miles) of which are paved. International airports include Khartoum International Airport and Port Sudan New International Airport. A new airport-hotel complex, located 40 km from downtown Khartoum and capable of handling 7.5 million passengers each year, is slated to replace Khartoum International. However, construction has been stalled for several years, and in December 2014, Sudan signed a 20-year, $700 million loan agreement with China to finish the 86,000 square meter terminal and runway complex.

Media & Communications

The news industry in Sudan is considered highly restricted, particularly after the 1989 coup that brought President Bashir to power. Before 1989, Khartoum had twenty-two daily newspapers, with nineteen in Arabic and three in English. Many of these newspapers were banned and journalists were dismissed or even arrested following the coup by Bashir.

Though the interim constitution in Sudan allows for freedom of thought, expression, and press, it is only allowed as regulated by the government, and is thus subject to restrictions. The government has openly assaulted, imprisoned,

exiled, and murdered journalists for releasing press critical of the government. Many foreign journalists have been forbidden entry, particularly those attempting to monitor the Darfur crisis. Despite these harsh restrictions, there are some voices of the opposition that are heard.

Sudan TV is a government-owned station that runs government-mandated stories portraying policy in a positive light. Government-run radio is largely the same, and most stations continue to be run by the state. These stations broadcast biased news, music in line with Muslim moral code, and cultural and international programs. There are a few opposition radio stations, but many of them are underground and only operate until their whereabouts have been discovered. There are generally more independent newspapers than other forms of press.

As of 2012, there were an estimated 7.2 million Internet users, with 18,472 fixed-broadband subscriptions and 5.6 wireless broadband subscriptions. Also in 2012, there were 27.7 million registered cellular phone users.

SOCIAL DEVELOPMENT

Standard of Living

One of the poorest countries in the world, Sudan ranked 166th out of 187 countries on the 2014 Human Development Index, which measures quality of life indicators. In 2015, the average life expectancy was nearly 66 years for women and 61 years for men.

Water Consumption

It is estimated that the annual renewable water resources of Sudan comprise approximately 149 cubic kilometers (35 cubic miles). Main sources of water include the Nile River system (comprising the White Nile, Blue Nile, and Main Nile Rivers), as well as the Nubian Sandstone Basin, the largest aquifer in the country, and the Umm Rwaba Basins. In 2012, 76.4 percent of the population did not have access to adequate sanitation systems and 45.5 percent lacked access to safe drinking water.

Education

Education is mandatory and free in Sudan between six and 13 years of age. Elementary school lasts for six years, while middle school and high school consist of three years each. Schools are mostly located in northern and central towns and cities; in the west, violence has impeded both the building of schools and students' attendance. In the early 21 century, before South Sudan's secession, it was estimated that only between 20 and 30 percent of youth were enrolled in school, with only 12 percent of students continuing past the fourth-grade level. As of 2012, the average amount of time each students spends in school is approximately seven years.

In 1990, President Bashir made Arabic the language of instruction and elements of Islamic faith and culture integral to the curriculum. This has been met with controversy among non-Muslims, particularly in the country's former south before secession. In 2015, the average literacy rate was 75.9 percent, but higher among males (83.3 percent) than among females (68.6 percent). The school dropout rate is also higher for female students than male.

Of Sudan's 32 universities, the largest and most prestigious are located in the north, particularly in Khartoum. These include the University of Khartoum and the College of Fine and Applied Arts at the Sudan University of Science and Technology. Though women are allowed to study at this level, they are restricted to certain disciplines, such as medicine, law, economics, and applied arts. There are also colleges and numerous vocational institutes in Sudan.

Women's Rights

Tradition and Muslim law limit the role of the woman in Sudanese society. Most women are still limited to traditional roles such as housekeeper, caregiver, cook, and purveyor of homemade goods. Sudanese women do not go much further in school than the elementary level and generally marry at very young ages, often times to men who are already married. Under Sharia, polygamy is legal and a man may take up to four

wives. Women are also expected by law to cover their heads with scarves. However, local authorities rarely enforce this rule, and women frequently walk the streets with their hair uncovered and wearing jeans.

Nevertheless, women can still be subjected to corporal punishment, such as flogging, for violating Article 152 of Sudan's Criminal Penal Code of 1991, which has been incorporated into the 2009 Society Safety Code and remains in effect in 2015. The law calls for punishment of those who perform any "indecent act or act contrary to public morals" that generally upset "public feelings." Such broadly worded phrasing has led to individual interpretations by local authorities and have resulted in floggings and fines for women who do wear pants or who have failed to cover their hair. Amnesty International estimates that, in Khartoum alone, 40,000 to 50,000 women are arrested, tried, and disciplined annually.

By law, women are required to have their husbands obtain a visa for them if they are to leave the country. They are never allowed to procure visas for themselves or for their children. Such a measure prevents women from leaving the country without the permission, or knowledge, of their husbands. Under Sharia, a Muslim man may marry any woman he pleases, regardless of religion or race. Immediately upon marriage, his new bride automatically becomes a Muslim. However, a Muslim woman may not marry a non-Muslim man, unless he first converts to Islam.

Female circumcision is still practiced in Sudan, and it is estimated that almost 90 percent of Sudanese women have undergone the procedure. Often, the technique is ritualized and conducted by a layperson, not a doctor; neither sterile instruments nor anesthesia are used. Severe illness and death from the procedure are not uncommon. The reasons for the continued practice of what has been called "genital mutilation" by human rights groups can be traced to tradition, cultural identity, religious obligation, and even monetary considerations. Women who have been circumcised often bring a higher bride price because they are considered hygienic and conform to the interpreted expectations of the Koran, which some Sudanese feel calls for female circumcision. However, circumcision makes both intimate relations and childbirth extremely difficult and painful for those who have undergone the procedure. It is a practice that the United Nations and numerous human rights organizations have condemned.

Other areas in which Sudanese women are treated unequally include property rights, divorce rights, and economic rights. When a woman is widowed by her husband, she is only entitled to inherit one-eighth of his total property. One-third of the property goes the female children, while the remaining property goes to the male children. Divorce is next to impossible for a woman to achieve, but men may easily divorce their wives. Pregnancy out of wedlock is illegal and can even be tried as the federal offense of adultery, punishable by several years in prison.

Beyond the legal inequalities faced by women in Sudan, physical and emotional abuses are rampant throughout the country, particularly in the conflict-ridden Darfur region. The crime of rape is punishable by law with a sentence of 100 public lashes or ten years in prison, if convicted. Still, despite the high number of women who confessed to having been sexually assaulted, few came forward to file reports. This is due to the stigma family members associate with rape and the blame that is often placed on the victim as instigator, potentially resulting in her own imprisonment and execution. Under Sudanese law, engaging in sexual relations outside marriage is considered a capital offense and can result in death by stoning. Furthermore, in the Darfur region, the vast number of assaults described by women involved "uniformed men," and accusing the military is generally not an option.

Health Care

Sudan's health care system is very basic, and does not meet the needs of the population. Even in more developed areas, such as the urban areas of the north, there are shortages of facilities, supplies, and trained personnel. According to the Central Intelligence Agency, there are 0.28 physicians and 0.8 hospital beds to every 1,000 people. Though medicine and medical treatment are nominally free, the government spends only a fraction of its budget on health care. Although in 2013, these expenditures represented 6.5 percent of the country's GDP.

War, unclean drinking water, poor sanitation, famine, childhood malnutrition, and refugee crises have exacerbated an already unstable and underfunded system. Preventable diseases such as tuberculosis, malaria, dysentery, meningitis, and hepatitis are common; the number of AIDS cases is also growing. Traditional, folkways medicine is often the only recourse for many poor, rural people.

GOVERNMENT

Structure

Since winning its independence from the United Kingdom and Egypt in 1956, Sudan has undergone decades of turmoil marked by coups, autocratic governments, and a lengthy civil war. It has also experienced strained ties with its neighbors and in the international community for its ostensible support of terrorists.

In early 2005, the government and rebels agreed to greater autonomy for the southern half of the country, with the eventual goal of independence from the Arab-dominated north, which was achieved with the secession of South Sudan in 2011. The violent conflict Darfur, where it is thought that the government-supported Arab militias against African rebels claimed approximately 300,000 lives and created a diaspora of approximately three million refugees.

A Comprehensive Peace Agreement (CPA, or Naivasha Agreement) was achieved on January 9, 2005, which ended the Second Sudanese Civil War and determined the shape of the Sudanese government, allowing for the eventual independence of southern Sudan by popular referendum. Following South Sudan's ultimate secession in 2011, the government of Sudan changed. A president who is popularly elected to five-year terms heads the executive branch. He or she is also the prime minister and the chief of the armed forces. The president's responsibilities include the appointment of local governors and cabinet members, pending legislative approval.

The legislative branch is now bicameral and consists of the lower house, known as the National Assembly, and an upper house, known and the Council of States, which has 50 seats indirectly elected by state legislatures. The National Assembly's 354 seats, which were previously elected positions, became six-year-long appointed positions, based on a power-sharing formula involving the National Congress Party (52 percent); other Arab political parties (14 percent), like the Sudanese Ba'ath Party, Sudan People's Liberation Movement–North (28 percent), and other political parties (six percent), like the United Democratic Front.

Political Parties

Though political parties are now allowed to function, they must be approved by the government and follow strict guidelines meant to preserve the status quo. The National Congress Party is the official party of Sudan and is led by Omar al-Bashir, who became president of Sudan in 1989 after staging a coup d'état against former Prime Minister Sadiq al-Mahdi. The National Congress Party has been accused of funding Arab militias such as Janjaweed to suppress the African, non-Muslim population of Darfur.

The Sudan People's Liberation Movement (SPLM) is the political arm of the guerilla movement that has successfully fought for independence from the north. (The government of Sudan and the Sudan People's Liberation Movement in 2005 signed a peace treaty known as the Comprehensive Peace Agreement. Its aim was twofold: to end the Second Sudanese Civil War and to begin establishment of an autonomous Southern Sudan.) When South Sudan seceded by popular vote in 2011, a portion of the SPLM split, so that it might continue to take part in northern politics. They became Sudan People's Liberation Movement–North. Other political parties include the Popular National Congress, the Democratic Unionist Party, and the Umma Party.

In the April 2015 elections, the first held since the secession of South Sudan, incumbent president Omar al-Bashir of the National Congress Party won with 94.5 percent and 5,252,478 votes, with Fadul al-Sid Shuaib of the Federal Truth Party achieving 1.43 percent and 79,779 votes. Approximately fifteen candidates ran against incumbent Bashir; most of them were largely unknown figures. The next elections will be held in 2020.

Local Government

Sudan is divided into eighteen states, each presided over by a governor (known as a "wali"), as well as several state ministers and provincial ministers. The central government maintains tight control of the local governments.

Judicial System

The highest court in Sudan is the Supreme Court, which consists of approximately seventy judges—all appointed by Sudan's president—who operate in panels of three. Other courts include the Court of Appeal, Constitutional Court, Public Courts, and District Courts. All levels of the Sudanese judicial system follow Sharia law.

Taxation

The top corporate tax rate in Sudan is 35 percent, and taxation rates largely depend on the corporation's activities. For example, the agricultural sector is exempt from taxation, while industrial services are taxed at a rate of 10 percent. Cigarettes and tobacco-related businesses are taxed at 30 percent, and those in the oil and gas industry pay the greatest rate, 35 percent. Personal income tax is levied at 15 percent. Sales tax is currently 10 percent, and a value-added tax (VAT) is levied at 15 percent, with a special rate of 20 percent for services such as telecommunications.

Armed Forces

The Sudanese Armed Forces comprises a navy (which includes marines), a land force, an air force, and a popular defense force. In 2014, there were approximately 109,300 active military personnel, of which 17,500 were paramilitary forces. There are another 85,000 reserves.

Foreign Policy

Two years after Sudan achieved independence in 1956, General Ibrahim Abboud (1900–1983) seized power in a coup and instituted policies that favored the north's economy and Islamic law. He exiled Christian missionaries in what is now South Sudan and replaced their teachings with the Koran and Arabic as official doctrine. The alienated south was helpless to respond, save a few rebel groups. However, his policies deteriorated with the price of international goods, and he was ousted in the 1960s. A transitional government replaced him until Gaafar Nimeiry (1930–2009) seized power in 1969.

Conflict in what is now South Sudan, as well as a few attempted coups plagued Nimeiry's early presidency. This forced him to reach an agreement with the then unified Southern Sudan Liberation Movement (SSLM). The Addis Abba Agreement, signed into law in 1972, gave southern Sudan unprecedented autonomy to govern itself. The legislation quelled fighting between southern rebels and the government. Nimeiry gradually transformed the Sudanese constitution to resemble Sharia and reversed everything in the Addis Abba Agreement, thereby nullifying Southern Sudan Autonomous Region. This resulted in civil war and lead to Nimeiry's ousting in 1985. After widespread political unrest, Omar al-Bashir (1944–) and his Revolutionary Command Council for National Salvation (RCC) seized power in 1989 from the democratically elected Prime Minister Sadiq al-Mahdi (1935–), who had begun negotiations with southern rebel groups.

The RCC introduced a brutality aimed at eliminating any opposition. It imprisoned educated elites responsible for past uprisings and set out to destroy the southern opposition. Allying with a western Sudanese/eastern Chad-based militant Islamic militia—comprised largely of men from the Guhayna and Baggara tribes—called the Janjaweed, the Sudanese government

largely ignored the annihilation of hundreds of thousands of southern and western Sudanese, who were systemically raped, beaten, and murdered in what is now referred to as the Darfur Genocide. In addition to rape, torture, and murder, Janjaweed, along with the Sudanese Army, looted and burned entire villages, and poisoned water supplies, making entire areas uninhabitable. In an attempt to gain the support of the Middle East, Bashir also aided Iraqi leader Saddam Hussein (1937–2006) during the Gulf War (1990–1991). This policy alienated him from the international community and drove Sudan further into economic peril.

Sudan's foreign policy in the early 21st century has prioritized relations with other Muslim countries. The country has also worked with regional states to increase stability and combat terrorism. However, relations with neighboring nations have often been contentious, at best. For example, in May 2008, Sudan broke off diplomatic relations with Chad after claiming the country was helping rebels in Darfur attack the Sudanese capital. (Chad had previously denounced the Sudanese government for its role in the conflict.) Sudan has also maintained strained relations with the Western world, particularly the United States, despite relying on Western Europe and the U.S. for aid. In 2005–2006 alone, the U.S. donated $2.6 billion (USD) in aid to Sudan in peacekeeping and humanitarian efforts. Between January and August of 2015, the United States Agency for International Development (USAID) sent $157,227,725 for the same purpose, some of which was sent to Sudan's Humanitarian Aid Commission to assist with displaced persons from ethnic conflicts in Abu Karinka and the three new refugee sites in the White Nile State, which already accommodates seven other refugee sites.

Despite the humanitarian crisis, in March 2009, Bashir announced that Sudan would expel all international aid workers from Sudan within one year. It is estimated by the United Nations (UN) that this would endanger an estimated 1.1 million refugees in the embattled Darfur region, where an estimated 300,000 people have been killed since 2003. The conflict in Darfur has also led to trade embargoes and economic sanctions against Sudan, although Russia has come to Sudan's aid beginning in December 2014 and has promised increased military aid to the Sudanese government.

Despite the International Criminal Court's two outstanding warrants for President Bashir, one from 2009 and another from 2010, the Sudanese president's June 2015 attendance of the African Union Summit in South Africa did not result in his arrest, even though South Africa is a member of the ICC and, therefore, was obliged to take Bashir into custody. South Africa's adherence to the immunity of visiting diplomats sent the issue to the country's High Court, which eventually ruled that Bashir should have been detained. However, he had already departed from Pretoria. South Africa's failure to act sparked international outrage.

Human Rights Profile

International human rights law insists that states respect civil and political rights and promote an individual's economic, social, and cultural rights. The United Nations Universal Declaration on Human Rights (UDHR) is recognized as the standard for international human rights. Its authors sought the counsel of the world's great thinkers, philosophers, and religious leaders and were careful to create a document that reflects the core values shared by every world culture. To read this document or view the articles relating to cultural human rights, visit www.ohchr.org/EN/UDHR/Pages/Introduction.aspx.

Sudan is most often associated with the ongoing conflict and humanitarian crisis in Darfur, which began as protests against the area's marginalization and an appeal to stop nomadic groups from attacking and displacing sedentary farmers. The conflict has gained international attention through the efforts of human rights activists to shed light on the atrocities committed in this western region of the nation. Due to the conflict among the government military forces; the nationally aligned Janjaweed militia;

tribal militias, like the Ma'aliya and Rizeigat; and the unified rebel groups, the Justice and Equality Movement (JEM) and Sudan Liberation Army (SLA), an estimated 400,000 people in the region have been killed since the conflict first began in 2003. An additional three million have been dispersed from their homes in Darfur to other regions in the nation. In addition, an estimated 262,900 are now living in twelve refugee camps, also plagued by ethnic violence, in Chad. Government-directed bombings by Rapid Support Forces intensified in April 2014 in the Nuba Mountains of Southern Kordofan, destroying schools, religious buildings, health centers, and water supplies. And between January 2014 and August 2105 alone, 61 peacekeepers from the African Union-UN Hybrid Operation in Darfur (UNAMID) have been killed, while several other aid workers have been detained by unidentified armed militia for as long as 128 days. The UN has called on the Sudanese government to investigate the detentions, but no action has yet been taken. Ultimately, the Darfur conflict has been condemned by the Western world as an act of genocide.

The humanitarian crisis is further complicated by clashes, in 2014 and 2015, between members of the Ma'aliya and Rizeigat tribes, in Abu Karinka, part of East Darfur. The violence has destroyed an estimated 660 homes and created approximately 24,000 internally displaced persons.

In 2015, USAID's Office of Foreign Disaster Assistance acknowledged three new refugee sites in Sudan's White Nile State, where there are already an estimated 88,700 South Sudanese refugees distributed over seven established camps within the region. With the 13,000 additional South Sudanese asylum seekers, overcrowding has become a serious concern, but has not been addressed by the Sudanese government.

In addition to the mass murders in Darfur, Human Rights Watch and Amnesty International (AI) have accused the government of committing the crimes of arbitrary arrest and detention, manipulating the election system in their favor, and embezzling funds for government-sponsored violence. Today, many call for the ousting of Bashir and for justice to be served in the international legal system. In 2009 and 2010, the International Criminal Court (ICC) issued an arrest warrant for Bashir, charging him with war crimes, crimes against humanity, and genocide in connection with atrocities in Darfur. He is the first leader in history to be so charged while still in office.

Migration

Between January and August of 2015, there were an estimated 1,976,000 internally displaced persons in Sudan, and according to the UN, some 6.9 million Sudanese who are in need of humanitarian aid. Many Sudanese refugees, particularly those from the Darfur region, have fled to neighboring Chad and, in 2015, numbered 368,290. In response, Chad is attempting to transition these refugees out of camps and into host communities. According to the CIA, for every 1,000 residents, Sudan has lost 4.29 people.

ECONOMY

Overview of the Economy

With the secession of South Sudan, Sudan has lost three-quarters of its oil production and the related transit feeds, as the oil fields first discovered in 1978 are located in what is now the new country. This remains a lingering point of tension between the two nations, since oil was Sudan's greatest economic generator and spurred significant economic growth since 1999. Moreover, Sudan has been subjected to U.S. sanctions because of the violence in Darfur. Austerity measures and the search for other income sources, like the exploration of gold mining and the expansion of the gum Arabic trade represent Sudan's current path forward.

Still battling inflation, which soared to 47 percent in 2013, the country's economy continues to reel. However, it also experienced some modest growth, according to CIA data. In 2014, the country's gross domestic product (GDP) was $159.1 billion (USD), which represented a 3.4 percent growth rate from the previous year. The gross domestic product per capita was an estimated at $4,300 (USD). Those living along the Nile corridor are generally more prosperous than those living in regions that do not have ready access to the river.

Industry

The industrial sector is not well developed in Sudan. However, with the loss of oil-related income, Sudan has been forced to explore new income generators. Consequently, the industrial production growth rate increased by 2.9 percent in 2014. Industry now accounts for 35.6 percent of the GDP and employs around seven percent of the labor force.

Light industry mostly depends on the products of the agricultural sector, such as sugar cane and cotton. However, manufacturing is growing, and now includes construction materials, beverages, soap, cigarettes, textiles, and paper. Gold mining and processing is another industrial sector the Sudanese government is currently expanding.

Labor

The labor force numbers almost 11.92 million, with 13.6 percent unemployment (2014 estimates). Approximately 46.5 percent of the population lives below the poverty line, according to CIA statistics.

Energy/Power/Natural Resources

Gold has become Sudan's most valuable natural resource, since the loss of its southern oil fields. Small deposits of chromium, copper, iron ore, zinc, silver, tungsten, uranium, talc, and asbestos are also present.

The Nile River is a significant source of hydropower; dams currently produce 46 percent of the country's energy. The Nile also creates fertile areas that allow for extensive cultivation.

Lack of safe drinking water and desertification are two of the most pressing environmental problems in Sudan. The process of desertification has increased because of overgrazing, poor agricultural practices that have degraded the soil and the use of wood as a fuel supply by a large portion of the population. The civil war, and its attendant violence, has impeded protection of wildlife, which has been widely poached. Moreover, an estimated 1 million landmines are scattered throughout the country, endangering all life, both human and animal.

Fishing

The country's rivers, tributaries, related swampland, and Red Sea coast are exploited for fish. There are generally three levels of fishing: subsistence, artisanal, and commercial. Common catches include wild mollusks and finfish, like sardinella, mullet, and red bass. Often, fish are sun-dried, without salt preservation, and there is frequent spoilage and loss. There is fish farming in Sudan, but the country lacks trained personnel who can sustain production. According to the Sudanese government, an annual 56,000 tons of fish are caught in the country, with some are exported to Zaire and Egypt.

Forestry

Forests are exploited for timber, and charcoal is an important byproduct. Deforestation is an issue in the country as forests tend to be cleared to create agricultural land. Tree species in Sudan include mahogany, eucalyptus, and teak.

Mining/Metals

Sudan's greatest natural resource, since losing its oil reserves with the secession of South Sudan, has been its gold. In 2013, the British Columbia-based corporation, Orca Gold, acquired a 7,046-kilometer land block with three mineralized zones in Sudan portion of the Arabian-Nubian Shield. With proceeds from the work of similar corporations and independent artisan miners working in the Nile River State, Sudan made $2.5 billion (USD) in gold exports and related fees in 2014 alone.

Agriculture

Agriculture is central to the Sudanese economy, but is prone to drought. Roughly, 80 percent of the labor force is engaged in agriculture, which accounted for 26.8 percent of the GDP in 2014. Cotton is the major cash crop. Grains, root crops, nuts (especially peanuts), sugarcane, sorghum, millet, wheat, sesame seeds, and gum arabic are also important, as are cassavas, papaya, bananas, and sweet potatoes.

Animal Husbandry

Sudan continues to be one of the largest exporters of sheep on the African continent. In To enhance production, the country seeks to improve veterinary care and access to water as well as put price controls on fodder and waive taxes for farmers. In 2010, a year after the government began allowing private veterinarians to distribute medicines and necessary vaccines to independent and localized herders, it was estimated Sudan had 130 million sheep, goats, cattle, camels, and poultry. Livestock continues to represent a vital form of meat and dairy, provides modes of transport, and serves as an export commodity. The industry meets both domestic demand and accounts for some of Sudan's trade with Saudi Arabia as well as other Middle Eastern nations. For example, in 2010, 200,000 cattle were exported from Sudan to Malaysia.

Tourism

Ongoing warfare and a destroyed and undeveloped infrastructure have previously restricted Sudan from realizing its potential as a tourist destination. Nonetheless, archaeological sites in Sudan draw some visitors. These include the ruins of the ancient kingdom of Meroe and numerous ruins from the Pharaonic period. Many of the artifacts are exhibited in museums in Khartoum. The Sudan National Museum, the Natural History Museum, and the National Museum for Ethnography, all in Khartoum, have the most extensive collections.

Kristen Pappas, Michael Aliprandi, Alex K. Rich, & Savannah Schroll Guz

DO YOU KNOW?

- The collection at the National Museum in Khartoum includes artifacts from the ancient kingdom of Kush, mentioned in the biblical book of Genesis.

- Many ancient monuments from northern Sudan had to be dismantled and reconstructed elsewhere to save them from the flooding caused by the Aswan High Dam in Egypt.

- Since the 1950s, Sudan has produced 80 percent of the world's gum Arabic, an essential element of soft drinks like Coca Cola. In 2007, in response to sanctions leveled against the country, Ambassador John Ukec Lueth Ukec threatened to stop the flow of gum Arabic exports.

- The name "Khartoum" means "elephant's trunk," which is perhaps a reference to the city's once-thriving ivory trade. It may also reference the shape of the nearby confluence of the White Nile and Blue Nile rivers; the island at the center of the convergence, when seen in conjunction with the northward-flowing Nile and westward-flowing Blue Nile, looks like an elephant with its trunk outstretched.

Bibliography

"Children in Sudan: Slaves, Street Children and Child Soldiers." New York: *Human Rights Watch*. 1995.

Andrew S. Natsios. "Sudan, South Sudan, and Darfur: What Everyone Needs to Know." Oxford, UK: *Oxford UP*. 2012.

Don Cheadle and John Prendergast. "Not on Our Watch: The Mission to End Genocide in Darfur and Beyond." New York: *Hyperion*. 2007.

Fergus Nicoll. "The Mahdi of Sudan and the Death of General Gordon." Charleston, SC: *History Press*. 2005.

Gabriel Warburg. "Islam, Sectarianism, and Politics in the Sudan since the Mahdiyya." 2nd ed. London, UK: *C. Hurst & Co Publishers Ltd*. 2003.

James Copnall. "A Poisonous Thorn in Our Hearts: Sudan and South Sudan's Bitter and Incomplete Divorce." London, UK: *Hurst*. 2014.

John Young. "The Fate of Sudan: The Origins and Consequences of a Flawed Peace Process." London, UK: *Zed Books*. 2012.

Joseph Akol Makeer. "From Africa to America: The Journey of a Lost Boy of Sudan." Oklahoma City: *Tate Publishing & Enterprises*. 2008.

Julie Flint and Alex de Waal. *"Darfur: A New History of a Long War."* London, UK: *Zed Books*. 2008. African Arguments Ser.

P.M. Holt and M.W. Daly. "A History of the Sudan: From the Coming of Islam to the Present Day." 6th ed. New York: *Routledge*. 2014.

Robert O. Collins. "A History of Modern Sudan." Cambridge, UK: *Cambridge UP*, 2008.

Simon Broughton and Mark Ellingham. "World Music." 2nd ed. London, UK: *Rough Guides*. 2000.

Works Cited

"About the Film." The Lost Boys of Sudan. *Trans Art Media*. 2003. http://www.lostboysfilm.com/about.html.

"Cemetery 117." Wikimedia/Creative Commons. *Wikipedia*. 21 Jun. 2015. http://en.wikipedia.org/wiki/Cemetery_117.

"China, Sudan sign $700m loan for new Khartoum airport." *Sudan Tribune*. Sudan Tribune, 16 December 2014. http://www.sudantribune.com/spip.php?article53371

"Contemporary Art in Sudan." *Contemporary Sudanese Art*. Michael Hüther, 13 Dec. 2003. Web. http://www.m-huether.de/sudan/sudart/

"Darfur." *Save Darfur*. United to End Genocide, 2015. http://savedarfur.org/the-conflict/darfur/.

"Events of 2015." World Report 2015: Sudan. *Human Rights Watch*. 2015.

"Female genital mutilation still rampant in Sudan." *Sudan Tribune*. 20 Nov. 2005. Web. http://www.sudantribune.com/spip.php?article12647.

"Gebel Barkal and the Sites of the Napatan Region." *UNESCO World Heritage List*. UNESCO/World Heritage Convention, 2015. http://whc.unesco.org/en/list/1073.

"History of the Sudan." *Encyclopædia Britannica*. Encyclopædia Britannica, Inc., 2015. http://www.britannica.com/EBchecked/topic/1251910/history-of-the-Sudan.

"Lord Horatio Kitchener (1850–1916)." *BBC History*. 2014. http://www.bbc.co.uk/history/historic_figures/kitchener_lord.shtml.

"Mission Arts Sudan." *Arts Sudan*. Arts Sudan, 2009. http://www.artsafrica.org/sudan/index.html.

"Napata." *Encyclopædia Britannica*. Encyclopædia Britannica, Inc., 2015. http://www.britannica.com/EBchecked/topic/402807/Napata.

"Nuba." *Encyclopædia Britannica*. Encyclopedia Britannica, Inc., 2015. http://www.britannica.com/EBchecked/topic/421474/Nuba.

"Nuer." *Encyclopedia Britannica*. Encyclopedia Britannica, Inc., 2015. http://www.britannica.com/EBchecked/topic/422112/Nuer.

"Sawākin." *Encyclopedia Britannica*. Encyclopedia Britannica, Inc., 2015. http://www.britannica.com/EBchecked/topic/525891/Sawakin.

"Sudan." *U.S. Department of State*. U.S. Department of State, 2015. http://www.state.gov/p/af/ci/su/.

"Sudan country profile—Overview" *BBC News*. 18 Jun. 2015. http://www.bbc.com/news/world-africa-14094995.

"Sudanese Arabic." *Wikipedia*. Wikimedia/Creative Commons, 29 May 2015. http://en.wikipedia.org/wiki/Sudanese_Arabic#Greetings_in_Sudanese_Arabic.

"Sudanese Food." *Embassy of the Republic of Sudan, Washington, DC.* www.sudaneseembassy.org, 2015. http://www.sudanembassy.org/index.php?option=com_content&id=39&Itemid=57. https://www.hrw.org/world-report/2015/country-chapters/sudan.

Alexandra Barton. "Water Crisis—Sudan." *The Water Project*. The Water Project, 2015. http://thewaterproject.org/water-in-crisis-sudan.

Amal Habani. "Arrested and Beaten for Wearing Trousers." *Amnesty International Human Rights Now Blog*. Amnesty International, 31 Mar. 2015. Web. http://blog.amnestyusa.org/africa/arrested-and-beaten-for-wearing-trousers-stop-the-public-flogging-of-women-in-sudan/.

David A. Graham. "How a Suspected War Criminal Got Away." *The Atlantic*. The Atlantic Monthly Group, 16 Jun. 2015. Web. http://www.theatlantic.com/international/archive/2015/06/omar-bashir-sudan-icc/395930/.

David Smith. "ICC chief prosecutor shelves Darfur war crimes probe." *The Guardian*. The Guardian News and Media Limited. 14 Dec. 2014. http://www.theguardian.com/world/2014/dec/14/icc-darfur-war-crimes-fatou-bensouda-sudan.

Helen Chapin Metz, ed. "Kush, Meroe, and Nubia. Excerpted from *Sudan: A Country Study*." Washington, DC: Federal Research Division of the Library of Congress, 1991. *Sam Houston State University*, 2015. http://www.shsu.edu/~his_ncp/Sudan.html.

UN Office for the Coordination of Humanitarian Affairs. "Sudan 2014 Population Displacement in Darfur: Darfur Humanitarian Update." *Relief Web*. UN Office for the Coordination of Humanitarian Affairs, 26 May 2014. http://reliefweb.int/report/sudan/sudan-2014-population-displacement-darfur-darfur-humanitarian-update 26 may-2014.

UN Refugee Agency. "Sudan: 2015 UNHCR country operations profile—Sudan" *UNHCR*. United Nations High Commission for Refugees, 2015. http://www.unhcr.org/pages/49e483b76.html.

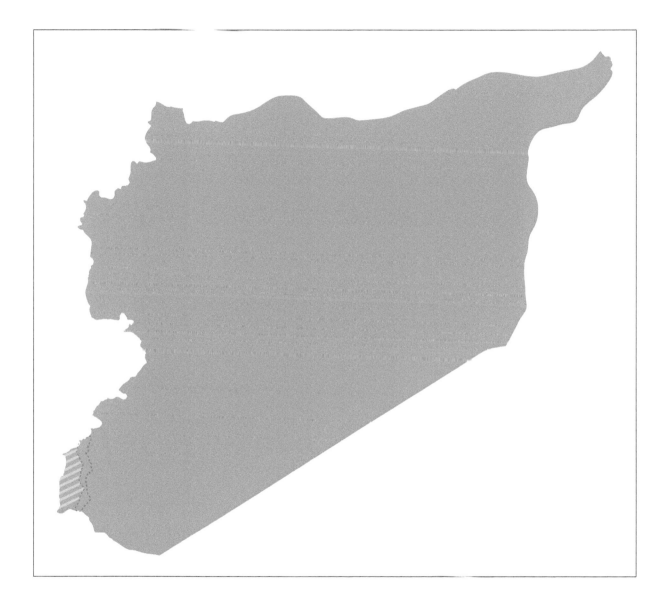

Introduction

The Syrian Arab Republic, or Syria, is a Middle Eastern country that borders Turkey, Iraq, Jordan, Israel, Lebanon, and the Mediterranean Sea. Syria's is a complex, modern culture informed by a diverse population, and it includes some of the world's oldest continuously inhabited cities.

Since 2011, Syria has been racked by civil war, which has become known as the Syrian Revolution. The conflict was sparked by the Arab Spring demonstrations of early 2011, during which Syrians challenged the ban of political parties and the existence of the Emergency Law, which facilitated arbitrary arrests and detainments. Protesters also demanded the removal of corrupt government officials, including President Bashar al-Assad. While the Assad government, including the legalization of some political organizations and the repeal of the Emergency Law, made some compromises, Assad was not deposed. General demonstrations against Assad's repression developed into armed confrontations, during which government forces responded with violence. As of January 2015, the death toll reached 220,000, and has continued to climb. With 11.6 million refugees, of which 7.6 million are internally displaced, Syria's civil war has produced one of the largest humanitarian crises in the world. In December 2012, 130 nations recognized the Syrian National Coalition, based in Doha, Qatar, as the legitimate representative of the Syrian people.

Further complicating humanitarian matters in Syria is the rapid expansion of the Islamic State of Iraq and the Levant (ISIL). Since March

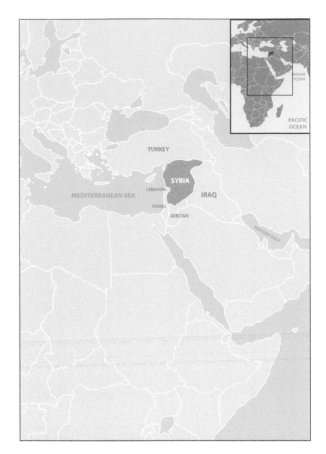

2015, ISIL has controlled territory in both Syria and Iraq, where it has perpetrated war crimes and ethnic cleansing, according to the UN. ISIL has also contributed to escalating violence in the Syrian civil war.

GENERAL INFORMATION

Official Language: Arabic
Population: 17,064,854 (2014 estimate)*
Currency: Syrian pound
Coins: The Syrian pound comes in coin denominations of 1, 2, 5, 10, and 25.
Land Area: 183,630 square kilometers (70,899 square miles)
Water Area: 1,550 square kilometers (598 square miles)
National Anthem: "Ḥumāt ad-Diyār" ("Guardians of the Homeland")

* As of July 2015, an additional 18,900 Israeli settlers inhabit the Golan Heights

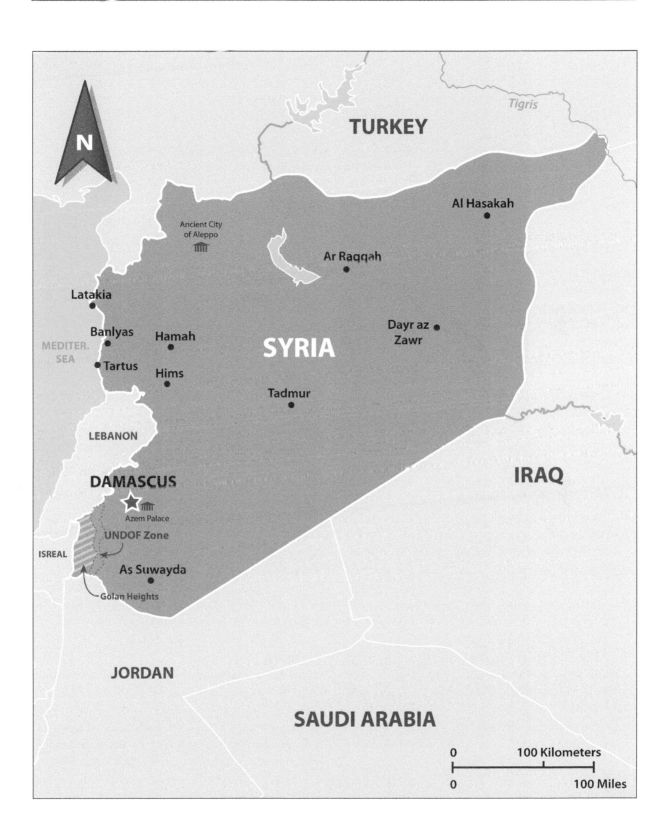

TURKEY

Tigris

Al Hasakah

Ancient City
of Aleppo

Ar Raqqah

Latakia

Dayr az
Zawr

Banlyas

Hamah

SYRIA

MEDITER.
SEA

Tartus

Hims

Tadmur

LEBANON

DAMASCUS

IRAQ

Azem Palace

UNDOF Zone

ISREAL

As Suwayda

Golan Heights

JORDAN

SAUDI ARABIA

0   100 Kilometers

0   100 Miles

Principal Cities by Population (2014):

- Aleppo (2,132,100)
- Damascus (1,711,000)
- Homs (750,501)
- Hamah (460,602)
- Latakia (383,786)
- Hasakah, also Al-Hasakah (251,570)
- Dayr az-Zawr, also Deir ez-Zor (239,196)
- Rakka, also Al-Raqqah (220,268)
- Qamishly, also Al-Qamishli (184,231)
- Tartus, also Tartous (162,980)

Capital: Damascus
Time Zone: GMT +2
Flag Description: The Syrian flag features three horizontal bands of red (top), white (center), and black (bottom). In the center of the white band are two small, green five-pointed stars.

Population

Once developing at one of the fastest international rates, Syria's population growth in 2015 has stalled at an annual rate of –0.16 percent. Population density is approximately 99 people per square kilometer (approximately 258 per square mile) and is most dense in the western portion of the country. Nearly 58 percent of the population lives in urban areas, while the Syrian Desert, in the southeast, is the least dense. Aleppo is the largest city, with a population of over two million, followed by Damascus at over 1.7 million. Other major population centers include Homs, Hamah, and Latakia.

Arabs make up 90.3 percent of the population. The Kurds, who generally occupy rural areas, are the largest minority. Armenians, Jews, and Palestinian refugees are also represented. The Bedouin, nomadic tribesmen who tend livestock, have decreased greatly in number as the government has sought to make them settle.

Languages

The vast majority of the Syrian population speaks Arabic, a Semitic language. Arabic can be divided into three forms: classical Arabic, the language of the Koran; Modern Standard Arabic, which is used on the radio and in newspapers throughout the Arab world; and the dialects spoken in each Arab country. Syrian Arabic, which shares characteristics with Lebanese Arabic, varies throughout the country. The differences of grammar, accent, and colloquialisms within the dialect are such that the origins of the speaker are discernible.

Native People & Ethnic Groups

Most ethnic groups represented in Syria have long histories in the country itself or in the region. The modern population largely lacks a national identity and is divided by ethnicity; rural versus urban backgrounds; and, above all, religious persuasion. Loyalty is given to one's family and group rather than to an overarching national ideal, and there is often extreme distrust between groups. The government has attempted some Arabization of non-Arab groups, but in general, the groups hold to their native customs and beliefs. In 2015, Arabs make up an estimated 90.3 percent of the population.

The largest minority ethnic group is the Kurds, who, along with Armenians, make up roughly 9.7 percent of the population and inhabit the northeastern region of the country, near the borders of Turkey and Iraq. The Kurds share similar religious beliefs with the Arab majority ethnic group. The Kurdish language has restrictions placed on it by the Syrian government; for instance, children's names, names of businesses, and place names must be in Arabic, and Kurdish language books are banned from publication.

Religions

Islam is the dominant religion, and 74 percent of the population adheres to Sunni Islam. Sunnis are found throughout the country and form a majority in most regions. The Alawites are the largest religious minority and, together with the Ismaili and Shia, account for 13 percent of the population. Interestingly, Alawites practice a unique offshoot of Shia Islam, the precepts of which are largely kept secret. Once repressed, their lot has improved over the last three decades, since the major politicians of the period have come from this minority. They generally live in rural areas of the province of Latakia. Other Muslim sects include the Druze, who represents three percent of the total population. Greek Orthodox, Syrian Orthodox, Armenian Orthodox, and Nestorians are four of the Christian sects, which collectively represent 10 percent of the population. The Christian and Jewish populations tend to inhabit urban centers, particularly in Damascus and Aleppo.

Climate

Syria has hot dry summers and cool wet winters. The highest precipitation levels are along the Mediterranean coast and in the mountains, with annual rainfall of between 75 and 100 centimeters (between 29 and 39 inches). The rainy season is between October and May. Precipitation decreases along an arc running east into the desert, which receives less than 2.5 centimeters (1 inch) per year. Snowfall occurs in the higher mountains. Sandstorms and droughts are both common.

Summer highs for Damascus, located in the southwest, reach an average maximum of 40° Celsius (104° Fahrenheit). Winter lows reach an average minimum of 4° Celsius (32.9° Fahrenheit), and the city and surrounding areas generally experience 20 centimeters (7.9 inches) of precipitation. The northwestern city of Aleppo has similar temperatures but receives more rainfall. Summer temperatures in the eastern desert can surpass 45° Celsius (113° Fahrenheit).

ENVIRONMENT & GEOGRAPHY

Topography

Syrian territory is comprised of several zones. The coastal zone that runs approximately 193 kilometers (120 miles) along the Mediterranean is 32 kilometers (20 miles) wide and is characterized by promontories and sand dunes. Two mountain ranges run parallel to this zone: the low Jabal an Nusayriyah—on average, 1,212 meters high (3,976 feet)—and the Anti-Lebanon

Mountains, which continue along the border with Lebanon some 93 miles and terminate in the hills of the Golan Heights. Mount Hermon, Syria's highest point, rises 2,814 meters (9,232 feet) from this range. The country's lowest point is an unspecified area near Lake Tiberias, also known as the Sea of Galilee, and is around 200 meters (656 feet) above sea level.

The rest of Syria is a large plateau containing the northern plain of Al Jazirah (Arabic for "the island"), the Euphrates River basin, and several desert areas, such as the southeastern Syrian Desert and the Homs Desert. The Euphrates River, which flows into Syria from Turkey then into Iraq, is the country's longest river. The Euphrates and its tributaries feed some of the richest agricultural land in the country. Lake Assad is a man-made reservoir, created in 1974, which utilizes the waters of the Euphrates. Lake Jabboul, near Aleppo, and Lake Qattineh, near Homs, are Syria's only natural lakes.

There are also several oases in Syria. The most important, fed by the Baradā River, is the Al-Ghūtah Oasis. Measuring 375 square kilometers (145 square miles), it has supported the city of Damascus since ancient times.

Plants & Animals

In Syria, the Arabian Oryx and the Syrian Hamster (one of the few endemic species) are listed as endangered, as is the Asian elephant. The Syrian elephant, which once roamed the terrain, went extinct around 100 BCE. Other common animals include the herbivorous hyrax (which resembles a North American groundhog), along with long-eared hedgehogs, various species of bats (fruit and horseshoe varieties are common), shrews, hyenas, foxes, gray wolves, jackals, cheetahs, hares, hamsters, gerbils, voles, various weasels, gazelle, and wild goats, among many others. Wild boar can be found in mountain forests. Among the bird species are falcons, eagles, and various types of wetland birds that breed in the country's river basins.

Syria also has a limited range of vegetation because of its largely arid conditions. It is estimated that 41 percent of the land supports grass and shrub, like buckthorn and tamarisk, and, in less dry areas, scattered trees. During a brief period in the spring, these areas are generally covered with wild flowers. Along the coast, reed grasses often grow. The largest forests, which make up only one percent of the total land, are found in the Anti-Lebanon Mountains. Oak, pine, fir, and cypress trees grow there. Along the Mediterranean coast grasses, shrubs and a few trees are found, while oases support palm and banana trees.

CUSTOMS & COURTESIES

Greetings

Syrians speak a variety of languages, including Kurdish, Armenian, Aramaic, Circassian, French, and English, but the official and most widely spoken language is Arabic. There are also several regional dialects of Arabic, with the North Levantine dialect (also known as Syro-Lebanese Arabic) being the most popular.

Most Syrians greet one another by saying "Murhuba" ("Hello") while shaking hands. Other common phrases include "Kayf haalak" ("How are you"), used for men, and "Kayf haalek," used for women. A more formal greeting consists of "As-salaam alaykum" (Peace be upon you"), with the appropriate response being "Wa alaykum as-salaam" ("And unto you, peace"). If men are particularly close, they might embrace upon greeting. Women who are close will often exchange kisses on each side of the cheek. Some Muslims will not shake hands or otherwise touch a member of the opposite sex unless that person is their spouse or child. Instead, these individuals will raise a hand to their chest as a method of greeting.

Gestures & Etiquette

Perhaps the most dominant feature of Syrian social etiquette is to always treat one another kindly. Prior to engaging in discussions of business or other serious matters, Syrians usually greet one another politely and ask about the health of each other's families. Another important rule of etiquette for Syrians is removing shoes before entering a mosque, and most families observe this rule in their homes. Guests are also expected to follow this practice. Keeping indoor spaces clean—especially ones that are concerned sacred—is very important to Syrians.

The concept of the "evil eye" is also present in Syria. The evil eye is thought to be an evil manifestation that can bring bad luck. In fact, Syrians are wary of complimenting another person or their children, as the praise may put the evil eye on the person or child. Although some regard this concept as folklore, some Syrians still take what they believe are proper precautions to ward off this ominous threat. In order to counter the evil eye, Syrians adorn themselves with things such as jewelry or charms in the shape of the iconic hand of Fatima. Other Syrians hang Esfand (known in North America as wild rue) throughout their homes, or they also burn it. When the tiny seeds pop, much like popcorn, a fragrant smoke is released that people direct towards their head to both remove and ward off the evil eye.

Interactions with the opposite sex are also different in Syria in comparison to Western countries. Public displays of affection are not common in Syria and generally frowned upon. Women also tend to show less skin than women in Western countries do, although the country has no official legislation on dress and public attire.

Eating/Meals

As a predominantly Muslim country, many eating customs in Syria pertain to Islam. For example, Muslim Syrians refrain from consuming pork or alcohol and fast during the holy month of Ramadan. During this holy period, eating in public is frowned upon, and this expectation extends to visitors and non-Muslims. Food is also consumed with the right hand, as the left hand is associated with personal cleansing and thus considered impure. Hands are also generally washed before and after eating.

An interesting development in the dining culture of Syria is the history and lasting presence of street food. Syria is known for having an abundance of street vendors. One of the most common items one can find in urban areas is shawarmah (also shāwarmā), a dish either made from finely shaved pieces of meat (either beef or lamb) or, less frequently, chicken. The meat or chicken rotates on a spit and the outer layers are shaved off for each sandwich. The sandwich, much like a gyro, is commonly served inside pita bread and can be accompanied by sliced tomato, onions, pickles, pepper, and a garlic sauce.

Coffee is a key feature of almost every Syrian meal and is perhaps Syria's most common social drink. While coffee is served in homes, there are also many coffeehouses dotting the Syrian cityscape. Turkish coffee, a thick, dark liquid that can be served bitter or sweet, is usually served in theses coffeehouses. The process for making Turkish coffee involves boiling grounds in water at least three times (without allowing it to scald or boil over), then further reducing the liquid to create a thicker, richer coffee. It is made in a small batches of three to five shots at a time. It is generally served in small, espresso-style cups and sugar is sometimes added.

In the rural areas of Syria, Arabic coffee is served. The Bedouin, a nomadic group, are well known for serving this beverage. The process for making Arabic coffee begins with roasting green coffee beans until they are golden (often in an ordinary oven, but traditional roasting occurred over an open fire in a pan called a ta-waa) and then pounding the beans into a fine powder. The coffee is then boiled in a small pot and complimented by cardamom, whose pods either are roasted and ground with the coffee beans or can be added to the pot as it boils. Sometimes, a pinch of saffron and several dashes of rose water are also added to the coffee. The finished product is served in special cups and is often lighter in color than traditional coffee preparations. Dates frequently accompany coffee, as their sweetness offers a pleasant counterpoint to the coffee's bitterness. Many Syrians, especially the Bedouin, enjoy a cup of coffee after their meals, as it helps with digestion and provides additional time for conversation.

Visiting

Hospitality is a fundamental value of Syrian culture. Entertaining guests—both new and old—is an important event for Syrians and any invitation into a Syrian's home should be accepted if possible. Syrians will go out of their way for guests, cooking lavish meals, serving fruits, pastries, and other desserts, as well as tea and coffee. Syrians will gently coax their guests into eating as much as possible, and if guests are unable to clear their plates, it is generally considered the sign of a successful event. Dessert, tea, or coffee will usually follow. Syrian hospitality might also extend to inviting guests to relax, take a nap, or even stay the night. Guests either are customarily expected to return the favor by inviting over their hosts for a similar event, or are expected to bring some sort of small gift, such as pastries, fruit, or flowers.

LIFESTYLE

Family

Syria follows the tradition of other Middle Eastern cultures by placing family as the core building block of society. Large and extended families, with sons and their immediate families often living with parents, were historically common. Traditionally, men were the head of the household and the sole providers working outside the home; women stayed at home, tending to the domestic necessities of cooking, cleaning, and child rearing. Daughters were expected to help with domestic tasks, while sons enjoyed what was considered a more leisurely life. However, sons were also expected to assist with agricultural chores or take on an apprenticeship.

These traditions are now changing. As Syria transitioned into the 21st century, more women were entering the workforce. In fact, women made up an estimated 33.7 percent of the workforce heading into the last decade of the 20th century. This included positions of authority in parliament, the military, and the police force. Women also have been pursuing careers in law, medicine, and engineering. The ruling Arab

Socialist Ba'ath party also promotes secular public politics, and consequently, traditional attitudes are changing towards issues like the use of veils in public and women's unescorted public movements. Since the Syrian Civil War began in 2011, women's responsibilities have increased, with some women becoming sole breadwinners for their families following the death or disability of their husbands.

Housing

In the urban centers of Syria, especially Damascus and Aleppo, townhouses are common residences for the middle and upper class. If the family is Muslim, the houses may be divided into two sections: a salamlik, an area for the male family members to entertain guests and business colleagues, and a haramlik, the area that is considered the private space for women and the family. Traditionally, only males from the immediate family are allowed in the latter area. These homes usually feature courtyards adorned with intricate tilework, fountains, and gardens. Ceilings adorned with fresco paintings, sculpted stucco, and chandeliers are examples of typical decorative interior elements.

Rural Syrian homes are often described as beehives due to their rounded shape. This architectural style is believed to date back over 1,000 years. The structures are generally made of mud and in some locations are adjoined with walls to create an inner courtyard. The interiors are quite simple and may feature handcrafted wall hangings and pictures of religious sentiment.

With the military sieges accompanying the Syrian Civil War, the UN has estimated that Syria has more than 7,600,000 displaced nationals within its borders. Because their homes have been damaged or otherwise made uninhabitable, many have moved to temporary living quarters, like Damascus' Yarmouk Camp, an unofficial refugee camp that had traditionally been home to a large Palestinian population. After the Islamic State of Iraq and the Levant (ISIL) took control of the Yarmouk in April 2015, many Syrians have fled to camps outside the country, like Shatila in southern Beirut. Such events have had a significant impact on the housing situation within Syrian borders.

Food

Syrian cuisine is similar to other neighboring Middle Eastern and Arabic cuisines and can be heavily dependent upon fresh vegetables and fruits, beans and grains, meats, and spices. Certain Syrian dishes are distinctly made with olives and wheat as staples and have been influential in the culinary traditions of Palestine, Jordan, and Lebanon. Olive oil is also a staple ingredient and olives are served as snacks and appetizers throughout the day. Breads are also a part of most meals. Generally, Syrian breads do not utilize yeast. The most common type of bread is unleavened Arabic bread called khobz or khubz (known in Western culture as pita bread). This type of bread is served with almost all meals and is used for dipping into various spreads that accompany meals, such as hummus and baba ghannuj. It is also used as a scoop for meat and fish dishes. Different types of thin flat breads, like manoushi, are also very common.

For breakfast, it is common to have fresh fruits or vegetables, as well as falafel (ground chickpeas formed into balls and fried), eggs, and labneh (a thick, lightly salted yogurt, with whey removed), accompanied by fresh juice and sweetened tea. Lunch, usually the largest meal of the day, often includes numerous dishes. A variety of dips is served, accompanied by rice and breads, and meat, poultry, or fish dishes. Kebbah (or kibbeh) is a common main dish and is made from ground meat (lamb or beef), cracked wheat, cinnamon, onion, black pepper and a few other spices, including cinnamon, nutmeg, cloves, and allspice. Sometimes it is formed into balls and stuffed with pine nuts, but it can also be formed into something similar to a casserole. A common chicken dish is shish taouk: cubes of marinated chicken that are either baked, grilled, or broiled and are usually served with a garlic-based dipping sauce. Close to the Mediterranean coastline, fish is often served as a main dish. Dinner is traditionally not a big meal for Syrians. In the past, before the time of refrigeration, they would often use the leftovers from lunch to create stews and soups. Today, Syrian dinners resemble the European style, three-course meal.

Life's Milestones

A birth in Syria is a celebrated thing. While celebrations for sons in the past have been more lavish than celebrations for daughters, this tradition is changing. A ceremony called sabu'ah is usually held seven days after the birth of the child. This event is similar to a naming ceremony, as the baby's name is officially announced to the community on this day. During the ceremony, special songs are sung and freshly grown wheat is offered as a wish for speedy growth, as well as other symbolic gestures.

While there are a variety of religions present in Syria, the most widely practiced is Sunni Islam. In this tradition, when a death occurs, funerals are quick affairs and burial usually occurs within twenty-four hours. Female family members wash the body, usually, a task known as *mghassel*. The body is then dressed in two to four pieces of satin or linen cloth. The men of the family and community then take the body to the local mosque, where prayers are recited over the body. Unlike in some Christian traditions, there is no viewing of the body. Immediately following this part of the ceremony, the body is taken to the cemetery where it is buried, wrapped only in the linen or satin cloth. Particularly in rural communities, a ram or bull is sacrificed in the name of the deceased following burial. Moreover, before the animal is slaughtered, prayers are recited and the knife is blessed as part of the sacrificial offering. The family may also invite the poor to a meal of meat and bulger, both at the time of the person's death and forty days afterward, when the tombstone is also placed. Muslim widows will often don white for a period and then will join other mourners of the dead by wearing black, although younger generations have begun to move away from this observance. In the hours following burial, particularly during the wake, mourners do not speak to the deceased's family members when visiting. Instead, they sit silently for a few moments with family members, nod respectfully, and quietly recite the *fateha* (the first verse of the Koran) three times before leaving. While some practitioners of Sunni Islam discourage grave visitation, some, often women, do visit and care for them.

CULTURAL HISTORY

Syria shares a common culture with other Arab countries. The single most important literary work is the Koran, which has given rise to unique achievements in architecture, both religious and domestic, as well as a strong oral tradition and deeply ingrained customs, such as hospitality.

Architecture

The architecture of Syria has been influenced by a variety of cultures, mainly the empires of the Romans, Byzantines, and Ottomans. Syria benefited from the political and economic stability afforded by its Roman rule from around 64 through 395 CE, and during that time, the country's architecture flourished. The Byzantine Empire, which ruled the area for over two centuries, introduced a Hellenistic architectural style, evident in the Basilica St. Simeon Stylites (or Qalaat Semaan), a church and pilgrimage site constructed in the fifth century. On May 28, 2015, the basilica was captured by People's Protection Units (YPG) and their female division (YPJ), Kurdish forces created to oppose ISIL, which objects to the reverence of such locations. During its seizure, there was little damage to the country's oldest surviving Byzantine church. Under the rule of the Ottoman Empire (during the 16th through the 20th century), Islamic architecture flourished in Syria, and many mosques, such as the Tekkiye Mosque in Damascus, and khans (inns) were constructed.

Dance

The development of classical dance is intertwined with the history of classical music. Young women often performed dance routines to accompany classical music in the royal courts.

This style of dance is similar to Western modern dance as both styles attempt to convey emotions and/or a story through movement. Classical Syrian dance also includes some shaking of the hips and shoulders.

A very old and well-known form of dance that has been popular in Syria for centuries is raqs balladi, or belly dance. The origins of the dance are disputed and range from a birthing ritual or a temple dance, to an instructional method by which young brides may seduce their new husbands. Nonetheless, the jubilant dance, which features snake-like movements and shaking of the hips and shoulders, remains a central feature of most Syrian celebrations. Occasionally, metal finger cymbals (sagat) are employed as part of the performance.

Folk dances are extremely popular in Syria, with the most famous being the dabkah, a type of line dance performed in Syria, Lebanon, Jordan, and Palestine. The leader at the front of the line cues the following dancers' movements both verbally and with certain motions. In Syria, the performance of the dance changes slightly according to the gender of the dancers.

Bedouins, along with Kurds, Turks, and Armenians, have formed their own dances and renditions of the dabkah, including the ardah (meaning 'display' or 'parade'), a war dance performed by men that was once intended to reveal their prowess and lift their morale before combat. The men configure themselves into two lines facing one another while holding either a sword or a camel prod. The dance is similar to the dabkah, in that the dancers follow the cues from a leader. The two lines are in a sort of mock battle with one another. The losing side lowers their swords or camel prods in defeat at the conclusion of the dance.

Music

Syrian music is located within the larger category of classical Arabic music, which blends musical traditions from Persian, Arabian, and Hellenistic styles. Classical Arabic music features both instruments and vocals. The instruments usually found in classical Arabic music include: the oud, a five- or six-stringed instrument similar to a lute; a qanun, a flat, stringed instrument, which resembles a zither and is played on one's lap; the kamanjah, a four-stringed instrument, played with a bow and shaped like a long-necked lute; a ney, a flute-like instrument; a riq, a tambourine; and a darabukah, a ceramic, vase-shaped drum. While the instruments are an important element to the music, the voice is essential. A good singer can take listeners to a state of tarab, or musical ecstasy.

A special form of Arabic music that emerged in Muslim Spain and was heavily influenced by Arabic poetry is the muwashshah (plural being muwashahat). The songs are organized in a call and response format—verses are sung in classical Arabic and the chorus is sung in colloquial Arabic. A special formation of the tradition, called Qudud Halabiya, originated in Aleppo in northern Syria. Although the songs are not explicitly songs of devotion, they have become an essential part of Sufi rituals, called zikr (also dhikr). (Sufism is a mystical sect of Islam.) One of the most important performers of traditional muwashahat music is Aleppo-born Sabah Fakhri (1933–), one of the few Syrian singers to garner international acclaim. Perhaps the most popular Arab musician to hail from Syria, however, is Farid al-Atrash (1910–1974). Known as the "king of the oud," his name is still synonymous with classic Arabian music throughout Syria and the Arab world.

Literature

The literature of Syria has ancient roots. Some of the world's oldest texts have been found in modern-day Syria. The subjects of these texts, most commonly written in a Semitic language, are quite varied. Throughout the centuries, Syria's intellectual elite produced many important philosophical texts, on par with the ancient Greek schools of Athens and Alexandria. With the spread of Islam, Syrian literature continued to enjoy a leading role in the production and proliferation of Arabic literature. Early Syrian writers produced important works in the sciences and poetry, as well as traditional biographies and narratives. Poetry has long held an important place in Arabic culture. Its role as one of the highest modes of expression continued with the establishment of Islam as the region's dominant religion.

During the Umayyad period (661–750), three important poets emerged, all of whom were Bedouin and supported by the royal court: al-Akhtal (c. 640–710), al-Farazdaq (c. 641–c.730), and Jarir (c. 650–c. 729), whose poems were mainly written in qasida (ode) style. These three contemporaries often directed satirical poetry at one another. This "war of words" was said to have lasted 40 years, and this style of poetry earned a distinguished place in the cannon of Arabic literature. All three poets are credited with bringing together the traditional Bedouin culture of the region with the emerging Muslim society.

Although frequently repressed and sometimes forced into exile, contemporary Syrian literary figures have nonetheless achieved international recognition for their works. These poets, writers, and playwrights include magical realist Salim Barakat (1951–), who is of mixed Kurdish and Syrian descent; the poet Ali Ahmad Said Esber (1930–), known by his penname Adunis; feminist novelist Ulfat Idilbi (1912–2007); controversial novelist and screenwriter Khaled Khalifa (1964–), whose works have been banned by the Syrian government; novelist and poet Colette Khoury (1931–), whose work includes erotica, a taboo genre in Syria; social realist novelist Hanna Mina (1924–); satirical playwright Saadallah Wannous (1941–1997); and writer and journalist Samar Yazbek (1970), a member of the minority Alawi community and winner of the PEN/Pinter Prize for her book *A Woman in the Crossfire*.

CULTURE

Arts & Entertainment

Syria has a lively cafe culture; men meet to drink coffee or tea, smoke flavored tobacco from a water pipe, and socialize. A café tradition, though one that is dying out, is the performance of the hakawati, a storyteller and actor who recounts the epics and fables of Arabic culture for the café patrons.

Modern Syrian literature often focuses on political issues, including women in society and the French occupation, creating a language with which Syrians promote and explore their own national identity. Syria's foremost authors, some of whose books are available in English, are Hanna Mina (1924–), Zakariya Tamer (1931–), Halim Barakat (1933–), and Ulfat Idilbi (1912–2007).

Ulfat Idilbi is one of Syria's most cherished female writers. Born in Damascus and married to a physiologist, she insisted on taking her husband's last name, as she believed the tradition of women retaining family names was patriarchal. Her writing career began when she was just a teenager, and her best-known work is *Dimashq ya Basmat al-Huzn* (*Sabriya: Damascus Bitter-Sweet*, 1995). The novel follows the trajectory of Sabriya, a woman coming of age during the 1920s who experiences the French occupation and the emerging Syrian nationalist movement. *Sabriya* also tells the story of a woman growing up in a patriarchal society. The novel received accolades in Syria and abroad and has since been adapted into a television series.

One important and extremely popular Syrian poet was Nizar Qabbani (1925–1998), a native of Damascus. His romance poetry is praised because it focuses on the feelings of women, and his attention to topics concerning gender roles is partly a result of his sister's suicide—an event that deeply shook him. Seeking to avoid a forced marriage to a man she did not love, Qabbani's sister took her own life, and for this reason, Qabbani's poetry consistently rallied for women's social freedom. Later, in "Bread, Hashish and Moon" of 1954, he also criticized Arab societies that he felt were succumbing to rampant drug use and given to backward thinking. The poem spurred the Syrian parliament to discuss his prosecution, although no charges were filed. Qabbani's poetry is known for its use of simple, yet eloquent language, which is seen in juxtaposition to the elevated and often inaccessible language of classical Arabic poetry.

Syrian cinema, though still a fledgling industry, has begun to receive worldwide attention. An international film festival and a theatre festival had been held in Damascus, where filmmakers could screen work related to important political and social issues. However, the last film festival was held in 2010, the year before the Arab

Spring demonstrations erupted in civil war. However, one of the leading figures of Syrian film is still Durayd Lahham (1934–), an actor, director, and screenwriter. He began his career as a comedic actor in the Syrian arts community. However, events such as Six-Day War of 1967 compelled him to focus his work on subjects of a political nature. One of his most acclaimed films is *Al-Hudud* (*The Border*, 1987). The film addresses the idea of pan-Arabism, chronicling the main character's experience of losing a passport and facing restricted travel between two Arab countries.

Annual arts festivals include the Bosra Festival of folk music and the Palmyra Festival, which highlights camel and horse races and traditional singing and dancing. Both of these festivals have also been suspended since the outbreak of war.

Cultural Sites & Landmarks

Syria is home to five World Heritage Sites as designated by the United Nations Educational, Scientific, and Cultural Organization (UNESCO). They include the ancient cities of Aleppo and Damascus, and the ancient ruins of Bosra and Palmyra. Also included are two significant castles: the crusader fortress of Crac des Chevaliers and Qal'at Salah El-Din, or Citadel of Salah Ed-Din. Because of the Syrian Civil War and its related skirmishes and airstrikes, many of these sites have been moved to UNESCO's Endangered Heritage List.

Aleppo, a northwestern city located along the path of many ancient trade routes, was ruled by a variety of world powers throughout history, including the Hittites, Egyptians, Arabs, Mongols, Mamluks, Persians, and Ottomans. Because of its diverse past, the city is the site of many ancient structures, including a 13th-century citadel and the 8th-century Great Mosque of Aleppo, whose minaret—built in 1090—was destroyed by bombs in April 2013. These structures both are found in the old section of the city. Within this quarter, which features narrow cobblestone roads built in a grid style of the Greeks, is one of the world's most famous

covered bazaars. Aleppo is considered one of the oldest inhabited cities in the world but is now at risk from overpopulation.

The capital of Damascus, believed by some scholars to be the oldest continuously inhabited city, is located in the southwestern part of Syria. The city is also affectionately called al-Fayha ("the Fragrant"), most likely due to the prevalence of orchards and lush gardens throughout the city. The city contains over 120 monuments, including the 8th-century Great Mosque of the Umayyads, the Citadel of Damascus, and Azem Palace, which houses the Museum of Arts and Popular Traditions. Many of these landmarks and monuments are contained within the Old City of Damascus, which has seven city gates, one of which dates back to Roman times. In 2008, Damascus was named the Arab Capital of Culture, a rotating distinction initiated in 1996 by the Arab League of the UNESCO Cultural Capitals Program.

Bosra, another Syrian city that has been passed through the hands of several different rulers, is no longer inhabited due to both earthquakes and unsatisfactory Turkish rule in the 12th century. The Romans designated Bosra as the capital of its province, Arabia. Because of this Roman presence, the remains of a second-century Roman theatre still stand. The city is also home to significant Christian ruins and mosques. Similarly, the ancient city of Palmyra is also an ancient city that fell into disuse and became a major archaeological site. One of the notable ruins within the "city of palm trees" is the Temple of Bel, whose façade was significantly damaged by a mortar bomb in April 2013, while its great sandstone columns have been chipped by shrapnel. Bel is a god whom the Palmyrians thought controlled the celestial bodies. Worship of Bel showed a resemblance to a monotheistic religion. The temple sits among many other ruins, including architecture, which shows a fusion between Mesopotamian, Persian, and Corinthian styles.

The castles of Crac des Chevaliers and Qal'at Salah El-Din, recognized as a collective World Heritage Site in 2006, represent important examples of fortified architecture in the Near

East. The first castle dates back to the time of the Crusades (11th to through the 13th centuries) and was considered one of the best-preserved medieval castles in existence until it was shelled by the Syrian Arab Army in August 2012 and hit by airstrikes in July 2013 during the Siege of Horns, part of the Syrian Civil War. The Citadel of Salah ed-Din dates back to the 10th century and retains the name of the Sultan Saladin (c. 1138–1193 CE), credited with recapturing the Holy Land from the crusaders.

Libraries & Museums

Syria's ancient history and culture is showcased in several museums, most notably the National Museum, which contains some of the world's most important archaeological discoveries. Among the Damascus-based museum's many highlights are portions of the Dura-Europos Synagogue, found in 1932 and thought to be the oldest preserved synagogue, with an Aramaic inscription dating it to at least 244 CE. Its figurative paintings are currently on display in the museum as part of a complete Dura-Europos facsimile reconstruction.

The Al-Assad National Library, founded in 1984, is located in Damascus and houses over 40,000 printed resources within its nine floors. Other libraries include the University of Damascus Library, established in 1903 and boasting 169,000 volumes and 3,830 current periodicals, and the Arab Academy of Damascus Library, which contains 15,000 volumes and 500 manuscripts.

Holidays

Many of Syria's holidays are religious in nature and accord with the Islamic calendar. The most important celebrations are the fasting month of Ramadan, ending with Eid al-Fitr, when people gather for feasts and wear new clothes. Eid al-Adha is celebrated in a similar way and commemorates Abraham's willingness to sacrifice his son Isaac (other accounts indicate the holiday commemorates the parting in Mecca of Abraham and his first son Ishmael, a prophet and ancestor of Muhammad). Muharram commemorates

the flight of Muhammed and his followers from Medina to Mecca and initiates the Muslim New Year.

The most important secular holidays are Revolution Day (March 8), which celebrates the Ba'ath party's rise to power; Evacuation Day (April 17), commemorating the French withdrawal from Syria in 1946; and Martyr's Day (May 6), which marks the bloody struggle for independence from the Ottomans.

Youth Culture

The majority of Syrian youth were hopeful when Bashar al-Assad took office in 2000. After all, Syria was a very young country—the majority of the population in 2009 was younger than the 43-year-old president—and many anticipated the young president would institute reforms and generally breathe fresh air into the country. When President al-Assad assumed office in 2000, the unemployment rate was at a then-staggering 20 percent. By 2011, it was even higher—48 percent—for those 15 to 24 years of age. The official overall unemployment number in 2014 stands at 33 percent, although the civil war and its attendant diaspora have likely affected the accuracy of such statistics. Violence, worsening inflation, and the ever-rising unemployment figures have pushed many young Syrians to seek education and employment abroad, but those who do so are of a privileged social class with the means to escape. Others are internally displaced, fleeing violence with their families; many seek asylum in Lebanon.

SOCIETY

Transportation

Syria has developed and extensive road networks and major highways connect Aleppo, Damascus, and Baghdad in Iraq. Popular modes of public transportation include buses, minibuses, and trains, while taxis are commonly used for local transport. The rail system, solely diesel-electric traction, also connects Syrians to their northern neighbor, Turkey; their eastern neighbor, Iraq;

their southwestern neighbor Jordan; and their western neighbor, Lebanon. In 2014, a proposed track extension will connect Syria's seventh largest city, Dayr az-Zawr, and Al'Qa'im, Iraq, which 400 kilometers (248.5 miles) north of Baghdad.

Syria also has three international airports, in Damascus, Aleppo, and Latakia. A number of domestic airports are scattered throughout the country. Syrian Arab Airlines is the national carrier.

Syria's west coastline on the Mediterranean Sea also has encouraged the development of ports. Latakia is Syria's largest port, while Tartus—also a popular vacation spot—is the country's second largest port. Between 1995 and November 2003, the United Nations (UN) used these ports to ship food to Iraq as part of its Oil-for-Food Program. However, this program ended in 2003, following allegations of corruption and kickbacks, of which Syrian officials and public figures were named as beneficiaries.

Traffic moves on the right side of the road in Syria.

Transportation Infrastructure

Beginning in the 1980s, transportation infrastructure in Syria underwent widespread development. In 1991, legislation was passed that allowed for private sector investment in the transportation sector, which also helped to spur infrastructure development in Syria. Road networks in the country were increased from approximately 19,819 kilometers (12,314 miles) in 1980 to 68,157 kilometers (42,350 miles) in 2014. As of 2013, it was estimated that 61,514 kilometers (38,223 miles) of roads were made of asphalt.

Media & Communications

The Syrian government owns and controls the media. As of 2013, Freedom House, a media watchdog group, classifies Syria as "Not Free," giving it a score of 88 out of 100. Article 38 of Syria's constitution provides for freedom of speech. However, any material that is critical of or threatening toward the administration and the ruling party is forbidden. Self-censorship is widely practiced, and it is rare for a foreign journalist to be recognized officially by the government. This restricting environment of censorship was lifted slightly with the appointment of President Bashar al-Assad (1965–) in 2000. Following his rise to power, private publications were allowed into circulation. This small allowance of press freedom was short-lived, after a law was passed that placed numerous restrictions on the media.

The issue of freedom of the press has not seen much progress in the last several years, with the most significant improvements being the allowance of television programs featuring debates on taboo issues and interviews with leaders from the Ba'ath party's opposition.

Television and radio are also mostly state-run. While FM broadcasters have been allowed to be run privately—the first one debuted in 2005—they are still not allowed to broadcast any news or content of a political nature. The state-run Syrian TV operates in Arabic, French, and English. Many Syrians have turned to satellite television to gain access to a set of more nuanced opinions. Syrians also are avid Internet users; as of 2013, roughly 26.2 percent of Syrians used the Internet. However, Reporters without Borders heavily criticizes Syria for its harsh censoring of websites and blocking of many news websites not run by the government.

SOCIAL DEVELOPMENT

Standard of Living

Life expectancy is about 77 years for women and 72 years for men. In 2014, the country ranked 118th out of 187 countries on the UN Human Development Index.

Water Consumption

The main sources of water in Syria are groundwater (including aquifers and springs) and surface water in the form of 16 rivers (the largest being the Euphrates River) and five lakes. In 2012, 92.3 percent of the country's urban population and 87.2 percent of its rural had access to improved water systems. In 2012, 96.2 percent of the country's urban population and 95.1 percent of its rural population were connected to sewage systems.

Education

Primary education, lasting six years, is free and compulsory. It is followed by six years of secondary education, divided into lower and higher levels. There is also vocational training at the secondary level. Since 2000, the Syrian government has significantly increased education expenditures, which represented 4.9 percent of the GDP in 2007.

In 2015, the literacy rate was estimated to be 86.4 percent and was significantly higher for males (91.7 percent) than for females (81 percent). The overall literacy rate shows a marked improvement from the early 1980s, when an intense government-sponsored literacy campaign began.

Four universities operate in Syria: Damascus University, the largest; Aleppo University; Tishreen University in Latakia; and Al-Baath University in Homs. Among the institutes and colleges are the Higher Institute of Applied Sciences and an Arabic Languages Academy in Damascus.

The 2009 *Global Gender Gap Report*, published by the World Economic Forum, ranked countries according to their attainment of gender equality in areas such as education, economic opportunities, and health. Syria ranked 121st out of 134 countries; however, in the category of educational attainment, the country ranked a bit higher, at 104th out of 134. In the 2014 rankings, Syria was 139th of 142 countries.

Women's Rights

The Syrian constitution ensures gender equality and many Syrian women are active in all facets of public life, particularly in the political arena. The 2007 elections resulted in 31 of the 250 seats in parliament taken by women. However, in the 2012 elections, the number has dropped to twelve, although there were 710 females among the 7,195 candidates. The Arab Women Parliamentarians Project, which is supported by the Syrian Commission for Family Affairs, the General Women's Union, and the UN Development Fund for Women (UNIFEM), has assisted these women in their pursuit of top-level positions, and a reported 55 percent have participated in the activities of the project. The increasingly active role of women in government has lead to a better status for Syrian women.

As of 2013, Syrian women make up nearly 13.4 percent of the workforce, and these numbers are growing as women continue to pursue higher education. In 1985, legislation was passed that provides women with longer maternity leave, permits breastfeeding in the workplace, and protects pregnant women from jobs that could harm their fetus. While universities do not practice gender discrimination, the majority of women enter into programs such as education, languages, humanities, social sciences, computer science, and medicine. Programs such as these are believed to be more in line with what is "acceptable" work for women. However, larger numbers of women are pursuing careers in law, medicine, and engineering. Women are also allowed to own their own companies, but make up only an estimated three percent of the total number of operating businesses.

Despite these achievements, there are personal status laws and penal code provisions that are unequal in their treatment toward women. One particularly discriminatory provision is the allowance of a judge to defer punishment against a rapist if he marries his victim. Honor crimes are also judged more leniently than other assault and murder charges. The Syrian Women's Observatory noted at least ten honor crimes in 2008. That same year, the minister of social affairs declared the Syrian Women's Association, which was founded in 1948, illegal. The Social Initiative Organization was also forced to cease working and the ministry would not allow five non-governmental organizations (NGOs) to receive licenses.

Health Care

Before the war, Syria had a socialized medical system that extended health care to all of its citizens for free or at nominal cost. The Ministry of

Health also restricted the prices charged by private hospitals. Both state-run and private hospitals are concentrated in the major urban centers, so the rural population receives less adequate medical care, generally from basic health clinics. Overall, Syria has always suffered from a shortage of doctors, nurses, and dentists. The civil war has only exacerbated the system's essential problems. Since the violence began, 70 percent of drugs have become unavailable and an estimated 60 percent of hospitals and clinics have been severely damaged, even razed. Nearly half Syria's doctors have fled the country, leaving a few cash-strapped aid organizations to treat an estimated eights million sick or injured homeless Syrians. As of a result of such conditions, in 2014, previously eradicated diseases, like measles, have begun surging back, while those with injured limbs—salvageable under normal circumstances—are forced into amputations due to the absence of necessary equipment and medical facilities.

GOVERNMENT

Structure

Syria began the 20th century under Ottoman rule. Following the dissolution of the empire, it came under the rule of the French. This period, known as the French Mandate Period, lasted until the end of War World II. A period of instability followed, marked by political tensions within Syria and with its neighbors. In 1970, General Hafez al-Assad, who belonged to the Alawite minority, took power of the country in a coup and remained its president until his death in 2000. His oldest living son, Bashar Al-Assad, is currently Syria's president and has been since 2000.

According to the constitution of 1973, Syria is a democratic socialist republic, but in reality, it is largely a single-party system, consistently controlled by the Ba'ath Party. The president is elected by popular vote to a seven-year term. As head of the executive branch, the president wields considerable powers. He appoints the prime minister, the council of ministers over which the prime minister presides, the Supreme Court justices, as well as several vice presidents if he chooses. He is also commander-in-chief of the armed forces, secretary of the Ba'ath Party, and can choose to put important national issues to a popular referendum.

The Syrian legislature is called the People's Assembly, a unicameral body of 250 officials elected by popular vote every four years.

Political Parties

The Ba'ath Arab Socialist Party has dominated the Syrian political system for the last several decades. Five other parties, socialist or communist in nature and with a philosophy of pan-Arabism, form the National Progressive Front (founded in 1972) with the Ba'ath Party. In 2005, the Syrian Social Nationalist Party became the first non-socialist and non-pan-Arabism political party officially recognized by the government. Established by former president Hafiz al-Assad, the NPF offers a limited level of participation in government for political organizations other than the ruling Ba'ath Party.

In 2007, the Ba'ath Arab Socialist Party won 134 of the 250 seats in the People's Council of Syria. The Arab Socialist Union won eight seats, while the Socialist Unionists won six. Eighty-one seats were won by independents.

In 2012, the most recent election, the National Progressive Front (NPF) won 168 seats in the People's Council: the Ba'ath Party gained 134, the Socialist Unionists eighteen, the Wissal Farha Bakdash faction of the Communist Party won eight, the Yusuf Faisal faction of the Communist Party won three, the Nationalist Vow Movement won three, and the Arab Socialist Union won two. The Popular Front for Change and Liberation, a coalition of parties, collectively won five seats and became the opposition power in the People's Council of Syria. Seventy-seven seats went to non-partisan independents.

Local Government

Syria comprises fourteen governorates (muhafazat), each of which is overseen by a governor (who is appointed by the Ministry of the Interior) and a council. The governorates are further divided into 65 districts (manatiq), one of which is Damascus. Additional administrative subdivisions include counties and villages, each of which is governed by locally elected councils.

Judicial System

The highest court in Syria is the High Constitutional Court, which rules on electoral issues and the constitutionality of legislation. Members include the president and four judges he appoints to renewable, four-year terms. Secular courts include civil and criminal courts, under the purview of the Ministry of Justice, and the Court of Cassation, the country's highest court of appeals. Religious courts include the Sharia courts, doctrinal courts, and spiritual courts. Special courts include military courts and the Economic Security Court. Prior to April 21, 2011, the date on which President Assad abolished it by legislative decree number 53; Syria had a Supreme State Security Court, which tired political and national security cases.

Taxation

The top income tax levied in Syria is 22 percent, and the top corporate tax is 28 percent. Other taxes include property transfer taxes and estate/inheritance taxes. As of 2010, there was no value-added tax (VAT). Civil conflict has made tax collection and policy enforcement highly problematic.

Armed Forces

The armed forces of Syria comprise the Syrian Arab Navy, Syrian Arab Army, and Syrian Arab Air and Defense Forces. After a significant number of civil-war-related casualties and desertions, active personnel are reported to number between 150,000 and 178,000, down from the previous figure of 325,000. Because of diminishing troops, several hundred thousand reservists have been called to duty. Government-organized checkpoints and home raids have been executed so that reservists, who fail to comply with call-up orders, can be located. In addition, civil servants, who evade deployment, are slated for dismissal.

Foreign Policy

Syria holds membership in numerous international organizations, including the UN, the Non-Aligned Movement (NAM), and the International Monetary Fund (IMF), and served as a nonpermanent member of the UN Security Council (UNSC)—a two-year term which ended in 2003. Syria also holds membership in significant regional organizations such as the Organization of Arab Petroleum Exporting Countries (OAPEC) and the Arab League, and maintains an influential role in the Middle East, particularly in the Israel-Palestinian conflict. Since 1948, Syria has been constantly at war with Israel and is involved in a dispute with Israel over the conflicted Golan Heights region. Although Syria denies that it materially supports organizations such as Hezbollah, many believe Syria provides them with both weapons and funding. Syria's power over Lebanon is believed to be dwindling due to the election of a largely anti-Syrian parliament in Lebanon in 2005.

Despite its government's strong pan-Arab views, Syria's closest ally in the region may be Iran. The alliance dates to the 1970s, when Syria's version of the Ba'ath party took a different form than Iraq's version. This resulted in strained relations between Syria and Iraq and closer relations between Iran and Syria. During the Iran-Iraq war (1980–1988), Syria, unlike other Arab countries, supported Iran. Iran sends Syria millions in aid each year to assist in the upkeep of Syria's Shiite holy sites, which attract thousands of Iranian tourists each year. The U.S. invasion of Iraq in 2003 also brought the two countries closer. One of the strongest uniting forces between the two is their opposition to Israel. Iran is also public supporter of Hezbollah, but the extent to which it supports the organization materially is debated. Syria's close relations with Shiite Iran are troublesome to its predominately-Sunni Arab neighbors, Egypt, Jordan, and Saudi Arabia. The countries have felt threatened due to the strong ties between Iran and Syria, fearing the relations will strengthen the influence of Shiite Iran over the region.

Relations between the U.S. and Syria have been strained at best. Because of Syria's strong anti-Israel stance, the two nations have fundamental differences on some of the most important issues facing the Middle East region. The US has long accused Syria of supporting Hamas and Hezbollah, anti-Israel organizations, which the US lists as terrorist groups. Following the terrorist attacks of September 11, 2001, relations between the two improved slightly, as Syria divulged information about members of al-Qaeda. Friendly relations between the two were short-lived as President Bashar al-Assad was one of the Arab world's most vocal critics of the U.S. invasion of Iraq. The U.S. suspects that Syria has allowed both fighters and weaponry across the border into Iraq in 2008. In addition, the U.S. has accused Syria of providing shelter to some of the members of Saddam Hussein's dissolved regime. Because of the Syrian Civil War, the U.S. suspended its embassy in 2012, and following chemical weapons attacks on rebels in Damascus by Assad loyalists, the U.S. has threatened to destroy chemical and biological weapons installations in August 2013, although no U.S. strikes have been made.

Since late 2011, the U.S., the European Union, Turkey, and the 21 member-countries of the Arab League have all leveled sanctions against Assad and Syria. As of December 2012, 130 countries acknowledged the Syrian National Coalition as the true representative of the Syrian people.

Human Rights Profile

International human rights law insists that states respect civil and political rights and also promote an individual's economic, social, and cultural rights. The United Nations Universal Declaration on Human Rights (UDHR) is recognized as the standard for international human rights. Its authors sought the counsel of the world's great thinkers, philosophers, and religious leaders and were careful to create a document that reflects the core values shared by every world culture. To read this document

or view the articles relating to cultural human rights, visit www.ohchr.org/EN/UDHR/Pages/Introduction.aspx.

Since the Syrian Civil War broke out in 2011, the Syrian government has been accused of censorship and war crimes. Not only has the UN accused the Syrian government of using chemical weapons against its citizen opposition, it has also been accused of shelling areas the UN was slated to inspect, so that investigations would be further delayed and evidence eliminated. As of April 2015, an estimated 310,000 people have been killed as a result of the fighting, and humanitarian agencies have accused Assad's government and ISIL of perpetrating massacres. In May 2015, Amnesty International reported that Syrian governmental forces were dropping what are called "barrel bombs"—55-gallon drums filled with explosives, nails, and shrapnel—on schools, hospitals, mosques, even crowded markets in areas held by rebel forces, like Aleppo.

In order to control information leaving the country's borders, Assad has called for a foreign media blackout. Freedom House reported that, in February 2012, Syrian forces overran the Damascus-based non-governmental organization the Syrian Center for Media and Freedom of Expression, and arrested 14 people, including with the organization's chief. In addition to detention and harassment by government forces, the watchdog group Committee to Protect Journalists has reported that 30 correspondents were killed within Syrian borders in 2012 alone.

Even before the Arab Spring protests and ensuing civil war, Syria restricted freedom of speech, assembly, and political association, which was, in part, what brought Syrians to the streets to protest during Arab Spring in 2011. Ethnicities, such as refugees from neighboring countries and the Kurds, are also targeted and refused certain rights. Other documented human rights abuses include corruption in the political and judicial systems, restrictions of the freedom of religion, the sanctioning of torture, and denial of fair trial. Syria also forbids international monitoring agencies from entering prisons or detention centers.

In direct violation of Articles 2 and 19 of the UDHR, the Syrian Security Services—even before the outbreak of civil war—continued to arrest and imprison people based upon their political activities and their membership in certain groups. In 2008, over 75 such detainees were sentenced. The charges ranged from belonging to the Muslim Brotherhood, participating in Kurdish political activism, speaking out against the government, and belonging to other forbidden political groups. One particular case, which received heightened media attention, involved political activist Kamal al-Labwani, a doctor and founder of the Democratic Liberal Gathering. He was sentenced to 12 years imprisonment for endorsing peaceful reform in Syria abroad. On April 23, 2008, the Syrian Military Court added another three years to the 12-year sentence he is already serving for supposedly insulting prison authorities. Similarly, Habib Saleh, a writer and political analyst, was arrested on May 7, 2008, on charges of criticizing the government and supporting the opposition.

The Kurds are a constant target of Syria's security forces. As Syria's biggest non-Arab ethnicity, the group has long faced discrimination. In violation of Articles 2 and 27, many Kurds who are born in Syria are still denied citizenship. Syrian authorities also attempt to prevent the teaching of Kurdish in schools. Syrian security forces opened fire on a group of Kurds who were celebrating the New Year on March 20, 2008, killing three people. Kurdish political demonstrations are also the focus of security forces attacks; on September 14, 2008, over 50 Kurds were given six-month jail sentences for their participation in political demonstrations. The activists were protesting the assassination of Sheikh Ma'shuq al-Khaznawi, a former leader in the Kurdish community.

Syria has also faced a growing refugee problem, as asylum-seekers from both Iraq and Palestine have been increasing in number, although the civil war has staunched this flow and significantly damaged some of the entrenched Palestinian camps in Damascus. An estimated 1–1.5 million Iraqi refugees have sought shelter in Syria. While Syria does give the refugees access to hospitals and schools, they are refused the right to work due to the rising Syrian unemployment rate.

ECONOMY

Overview of the Economy

Syria has traditionally had a weak, mixed economy, which has been further destabilized by the chaos of war and the economic sanctions imposed by countries critical of Assad's response to dissidents. Western bans on Syrian oil exports have staunched the flow of much-needed revenue, while hyperinflation has severely devalued the national currency. In 2013, the Syrian pound was down to one-sixth of its pre-2011 value. Previously the country's economic center, Damascus has been the site of relentless shelling and sniper fire, with many businesses damaged and looted and public markets (souks) similarly plundered. Consequently, the black market has begun to thrive. In 2013 alone, Syria's foreign currency reserves fell to between $2 and $5 billion (USD), some $13 to $15 billion (USD) lower than it had been just two years before. Syria now depends largely on credit from its remaining allies, Russian, Iran, and China.

The Syrian gross domestic product (GDP) was $107.6 billion (USD) in 2011, the last time accurate economic statistics were available. Its per capita GDP was an estimated $5,100 (USD) that same year. The country's labor force was estimated to be around 4.022 million in 2014. Unemployment stood at 33 percent in 2014, although these statistics may not incorporate Syrians displaced by the war and unable to find work. The unemployment rate therefore may be much higher. Far fewer women than men are employed overall, particularly in urban areas, although some women have been forced to be their family's sole breadwinner due to complications created by war. The country's major export markets in 2013 were Iraq, Saudi Arabia, Kuwait, the United Arab Emirates, and Libya.

Industry

Industry occupies 16 percent of the work force and, in 2014, represented 22.7 percent of the GDP. The processing of textiles, petroleum, seed oils, chemicals, building materials, auto assembly, and food processing are all part of the industrial sector. Of these, the largest is textiles, yielding products made of cotton, silk, and wool.

Oil has been a major export for the last three decades, though the oil is not of the highest quality and the reserves currently being exploited might soon be exhausted. Syria also gains revenue by having oil pipelines run across its territory. The natural gas industry, smaller than the oil industry, is also important.

Labor

In 2014, the labor force of Syria was comprised of 4.002 million workers. As of 2008, 67 percent worked in the services sector, 16 percent worked in the industrial sector, and 17 percent worked in the agricultural sector.

Energy/Power/Natural Resources

Syria has modest reserves of crude oil and natural gas. Minerals found in large quantities are phosphate, salt, and crude asphalt. Sand (silica), gypsum, and gravel have also been mined for construction materials. Two of the country's most important natural resources, however, are its fertile land and its waterways' capacity to generate hydroelectric power.

Among the environmental problems that Syria is facing are industrial pollution of rivers, untreated wastewater from urban centers, and poor land management. The latter problem has led to soil erosion and desertification and threatens vital ecosystems such as the Al Ghutah oasis, which is decreasing in size.

Fishing

Syria has a small fishing industry, and its aquaculture is primarily conducted in freshwater. Fish farming itself—established in the late 1950s by the Aquatic Life Service (now the Directorate of Fisheries Resources), part of the Ministry of Agriculture—consists principally of pond culture and cage culture and accounts for approximately 50 percent of the country's overall production. Some unconventional methods have been employed to foster a viable expanded aquaculture model, and this has included using salinized irrigation and drainage canals for raising fish. Still, the main fish species produced commercially are carp and tilapia. Commercial fishing also takes place in Syria's inland rivers, farms, and lakes, as well as on the Mediterranean coastline.

Forestry

Approximately 2.4 percent of Syria is forested, making its forestry industry virtually non-existent. After the dissolution of the Ottoman Empire, the forests that once belonged to the Sultan reverted to the state. Therefore, all Syrian forests are state owned, and, to date, few conservation or management efforts have been made. Common tree species include Turkish and Aleppo pines; Cilician fir; Turkey, kermes, and Palestine oak; cedar of Lebanon, Mediterranean cypress, and common chestnut.

Mining/Metals

Phosphates represent a valuable export for Syria, with the country exporting 3.2 million tons in 2008. The following year, Syria became the world's ninth largest producer of phosphate rock. The phosphate industry is expected to grow over the course of the early 21st century. Other vital natural resources include chrome and manganese ores, iron ore, rock salt, natural crude asphalt, silica, gypsum, and marble.

Agriculture

Agriculture represents 16.4 percent of the GDP and occupies 17 percent of the work force, though Syria's climate does not create ideal growing conditions. One-quarter of the land area is under cultivation, and the potential for irrigation projects in currently fallow areas could lead to greater land development. The government has implemented programs to discourage poor soil management, since reliance on fertilizers and failure to rotate crops has decreased the land's productivity. Major crops include cotton, wheat, barley, lentils, chickpeas, olives, sugar beets, citrus and other fruits, dates, corn, tobacco, and olives.

Animal Husbandry

Grazing land comprises 45 percent of Syria's land area, and sheep—Syria's most valuable livestock thanks to the high price brought by mutton from the Awassi breed—are most often the ones who graze the land. Goats and cattle are the other most common livestock. While chickens are kept for both their egg production and potential for meat, buffalo are also raised, along with camels and mules, which are employed as beasts of burden. Butter and ghee (clarified butter), sheep's milk and meat, along with cheese and eggs represent Syria's most abundant output.

Tourism

The Syrian Civil War has made travel to the country extremely dangerous. As of mid-2015, over 200,000 people have died because of the violence, which has included bombings, airstrikes, and persistent gunfire. Foreign nationals, particularly Westerners, have also been frequent targets of kidnappings and executions. Before the war, tourism did generate some substantial income for the country. In 2004, for example, an estimated 5.8 million tourists visited Syria, generating $1.8 billion USD and employing 92,000 people.

Certainly, many of Syria's most interesting tourist sites are archaeological, and artifacts from these sites have been exhibited in important collections throughout the country, particularly in the National Museum of Damascus. The ancient Canaanite city of Ugarit has traditionally been a large draw, as is the Church of St. Simeon the Stylite and the early Christian ruins, called the Dead Cities, which are scattered across Syria. Sadly, the once well-maintained Roman amphitheater at Bosra and the ruins of Palmyra are currently all on the UNESCO endangered list, as they have been damaged by gunfire and bombings. Mosaics at the Roman ruins at Apamea have been severely effaced by both shelling and subsequent bulldozing. The once well-preserved crusader castle, the Crac des Chevaliers (Castle of the Knights), is also currently on UNESCO's endangered sites list for having taken a direct hit during shelling. Numerous other sites have been physically damaged, occupied by troops, or otherwise looted, and there is a burgeoning black market in antiquities.

The cities of Damascus, Aleppo, and Hama all have old quarters filled with sacred and domestic architecture. However, many of these communities have since been leveled. A fire that started during a conflict between rebel forces and regime troops, for example, ravaged the covered market in Aleppo.

In early 2014, the London *Telegraph* estimated that, once fighting ceases, it may take five years before the country will again be prepared for tourists. However, some damage is irreversible. The single most famous building in Damascus is probably the Umayyad Mosque, one of the holiest sites in Islam and the former location of both a Roman temple and a Christian church. It now stands in ruins, with its 11th-century minaret having been destroyed in April 2013. Amid the violence and in the absence of paying work, some tour guides and bus drivers, who previously ferried tourists through Damascus, are now being paid to take refugees to Lebanon, although this is an extremely dangerous activity, since they must pass through both government and dissident lines.

Kianoosh Hashemzadeh, Michael Aliprandi, &
Savannah Schroll Guz

DO YOU KNOW?

- Saint Simeon the Stylite stood atop a pillar for 37 years out of religious devotion in what is now northern Syria, near Aleppo. After his death, a church was built in his honor, the ruins of which still include a small portion of the pillar.

- The world's earliest known musical texts and one of the earliest alphabets were both unearthed on tablets at the ancient site of Ugarit, near Latakia on the Mediterranean coast. Scholars date them to between the 14th and 12th centuries BCE. Texts are in the Ugaritic language, which is linguistically related to Hebrew, Aramaic, and Phoenician.

- The head of Saint John the Baptist (Yaḥyā ibn Zakarīyā) was reputedly interred in the Umayyad Mosque in Damascus.

- According to the Christian Bible, St. Paul's conversion to Christianity occurred on the road to Damascus, and he is reputed to have lived on a street in the old city referred to in the Bible as the "street called Straight."

Bibliography

Christian C. Sahner. "*Among the Ruins: Syria Past and Present.*" Oxford, UK: *Oxford UP*. 2014.

Dalal Kade-Badra and Elie Badra. "Flavours of Aleppo: Celebrating Syrian Cuisine." Vancouver, BC: *Whitecap Books*. 2013.

David W. Lesch. "Syria: The Fall of the House of Assad." New Haven, CT: *Yale UP*. 2012.

Fouad Ajami. "The Syrian Rebellion." Stanford, CA: *Hoover Institution Press*, 2012.

John McHugo. "Syria: A Recent History." London: *Saqi Books*. 2015.

Lena Jayyusi, ed. "On Entering the Sea: The Erotic and Other Poetry of Nizar Qabbani." 2nd ed. Brooklyn, NY: *Interlink Books*. 2013.

Malu Halasa, Zaher Omareen, and Nawara Mahfoud, eds. "Syria Speaks: Art and Culture from the Frontline." London: *Saqi Books*. 2014.

Miriam Cooke. "Dissident Syria: Making Oppositional Arts Official." Durham, NC: *Duke University Press*, 2007.

Samar Yazbek, ed. "A Woman in the Crossfire: Diaries of the Syrian Revolution." Transl. Max Weiss. London: *Haus Publishing*. 2012.

Ulfat Idilbi. "Sabriya: Damascus Bitter Sweet." 2nd ed. Brooklyn, NY: *Interlink Books*. 2003.

Works Cited

_____. "Death Everywhere: War Crimes and Human Rights Abuses in Aleppo." *Amnesty International*. 4 May 2015. http://www.amnestyusa.org/research/reports/death-everywhere-war-crimes-and-human-rights-abuses-in-aleppo.

"Aleppo." *Encyclopaedia Britannica*. Encylopaedia Britannica, Inc., 2015. http://www.britannica.com/place/Aleppo.

"Bostra." *Encyclopaedia Britannica*. Encylopaedia Britannica, Inc., 2015. http://www.britannica.com/place/Bostra.

"Damascus." *Encyclopaedia Britannica*. Encylopaedia Britannica, Inc., 2015. http://www.britannica.com/place/Damascus.

"Duraid Lahham Official Website." *Duraid Lahham*, 2005. http://www.duraidlahham.com/indexa.htm.

"Palmyra." Encycolpaedia Britannica. *Encylopaedia Britannica, Inc.,* 2015. http://www.britannica.com/place/Palmyra-Syria.

"Syria." Freedom of the Press 2013. *Freedom House*. 2015. https://freedomhouse.org/report/freedom-press/2013/syria#.VdDg_GBRHIU.

"Syria Profile—Overview." *News: Middle East*. BBC, 25 June 2015. http://news.bbc.co.uk/2/hi/middle_east/country_profiles/801669.stm.

"Syria." *Human Rights Watch*. Human Rights Watch, 2015. Web. https://www.hrw.org/middle-east/n-africa/syria.

"Syrian Arab Republic." *Amnesty International Report 2014/15*. Amnesty International, 2015. https://www.amnesty.org/en/countries/middle-east-and-north-africa/syria/report-syria/.

"Syrian Arab Republic." *UNdata*. United Nations Statistics Division. 2015. https://data.un.org/CountryProfile.aspx?crName=Syrian%20Arab%20Republic.

"Temple Of Bel Damaged By Mortars as Syria Violence Hits Ancient Archeological Site In Palmyra" *The World Post. TheHuffingtonPost.com, Inc.,* 3 Jun. 2013. http://www.huffingtonpost.com/2013/04/03/temple-of-bel-damaged-syria_n_3005392.html.

"Women's Defense Units (YPJ) Internal System." *People's Defense Units Official Website*. YPJ Headquarters Leadership/Fermandariya Bîryargeha YPJ, 3 May 2015. http://ypgrojava.com/en/index.php/ypj.

"World Heritage List: Syria." UNESCO World Heritage Convention. *UNESCO World Heritage Centre.* 2015. http://whc.unesco.org/en/statesparties/sy.

Alyssa Cogan. "Voices of Syria's youth: What it's like to grow up as a refugee." *MercyCorps.org.* Mercy Corps, 20 Jun. 2014. Web. http://www.mercycorps.org/articles/turkey-iraq-jordan-lebanon-syria/voices-syrias-youth-what-its-grow-refugee.

Barbara Plett. "Syria's Youth Look to Bashar." *BBC News.* BBC, 22 Aug. 2000. http://news.bbc.co.uk/2/hi/middle_east/891754.stm.

Carole Kerbage. "Syrian Women: From the Kitchen to the Workforce." *Al Monitor: The Pulse of the Middle East.* Al-Monitor, 30 Sept. 2013. http://www.al-monitor.com/pulse/culture/2013/09/changing-gender-roles-among-displaced-syrians.html#.

J. Rolley. "Forest conditions in Syria and Lebanon." FAO Corporate Document Repository. *Food and Agriculture Organization of the United Nations.* 2015. http://www.fao.org/docrep/x5343e/x5343e06.htm#.

Lizzie Porter. "Syria three years on: what for the future of tourism?" *Telegraph Travel.* Telegraph Media Group Limited, 19 Mar. 2014. Web. http://www.telegraph.co.uk/travel/destinations/middleeast/syria/10708151/Syria-three-years-on-what-for-the-future-of-tourism.html

M. Paul Lewis, M. Paul, Gary F. Simons, and Charles D. Fennig, eds. "Languages of Syria." *Ethnologue: Languages of the World.* 18th ed. Dallas, Texas: SIL International, 2015. Web. http://www.ethnologue.com/country/sy/languages.

Michael Slackman. "An Arab Artist Says All the World Really Isn't a Stage." *New York Times.* The New York Times Company, 19 Aug. 2006. http://www.nytimes.com/2006/08/19/world/middleeast/19lahhman.html?ex=1313640000&en=0bae426f0a20a241&ei=5090&partner=rssuserland&emc=rss&_r=0.

Peter Clark. "Ulfat Idilbi: Renowned Syrian Fiction Writer, Lecturer and Feminist." *The Guardian.* Guardian News and Media Limited, 19 Apr. 2007. Web. http://www.theguardian.com/news/2007/apr/19/guardianobituaries.booksobituaries.

Rhett A. Butler, Rhett A. &and Jeremy L. Hance. "Largest Cities in Syria, Ranked by Population." *Mongabay.com.* Mongabay, 2015. http://population.mongabay.com/population/syria.

Ruth Sherlock, Ruth. "UN accuses Isil jihadists of 'ethnic cleansing.'" *Telegraph.* Telegraph Media Group, Limited, 25 Aug. 2014. Web. http://www.telegraph.co.uk/news/worldnews/middleeast/iraq/11055125/UN-accuses-Isil-jihadists-of-ethnic-cleansing.html.

UN Women. "New study to examine women's role in peace and security over the past 15 years." *UN Women.* 10 Sept. 2014. http://www.unwomen.org/en/news/stories/2014/9/launch-of-global-study-on-resolution-1325.

World Economic Forum, ed. "Syria." *The Global Gender Gap Report 2014.* World Economic Forum, 2015. Web. http://reports.weforum.org/global-gender-gap-report-2014/economies/#economy=SYR.

Zachary Laub, Zachary & and Jonathan Masters. "Syria's Crisis and the Global Response." *Council on Foreign Relations.* Council on Foreign Relations, 11 Sept. 2013. Web. http://www.cfr.org/syria/syrias-crisis-global-response/p28402#p6.

Ancient ruins of Roman amphitheater in Dougga, Tunisia

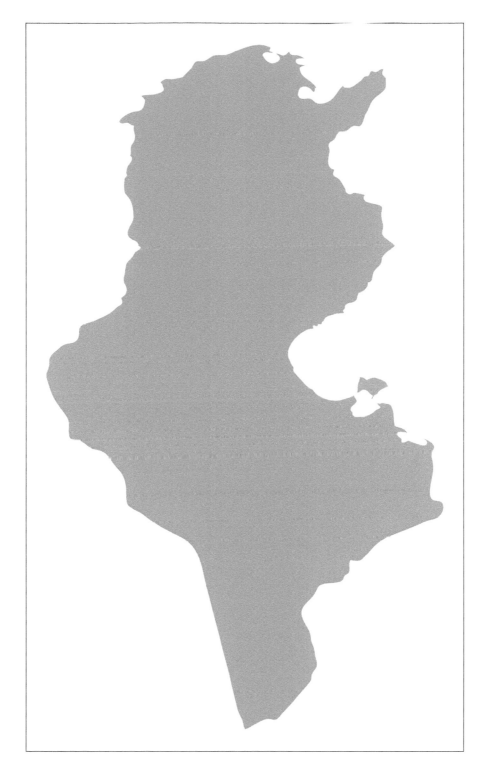

TUNISIA

Introduction

The Republic of Tunisia is a Northwest African nation located on the Mediterranean Sea. Its neighbors are Algeria and Libya. The region is called the Maghreb, which is the Arabic name for northwestern Africa.

The land's cultural heritage stretches back to the time of ancient Carthage, whose ruins lie near the modern capital of Tunis. At various times, the country was governed by the Romans and the Ottomans. It is a member of the Arab League and African Union, and has established trade agreements with the European Union. Tunisia has been a de facto single-party state since gaining independence from France in 1956, but this changed in 2011.

In December 2010, following the self-immolation of a street vendor protesting the country's rampant poverty and repressive regime, The Jasmine Revolution—which gave rise to the larger Arab Spring—commenced and lasted for three weeks and six days, from December 17, 2010 to January 14, 2011. Subsequent protests forced President Zine al-Abidine Ben Ali, who had been in office for 23 years, to flee in January 2011, and a constitutionally-appointed interim president, Fouad Mebazaa, took office. Mebazaa, along with Prime Minister Mohamed Ghannouchi, then dissolved Ben Ali's party, the Constitutional Democratic Rally (CDR).

On October 23, 2011, the first free and democratic elections were held, and the Islamist Ennhada party won a majority of the interim government's legislative seats. However, after two assassinations of government officials by militant Islamic sympathizers and with widespread concern that extremism would take hold in Tunisia, the Ennhada was voted out of majority rule in October 2014 and a decidedly secularist president was elected. In 2014, Tunisia adopted a new constitution and established a unicameral legislative body, yet it continues to face political unrest, terrorist upsurges, and challenges to both civil liberties and human rights.

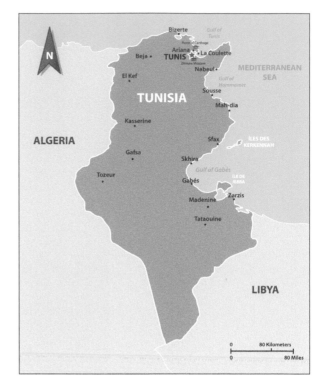

GENERAL INFORMATION

Official Language: Arabic
Population: 11,037,225 (2015 estimate)
Currency: Tunisian dinar
Coins: 1,000 millimes equal one dinar. Coins are issued in denominations of 5, 10, 20, 50, 100, 200, and 500 millimes, and ½, 1, 2, and 5 dinars.
Land Area: 155,360 square kilometers (59,984 square miles)

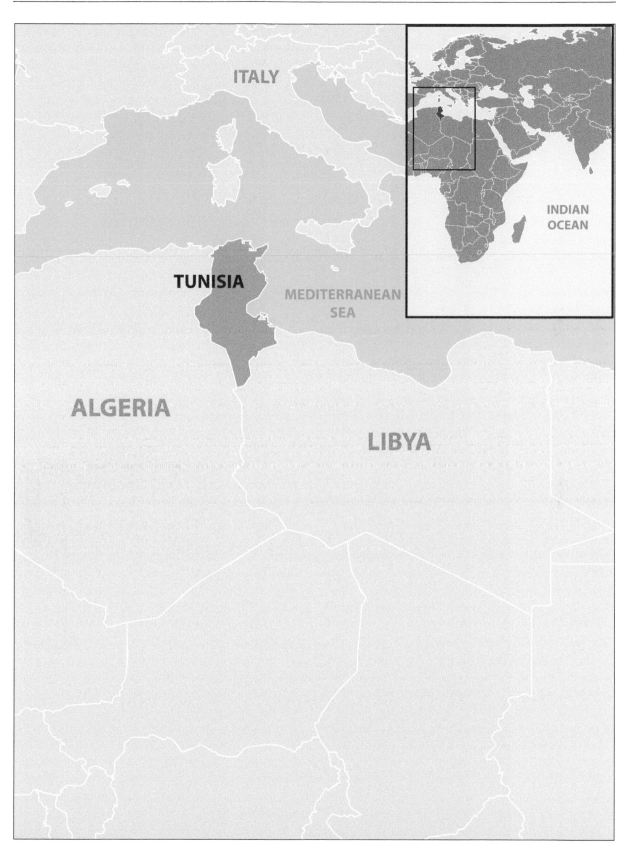

Principal Cities by Population (2014):

- Tunis (651,183)
- Sfax, also Safāqis (330,440)
- Sousse, also Sūsa (271,428)
- Ettadhamen-Mnihla, also At-Tadaman (196,298)
- Kairouan, also Al Qairawān (186,653)
- Gabès, also Qābis (152,921)
- Bizerte, also Banzart (142,966)
- Ariana, also Aryanah (114,486)
- La Soukra (129,693)
- Gafsa, also Qafṣa (111,170)

Water Area: 8,250 square kilometers (3,185 square miles)
National Anthems: "Ḥumāt al-Ḥimị" (Arabic, "Defenders of the Homeland")
Capital: Tunis
Time Zone: GMT +1
Flag Description: The Tunisian flag is bright red with a centered white circle depicting a red crescent and star. The red symbolizes Islam, and the crescent and star are also common Islamic symbols associated with the Ottoman Empire.

Population

Tunisia has a relatively youthful population; around 36 percent are under the age of 25, while 45 percent are between 25 and 54 years old. The estimated median age is just over 31 years. Most of the population is urban, living near the fertile, coastal areas. The geographic concentration is a necessity. The Atlas Mountains and the Sahara Desert lie to the south, and both are harsh environments.

At 98 percent, Arabs are the dominant ethnic group in Tunisia, though many people are also of Berber background. Additionally, there is a very small Jewish minority—about 1 percent—whose families have lived in Tunisia since ancient times. A European minority of less than one percent also calls Tunisia home.

Languages

Arabic is the official language of Tunisia, and is spoken by the large majority of the population. The local dialects of Arabic are similar to those spoken elsewhere in the Maghreb (northwest Africa), but differ greatly from those spoken in the Middle East. Use of the various Berber languages, like Tashelhit and Atlas Tamazight, has dwindled, but these are still spoken by a small portion of the population. A strong French influence exists from the era of French colonialism, and French remains widely spoken, though Arabic is the official language.

Native People & Ethnic Groups

The modern population of Tunisia is largely Arab (98 percent), but there is a large Berber population. The Berbers (from whose name comes the geographical term "Barbary Coast"), were known to Europeans as "Moors" during the Middle Ages. Despite Arab predominance, Berber languages continue to be spoken, especially in rural areas.

Culturally, Tunisia is part of the Maghreb ("the West" or, literally, "sunset"), the coastal region of North Africa lying between the Mediterranean coast and the Atlas Mountains. The term applies usually to Tunisia, Morocco, Algeria, Libya, and Mauritania, and these peoples are of Arab and Berber background.

Religions

The overwhelming majority (99.1 percent) of Tunisians are Muslims. While there are also small Shia and Sufi communities, almost all Tunisians belong to the Sunni branch of Islam and specifically to the subdivision that adheres to the Malikite madhhab (one of the branch's four major interpretations of Sharia law). The constitution allows for freedom of religion and practice of that religion, unless it disturbs the public order. However, Islam is the official religion, and the president is required to be a Muslim. Islamic prayer leaders receive government salaries, and the Grand Mufti of the Republic, the most senior Islamic official, is appointed by the president. There are, however, many restrictions on the practice of religion. No foreign religious groups, for example, may seek to gain converts. The government also is opposed to Islamic fundamentalism and maintains strict controls on the use of mosques and women's wearing of the hijab, or head covering.

Approximately 1,700 Jews live in Tunisia; the majority, around 1,000, live on the island of Djerba, where there has been a Jewish community for 2,500 years. Around 700 Jews live in and around Tunis and are descended in part from Southern Europeans who settled there during the Renaissance.

Climate

Tunisia has a temperate, Mediterranean climate in the northern, coastal region. Here, winters are mild and moderately wet, while summers are often hot and dry. For this reason, the most pleasant times of year are spring and fall. The average summer temperature is 32° Celsius (90° Fahrenheit), although in July and August, temperatures can reach as high as 42° Celsius (104° Fahrenheit). The average winter temperature along the coast is a pleasant 20° Celsius (68° Fahrenheit). On average, Tunisia receives about 500 mm (19.68 in) of precipitation annually.

The interior has an African climate; southern Tunisia is arid, blending into the Sahara Desert in the extreme south. The southern region may receive as little as 150 millimeters (6 inches) of rain per year, though parts of the Sahara are essentially rain-free. Daily temperatures in southern Tunisia regularly climb to 45 °C (113 °F).

ENVIRONMENT & GEOGRAPHY

Topography

Tunisia has several sharply defined geographical regions. The north is a fertile coastal zone, lying between the Mediterranean Sea to the east and the rugged but fairly low Atlas Mountains to the west. The Atlas Range's highest point in Tunisia is Jebel ech Chambi, at 1,544 meters (5,066 feet) above sea level.

The long coastline (1,148 kilometers, or 713 miles) forms part of the famous "Barbary Coast," taking its name from the Berber peoples. The Tunisian portion possesses many excellent

harbors, including Bizerte (once the site of a French naval base and currently the northernmost city in Tunisia). Tunisia is also relatively close to Sicily, which lies only 130 kilometers (81 miles) away.

The central part of the country is a semi-arid plain, with many salt flats and the huge salt lake known as Chott Djerid, which is also the country's lowest point at 17 meters (56 feet) below sea level. The southern region of Tunisia is covered by the Sahara Desert and dotted with occasional oases.

Plants & Animals

Rich plains as well as Mediterranean-style woodlands and steppe cover Tunisia's coastal region. Large mammals are rare. Smaller species common to the North African coast are Barbary sheep, gazelles, and the wild boar. Bou-Hedma National Park—on UNESCO's tentative list of World Heritage Sites since 2008—contains many wild animals, including endangered species such as the scimitar-horned oryx. The monk seal, which once lived along the Tunisian coast, is now locally extinct.

Heading southward, toward the Sahara, the country becomes increasingly dry. In this steppe region, one can find numerous small mammals such as gerbils and jerboa. The ostrich was once common, but became extinct in the 20th century. Few species are found in the vast Sahara Desert itself.

CUSTOMS & COURTESIES

Greetings

Greetings are extremely important in Tunisia, and people attach a great deal of significance to them. Thus, failing to acknowledge someone is considered rude, and children are taught from a young age to greet their elders as a sign of respect. When greeting someone, the expression "Asslema" ("Peace be upon you") is commonly used. A more formal version of this greeting is "as-salam alaykum," to which the appropriate response is the equally formal "wa alaykum e-salam," which translates to "and upon you, peace." Greetings also differ between countryside and cities, the origins of which come from a combination of Berber and Islamic traditions.

In the countryside, men greet each other with a handshake, followed by placing the hand on one's own heart to signify sincerity. Additionally, men will often kiss each other once on each cheek while shaking hands. This gesture occurs whether two people know each other or are meeting for the first time. While women would also kiss each other once on each cheek, it is considered improper for men and women to greet each other with a kiss. It is also important to note that when shaking hands, the right hand is always used, as the left hand is associated with the cleansing of the body in Muslim culture and thus thought to be impure.

Generally, less conservative traditions are adhered to in urban areas, and men may kiss women on the cheek; this is especially true among young people. This shows the influence of the French, who greet each other in a similar way. However, in Tunisia, as opposed to France, men may also kiss men on the cheek, though this is becoming less common. Depending on the situation and the individuals, people meeting for the first time may kiss or just shake hands. When meeting the friend of a good friend, for example, kisses are usually given. (In business situations, there is only a handshake, with no kissing involved.)

Gestures & Etiquette

Tunisians are known for their warmth and hospitality, both of which are important in Tunisian culture. In general, Tunisians welcome foreign visitors from all origins and ethnicities, and try their best to make them feel at home. Even in shops, it is not uncommon to be invited to sit down and drink tea with the proprietor.

Nonetheless, Tunisia is a Muslim state, and certain etiquette, such as refraining from wearing revealing attire, is expected. Additionally, during the Muslim month of Ramadan, in which fasting occurs during the day, it is considered disrespectful to eat within view of someone who is fasting. Therefore, non-fasting Tunisians are typically discreet, and restaurants that are operating often obstruct the view from the street.

Tunisians commonly use a lot of imagery, symbolism, and colorful proverbs in their speech to convey meaning and are known for having a subtle, sarcastic sense of humor. In fact, there is much that is not explicitly spoken in Arabic culture, but communicated through implication. In addition, Tunisians are great gesticulators, much like the Italians, and many messages are communicated exclusively through hand gestures. For example, pointing upward with all the fingers and thumb together, while the palm faces the body, signifies "wait" or "good," depending on the context. While it is considered rude to point at someone and winking at someone is also considered impolite, Tunisians do beckon others by waving the fingers toward the body while the palm is turned downward—an orientation opposite the North American beckoning gesture. Also important to note is that the symbol for okay in many Western countries means the opposite in Tunisia, indicating something is unpleasant or a 'zero.'

Eating/Meals

Mealtime is a very important part of Tunisian tradition, and dining typically occurs at home among family and friends. Generally, meals are usually eaten in a relaxed way with not much talking.

The midday meal is typically the largest meal of the day and is traditionally followed by a nap. If possible, people return home for this meal and continue working afterward. In the summertime, workers may be given a special schedule, whereby they start earlier in the morning and are released in the afternoon. Since Tunisia has a particularly hot climate, this affords people the opportunity to stay in after their meal and nap. Later, in the early evening when it's cooler, they may go out to a café and return home for the evening meal, which is generally smaller than the midday meal. Dessert usually consists of native seasonal fruits, such as dates, figs, peaches, or tangerines, or a cake or pastry served with green mint tea in the afternoon.

The older tradition, still practiced in rural Tunisia, is for the family and guests to remove their shoes and sit on the carpet or on low wooden chairs around a low table, sometimes but not always circular, and to share meals from communal dishes. This is a way to show friendship and strong ties. Usually fried hot green peppers are served, and olives are always on the table. After the couscous, fresh fennel is served to cleanse the mouth and help with digestion. In cities, people generally eat around regular tables and sit on chairs, using individual plates.

Visiting

In Tunisia, visiting unannounced is considered quite normal. Generally, guests are always well received, as hospitality is a key value held by all Tunisians. In fact, many Tunisians prepare additional food at mealtimes to prepare for such visits.

When someone is invited for dinner or lunch, the table has to be covered with food. This shows the guest that he is very welcome and appreciated in the house. Additionally, the piece of meat that is given to the guest is special, usually the best cut available. The old tradition, still practiced in rural communities, is to honor a guest by slaughtering a lamb (or goat), often in the guest's presence, and preparing it with couscous. Veal is usually reserved for weddings and other large celebrations due to the animal's size.

During Ramadan, visiting becomes even more important. Every night, the fast is customarily broken with a substantial meal featuring traditional Tunisian dishes. A special work schedule is also in effect, cutting the workday in half. At the end of Ramadan is Eid al-Fitr (Festival of the Breaking of the Fast), a celebration that typically lasts up to three days. During this time, it is common for neighbors to visit and exchange homemade pastries, and families will usually gather at the home of the oldest or most respected relative.

LIFESTYLE

Family

Family remains an important institution in Tunisia, and families stay connected throughout life. Familial ties are strong, and older siblings are always shown more respect. In sickness and strife, or in peace and prosperity, visiting family is always expected, and it is considered rude to neglect one's relatives.

Families sometimes live in clusters within neighborhoods. Very often, especially in earlier times, one entire street might be inhabited by the same family and would even bear that family's name. In modern times, kinship clusters have loosened due to urban migration and emigration, and the increasing number of youth who leave home to study. However, the bond of family remains strong, even when relatives are separated.

Housing

The traditional Tunisian house consists of a square inner courtyard, often open-air, surrounded by the rooms of the house. A long passageway connects the front entrance to the rest of the house, and windows are often covered with iron bars or wooden shutters. In earlier eras, all of this served to keep the women of the family safe from the eyes of strangers. Traditional Tunisian houses, especially in coastal towns, are of cement and stucco construction, with many painted white. Generally, roofs are flat and can serve as terraces. In the oasis town of Tozeur, the exteriors of houses are covered with the locally produced yellow bricks, which are often arranged in intricate patterns and geometric designs.

Distinctive characteristics of traditional Tunisian houses are the arched doorways and heavy wooden doors dotted with metal studs, which often form an ornate pattern. Frequently, these doors are painted a stunning blue, as is the case with most of the doors and shuttered windows in Sidi Bou Saïd (an enclave, or town, outside the capital of Tunis). On the interior, floors are usually of ceramic or stone tile, which helps keep the floors cool in the hot climate. Tunisian carpets are brought out to cover the floors in cooler months. With the arrival of the French in the 19th century, European-style dwellings became more popular, and after independence, Tunisia continued to modernize. Modern Western-style apartments are now common in urban areas, and many urban Tunisians have moved into houses in the suburbs that combine Western and Tunisian architecture.

One can see the relics of an ancient Berber way of life on the plateaus of Matmâta in southern Tunisia. The traditional Berber dwelling in this arid region is comprised of a pit dug into the ground to form a central patio and a series of subterranean caves off to each side that serve as rooms. Alternately, it can simply consist of caves dug into a mountainside. One advantage to this type of housing is the natural temperature regulation: they stay at a consistently comfortable temperature despite the conditions outside. Today, many of the Berber inhabitants of the region have moved into modern houses, but at least 100 subterranean dwellings remain in use. In southern rural areas, dwellings may be as simple as tents made from camel and goat hair, which are the traditional residences of the desert-dwelling Bedouin people in this part of Tunisia.

Food

Tunisia's cuisine is largely influenced by traditional Mediterranean and Middle Eastern ingredients, and the country's rich agricultural tradition and long Mediterranean coastline. Thus, common ingredients include olives; fresh seafood and meats; chickpeas; widely varying vegetables; nuts; fruits, such as citrus, figs, and dates; and fragrant spices, such as cumin, caraway, coriander, and hot pepper.

Harissa is a popular spicy red pepper paste used throughout Tunisia. It is made by roasting (or, traditionally, drying on rooftops) a variety of red peppers, like serranos and sweet red bells, and then grinding them with olive oil, garlic, coriander, and caraway. The final product has the consistency of a thick dip or paste and is eaten alone with olive oil and bread, spread on sandwiches or crêpes, or used to season stews and other dishes. Considered a common condiment of sorts, harissa, along with olive oil, olives and bread, is found on restaurant tables in Tunisia in the same way salt and pepper adorn restaurant tables in Western countries.

The most popular national dish is couscous, a very fine, round semolina pasta of Berber origin. Couscous is traditionally steamed in a special two-tiered pot over a stew made with lamb, fish, or beef. Some of the stew liquid is added to the couscous at the end to give it flavor. Generally, Tunisian couscous is spicy, as it is often mixed with a harissa and tomato base. A common snack or appetizer is the brik (pronounced breek), which consists of very thin dough filled with a raw egg, deep fried until golden and crispy (the egg cooks, but the yolk remains runny). Tunisian tuna and harissa are often added.

Other traditional dishes include salade méchouia, a piquant cold salad made from roasted long green peppers and tomatoes, mashed together with garlic, onions, olive oil, and spices, such as coriander. It is often served before a meal in restaurants or at home, on a plate garnished with olives, olive oil, Tunisian canned tuna, and a boiled egg. A tagine (or tajine) is deep ceramic dish with a conical lid, but in Tunisia, it can also refer to a popular egg-based casserole, similar to a thick frittata, which may be baked in such a dish. Tagines can contain almost any combination of ingredients: ground meat or chicken, potatoes, ricotta cheese, spinach, eggplant, peas, or other vegetables.

Tunisians are famous for eating lots of bread with their meals, and baguette making there is often considered an art. (In fact, the prize for the best Parisian baguette in 2008 went to a Tunisian.) Tunisian pastries are heavily influenced by Turkish confections and traditional Arab pastries. Baklava and other filled phyllo dough treats are quite common, as are sweet rolled balls made of almond or pistachio pastes and flavored with rose, orange blossom, or geranium water. One distinctly Tunisian sweet is the makroudh, a syrupy sweet, date-filled fried semolina pastry originating in Kairouan. Such sweets may be accompanied by a sweet hot green tea flavored with mint, a Tunisian favorite.

Life's Milestones

Because Tunisia is a predominantly Muslim culture, there are many religious rituals concerning life's major events. Beginning at birth, circumcision is a common custom for males and is typically followed by a celebration involving family and friends. Traditionally, a lamb or calf is slaughtered on the threshold of the house for the occasion.

Marriage is an elaborate ceremony that traditionally lasts a week, with every day characterized by special events, such as the groom bringing gifts to the bride's house. On the day before the wedding, the bride receives henna decoration on her hands and feet in the company of women friends. The wedding celebration itself is a huge event, and many guests are invited. Traditionally, the bride is costumed in a heavy dress and makeup, and the couple is seated on a dais (raised platform) where guests approach to congratulate them.

When there is a death in the family, the period separating death from burial is typically short. Traditionally, family and friends gather in a house, with women and men separated in different rooms. People dress in normal colors, as it is not customary to wear black at Tunisian funerals. Forty days after the burial, the family and friends organize a party centered on remembrance, which traditionally features the reading of the Koran (Islam's holy book) and Koranic chants. A traditional couscous, made with lamb, raisins, and sometimes boiled eggs, may be prepared for both the funeral and the subsequent remembrance ceremony.

CULTURAL HISTORY

Art

Due to its long history of conquest and assimilation—the region has been invaded and occupied by the Romans, Vandals, Byzantines, Arabs, Turks, Spaniards, and French—Tunisia has a uniquely diverse and rich artistic tradition. The original inhabitants of the region were the Berbers, whose art included jewelry, leather, and carpet weaving. Carpet making would develop into a renowned tradition in Tunisia. There are two main types of carpets: those woven by the nomadic Berbers, and the hand-knotted carpets of Kairouan, considered the oldest Islamic settlement and the holiest city in Tunisia. The Berber carpets are of a more rustic design, are made from longhaired sheep's wool of white or beige, and bear warm-toned geometric patterns, simplified animal shapes, or folkloric motifs. The Kairouan carpets are more refined, with deeper colors and more intricate and regular patterns, similar to classical Persian rugs. This style was introduced to Kairouan in the 19th century by the Turks.

Ceramics and mosaics would become an important part of Tunisia's artistic heritage, beginning with the Phoenicians and the Carthaginian Empire and extending into Roman and Early Christian times. Some of the world's earliest mosaics, made from terra cotta, have been unearthed in Tunisia and date back to the fifth century BCE. Tunisia, in fact, proclaims to have the finest collection of mosaics in the world (particularly Roman), with many dating between the second and fourth centuries CE. Many of these mosaics display scenes of hunting and games, mythological images and legends, and portraits.

Following Arab invasion, Tunisian art was largely Islamic in nature and often characterized as Arabesque (a geometric form of Islamic art influenced by Persia and the Near East). A common motif in Tunisian art, especially in jewelry, is the hamsa (Arabic for "five"), also known by the Islamic name Hand of Fatima or Eye of Fatima. It is an ancient symbol, common throughout the Muslim and Jewish world, and is believed to protect the bearer from the "evil eye." The shape is of a stylized hand, often set with a jewel in the center of the palm to suggest an eye.

Architecture

Tunisia's architectural diversity ranges from grand Islamic architecture, such as mosques with their high minarets, domed roofs, and interior décor of intricate ornamental detail, to preserved Roman architecture, including ancient baths and a second-century amphitheater in Carthage. A distinct Ottoman influence is evident in a hammam, or public bathhouse (also known as Turkish baths, a variant of the ancient steam baths). Many cities, such as Kairouan and Sousse, have retained much of the original fortifications that surrounded and protected them in medieval times. The kasbah (fortress) was the main center of defense for the medieval city. A distinctive and typical piece of architecture that can be seen in the countryside is a zaouia (also zawiya), a small, white dome-roofed building that serves as the tomb of or shrine to a marabout, a scholar of the Koran or holy man.

In cities such as Tunis, the capital, the traditional Islamic architecture melds with the French colonial style and modern aesthetics. The straight, broad streets, apartment buildings, and cafés are reminiscent of Europe, as are the National Theater and the Catholic cathedral. As Tunisia has become a popular resort destination, many modern seaside villas and hotels have been developed. Many of these combine modern Western-style construction with Tunisian architectural accents, such as arched doors and windows, white stucco exteriors, patios and gardens.

Music

Like all of Tunisia's arts, its traditional music was a result of the influence of various cultural elements. Maluf (or malouf) is considered the basis of traditional Tunisian music. It contains elements of classical Arabic music and North African/Berber rhythms, but has evolved special modes and rhythms that are unique to Tunisia. It is based on a special form of Arabic music that evolved in Muslim Spain in the ninth century CE, also known as Arab Andalusian music (Andalusia refers to a historic region of Spain). As the Muslims fled Spain to North Africa during the 13th through the 15th centuries, they brought this style of music with them. Later, when the Ottoman Empire extended into Tunisia, Turkish styles were added to traditional maluf.

In the late 19th century, during French colonial rule, maluf began to decline in popularity. Baron Rodolphe d'Erlanger (1872–1932), a Paris-born painter and musicologist who lived in Tunis, is often credited with preserving maluf by compiling a collection of this traditional music in written and recorded form. His definitive, six-volume *La Musique Arabe* was published between 1930 and 1959. In 1934, the Rachidia Institute was founded to preserve the patrimony of maluf music. The Rachidia transformed the original maluf, taking it from a simple improvisational folk style, performed by small ensembles of traditional Tunisian instruments, to the level of high art, performed by larger orchestras incorporating a wider variety of classical Arabic and Western instruments. Many modern musicians study at the Rachidia Institute, and although maluf is no longer itself a widely popular form of music (except at weddings and cultural events), it forms an important foundation for modern Tunisian music.

Interesting to note is that heavy metal music is extremely popular among younger Tunisians, and Tunisian metal bands, like Carthagods, Myrath, and Embers of Revenge, have been covered by music journalists in America as part of the genre called African Metal.

Literature

Modern Tunisian literature, like the literature of other parts of the Maghreb, is usually written in either Arab or French and often reflects the country's colonial experience. In the early 20th century, a Tunisian and Arabic sensibility developed in direct opposition to the French colonial literary movement. Abu Al-Qasim Al-Shabbi (1909–1934) was revolutionary in his approach to poetry, which rejected Western conventions and sought unique Arab forms inspired by a host of influences. The result was an Arab realism. Poet Mustafa Khrayyef (1909–1967) wrote poems documenting Tunisian history; his brother, Bashir Khrayyef (1917–1983) was a novelist best known for his work *Al-Dadl h f 'ar j nh* (*Dates on Their Stalks*, 1969), which chronicles the lives of the southern Tunisian working class. Of the same generation, 'Al al-D ' j (1909–1949) became a noted short story writer, focusing on the daily lives of Tunisians. His works are collected in a volume titled *Sleepless Nights* (1991). Another short story writer was Hasan Nasr (1937–), who wrote stories about characters trying to resolve the conflict between the past and present.

One of Tunisia's most pre-eminent novelists was Mahm d al-Mis'ad (1911–), most famous for his novels *al-Sudd* (*The Dam*, 1955) and *Haddatha Abu Hurayra q la* (*Thus Abu Hurayra Narrated*, 1973). Muhammad al-'Ar s al-Matw is another writer who chronicled the lives of Tunisians under colonial rule.

CULTURE

Arts & Entertainment

Tunisia enjoys a vibrant modern arts culture that is both forward thinking and rooted in tradition. For example, the arts remain an important vehicle for the expression of a uniquely Tunisian identity, but also serve as an important forum for the discussion of social problems. However, open criticism of the government is still largely censored, despite post-revolution reforms, so historical, philosophical, and international political issues are largely explored. Contemporary Tunisian literature, though not necessarily cohesive, also deals with issues such as women, sexuality, and feminism in Islam.

Tunisian cinema, which emerged in the 1920s, has blossomed in the early 21st century. One notable contemporary female director is Moufida Tlatli (1947–), whose films *The Silences of the Palace* (1994) and *La Saison des Hommes* (2001) address the historic and contemporary repression of women in a male-dominated society. Another well-known director is Férid Boughedir (1944–), whose film *Halfaouine* (1990) tells the story of a boy coming of age in Tunisia in the 1950s. The Journées Cinématographiques de Carthage (Carthage Film Festival) is one of several film festivals in Tunisia (and the oldest in Africa). It is held every two years and features Arab and African films.

Music is an important aspect of Tunisian culture, and many modern artists reflect Tunisia's diversity and cultural progressiveness. Anouar Brahem (1957–) is one of Tunisia's most respected and internationally renowned musicians. He plays the oud, a key instrument in classical Arabic music. However, he has taken it out of the context of orchestras and ensembles and made it a solo instrument. His music explores new ground through his collaborations with jazz artists and musicians from different ethnic traditions.

Tunisia is also home to several significant festivals, including the International Carthage Festival, a month-long arts festival featuring music, dance, theater, and film, and the Tabarka Festival, which demonstrates the embracing of other cultures in Tunisian society. Another cultural festival of note is the International Festival of the Sahara in Douz, southern Tunisia, which celebrates Bedouin culture, and which features camel spectacles, Berber dance, and other folkloric traditions. In addition, there are a series of mini-festivals in the summer featuring Tunisian and international artists, with music workshops and other activities. These include the Jazz Festival, followed by the World Music, Latinos, and Raï Festivals. (Raï is a modern fusion of Algerian folk music with modern pop styles, with distinct Spanish, French, reggae and hip-hop influences.)

Tunisia has a long tradition of handcrafted pottery, and ceramics and painted tiles are commonly found in a Tunisian home. The two main producers of ceramics in Tunisia are Nabeul and Guellala on the island of Djerba. The pottery of Guellala is of a simple, ancient, and functional style, and largely consists of amphora-style water jugs, bowls, large olive jars, and other useful items, all produced in the original earthen tone of the natural clay. Nabeul is known for fine hand-painted and brightly glazed pottery, which includes sets of dishes, cups, vases, tagines, and other household items, as well as decorative tiles for use in construction or as wall hangings. Typical designs include geometric or stylized floral and animal (particularly fish) patterns. The island of Djerba is also known for fine silver and gold jewelry.

Cultural Sites & Landmarks

Tunisia's history, culture, and landscape are unusually rich and multilayered and range from medieval, Islamic, and colonial architecture, traditional Arab markets (called souks) and ancient Roman ruins, to sand dunes, green mountains, and pristine Mediterranean beaches. Tunis, the capital, holds much of this interest and is home to two World Heritage Sites, as designated by United Nations Educational, Scientific, and Cultural Organization (UNESCO). These include the ancient city of Carthage and the Medina of Tunis.

Considered one of the most historically significant landmarks in northern Africa, the ruins of Carthage are visible throughout the modern city of Tunis. Founded in approximately 814 BCE by Phoenician traders, Carthage was an important Mediterranean port city. After the Romans defeated Carthage in the Third Punic War (149–146 BCE), they destroyed and later rebuilt the city. As a result, many Roman structures have replaced the original buildings. The Medina of Tunis, or old town of Tunis (medina is Arabic for "city"), is located in the center of the capital. It hosts the city's vibrant souks, or marketplaces, as well as around 700 historical monuments. These include mosques—in particular the Al Zitouna Mosque (also Al-Zaytuna Mosque) from the ninth century—and schools dating from the city's medieval period.

Tunisia is home to some of the most extensive Roman ruins in northern Africa. Ancient sites of note are Utica, Dougga (also Thugga), and El Jem (also El Djem), the latter two recognized as World Heritage Sites. Utica was the oldest Phoenician colony in Tunisia, founded in the 12th century BCE. After the destruction of Carthage, Utica became the capital under the Romans. Still extant are columns, building foundations with marble and mosaic floors, and a sundial.

Dougga is often considered the best-conserved Roman town in North Africa. Originally a Berber settlement, Dougga passed through Punic (Phoenician) and Roman occupation before declining in the later Islamic period. The Amphitheater of El Jem is a well-preserved third-century Roman coliseum and the largest in North Africa with a capacity of around 35,000 spectators.

Other ancient sites in Tunisia include Kerkouane and Kairouan. Kerkouane, designated a World Heritage Site in 1985, is a rare example of a pure Phoenician city. It was abandoned in the third century BCE, before the Roman period, and was never rebuilt or reoccupied. The ruins of the houses, with their courtyards and sophisticated baths, offer a glimpse of life during the Carthaginian period. Kairouan, declared a World Heritage Site in 1988, is located in the dry, hot center of the country. It was established in 670 CE by Islamic general Uqba ibn Nafi (622–683), who was charged with converting North Africa to Islam. Many consider it to be the fourth-holiest site in Islam (after Mecca, Medina, and Jerusalem). The city is well known for its rich Islamic architecture, lively souks, and historic mosques.

Tunisia is also renowned for its landscape. In fact, many sites in the nation were chosen as settings for scenes in the *Star Wars* film series, most notably the subterranean cave dwellings in Matmâta in southern Tunisia. Many of the scenes in the films were inspired by the Berber architecture present in rural Tunisia, and several constructed sets, complete with buildings and facades, are still standing. Tunisia is also home to one natural World Heritage Site, Ichkeul National Park, home to Ichkeul Lake. The site is an important location for migrating birds, but is listed as endangered due to changes in its ecological balance.

Libraries & Museums

Artifacts from the Carthaginian and Roman periods are on display in Tunis at the Museum of Carthage and at the National Bardo Museum. The National Bardo Museum is housed in a 19th-century palace and displays Roman mosaics. The Museum at Carthage explores the artifacts of the Punic (Phoenician) and Roman eras. A third-century BCE sarcophagus of a priest and priestess is on display there, as are Punic masks and pottery and glass jewelry.

The National Library of Tunisia—established in 1885 and, prior to independence, called the French Library—has a collection of over one million books, including 40,000 manuscripts, one of which is a 10th-century document titled *Tafsir Yahia Ibn Sallam.*

Holidays

Tunisia's national independence holiday is March 20 and commemorates the country's liberation from France in 1956, while July 25 is Republic Day, memorializing the formation of the Tunisian nation. Eid El Jala', or Evacuation Day, celebrates the retreat of the French from Bizerta in 1962. A number of Islamic holy days are also official holidays. These include Milad un Nabi (the Prophet Muhammad's birthday), Eid al-Fitr (marking the end of Ramadan), Eid al-Idha (the Feast of the Sacrifice), and Hegire (Islamic New Year), which is based on the moon calendar.

Youth Culture

Tunisian youth are very much influenced by Western culture, particularly European culture. Nightclubs are very popular among teenagers and older youth, and Tunisia has become somewhat renowned for its dance club scene. Unlike in many other Muslim and Arab countries, girls and boys freely interact and go to clubs and cafés together, at least in the modern cities. Popular music among young Tunisians includes Arab and European pop music, techno and house music, as well as other popular genres, such as metal, hip-hop, and jazz. Reggae is also especially popular.

Internet usage is prevalent, and satellite dishes cover many Tunisian roofs, despite some restrictions on the media. Most Tunisian youth have cell phones—sometimes even more than one. It's also common to see young Tunisians—especially males—gather in coffee shops for socializing; a high unemployment rate among recent graduates contributes to this café culture. In addition, Tunisian youth love to dress in the latest fashions, especially Italian styles and designer brands. In general, young Tunisians are known for taking great pride in their appearance.

Football (soccer) is the country's main sport, and stadiums are full of enthusiastic soccer supporters during championships. Tunisia's national football team, nicknamed "Les Aigles de Carthage" (the Carthage Eagles), was Africa's Soccer Champion in 2004 and 2013. They have also qualified four times for the FIFA World Cup, but have not yet made it out of the round one match-ups. Many young Tunisians (boys in particular) are avid amateur soccer players.

SOCIETY

Transportation

A popular mode of transportation is the louage, special private cars that carry up to five people (or larger vehicles that can carry eight) at a very affordable cost. In general, Tunisian drivers are known to be aggressive, and Tunisia has a high rate of auto accidents. Tunisians drive on the right side of the road.

Transportation Infrastructure

There are 15 major airports in Tunisia (as of 2015), and Tunis Air connects to all major European airlines. There is a very limited railway system in Tunisia, built by the French during colonization (1881–1956) and operated by the Société Nationale de Chemins de Fer Tunisiens (SNCFT). It runs passenger trains to a few major cities. More popular and more far-reaching are the buses routes that connect the country. There is also an above-ground tram system in operation in Tunis.

Major cities in Tunisia are linked by paved roadways, with three major routes out of Tunis, to Bizerte, to Sousse, and to Beja. In addition, the Trans-African Highway passes through Tunisia and connects North African nations to western Africa.

Media & Communications

Tunisia has several major newspapers in both French and Arabic, including *La Presse, L'Action,* and *Le Temps* (French) and *Essahafa, Al-Horria, Assabah* (Arabic)—all government-owned.

In fact, most Tunisian newspapers receive government subsidies, including "opposition" papers. While a small number of independent papers are in operation, it has become difficult for them to receive and increase financing and distribution. Additionally, while the government insists that opposition papers are free from censorship and the new constitution designates freedom of the press as well as freedom of expression, the countless reports of the harassment and detention of journalists under the Ben Ali regime have not eased. Many journalists—the Tunisian Journalists' Syndicate (SJT) estimates well over 100—have gone into exile as a result. Moreover, a 2015 draft law that follows on the heels of recent terror attacks calls for 10-year prison sentences for those with "state secrets" and fines and imprisonment for those who criticize either the armed forces or the customs agents. Such measures may further alienate and silence journalists.

Tunisia has two national television networks, TV7 and Canal 21 (also *La Télévision Tunisienne* 2), which are operated by ERTT (Tunisia's national Radio and Television Establishment or *Établissement de la Radiodiffusion-Télévision Tunisienne*), and one private satellite network, Hannibal-TV. Many Tunisians have satellite dishes and receive broadcasts from other Arab countries or Arab channels from London. Programming from European nations, such as Italy and France, are also popular.

Free speech is guaranteed by the Tunisian constitution, and the official position is that Tunisian and foreign journalists, as well as opposition parties, are free to exercise this right. However, it is widely believed that there are no free media in Tunisia, and television and the press are tightly controlled by the government. There are frequent reports of harassment or intimidation of journalists and widespread censorship. The revolution appears not to have altered the government's practices in this area, as noted above and within the Human Rights segment of this chapter. In 2014, Freedom House, an independent reporting group, designated Tunisia's media as only "Partly Free."

Internet access is widely available in Tunisia—Internet usage was estimated at 44 percent of the population in 2014—but online journalism outlets and blogging sites are closely controlled by the government. Additionally, access to sites related to human rights or that contain anti-government content are routinely blocked. However, many apps are not, and during the Jasmine Revolution in 2010 and 2011, Twitter and Facebook played an enormous role in spreading the word about protests, while also providing a reporting gateway that allowed information to reach the global community in real-time.

Nevertheless, individual usage also continues to be monitored, despite the regime change and political reforms. Just as in 2004 un Ben Ali's administration, eight young Tunisians were arrested and sentenced to thirteen years in prison on charges of plotting terrorist acts merely for downloading files from the Internet, bloggers and journalists are still being prosecuted for statements critical of government officials. Specific examples appear within the Human Rights segment of this chapter.

In 2010, Reporters Without Borders noted that Tunisia, along with China and Iran, was employing sophisticated and effective Internet censorship technology—called Ammar 404—and was placed on their "Enemies of the Internet" list. Such filters were removed in 2011. However, in 2015, Reporters without Borders still ranked Tunisia 126 out of 180 countries in the World Press Freedom Index. This number is slightly higher than in 2014, when they ranked 133. However, Tunisia remains on the independent watchdog group's "Under Surveillance" list.

SOCIAL DEVELOPMENT

Standard of Living
Tunisia ranked 90th on the 2014 United Nations Human Development Index rating of 187 countries.

Water Consumption

Tunisia's water and sanitation infrastructure is well developed in urban areas, with 100 percent of the population enjoying access to improved water sources. In rural areas, however, improved water sources stand at just 90.5 percent. The disparity broadens further when it comes to sanitation: over 97 percent of Tunisia's urban population has access to improved sanitation facilities, while in rural areas, only 76.6 had this level of access. One of Tunisia's ecological problems is, in fact, raw sewage in waterways, and this is directly attributable to the inadequacy of current sanitation facilities.

Education

Tunisia has made great strides in literacy, particularly during the late 20th century. By the early 21st century, the average literacy rate had risen from 59 percent to 81.8 percent of the total population (nearly 90 percent of the male population and around just over 74 percent of the female population in 2015). Education in Tunisia is mandatory for the first nine years; females in Tunisia generally complete 14 years of education, while males complete 13 years. In later years, both French and English are taught.

Islam is a major part of the educational structure. All public schools must provide religious instruction in Islam. The public university system includes the Zeitouna Koranic School, a school for studying the Koran.

Women's Rights

Tunisia is widely hailed as being one of the most progressive Arab and Muslim states with regard to women's rights. Women made huge gains in 1956, just after Tunisia gained its independence from French colonial rule. Tunisia's leader at the time, Habib Bourguiba (1903–2000), sought to modernize the nation, and one of his first acts was to introduce the Code of Personal Status in 1956. This was a series of laws that sought to improve gender equality and gave Tunisian women more rights than the majority of women in the Muslim world, many

of which were even beyond European standards at the time. What was especially unusual was that these laws were imposed by the country's leader, Bourguiba—and subsequently reinforced by his successor, Ben Ali—and not sparked by any grassroots feminist movement. Bourguiba believed Tunisia could not move forward as a nation until women were granted equal status. He was strongly influenced by an earlier theologian and writer, Tahar Haddad (1899–1935), who advocated women's rights based on what he believed to be a true reading of the Koran.

Bourguiba's code ultimately gave women full legal status in society, including the right to vote, seek a passport, and have a bank account, as well as equal rights to education and work, including the right to own businesses. The code also gave women equal status in marriage and allowed women to file for divorce in court the same way men could. It abolished the tradition of "repudiation," by which a man could easily and unilaterally divorce his wife for any or no reason, while the wife had no recourse. It also gave women greater custody rights over their children and inheritance rights for their husband's or father's property. Furthermore, it outlawed polygamy, raised the legal marriage age, and required mutual consent between bride and groom for a marriage to take place. In the years that followed, women gained abortion rights, access to family planning services, and the right to receive child support payments following divorce.

Women also made substantial gains regarding equal opportunity and equal pay in the workforce, and they have significantly increased their representation in certain areas. For example, as of 2008, women constituted 31 percent of lawyers (compared to 10 percent in 1992) and 40 percent of university professors (compared to 22 percent in 1992); 57 percent of university students are also women (as compared to 37 percent in 1989). However, men are still more visibly represented, especially in government positions (as of 2005, women represented

37 percent of the nation's civil service). Women are also guaranteed equal access to education, but illiteracy among women remains higher than among men in the early 21st century. In 2015, male literacy was 89.6 percent, while female literacy was just 74.2 percent.

With election of the Islamist Ennhada Party in the 2011 post-revolution democratic elections, women have begun to worry about the continued status of these freedoms, even after Ennhada was voted out of the political majority in the 2014 elections. Renowned Tunisian feminists Munjiyah al-Sawaihi and Fawzia Zouari have expressed concern that the revolution, in which women played an active role, will effect a retrogression in women's rights and have cited events in Algeria and Iran as examples of changes that may yet occur.

Tunisia still remains socially conservative by Western standards, and as a result, women are widely held to different standards of behavior than men in family and social life. This is especially evident in rural areas, where a more traditional way of thinking presides. Abuses such as rape are vigorously punished—rapists typically receive life imprisonment or face the death penalty if the act was committed with threat or a weapon. However, domestic abuse remains a social issue, and is often perceived as an internal, or family, matter. Thus, enforcement has been criticized as being lax, and it is believed that social stigma has prevented cases from being reported. The government and women's groups such as the non-governmental organization National Union of Tunisian Women (UNFT) continue to push for reforms, and are working to raise awareness to stop domestic violence and violence against women.

Health Care

Tunisia has a modern health care system, and life expectancy at birth (74 years for men, and 78 years for women) is comparable to that of developed countries. Infant mortality, however, remains high, at just over 23 deaths per 1,000 live births (2015 estimate).

GOVERNMENT

Structure

Throughout its history, Tunisia has been part of many notable empires, including the Carthaginian, Roman, Byzantine, and Ottoman empires. In 1881, France established a protectorate over Tunisia. Under the leadership of reformer Habib Bourguiba, the Tunisians overthrew French rule in 1956 and established a republic the following year. The former Tunisian constitution was established in June 1959 and amended in both 1999 and 2002, following the 2002 Tunisian Constitutional Referendum, which eliminated the presidency's three-term limit. Following 2011 public protests, the ousting of President Ben Ali, the dissolution of Ben Ali's de facto ruling party, the Constituent Assembly— serving as an interim acting parliament—adopted a new constitution on January 26, 2014.

Tunisia's chief executive and commander-in-chief of the Tunisian Armed Forces is the president, who is elected by popular vote to a five-year term, with a two-term limit, as designated by the 2014 constitution. The president selects a prime minister and cabinet, who administer the government. The Assembly of the Representatives of the People—the unicameral legislative body that replaced Tunisia's interim Constituent Assembly installed during the post-revolution state of emergency—now has the right to recommend impeachment for a president who has violated the constitution.

Elected on October 26, 2014 the unicameral Assembly of Representatives (Majlis Nawwab ash-Sha'b) not only replaced the interim Constituent Assembly, but also fully supplanted the pre-revolution bi-cameral parliament, which had consisted of the upper Chamber of Advisors and lower Chamber of Deputies. The highest court remains the Cour de Cassation (Court of Cassation). Tunisia's legal system is a combination of French law and Islamic (Sharia) law. Sharia can come into play in cases of family law, relating to inheritance and child custody issues.

Political Parties

For the republic's first several decades, the Constitutional Democratic Rally (CDR), formerly known as the Socialist Destourian Party, was the only legal political party. Opposition parties were made legal in 1981, but still had little power; they included the Social Democratic Movement (MDS), the Popular Unity Party (PUP), the Union of Democratic Unionists (UDU), At-Tajdid (also called the Renewal Movement), the Liberal Social Party (PSL), the Green Party for Progress (PVP), the Democratic Progressive Party (PDP), and the Democratic Forum for Labor and Liberties (FDTL). The Islamic fundamentalist Renaissance Party (Al Nahda) had been illegal because it is a religious-based party. However, the Jasmine Revolution and subsequent dissolution of the CDR changed all this, leading to free and democratic elections in 2011, the first since independence in 1956.

In 2011, the conservative democratic Islamist Ennahda gained a majority (89) of the 217 constituent assembly member seats. Congress for the Republic (CPR) gained 29, the populist Current of Love (Aridha) achieved 26, the Democratic Forum for Labour and Liberties (Ettakatol) won 20, and the Progressive Democratic Party (PDP) gained 16 seats.

In the 2014 elections, Nidaa Tounes, or "Call of Tunisia," won the majority, with 86 seats. This time, the former majority Ennahda won 69, while 16 were achieved by the free-market economist party, Free Patriotic Union (UPL), achieved. The leftist political and electoral coalition the Popular Front won 15, liberalist and secular Afek Tounes won eight, and CPR won four.

Local Government

Tunisia is divided into 24 provinces, known as governorates. Tunis, the capital, is administered as its own governorate. The governors are appointed by the central government, as are local administrators. Municipalities elect their own councils and mayors.

Judicial System

Tunisia's legal system is based on French civil law and Islamic law. Cantonal courts consider criminal cases; courts of first instance consider civil, commercial, correctional, social, and personal matters; courts of appeal consider appeals; and the Court of Cassation is the highest court. The judicial system, even in the post-revolutionary climate, is not considered impartial, as evidenced by the case of a Tunisian journalist, Zied el-Heni, who was imprisoned after declaring state attorney Tarek Chkioua to be a liar.

While the Tunisian Criminal Procedure Code in the civil law system allows for a defendant to be present at trial, retain counsel, question witnesses, and appeal, there are instances where these codes are overlooked. Some have also expressed concern that defense attorneys are not always granted full participation by judges in trials.

Taxation

The government of Tunisia levies a graduated income tax, whose top level is 35 percent. It corporate taxes stand at 25 percent, with 35 levied on companies involved in financial transactions, telecommunications, insurance companies, and companies emitting hydrocarbons. Value-added, social security (one percent), professional training (two percent), and land registration taxes are also part of the tax revenue system. Capital gains is considered earned income and, therefore, taxed at the regular income tax rate, without special designation. Some foreign companies can take advantage of exemptions and reductions.

Armed Forces

Tunisia's military, founded in 1956, consists of an army, navy, air force, and a 12,000-member national guard. One year of compulsory service is required, although many Tunisians fail to serve that year. The United States performs joint military exercises with Tunisian armed forces and serves as Tunisia's largest equipment supplier. There are currently between 45,000 and 60,000 active personnel.

Foreign Policy

Since ancient times, Tunisia has served as a gateway between Europe, Africa, and the Middle East. Due to this intricate relationship, Tunisia has striven for positive international ties and balance as it has developed. Its approach to foreign policy has traditionally been one of moderation, pragmatism, and relative neutrality. However, though Tunisia is not involved in any major border or territory disputes in the early 21st century, and has not engaged in any major conflicts since gaining independence from France in 1956, this balance has not always been easy to achieve. Disputes with Libya occurred in 1976; 1980, when Libyan-trained rebels attempted to take Gafsa; and 1985, when Libya expelled Tunisian workers and threatened military action. True to its stated foreign policy principles, Tunisia did not engage Libya, but instead severed ties, eventually normalizing relations. Tunisia now has only a maritime dispute with Libya.

Tunisia has traditionally been a voice of balance and reason in the Arab-Israeli conflict; the country is willing to recognize Israel, but stresses the importance of diplomacy and negotiations. On the other hand, Tunisia offered refuge to the Palestinian Liberation Organization (PLO) for eleven years (1982–1993), which resulted in Israeli retaliation on Tunisian soil. Tunisia is a member of the Arab League of Nations and even served as its host from 1979 to 1990, when Cairo (in Egypt) was boycotted for having signed a peace treaty with Israel.

Tunisia also belongs to the Arab Maghreb Union (UMA), a political and economic union that includes Libya, Algeria, Morocco, and Mauritania. Relations have been tense at times, especially with Libya during the mid-1980s. Tunisia and Libya have since normalized relations, as previously noted, and the two countries have re-established trade. Additionally, Tunisia continues to work to ease tensions and strengthen ties among the Maghreb nations. Tunisia also belongs to the African Union (AU), with 52 other African states, and has supplied peacekeeping troops to war-torn nations, such as Somalia and Rwanda.

Tunisia signed an Association Agreement with the European Union (EU) in 1995 and maintains strong economic and political ties with Europe. A source of tension has been the high number of illegal Tunisian immigrants moving into Europe, particularly into France and Italy. The United States and Tunisia have maintained a cordial relationship since the 18th century. The U.S. considers Tunisia an important strategic ally, both for its location and its reputation as a moderate Muslim state strongly opposed to Islamic fundamentalism. Relations cooled briefly during the first Gulf War (1990–1991), when Tunisia opposed the US invasion of Iraq, but they remain strong to this day, despite Tunisia's questionable approach to democracy and poor human rights record. In fact, the U.S.-Tunisian Joint Military Commission meets annually to discuss security issues.

Terrorist attacks, like those at Tunisia's Bardo National Museum in 2015—for which a splinter-group of the Algerian-based al-Qaeda in the Islamic Maghreb has claimed responsibility—and Sousse will, no doubt, influence the future of Tunisian foreign relations, both in terms of the aid it seeks and the relations it maintains with the countries supporting such organizations.

Human Rights Profile

International human rights law insists that states respect civil and political rights and also promote an individual's economic, social, and cultural rights. The United Nations Universal Declaration on Human Rights (UDHR) is recognized as the standard for international human rights. Its authors sought the counsel of the world's great thinkers, philosophers, and religious leaders and were careful to create a document that reflects the core values shared by every world culture. (To read this document or view the articles relating to cultural human rights, visit www.ohchr.org/EN/UDHR/Pages/Introduction.aspx.)

In comparison with other Arab and Muslim states, Tunisia has the appearance of a more liberal, open society. Tunisia is often praised for its relative stability, modernity, economic growth, and progressive stance on women's rights issues. However, since the administration of Zine al-Abidine Ben Ali (1936–)—who deposed President Habib Bourguiba (1903–2000) in 1987 in a bloodless coup—the government has been accused of multiple human rights violations, a condition that has not improved since Ben Ali's ousting in 2011 during the Arab Spring. In fact, many consider Tunisia's government to be one of the most repressive in the Arab world, something that appears not to have changed significantly despite the regime change and new constitution.

On April 8, 2015, Tunisia's Council of Ministers drafted a law that grants additional powers to internal security forces, customs agents, and the military, while also restricting constitutionally-conferred liberties. For example, Article 5 of the new law calls for ten-year prison terms for anyone who obtains security secrets. The stringent punishment and broad terminology concern human rights groups, particularly since Tunisia does not have a method for distinguishing between classified and non-classified information. Therefore, journalists who report on political issues may, therefore, self-censor rather than risk criminal prosecution and prison. Even more troublesome are penalties for any criticism of the armed forces, customs agents, or internal security—another stipulation of the new law. Under a similar military justice code, Tunisian blogger Yassine Ayari was recently prosecuted for "defaming the army," following a Facebook post about Tunisia's former defense minister.

Among other potential violations to the UDHR, the new law proposes life imprisonment for anyone who damages or destroys police property and prescribes similarly harsh sentences for "disturbing the public order," a portion of the law that may potentially deter even peaceful public demonstrations. Each of the elements in the new law stand in direct opposition to the 2014 constitution, which grants freedom of speech and press.

Freedom of religion is similarly under siege, although this also occurred under former president Ben Ali's administration. Tunisia is a predominantly Muslim nation, with Islam as the official state religion. Muslim holidays are officially recognized as national holidays and the constitution only allows for a Muslim president. The practice of other religions is permitted, however, and interfaith dialogue is encouraged. The government generally respects religious freedom, and Tunisia is home to a small indigenous Jewish population (mostly on the island of Djerba) and a small number of Christians, Baha'i and other faiths. Nonetheless, there have been cases of abuse, especially concerning members of the Baha'i faith, Tunisian converts to Christianity, and Islamic fundamentalists.

Despite Tunisia's status as a Muslim state, the Tunisian government's relationship with Islam is complex. Although the government financially supports mosques, it also strictly controls their activities. Islamic fundamentalism is often targeted by the government, to the point of repression and persecution, and Islamic political parties (as well as any other religion-based political parties) are prohibited by law. Furthermore, women are forbidden to wear the hijab (Islamic headscarf) in government offices and public schools. There have been reports of police harassment of women wearing the hijab in public or of men perceived to be extremely religious. Suspected Islamists are dealt with harshly, with certain non-governmental organizations (NGOs) reporting that the family members of Islamic fundamentalists are frequently punished or blacklisted.

Migration

According to Tunisia's Office of Tunisians Abroad, there are approximately 1,223,213 Tunisians living abroad, mostly in Europe (84.4 percent) and primarily in France and Italy. Additionally, the government is trying to address internal migration concerns that bring rural populations seeking employment to urban centers. In 2009, the Tunisian government launched a program that would both decrease emigration and create jobs in regions throughout the country by offering grants to those seeking to create handicraft and industrial jobs. The efficacy of this program has not yet been assessed.

ECONOMY

Overview of the Economy

Since gaining independence in the 1950s, Tunisia has transitioned from its mostly agricultural economy to one based heavily on manufacturing, energy production, and tourism. This is the direct result of the government's pro-growth economic policies, which encourage foreign investment and infrastructure development. However, the Arab Spring, the ultimate ousting of President Zine al-Abidine Ben Ali, and the civil unrest that followed played havoc with Tunisian markets, investors, and tourism. Between 2012 and 2013, the country's political turbulence and many uncertainties lead to a series of downgrades to Tunisia's credit rating, something from which the country is still recovering. Nevertheless, Tunisia's gross domestic product (GDP) was a robust at $124.3 billion USD in 2014, with a per capita GDP of $11,300 USD. Services made up the largest sector, accounting for 62.3 percent of the GDP.

Industry

Tunisia's post-colonial leaders have focused on developing the country's manufacturing, which is based mostly in Tunis. Major industries include textiles and apparel, food processing, wood and paper products, petrochemicals, and industrial metals such as steel. Many international firms, including car-maker Peugeot, have offices in Tunis.

The country's trade is closely linked with North Africa and the Europe Union. France, once the colonial ruler, is now a major trading partner, though Tunisia trades extensively with other European Union members. The country is working with the EU to establish free trade between their jurisdictions, a move which is promoting economic reforms such as greater privatization.

Labor

Despite economic growth, and the increase in the size of the middle class, Tunisia continues to have extensive unemployment, estimated at 15.3 percent in 2014. The problem has been exacerbated by the 2012 and 2013 political upheavals, which have led to a series of downgrades to Tunisia's credit rating. As of 2014, 51.7 percent of the workforce was employed in service industries, almost 33.2 percent worked in industry, and 14.8 percent in agriculture.

Energy/Power/Natural Resources

Tunisia has many mineral resources. In recent years, energy sources such as petroleum and natural gas have been discovered, though not in the same quantities as in Middle Eastern countries. Other important minerals found in Tunisia include iron ore, lead, zinc, and salt.

The coastal regions have rich farmland. Much of the southern part of the country is covered by the Sahara Desert. The desert is growing in part because of human influence, through activities such as overgrazing and deforestation. Pollution is another problem, particularly raw sewage in waterways, which is due to insufficient sanitation.

Fishing

Since the first shellfish farm was established on Lake Bizarete in the 1960s, Tunisia has seen a steady growth in the fisheries sector. These numbers increased with the continued development of aquaculture. In 2011, the country produced 57.8 tons of fish and seafood products. Of this, 15,495 tons—valued at 153.7 million dinars ($77 million USD)—were exported between January and June of 2011 alone. Continued investment in aquaculture is expected.

Forestry

According to the UN, 6.5 percent of Tunisia is covered in forest. Of this, 690,000 hectacres (1,705,027 acres) has been planted. Most of Tunisia's naturally-occurring forest is in the Kroumirie Mountains in the north, where oak and pine grow. Reforestation efforts noted above are geared towards both production and dune stabilization.

Mining/Metals

Along with petroleum, Tunisia has many mineral resources. Important minerals include iron ore, lead, zinc, and salt.

Agriculture

Though it accounts for 8.7 percentage of the country's GDP, agriculture is important in the fertile coastal regions. Production includes grains, fruits, olives, and olive oil. However, tomatoes, citrus fruit, sugar beets, dates, and almonds are also common harvests in this region. Olives and olive oil are among Tunisia's main exports.

Animal Husbandry

Tunisian livestock farming takes place largely in the north, where both beef and dairy cattle are raised. Planting acacia, as recommended by Rome-based International Fund for Agricultural Development, has recently enhanced forage opportunities for livestock. Since the early 2000s, commercial poultry farming has gained a foothold within the economy.

Tourism

Tunisia has transformed itself into a major tourist destination, receiving around 6 million visitors per year (2006). A major boom came in the 1970s, thanks to the release of the original *Star Wars* film, shot partly on location in Tunisia. Tourism is now one of the country's most important industries. However, the industry did experience a sharp downturn in 2015, following the Bardo National Museum terrorist attack, in which 22 hostages—many of them tourists—were killed and another 50 were injured. The Sousse attack three months later, during which 38 people were killed—30 of them British—further effected a sense of instability in Tunisia's tourism industry. Nevertheless, spa-related and medical tourism by Western nationals is becoming increasingly popular, and the tide of these tourists has not been stemmed by recent violence.

Tunisia has made major efforts to protect its cultural heritage, in part for the enjoyment of tourists. The ruins of Carthage lie close to the site of modern Tunis and are a popular tourist destination. The Roman ruins at Dougga are an important archaeological site.

The country is home to several historic mosques, including Kairouan, established in the seventh century. Kairouan, also known as "The Great Mosque," became a UNESCO World Heritage Site in 1988. Tourists also visit Tunisia for the rich and cosmopolitan cultural offerings of Tunis, including arts festivals.

Jennifer Carlson, Eric Badertscher,
Micah Issitt, & Savannah Schroll Guz

DO YOU KNOW?

- Carthage means "New City" in the Phoenician language.

- Archaeologists have found evidence suggesting that the Mediterranean coast of Africa was occupied by early human and prehistoric civilizations as early as one million years ago. Evidence from early groups of *Homo sapiens* have been found in caves around Tunis and other portions of the Tunisian coast that date to at least 10,000 years ago.

Bibliography

Albert Memmi. "The Pillar of Salt." Boston: *Beacon Press.* 1992.

Anthony Ham and Abigail Hole. "Lonely Planet: Tunisia." London, UK: *Lonely Planet.* 2004.

Béatrice Hibou. "The Force of Obedience: The Political Economy of Repression in Tunisia." Transl. Andrew Brown. Cambridge, UK & Malden, MA: *Polity Press.* 2011.

Christopher Alexander. "Tunisia: Stability and Reform in the Modern Maghreb." New York: *Routledge.* 2010. The Contemporary Middle East Ser.

Christopher Daniel Jacobs and Peter Morris. "The Rough Guide to Tunisia." 8th edition. New York: *Rough Guides,* 2009.

David Soren, Aicha B. Khader and Hedi Slim. "Carthage: Uncovering the Mysteries and Splendors of Ancient Tunisia." *Simon & Schuster/ Touchstone Books.* 1991.

Kenneth J. Perkins. "A History of Modern Tunisia." 2nd ed. Cambridge, UK: *Cambridge UP*. 2014.

Kenneth J. Perkins. "Historical Dictionary of Tunisia." Lanham, MD: *The Scarecrow Press*. 1997.

Michael Willis. "Politics and Power in the Maghreb: Algeria, Tunisia and Morocco from Independence to the Arab Spring." Oxford, UK: *Oxford UP*. 2014.

Monia Hejaiej. "Behind Closed Doors: Women's Narratives in Tunis." Piscataway, NJ: *Rutgers UP*. 1996.

Mounira M. Charrad. "States and Women's Rights: The Making of Postcolonial Tunisia, Algeria, and Morocco." Berkeley: *U California P*. 2001.

Mustapha Tlili. "Lion Mountain." Transl. Linda Coverdale. New York: *Arcade Publishing*, 1990.

Nouri Gana, ed. "The Making of the Tunisian Revolution: Contexts, Architects, Prospects." Edinburgh, UK: *Edinburgh UP*. 2013.

Paula Holmes-Eber. Daughters of Tunis: Women, Family, and Networks in a Muslim City." Boulder, CO: *Westview Press*, 2002.

Robert Lang. "New Tunisian Cinema: Allegories of Resistance." New York: *Columbia UP*. 2014. Film and Culture Ser.

Works Cited

_____. "Tunisia charges editor with complicity in terrorist attack." *CPJ: Committee to Protect Journalists. CPJ: Committee to Protect Journalists*. CPJ, 23 Jul. 2015. Web. https://cpj.org/2015/07/tunisia-charges-editor-with-complicity-in-terroris.php.

_____. "U.S. Relations with Tunisia" *Bureau of Near Eastern Affairs Fact Sheet*. U.S. Department of State, 22 Aug. 2013. Web. http://www.state.gov/r/pa/ei/bgn/5439.htm.

"Festival International du Sahara Douz." *Festival du Douz*. 2015. http://www.festivaldouz.org.tn/.

"Institut National de la Statistique—Tunisie." *Tunisian Government Portal*, 2015. http://www.ins.nat.tn/indexfr.php.

"Middle East/North Africa: Tunisia." *Reporters Without Borders*. Reporters Without Borders, 2015. http://en.rsf.org/tunisia.html.

"Tunisia Country Profiles—Overview." *BBC News*. BBC, 30 Jun. 2015. http://news.bbc.co.uk/2/hi/middle_east/country_profiles/791969.stm.

"Tunisia." *World Factbook*. Central Intelligence Agency, 2015. https://www.cia.gov/library/publications/the-world-factbook/geos/ts.html.

"Tunisian Carpets and Tapestries." *Raken Style*. Raken, 2005. http://www.raken.com/style/eng/historique/tapis_tapisserie.asp.

Andrea Barron. "Tunisia as an Arab Women's Rights Leader." *The Globalist*. The Globalist, 12 July 2007. http://www.theglobalist.com/tunisia-as-an-arab-womens-rights-leader-part-1/.

Asma Ghribi. "A New Law Sends an Ominous Signal in Tunisia." *Foreign Policy*. FP, 5 May 2015. Web. http://foreignpolicy.com/2015/05/05/a-new-law-sends-an-ominous-signal-in-tunisia-arab-spring-bardo-tunis/.

Ben Bouazza and Paul Schemm. "Second Tunisia assassination could spell end to Islamist government." *Washington Post*. 26 Jul. 2013. https://www.washingtonpost.com/world/second-tunisia-assassination-could-spell-end-to-islamist-government/2013/07/26/0708bf2a-f636-11e2-aa2e-4088616498b4_story.html.

Charles O. Cecil. "Tunisia's Center of Ceramics." *Saudi Aramco World* 54.2 (March/April 2003). https://www.saudiaramcoworld.com/issue/200302/tunisia.s.center.of.ceramics.htm.

Committee to Protect Journalists. "Attacks on the Press 2007: Tunisia." *CPJ: Committee to Protect Journalists*. CPJ, 5 February 2008. http://www.cpj.org/2008/02/attacks-on-the-press-2007-tunisia.php.

European Jewish Congress. "Latest News from the Community." *The Jewish Community of Tunisia*. European Jewish Congress, 2010.

Hédi Slim, Ammar Mahjoubi, Khaled Belkhoja, & and Abdelmajid Ennabli. *Histoire Générale de la Tunisie, Tome I: L'Antiquité*. Tunis: Sud Éditions, 2003.

Hichem Djaït, Mohamed Talbi, Farhat Dachraoui, Abdelmajid Dhouib, M'hamed Ali M'rabet, and Faouzi Mahfoudh, "Histoire Générale de la Tunisie, Tome II: Le Moyen-Âge." Tunis: *Sud Éditions*, 2005.

Marouen Achouri. "Tunisian Judicial System In Need of Serious Reform." *Al Monitor: Pulse of the Middle East*. Al-Monitor, 22 Sept. 2013. Web. http://www.al-monitor.com/pulse/politics/2013/09/tunisia-judicial-judges-reform.html. Amnesty International. "Tunisia: Amnesty International Report 2014/15." *Amnesty International*. 2015. https://www.amnesty.org/en/countries/middle-east-and-north-africa/tunisia/.

National Union of Tunisian Women. Union Nationale de la Femme Tunisienne, 2012. www.unft.org.tn.

Official Website of the National Union of Tunisian Women. National Union of Tunisian Women, 2015. www.unft.org.tn.

Ray Takeyh, Ray. "Close, but No Democracy" *Council on Foreign Relations*. Council on Foreign Relations, 2015. http://www.cfr.org/publication/7594/close_but_no_democracy.html.

Thorne Anderson, Thorne. "The Musical Pulse of Tunisia." *Saudi Aramco World* 52. 4 (July/August 2001). http://www.saudiaramcoworld.com/issue/200104/the.musical.pulse.of.tunisia.htm.

U.S. State Department. "Tunisia: International Religious Freedom Report." *Bureau of Democracy, Human Rights, and Labor. U.S. State Department Website*, 2015. http://www.state.gov/g/drl/rls/irf/2002/14016.htm>.

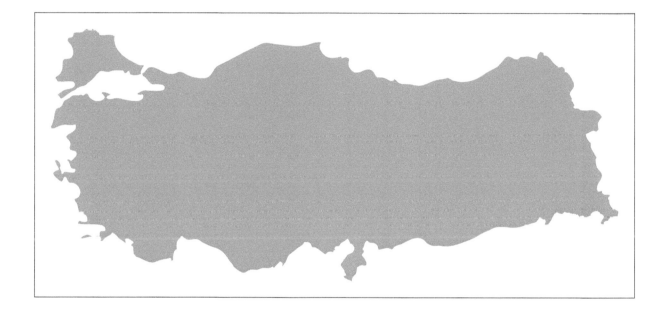

TURKEY

Introduction

The Republic of Turkey occupies a strategic position between Europe and the Middle East. It has been an independent nation since 1923, though several civilizations have flourished in the territory for thousands of years. It was a political and cultural center for both the Byzantine and Ottoman empires.

Under the leadership of Mustafa Kemal Atatürk (1881–1938), modern Turkey was born as a Westward-looking and secular republic. In the early 21st century, Turkey is seeking membership in the European Union. Although it faces continued challenges from EU members, if successful, it will be the first country with a largely Muslim population to have joined.

The country continues to face violent unrest from the Kurdish separatist group the Kurdistan Workers' Party (Partiya Karkerên Kurdistanê, or PKK), which is based in southeastern Turkey and northern Iraq. NATO and more than twenty other countries have designated PKK a terrorist organization. In mid-August 2015, after continued violence and Turkish-led airstrikes on PKK sites in Turkey and Iraq, Turkish president Recep Tayyip Erdoğan vowed to eradicate the PKK within Turkish borders.

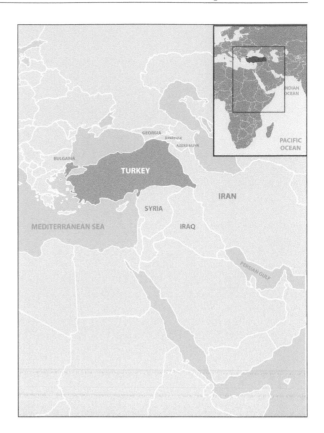

GENERAL INFORMATION

Official Language: Turkish
Population: 79,414,269 (2015 estimate)
Currency: Turkish lira

Coins: Available in the following denominations: 1, 5, 10, 25, 50 kuruş and 1 lira
Land Area: 769,632 square kilometers (297,156 square miles)
Water Area: 13,930 square kilometers (5,378 square miles)
National Motto: "Egemenlik, kayıtsız şartsız Milletindir" ("Sovereignty unconditionally belongs to the Nation")
National Anthem: "İstiklâl Marşı" ("Independence March")
Capital: Ankara
Time Zone: GMT+2
Flag Description: The Turkish flag is all red. Just to the left of the flag's center is a white crescent moon with a white, five-pointed star just to the right of the crescent's opening.

Population

In 2015, the population of Turkey was estimated to be 79,414,269. Turkey has a young, growing population, with just over seven percent over

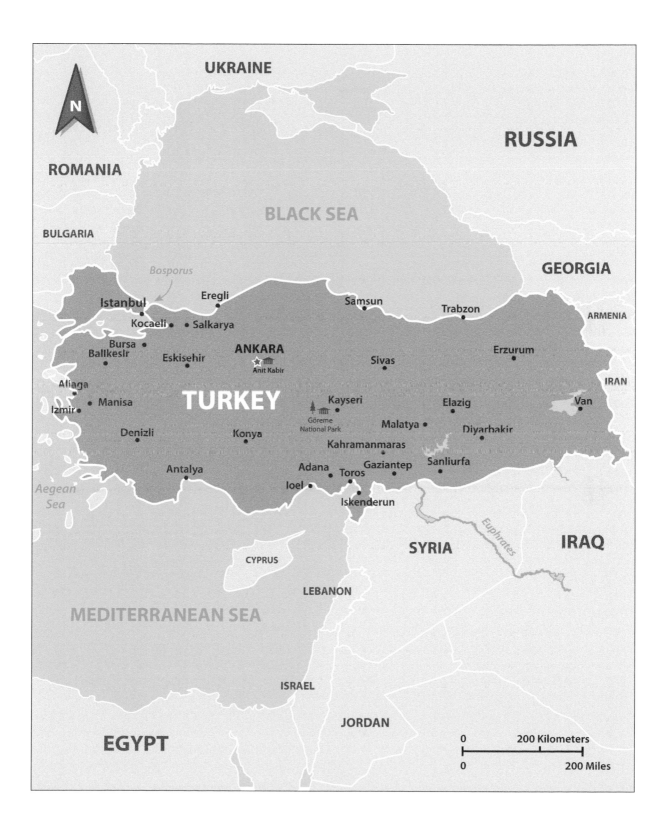

Principal Cities by Population (2014):

- Istanbul (14,100,000)
- Ankara (4,587,558)
- Izmir, also İzmir (2,847,691)
- Bursa (1,800,278)
- Adana (1,663,485)
- Gaziantep, also Antep (1,510,270)
- Konya (1,174,536)
- Antalya (1,068,099)
- Diyarbakir (930,266)
- Mersin (915,703)

65 years. The median life expectancy is just over 74 years old, with the female median age being 77 and the male just over 72 years. As of 2015, the average number of children born to each Turkish woman was 2.05, and there were 18.87 infant deaths per 1,000 live births.

In the space of approximately half a century, the population of Turkey shifted from predominantly rural to predominantly urban. As of 2015, 73.4 percent of the population lives in urban areas. The most densely populated areas are along the coasts. The northern and western regions of the country tend to be more economically developed, while the southern and eastern regions are less so.

Languages

Turkish is the sole official language of the country. It belongs to the Altaic language family, which originated in Central Asia. Like many aspects of Turkish life, the Turkish language was reformed during the early days of the republic. The Arabic alphabet was exchanged for a modified Latin alphabet, and many non-Turkish words were purged. Such reforms had wide-ranging effects, including a rupture with the language of the Ottoman Empire and the script of the Koran.

Kurdish and Arabic are the second and third most commonly spoken languages. It is difficult to find reliable, accurate information on the percentage of the population that speaks Kurdish, as census efforts in the country tend to avoid data pertaining to the country's minority ethnic groups. Armenians and Greeks speak their own languages respectively, while the Jews in Turkey speak a medieval Spanish derivative called Ladino.

Native People & Ethnic Groups

As mentioned, information on ethnic groups in the country is difficult to find, as Turkish censuses do not gather information on ethnic minorities. It is estimated, however, that, as of 2014, between 70 and 75 percent of the population is Turkish, though ethnic Turks actually constitute a lesser and uncertain proportion, perhaps as little as 25 percent. Kurds continue to make up the largest minority, at 18 percent of the population. There are also small groups of Arabs, Armenians, Greeks, and Jews, as well as various ethnic groups from the Caucasus, which together represent between seven and 12 percent of the population.

Some of the oldest civilizations in the world were established in Asia Minor. Waves of different groups followed, from the Hittites and Phrygians to the Greeks and Romans. Ethnic Turks first arrived from the Central Asian steppe in the 11th century, bringing Islam with them.

The 1923 Treaty of Lausanne defined "minorities" in Turkey as being religion-based (instead of ethnically, linguistically, or culturally based). In theory, the treaty granted full citizenship rights to non-Muslim persons living in Turkey; however, the treaty has historically applied to only three of Turkey's many ethnic groups: those of Armenian, Greek, and Jewish descent.

Several of the minorities still present in Turkey once had much larger populations. Both the Greeks and the Armenians exemplify this trend, and both populations underwent forced relocations during the early 20th century. Many Greeks moved to Greece following Turkey's war for independence, and many Armenians left eastern Turkey as the Ottoman Empire was dissolving. A deep ethnic wound still pains the country and its relations with other nations; the Armenians maintain that hundreds of thousands of (and some sources say over one million) Armenians perished from starvation, disease, and mass murder during forced removals from

Turkish territory, and they have repeatedly sought to have these deaths recognized as genocide. The Turkish government does not accept the term "genocide" in association with the claims, arguing that the Armenian deaths were war casualties.

One of the most persistent sources of conflict in modern Turkey has been between the indigenous ethnic Kurds, who have an ancient history in the southeastern part of the country, and the Turkish majority. With the founding of the republic, there was an attempt to downplay the ethnic and cultural differences of the Kurds and other ethnic minorities. The Kurdish language was banned, even in private use, until 1991. While a ban on Kurdish language in the education system was lifted in 2003, Kurds were still banned from giving their children Kurdish names. In the early 21st century, numerous politicians and political figures have been arrested and sentenced to prison terms for delivering political speeches and propaganda in Kurdish.

In 1984, the Kurdistan Workers' Party (PKK) began a terrorist campaign intended to create an independent Kurdistan. Warfare between the Turkish military and Kurdish guerillas continued intermittently through most of the 1990s. The leader of the PKK was captured in 1998, and a truce declared in 2000. However, in 2015, southeastern Turkey has again become the site of increased violence between the PKK militants and the Turkish government. In mid-August 2015, the PKK claimed responsibility for a bombing that resulted in the deaths of four Turkish police officers and a soldier in Sirnak, a Kurdish-dominated region of Turkey. This, along with other episodes of violence that have resulted in the death of 50 people, has caused the Turkish armed forces to retaliate by bombing the PKK militants' bases in southeastern Turkey, using U.S. F-16s stationed at Incirlik Airforce Base. The U.S. fighter planes are at Incirlik to combat ISIS, although the PKK has accused Turkey of colluding with ISIS against the Kurds. Turkey has denied this accusation.

Religions

Though Turkey is a conservative country, influenced by moderate Islam, it is committed to a secular society. Nevertheless, there are still frequent tensions between the secular government and those who want religion to have a greater role in public life.

Because the country does not take into account religious affiliations when recording census data, exact statistics on religious affiliations can only be estimated.

Most Turks are Sunni Muslims, as are roughly two-thirds of Kurds. The remainder of the Kurds and nearly all Muslim Arabs belong to the persecuted Alevi religious community, which has a belief system distinct from that of Shia Muslims; Alevis take a philosophical and humanist approach to their religion and believe in a democratization—rather than segregation—of the sexes. Perhaps 20 percent of the Sunni majority practice a mystical form of the religion called Sufism, to which the renowned dervishes belong.

Syrian Orthodox Christians, who are ethnically Arab, comprise the largest Christian community. Greeks and Armenians within the country belong to their respective branches of the Orthodox faith.

Climate

The climate along the Mediterranean and Aegean coasts is subtropical. It is characterized by long, warm summers and wet, but mild winters. A similar, though wetter, climate prevails along the Black Sea. On the arid central Anatolian Plateau, summers are hotter and drier and winters are much colder, giving this region a continental climate. Precipitation generally falls as snow. Winters in the eastern highlands are longer and harsher, and summers are hot and dry.

Turkey lies on an active seismic belt, the Anatolian Plate, along which run the strike-slip lines (that is, faults that move laterally and have little, if any, vertical motion) known as the North Anatolian Fault and the East Anatolian Fault. The country is also situated in an area where the Eurasian, African, and Arabian tectonic plates meet. Earthquakes range from slight tremors to devastating natural disasters. Aftershocks are common following moderate and intense earthquakes. The worst recent earthquake, which killed an estimated 15,000 people, was centered in northwestern Turkey in 1999. More recently, on October 23, 2011, a 7.1-magnitude quake struck near the city of Van in eastern Turkey. Officially classified as "severe," the Van quake killed 604, injured 4,152, and significantly damaged or entirely leveled 2,200 buildings.

ENVIRONMENT & GEOGRAPHY

Topography

Only a small portion of Turkey's land, called Thrace, lies in Europe and includes the Gallipoli Peninsula. (One quarter of Thrace's total expanse lies in Turkey; one-tenth is in Greece, and the remainder is in Bulgaria). The Bosporus Strait, the Sea of Marmara, and the Dardanelles, forming a waterway that links the Black Sea and the Aegean, separate the Asian side from the Europe.

Turkey is divided into seven natural regions: the Pontus and Taurus mountain ranges, the central Anatolian Plateau, the eastern highlands, the Arabian Platform, and the Black Sea, Aegean, and Mediterranean regions. The coastlines along the three major seas account for three-quarters of Turkey's border.

The Pontus and the Taurus are the most significant mountain ranges, and they provide substantial barriers between the seas and the inner plateau. The Pontus range runs parallel to the Black Sea and gains in elevation along its eastern portion. The Taurus generally parallels the Mediterranean until the coast turns south along the Arabian Platform. These two mountain ranges meet in Eastern Anatolia, forming the Anti-Taurus. It is here that Turkey's highest peak, Mount Ararat, rises to an elevation of 5,165 meters (16,945 feet).

Of the many rivers in Turkey, three of the most important flow from the Anti-Taurus range: the Tigris, the Euphrates, and the Aras. Other rivers include the Gediz and the Büyük Menderes, which empty into the Aegean; the Ceyhan and Seyhan, which empty into the Mediterranean; and the Sakarya and Turkey's longest river,

Kizilirmak, which empty into the Black Sea. The largest lake, Lake Van, is located in the east.

Turkish territory also includes several small islands off the Aegean coast.

Plants & Animals

Vegetation on the arid Anatolian Plateau is characterized by a variety of grasses and small stands of trees, including oak and juniper. Shrubs and trees, such as oak and pine, are found along the Aegean and Mediterranean coasts. In contrast to the dense forests of the eastern Pontus Mountains, where valuable hardwood trees like walnut and maple are found, the typical Mediterranean growth is sparse.

Turkey is home to 116 animal species, most of them Asian. Common species include boar, deer, gazelle, wolf, fox, and bear. Seventeen of these animals are endangered, the Mediterranean monk seal critically. There are five species of mammals found only in Turkey, all of them rodents. These species include the woolly dormouse, Anatolian vole, Doğramaci's vole, the Asia Minor spiny mouse, and *Crocidura arispa*, commonly known as the jackass shrew.

The heavy impact of human settlement and cultivation usually keeps larger animals confined to the less exploited regions. The number of tourists visiting Turkey has had a negative impact on some ecosystems.

CUSTOMS & COURTESIES

Greetings

A firm handshake is a common greeting in Turkey, especially in business settings. However, a man should not shake a woman's hand unless she offers it first. A warmer variation, frequently used on social occasions, is the two-handed handshake, in which one party uses both hands to clasps the hand of the other. In addition, Turks will often embrace and kiss both cheeks when meeting and parting with a close friend. At family gatherings, it is also customary for young people to kiss the back of the hand of an elderly family member and then touch it to their foreheads as a sign of respect. Lastly, when joining a small group, each member of the group is typically greeted individually, beginning with the eldest.

The traditional greeting is "Merhaba" ("Hello"), followed by "Nasilsiniz" ("How are you?"). A less formal greeting, and common among youth, is "Selam" ("Salute"). Among friends, greetings are followed by polite inquiries about family, health, and work. However, women in rural areas and traditional women may be uncomfortable talking to a man to whom they have not been formally introduced. In a business setting, more personal inquiries are replaced by general small talk as a preliminary to doing business. Additionally, going directly to the business at hand is considered rude, and small talk will accompany even a simple retail transaction.

Gestures & Etiquette

The traditional way of addressing someone is to use the first name, followed by the title bey for a man (as in Ahmad Bey), or hanim for a woman. A recent variation on this, mostly used by business people dealing with Europeans, is to use bey or hanim, or the more modern bay or bayan, followed by the surname. As a matter of respect, elderly people are often addressed by adding amca (uncle) or teyze (aunt) to their first name (as in Ahmad Amca).

Traditional ideas concerning modest behavior for women continue to influence Turkish culture. Religiously conservative women may cover their face and mouth with their headscarf in the presence of non-family members, and it is common to see people of the same gender holding hands on the public street. However, public displays of affection between persons of the opposite sex are rare. Additionally, many women are uncomfortable sitting next to a man on public transportation and will stand rather than sit between two men.

Some of the practical courtesies in Turkey are influenced by Muslim culture and include the removal of shoes before entering a mosque and the covering of the head for women. Many mosques also enforce a dress code that forbids visitors from entering the building wearing shorts or other attire deemed immodest. Larger mosques provide robes or sarong-like wraps for the benefit of visitors who are not appropriately dressed. It is also generally considered offensive to use the left hand to pass something, and objects are passed from person to person with the right hand or both hands. This is because, in Muslim culture, the left hand is traditionally used for the cleansing of the body and is thus considered impure. Additionally, some postures that are common in Western culture are considered rude in Turkey, such as showing someone the soles of one's feet or shoes, or crossing the arms while facing someone.

Eating/Meals

The brewing and serving of tea play an important role in Turkish culture. Outdoor tea gardens are common, and a visitor to a home or a place of business will typically be offered tea on arrival. In commercial or retail districts, small tea stalls provide tea and other beverages to businesses, often bringing the beverages through the street or the bazaar on a tray. Whether in a home or in a restaurant or café, tea is brewed samovar-style (a samovar is a traditional container used to heat water). This means that a small pot of very strong tea is kept hot over a larger pot of boiling water and served in tiny tulip-shaped glasses with saucers. Generally, tea is served with cube sugar on the side.

Breakfast typically includes fresh bread with butter and preserves, olives, yogurt, sliced tomatoes and cucumbers, as well as dried fruits. Salty cheeses are also an essential part of breakfast table. The most prevalent cheeses include Beyaz peynir, a salty white cheese made of indigenous sheep's milk, and kasseri (or kaşar), a slightly hard yellow cheese also made from sheep's milk. Kaymak, a dairy product much like clotted cream, is often spread on fresh bread and topped with honey or jam. In fact, fresh bread is generally part of every meal, and bakeries typically bake it in the morning for breakfast and lunch and again in the afternoon for dinner. Types of bread include a long sourdough loaf similar to a French baguette; several varieties of griddle-baked breads; and pide, a leavened flatbread usually topped with tomatoes, onions, meat, and herbs and different from the more widely recognized pita. Simit, bread that is shaped like a bagel and covered with sesame, poppy, sunflower, or flax seeds, is a popular mid-morning snack. It can be purchased from street vendors and in small convenience stores.

Many restaurants specialize in a certain type of food. Some serve only fish or meat with a limited number of side dishes. For example, çorbaçi specialize in soup, while kebapçi and köfteçi serve grilled meats. Esnaf lokantası (tradesmen's restaurants) are designed to move patrons in and out quickly. For this reason, they often specialize in lunch and serve a variety of home-style dishes that, occasionally, have been prepared in advance and are kept warm over steam tables. Other lokatansi have a limited menu, with items that can be speedily prepared to order. Many foods are traditionally eaten with the fingers or scooped up with bread, though utensils are commonly used as well.

Visiting

Hospitality is an important part of Turkish culture. Because Turkish entertainment happens in public places, such as restaurants, an invitation to a Turkish home is a great honor and is taken very seriously. As such, informal or unannounced visits are customarily not appropriate for anyone other than a family member.

Turkish people typically remove their shoes on entering their homes and often provide an assortment of slippers for guests. Visitors are offered something to eat or drink. In a traditional household, this offer may be preceded by an offer of eau de toilette. If the visitor accepts, a small amount of lemon or lavender scent is traditionally poured into cupped hands, which the visitor then rubs on the face, hands and wrists, the purpose of which is to cool and refresh.

Once inside the house, guests are seated according to relative importance, usually in terms of age and social status. Thus, the most honored (or oldest) guest is given the seat farthest away from the door, with the host taking the seat closest to the door. At a dinner party, the host will offer additional servings of food many times. While it is polite to say no to the first offer, the expectation is that the guest will accept on the second offer. In a traditional home, the host may not sit down and eat with the guests, but will stand and serve everyone at the table.

LIFESTYLE

Family

A traditional rural household is composed of a man and his wife, their adult sons and their wives, and their young children and grandchildren. When the male head of the household dies, a traditional household is then subdivided into smaller households headed by the adult sons. With the advent of modernization, an increasing number of men are finding work in urban areas, and their families remain at home in the villages to work the family land. However, extended family ties remain close, even among the urban population, though the traditional extended-family household is impractical within the constraints of urban housing. Even within the city, it is rare for a person to live alone.

Arranged marriages are still common in rural areas and among more traditional religious families. Although the country is predominantly Muslim, only civil marriages are legal. Additionally, many couples have two marriage services: the legal civil service, followed by a religious service to satisfy more traditional family members. Polygamy, or plural marriages, which were legal under Islamic law, was outlawed in 1925 as part of Atatürk's Westernizing reforms. However, polygamy still occurs and the question of legitimacy and legal rights for the children of such marriages is an ongoing social problem.

Housing

The traditional townhouse in Turkey was two stories tall and built around an interior courtyard or garden. The second story typically had large windows with wooden grills, and since these often project out over the street, the design both captures sun to create brightly lit rooms, but also creates a shadowy tunnel effect on narrow streets. Generally built of wood or stone, most houses were whitewashed on the exterior and have red tile roofs. Traditional houses are still common in smaller cities and in the older neighborhoods of larger cities. New apartment buildings in larger cities are mostly built of brick or concrete in the "modern" style popular during the 1950s and 1960s in North America.

A typical village house is two stories high, with a flat roof that is used much like a patio. Traditionally, the lower floor was used to shelter animals and for storage. Many of these rural or village houses are built from different materials, largely depending on the region's climate and terrain. The most commonly used materials are stone, wood, and sun-dried brick. In recent years, concrete block has become the preferred material for those who can afford it. Additionally, as towns on the Aegean and Mediterranean coast, such as Bodrum, become more popular as resort areas, a growing numbers of luxury condominiums are being built.

Food

Turkish cuisine is a distinct cuisine with notable Mediterranean and Middle Eastern influences. It evolved from the culinary traditions of the Ottoman Empire as well as the culinary attitudes of the region's indigenous peoples. It is largely based on meats, such as lamb and fish, and other staples, like yogurt and olive oil. A wide variety of vegetables, most notably tomato, eggplant, and onion, feature prominently in Turkey's cuisine. Although very few Turks are vegetarians, the portions of meat are typically smaller than those served in North America, and vegetables are often the largest part of the meal. As in most Islamic countries, no pork is eaten.

The most common way to prepare meat is roasting or grilling over a hot charcoal fire. Both methods are used to create the style of meat known as "kebab." The best-known dish in this style is shish kebab, which consists of pieces of lamb roasted on a skewer. Other common kebab dishes are döner kebab, which is lamb roasted on a vertical spit and served in slices, often on flatbread, and köfte kebab (or Şiş köfte), which is ground lamb meatballs. Other typical dishes include pilaf, which generally consists of rice, and börek, which is a pastry made from thin sheets of dough that is filled with meats, cheeses, or other ingredients.

One famous eggplant dish is imam bayaldi ("imam fainted"), which is eggplant stewed in lavish amounts of olive oil. According to legend, the new bride of an imam used all the olive oil that she had brought as part of her dowry to cook eggplant for him the first night they were married. Accounts differ on whether the imam fainted because the dish was so delicious, or because his bride was so extravagant.

Turkish coffee is not as common as tea. It is generally very expensive and is usually served after a meal. Each cup is brewed individually by boiling coffee, water, and sugar together in special pot with a long handle. The resulting brew is very strong and thick, and as it sits, the grounds settle to the bottom of the cup. The dregs at the bottom of the cup are often used in fortune telling after the coffee is drunk.

Life's Milestones

Most Muslim boys in Turkey undergo circumcision, called "sünnet" usually around the age of four. Treated as a ritual rather than an operation, circumcision is the occasion of a major celebration. The boy is dressed in special clothes that resemble those of an Ottoman prince and receives presents from friends and relatives. It is also common for municipalities to organize group circumcision parties for poor families.

Military service is mandatory for Turkish men and lasts for a period of six to 12 months, beginning at 21 years of age. On the day that a young man departs for his service, friends, and family see him off in a public display sometimes called a "soldier wedding." Gathering in the parking lots where buses wait to take them to camp, the young men dance to drum and pipe under waving Turkish flags. In smaller communities, the whole town may turn out for such an event.

Most Turkish Muslims, whether religiously conservative or not, try to visit Mecca at least once in their lifetimes. Known as the Hajj, this pilgrimage to Mohammed's birthplace is one of the five religious pillars, or obligations, of Islam. Making the pilgrimage often marks a fundamental change from a Westernized lifestyle to a more traditional one.

CULTURAL HISTORY

Art

Modern-day Turkey was created at the end of World War I from the Turkish-speaking provinces of the Ottoman Empire (1299–1923). The country is the cultural heir not only of the Ottomans, but also of the Byzantine Empire (which lasted from roughly the fourth to the 15th centuries CE) and the Islamic Golden Age (a renaissance of Islamic art between the eighth and 13th centuries CE).

The influence of Islam on Turkish art is evident in the prevalence of geometric designs, and the emphasis on certain artistic effects, such as color, abstraction, and balance. This is because Islam, as decreed by the hadith (reports of Muhammad's verbatim teachings), prohibits the representation of either the human or animal forms. In the case of Ottoman Turkey, a display of floral designs was added to the design vocabulary, with the tulip becoming a particularly prominent symbol. (The Tulip period is a period in Ottoman history dating 1718–1730, during which European movements, such as the Baroque, became a strong influence on the arts.) These patterns began to appear in a wide range of traditional art forms, including rugs, the famous glazed ceramics from the potteries at Iznik, and silk textiles.

In addition to carpet weaving, ceramics, jewelry, and silk embroidery, another traditional art to develop in Turkey is ebru. Often considered a distinct Turkish art form, ebru refers to paper marbling—in which marbled patterns are reproduced on paper—and emerged in Turkey during the 15th century. This decorative art form was traditionally used in bookmaking, as well as calligraphy. In fact, the so-called "art of the book" was the most elaborate of the Ottoman arts, reflecting the importance of the book in Islamic culture. Each illustrated manuscript was an expensive and unique production, requiring the talents of a range of artists, brought together in the nakkashane, or imperial studio. The most revered of these artists were the calligraphers. They not only copied texts in a variety of scripts with different graphic and emotional qualities, but also turned imperial and common documents into works of art. Other artists involved in producing manuscripts included illuminators, painters, and bookbinders.

Painting began to emerge fully as an established prominent art in Turkish culture in the 19th century, following the increasing Westernization of the Ottoman Empire. This largely coincided with the formal founding of a school of fine arts (which would become the Mimar Sinan University of Fine Arts in Istanbul) by pioneering Turkish painter Osman Hamdi Bey (1842–1910). While early Turkish painters focused mostly on landscape painting, they soon introduced more modern influences into their art, most notably impressionism, followed by abstract and cubist art.

Architecture

Ottoman architecture is in many ways an extension of the Byzantine style of architecture that emerged from the Roman Empire in the 4th century CE and Persian architectural styles. Like the Romans, the Ottomans built a distinctive style of public architecture throughout their empire. The central structure of an Ottoman city was often the mosque, which was typically built on a standard pattern of a large single dome surrounded by slender minarets and a colonnaded courtyard. This dome structure continued to be a prominent feature of Turkish architecture, revealing the blend of Western and Eastern elements.

During the Westernization of the Ottoman Empire in the late 19th and early 20th centuries, Turkish architecture was influenced by the ornamental styles of the baroque movement, among other European styles. This blend of styles is often seen in the architecture of mosques and public buildings and the use of grand fountains and other such decorative elements. This period was followed by an emergence of neoclassical traditions and an attempt to establish a national style of architecture.

Perhaps the most famous Turkish architect is Mimar Sinan (1489–1588), who began his career as a member of the elite Turkish troops called the Janissaries (the personal soldiers of the sultan). Becoming skilled at engineering and architecture while serving in the army, he was soon appointed royal architect. He built more than 300 buildings throughout the Ottoman Empire (including an estimated eighty-four mosques) for three sultans, beginning with Suleiman I (1494–1566). His buildings are notable for his skillful use of the characteristic Ottoman dome and its relationships to the structures around it. His best-known building is perhaps the Suleiman Mosque (Süleymaniye Mosque) in Istanbul, while his masterpiece is considered to be the Selimiye Mosque in Edirne.

Music

Historically, Turkish music was divided between the classical music of the Ottoman court—often called sanat or klasik—and traditional Turkish folk music. This was typically played among the rural population and was popular at weddings, festivals, and funerals. Classical music was considered refined and elite and largely based on the classical music and styles of Arabian and Persian classical music. Turkish folk music is more lively and unrestrained and has numerous varieties and regional differences. In addition, the traditions of this mostly rural music were typically not written down, but generally passed along by Turkish troubadours (often called the "asiklar"). Turkish music also features many distinct traditional instruments, such as the Turkish bağlama, a type of stringed lute considered fundamental in Turkish folk music.

Two other forms of specialized music stood outside the classical/folk divide: mehteran, typically played by Ottoman military marching bands, and the music of the whirling dervishes. In the 16th century, military marching bands

were otherwise unknown. The shrill marching music of the mehteran (the name for the Ottoman military band), produced by a combination of horns and percussion, added to the terror caused by the ferocious army. The Ottomans abandoned the music in the 19th century following Sultan Mahmud II's massacre of the janissaries, who formed the core of the bands. In 1953, the Turkish Armed Forces revived the mehteran tradition for ceremonial occasions.

Dance

The so-called "whirling dervishes" are members of the Mevlevi Order of Sufis, an order that was founded in Turkey in the 13th century. (Sufism is described as a mystic sect of Islam.) The dervishes dance the sema as an act of devotion, spinning continuously in place to complex vocal and instrumental compositions called ayin. This ritual is also referred to as Sufi or Dervish whirling and is considered a type of meditation. Together, the spiritual dance and music are meant to replicate the heavenly bodies spinning to the music of the spheres.

In 1925, the Sufi orders, which had been politically influential under the Ottomans, were banned as part of a national move toward a secular state. In particular, the dancing lodges (tekke) of the Mevlevi Order of Sufism were closed. For roughly 40 years, devout Sufis practiced their devotions in strict secrecy, posting guards against police raids whenever they gathered for their ritualistic dances and worshipping. Although the order still does not officially exist, and laws against the open practice of Sufism remain on the books, the government restored the Mevlevi lodge in Galata as a museum in 1970. Dervishes are now allowed to perform as a tourist attraction at the museum and other venues, including an annual dervish festival each December in Konya, which was the spiritual home of the Mevlevi Order.

Literature

As with music, Turkish literature was historically divided between a court-based literary tradition, which was influenced by Arabic and Persian genres and styles, and an oral folk tradition. The dominant form of the written literary tradition was Ottoman Divan (or Diwan) poetry (also called court poetry), which was strictly metered, highly symbolic, and often combined Sufi mysticism with erotic imagery. The literary tradition also included historical and philosophical writing, but no tradition of prose literature developed until the 19th century.

The folk tradition included epics, an oral poetry form generally written in quatrains (four-line stanzas), and a series of lively folktales. Often humorous, these tales typically centered on stock characters, the most famous of which are Keloğlan (literally, "bald boy"), a young man faced with the problems of village life, and Nasreddin, a Muslim imam who is both a trickster and a "wise fool" character.

In the 19th century, reformers began purging Arabic and Persian influences from Ottoman Turkish literature. They combined themes from the folktales with Western literary traditions to create the first Turkish novels and short stories. This was followed by a nationalistic period—the National Literature movement—in the early 20th century. The literature of this period was characterized by simple language and structure (particularly poetry), and was influenced by the developing idea of a national Turkish identity (as opposed to Persian, Arabic, or Ottoman).

CULTURE

Arts & Entertainment

Many of the richest cultural expressions in Turkey derive from Ottoman times, when massive architectural projects were undertaken. These buildings are often decorated with intricately detailed tiles, representing one of the foremost arts of the period. When the Republic of Turkey was founded in 1923, Mustafa Kemal Atatürk and other leaders of the new country were determined to create a modern, secular state. Their goal was a unified culture that emphasized Western influence and "Turkishness," replacing the previously dominant Islamic culture and its Arabic and Persian roots.

This idea of nationalism specifically favored the folk arts of rural Anatolia (a region in western Asia, which now mostly comprises modern-day Turkey). Folk music from the Anatolian region of Turkey received both the dubious benefits of government encouragement and widespread exposure on radio and television. Official musicologists collected folk music in the field, creating an invaluable archive of recordings. The classical music genre of the Ottoman Empire, with its reliance on Arabic, Byzantine, and Persian musical modes, was specifically attacked, and classified as an elite, urban form divorced from its Turkish cultural roots. In the early 1970s, Turkish classical music returned to favor, and a state music conservatory was founded in 1976. This gave classical musicians the same quality of state-supported training as that given to folk musicians.

Twentieth-century Turkish literature offered several names of international stature, when the novelist Yaşar Kemal (1923–2015) and the poet Nazim Hikmet (1902–1963) earned prominent reputations. The most well known writer in contemporary Turkey is novelist Orhan Pamuk (1952–). He won the Nobel Prize in Literature in 2006, becoming the first Turk to win a Nobel Prize. His works include the novels *Snow* (2002), *My Name is Red* (1998), *The New Life* (1995), *The Museum of Innocence* (2008), as well as the memoir *Istanbul: Memories and the City* (2003).

Turkish literature also replaced music at the forefront of Turkey's ongoing struggle with questions of national identity in June 2005, when a new penal code, article 301, made it illegal to insult "Turkishness," including the nation's government institutions. Since it became law, thousands of people have been charged with offences against section 301, a large number of them publishers, journalists, and other writers. These include Pamuk, novelist Elif Şafak (1971–), author of the bestselling *The Bastard of Istanbul*, and Turkish-Armenian journalist Hrant Dink (1954–2007). Most of the high profile arrests have been related to the 1915 Armenian Genocide, an issue that is still sensitive in Turkey. On April 30, 2008, the language of article 301 was amended to make it illegal to insult Turkey, Turkish ethnicity, or the Turkish government, rather than "Turkishness." The law remains a point of contention in Turkey's ongoing attempts to become a full member of the European Union.

Traditional carpet making is still practiced in Turkey, and carpets and kilims (flat-woven carpets) are made with a variety of methods and patterns. The more valuable carpets are made by hand with traditional dyes and materials. Carpets and kilims are now the most widespread visual art in the country, and rural rug cooperatives provide young women with training in creating handmade rugs, as well as a market for their work. Traditional Turkish arts, such as Iznik-inspired pottery, alabaster work, and both knotted and woven carpets, are also still practiced with an eye to creating for the tourist trade, often with government support.

Turkish people follow their national football (soccer) teams fervently. Popular teams include Fenerbahçe, Beşiktaş, and Galatasaray. Traditional oil wrestling, which is the occasion for an annual festival in western Turkey, is also a respected sport.

Cultural Sites & Landmarks

Located at the crossroads between Europe, Asia, and the Middle East, modern Turkey is home to the cultural remains of many former empires. The Hittites, Persians, ancient Greeks, Romans, and Ottomans all occupied the region. In addition, Turkey is home to nine protected World Heritage Sites, as designated by the United Nations Educational, Scientific, and Cultural Organization (UNESCO). These sites are catalogued due to their natural or cultural importance.

The Göreme National Park, in the region of Cappadocia, is one of the most popular cultural sites in Turkey. Ninth-century Christians carved more than thirty chapels and monasteries out of the area's soft volcanic material, both underground and into cliff sides. Many of the churches are decorated with Byzantine frescos of the life of Christ and the early saints. The surrounding area is also honeycombed with underground cities and cliff-side dwellings that date from as early as the ancient Hittites (c. 1600 BCE–c. 1178 BCE) through the 1960s, when the Turkish government outlawed them. The site is also famous for its "fairy chimneys," which are conical formations of rock. Together, the national park and the surrounding landscape were listed as a World Heritage Site in 1985.

In 1870, German archaeologist Heinrich Schliemann (1822–1890) located the site of the fabled city of Troy, using the physical descriptions in Homer's epic poem of the Trojan War, the *Iliad*. Although later archeologists have condemned Schliemann's excavation methods, his discoveries made Troy one of the most famous archeological sites in the world. Still an active archaeological dig, portions of the site are open to the public, including a small museum and a fanciful wooden recreation of the Trojan Horse, the device that Homer's Greeks used to breach the walls of Troy. The archaeological site was listed as a World Heritage Site in 1998.

Other World Heritage Sites include the Divriği Great Mosque and Hospital, built in the 13th century and renowned for their architecture and carvings; the archaeological site of Hattusha, an ancient Hittite capital; Mount Nemrut, officially listed as Nemrut Dağ, a mountain whose summit contains the mausoleum (tomb) of Antiochus I (69–34 BCE), as well as various statues, and dates to the first century BCE; the city of Safranbolu, recognized for its Ottoman architecture; and Hierapolis-Pamukkale, which are important natural landscapes that feature hot springs, petrified waterfalls, and ancient ruins.

Ephesus is the best-preserved Roman city east of the Mediterranean. It appeals not only to tourists interested in classical ruins, but also to those interested in early Christian sites. Founded in the 10th century BCE by the Greeks, the city became the chief port of the Aegean under Roman rule and the capital of Roman Asia. It was also an important city for early Christianity, and Paul the Apostle (Saint Paul), a famous Christian missionary, used it as a base for his missionary work for several years. It is also believed that both the Saint John the Apostle, one of the twelve disciples of Jesus Christ, and Mary the mother of Jesus, lived in or near the city at the end of their lives.

The Gallipoli National Historic Park was created to commemorate the Gallipoli campaign of World War I, in which more than 500,000 Turkish and Allied soldiers died. The campaign was a nation-building event for both Turkey and the then-British possessions of Australia and New Zealand. Thousands of Australians and New Zealanders visit the park each year on Anzac Day (April 25), when Turkey honors the Australian and New Zealand Army Corps (ANZAC) forces who died in the campaign. The war memorial is unusual in that it honors the dead from both sides of the battle.

The Anitkabir, Atatürk's mausoleum, monument, and museum, is the most-visited site in Ankara. The huge complex is the greatest example of modern Turkish architecture. Nearby, an equestrian statue of Atatürk can be found in Ulus Meydani (Ulus Square).

Libraries & Museums

Aya Sofya (also Hagia Sophia) in Istanbul was originally built as a Byzantine church between 532 and 537 CE during the reign of Justinian I (c. 483–565). After the Ottomans conquered Constantinople in 1453, Sultan Mehmet II (also known as "Mehmed the Conqueror," 1432–1481) converted the church into a mosque. He covered the figurative golden mosaics that decorated its dome and upper walls with plaster and whitewash. In 1932, modern Turkey, under the leadership of the country's founder, Mustafa Kemal Atatürk, opened the mosque as a museum honoring both its Muslim and Christian heritage. The surviving mosaics have been uncovered and restored.

In 1948, the National Library of Turkey ("Millî Kütüphane") opened its doors in Ankara. Publisher of the Turkish National Biography, its collection includes some 26,000 manuscripts, Turcica (materials relevant to Turkish studies), translations of Turkish literature, and a repository for legal deposit publications. Also in Ankara is

the Bilkent University Library, which is open to the public.

Holidays

Secular holidays in Turkey include Atatürk Commemoration Day, which is also Youth and Sports Day (May 19); Victory Day (August 30), which celebrates the country's triumph in the Turkish war of independence (1919–1923); and Republic Day (October 29). Seker Bayrami (literally "sugar feast"), the three-day festival that concludes the holy fasting month of Ramadan, and Kurban Bayrami ("feast of the sacrifice"), when animals are sacrificed and alms are given to the poor, are two of the most widely celebrated Islamic holidays.

Youth Culture

As a result of a high birth rate, Turkey has an increasingly youth-driven culture and nearly 42 percent of the population is under 25 years old. Although conservative Islam has recently increased in Turkey, it remains very much a secular Muslim country, as reflected by the culture of its youth. This trend may be seen in the increasing diversification and wide demand for popular music in Turkey at the turn of the twenty-first century.

Turkey's most common pop music, the hugely popular arabesk, is in many ways a revolt against the officially sanctioned dominance of folk music. It is a synthesis of Turkish folk music and Middle Eastern musical styles—including Arabic belly dancing music and Egyptian film music. Arabesk uses subject matter and lyrics that reflect the migration of village and rural Turks into the city and other urban areas. It is also known as "minibus music" because it is the preferred music of the crowded dolmuş (minibuses) that transport Turkish workers to their jobs each day. Arabesk recordings now outsell those of every other genre of Turkish music.

In addition to arabesk, Turkey has a strong indie music community, producing alternative Turkish versions of rock, electronica, hip-hop, rap, and house music (electronic dance music). The Turkish popular music scene has produced several international pop stars, including the German-born Turkish phenomenon Tarkan Tevetoğlu (1972–). Known simply as Tarkan, he has achieved an international reputation and the media moniker as the "Prince of Pop." In fact, *The Washington Post* compared Tarkan's effect on Turkish audiences to that of Elvis Presley on American audiences in the mid-20th century.

SOCIETY

Transportation

The U.S. Department of State recommends driving defensively in Turkey and encourages visitors to avoid driving at night. It is also recommended that drivers and passengers always wear seat belts and that children ride in the back seat of the vehicle. In addition, it should be noted that drivers use the right hand side of the road in Turkey and often use their horns and headlights to communicate with other vehicles.

Car ownership remains a relative luxury in Turkey, with roughly 16,751,754 million registered cars in a population of more than 80 million people. As a result, there is a wide variety of public transportation available in major cities. Taxis are common, but it is recommended that visitors use the backseat of taxis as opposed to riding in the front passenger seat as it greatly reduces risk of injury if an accident takes place. In addition to official bus systems, most cities also have the dolmuş, a small van that operates as a type of shared taxi and has set routes. They operate by picking up and letting off passengers anywhere along their designated routes.

Metros, trams, and light rail systems are also experiencing an upsurge in Turkey. Twelve cities, including Istanbul, Eskisehir, Adana, and Konya, have one of these three systems in place. Ankara also has a light rail-style metro, known as the "Ankaray," which complements its growing underground subway system.

Although there are flights between major cities, most Turks travel across the country on one of the hundreds of inter-city bus lines. The buses are quite luxurious by American standards and are often staffed by a steward who provides water and snacks to the passengers (and brews tea for the driver).

Many international flights into Turkey land at Atatürk International Airport in Istanbul, although there are sixteen international airports throughout the country. Two other major airports are Ankara's Esenboğa Airport and Adana's Şakirpaşa Airport.

Transportation Infrastructure

The Marmaray rail tunnel, which runs under the Bosphorus Strait and whose first phase became operational in October 2013, connects the European and Asian sides of Istanbul. As of 2014, it boasted a daily ridership of 148,034. The Marmaray rail project also includes long-range plans to enhance suburban rail lines running along the Sea of Marmara, in order to increase commuter access. Istanbul also has several ferries across the Bosporus strait, the Golden Horn (the inlet which divides the city), and the Sea of Marmara (also known as the Sea of Marmora).

Media & Communications

The government monopoly on broadcasting was abolished in 1994. However, the government still oversees broadcasting content and infrastructure by way of a regulatory body known as the Radio and Television Supreme Council (RTÜK). In addition to government-sponsored Turkish Radio and Television networks (TRT), there are now 63 private television networks and more than 1,078 private radio stations. Additionally, there are currently 37 national dailies and two national news weeklies, all owned by a variety of publishing groups. Recent surveys, however, suggest that less than 10 percent of the population actually reads newspapers, and weekly celebrity magazines and satirical cartoons reach a much wider audience.

Cell phone service is available throughout the country through two major systems, accounting for roughly two-thirds of the telephones in Turkey. Roughly, 67 million Turks have a cell phone, and cell phones must be registered with the government. This measure was officially designed to help prevent the use of cell phones in terrorist activity and to unofficially stop the importation of inexpensive phones. The Internet is widely available in public locations, such as schools, libraries, and Internet cafés. With some restrictions, the government encourages its use, and in 2014, an estimated 46.6 percent of the population regularly uses the Internet.

SOCIAL DEVELOPMENT

Standard of Living
In 2014, Turkey's Human Development Index rank was 69 out of 187 countries.

Water Consumption
Turkey borders several large bodies of water, including the Mediterranean Sea to the west and southwest and the Black Sea to the north. It is estimated that Turkey has 112 billion square meters of exploitable water resources. The water resources of the country are vulnerable to drought conditions, which tend to occur every 15 years, on average. Water pollution from industrial run-off is probably Turkey's most pressing environmental problem. Urban areas have 100 percent access to improved drinking water sources, while rural populations have 98.8 percent access. Just over 97 percent of urban populations and 75.5 percent of rural populations enjoy improved sanitation facilities.

Education
Public education in Turkey consists of five divisions ranging from preschool to university (or post-secondary). Only primary and secondary education is compulsory. Students must pass a competitive national exam to gain entrance into universities. High schools are divided into lyceums—that offer a general education and college prep—and vocational schools.

There are currently 179 institutions of higher education, 104 of which are state-run universities, 71 are privately funded universities, and four are military academies. Some of the most prestigious include the University of Istanbul, the Middle East Technical University, and Bilkent University in Ankara.

As of 2015, the literacy rate in Turkey was estimated to be 95 percent, with 98.4 percent of men and 91.8 percent of women able to read and write. Education is compulsory from ages six to 18, financed by the state, and lasts an average of 12 years. Educational expenditures generally account for 2.9 percent of the country's gross domestic product (GDP).

Women's Rights
The position of women in Turkish society is emblematic of the state's balancing act between Western-style modernity and Islamic tradition. Since the Republic of Turkey was founded in 1923, women have had equal status under Turkish law. One of the principle goals of Atatürk's reforms was the emancipation of women, based on the principle that Turkey was to be a secular state not bound by the principles of Islamic law (Shari'a). A series of reform acts beginning in 1926 gave women the right to vote, hold political office, and inherit property in their own right. Polygamy was also abolished, and civil divorce laws replaced the traditional right of divorce by a simple statement of repudiation, giving women new protections. The first women were elected to seats in the Turkish parliament in 1935, and the first woman prime minister, Tansu Penbe Çiller (1946–), held office from 1993 to 1996.

Over time, these reforms have benefited the educated middle and upper class women of the cities, though social and official discrimination continue to exist. Official equality has less effect on the lives of rural and working class women. Despite compulsory education for all children between the ages of six and eighteen, rural women are less likely to attend school than their urban counterparts, in part because the state schools are co-educational. In the extreme east and southeastern regions, in particular, women still face domestic violence, forced marriages, and so-called "honor killings—in which women are killed by male family members as a result of behavior that is seen as a detriment, or dishonor, to the family's reputation. Such behavior can range from loosely defined "disobedience," to giving birth to an illegitimate child as the result of rape.

Women's dress has been an issue in the political conflict between secularists and conservatives. With the Hat Law of 1925, Atatürk banned both the turban and the fez for men and, with the 1934 "Prohibited Garments" law, banned the veil and headscarves traditionally worn by Muslim women. Under this law, wearing the hijab or headscarf in public—especially in government buildings, hospitals, and schools—was illegal. However, a constitutional amendment was passed in February 2008, making it legal for women to wear headscarves on university campuses, and the change resulted in tremendous controversy. Supporters of the change hailed it as expansion of freedom of religion. Those who opposed the measure saw it as an attack on political secularism, and feared increasing pressure on those women who choose not to wear the scarf. On June 5, 2008, Turkey's Constitutional Court reversed the amendment, saying it violated the constitutional principle of secularism. However, in 2013, the ban was again lifted, and women who work in civil service jobs may now wear the hijab at work.

Health Care

The Ministry of Health is responsible for the country's health program, which extends free medical services to the population in government-run hospitals. Where it is available, service is generally adequate. However, it tends to be concentrated in cities and towns. Private clinics and hospitals attract wealthier citizens, as well as doctors and nurses seeking higher salaries. In 2013, health care expenditures accounted for 5.6 percent of the GDP, and in 2011, there were 1.71 physicians and 2.5 hospital beds for every 1,000 people.

GOVERNMENT

Structure

The Republic of Turkey was officially founded on October 29, 1923. Since then the military has stepped in three times, most recently in 1980, because it considered the secular nature of the republic to be threatened. A new constitution, designed to defend Atatürk's principles and increase the powers of the central government, was approved by a national referendum in 1982. It was amended in 2001, 2007, and 2010. Specifically, in October 2007, voters approved a constitutional amendment that called for direct elections of the nation's president.

As set out in the new constitution, the executive branch is presided over by a president, who is elected to five-year term and must not maintain any ties with his or her political party. This president may be elected to a second term. As head of state, the president is responsible for upholding the constitution; appointing the prime minister and the judges of the Constitutional Court; and presiding, along with the prime minister, over both the Council of Ministers and National Security Council.

The Grand National Assembly (Türkiye Büyük Millet Meclisi) is the unicameral legislative branch of the government. Its 550 members are elected every four years, and it is from this pool that the prime minister is chosen. The prime minister presides over the Council of Ministers and ensures, with the Council, that government policy is carried out. He is also an integral part of the National Security Council. The president has veto powers over legislation proposed by the National Assembly.

Political Parties

Turkey has operated under a multi-party system since 1945, and there are currently four main parties represented in the National Assembly, following the June 2015 elections: the Justice and Development Party (AKP, 258 seats); The Republican People's Party (CHP, 132 seats); Nationalist Movement Party (MHP, 80 seats); and People's Democratic Party (HDP, 80 seats).

More specifically, in the 2015 elections, the Justice and Development Party (AKP) won 40.87 percent of the vote. The AKP is a conservative party that advocates a free market economy, as well as Turkey's membership to the European Union. Ahmet Davutoğlu, who has been prime minister of Turkey since August 2014, leads it. Recep Tayyip Erdoğan, founder of the AKP and former prime minister, became president of Turkey in August 2014.

The Republican People's Party (CHP) won 24.95 percent of the vote in the 20015 elections. Founded in 1923, the CHP is a centre-left social democratic party. The Nationalist Movement Party (MHP), founded in 1969, won 16.29 percent of the vote in 2015. The MHP falls on the far right of the political spectrum in Turkey and advocates Turkish nationalism. The left wing, pro-Kurdish People's Democratic Party, founded in 2012, won 13.12 percent of the 2015 vote.

Local Government

Turkey is divided into 81 provinces that are divided, in turn, into districts and sub-districts (ilçe). A governor (vali), appointed by the Ministry of the Interior and approved by the president, oversees each province and acts as head of the provincial assembly, which is elected to five-year terms. Provinces are further divided into districts, which are overseen by an elected mayor, as well as an elected assembly. Local government is responsible for providing health and social assistance programs, education, basic law enforcement, and drinking water, among other services.

Towns in Turkey are divided into villages, which are overseen by an elected official and village assembly. In order to be considered a village, the area must have more than 150 persons residing in it.

Judicial System

The court system of Turkey includes civil and criminal courts at the city and district levels, as well as administrative courts and regional administrative courts. Military courts have a separate jurisdiction, as determined by the 1982 constitution, but they can try civilians during periods of martial law. The highest courts mentioned in Articles 138 to 160 of the constitution include the Constitutional Court, which examines the constitutionality of enacted laws; the Court of Cassation, which offers final rulings and is divided into civil and criminal chambers; and the Council of State, which is the country's highest administrative court and is specifically defined by Article 155 of the constitution. The Turkish Court of Accounts audits the Turkish government's revenues, expenditures, and budgets.

Taxation

The government of Turkey levies a progressive income tax that ranges from 15 to 35 percent, depending on a person's income. There is a flat corporate tax rate of 20 percent. Other taxes levied include inheritance taxes, value-added taxes (VAT), environmental taxes, and property taxes. Capital gains taxes are added to the general income of individuals and corporations and taxed at the aforementioned rates.

Armed Forces

The Turkish Armed Forces (TAF) consists of an army, navy, and air force. The gendarmerie, which supplements local police forces and assists in maintaining public order, and the coast guard each have law enforcement and military duties: During peacetime, they are under the Interior Ministry's purview; during war, they operate under the army and navy. Conscription begins at age 21 and lasts between six and 12 months, depending on the education level achieved before entering. With 685,862 active personnel and three million reserves, the TAF is the second largest armed force in the North Atlantic Treaty Organization (NATO), second only to the United States forces (2012).

Foreign Policy

Turkey's foreign policy reflects its unique position at the juncture between Europe, Asia, and the Middle East. Since its formation in 1923, the Turkish Republic has been politically closer to Europe than to the Arab-dominated Middle East or the Iranian theocracy, even though a majority of its population is Muslim. It has strengthened its relations to Europe and the West through its membership in organizations such as the Council of Europe, the Organization for Security and Co-operation in Europe (OSCE), and the

Organization for Economic Co-operation and Development (OECD). Turkey is also a founding member of the UN. Additionally, since the collapse of the Soviet Union in 1991, Turkey has established close relationships with the newly independent states of Central Asia, whose populations are largely Turkic speaking.

Recently, much of Turkey's foreign policy centers on two major goals: joining the EU and halting the spread of Muslim extremism by battling ISIS in Syria. Turkey was approved as a candidate for EU membership in 1999, and the country immediately began to introduce human rights and economic reforms designed to bring Turkish law into compliance with EU standards. Following a positive report by the European Commission, Turkey began accession negotiations with the EU in October 2005, with the goal of achieving membership by 2015. Unresolved issues that continue to delay EU membership include the disputed state of North Cyprus, European concerns about the role of Islam and the military in Turkish politics, controversy over article 301 of the Turkish Constitution, and the objections of several existing EU member states, including Austria. At the same time, Turkish proponents of EU membership face opposition at home from Turkish Islamicists. Ultimately, EU president Jean-Claude Juncker, elected in 2014, has stated that Turkey has "turned its back on European democratic values," and, under his tenure, will not be allowed to join the union.

In 2015, Turkey made a commitment to the United States to help battle ISIS in Syria and Iraq. The US has recently delivered F-16 fighter jets to Turkey's Incirlik Airforce Base for this purpose. However, in addition to bombing ISIS targets, Turkey has also made significant airstrikes on PKK targets in southeastern Turkey in retaliation for violence and bombings perpetrated by the Kurdish separatist group. As of August 2015, Turkey's true motives for bringing in US weaponry and pledging to fight Islamic extremism has been called into question by the Kurds, whose own efforts to battle ISIS have been thwarted by the Turkish government's recent air raids.

Turkey has long-standing disputes with Greece over the extent of territorial waters and the control of underwater resources in the Aegean Sea, the ownership of uninhabited islands near the Turkish coast, airspace, and most notably the island of Cyprus. In 1974, Turkish forces invaded Cyprus with the goal of protecting Turkish Cypriotes following a Greek-supported military coup. The southern part of the island is Greek, but Turkey maintains about 35,000 troops in the northern "Turkish Cyprus," which only Turkey recognizes as a sovereign state. Turkey also has a problematic relationship with Iraq, on its southeastern border. Iraq accepted hundreds of thousands of Kurdish refugees following the separatist violence of the 1980s and 1990s (leading to an escalation of ethnic violence in Turkey). Turkey supported the UN action against Iraq in the first Persian Gulf War and, in 2003, allowed United States forces to use Turkish airspace in the Iraq War.

Turkey has been an ally of the U.S. since the 1950s, when it joined the North Atlantic Treaty Organization (NATO) as a defense against Soviet expansion. Turkey was also the first of the Islamic countries to express support for the U.S. following the attacks of September 11, 2001. Turkey not only trained troops to fight against the Taliban, but also sent its own troops to Afghanistan. However, U.S.-Turkey relations became strained in 2003, when Turkey refused to allow U.S. troops to attack Iraq from within the county, fearing that weakening Iraq would lead to an independent Kurdish state. Turkey and the US have also been at odds over Turkey's denial of the Armenian Genocide—the widespread massacre of Armenians between 1915 and 1923—which only 26 countries have officially recognized as of 2015.

Human Rights Profile

International human rights law insists that states respect civil and political rights and promote an individual's economic, social, and cultural rights. The United Nations Universal Declaration on Human Rights is recognized as the standard for international human rights. Its authors sought the counsel of the world's great thinkers, philosophers, and religious leaders and were careful to create a document that reflects the core values shared by every world culture. (To read this document or view the articles relating to cultural human rights, visit www.ohchr.org/EN/UDHR/Pages/Introduction.aspx.)

Turkish constitution generally upholds Article 2 of the UDHR, defining Turkish nationality in terms of citizenship rather than ethnicity, and prohibiting discrimination based on race, gender, religion, disability, language, or social status. Nonetheless, Turkey has a history of discrimination and even violence against its ethnic and religious minorities, like the Kurds and Armenians. The reform of Turkey's constitution and penal code has been an ongoing issue in its negotiations to join the EU.

Turkey's most active problems are with the Kurdish minority, which roughly comprises 20 percent of the population. The 1980s and 1990s were marked by civil war in southeastern Turkey between Turkey and the radical Kurdish organization known as the Kurdistan Workers' Party (PKK), which wanted to form an independent Turkish state. Thousands died because of violence from both sides of the conflict, and more fled into exile. In 2000, the Turkish parliament passed laws granting more rights to Kurds, and the PKK abandoned its revolutionary activity.

However, the brief improvement in relations did not last, and the PKK resumed guerilla activities against the Turkish government in 2004 under the name of the People's Congress of Kurdistan (KGK). In 2007, the Turkish army retaliated with military action against Kurdish strongholds in northern Iraq. Tensions flared again in 2013 and reached a boiling point in 2015, with violence erupting from adherents of the revived PKK. The Turkish government has responded in kind, employing airstrikes on the Kurdish separatist group's enclaves in southeastern Turkey, Syria, and northern Iraq.

Other significant minorities, including Greeks, Armenians, Jews, Circassians, Georgians, and Laz, continue to experience degrees of discrimination in the modern Turkish state. Most notably, the massacre of the Armenians by the Ottomans in the early 20th century remains an incendiary subject for both Armenians and Turks.

Although Turkey is a secular state, most Turks are Sunni Muslims. Both the Muslim majority and the various religious minorities complain of restrictions on the freedom of religion called for in Article 18 of the UDHR, and the growing strength of Islamist political parties is seen as a threat by many Turkish minorities. At the same time, strong measures taken to protect political secularism, such as criminal charges for reading Islamic prayers at political rallies, are seen by conservative Muslims as attacks on freedom of religion.

Turkish prisons have been infamous for their disregard of the freedom from torture and cruel and unusual punishment called for in Article 5 of the UDHR. Although international human rights organizations continue to report a high incidence of such problems every year, observers agree that the Turkish government has put measures in place to control the problems and that situation has improved in recent years.

The freedom of opinion and expression called for in Article 19 of the UDHR is under continuous pressure by the government. There are significant restrictions on the use of minority languages, like Kurdish, in broadcasts, and a number of journalists and political figures have been imprisoned. In addition, numerous private stations have had their licenses to broadcast suspended as a result of reporting on politically sensitive subjects, including Kurdish separatism, the rise of Islamic-based political parties, and the role of the military in the Turkish government. Other journalists have been imprisoned for insulting "Turkishness." Despite government restrictions, journalists criticize both policy and leaders on a daily basis and biting satirical cartoons are a standard feature of the Turkish press.

Following the July 25, 2015 airstrikes on PKK centers in southeastern Turkey, Syria, and Iraq, Turkey's High Council for Telecommunications blocked hundreds of news sites, according to the watchdog group Reporters without Borders. Some of these sites, like the left-wing Sendika.org, remain inaccessible in Turkey. Even Twitter was blocked for several hours on July 22, following the suicide bombing in Suruç and a subsequent, court-ordered ban on images from the event. Such actions are evidence of the government's continued control of the media, citizens' access to it, and the distribution of real-time information.

ECONOMY

Overview of the Economy

Turkey's gross domestic product (GDP) was $1.508 trillion (USD) in 2014, and its per capita GDP was $19,600 that same year. Inflation, which has long been a scourge of the economy, has steadily declined over the last several years. The labor force is estimated at 27.56 million people, with unemployment around 9.9 percent (2014). Germany, Iraq, the United Kingdom, Russia, Italy, and France represent Turkey's principal export markets.

Industry

Iron, steel, clothing, and transport equipment lead the market; paper, cement, and refined petroleum, mainly for domestic consumption, are also widely produced. The food-processing industry is dominated by sugar, olive oil, meat, and other animal products.

The chemical industry enjoys the advantage of high-quality minerals exploited in the country. Caustic soda, chlorine, and sodium phosphates are just a few of its products.

Labor

Just over 26 percent of the Turkish labor force is engaged in industry, a sector that accounts for almost 27 percent of the GDP.

Approximately 25.5 percent of the labor force works in the agricultural industry, which makes up 8.2 percent of the country's GDP. A little over 48 percent of the labor force works in the services industry, which accounts for almost 65 percent of the national GDP.

Energy/Power/Natural Resources

Turkey has deposits of fossil fuels, including petroleum and natural gas. Coal is the most prevalent, most of which is lignite, a low-grade type

that Turkey has substituted in favor of cleaner fuels. None of these deposits is adequate to meet domestic demand.

Major dam-building projects are set to further increase Turkey's hydroelectric power production. Many of the power plants derive their energy from the Euphrates. The four largest hydroelectric stations are Atatürk Dam, Karakaya Dam, Ilisu Dam, and Birecik Dam.

Mining/Metals

Copper, chromite, bauxite, iron, and manganese are a few of the mineral deposits found in Turkey. Although mining these minerals does not account for a substantial sector of the economy, since they do not exist in vast quantities, the extraction process is vital for furnishing other sectors with raw materials. Also notable is that Turkey exports a great deal of natural stone and is a world leader in the export of marble and travertine (a type of limestone popular in high-end construction).

Agriculture

Though subsistence agriculture declined during the latter half of the 20th century, its importance to the economy cannot be underestimated. Not only does it engage a significant portion of the labor force (roughly 25 percent) it also provides raw materials for the industrial sector. Moreover, unlike most countries, Turkey produces enough food to feed its population. Agriculture makes up 8.2 percent of the country's GDP.

Generally, Turkey's land surface is highly cultivated. Cereals make up the major cash crop, but cotton, olives, citrus, and vegetables, particularly sugar beets have high yield. Hazelnuts and pulses, like lentils, make similarly positive returns. Crops that are more specialized include tobacco and tea.

Animal Husbandry

Animal husbandry is an integral part of the agricultural sector and particularly important in more mountainous regions. Sheep, raised for meat and for wool, are the most common livestock; in 2013, there were an estimated 27,425,233 head of sheep in the country. Cattle and goats are prevalent as well. Livestock accounts for one quarter of the total value of agricultural production.

Tourism

Tourism is a vital economic sector. In 2014, an estimated 41,263,670 foreign tourists visited Turkey, generating $29.5 billion USD in revenue. However, the number of tourists visiting Turkey has had a negative impact on some ecosystems.

The country offers a plethora of cultural sights, from ancient Greek and Roman ruins and museums housing their artifacts to the Byzantine and Ottoman architecture of Istanbul. The Aegean and Mediterranean coastlines are particularly favored by tourists, and these areas offer the most developed infrastructure. Finally, Cappadocia, in central Anatolia, is popular for both its lunar-like stone formations and underground cities and churches.

Pamela Toler, Michael Aliprandi, Ellen Bailey, & Savannah Schroll Guz

DO YOU KNOW?

- "Yogurt" (also yoghurt and yoğurt) is one Turkish word that has been taken into the English language.

- Legend has it that the remains of Noah's Ark rest on Mount Ararat in eastern Turkey.

- Aya Sofya (also Hagia Sofia) in Istanbul was first a church, then a mosque, and is now a museum. It was once also the largest enclosed space in the world.

- The ruins of Troy are located in western Turkey.

- Turkey was the first nation to celebrate Children's Day, which was officially established by Mustafa Kemal Atatürk in 1929. Currently known as "Sovereignty and Children's Day" and celebrated annually on April 23, the holiday is now recognized by the United Nations.

- The Anglicized version of Ankara is "Angora."

Bibliography

"Turkish Culture Portal." *Turkish Cultural Foundation.* 2015. http://www.turkishculture.org/.

Arin Bayraktaroglu. "Culture Shock! Turkey: A Guide to Customs and Etiquette." Tarrytown, NY: *Cavendish Square.* 2009.

Aliza Marcus. "Blood and Belief: The PKK and the Kurdish Fight for Independence." 2nd ed. New York: *New York University Press.* 2007.

Andrew Mango. "The Turks Today." Woodstock, NY: *Overlook Press.* 2006.

Bruce Clark. "Twice a Stranger: The Mass Expulsions that Forged Modern Greece and Turkey." Cambridge, MA: *Harvard UP*, 2009.

Charlotte McPherson. "Turkey—Culture Smart!: The Essential Guide to Customs & Culture." London: *Kuperard.* 2014.

Dan DeLuce. "Turkey Enters the War Against the Islamic State." *Foreign Policy.* FP, 23 Jul. 2015. https://foreignpolicy.com/2015/07/23/turkey-enters-the-war-against-the-islamic-state/.

Erik J. Zürcher. *Turkey: A Modern History.* New York: I.B. Tauris, 2004.

Esin Atil, ed. "Turkish Art." Washington, DC: *Smithsonian Institution Press & Harry N. Abrams, Inc.* 1980.

Gamze B. Bulut and Nevin Gezgin. "Turkish Culinary Art: A Journey through Turkish Cuisine." Clifton, NJ: *Blue Dome Press.* 2014.

Nicole Pope and Hugh Pope. "Turkey Unveiled: A History of Modern Turkey." 2nd ed. Woodstock, NY: *Overlook Press*, 2011.

Orhan Pamuk. "Istanbul: Memories and the City." New York: *Knopf*, 2006.

Works Cited

"Countries that Recognize the Armenian Genocide." *Armenian National Institute.* Armenian National Institute, Inc., 2015. Web. http://www.armenian-genocide.org/recognition_countries.html.

"*DK Eyewitness Travel Guide: Turkey*." London: *DK Publishing, Inc.*, 2014.

"Erdogan vows to continue offensive until PKK's end." Al Jazeera. *Al Jazeera Media Network*. 11 Aug. 2015. http://www.aljazeera.com/news/2015/08/turkey-carries-fresh-air-strikes-pkk-targets-150811085229832.html.

"Middle East: Turkey." World Fact Book. *Central Intelligence Agency*, 30 Jul. 2015. https://www.cia.gov/library/publications/the-world-factbook/geos/tu.html.

"Number of Registered Motor Vehicles in Turkey Up." Anadolu Agency. *Anadolu Agency News Academy*. Web. 17 Oct. 2012. http://www.aa.com.tr/en/rss/91493—number-of-registered-motor-vehicles-in-turkey-up.

"Turkey Country Profile" *News*. BBC, 22 Mar. 2012.

"Turkey Facts." National Geographic. *National Geographic Society*, 2015. http://travel.nationalgeographic.com/travel/countries/turkey-facts/.

UNESCO. "Turkey: Properties inscribed on the World Heritage List." World Heritage CentreCenter. *UNESCO World Heritage Center*, 2015. http://whc.unesco.org/en/statesparties/tr.

"U.S. Relations with Turkey." *Bureau of European and Eurasian Affairs Factsheet. U.S. Department of State*, 24 Feb. 2015. http://www.state.gov/r/pa/ei/bgn/3432.htm. http://news.bbc.co.uk/2/hi/europe/country_profiles/1022222.stm.

Amanda Paul and Demir Murat Seyrek. "Freedom of religion in Turkey—The Alevi issue." *European Policy Centre*. EPC, 24 Jan. 2014. http://www.epc.eu/pub_details.php?pub_id=4093

Annette Hagedorn and Norbert Wolf. "Islamic Art." New York: *Taschen America*, 2009.

Barry Turner, ed. "Turkey: Türkiye Cumhuriyeti." Statesman's Yearbook Online. *Palgrave Macmilan.*, 2015. http://www.statesmansyearbook.com/entry?entry=countries_dc_tr&x=12&y=8

C.W. Ceram, *Gods, Graves and Scholars: The Story of Archeology*. 3rd Rev. ed. New York: Alfred A. Knopf, 2001.

David Levinson, ed. *"Encyclopedia of World Cultures: Africa and the Middle East."* Vol. IX. Boston: *G. K. Hall & Company.*, 1995.

Jenny White. "An Insider's Guide to Eating like a Turk." *Gourmet* (October 2008): 64-69.

Manfred Korfman. "Was There a Trojan War?" *Archaeology* 57.3 (May/June 2004). Web. http://www.archaeology.org/0405/etc/troy.html.

Mustafa Üstünova and Kerime Üstünova. "Soldier Weddings in Kaynarca." *Journal of Folklore Research*. 43. 2 (May–August 2006): 175-185.

Neil Arun. "Turkey v Islamic State v the Kurds: What's going on?" *BBC News*. BBC, 10 Aug. 2015. http://www.bbc.com/news/world-middle-east-33690060. New York. John Wiley & Sons, 1997.

Roff Smith. "Why Turkey Lifted Its Ban on the Islamic Headscarf." *National Geographic*. National Geographic Society, 12 Oct. 2013. Web. http://news.nationalgeographic.com/news/2013/10/131011-hijab-ban-turkey-islamic-headscarf-ataturk/.

Roger Axtell, Roger. *Gestures: The Do's and Taboos of Body Language around the World*.

Terry Richardson and Marc Dubin. *The Rough Guide to Turkey*. London: Rough Guides Ltd., 2013.

William Dalrymple. "What goes round…." The Guardian. *The Guardian News and Media Limited.* 5 November 2005. http://www.guardian.co.uk/books/2005/nov/05/featuresreviews.guardianreview26.

The Jumeirah Mosque in Dubai, United Arab Emirates

UNITED ARAB
EMIRATES

Introduction

The United Arab Emirates (UAE) is a collection of seven small emirates, or states, located in the Middle East on the eastern coast of the Persian Gulf on the Musandam Peninsula. The Arabic name for the United Arab Emirates is Dawlat al-Imarat al-'Arabiyah al-Muttahidah.

The seven emirates (so named because emirs rule them) are Abu Dhabi, Ajman, Dubai, Fujairah, Ras al-Khaimah, Sharjah, and Umm al-Quwain. These once-independent sheikdoms were previously known as the Trucial States, an informal British protectorate, from 1820 to 1971. Before the emirates signed the 1820 treaty with Britain, the area along the southeastern Persian Gulf coast and Strait of Hormuz, was dubbed the "Pirate Coast" for the number of raiders—later identified as agents and even members of the Sharjah and Ras al-Khaimah ruling families—seizing British-identified cargo ships.

After gaining independence from Great Britain on December 2, 1971, six of the seven emirates became the United Arab Emirates, with the seventh, Ras al-Khaimah, joining the group on February 10, 1972. The largest emirate by far is Abu Dhabi, which lies along the Persian Gulf. The remaining emirates are located on the Musandam Peninsula, the body of land that separates the Persian Gulf from the Gulf of Oman.

The UAE, whose citizens are called Emiratis, is now considered the most liberal of the Persian Gulf states, though it is still conservative by Western standards. Since 1971, when the union was formed, it has also been one of the most stable countries in the Arab world, enjoying both economic prosperity and peaceful international relations. Even the widespread revolts of Arab Spring did not trouble the union, although, in response to activists' demands for a parliament with full legislative powers, the government did slightly expand voting eligibility and invest $1.6 million (USD) to upgrade the states' infrastructure.

GENERAL INFORMATION

Official Language: Arabic
Population: 9,445,624 (2015 estimate)
Currency: Emirati dirham
Coins: Coins are in denominations of 1, 5, 10, 25, 50 fils, and 1 dirham, which is equal to 100 fils.
Land Area: 83,600 square kilometers (32,278 square miles)
National Anthem: "Ishy Bilady," or "'īšiy bilādī" ("Long Live My Nation")
Capital: Abu Dhabi

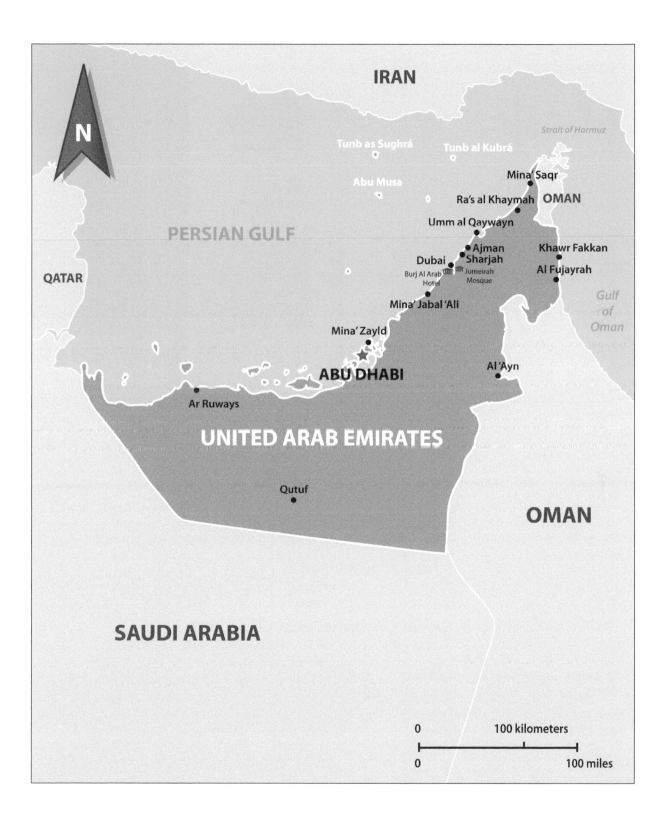

Principal Cities by Population (2013):

- Abu Dhabi (2,450,000)
- Dubai (2,106,177)
- Sharjah (801,004)
- Al-Ain, also al-'Ayn (518,316)
- Ajman, also 'Ağmān (238,000)
- Ras al-Khaimah, also Ra'sal-Khaymah (263,217)
- Fujairah, also Al Fuğaira (152,000)
- Umm al-Quwain (72,000)

Time Zone: GMT +4

Flag Description: The national flag consists of a vertical red band on the left (hoist) side, with equal horizontal bands of green (top), white (middle), and black (bottom). Green symbolizes fertility, white symbolizes neutrality, black represents oil prosperity, and red is symbolic of unity; the four colors also stand for the Pan-Arab colors, representing Arab unity.

Population

Since the land in the UAE is almost entirely desert, the population density is highest along the coast or near the interior oases. Most of the people living in the emirates are not actually citizens, and that rate is increasing; as of the July 2015, UN data reveals that approximately 85 percent of the population was immigrants. Many of the non-Emirati are also foreign workers or citizens of nearby Arab countries. The Abu Dhabi emirate is the largest by population, with the Dubai emirate as second largest.

In 2015, the average life expectancy in the United Arab Emirates is 77 years—80 years for women and 75 years for men. The birth rate stands at 15.43 births per 1,000 people, with approximately two children born to each woman. However, the infant mortality rate averages 11 deaths for every 1,000 live births.

Languages

Arabic is the official language, though English and Farsi are also widely spoken. Other languages include Hindi and Urdu.

Native People & Ethnic Groups

Bedouin Arab tribes were the first inhabitants of the region. Today, native Arabs are a minority in the UAE, due to the large number of foreign workers employed in the nation's petroleum industry. An estimated half of the population of the United Arab Emirates is comprised of a combination of south Asians (including Filipinos), eastern Indians, and Pakistanis; more specifically, approximately 1.75 million residents are from India, while an estimated 1.25 million hail from Pakistan. Asian expatriates, representing namely the Philippines, China, and Korea, number close to 1 million. Iranians and other non-national Arabs comprise another 20 percent of the population, and Egyptians account for 10 percent of the population. In addition, Bangladeshis number about 500,000, while Western expatriates—namely from United Kingdom, Europe, Australia, and Africa—also equal about 500,000. The country's foreign residents are mostly male workers and their families.

Religions

Most of the country's people, around 76 percent, are Sunni Muslims. However, there are also some Shi'ite Muslims in Dubai and Sharjah. Christians represent 9 percent of the population. Hinduism and Buddhism represent just over 10 percent, while less than 5 percent of the population is divided among the following faiths: Parsi, Baha'i, Druze, Sikh, Ahmadi, Ismaili, Dawoodi Bohra Muslim, and Judaism.

Climate

The climate of the United Arab Emirates is overwhelmingly hot and dry, with a slight increase in humidity near the coast. The average rainfall, most of which occurs between December and March, is between 10 and 15 centimeters (four and six inches) annually.

The average temperature in January is about 19° Celsius (66° Fahrenheit), while in July the temperature is around 35° Celsius (95° Fahrenheit). However, the temperature in the summer can reach as high as 45° Celsius (115 degrees Fahrenheit) at the coast, and a blistering 49° Celsius (120° Fahrenheit) in the interior desert. The shamal, a wind that stirs up dust and sand, blows from the north and northwest during the winter and early summer.

ENVIRONMENT & GEOGRAPHY

Topography

The United Arab Emirates is bordered by Qatar to the northwest, Saudi Arabia to the west and south, and Oman in the east and the northeast.

Aside from the coast and a few salt flats in the western part of the country, the United Arab Emirates is almost completely desert. The Matti Salt Flat stretches to the south into Saudi Arabia, but otherwise, the country is barren. It is home to some of the largest sand dunes in the world.

The largest oases include Al-'Ayn (meaning "the spring"), which is east of Abu Dhabi. The northern portion of the Al Hajar Mountains lies east of the Musandam Peninsula, and continues into Oman. The United Arab Emirates' highest point is in this range, at Jabal Yibir, 1,527 meters (5,010 feet) above sea level.

There are numerous shoals and islands off the coast. The country's largest harbors, Dubai's Porta Rashid (or Mina Rashid) and the Port Jebel Ali (or Mina Jabal Ali), are both manmade. There are, however, three natural deepwater harbors in the Gulf of Oman, at Dibba al-Hisn, Khawr Fakkan (or Khor Fakkan), and Kalba.

Plants & Animals

Since most of the UAE is desert, the country's plant and animal life is limited. While the most prevalent animals are donkeys, sheep, and camels, UAE also boasts Arabian Oryx, Sand Gazelle, and Arabian Mountain Gazelle. In the Persian Gulf and in the Gulf of Oman, there are also significant populations of dugong, or sea cows. Very little of UAE's land will support vegetation (just an estimated 1 percent), although shrubs and grasses appear in desert areas. Aside from date palm groves, most of the vegetation is located on the coast, near the mountains, or within oases. These areas generally include acacia, eucalyptus, and tamarisk trees.

CUSTOMS & COURTESIES

Greetings

The United Arab Emirates is, primarily, an Arabic-speaking, Muslim nation. Therefore, as in the rest of the Arab world, the most common form of greeting is the phrase "As-salamu alaykum" ("Peace be unto you"). However, this greeting may differ depending on the person being addressed. For example, the word "Alayka" is used if speaking to one male, but "Alayki" is spoken to one woman, and the "Alaykum" form is correct for a group of people. The proper response is "Wa alaykum as-salaam" ("And peace be upon you"). This greeting is also used when leaving the company of others and may be accompanied by a handshake and a series of embraces or kisses upon the cheek.

A man may also shake a woman's hand if she puts her hand forward first; otherwise, a spoken greeting will suffice. Although English is commonly spoken throughout the UAE, the English-language greeting of "Hello" is not advisable because it shows disrespect toward local customs and Islamic tradition.

Gestures & Etiquette

There are many significant differences between Arab and Western cultures where gestures and etiquette are concerned. Placing one's hand over the heart or prolonging a handshake are both gestures of sincerity that are common to both cultures. Common to the UAE is the gesture of greeting in which two men hold each other's right hand, while placing the left hand on the other's right shoulder, followed by a kiss on the cheek. However, in Muslim culture, showing the sole of one's foot and using one's left hand in any context except for hygiene is considered disrespectful. Likewise, pointing and giving the "thumbs up" sign are also considered rude.

Because of the restrictions of Islamic law and social custom, there are several Western behaviors are avoided in the UAE, including smoking, drinking alcohol, and cursing (even in English) in public. For women, these restrictions are even tighter, including avoiding wearing revealing clothing, such as low-cut tops, short sleeves, and short skirts. Business etiquette is also slightly different in the UAE. In general, the business casual style of work-wear in the West does not exist. Both men and women are expected to dress well when doing business (suit and tie for men and pants suits or modest dresses for women).

During Ramadan, an annual month-long period of religious fasting and devotion, there are other forms of etiquette related to this custom. These include refusing food or drink during the day (in public), and refraining from dancing, singing, drinking alcohol, or smoking between sunrise and sunset.

Eating/Meals

Meals in the UAE are family gatherings held in the morning, at midday, and in the evening, with the largest meal occuring at midday. Coffee and tea are frequently served during each meal. Middle Eastern and Asian cuisines—including those of Lebanon, Iran, India, and Pakistani, as well as China, Thailand, and the Philippines—are very common in the modern UAE diet. Meals are customarily served on the floor on a large placemat surrounded with such items as rice, dates, fruit, and hot drinks. Seated on the floor with their legs crossed under them, diners eat with the right hand only (since the left hand is associated with the cleansing of the body) and do not typically use utensils. Most meals end with coffee or tea and possibly a shisha (hookah) pipe with perfumed tobacco.

Whenever possible, the entire family will eat together. However, this custom, like many in the UAE, is changing, as the country becomes more Westernized and modern. As a result, it is not uncommon for Emiratis to eat lunch in a fast food restaurant or any one of the country's many hotels and resorts. Muslims must also be very conscious of the ingredients found in pre-packaged or fast food since these items may con-

tain items that are not allowed, such as pork and foods that are not prepared according to Islamic law. During Ramadan, certain rules of eating and meals change. After sunset, it is customary for families to gather with their community to break their fast (this is known as iftar or ifṭār) by eating dates and other delicacies.

Visiting

Important practices show a guest's respect toward an Emerati host. Entering a home barefoot, being respectful to women, and dressing conservatively are all-important points of etiquette in the UAE. If a guest is served coffee, sweet tea, or other refreshment, it is customary to accept the first cup, drink it, and then gesture for a second cup. A host's belongings should not be openly admired, since it may be expected that the guest wishes it as a gift.

When seated, it is improper to reveal the soles of one's feet, or to speak about the host's wife, daughters, or female relatives. It is also considered rude to use forceful language and gestures in conversation. When dining, guests do not eat or pass food with the left hand.

LIFESTYLE

Family

In traditional Islamic society, the family is the most important social institution, and family members are expected to represent their families respectfully in all actions and deeds. Families in the UAE follow this familial obligation. Within the family unit, it has always been customary in the UAE that women are responsible for the care and education of their children. However, in recent years, as the UAE has become more influenced by Western traditions, this traditional viewpoint has begun to change. As a result, both father and mother share some of the responsibilities of child rearing. UAE family life commonly includes extended family members as well. It is also not uncommon for a man to be polygamous, meaning that he has multiple wives, but women do not have the same right.

Housing

A typical home has separate areas for men and women, as well as separate entrances. Many homes in the UAE are built around a central courtyard, where men and women come together with their families. Badgeers (also badgirs), or windtowers, provide air conditioning for homes across the UAE, but electric air conditioning is also very common.

Emiratis have access to many of the same furnishings and conveniences as Europeans or Americans. In rural areas, traditional homes made from palm fronds, mud, coral, and other natural, regionally available materials are being replaced by modern dwellings, many of which are given to residents by the government.

Wealthy Emiratis typically live in ornate, five-bedroom villas or may purchase a two- or three-bedroom condominium in one of the many luxury high rises that have become the signature of urban centers like Dubai and Abu Dhabi. In 2015, non-Emiratis who wished to purchase a home in the UAE more often financed their homes, while Emiratis preferred to pay in cash. Non-Emiratis purchasing homes within the UAE is becoming increasingly common, as many international businesspersons and travelers spend a great deal of their time in the country. New homeowners may have to wait as long as three years between the time they contract to build a new home and its point of completion.

In the summer of 2009, the Abu Dhabi emirate announced plans to construct 17,000 villas in twenty-three locations to house the local population. The development of the Emirati housing project is expected to last five years, and includes plots given to Emirati families. Another plan to build 50,000 homes for Emiratis over 20 years was announced earlier.

Architecture, home building, and city planning continue to be a vital part of both UAE's identity-construction and economy. Each year at Cityspace Abu Dhabi, in the expansive Abu Dhabi National Exhibition Centre, architects, designers, and developers exhibit their plans for innovative commercial spaces and residential housing projects for the benefit of investors and fellow developers willing to bring their ideas to fruition.

Food

The cuisine of the UAE is similar to most other Arab cuisines, with some distinct culinary influences from neighboring Asian, Middle Eastern, and Mediterranean cultures. Common ingredients include fruits and vegetables such as dates, oranges, pomegranates, bananas, onions, carrots, tomatoes, asparagus, and spinach; seafood such as various types of fish and shrimp; camel meat, lamb, and poultry. Pork is prohibited by Islamic law, but may still be found in certain areas catering to non-Muslims; nuts such as pistachios and almonds; dairy products such as yogurt and feta cheese; rice and flatbreads; and spices such as cardamom, saffron, turmeric, thyme, and cinnamon. The national dish is considered to be shawarma, an Arabic-style sandwich made with meat, vegetables, and sauce usually tahini (made of sesame seeds) or amba (made of spicy pickled mango). Traditionally, it is made with lamb or goat, hummus, pita bread, and cucumber and tomato, over which the chosen sauce is drizzled.

Many dishes that are common in the UAE are also Western favorites, such as tabbouleh (made from wheat, mint, parsley, tomatoes, and lemon juice) and hummus (crushed chickpeas with olive oil, tahini, garlic, and lemon). A typical breakfast may include dates with coffee and warm, Bedouin-style breads, like khameer (fried dough) or chebab (similar to American pancakes, but made with cardamom and saffron). The midday meal is the most important meal of the day, and may include a main dish, such as lamb, as well as rice, cooked vegetables, and salad. Often, the vegetables and meat are cooked together in a sauce and served over rice. Kebabs, which are meat and vegetables cooked and served on a skewer, are also extremely popular meals. Gahwa (spiced coffee) or red tea with mint is often served following the meal to aid digestion.

Life's Milestones

There are several common traditions in the UAE that celebrate some of life's passages. Shortly after a child is born, the father will offer the first prayer the baby will ever hear during its life. While birthdays are not commonly celebrated, weddings are expensive and lavish affairs where many guests (sometimes hundreds) will celebrate and feast for several days and nights. A Bedouin marriage lasts for a full week and involves many traditional rites, such as the negotiation between the groom's and bride's families; a ritual decorating of the bride; music and dancing (including the sword dance known as al-Ardha); dowries and jewelry; and many gifts exchanged between families.

Funeral rites for Muslims in the UAE typically follow Islamic custom, including washing the body, wrapping the body in a shroud, and burial within as short a period as possible, usually twenty-four hours. The traditional mourning period is three days, but for widows, that period lasts four months and 10 days.

CULTURAL HISTORY

Art

The United Arab Emirates (UAE) is a relatively young country, having been established as a sovereign nation in 1971. Therefore, its cultural history must be considered in three ways: first as a nation whose cultural and artistic heritage comes from the Islamic legacy of the region (the Arabian Peninsula in the Middle East); second, as a place whose local culture is heavily influenced by expatriates and foreign workers; and finally, as a nation whose native population is much smaller than that of its international community. As a result, the artistic culture of the UAE often includes works that reflect a modern, yet respectfully traditional, Islamic nation that is open-minded about Western culture and other influences.

The primary cultural identity of the UAE in the 21st century may come from the efforts of the nation's wealthy financiers to build art galleries and attractions designed to draw the attention of people around the world. There are many projects currently underway to position the UAE as an international cultural destination. Included among these are the Sheikh Zayed Book Awards, a prestigious, annual prize-giving contest to promote modern Arab literature, and the construction of arts and culture centers designed by famous international architects, such as Canadian-American Frank Gehry (1929–) and Iraqi-British Dame Zaha Mohammad Hadid (1950–).

Architecture

The UAE is building a cultural identity by becoming a showcase for modern architecture. Because of the very high population growth rate, many modern marvels of architecture have been built or planned within recent decades.

In Dubai, the largest of the seven emirates, or states that make up the country, the Burj Al Arab hotel towers over the water at 321 meters (1,053 feet), from its foundation on a man-made island. Designed by British architect Tom Wright and shaped like the mast and sail of a ship, it is the fourth tallest hotel in the world. The tallest, the Rose Tower, which is also the world's third tallest hotel at 333 meters (1,093 feet), is also located in Dubai. Until 2012, it was the world's tallest hotel, until JW Marriott Marquis Dubai, which stands at 72 stories and 355 meters (1,165 feet), and Mecca Royal Clock Tower Hotel in Saudi Arabia, which reaches a staggering 601 meters (1,972 feet), supplanted it.

More recently, the UAE received world attention because of plans to build the Palm Islands, three giant island-cities in the Persian Gulf, each shaped like a palm tree and topped by a crescent shape. Of the three projects, known as Palm Jumeirah, Palm Deira, and Palm Jebel Ali, only Jumeirah has been completed as of November 2014. Jebel Ali and Deira, begun in 2002, have been on hold since the financial crisis of 2008. Between Palm Jumeirah and Palm Deira, two other archipelagoes are planned: "The World," comprised of some 300 artificial islands arranged in the shape of the world map, and "The Universe," slated for completion between 2023 and 2028, which will mimic the shape of the Milky Way and solar system.

Another example of the modern design in the UAE is the Mall of Emirates, a 223,000 square meters (2.4 million square feet) shopping mall. More of a retail novelty than an architectural wonder—it contains an indoor ski slope—the mall is a testament to the nation's contemporary approach to architecture. Such attractions have helped create the image of the UAE as one of the world's most intriguing tourist destinations and one of the world's biggest spenders in terms of urban development.

In August 2015, Dubai's ruler, Sheikh Mohammed bin Rashid, issued laws initiating a Dubai Foundation for the Museum of the Future and the funding of several research centers dedicated to advancing science and technology. Portions of the Museum of the Future—a shiny, silver, ovoid building, open in the center and inscribed with calligraphy—will be created using innovative 3D printing technology. The museum will cost an estimated $136 million (USD) and is set to be completed in 2017. It will serve as a test-site for new inventions and tech start-ups.

However, the traditional Arabic and Islamic cultures are also very visible in the UAE. A tomb in the Hili Archaeological Gardens near the city of Al-Ain dates back to approximately 3000 BCE. The Jumeirah Mosque in Dubai is considered one of the Middle East's most beautiful mosques. It was built in the 1970s in a medieval Islamic style known as Fatimid, named after the Fatimid Islamic Caliphate (909–1171 CE).

Music & Dance

Traditional music and dance are still very much a part of the multicultural UAE lifestyle, but have been affected by encroaching modernism. For example, variants of the African six-stringed tambura (or tanpura) and the British bagpipe are commonly used in regional music rooted in Bedouin culture. Similarly, traditional dances, such as the ayyalah and liwa, are still performed at celebrations, family events, and cultural expositions.

The nightlife that the UAE has become known for during its brief history is more likely to feature a mix of Western and Arab popular music. Western music styles, such as electronica, rhythm and blues (R&B), reggae, rock, and hip-hop, have become absorbed into UAE culture in a way that has created something uniquely identifiable with the country's culture.

CULTURE

Arts & Entertainment

The culture of the UAE is a mixture of traditional Arabic cultures, similar to the country's Persian Gulf neighbors. Camel and horseracing are very popular sports in the country. Top racing camels command high prices, much like prized thoroughbred horses. There are several camel racetracks in the emirates, including Digdaga in Ras al-Khaimah and Nad Al Sheba in Dubai. The Dubai World Cup thoroughbred horse race is held in the UAE each March. Sports such as football (soccer), tennis, and golf are also popular.

Cultural Sites & Landmarks

The UAE's cultural sites and landmarks vary between the historic and the modern. For a nation steeped in wealth and luxury, it is interesting to note that efforts have been made to maintain an interest in its past, rather than merely on its present and future. Natural attractions are also on display whenever possible throughout all seven emirates.

The capital, Abu Dhabi, offers a glimpse into the history of the region prior to the oil boom. At Dhow Harbor, artisans still practice the art of shipbuilding, while a reconstructed nomadic Bedouin camp is on display at Heritage Village. The city is also home to fortifications built in the 18th and 19th centuries, including Al Maqta'a Fort and Qasr al-Hosn, the city's oldest stone building. Meanwhile, Sir Bani Yas Island is a nature preserve and sanctuary that is home to many rare species of fauna, including gazelles, Arabian oryxes, llamas, spotted deer, and as many as 86 species of birds, as well as many types of regional plants, such as citrus and olive groves. Another popular natural attraction in

Abu Dhabi is the Liwa Oasis, where agricultural greenery lies juxtaposed against the famous towering sand dunes of the Arabian Peninsula.

Like other large cities in the UAE, the souks (or markets), with their local shopkeepers and traders, can be exciting places to shop (and bargain). Other important landmarks in the city include the Deira Clocktower; the Heritage Village of Hatta, in the Hatta Mountains (in rural Dubai), and Burj Khalifa (previously known as the Burj Dubai), a skyscraper that is the tallest man-made structure ever built at 829.8 meters (2,722 feet). Dubai is mainly known for its shopping tourism and contains numerous shopping destinations such as malls. (See also the Architecture section of this culture profile.)

The northern emirates of Sharjah, Ajman, Umm al-Quwain and Ras al-Khaimah are not as wealthy as Abu Dhabi or Dubai, but offer their own contributions to the country's culture and heritage. In Sharjah, for example, is the King Faisal Mosque, the largest in the nation. In all four emirates, forts that once protected the region are all open to the public. Umm al-Quwain is the site of two archaeological sites—Tell Abraq and al-Dur. Both are of major historical importance because of their glimpse into pre-Islamic life in the emirates thousands of years before the oil boom. The same may be said of Shimal, an archaeological site in Ras al-Khaimah. The eastern emirate of Fujairah is also full of important historical and natural attractions, including the ruins of Al Hayl Castle and an old town.

Libraries & Museums

In Dubai, the past is on display at the Dubai Museum, in the restored Al Fahidi Fort. The fort is the city's oldest building that once served as the residence of rulers and the seat of government. Exhibits range from musical instruments and traditional garb to a replica of an ancient Quran school and a display on pearl diving and other traditional fishing practices.

For the most part, each emirate has a museum dedicated to that region's history and Arab heritage. They include the Umm al-Quwain Fort and Museum, located in the emirate of Umm al-Quwain; Fujairah Museum, located in the emirate of Fujairah; the archaeological and ethnological National Museum of Ras al-Khaimah, located in the northern emirate of Ras al-Khaimah; Ajman Museum, situated in an 18th-century fort; and the Al-Ain Museum, an archaeological and ethnological institute located in Al-Ain, Abu Dhabi's second largest city.

The city of Sharjah, the seat of government in the emirate of the same name, also houses numerous museums and historic buildings, including the Sharjah Museum of Islamic Civilization, the Sharjah Heritage Museum, the Sharjah Science Museum, the Sharjah Police Museum, and the Sharjah Calligraphy Museum. In 1998, UNESCO named the city as the cultural capital of the Arab world.

Three new museums will open in Abu Dhabi in 2017. The 450,000-square-foot Guggenheim Abu Dhabi, designed by Frank Gehry; a branch of the Louvre, designed by Jean Nouvel; and Zayed National Museum, designed by Norman Foster and the result of a collaboration between the UAE and the British Museum, are all part of a $27 billion (USD) Emirati cultural initiative to make the country an arts and culture capital as well as a must-see global destination.

Holidays

The UAE observes two secular holidays: National Day (December 2), which celebrates the formation of the United Arab Emirates in 1971, and New Year's Day (January 1).

Other holidays reflect the majority Muslim population and follow the lunar calendar, so the dates vary from year to year. They include the Prophet Muhammad's Birthday, the Islamic New Year, the end of Ramadan (Eid al-Fitr), and the Ascension of the Prophet (Leilat al-Meiraj).

Youth Culture

The UAE is a highly multicultural nation, influenced by both Arab and Western traditions. This is particularly so in the highly populated cities of Abu Dhabi and Dubai—the first and second most populous cities, respectively. In these cities, youth activities are similar to those found in other cultures and include shopping and socializing. In addition, like many other youth cultures, the youth of the UAE are technologically savvy, and cellular telephones and Internet are both as popular and important for young Emiratis as for youth anywhere. Additionally, because of the numerous tourist attractions in the UAE, much of the local youth culture takes place in nightclubs that cater to tourists, expatriates, and wealthy Emiratis.

Although popular music and dance from Lebanon and the Gulf region are particularly popular, young Emiratis also have the opportunity to enjoy the many Western entertainers that play locally. In addition, because of the large number of people from foreign cultures who live and work in the UAE, youth culture is virtually multinational in character. As the country continues to transition into one of the Arab World's arts and culture capitals, it is likely that the youth will play a major role in determining the character and content of future Emirati pastimes.

SOCIETY

Transportation

Vehicles are the main mode of transportation in the UAE, and the country has an extensive road network. Road accidents and congestion have become concerns in the early 21st century, particularly in larger cities such as Dubai. Vehicles drive on the right-hand side of the road, and the use of front seat belts is compulsory.

Taxis are also cost effective and abundant and public bus transportation is available in certain emirates. In 2015, the public transportation system in Dubai, operated by the Road & Transport Authority (RTA), consisted of over 734 buses operating over seventy-nine routes. In certain cities, such as Dubai, water taxis are widely used and generally available. Dubai, a developing metro system subway system, with two functioning lines and plans for three more will increase urban accessibility. The archipelago Palm Jumeirah, near mainland Dubai,

has a monorail, and the Dubai Tram runs 14.5 kilometers (9 miles), from Dubai Marina to the Burj Al Arab hotel complex and the Mall of the Emirates.

Previously, UAE lacked railroads. However, the government is changing this, beginning with the 2009 creation of Etihad Rail, which will facilitate the construction of and ultimately oversee the nation's freight and passenger railway system. In 2011, the country ordered seven diesel locomotives to pull cargo to export points along the first 264-km (164 miles) segment of railway. The overall goal is not only to link major industry and population centers, but to connect also to Gulf Cooperation Council nations' rail lines.

In Abu Dhabi, there is an even more ambitious plan: Masdar City will become the region's first carbon-neutral city. Within Masdar City, no personal vehicles will be allowed. Instead, residents and visitors will use a small rapid transit system to traverse the city. While there is some skepticism about the plans for Masdar City, it may become a showcase for green living in desert climates.

Transportation Infrastructure

During its brief history as an independent nation, the UAE has continued to build an impressive road-based transportation system. It links all major cities and enclaves within its borders and connects the UAE to its neighboring nations. It has also maintained its maritime transportation infrastructure for sea transport within the Persian Gulf Region, as there are five major seaports. Like most other aspects of this country, these, too, are being developed as more and more of the region's oil wealth provides funds for continued development. In addition, there are seven international airports in the UAE (and twenty-one airports overall) with plans to build several more in the next few decades; Al Maktoum International Airport, in Jebel Ali, opened in June 2010. It is part of a larger planned project, Dubai World Central, a residential, commercial, and logistics center that is also expected to be the world's largest passenger and cargo hub when fully complete in 2021. In December 2014, a few airlines began offering passenger service from the airport, although the facility will ultimately have the capacity to move 12 million tonnes (13 million short tons) of cargo and 260 million passengers.

Media & Communications

Media and communications services are very important in the UAE. Etisalat, a powerful company that also provides services in Asia, Africa, and throughout the Middle East, has monopolized the telecommunications infrastructure. In 2005, the Emirates Company for Integrated Telecommunications (ETIC) was launched and rebranded with the name 'du' in early 2006. These organizations are considered to offer the finest systems in the Arab world, with the lowest mobile telephone rates and highest capacity for Internet connectivity per capita. As of 2014, there were approximately 26 television stations and 20 radio stations in the UAE. As of 2013, approximately 88 percent of the population was considered Internet users.

Despite this impressive system, however, there is still a high amount of censorship in the UAE. Nearly all television and radio stations are government-run, and Internet and media censorship in the UAE is on par with the rest of the Middle East. As a result, writers, editors, and other associated media will often practice self-censorship. Media operations in the UAE have been bolstered by the creation of Dubai Media City, which hosts hundreds of international news agencies, publishers, Internet content providers, and other businesses who operate tax-free. Dubai Media City supposedly offers more relaxed requirements. A company operating in the zone may be fully owned by an international company and, therefore, is free from certain restrictions on state-run companies. Despite this, there have been several incidents involving censorship of content, and filtered sites usually redirect to a page with a message from du indicating the site's blocked status. Since 2008, the UAE has been listed as "Under Surveillance" by the watchdog group Reporters without Borders.

SOCIAL DEVELOPMENT

Standard of Living
The UAE ranked 40th out of 187 countries on the 2014 United Nations Human Development Index, which measures quality of life indicators. Only Qatar (31) and Saudi Arabia (34) ranked above UAE.

Water Consumption
The United Arab Emirates' per-capita water usage is among the highest in the world. A 2010 water report, in fact, revealed Abu Dhabi to have the world's highest per capita water consumption rate—with individuals using between 525 and 600 liters per day. In 2013, per capita consumption was still 82 percent above the global average and three times that of countries within the European Union. Desalinated water constitutes over 80 percent of all water consumption in the UAE (some 2010 estimates place that number as high as 98 percent) and there are thirty desalination plants in operation in the country. Water demand and consumption remains a serious concern in the water-scarce nation; such a reliance on desalination can have adverse environmental effects, particularly in terms of the large amount of energy expended in the process. A Water Resources Management Strategy to control water wastage was launched by the UAE's Federal Water and Electricity Authority (FEWA) in early 2010. In 2014, the UAE celebrated World Water Day, endorsed by the UN and intended to increase awareness about the problem of global water shortages.

Education
The education system in the UAE is four-tiered, and all citizens have access to primary and secondary education, spanning 14 years (this also includes kindergarten and a preparatory stage between attending primary and secondary schools). Education, in fact, is compulsory and universal until the ninth grade. In addition, for UAE residents, it is free for both males and females up to and including the post-secondary

level. In 2006, foreign nationals were permitted to attend UAE's public schools, although they are required to pay a fee. According to recent statistics, approximately 40 percent of students receive private schooling. In 2014, the Ministry of Education developed the long-range program, "Education 2020," which aims to foster greater critical thinking skills in students and proposes enhancements to math and science curricula.

Higher education is also free for UAE nationals. The United Arab Emirates University, located in Al-Ain and founded in 1975, is considered the flagship school of higher education, as it is the oldest of the state-sponsored higher education institutions. As of the 2006/2007 academic year, less than a quarter of enrolled students at the university were male, while female students represented 79 percent of the student body. Many other institutes of higher learning have since opened, including Zayed University, established in 1998; Abu Dhabi University, established in 2003; and a system of Higher Colleges of Technology (HCTs), of which there are twelve. As of 2015, there were over 115 universities or institutes of higher learning, including satellite campuses of NYU and the Paris-Sorbonne.

The average literacy rate in the United Arab Emirates is 93.8 percent (95.8 percent among women and 93.1 percent among men).

Women's Rights

Equal status for women is not the norm in Arab society. For example, in Saudi Arabia, women are not allowed to sit in the same classrooms as men and have limited options regarding what they can study, nor are they allowed to vote. However, the UAE is not a typical Arab nation and is much more modernized than many of its neighbors, particularly in the treatment of women. The United Arab Emirates' government is committed to women's rights and enhancement, with the country's constitution guaranteeing equal rights for both women and men. As a result, women are given equal legal status as men in almost all areas of society, as well as the same rights to education and work opportunities. In

fact, the World Economic Forum's 2014 Global Gender Gap report indicated that the UAE leads all other countries in the Gulf region when it comes to gender equality issues.

Within the Emirates, there are several national and international organizations dedicated to the health and welfare of women in society. These include the UAE Women's Federation (created by the founder of the country) and several women's development societies. There have also been numerous efforts within the UAE to ensure that the progress of women in society is strengthened, and that women are given the resources they need to become more educated and effective citizens. Such efforts have led to a massive increase in the number of educated and professional Emirati women since the country's founding. Within the professions, it is very common that women fulfill the same roles as men, including as business owners, managers, and other levels of authority. Notable, too, is that there are currently four female fighter pilots and over thirty women in the country's special security forces. Moreover, in September 2014, the UAE established the first women's military training college, the Khawla bint Al Azwar Military School. Women fill five UAE cabinet positions, and, of them, Sheikha Lubna Al Qasimi, Minister for International Cooperation and Development, has been listed among *Forbes* magazine's 100 most powerful people. As of 2014, 71.6 percent of students in post-secondary institutions are women. Strides continue to be made in advancing women professionally, and in 2015, the UAE government established the Gender Balance Council to further increase women's public sector participation.

Despite these freedoms, there are still restrictions on women in the Emirates. However, these restrictions are mostly cultural and related to Islamic law (Sharia) and custom rather than civil law. For instance, a woman may not marry more than one man, but men are permitted up to four wives. An Emirati husband can also forbid his wife and children from traveling. In addition, the government reserves to the right to imprison or deport non-citizens if they bear children out of wedlock. Because of these restrictions, the conditions for women in the UAE are still considered archaic and in need of improvement. Discriminatory practices in employment, domestic violence, and human trafficking for the intent of sexual exploitation, though not prevalent, have also all been reported.

Health Care

Hospital services are free to citizens of the United Arab Emirates. An increasing number of privately owned clinics and hospitals provide care for the country's large population of foreign workers and non-nationals. Most health-care facilities are located in Abu Dhabi and Dubai. In 2013, healthcare expenditures accounted for 3.2 percent of the GDP.

GOVERNMENT

Structure

The government of the United Arab Emirates is a federation led by the ancestral families of the seven emirates. On the national level, it is made up of the Supreme Council of Rulers, comprised of the rulers of the seven emirates. The council elects a president and a vice president for the union; these officials serve five-year terms. The president then appoints a prime minister and a cabinet.

The United Arab Emirates has a unicameral legislature called the Federal National Council, which consists of forty members who serve five-year terms. Population apportions the number of representatives for each emirate. For example, Abu Dhabi and Dubai both have eight, while Umm al-Quwain has four. Voters elect the members from each emirate. A provisional constitution was ratified in 1971 and made permanent in 1996. There are no political parties within the country, and democratic elections for the Federal National Council only began in 2006.

The laws of UAE are mixture of Western civil and Islamic law (or Sharia). The Supreme Court deals with national-level cases. There are also lower, local courts to deal with emirate-specific issues. However, domestic and religious disputes are resolved in a separate Islamic court.

The two most powerful emirates are Dubai and Abu Dhabi, and consequently their armed forces are somewhat more independent. In all, the UAE has approximately 65,000 troops.

Political Parties

The United Arab Emirates does not have political parties. Such parties are, in fact, illegal.

Local Government

Each emirate maintains its own form of local governance, each of which varies in scope and size. The populous emirate of Abu Dhabi, for instance, maintains an executive council that has been chaired by the crown prince of Abu Dhabi, Mohammed bin Zayed bin Sultan Al Nahyan, since 2004. This council oversees departments similar to government ministries. The emirate is subdivided into regions, and its main cities, Al-Ain and Abu Dhabi, are governed through municipalities, each with a municipal council. Executive councils are present in the emirates of Sharjah and Dubai as well. All emirates maintain a similar form of municipal and departmental governance. The ruler of each emirate (called emirs) may also designate certain forms of governance or authority in remote or small settlements within their emirate, some of which may be tribal-based.

Judicial System

The UAE has a federal judicial system that only excludes the emirates of Ras al-Khaimah and Dubai, who maintain independent systems. The courts are subdivided into criminal and civil divisions and consist of three stages: courts of first instance, courts of appeal, and the Federal Supreme Court, over which five judges preside. Each emirate also maintains Sharia courts, which rule in accordance with Islamic law.

Taxation

In the absence of federal tax legislation, each emirate maintains its own tax laws and regulations. There is no tax on personal income and capital gains. In addition, there is no value-added tax (VAT) or federal corporate tax in the United Arab Emirates (each emirate has its own laws, if any, regarding taxes levied on corporate profit). The only entities that are taxed are petrochemical, oil, and gas companies as well as foreign banks. In addition to paying a flat tax of 55 percent, oil, gas, and petrochemical companies must also pay production royalties to the emirates in which they operate. In Abu Dhabi, Dubai, and Sharjah, foreign banks pay a 20 percent flat tax on income earned within the emirate itself, not the bank's overall income. Also within emirates, service fees or duties may apply, as may property taxes.

Armed Forces

In 1951, the emirates combined their military forces, creating the Union Defence Force. The deployment of this force is at the discretion of the Supreme Council. It consists of an air force and air defense, the Critical Infrastructure Coastal Patrol Agency (CICPA), a navy, land forces, and a presidential guard, which is relatively small. According to the United States Department of State, the armed forces of the UAE have approximately 65,000 active personnel. Service lasting approximately two years is compulsory for men, ages eighteen through thirty. Men who have graduated from secondary school are required to serve only nine months. Women may also serve, and generally train for nine months. Their service, however, is on an entirely volunteer basis.

Foreign Policy

The UAE is a member of the United Nations (UN), the Arab League, and the Gulf Cooperation Council (GCC). As part of the Arabian Peninsula and Persian Gulf Regions, the UAE has been involved in several of the most notable international crises in the region since the 1970s. These include the Iran-Iraq War in the 1980s, the Persian Gulf War in the early 1990s, and the 2003 U.S.-led Iraq War. In particular, the UAE sided against Iraq after the Iraqi invasion of Kuwait in 1990 and, afterward, allowed foreign powers to use military facilities within its borders to fight

Iraq. Despite this, in 1997, the UAE gave foreign aid to Iraq and disapproved of the economic and financial blockades against Iraq. In 2000, the UAE, along with several other Arab nations, urged Iraq to comply with UN regulations.

The UAE has maintained friendly ties with the U.S. throughout its recent history. The UAE's embassy in Afghanistan was closed following the September 2001 terrorist attacks against the US, but was reopened in 2002. After the U.S.-led invasion of Iraq, the UAE refused to participate, but later allowed the US to use an Abu Dhabi air base for personnel and aircraft. Despite its pro U.S. stance, however, the UAE has also used its ties to the US as a way of encouraging a solution to the Arab-Israeli Conflict and for cautioning foreign restraint in the region. The UAE also maintains important ties with Egypt, China, Japan, the U.S., the United Kingdom (UK), India, and Pakistan.

Since the early 1970s, Iran and the UAE has maintained a boundary dispute over Abu Musa, an archipelago in the Strait of Hormuz, as well as the Greater Tunb and Lesser Tunb islands, also in the Strait of Hormuz. According to the UAE, these territories are rightfully owned by the UAE, however, since 1971, they have been occupied by Iran. Both Iran and the UAE assert their historical rights to the islands, but until an international court decides their fate, they will be occupied and held by Iran. Despite its tensions with Iran, the UAE has remained an ally and strong economic partner since becoming an independent nation. It is also friendly with Oman and Saudi Arabia, its immediate neighbors. Diplomatic relations were established with South Korea in June 1980, and the UAE became the third largest supplier of oil to the country in 2014.

Human Rights Profile

International human rights law insists that states respect civil and political rights and promote an individual's economic, social, and cultural rights. The United Nations Universal Declaration on Human Rights is recognized as the standard for international human rights. Its authors sought the counsel of the world's great thinkers, philosophers, and religious leaders and were careful to create a document that reflects the core values shared by every world culture. (To read this document or view the articles relating to cultural human rights, visit www.ohchr.org/EN/UDHR/Pages/Introduction.aspx.)

International human rights agencies and watchdog groups have strong concerns regarding the UAE's human rights record. In particular, it has been demonstrated that the UAE does not allow political freedom or hold open elections. It also does not allow freedom of expression, freedom of assembly, or freedom from discrimination based on sex, religion, or nationality. It is a destination for human trafficking of men, women, and children from around the world for uses in involuntary labor and sexual exploitation, and does not offer protections of fair and safe employment conditions for guest workers, which make up 95 percent of the private sector labor force. Often these foreign workers, many of them female and from countries like Ethiopia, Eritrea, Iran, and East, South, and Southeast Asia, are forced into uncompensated labor and abuse. Male foreign guest workers, who are frequently employed in the construction fields, are similarly forced to work without pay through debt bondage to repay fees that brought them to the country.

The UAE constitution allows for freedoms of expression, religion, and assembly, but in practice, that is not always the case. For example, there is intolerance for anything that demeans Islam or is otherwise not acceptable to the government. In 2007, an incident involving the temporary closure of a Pakistani television channel stationed at Dubai Media City raised awareness of how extensive UAE censorship can be when tested. The official religion of the UAE is Islam, and the vast majority of the emirates are Sunnis. While Sunnis enjoy considerable benefits from the state, such as funding for mosques, all other religions are privately funded, and there are restrictions on their assembly and proselytizing activities. (For example, it is a crime to hand out non-Muslim literature).

The UAE, while casting itself as a modernized and tolerant country, does not always follow fair and equal practices for all citizens, despite the country's constitutional promises. As is common in Arab nations, there is very little genuine equality between the sexes, although great strides are being made in women's educational and professional lives. Muslim women still face many restrictions. For example, while Muslim males may marry someone outside their faith, Muslim women must marry within their faith. In terms of political freedoms, there are no open elections in UAE society, nor are there any choices for political engagement outside of the country's ruling families. Additionally, according to Amnesty International (AI), homosexuality among males is illegal in the UAE and punishable by execution. Labor practices are quite restrictive in the UAE as well. Guest laborers commonly face oppressive working conditions, such as passport seizure, pay decreases, or delays, debt bondage for sponsorship fees, and general labor discrimination.

The worst human rights abuses in the UAE, however, are largely condemned publicly by the government, especially the sexual and employment exploitation of women and children. According to the U.S. State Department, the United Arab Emirates is considered a Tier 2 nation, which means that it is no longer on its Watch List. Moreover, in January 2015, the government expanded the victim protection clauses of Federal Law 51, in order to preclude punishment of sex trafficking victims who had traditionally been imprisoned and fined for unlawful sexual relations. In 2014, the UAE government pursued legal action against perpetrators in fifteen sex trafficking cases.

Despite this, there are relaxed punishments throughout the UAE that enable so-called international sex tourism. It is reputed that women from all over the world are brought to Dubai to become prostitutes and that Dubai, specifically, is considered to be a hotbed of this type of illegal exploitation. Many people believe that the UAE government ignores prostitution because it is considered to be good for the local business economy.

In recent years, the UAE has had to crack down on illegal exploitation of children forced into becoming camel jockeys. In 2006, a lawsuit was filed against Dubai's leader, accusing him of kidnapping minors from Bangladesh, Sudan, and southern Asia to use as camel jockeys.

Migration

An overwhelming number of people residing in the UAE are of foreign origin, and immigration and labor migration remain key issues in the Middle Eastern nation. With the onset of the global economic crisis in 2008/09, the construction sector slowed considerably, and many migrant workers who came to the UAE for employment are without the funds to return home. In addition, in the wake of reports from organizations such as Human Rights Watch, the government has made steps to improve the housing and working conditions of immigrant laborers in the UAE. Lastly, Israeli citizens are forbidden to enter the country. Overall, in 2015, for every 1,000 people, 12 emigrated from the country.

ECONOMY

Overview of the Economy

The economy of the United Arab Emirates is dominated by oil production. The wealthiest emirates are Abu Dhabi and Dubai. In fact, Abu Dhabi boasts one-tenth of the world's oil reserves, and it accounts for half of the entire country's revenue. Abu Dhabi's oil reserves are predicted to last until the end of the 21st century. The country also provides a large portion of the world's natural gas reserves.

The UAE is a relatively wealthy country, and its efforts to diversify economically have reduced, by 25 percent, the country's reliance on oil production as its sole income generator. In 2014, the gross domestic product (GDP) was estimated to be $599.8 billion (USD), with a per capita GDP of $64,500.

Industry

Petroleum plants and refineries dominate the United Arab Emirates' industrial landscape. In Abu Dhabi, there are also ammonia plants, while

Dubai has a dry dock that functions as a trade center. Sharjah also has factories for paint and plastic pipes.

The Mina Jebel Ali Free Zone was developed in the 1980s to encourage foreign industry to relocate to UAE. Historically, Dubai was a route for smuggling gold into India. Today, it is an important trading center for the Persian Gulf. Many of the country's major imports, including machinery, animals, and food, are re-exported to neighboring countries.

Labor

In 2014, 85 percent of the labor force was comprised of foreign workers. To counter the large percentage of non-nationals in the workforce, the UAE government has begun to offer incentives to companies that hire UAE citizens. Unemployment has increased, especially in light of the 2008–09 global economic crisis; in 2009, an estimated 40,000 Emiratis were unemployed, the highest since the country was established in 1971. The continued unemployment problem has especially affected those aged fifteen to twenty-five, and in 2014, their unemployment numbers rose to 8 percent. The sector with the greatest number of non-Emirati workers was construction, which accounted for 32.5 percent of the total workforce in 2014. By comparison, 86.4 percent of Emiratis work for the government.

Energy/Power/Natural Resources

The United Arab Emirates' most valuable natural resource is oil. It was discovered in Abu Dhabi in 1958, and later in Dubai in 1969. In each emirate, the government is a controlling interest in the oil companies. However, the British, French, Japanese, and American governments all have interests in these international oil companies.

The main offshore field in Abu Dhabi is Umm ash-Shaif. The emirate also shares an offshore oil field, Al-Bunduq, with neighboring Qatar. Dubai, which produces approximately one-third of the country's petroleum, has offshore oil fields in Haqlfath, Fakah, and Rashid. In 1974, natural gas was also discovered in the Sharjah Emirate.

Fishing

Since the turn of the 21st century, the commercial fishing industry in the United Arab Emirates has seen a drop in its total fish catch, particularly in the emirate of Abu Dhabi. As a result, the number of registered fishing boats in the country has decreased over 25 percent from 1999, and the government's fisheries department has begun promoting aquaculture and sustainable fisheries development. The eastern coast remains the country's primary fishing region, and there are about twenty commercial species in UAE waters, including red mouth grouper, skipjack tuna, deep-water red snapper, and yellowfin tuna.

Agriculture

Agricultural production in the United Arab Emirates is a constant struggle against the region's lack of water and intermittent locust swarms. The country can nearly meet its own domestic demand for fruits and vegetables, but still must import grains. Agricultural production is concentrated around Diqdaqah in the Ras al-Khaimah Emirate, the coastal area of the Fujayrah Emirate, Falaj al Mualla in the Umm al-Quwain Emirate, and Wadi adh Dhayd in the Sharjah Emirate. The total cultivates land currently stands at 160,000 hectares (395,369 acres). Commercial crops include dates, tomatoes, and cucumbers. Irrigation using wells and pumps is very important to agriculture in the United Arab Emirates. The Arid Lands Research Center in Al-'Ayn is studying methods for raising crops in desert conditions.

Animal Husbandry

Al-'Ayn Dairy, the first established dairy in the country, was founded in 1981. In 2009, they recorded a milestone in the country, with the production of approximately 30 million liters (7,925,161 gallons) of milk. (By comparison, the US dairy industry produces over 20 billion gallons.) In general, the United Arab Emirates has begun producing enough poultry, fish, eggs, and dairy to feed its population. In 2013, the Abu Dhabi Department for Food Monitoring was created by UAE's Executive Council. Its purpose is to enhance meat and dairy production by disseminating 'best practices' directives, providing veterinary assistance and vaccinations for large animals, and advising farmers on ways to reduce waste.

Tourism

The United Arab Emirates, especially Dubai, is a popular destination for British tourists. In 2004, more than 600,000 British nationals visited that emirate alone.

Despite the decentralized character of the emirates, there is a highly developed inter-emirate highway system to facilitate travel throughout the country. There are also seven international airports, three in Abu Dhabi, two in Dubai, one in Fujairah, and one in Sharjah.

In Dubai, tourists enjoy desert safaris, traveling across the dunes in all-terrain vehicles or SUVs (an activity known as "dune bashing"), and sand dune skiing. In 2000, the government instituted the Dubai Shopping Festival, which functions like a gigantic duty-free market for tourists. It usually occurs in February. The Dubai Desert Classic, a golf tournament, also occurs in February, as does the Al-Ain Classical Music Festival. For racing enthusiasts, both the UAE Desert Challenge Motor Rally and the Formula One Abu Dhabi Grand Prix are held in November, while the Dubai Film Festival follows in December.

Chris Belanger, Barrett Hathcock, &
Savannah Schroll Guz

DO YOU KNOW?

- Ajman, the smallest of the country's seven emirates, has an area of only 260 square kilometers (100 square miles), but a population of 361,160. Ninety-five percent live in Ajman city.

Bibliography

"Images of Dubai & the UAE." Dubai: *Explorer Publishing*, 2006.

"Time Out Dubai, Abu Dhabi & the UAE." 2nd ed. London: *Time Out Guides*. 2005.

Caroline Stone. *"DK Eyewitness Books: Islam."* New York: *DK Publishing*. 2005.

Elinor LeBaron. "Dubai and the United Arab Emirates: Practical Tips for Travelers." Washington, DC: *Gulfscape Arabia*, 2015.

Jenny Walker. "Oman & the United Arab Emirates." Hawthorn: *Lonely Planet Publications*. 2013.

Julia Johnson. "United Arab Emirates." Philadelphia: *Chelsea House Publications*. 1999. Major World Nations Ser.

Liz Sonneborn. "United Arab Emirates: Enchantment of the World." 2nd ed. New York: *Children's Press*, 2008.

Margaret K. Nydell. "Understanding Arabs: A Contemporary Guide to Arab Society." Boston: Intercultural Press. 2012.

Oscar Eugenio Bellini and Laura Daglio. "New Frontiers in Architecture: The United Arab Emirates Between Vision and Reality." Muncie, IN: *White Star*, 2010.

Philip Jodidio. "Architecture in the Emirates." Los Angeles: *Taschen America*. 2007.

Works Cited

"Cityscape AbuDhabi." *Informa Exhibitions*. 2015. http://www.cityscapeabudhabi.com/.

"Farming is a niche occupation in UAE." *The National*. Abu Dhabi Media, 25 Jan. 2013. http://www.thenational.ae/thenationalconversation/editorial/farming-is-a-niche-occupation-in-uae.

"The Gulf States: Buying up art and culture." *Economist* 382.8515 (8 Feb. 2007): 46-47. http://www.economist.com/node/8677161.

"United Arab Emirates." Explore Middle East and North Africa. *Human Rights Watch*. 2015. https://www.hrw.org/middle-east/n-africa/united-arab-emirates.

"United Arab Emirates." Office to Monitor and Combat Trafficking in Persons: 2015 Trafficking in Persons Report. *U.S. Department of State*. 2015. http://www.state.gov/j/tip/rls/tiprpt/countries/2015/243557.htm.

"United Arab Emirates profile—Overview." *BBC News*. 24 Feb. 2015. http://www.bbc.com/news/world-middle-east-14703998.

"Women in the UAE." *The UAE*. Embassy of the United Arab Emirates Washington DC, 2015. http://www.uae-embassy.org/uae/women-uae.

_____. "U.S. Relations with United Arab Emirates." Bureau of Near Eastern Affairs Fact Sheet. *U.S. Department of State*. 11 Jun. 2013. http://www.state.gov/r/pa/ei/bgn/5444.htm.

Art Murray. "From nomads to knowmads: Knowledge cities rise from the desert sands." *KM World* 18.1 (Jan. 2009): 17. http://www.kmworld.com/Articles/Column/The-Future-of-the-Future/The-Future-of-the-FutureFrom-nomads-to-knowmadsKnowledge-cities-rise-from-the-desert-sands-52040.aspx.

Asa Fitch. "Dubai Unveils Plans for Museum Of The Future." *The Wall Street Journal*. Dow Jones & Co, Inc., 4 Mar. 2015. http://blogs.wsj.com/dispatch/2015/03/04/dubai-unveils-plans-for-a-museum-of-the-future/.

Binsal Abdul Kader. "Abu Dhabi takes steps to reduce water consumption." *Gulf News*. Al Nisr Publishing LLC, 20 Mar. 2014. http://gulfnews.com/news/uae/environment/abu-dhabi-takes-steps-to-reduce-water-consumption-1.1306746.

Jane Ingram Allen. "Selling the Other Asia." *Art in America* 97.1 (Jan. 2009): 28-29.

Juliet Highet. "Abu Dhabi's Vision." *Middle East* (Aug. 2008): 56-58.

Kevin Whitelaw. "A Cultural Oasis. (Cover story)." *US News & World Report* 144.17 (16 June 2008): 38-39.

Martin Croucher. "Unemployment rates among young Emiratis increasing but national service can help." *The National UAE*. Abu Dhabi Media, 28 Mar. 2014. http://www.thenational.ae/uae/government/unemployment-rates-among-young-emiratis-increasing-but-national-service-can-help.

Megan K. Stack. "In Dubai, the Sky's No Limit." *LA Times*. 13 Oct. 2005. Web. http://articles.latimes.com/2005/oct/13/world/fg-dubai13.

Rachel Aspden. "Written in the sand: Observations on Abu Dhabi." *New Statesman* 137.4893 (21 Apr. 2008): 18-19. http://www.newstatesman.com/society/2008/04/abu-dhabi-arab-writers.

Sana'a's Old City in Yemen

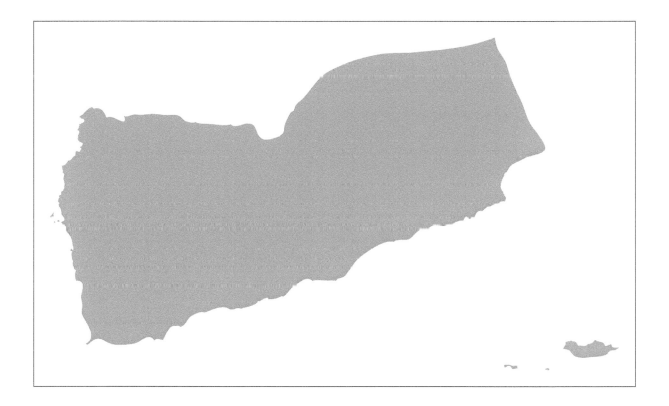

Yemen

Introduction

Yemen is a mountainous country in the southwest region of the Arabian Peninsula. Officially known as the Republic of Yemen, the country was formed on May 22, 1990, when the Yemen Arab Republic, or North Yemen, joined with the People's Democratic Republic of Yemen, or South Yemen.

Because of its strategic location on the Arabian Peninsula and its valuable port city of Aden, Yemen has been an object of geopolitical and economic interest for a number of major foreign powers, including the United States, Great Britain, and Russia. It has also been involved in political and border disputes with its neighbors, Oman and Saudi Arabia.

Yemen has long been an important part of the Arab world. Since the 1st century BCE, the region played a vital role in ancient trade routes—particularly the Incense Road—thanks to the country's once plentiful frankincense and myrrh trees. The region has often been referred to as one of the most beautiful in the world, and its numerous cultural sites and landmarks are a testament to this. The country is home to four UNESCO World Heritage Sites, although several are now damaged as a result of the civil unrest that erupted in 2015.

Yemen is fraught with conflict, much of which goes well beyond problems Yemenis demonstrated against during the Arab Spring of 2011. Two years before sectarian rebels deposed him, Yemeni president Abd Rabbuh Mansur Hadi indicated that his country faced "three undeclared wars": Al-Qaeda, the Islamic State of Iraq, and the Levant (ISIL), pirates in the Gulf of Aden, and Houthi rebels in the north. Indeed, since January 2015, Yemen has been in a state of chaos following a coup by the armed rebels known as Houthis, who belong to the group Ansar Allah (Supporters of God). As of August 2015, Houthis hold the country's capital, Sana'a, as well as a great deal of northern Yemen.

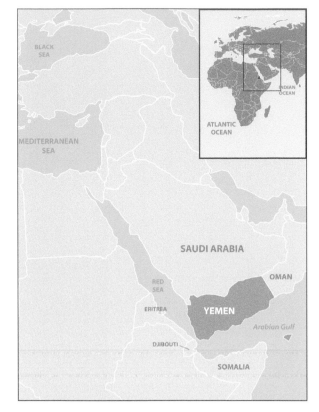

GENERAL INFORMATION

Official Language: Arabic
Population: 26,737,317 (2015 estimate)
Currency: Yemeni riyal
Coins: 100 fils equal one riyal. Fils have essentially disappeared from circulation and coins are issued in denominations of 1, 5, 10, 20, and 50 rials.

Principal Cities by Population (2013):

- Sana'a (1,937,451)
- Aden (760,923)
- Sa'dah (741,000)
- Ta'izz (also Taiz) (615,222)
- Hodeidah (also Al Hudaydah) (400,000)
- Ibb (212,992)
- Al Mukalla (182,478)
- Dhamar (146,346)
- 'Amran (90,792)

Land Area: 527,968 square kilometers (203,849 square miles)
National Anthem: "Nashīd al-Yaman al-Watanī" ("United Republic")
National Motto: "Allāh, al-Watan, ath-Thawrah, al-Wahdah" ("God, Country, Revolution, Unity")
Capital: Sana'a
Time Zone: GMT +3
Flag Description: Yemen's flag is a horizontal tricolor of red, white and black, the colors of Arab unity. The red (top) symbolizes the blood of martyrs, white (middle) symbolizes the country's bright future, and black (bottom) symbolizes the country's dark past.

Population

The majority of people living in Yemen are Arabs, although there are some non-Arab minority groups living in the south. These groups include Pakistanis, Somalis, and Indians. Yemen has, for the most part, a rural and agricultural society. Most Yemenis live in small towns and villages across the country. Only 34.6 percent (2015 estimate) of the population lives in urban areas.

A large number of the male population of Yemen has traditionally worked abroad in other oil-rich Arab countries in the petroleum industry. Their remittances make a significant contribution to the country's GDP.

The median age of the population is 18.6 years, and in 2015, the population of people under the age of fourteen was 41.09 percent. Some estimates indicate that the Yemeni population is growing at an extreme rate, and for a country with about 2.2 percent arable land and limited fresh water resources, that puts an extraordinary strain on already limited resources.

Languages

Arabic is the country's official language and the most widely spoken.

Native People & Ethnic Groups

Yemen was the home of a number of ancient civilizations, including the Minaeans, Hadhramauts, Qatabans, Ausans, Sabaeans, Himyarites, as well as the Ethiopian, Persian, and Ottoman empires. The Zaydi (Shia) and Sunni branches of Islam were established there in the seventh century.

The modern Yemeni people are descended from tribes of Semitic Arabs and the country is said to be tribal in nature, with the two major tribes being the Bakil and the Hashid, both Zaydi Islam groups. Tribalism is strongest in the north of the country. The Houthi tribe (also in the north) is in the midst of a conflict with the central Yemeni government in Sana'a; the Bakil tribe supports the Houthi. The Hashid tribe (which finds their home in the highlands in the north and northwest) has aligned themselves with the central government.

While Yemeni society tends to be centered on village and town life, a nomadic people called the Bedouin dwell in the northeastern region of the country.

Religions

Most people in Yemen practice Islam (99.1 percent), and follow the Sunni Muslim branch of Islam (65 percent). A smaller percentage of the population is Shiite or Zaydi Muslims (35 percent). Religious minorities (0.9 percent) in the country include Baha'i, Christians, and Hindus; nearly all of the Yemeni Jewish population immigrated to Israel after that country was founded in 1948.

Climate

Most of Yemen experiences an arid, desert climate, with variable temperatures. The country's coastal areas have a hot and humid climate and little precipitation, particularly in the eastern portion of the country. Temperatures in the humid coastal Tihama region can reach around 45° Celsius (113° Fahrenheit), with the humidity ranging from 85 to 98 percent. The region receives only 150 to 400 millimeters (6 to 16 inches) of precipitation per year.

In the western part of the country, the higher elevations tend to experience cooler temperatures (generally between 15° and 22° Celsius, or 51° and 71° Fahrenheit) and more regular rainfall, although areas in the north are subject to droughts. The highest areas of Yemen receive an average of 1,000 millimeters (40 inches) of precipitation per year, and sometimes experience frost. Yemen's central plateau experiences hot summers, with temperatures around 33° Celsius (91° Fahrenheit), and cold winters with freezing temperatures.

ENVIRONMENT & GEOGRAPHY

Topography

The Red Sea lies to the west of Yemen, and the Arabian Sea and the Gulf of Aden form the southern border. Neighboring countries include Saudi Arabia to the north and Oman, which lies to the northeast. Yemen also includes three islands: Kamaran, Perim, and Socotra.

Sana'a, the country's capital, is located in the northwest of Yemen. The city sits on the narrow plateau of a mountain range.

The highest point in Yemen is the peak of Jabal an Nabi Shu'ayb, at an elevation of 3,665 meters (12,027 feet). While much of the landscape in northern Yemen is made up of desert, arid hills, or mountainous country, it also includes a small coastal area known as Tihama, part of the Red Sea coastal plain (which continues north into Saudi Arabia) on the Bab-el-Mandeb Strait. Yemen's Tihama region is only 25 to 65 kilometers (15 to 40 miles) wide and often experiences over 85 percent humidity.

The southern part of Yemen features large spans of desert known as the Empty Quarter, or "Rub'al Khali," and occasional fertile valleys.

The western portion of the desert averages around 900 to 1,200 meters (3,000 to 4,000 feet) in elevation. The southern coastal plain is narrower than the Tihama, measuring from five to 65 kilometers (3 to 40 miles) wide.

Yemen is a dry country, with no permanent rivers or lakes. However, it does have wadis, or dry riverbeds, where flash floods may pass after rainfall. These wadis tend to be dry for most of the year. Many wadis can be found at higher elevations in the western highlands of Yemen.

Plants & Animals

The most biologically diverse region of Yemen is the western highlands, where there tends to be more water available. Overall, 400 vascular plant species can be found within Yemeni borders. Cacti, the tamarisk, and other flowering tropical plants are found in the tropical habitats of the Tihama. The dragon's blood tree, desert rose, and bitter aloe are also indigenous to the country. Yemen has been mostly deforested by people who use wood for fuel and construction.

Domesticated animals, such as sheep, goats, and camels, are the most common animals found in Yemen. However, the country also boasts smaller rodents, like the black-tufted gerbil, and several species of bats, including the Lanza's Pipistrelle. Hyenas are found primarily in lower-lying areas in the southern part of the country. One of Yemen's largest native animals is the gelada baboon, which lives in mountain habitats in the northern and northwestern parts of the country.

In general, environmental awareness is not dominant in the national consciousness, and there are few measures in place to protect the environment. There is a high level of air and water pollution in the country.

CUSTOMS & COURTESIES

Greetings

Greetings in Yemen vary based on regional dialects and the preferences of particular villages and communities. For example, a village culture in the north may say "Sabah-tu" ("Good morning"), while another may simple use "Marhaban," which is a version of "Welcome." Generally, the most common, and usually appropriate, phrase is the traditional Muslim greeting "As-salaamu Alaikum," which roughly translates to "Peace upon you (plural)." The response to that greeting is "Wa-alaikum Salaam" ("And unto you be peace"). In Yemen, this greeting is most often used between people who see each other quite frequently, for strangers, and for daily or brief interactions. Additionally, it is always used when entering a home or for formal, social or professional introductions.

An additional extended phrase, "Wa Rahmatu-llah" ("And the mercy of God") is often added to the greeting of peace when one wishes to express additional sentiment or respect. An even further extended version would be to add "Wa Barakatuh" ("And the blessings") to the very end of that phrase. This makes the full greeting "As-salaamu Aliakum wa Rahmatu-llahi wa Barakatuh," which translates to "May the peace, mercy and blessings of God be upon you (plural)." This phrase demonstrates the highest level of respect and affection for the recipient. Typically, the common reply to this would be "Wa Laikum As-salaam wa Rahmatu-llahi wa Barakatuh." It is also quite typical that one may begin the shortened phrase only to have the respondent elaborate on the greeting by adding another phrase.

Typically, all greetings, or salaamat, are followed by questions that range from a general "Kyaf Haluk" ("How are you?") to the more specific line of questioning, that encompasses family, health, and other such personal matters. Regardless of the question, the answer, "Alhamdulilah" ("All Praises are due to God"), is always used. Even in the greetings, the cultural preference to highlight characteristics of piety, or religious reverence, and humility are evident from the first interaction between two people. This is an essential concept in Islam and has become ingrained in Yemeni culture.

Gestures & Etiquette

Yemeni cultural norms and practice dictate that men and women without familial ties are

Yemeni peasant

restricted from both physical and social interaction. As such, it is rare that men and women have any form physical contact in public. These norms are based primarily on shared religious interpretation and Islamic law. Furthermore, it is important in Yemeni culture not to greet someone of the opposite gender until a greeting is initiated, especially as a man greeting a woman. That includes verbal greetings and physical greetings, such as handshakes.

These social customs are generally practiced in all situations. For example, when paying, it is not considered rude for a woman to place money on a countertop or a taxi dashboard in order to avoid contact with a man. Likewise, for men, it is a sign of respect to avoid contact with women in shared public spaces, such as moving from the path when a woman is walking. In addition, many public spaces have a system for gender separation already established. For example, restaurants provide separate seating for women and for families, and general and often larger sitting areas are predominately reserved for men. Women or men accompanied by women (usually family members) are often provided seating on a separate floor or in sections that are curtained off. Likewise, in universities and classrooms, men and women are given separate seating. Overall, it is rare for Yemeni women to eat in restaurants or other public establishments in northern cities.

A common gesture used in Yemeni culture is one that indicates patience. Loosely or informally translated as "Wait a moment," it is demonstrated by touching all five fingers of one hand together at their tips, with fingers directed upwards, and often shaking the hand downward. Depending on the context, it could also mean, "I'm coming," "Hold on" or "Just a little."

Eating/Meals

Lunch is typically the largest meal of the day in Yemen. More often than not, lunch is spent at home with family and takes place after the noontime prayer. The most common afternoon meals typically consist of roasted chicken and rice; foul (a bean dish, similar to American chili, also commonly served in the evenings); saltah (a Yemeni stew), widely considered the national dish of Yemen; kebabs (grilled lamb), and bread.

In Sana'a, and other larger cities, many quick meal options are available for those who cannot make it home during the day. For example, one can purchase a sandwich from street vendors, such as a potato and egg sandwich, a falafel sandwich, or a shawarma sandwich (a shaved lamb sandwich, much like a gyro). Fresh juice stands are also very common and popular. They serve as fast food stations between meals and in the evenings, when many restaurants have limited menus or are closed.

Most meals in Yemen are traditionally served "family style," in which food is shared in communal dishes and plates. It is also common for people to eat with their hands—more specifically, their right hand, which is the preferred hand in Muslim culture (the left hand is associated with the cleansing of the body and is thus considered impure). It is often considered rude to eat with the left hand, especially from a shared plate.

Many dishes served in Yemen are typically accompanied by bread. Often, the bread may act as the appropriate utensil. Sorghum flat bread remains one of the more popular breads served throughout the country. Typically, a diner will tear a piece, fold it, and then use it as either a scoop or utensil for whatever dish it accompanies. Additionally, because meals are commonly shared, washing one's hands before eating is significant in Yemeni culture, as well as other Muslim cultures. Generally, every restaurant and household will either have a sink or provide a basin and water in the dining area for this purpose.

Visiting

When entering a Yemeni home, a guest is expected to remove his or her shoes. This is an important aspect of social etiquette and respecting personal or home space. In addition, male non-family members are expected to refrain from initiating interaction or contact with the women of the household. In fact, it is common for women to neither interact with nor eat with men who are not considered family.

It is common for a host to offer their guests tea, coffee, or other snacks, and it is expected that a guest partake of these offerings. Sitting on the floor, typically on floor pillows or mafraj furniture (a low, firm couch that outlines the walls of a room), is also commonplace. Additionally, when eating, plastic, cloth or paper is usually laid out on the floor for the meal. Visitors are, for the most part, restricted to family gathering spaces, which is usually centered in the mafraj-furnished area. The kitchen, which can be a gathering space in Western culture, is considered more of a functional space, rather than a family or social room in the household.

A daily opportunity for visiting and socializing in Yemen is the communal qat chew. Qat (or khat) leaves (*Catha edulis*) act as a mild stimulant and are chewed in order to create feelings of euphoria. It is traditionally chewed directly after Asr (afternoon prayer) until Maghrib (evening prayer), which usually corresponds to the end of the workday. Typically, more adult men chew then women, largely because of the added expense and social acceptability, and because women generally have less leisure time.

Additionally, men and women hold chewing sessions separately.

In the recent decades, qat chewing has moved from being an elite activity to a distinguishing cultural pastime. Daily "chews" can include between 10 and 50 people, though they tend to occur in smaller groups. A popular social event, some women also attend qat chewing for the company and dance, rather than the activity of qat chewing itself. Qat can also play a role in special events, where the host provides the leaves for a wedding, a religious festival, or other milestone events.

There have been several studies on the physical and, to a lesser degree, social effects of the popularization of qat chewing in Yemen. The official stance of the government is that it is a harmless tradition, a sentiment shared by the majority of the Yemeni population. However, some medical professionals associate it with medical ailments, such as lesions, and have studied qat's effect on heart rate and blood pressure.

Additionally, for some families, it has become a serious strain on household income and can have other adverse social effects, such as general lethargy and decreased productivity. Regardless, the qat crop remains the highest grossing agricultural product in Yemen, and qat farms outnumber other agricultural operations.

LIFESTYLE

Family

Families in Yemen are typically large. While the minimum age for marriage has been recently contested—it was, at one time, 15 years of age—the official stance of ulama (Muslim religious scholars) is that the onset of women's puberty is nine years of age, and marriages can, at this point, be consummated. As a result, it is common for Yemenis to marry young. A population that marries young results in families that include greater numbers of children. In fact, the average Yemeni household has between six and seven children.

A family is an essential unit in Yemeni society. For example, families are highly involved in the choosing of a spouse, and marriages typically require the approval of both families of the bride and groom. Their blessing is socially required before announcing and planning a marriage. Furthermore, some communities would not even recognize a marriage, though legally obtained, without familial involvement.

Families and households are, for the most part, nuclear (typically consisting of a mother, father and their children), though there is cultural emphasis on close ties with extended family members. In fact, there are some instances where marriage occurs between first cousins. These types of marriages offer security in knowing the history and background of your spouse, in addition to keeping wealth within a family. Instances, in which a husband's parents live within the household, if they are beyond an age or situation to support themselves, are also common. This is also considered a traditional Islamic practice.

Additionally, families often try to live in close proximity to each other for support, safety, and financial purposes. As such, co-residency between brothers can be commonplace. This residential practice allows the female members of the household to assist each other in domestic tasks. Furthermore, spatial limitations and financial limitations factor into the building or establishing of separate housing structures in walled cities. In these situations, extended family members co-habiting in the same household is often the only option.

Housing

There are many different and unique types of houses in Yemen, featuring both ancient and modern Yemeni building practices. Generally, climate, geology, and the availability of local materials figure prominently in the construction of Yemeni houses. For example, mud brick homes are most common in the southeastern Hadhramaut (or Hadramout) region, while houses made of brick are more common in large cities such as Sana'a and Sa'dah. Building stones and sun-baked bricks and blocks, as well as gypsum and alabaster materials, are the most common building materials. In addition, houses made from wood, reed, or straw can also be found throughout the country. Generally, most residences in Yemen are still largely constructed by the homeowner, though with the importing of certain materials, this practice has decreased.

Among the most commonly used materials in local or rural housing construction in Yemen are mud bricks. These bricks, made from mud and straw, are typically made in wooden molds in large yards outside of a particular town or village. Sixteen workers can make about 8,000 bricks a day. The bricks are stacked for a week to dry and harden, and are then stacked on a solid stone foundation. The mortar, or paste, used to cement the bricks together is typically made of the same mud, but with a different grass and straw mixture.

Generally, one story is built per year so that the mortar can dry. When the desired height has been reached, the roof is applied. Typically, the roof is made of rich soil and straw, with plaster being used to seal the mud. Several coats are usually applied, with cement sometimes used as a final coat. Finally, limestone is made into putty to reinforce the most vulnerable external walls. Each layer of plaster is thoroughly polished over a period of months, completing the structural assembly of the house. Next, external decorations are applied, often consisting of shaped or sculpted stone and mud, with additional mud and plaster applied for more refined or distinct decorations. Lime is also used to create a tile-like ceramic finish that is often painted.

This particular style of building takes a considerable amount of maintenance. However, it is considered a more suitable building style for arid climates in regions such as Hadhramaut. In addition, since the skills of masonry are often passed down through the generations, this building style has become a part of local village or community culture. Nonetheless, as modern materials become more readily available, maintaining traditional building practices is becoming more difficult, since they require more effort to maintain.

Food

The roots of Yemeni cuisine date back to ancient times, when the region was particularly important in the spice trade. Popular spices and herbs that have been incorporated into traditional Yemeni cuisine include coriander, caraway, fenugreek (used in curry), and mint. In addition, common ingredients found in staple Yemeni dishes include lentils, beans, rice, honey, eggplant, and other native vegetables (dairy products are often not common). Chicken and lamb are popular meat choices over beef and are commonly served grilled or boiled. Fish forms a significant part of the diet in coastal regions. Bread is commonly served with most meals.

A staple food in Yemen's capital, Sana'a, is saltah. It has become a signature lunch meal in many places throughout the country, yet remains primarily a Sana'ani dish. Saltah is a stew containing fenugreek (hulbah in Arabic); tomato; onions; beef, lamb, or chicken; egg, potatoes, and sometimes okra, which collectively adds to the dish's stew-like consistency. It is typically prepared in a special bowl called a madr or makli, and is usually eaten with sorghum flat bread. It often precedes an afternoon of chewing qat.

A special treat that makes for a fine dessert or breakfast is a dish called bint al-sahn, which literally means "daughter of the plate." Bint al-sahn (also known as sabayah) is a flaky cake-pie made in a large, round plate about two to three inches deep. It is prepared with flour, milk, eggs, butter (or ghee, clarified butter), yeast, and honey. It is often brushed with honey and sesame or black cumin seeds before being placed in the oven. It is usually brushed again with honey once it comes out. Though not considered a daily treat, the dish is very much a staple of Yemeni cuisine.

Finally, Yemen is also known for its coffee, called qahwah in Arabic, and known in Yemen as Qishr (or Kishr). In many places in Arabia, coffee is traditionally served at the end of a meal, often accompanied by a sweet dish. Yemen is particularly acknowledged for its unique coffee, some of which is brewed with ginger, giving it a distinctive taste. Yemen is especially renowned for its mocha coffee, which also has a unique taste. This style of coffee, in fact, became a highly profitable international export for Yemen. However, due to competing markets, water scarcity, and lack of infrastructure, exportation and production had drastically decreased by the 20th century.

Life's Milestones

The biggest milestone for both men and women is marriage and childbearing. For most young women, marriage is a primary goal, with education often curtailed in order to reach it. Likewise, for young men, there is pressure to find work that will provide for a family. Because of this, most women marry men who are older—on average, by six years—as they have had more time to build an income and career.

Demonstrating fertility is an important status builder in Yemeni culture. There is significant social pressure to have children very early in marriage, as it establishes status within the family and community. Efforts to increase literacy and access to education have effectively increased the median age for marriage among women, especially in urban environments. Nonetheless, children are still celebrated.

Weddings themselves are gender separate. They often include the entire community of a given area and feature music and dancing, depending on the family's preference. Men typically perform a traditional dance with their jambiyas (daggers) drawn and drum along in accompaniment. The women's celebratory events are typically private and held in halls, tents, or homes. Men's celebrations are in semi-public tents or in the streets of their city or town.

CULTURAL HISTORY

Art

Ancient Yemeni art and culture receives little attention in comparison to other Arab countries. However, Yemen has been considered an important seat of culture throughout the history of the Arab world. In fact, Yemen played an important role in ancient trade routes—particularly involving incense. The influence of Rome, Greece, and other ancient cultures is reflected in Yemeni bronze and stonework, most notably, in their statues. Other important Yemeni traditional arts included decorative textiles and pottery, both mainstays of nearly all ancient civilizations. However, textiles were particularly encouraged in the ancient Islamic world, as they were often highly regarded as gifts and sparked competition among Islamic caliphs (rulers) and other such nobility. Historically, a person's geographical origin could often be determined by the style of their embroidered costumes or clothing.

Traditional art and culture is still present in the embroidered traditional clothing and style of dress still popular in contemporary Yemeni culture. For example, the jambiya (also janbiya), a half-moon-shaped knife, is a staple accessory worn daily by Yemeni men on a waist belt. More decorative pieces then actual weapons, these knifes are commonly unsharpened and always carried in their holsters. The artistry of a jambiya varies greatly, from the very expensive (these may include silver embroidery and detailed workmanship) to the inexpensive (smaller pieces made from less expensive materials). Most often, the knife has a wooden handle with a metal shaft. Typically, the sheath, made of a wood casing covered with leather, is decorated with patterns of metalwork or thread embroidery.

Architecture

Yemeni architecture has remained a prominent feature of the country's rich artistic heritage. In fact, two of Yemen's historical cities, Sana'a and Sheba, were listed as World Heritage Sites by the United Nations Educational, Scientific, and Cultural Organization (UNESCO), particularly for their architecture. However, in June 2015, Saudi airstrikes on Sana'a's Old City, particularly its Al-Qasimi district, destroyed five of the 11th-century white-trimmed tower houses that are part of the UNESCO's World Heritage Sites. Just a few weeks before this, the Ottoman-era Al-Owrdhi historical compound, just outside the Old City, was similarly damaged by bombing.

Generally, however, traditional Yemeni architecture is characterized by functionality and harmony, an aesthetic combination that is still valued today. There are several initiatives that provide incentives and means for Yemenis to continually restore their homes and maintain time-honored traditions, even in the face of widespread poverty and airstrikes that endanger such efforts.

Though different regions and cities are characterized by their own techniques and styles, some distinct features are consistent with most Yemeni buildings and traditional Yemeni architecture. These features include multi-storey, mud-brick buildings, mosque minarets, and decorative, yet functional, windows. In addition, many Yemeni façades, minarets, and windows are ornamented with gypsum (a soft mineral) that is ground into lace-like fretwork, a task that involves the work of skilled artisans. Windows themselves are important functional and artistic features in traditional Yemeni architecture. They are characterized by arches and plaster designs within the arched frames. Historically, window-sills were built low to the ground because most Yemeni homes have very little furniture (pillows were often used instead).

Another unique feature of Yemeni architecture is the decorative wooden door. These doors are carved, often with much detail, from either local or imported wood. They are commonly fastened with bowtie-shaped hinges, and large metal nails are arranged in patterns. The wood is often quite thick and heavy, depending on local wood quality and affordability. Additionally, the building façade (outer walls or appearance) of many Yemeni buildings is often plastered, outlining windows and forming designs.

Yemeni architecture also varies by region due to the availability of building materials and their functionality. For example, the Old City of Sana'a is distinguished for its brick and stone buildings, which are now endangered by bombing, while the historic city of Shibam is championed for its mud buildings. In Shibam, buildings range in height from six to nine stories. These tall buildings are functional, and serve to shade the narrow streets below them. This function is especially important in the deserts of Hadhramaut, where Shibam is located. Additionally, narrow streets are common in Yemeni cities, and many streets of Sana'a are about the width of a small vehicle.

Music

Yemeni poetry has been important to the development of the country's traditional music, as well. In fact, many ancient poets began to incorporate instruments in their poetry recitations, with different melodies and rhythms used for different occasions. Traditional lutes ('ud and qambus), kettledrums (tasah and marfa') and flutes (shubbabah or qassabah) are some of the instruments first used to accompany sung verse. Generally, however, many Yemenis believe, due to Islamic law, that listening to instrumental music can lead to forms of debauchery. As such, it is often restricted and remains an issue debated in Yemen and among Muslims around the world.

Literature

Literature, most notably poetry, has a rich history in Yemen, and poetry perhaps represents the most significant artistic heritage of Yemeni culture. In fact, it is believed that the literary rate of ancient Yemen was very high (particularly during Sabaean rule from roughly 2000 to 700 BCE). The thousands of inscriptions that have survived from the ancient world evidence this. Polemic, or argumentative, poetry was particularly popular in Yemen and was historically used as a tool to spread Islam in the ancient Arabic world. For this reason, poets have been historically held in high esteem in Arab culture.

One of Yemen's most celebrated poets is Waddah al-Yaman (d. 709 CE). Considered the national poet of Yemen, Waddah is one of the most famous Arabic poets of the Umayyad period (661–750 CE) and is renowned for his poetic themes of romance and eroticism. However, Yemen's most famous poet may be Abdullah al-Baradouni (1929–1999). His poetry typically deals with national issues and is often critical of the government, which led to the poet's imprisonment. The anniversary of al-Baradouni's death, August 30, is now celebrated and observed nationally.

Today, the tradition of spoken verse remains a popular cultural heritage. It is particularly being employed as a tool to empower the poor and to fight illiteracy—particularly among women. (Yemen remains one of the poorest countries in the Middle East in the early 21st century.) Well-known poets often record their recitations and distribute them nationally, and spoken poetry still figures prominently in the communication, politics, and traditions of local tribes. In rural areas, local poets often enjoy privileged status. The subject matter of their verse ranges from parables and traditional or historic stories, to wedding songs, stories of Islam, and current events. Islamic law also dictates that the tradition of poetry recitation is gender-specific, and recitation circles are typically separated by gender.

Literature, outside of poetry, was largely underdeveloped in Yemen. Short story and novel writing did not emerge until the 20th century. Modern Yemeni fiction writers include Mohammad Abdul-Wali (1940–1973), who authored short stories and two novels. Zaid Muti' Dammadj's (1943–2000) novel *The Hostage* helped focus attention on contemporary Yemeni literature. Women have traditionally been under-represented in Yemeni literature, although poets Laila Elhan (1989–) and Sawsan al-Areeqe and writers Huda Ablan, (1971–) and Nadia Alkowkabani (1968–) are representative of a new, more inclusive generation of Yemeni's literary figures. In 2004, the city of Sana'a established the Sana'a Story Festival, which promoted the publishing industry and writing in Yemeni culture. In its final year, 2008, the Ministry of Culture co-organized the event, which brought 200 Yemeni and Arab authors to participate in the festival.

CULTURE

Arts & Entertainment

Contemporary Yemeni art has also recently begun to receive international attention. In 2000, the British-Yemeni Society organized an exhibi-

tion titled *Visions of Yemen*, which featured the work of fifteen Yemeni artists. Appearing in the UK cities of London, Cardiff, and Birmingham, the show was one of the first major exhibitions of Yemeni paintings, and from the show, 55 works were sold. Increasingly, more artists that are Yemeni are developing modern techniques in their art, referencing not only Yemeni heritage, but also politics and current issues. Renowned contemporary artists include Nasser Al-Aswadi (1978–), who has had several art exhibits in both Yemen and France, and Fuad Al-Futaih (1948–), largely considered Yemen's most famous modern artist and known for his portrayals of Yemeni women.

Cultural Sites & Landmarks

Yemen has often been referred to as one of the most beautiful nations in the world, and its numerous cultural sites and landmarks are a testament to this. The country is home to four UNESCO World Heritage Sites, including the now endangered Old City of Sana'a, which was bombed by Saudi airstrikes in 2015. Inhabited for over 2,500 years, Sana'a's narrow streets often limit transportation to walking, bicycling, and the occasional motorcycle taxi. The Old City is fortified, and it shelters mosques, as well as the city's largest souq (market), called the Souq al-Milh (Salt Market), and the 1,000-year-old Bāb al-Yemen (the Yemen Gate), which was once an important defensive structure.

Another World Heritage Site is the walled city of Shibam, located in the western Hadhramaut desert region. It has been referred to as the "Manhattan of Arabia" for its 500 tower structures, dating back to the 16th century. In 2008, flooding severely damaged some of the buildings, which are made of mudbrick, and caused them to collapse. Moreover, in March 2009, Al-Qaeda bombings effected further damage. The historic town of Zabid, on the eastern coastline, was inscribed as a World Heritage Site in 1993. It has played a historic role in Arab and Muslim history and was the capital of Yemen from the 13th to the 15th centuries. It is also considered a center of Islamic education.

The final World Heritage Site is the Socotra Archipelago, a small archipelago, or group of islands, in the Indian Ocean. UNESCO recognized it in 2008 for its environmental heritage. The archipelago includes Socotra and three smaller islands: Abd al Kuri, Samhah, and Darsah. Between the smaller islands, there are roughly 400 people, while on Socotra there are over 40,000 people. The major cities on the island are Hidibu and Qualansiya, where the population is largely concentrated. The archipelago is emerging as a popular ecotourism destination.

Yemen is home to a small Jewish minority in the northern mountain region. Though Judaism has existed in Yemen for over 1,500 years, Jews were always a minority in the region. The population significantly decreased with the advent of the Israeli state, to which many Yemeni Jews migrated. However, there remain small pockets of Jewish communities in cities such as Sa'dah. Jewish culture and practice, particularly concerning music, clothing, dance, and language, is quite evident in these communities. Additionally, the culture of these Yemeni Jewish communities is also quite distinct from their Muslim neighbors and the global Jewish community as a whole.

Although Yemen has many attractive tourist sites—and the geology and scenery is widely regarded—the tourist industry is not well developed. Tourists, in particular, are often targeted for questioning at security checkpoints and are required to travel with tourist papers.

Libraries & Museums

The National Museum of Yemen, in Sana'a, was founded in 1971 and is housed in the renovated Dar as-Sa'd (House of Happiness) in Sana'a. It contains numerous artifacts, as well as manuscripts and traditional crafts. The Museum of Art and Crafts is located in the Dar al-Shukr (House of Gratefulness) and features artifacts that reflect Yemen's daily life. Old University Museum has a large display of mummies and both the Taiz National Museum and Seiyun Museum are housed in palaces that highlight lifestyles, national history, and social artifacts.

Holidays

Since the majority of the population in Yemen is Muslim, the country celebrates all major Islamic holidays, including Islamic New Year on January 31. Yemen celebrates the unification of the north and south on Unity Day, which is held on May 22.

Youth Culture

Yemen has a significant youth population, with 41 percent of its population under the age of fifteen. During adolescence, gender roles become more clearly defined within households. Girls have responsibility that is more domestic and have limited mobility outside of the home. In rural homes, women play a role in the daily operations and maintenance of family land. Boys at this age typically have more leisure time. Their responsibilities are often limited to school, whereas girls have domestic responsibilities in addition to school.

The government has recently recognized this youth population surge and has begun focusing on youth services and initiatives. Engaging youth has become particularly important in the early 21st century. The significant population growth in past decades in Yemen has made it difficult for youth to find employment once they complete their education. There is also a growing issue of over-education or qualification, as the market frequently calls for vocational labor. Unemployment among those ages 15 to 24 is 26 percent for males and 74 percent for females.

As a leisure or recreational activity, most young men play pick-up football (soccer), as there are few facilities and resources for other gaming activities. Young women may take to crocheting, practicing henna designs (henna is dyestuff prepared from the henna plant), or other indoor activities and handicrafts. However, girls have significantly less free time than boys do. Additionally, according to the CIA, 1,334,288 children are engaged in some sort of child labor and are often forced to join in the process of locating clean water for the family household.

Though Internet usage is low in Yemen, the website Facebook remains popular among Yemeni youth and has become one of the top twenty most popular social network sites (SNS) in Yemen. However, young Yemeni women are careful not to upload photos to the site, for fear of misuse. It is standard in northern Yemen for women to wear niqab (face covering), and they often maintain this practice in their online avatars.

SOCIETY

Transportation

The most popular and inexpensive form of public transport in Yemen are buses. These consist of intra-city buses and rural routes between cities and towns. Typically, a bus is in actuality a mini-van that usually seats six to eight adults, or fifteen for longer distances. However, large coach buses seating about forty are commonly available from one major city to another. Generally, roads in the cities are well kept, while those in rural areas are more treacherous, often wrapping around mountains in the country's northern regions. Additionally, motorcycles are prevalent in cities, where they are more practical for navigating the narrow streets.

It is important to note that rules regarding gender separation are also maintained in public buses in the inner city. It is expected that if a woman enters a bus, she only sit next to other women or by herself. If there are no other women on the bus, and there is no space for the woman to sit by herself, she may simply wait for another bus or place a bag between herself and the man next to her. For long distances, it is quite rare for women to travel alone.

By law, cars in Yemen should travel on the right-hand side of the road.

Transportation Infrastructure

Yemen's road system is not well developed, but in cities, such as Sana'a, the roads are well maintained, as are those between Ta'izz to Mokha. Recent Saudi airstrikes have created damage to these roadways, however, and repairs have been slow. There are roads between Aden and Sana'a and Aden and Mukalla. Most mountain roads are treacherous, and roads in the desert are defined by the tire tracks of previous vehicles; these are best traveled by four-wheel drive.

In Yemen, there are 57 airports, only 17 of which are paved. Five of these airports are international: Aden International, Sana'a International, Ta'izz, Riyan Mukalla Airport, and Hodeida. Yemenia is that nation's principal airline. In March 2015, flights in and out of Yemen were suspended due to Saudi air strikes against Houthi fighters in Yemen. The flight suspension stranded thousands of Yemenis outside the country and trapped many Pakistanis and Indian nationals inside Yemen's borders. Local ferries are still available for travel between coastal cities.

Media & Communications

The media in Yemen are largely influenced by the government. The government has control over printing presses and owns the country's one television station and all radio stations. As such, according to Human Rights Watch, the press has often been subjected to intimidation and threats by both government and non-governmental parties. Many newspapers, such as *al-Thawra,* are also government-controlled. The weekly *Yemen Times* and the daily *Yemen Observer* are two popular English-language newspapers, which also have an online presence. Generally, music from Egypt is played on the radio, and television programs from Oman and Saudi Arabia make up the majority of programming available in Yemen.

According to Reporters without Borders, 12 journalists were arrested in 2007, and in 2009, the BBC reported (from Reporters without Borders and the Committee to Protect Journalists) that the government had harassed journalists at *al-Ayyam* newspaper, as well as confiscated and destroyed certain editions deemed harmful to national unity. In March 2015, CNN reported that a 28-year-old freelance Norwegian journalist, on assignment from the Norwegian newspaper *Bergens Tidende,* was detained by Houthi authorities in Sana'a for taking photographs of the destruction wrought by Saudi airstrikes. He was released after nearly a month in detention.

As recently as 1999, the Internet was only available through a government company. While that has changed, it is still extremely rare for the average person to have Internet access in their home. In fact, as of 2013, only 20 percent of the population used the Internet, and there is limited or no access in rural areas. There are, however, Internet cafés in major cities such as Sana'a and Aden.

The CIA estimates that, in 2014, 17.1 million people have mobile phones. There are four popular cell phone companies, all of which are government-affiliated. Prepaid phone card systems are also widely available. Local phone usage is reasonably priced, but international calls are quite expensive, whether made from cellular pre-paid phones or from call stations.

SOCIAL DEVELOPMENT

Standard of Living
Yemen ranked 154th on the 2014 United Nations Human Development Index of 187 countries.

Water Consumption
In Yemen, only 55 percent of the population has access to improved water sources, with 72 percent in urban areas and 46.5 percent in rural areas. Improved sanitation is also available only to 53.3 percent of the population, with 92.5 percent enjoying this access in urban areas and 34 percent in rural areas. In the country's capital Sana'a, only 40 percent of households are connected to the municipal water supply. The rest of the city's population must purchase water from tanker trucks that sell supplies at exorbitant rates. According to UN statistics, the lack of access to clean water results in the death of 14,000 children each year. Many others are chronically malnourished and unable to attend school because they are persistently searching for enough water to meet family needs.

As of 2010, the state of the water supply in the capital, Sana'a, was in critical condition, with over 80 percent of the nation's water supply already extracted from fossil reserves in the Sana'a Basin; these reserves are expected to be depleted by 2017. In 2015, 13 million Yemenis struggle to find clean water, and an estimated 14.7 million rely on water provided by humanitarian aid organizations to survive. Poor management practices and over drilling—combined with an outdated system of leaky pipes that waste an estimated 60 percent of water carried—have been blamed for the crisis' magnitude.

According to the *Times Online*, Yemen is poised to be the first country in the world to run out of water. Many wells are as deep as 200 to 300 meters (656 to 984 feet), with some wells in Sana'a as deep as 800 to 1,000 meters (2,624 to 3,280 feet), which requires oil well equipment to access. Many wells have dried up because the water table has dropped. In Ta'izz, tap water is only available every forty-five days. Those in mountainous regions climb to springs and wait in line for water. Of the water that is accessed, the overwhelming portion of it is used for agriculture (80 to 90 percent). The most prevalent crop is qat, accounting for nearly 40 percent of Yemen's agricultural output. However, the production of one "daily bag" of qat—that is, the amount one person usually chews in a day, which usually runs between $2 and $14 USD based on quality—requires more than 500 liters (130 US gallons) of water.

Desalinization plants have been considered, but no plans have been developed, and the government's decentralization plans for water management have still not been realized even in 2015, five years after the situation was deemed critical. Water rights have become a security issue, with armed conflict reported in some areas. With the increased presence of al Qaeda in Yemen and Houthi outbreaks, some have expressed concern that Yemen's water shortage could be a leverage point for extremists seeking to build support.

Education
Before the Houthi seizure of power, Yemen's Ministry of Education oversaw Yemen's educational system. Each governorate in the country was responsible for managing its own district offices, and those offices managed schools within

their districts. The governorates reported directly to the Ministry of Education. The ministry has a great deal of control over school affairs, including curriculum, textbooks, and teacher training and hiring.

Literacy is a problem in Yemen. In 2015, 55 percent of adult women in Yemen cannot read or write, and it is estimated that only 70 percent of the adult population is literate. Most Yemenis attend school an average of nine years. The urban male population is the best educated, followed by the rural male population. Urban women are, in general, better educated than rural women are, although women lag far behind men in education. This is due in part to cultural attitudes toward women in the country. Students in Yemen obtain their religious education alongside basic education.

In 2009, over 220 of the country's 725 schools were closed for five months due to fighting between Houthi rebels and government forces. Many of these schools were either destroyed or looted, and the country sought aid from non-governmental sources to provide shelter and supplies for the more than 120,000 students returning to school. Circumstances have not improved since the Houthis have overtaken Sana'a and a great deal of northern Yemen, as this has incurred the ire of Saudi Arabia, whose air raids in support of President Hadi's government have made daily life in occupied areas extremely dangerous.

Women's Rights

Social and cultural values in Yemen require that women live in seclusion, and education of women is often discouraged. Many women marry at a young age and are responsible for managing their husbands' households. Most women who work outside the home are employed in the agricultural industry. Women living in the south and in the Tihama region tend to experience more freedom than women who live in towns in the northern part of the country.

Legally speaking, women in Yemeni society have equal rights. In practice, however, there is inequity, especially regarding litigation and law enforcement. Yemen, in fact, would be considered

in violation of Article 16 of the UDHR, which requires for equality in marriage and divorce. For example, women must sue for divorce, while men are not required to do so. Likewise, inheritance is inconsistent between daughters and sons, and daughters receive significantly smaller inheritances. Additionally, women are subject to sexual abuse in prison and are only released into the custody of a male relative. This means that if no male relative is available, the woman's prison term is extended.

Though women legally have equal status in terms of suffrage and the right to work, among other areas, the reality is a system of institutionalized discrimination. For example, women's organizations are strictly monitored. Those organizations attempt to provide some of the services to which women have a right, but cannot readily access, including health services and education, which are both particularly important in rural areas.

Additionally, female circumcision also referred to as female genital mutilation—the process by which all or part of a woman's external genitalia is removed and the vaginal opening is partially sewn closed—is still practiced in Yemen. As of 2014, approximately 24 percent of Yemeni women have undergone the practice, which is considered a rite of passage and makes female children more highly prized as potential brides because they are perceived as cleaner. However, hemorrhaging, infection, and death following the procedure, which is often carried out in non-sterile conditions, are not uncommon, as is emotional trauma following the procedure.

In addition, the number of girls being withheld from receiving an education in Yemen remains high in the 21st century. In many cases, parents are withholding their daughters from attending school, largely due to poverty and tradition. As of 2015, while 80 percent of males were literate, only 55 percent of females could read and write.

Health Care

The Ministry of Public Health oversees the health care system in Yemen. Primary health care is provided by the government, which also has a referral system for other health services. Some primary health services include emergency care, family planning, and immunization.

Physicians and paramedics work in health clinics in towns and villages, and the country has a number of hospitals in its urban areas. However, resources and medical personnel are stretched extremely thin, and access to steady supplies of medicine and vaccines is often limited, particularly in rural areas. Humanitarian aid organizations provide a great deal of assistance in the medical sector. However, private health clinics are increasing in Yemen, yet such services are available only to those who can afford them.

In 2013, healthcare expenditures represented 5.4 percent of the country's GDP. For every 1,000 people, there is less than one doctor (0.2) and less than 1 hospital bed (0.7).

GOVERNMENT

Structure
Prior to 1990, Yemen was comprised of two separate countries, North and South Yemen. On May 22, 1990, the country of Yemen was created. The unification process involved bringing the institutions, laws, and political systems of the two countries into agreement with each other. Islamic law (Sharia) became the basis of the new country's legal system. In 1994, a civil war broke out due to conflicts between former northern and southern leaders; during this war, the former southern leaders tried to secede and form their own country.

Before the coup in January 2015 and its still-undetermined changes to the governing structure, Yemen had been a republic; its constitution was ratified in May 1991. The president, prime minister, and cabinet formed the executive branch of government. The president acted as head of state and the prime minister was appointed by the president and acted as head of government. The Yemeni legislature included two houses: the Shura Council, which has 111 members, and the House of Representatives, with 301 members. In 2001, several constitutional amendments strengthened the power of the executive branch, extending the president's term to seven years and giving the president the authority to dissolve parliament. The Shura, a house filled with presidential appointments, was doubled in size. Suffrage is universal for adults aged eighteen and older.

Political Parties
Before the 2015 coup, the largest political party in Yemen is the General People's Congress (GPC), which has held the presidency since unification and holds a majority in the House of Representatives. In 2006, an opposition coalition called the Joint Meeting Parties (JMP) fielded a candidate (Faisal bin Shamlan) that proved President Ali Abdallah Saleh's first real political challenge. The JMP was comprised of several parties, including the Islamist Islah party, the Yemeni Socialist Party, the Nasserist Unionist party, the Al-Haq party, and the Popular Forces Union Party. Other parties exist, but none has any real power given the dominance of the GPC.

Local Government
Yemen consists of 21 governorates (muhafazah) and one municipality (amanah). These are governorates are further divided in districts (muderiah), of which there are 333. While local governors and councils are directly elected, the power of the central government still has an impact on these local elections and often exercises its authority through these locally elected officials. Rural Yemen is more tribal in governance, and the central authority has little impact.

Judicial System
The 2014–15 coup by Houthi rebels has immobilized Yemen's constitutionally designated judicial system and replaced it with improvised tribal courts. However, before the overthrow, as designated by the 1991 constitution, the government's judicial branch was headed by a Supreme Court and included a separate system of commercial courts. The legal system, still based on Islamic law, or Sharia, now specifically follows the Zaydi branch of Islamic jurisprudence. However, the presumption of innocence and right to counsel provided for under the previous constitutional

government has not been recognized by Houthi proceedings thus far. While the constitution previously defined an independent judiciary, the executive branch traditionally exerted significant influence on judges, as they were appointed by and could be removed by the executive branch. Public confidence in the judiciary had been weak even before the government takeover.

Taxation

Yemen's personal income tax ranges between 15 and 20 percent, while corporate taxes range between 20 and 35 percent. Other taxes include a general sales tax, property tax, fuel tax, and a religious or practicing tax on wealth.

Armed Forces

The Yemen military is comprised of a land force; a coastal defense force, which includes the Marines; and an Air and Air Defense Force, known as al-Quwwat al-Jawwiya al-Yemeniya. There are also border guards and a strategic defense force.

Yemen has the second largest military force on the Arabian Peninsula. As of 2012, there is no conscription per se. However, there is a two-year service requirement for Yemeni citizens. The military consumes a large portion of the annual national budget; in 2012, its expenditures represented 4.2 percent of the GDP. Moreover, while troop levels are high, reports indicate the hardware and equipment are outdates and exists in insufficient numbers.

Foreign Policy

Yemen has had a tumultuous history in establishing itself as a unified state. Prior to 1990, Yemen existed as two states, Northern Yemen (the Yemen Arab Republic) and Southern Yemen (The People's Democratic Republic of Yemen). Southern Yemen broke from British colonial rule in 1967 and Northern Yemen from Ottoman rule in 1918. Both republics developed their own distinct cultures and were involved in a long series of conflicts. For example, Southern Yemen moved toward a communist government in the 1970s, causing many Yemenis to flee to Northern Yemen,

thus increasing the animosity between the two states. However, on May 22, 1990, the two states formally united to form the Republic of Yemen.

Since the unification, tensions have arisen with Yemen's northern neighbor, Saudi Arabia. These tensions are rooted in border issues, oil, and Yemen's position during the Gulf Crisis. As a member of the United Nations Security Council (UNSC), Yemen voted against the UN resolution to authorize military action to remove Iraqi forces from Kuwait prior to the Gulf War (1990–91). Saudi Arabia, on the other hand, supported foreign involvement in Iraq. As a result, many Gulf countries decreased or ended aid and diplomatic contact with Yemen, and a large number of Yemeni laborers were expelled from Saudi Arabia. This had a significant effect on the Yemeni economy, and Yemen is still trying to restore relations with its Gulf neighbors. (Yemen resolved its border dispute with Saudi Arabia in 2000, after both countries signed an International Border Treaty).

Yemen did not support the invasion of Iraq in 2003. However, the country offered to host reconciliation conferences in order to end sectarian violence. Otherwise, Yemen's relationship with the U.S. has generally been civil, although bilateral diplomatic ties have never been established. Yemen is, however, a recipient of aid from the U.S. Agency for International Development (USAID). Under the George W. Bush administration, Yemen had also been superficially cooperative with the US-led "war on terror," but did not readily turn over terrorists or halt suspected terrorist activity, which served to further cool U.S.-Yemeni relations.

Yemen has an established relationship with its southern neighbor Somalia. In fact, as of 2007, Yemen hosted over 110,000 Somali asylum seekers, having recognized them since the outbreak of civil war in Somalia in 1988. A majority of these refugees have settled in the southern city of Aden or refugee camps established by the Yemen government. Yemen also maintains strong relations with Djibouti, the neighboring country of Somalia, and recently settled a territorial dispute with Eritrea involving a Red Sea island group, the Hanish Islands.

Yemen does not have full membership status on the Gulf Cooperation Council (GCC). The GCC has resisted Yemen's membership, and only permits its participation by observers. The council includes Saudi Arabia, Oman, Bahrain, Kuwait, Qatar, and the United Arab Emirates (UAE). However, Yemen is a member of the Arab League and the Organization of the Islamic Conference (OIC). In addition, Yemen's UN membership dates back to September 30, 1947, when Northern Yemen was admitted.

Human Rights Profile

International human rights law insists that states respect civil and political rights and promote an individual's economic, social, and cultural rights. The United Nations Universal Declaration on Human Rights (UDHR) is recognized as the standard for international human rights. Its authors sought the counsel of the world's great thinkers, philosophers, and religious leaders and were careful to create a document that reflects the core values shared by every world culture. (To read this document or view the articles relating to cultural human rights, visit www.ohchr.org/EN/UDHR/Pages/Introduction.aspx.)

Yemen does not have an ideal human rights record. Between reports of kidnappings, deplorable prison conditions, and struggles for executive power and legislation, the country has failed to meet what is considered the minimum human rights standards.

For example, the violation of both Article 5 and 9 has been widespread. Article 5 deals with the torture and ill treatment of any human being, while Article 9 states that people are free from arbitrary arrest. Yet, according to the organization Human Rights Watch, the violation of both articles is prevalent in Yemen. The reports of torture derive mainly from prisons, while controversial figures in Yemeni society, largely political, have been subjected to unjustified arrest. In addition, Yemen has been accused of detaining and harassing journalists, a violation of Article 19. The independent administration of Sana'a University, the largest in the city, was challenged with the court-supported closure of the women's studies center in 1999.

As of March 2014, a multi-million dollar industry in the trafficking and exploitation of refugees and other migrants has developed in Yemen. Human Rights Watch indicates that, since 2006, so-called "torture camps" have existed in Yemen. Such camps are isolated and migrants seeking labor are often kidnapped and transported to the camps where their pain and misery is used to extort money from them or their families. Apart from a few camp raids in 2013, little else has been done to shut down their operations, and Human Rights Watch reports that bribery of government officials facilitates these activities.

Migration

Many men leave Yemen to work in places such as Saudi Arabia, sending remittances home to their families in Yemen. These remittances add up to a significant portion of the country's gross domestic product (4.43 percent in 2011, or $1.47 million). Issues have arisen of child trafficking and international aid organizations are assisting the Yemeni government in addressing these issues. Yemen is also a haven for refugees from both Somalia and Ethiopia, as it is a signatory on the 1951 Refugee Convention.

ECONOMY

Overview of the Economy

Yemen is a poor nation with few natural resources, increasingly scarce water resources, and little arable land. Before unification, both North and South Yemen faced economic problems. In the north, droughts hurt the agricultural industries, while shipping was harmed by the 1967 closure of the Suez Canal in the south. The city of Aden, which is located in the south, has been an important port since the opening of the canal in 1869.

Today, much of the country is in need of economic investment and development. The World Bank and the International Monetary Fund (IMF) are working to help the country lower its debt.

Oil provides the most significant source of revenue for Yemen. It represents an estimated 25 percent of the GDP and 65 percent of government revenue. In 2014, the estimated gross domestic product (GDP) was around $103.6 billion (USD). The per capita GDP for the same period was $3,800 (USD). The country's unemployment rate is around 27 percent.

Industry

Industry in Yemen accounts for around 26.8 percent of GDP (2014 estimate). Petroleum refining makes up a major part of the industrial sector. International companies from the United States and France have invested in the extraction of Yemen's petroleum resources, and oil exports have helped the country to lower its debt.

Other important industries in Yemen include natural gas production, crude oil production, petroleum refining, cotton-based textiles, leather goods, processed foods, commercial ship repair, cement, aluminum-based products.

Labor

The labor force in Yemen numbers about 7.26 million people in 2014, with an unemployment rate at about 27 percent. The vast majority of the population works in the agricultural sector (more than 70 percent, accounting for about 9.2 percent of the GDP). Less than 25 percent work in the industry and services sector. Civil service had become a desirable means of employment, as those jobs have seen wage increases in the early 21st century, where other wages have not.

Energy/Power/Natural Resources

First discovered in 1985 in the eastern highlands, oil is Yemen's most important and profitable natural resource. Foreign oil companies from the United States and other countries have set up refineries and pipelines to export the oil.

Natural gas, fish and seafood, rock salt, and other metal and minerals are among Yemen's less important resources.

Fishing

Fishing is an underdeveloped industry in Yemen. The government has eased export restrictions in this sector, and as a result, non-fillet fish are one of the country's top five exports, after crude petroleum, petroleum gas, refined petroleum, and coal tar oil. The World Bank, in conjunction with the Yemeni government, is supporting the Fisheries Management and Conservation Project, an effort to develop the fishing industry infrastructure necessary to expand this industry.

Mining/Metals

Yemen has limited veins of coal, iron ore, and copper, which themselves are not commercially valuable. There are also vast reserves of nickel, silver, gold, zinc, and cobalt, along with zeolite (used to trap heavy metals and neutralize radiation); talc; scoria (a vesiculated lava, like pumice); sandstone; perlite; magnesite; limestone; gypsum; feldspar; dolomite; various clays; and celestine (strontium sulfate, used in fireworks and the creation of metal alloys). Natural gas and crude oil are also abundant in the region.

Agriculture

Around 2.2 percent of the land in Yemen is arable. To water their crops, farmers have employed various methods of irrigation, including the use of diesel-powered pumps, wells, and wadi dams. Major agricultural products include qat, coffee, cotton, fruits, vegetables, grains, and pulses (a grain-legume, like lentils).

The best agricultural land in the southern portion of Yemen is found in the west, near Aden, and in the Wadi Hadhramaut valley in the east. In the Tihama, farmers raise tropical fruits and vegetables, such as bananas, citrus fruits, tomatoes, and papayas. Cotton is also raised there. At higher elevations, grains, such as millet and oats, along with nuts, figs, and melons are grown.

Many farmers in Yemen practice terrace farming in valleys with elevations of around 1,500 meters (4,900feet). They plant crops such as the qat shrub, coffee, apples, pears, and grapes. Corn, wheat, and sorghum also grow on terrace farms. Water shortages in the early 21st century, though, have contributed to the strain on Yemeni agriculture.

Interesting to note is that in 2015, qat is the largest source of income in rural areas, and the country's second largest revenue generator. Its production and distribution employ one in seven Yemenis.

Animal Husbandry

Along with other agricultural products, animal husbandry contributes about 9.2 percent to the country's GDP and assists in nutritionally sustaining Yemen's population. Sheep, goats, and cattle, donkeys, and camels comprise Yemeni farmers' primary livestock. In addition, since the 1970s, poultry farming has been pursued on a commercial level, with equal emphasis on eggs and broiler meat production. However, limited and ever-declining water resources are having a severe impact on this economic sector.

Tourism

Although it is a small part of Yemen's economy, tourism has become more important for the country. Yemen's tourism infrastructure includes guided tour operations and well over 300 hotels. It also has seen growth in the food service industry, with over 11,000 restaurants throughout the country.

Most tourists tend to visit the major cities, including Sana'a. Although there are improved transportation, hotel, and food services, parts of Yemen are dangerous for tourists because of tribal conflicts. In fact, many sites currently recommend against travel to Yemen due to increased reports of kidnappings, bombings, and the imminent danger of outright civil war.

Samira Abdul-Karim, Christina Healey, Anne Whittaker, & Savannah Schroll Guz

DO YOU KNOW?

- The Arabic word "Yemen" can mean "the right hand" and "prosperous" or "happy" in English.

- The ruins of the Great Dam of Marib, which was built somewhere between 1750 and 1700 BCE and lasted until 575 CE, can still be seen today in the northern part of the country, although in 2015, they have been severely damaged by Saudi airstrikes. A new dam was built near the ancient ruins and over the Wadi Dhana; it was dedicated to Sheikh Zayed Bin Sulṭān Āl Nayhān, the late ruler of the United Arab Emirates, in 1986. Āl Nayhān's tribe originated in Marib.

- Sana'a was chosen as the 2004 Arab Cultural Capital under the Cultural Capitals Program, an initiative by UNESCO to promote Arab culture and cooperation.

- The temple of the Queen of Sheba, a famous mythical queen, is thought to be located in Yemen.

Bibliography

_____. "Yemen Chronicle: An Anthropology of War and Mediation." New York: *Hill and Wang*, 2006.

Abir Ghattas. "Yemen's No Fly Zone: Thousands of Yemenis are Stranded Abroad." *Global Voices*. Global Voices, 15 Mar. 2015.

Charles Aithie and Patricia Aithie. "Yemen: Jewel of Arabia." Northampton, MA: *Interlink Pub Group*, 2009.

Chris Eboch. "Modern Nations of the World—Yemen." USA: *Lucent Books*, 2003.

Fernando Varanda. "The Art of Building in Yemen." London: *MIT Press*, 1982.

Gabriele Vom Bruck and Fred Halliday. "Islam, Memory, and Morality in Yemen: Ruling Families in Transition." England: Palgrave Macmillan, 2005. *Contemporary Anthropology of Religion Ser*. https://globalvoicesonline. org/2015/03/31/yemens-no-fly-zone-thousands-of-yemenis-are-stranded-abroad/#.

Janine A. Clark. "Islam, Charity, and Activism: Middle-Class Networks and Social Welfare in Egypt, Jordan, and Yemen." Bloomington, IN: *Indiana University Press*, 2004.

Lichtenthaler, Gerhard. "Political Ecology and the Role of Water: Environment, Society and Economy in Northern Yemen." Hampshire: *Ashgate Publishing*, 2003.

Madiha Al-Junaid. "Controversy Surrounds Alleged Houthi Courts in Amran." *Yemen Times*. 14 Aug 2014. http://www.yementimes.com/en/1807/news/4199/Controversy-surrounds-alleged-Houthi-courts-in-Amran.htm.

Mohammed Mukhashaf. "Despite conflict, qat is out the bag in Yemen." *Reuters*. Thomson Reuters, 14 Apr. 2015.

http://www.reuters.com/article/2015/04/14/us-yemen-security-qat-idUSKBN0N51F420150414.

Nathalie Handal. "The Poetry of Arab Women." 2nd ed. Northampton, MA: *Interlink Publishing Group*, 2015.

Paul Dresch. "A History of Modern Yemen." New York: *Cambridge University Press*, 2001.

Robert D. Burrowes. *Historical Dictionary of Yemen.* Lanham, MD: *The Scarecrow Press Inc*, 2009. Historical Dictionaries of Asia, Oceania, and the Middle East Ser.

Steven Charles Caton. "Peaks of Yemen I Summon: Poetry as Cultural Practice in a North Yemeni Tribe." *University of California Press*, 1993.

Tim Mackintosh-Smith. "Yemen: The Unknown Arabia." New York: *The Overlook Press*, 2014.

Victoria Clark. "Yemen: Dancing on the Heads of Snakes." New Haven, CT: *Yale UP*, 2010.

Works Cited

_____. "Yemen's Torture Camps." *Human Rights Watch.* Human Rights Watch, 25 May 2014. https://www.hrw.org/report/2014/05/25/yemens-torture-camps/abuse-migrants-human-traffickers-climate-impunity.

Alfred B. Prados and Jeremy M. Sharp. "Yemen: Current Conditions and U.S.

Relations." *CRS Report for Congress.* U.S. Department of State, 4 Jan. 2007. http://fpc.state.gov/documents/organization/81358.pdf

Anthony Tirado Chase and Abdul Karim Alaug. "Health, Human Rights, and Islam: A Focus on Yemen." *Health and Human Rights.* 8.1 (2004): 114-137.

Arwa Al-Rabee.' "Adolescent Reproductive Health in Yemen." *POLICY Project.* (January 2003): 1-16. http://www.policyproject.com/pubs/countryreports/ARH_Yemen.pdf.

Bill Heber Percy. "Visions of Yemen." *The British-Yemeni Society.* Al-Bab, July 2001. http://www.al-bab.com/bys/articles/percy01.htm.

Brad Carlile, "The Full-on Experience of Yemen." *Freeport Journal Standard.* 20 May 2001: C6. http://www.bradcarlile.com/travel/yemen.html

Charles Phillips & Alan Axelrod. "Yemenite Civil War, 1962-1970." *Encyclopedia of Wars.* Vol. 3. New York: Facts On File, Inc.

Daniel Martin Variscos. "On the Meaning of Chewing: The Significance of Qat (Cathaedulis) in the Yemen Arab Republic." *International Journal of Middle East Studies.* 18.1 (1986): 1-13.

Flagg W. Miller. "Public Words and Body Politics: Reflections on the Strategies of

Women Poets in Rural Yemen." *Journal of Women's History.* 14.1(2002): 94-122.

Habeeb Salloum. "Stories about Food in Yemen." *Things Asian.* Global Directions, Inc., 2015. http://www.thingsasian.com/yemen/food/stories

"Literature in Yemen Today." *Banipal: Magazine of Modern Arab Literature.* 36 (Autumn/Winter 2009).

Lizzie Porter. "Yemen: the Unesco heritage slowly being destroyed." *Telegraph Travel.* Telegraph Media Group Limited, 16 Jun. 2015. http://www.telegraph.co.uk/travel/destinations/middleeast/yemen/11678151/Ye

M. Azzam, "The Gulf Crisis: Perceptions in the Muslim World." *International Affairs.* (July 1991): 473-486.

Pamela Jermone, Giacomo Chiari, and Caterina Borelli. "The Architecture of Mud: Construction and Repair Technology in the Hadhramaut Region of Yemen" *APT Bulletin.* 30.2-3 (1999): 39-48.

Peter Kandela. "Women's rights, a tourist boom, and the power of khat in Yemen." *Lancet.* 355.9213 (2000): 1437.

Philip D. Schuyler, "Hearts and Minds: Three Attitudes toward Performance Practice and Music Theory in the Yemen Arab Republic." *Ethnomusicology.* 34.1 (1990): 1-18.

Steven Caton. "Salam tahiyah: greetings from the highlands of Yemen." *American Ethnologist.* (May 1986): 290-308.

Thomas B. Stevenson. "Migration, Family and Household in Highland Yemen: The Impact of Socio-Economic and Political Change and Cultural Ideals on Domestic Organization." *Journal of Comparative Family Studies.* 28.2 (1997): 14-55.

"Water scarcity in Yemen: the country's forgotten conflict." The Guardian. *Guardian News and Media Limited,* 2 Apr. 2015. http://www.theguardian.com/global-development-professionals-network/2015/apr/02/water-scarcity-yemen-conflict.

Yael Katzir. "Preservation of Jewish Ethnicity in Yemen: Segregation and Integration as Boundary Maintenance Mechanisms." *Comparative Studies in Society and History.* 24.2 (1982): 264-279. men-the-Unesco-heritage-slowly-being-destroyed.html.

"Yemen: 24 percent of Yemeni women experience genital mutilation." *News.* Female Genital Cutting Education and Networking Project, *FGMNetwork.* 12 Feb. 2007. http://www.fgmnetwork.org/gonews.php?subaction=showfull&id=1171338119&ucat=1&.

"Yemen." *Observatory of Economic Complexity.* Macro Connections/MIT/Alex Simoes, 2015. https://atlas.media.mit.edu/en/profile/country/yem/.

"Yemen Times." *Yemen Times.,* 2015. http://yementimes.com

"Yemen." *World Factbook.* Central Intelligence Agency, 2015.

"Yemen Crisis: Who is Fighting Whom?" *BBC News.* BBC, 26 Mar. 2015. http://www.bbc.com/news/world-middle-east-29319423. https://www.cia.gov/library/publications/the-world-factbook/geos/ym.html.

"Yemen." *Human Rights Watch,* 2015. https://www.hrw.org/middle-east/n-africa/yemen.

Appendix One:
World Governments

Commonwealth

Guiding Premise

A commonwealth is an organization or alliance of nations connected for the purposes of satisfying a common interest. The participating states may retain their own governments, some of which are often considerably different from one another. Although commonwealth members tend to retain their own sovereign government institutions, they collaborate with other members to create mutually agreeable policies that meet their collective interests. Some nations join commonwealths to enhance their visibility and political power on the international stage. Others join commonwealths for security or economic reasons. Commonwealth members frequently engage in trade agreements, security pacts, and other programs. Some commonwealths are regional, while others are global.

Typical Structure

A commonwealth's structure depends largely on the nature of the organization and the interests it serves. Some commonwealths are relatively informal in nature, with members meeting on a periodic basis and participating voluntarily. This informality does not undermine the effectiveness of the organization, however—members still enjoy a closer relationship than that which exists among unaffiliated states. Commonwealths typically have a president, secretary general, or, in the case of the Commonwealth of Nations (a commonwealth that developed out of the British Empire), a monarch acting as the leader of the organization. Members appoint delegates to serve at summits, committee meetings, and other commonwealth events and programs.

Other commonwealths are more formal in structure and procedures. They operate based on mission statements with very specific goals and member participation requirements. These organizations have legislative bodies that meet regularly. There are even joint security operations involving members. The African Union, for example, operates according to a constitution and collectively addresses issues facing the entire African continent, such as HIV/AIDS, regional security, environmental protection, and economic cooperation.

One of the best-known commonwealths in modern history was the Soviet Union. This collective of communist states was similar to other commonwealths, but the members of the Soviet Union, although they retained their own sovereign government institutions, largely deferred to the organization's central leadership in Moscow, which in turn deferred to the Communist Party leadership. After the collapse of the Soviet Union, a dozen former Soviet states, including Russia, reconnected as the Commonwealth of Independent States. This organization features a central council in Minsk, Belarus. This council consists of the heads of state and heads of government for each member nation, along with their cabinet ministers for defense and foreign affairs.

Commonwealth structures and agendas vary. Some focus on trade and economic development, as well as using their respective members' collective power to address human rights, global climate change, and other issues. Others are focused on regional stability and mutual defense, including prevention of nuclear weapons proliferation. The diversity of issues for which commonwealths are formed contributes to the frequency of member meetings as well as the actions carried out by the organization.

Role of the Citizen

Most commonwealths are voluntary in nature, which means that the member states must choose to join with the approval of their respective governments. A nation with a democratic government, therefore, would need the sanction of its popularly elected legislative and executive bodies in order to proceed. Thus, the role of the private citizen with regard to a commonwealth is indirect—the people may have the power to vote for or against a legislative or executive candidate based on his or her position concerning membership in a commonwealth.

Some members of commonwealths, however, do not feature a democratic government, or their respective governmental infrastructures are not yet in place. Rwanda, for instance, is a developing nation whose 2009 decision to join the Commonwealth of Nations likely came from the political leadership with very little input from its citizens, as Rwandans have very limited political freedom.

While citizens may not directly influence the actions of a commonwealth, they may work closely with its representatives. Many volunteer nonprofit organizations—having direct experience with, for example, HIV/AIDS, certain minority groups, or environmental issues—work in partnership with the various branches of a commonwealth's central council. In fact, such organizations are frequently called upon in this regard to implement the policies of a commonwealth, receiving financial and logistical support when working in impoverished and/or war-torn regions. Those working for such organizations may therefore prove invaluable to the effectiveness of a commonwealth's programs.

Michael Auerbach
Marblehead, Massachusetts

Examples

African Union
Commonwealth of Independent States
Commonwealth of Nations
Northern Mariana Islands (and the United States)
Puerto Rico (and the United States)

Bibliography

"About Commonwealth of Independent States." *Commonwealth of Independent States.* CIS, n.d. Web. 17 Jan. 2013.

"AU in a Nutshell." *African Union.* African Union Commission, n.d. Web. 17 Jan. 2013.

"The Commonwealth." *Commonwealth of Nations.* Nexus Strategic Partnerships Limited, 2013. Web. 17 Jan. 2013.

Communist

Guiding Premise

Communism is a political and economic system that seeks to eliminate private property and spread the benefits of labor equally throughout the populace. Communism is generally considered an outgrowth of socialism, a political and economic philosophy that advocates "socialized" or centralized ownership of the economy and the means of production.

Communism developed largely from the theories of Karl Marx (1818–83), who believed that a revolution led by the working class must occur before the state could achieve the even distribution of wealth and property and eliminate the class-based socioeconomic system of capitalist society. Marx believed that a truly equitable society required centralized control of credit, transportation, education, communication, agriculture, and industry, along with eliminating the rights of individuals to inherit or to own land.

Russia (formerly the Soviet Union) and China are the two largest countries to have been led by communist governments during the twentieth and twenty-first centuries. In both cases, the attempt to bring about a communist government came by way of violent revolutions in which members of the former government and ruling party were executed. Under Russian leader Vladimir Lenin (1870–1924) and Chinese leader Mao Zedong (1893–1976), strict dictatorships were instituted, curtailing individual rights in favor of state control. Lenin sought to expand communism into developing nations to counter the global spread of capitalism. Mao, in his form of communism, considered ongoing revolution within China a necessary aspect of communism. Both gave their names to their respective versions of communism, but neither Leninism nor Maoism managed to achieve the idealized utopia envisioned by Marx and other communist philosophers.

The primary difference between modern socialism and communism is that communist groups believe that a social revolution is necessary to create the idealized state without class structure, where socialists believe that the inequities of class structure can be addressed and eliminated through gradual change.

Typical Structure

Most modern communist governments define themselves as "socialist," though a national communist party exerts control over all branches of government. The designation of a "communist state" is primarily an external definition for a situation in which a communist party controls the government.

Among the examples of modern socialist states operating under the communist model are the People's Republic of China, the Republic of Cuba, and the Socialist Republic of Vietnam. However, each of these governments in fact operates through a mixed system of socialist and capitalist economic policies, allowing private ownership in some situations and sharply enforcing state control in others.

Typically, a communist state is led by the national communist party, a political group with voluntary membership and members in all sectors of the populace. While many individuals may join the communist party, the leadership of the party is generally selected by a smaller number of respected or venerated leaders from within the party. These leaders select a ruling committee that develops the political initiatives of the party, which are thereafter distributed throughout the government.

In China, the Communist Party elects both a chairperson, who serves as executive of the party, and a politburo, a standing committee that makes executive decisions on behalf of the party. In Cuba, the Communist Party selects individuals who sit for election to the National Assembly of People's Power, which then serves directly as the state's sole legislative body.

In the cases of China, Cuba, and Vietnam, the committees and leaders chosen by the communist party then participate directly in electing leaders to serve in the state judiciary. In addition, the central committees typically appoint individuals to serve as heads of the military and to lower-level, provincial, or municipal government positions. In China, the populace elects individuals to local, regional, and provincial councils that in turn elect representatives to sit on a legislative body known as the National People's Congress (NPC), though the NPC is generally considered a largely ceremonial institution without any substantial power to enact independent legislation.

In effect, most modern communist states are controlled by the leadership of the national communist party, though this leadership is achieved by direct and indirect control of lesser legislative, executive, and judicial bodies. In some cases, ceremonial and symbolic offices created under the communist party can evolve to take a larger role in state politics. In China, for instance, the NPC has come to play a more important role in developing legislation in the twenty-first century.

Role of the Citizen

In modern communist societies, citizens have little voice in selecting the leadership of the government. In many communist states, popular elections are held at local and national levels, but candidates are chosen by communist party leadership and citizens are not given the option to vote for representatives of opposing political parties.

In most cases, the state adopts policies that give the appearance of popular control over the government, while in actuality, governmental policies are influenced by a small number of leaders chosen from within the upper echelons of the party. Popularly elected leaders who oppose party policy are generally removed from office.

All existing communist states have been criticized for human rights violations in terms of curtailing the freedoms available to citizens and of enacting dictatorial and authoritarian policies. Cuba, Vietnam, and China, for instance, all have laws preventing citizens from opposing party policy or supporting a political movement that opposes the communist party. Communist governments have also been accused of using propaganda and misinformation to control the opinion of the populace regarding party leadership and therefore reducing the potential for popular resistance to communist policies.

Micah Issitt
Philadelphia, Pennsylvania

Examples

China
Cuba
Laos
North Korea
Vietnam

Bibliography

Caramani, Daniele. *Comparative Politics*. New York: Oxford UP, 2008. Print.

Priestland, David. *The Red Flag: A History of Communism*. New York: Grove, 2009. Print.

Service, Robert. *Comrades! A History of World Communism*. Cambridge: Harvard UP, 2007. Print.

Confederation/Confederacy

Guiding Premise

A confederation or confederacy is a loose alliance between political units, such as states or cantons, within a broader federal government. Confederations allow a central, federal government to create laws and regulations of broad national interest, but the sovereign units are granted the ultimate authority to carry out those laws and to create, implement, and enforce their own laws as well. Confederate governments are built on the notion that a single, central government should not have ultimate authority over sovereign states and populations. Some confederate governments were born due to the rise of European monarchies and empires that threatened to govern states from afar. Others were created out of respect for the diverse ideologies, cultures, and ideals of their respective regions. Confederations and confederacies may be hybrids, giving comparatively more power to a federal government while retaining respect for the sovereignty of their members. True confederate governments are rare in the twenty-first century.

Typical Structure

Confederate governments are typically characterized by the presence of both a central government and a set of regional, similarly organized, and sovereign (independent) governments. For example, a confederate government might have as its central government structure a system that features executive, legislative, and judicial branches. Each region that serves as members of the confederation would have in place a similar system, enabling the efficient flow of lawmaking and government services.

In some confederations, the executive branch of the central government is headed by a president or prime minister, who serves as the government's chief administrative officer, overseeing the military and other government operations. Meanwhile, at the regional level, another chief executive, such as a governor, is charged with the administration of that government's operations.

Legislative branches are also similarly designed. Confederations use parliaments or congresses that, in most cases, have two distinct chambers. One chamber consists of legislators who each represent an entire state, canton, or region. The other chamber consists of legislators representing certain populations of voters within that region. Legislatures at the regional level not only have the power to create and enforce their own laws, but also have the power to refuse to enact or enforce any laws handed down by the national government.

A confederation's judiciary is charged with ensuring that federal and regional laws are applied uniformly and within the limits of the confederation's constitutional framework. Central and regional governments both have such judicial institutions, with the latter addressing those legal matters administered in the state or canton and the former addressing legal issues of interest to the entire country.

Political parties also typically play a role in a confederate government. Political leadership is achieved by a party's majority status in either the executive or the legislative branches. Parties also play a role in forging a compromise on certain matters at both the regional and national levels. Some confederations take the diversity of political parties and their ideologies seriously enough to create coalition governments that can help avoid political stalemates.

Role of the Citizen

The political role of the citizen within a confederate political system depends largely on the constitution of the country. In some confederacies, for example, the people directly elect their legislative and executive leaders by popular vote. Some legislators are elected to open terms—they may technically be reelected, but this election is merely a formality, as they are allowed to stay in office until they decide to leave or they die—while others may be subject to term limits or other reelection rules. Popularly elected legislators and executives in turn draft, file, and pass new laws and regulations that ideally are favorable to the voters. Some confederate systems give popularly elected legislators the ability to elect a party leader to serve as prime minister or president.

Confederations are designed to empower the regional government and avoid the dominance of a distant national government. In this manner, citizens of a confederate government, in some cases, may enjoy the ability to put forth new legislative initiatives. Although the lawmaking process is expected to be administered by the legislators and executives, in such cases the people are allowed and even encouraged to connect and interact with their political representatives to ensure that the government remains open and accessible.

Michael Auerbach
Marblehead, Massachusetts

Examples
European Union
Switzerland
United States under the Articles of Confederation (1781–89)

Bibliography
"Government Type." *The World Factbook*. Central Intelligence Agency, n.d. Web. 17 Jan. 2013.
"Swiss Politics." *SwissWorld.org*. Federal Department of Foreign Affairs Presence Switzerland, n.d. Web. 17 Jan. 2013.

Constitutional Monarchy

Guiding Premise

A constitutional monarchy is a form of government in which the head of state is a monarch (a king or queen) with limited powers. The monarch has official duties, but those responsibilities are defined in the nation's constitution and not by the monarch. Meanwhile, the power to create and rescind laws is given to a legislative body. Constitutional monarchies retain the ceremony and traditions associated with nations that have long operated under a king or queen. However, the constitution prevents the monarch from becoming a tyrant. Additionally, the monarchy, which is typically a lifetime position, preserves a sense of stability and continuity in the government, as the legislative body undergoes periodic change associated with the election cycle.

Typical Structure

The structure of a constitutional monarchy varies from nation to nation. In some countries, the monarchy is predominantly ceremonial. In such cases, the monarch provides a largely symbolic role, reminding the people of their heritage and giving them comfort in times of difficulty. Such is the case in Japan, for example; the emperor of that country was stripped of any significant power after World War II but was allowed to continue his legacy in the interest of ensuring that the Japanese people would remain peaceful. Today, that nation still holds its monarchical family in the highest regard, but the government is controlled by the Diet (the legislature), with the prime minister serving in the executive role.

In other countries, the sovereign plays a more significant role. In the United Kingdom, the king or queen does have some power, including the powers to appoint the prime minister, to open or dissolve Parliament, to approve bills that have been passed by Parliament, and to declare war and make peace. However, the monarch largely defers to the government on these acts. In Bahrain, the king (or, until 2002, emir or hereditary ruler) was far more involved in government in the late twentieth and early twenty-first centuries than many other constitutional monarchs. In 1975, the emir of Bahrain dissolved the parliament, supposedly to run the government more effectively. His son would later implement a number of significant constitutional reforms that made the government more democratic in nature.

The key to the structure of this type of political system is the constitution. As is the case in the United States (a federal republic), a constitutional monarchy is carefully defined by the government's founding document. In Canada, for example, the king or queen of England is still recognized as the head of state, but that country's constitution gives the monarch no power other than ceremonial responsibilities. India, South Africa, and many other members of the Commonwealth of Nations (the English monarch's sphere of influence, spanning most of the former British colonies) have, since gaining their independence, created constitutions that grant no power to the English monarch; instead, they give all powers to their respective government institutions and, in some cases, recognize their own monarchs.

A defining feature of a constitutional monarchy is the fact that the monarch gives full respect to the limitations set forth by the constitution (and rarely seeks to alter such a document in his or her favor). Even in the United Kingdom itself—which does not have a written constitution, but rather a series of foundational documents—the king or queen does not step beyond the bounds set by customary rules. One interesting exception is in Bahrain, where Hamad bin Isa Al-Khalifa assumed the throne in 1999 and immediately implemented a series of reforms to the constitution in order to give greater definition to that country's democratic institutions, including resuming parliamentary elections in 2001. During the 2011 Arab Spring uprisings, Bahraini protesters called for further democratic reforms to be enacted, and tensions between the ruler and his opposition continue.

Role of the Citizen

In the past, monarchies ruled nations with absolute power; the only power the people had was the ability to unify and overthrow the ruling sovereign. Although the notion of an absolute monarchy has largely disappeared from the modern political landscape, many nations have retained their respective kings, queens, emperors, and other monarchs for the sake of ceremony and cultural heritage. In the modern constitutional monarchy, the people are empowered by their nation's foundational documents, which not only define the rights of the people but the limitations of their governments and sovereign as well. The people, through their legislators and through the democratic voting process, can modify their constitutions to expand or shrink the political involvement of the monarchy.

For example, the individual members of the Commonwealth of Nations, including Canada and Australia, have different constitutional parameters for the king or queen of England. In England, the monarch holds a number of powers, while in Canada, he or she is merely a ceremonial head of state (with all government power centered in the capital of Ottawa). In fact, in 1999, Australia held a referendum (a general vote) on whether to abolish its constitutional monarchy altogether and replace it with a presidential republic. In that case, the people voted to retain the monarchy, but the proposal was only narrowly defeated. These examples demonstrate the tremendous power the citizens of a constitutional monarchy may possess through the legislative process and the vote under the constitution.

Michael Auerbach
Marblehead, Massachusetts

Examples

Bahrain

Cambodia

Denmark

Japan

Lesotho

Malaysia

Morocco

Netherlands

Norway

Spain

Sweden

Thailand

United Kingdom

Bibliography

Bowman, John. "Constitutional Monarchies." *CBC News*. CBC, 4 Oct. 2002. Web. 17 Jan. 2013.

"The Role of the Monarchy." *Royal.gov.uk*. Royal Household, n.d. Web. 17 Jan. 2013.

Constitutional Republic

Guiding Premise

A constitutional republic is a governmental system in which citizens are involved in electing or appointing leaders who serve according to rules formulated in an official state constitution. In essence, the constitutional republic combines the political structure of a republic or republican governmental system with constitutional principles.

A republic is a government in which the head of state is empowered to hold office through law, not inheritance (as in a monarchy). A constitutional republic is a type of republic based on a constitution, a written body of fundamental precedents and principles from which the laws of the nation are developed.

Most constitutional republics in the modern world use a universal suffrage system, in which all citizens of the nation are empowered to vote for or against individuals who attempt to achieve public office. Universal suffrage is not required for a nation to qualify as a constitutional republic, and some nations may only allow certain categories of citizens to vote for elected leaders.

A constitutional republic differs from other forms of democratic systems in the roles assigned to both the leaders and the citizenry. In a pure democratic system, the government is formed by pure majority rule, and this system therefore ignores the opinions of any minority group. A republic, by contrast, is a form of government in which the government's role is limited by a written constitution aimed at promoting the welfare of all individuals, whether members of the majority or a minority.

Typical Structure

To qualify as a constitutional republic, a nation must choose a head of state (most often a president) through elections, according to constitutional law. In some nations, an elected president may serve alongside an appointed or elected individual who serves as leader of the legislature, such as a prime minister, often called the "head of government." When the president also serves as head of government, the republic is said to operate under a presidential system.

Typically, the executive branch consists of the head of state and the executive offices, which are responsible for enforcing the laws and overseeing relations with other nations. The legislative branch makes laws and has overlapping duties with the executive office in terms of economic and military developments. The judicial branch, consisting of the courts, interprets the law and the constitution and enforces adherence to the law.

In a constitutional republic, the constitution describes the powers allotted to each branch of government and the means by which the governmental bodies are to be established. The constitution also describes the ways in which governmental branches interact in creating, interpreting, and enforcing laws. For instance, in the United States, the executive and legislative branches both have roles in determining the budget for the nation, and neither body is free to make budgetary legislation without the approval of the other branch.

Role of the Citizen

In a constitutional republic, the citizens have the power to control the evolution of the nation through the choice of representatives who serve on the government. These representatives can, generally through complicated means, create or abolish laws and even change the constitution itself through reinterpretations of constitutional principles or direct amendments.

Citizens in a republic are empowered, but generally not required, to play a role in electing leaders. In the United States, both state governments and the federal government function according to a republican system, and citizens are therefore allowed to take part in the election of leaders to both local and national offices. In addition, constitutional systems generally allow individuals to join political interest groups to further common political goals.

In a constitutional democratic republic such as Guatemala and Honduras, the president, who serves as chief of state and head of government, is elected directly by popular vote. In the United States, a constitutional federal republic, the president is elected by the Electoral College, whose members are selected according to the popular vote within each district. The Electoral College is intended to provide more weight to smaller states, thereby balancing the disproportionate voting power of states with larger populations. In all constitutional republics, the citizens elect leaders either directly or indirectly through other representatives chosen by popular vote. Therefore, the power to control the government is granted to the citizens of the constitutional republic.

Micah Issitt
Philadelphia, Pennsylvania

Examples
Guatemala
Honduras
Iceland
Paraguay
Peru
United States
Uruguay

Bibliography
Baylis, John, Steve Smith, and Patricia Owens. *The Globalization of World Politics: An Introduction to International Relations.* New York: Oxford UP, 2010. Print.

Caramani, Daniele. *Comparative Politics.* New York: Oxford UP, 2008. Print.

Garner, Robert, Peter Ferdinand, and Stephanie Lawson. *Introduction to Politics.* 2nd ed. Oxford: Oxford UP, 2009. Print.

Hague, Rod, and Martin Harrop. *Comparative Government and Politics: An Introduction.* New York: Palgrave, 2007. Print.

Democracy

Guiding Premise

Democracy is a political system based on majority rule, in which all citizens are guaranteed participatory rights to influence the evolution of government. There are many different types of democracy, based on the degree to which citizens participate in the formation and operation of the government. In a direct democratic system, citizens vote directly on proposed changes to law and public policy. In a representative democracy, individuals vote to elect representatives who then serve to create and negotiate public policy.

The democratic system of government first developed in Ancient Greece and has existed in many forms throughout history. While democratic systems always involve some type of majority rule component, most modern democracies have systems in place designed to equalize representation for minority groups or to promote the development of governmental policies that prevent oppression of minorities by members of the majority.

In modern democracies, one of the central principles is the idea that citizens must be allowed to participate in free elections to select leaders who serve in the government. In addition, voters in democratic systems elect political leaders for a limited period of time, thus ensuring that the leadership of the political system can change along with the changing views of the populace. Political theorists have defined democracy as a system in which the people are sovereign and the political power flows upward from the people to their elected leaders.

Typical Structure

In a typical democracy, the government is usually divided into executive, legislative, and judicial branches. Citizens participate in electing individuals to serve in one or more of these branches, and elected leaders appoint additional leaders to serve in other political offices. The democratic system, therefore, involves a combination of elected and appointed leadership.

Democratic systems may follow a presidential model, as in the United States, where citizens elect a president to serve as both head of state and head of government. In a presidential model, citizens may also participate in elections to fill other governmental bodies, including the legislature and judicial branch. In a parliamentary democracy, citizens elect individuals to a parliament, whose members in turn form a committee to appoint a leader, often called the prime minister, who serves as head of government.

In most democratic systems, the executive and legislative branches cooperate in the formation of laws, while the judicial branch enforces and interprets the laws produced by the government. Most democratic systems have developed a system of checks and balances designed to prevent any single branch of government from exerting a dominant influence over the development of governmental policy. These checks and balances may be instituted in a variety of ways, including the ability to block governmental initiatives and the ability to appoint members to various governmental agencies.

Democratic governments generally operate on the principle of political parties, which are organizations formed to influence political development. Candidates for office have the option of joining a political party, which can provide funding and other campaign assistance. In some democratic systems—called dominant party or one-party dominant systems—there is effectively a single political party. Dominant party systems allow for competition in democratic elections, but existing power structures often prevent opposing parties from competing successfully. In multiparty democratic systems, there are two or more political parties with the ability to compete for office, and citizens are able to choose among political parties during elections. Some countries only allow political parties to be active at the national level, while other countries allow political parties to play a role in local and regional elections.

Role of the Citizen

The citizens in a democratic society are seen as the ultimate source of political authority. Members of the government, by contrast, are seen as servants of the people, and are selected and elected to serve the people's interests. Democratic systems developed to protect and enhance the freedom of the people; however, for the system to function properly, citizens must engage in a number of civic duties.

In democratic nations, voting is a right that comes with citizenship. Though some democracies—Australia, for example—require citizens to vote by law, compulsory participation in elections is not common in democratic societies. Citizens are nonetheless encouraged to fulfill their voting rights and to stay informed regarding political issues. In addition, individuals are responsible for contributing to the well-being of society as a whole, usually through a system of taxation whereby part of an individual's earnings is used to pay for governmental services.

In many cases, complex governmental and legal issues must be simplified to ease understanding among the citizenry. This goal is partially met by having citizens elect leaders who must then explain to their constituents how they are shaping legislation and other government initiatives to reflect constituents' wants and needs. In the United States, citizens may participate in the election of local leaders within individual cities or counties, and also in the election of leaders who serve in the national legislature and executive offices.

Citizens in democratic societies are also empowered with the right to join political interest groups and political parties in an effort to further a broader political agenda. However, democratic societies oppose making group membership a requirement and have laws forbidding forcing an individual to join any group. Freedom of choice, especially with regard to political affiliation and preference, is one of the cornerstones of all democratic systems.

Micah Issitt
Philadelphia, Pennsylvania

Examples

Denmark
Sweden
Spain
Japan
Australia
Costa Rica
Uruguay
United States

Bibliography

Barington, Lowell. *Comparative Politics: Structures and Choices*. Boston: Wadsworth, 2012. Print.

Caramani, Daniele. *Comparative Politics*. New York: Oxford UP, 2008. Print.

Przeworski, Adam. *Democracy and the Limits of Self Government*, New York: Cambridge UP, 2010. Print.

Dictatorship/Military Dictatorship

Guiding Premise

Dictatorships and military dictatorships are political systems in which absolute power is held by an individual or military organization. Dictatorships are led by a single individual, under whom all political control is consolidated. Military dictatorships are similar in purpose, but place the system under the control of a military organization comprised of a single senior officer, or small group of officers. Often, dictatorships and military dictatorships are imposed as the result of a coup d'état in which the regime in question directly removes the incumbent regime, or after a power vacuum creates chaos in the nation. In both situations, the consolidation of absolute power is designed to establish a state of strict law and order.

Typical Structure

Dictatorships and military dictatorships vary in structure and nature. Some come about through the overthrow of other regimes, while others are installed through the democratic process, and then become a dictatorship as democratic rights are withdrawn. Still others are installed following a complete breakdown of government, often with the promise of establishing order.

Many examples of dictatorships can be found in the twentieth century, including Nazi Germany, Joseph Stalin's Soviet Union, and China under Mao Tse-tung. A number of dictatorships existed in Africa, such as the regimes of Idi Amin in Uganda, Charles Taylor in Liberia, and Mu'ammar Gadhafi in Libya. Dictatorships such as these consolidated power in the hands of an individual leader. A dictator serves as the sole decision-maker in the government, frequently using the military, secret police, or other security agencies to enforce the leader's will. Dictators also have control over state institutions like legislatures. A legislature may have the ability to develop and pass laws, but if its actions run counter to the dictator's will, the latter can—and

frequently does—dissolve the body, replacing its members with those more loyal to the dictator's agenda.

Military dictatorships consolidate power not in the hands of a civilian but in an individual or small group of military officers—the latter of which are often called "juntas." Because military dictatorships are frequently installed following a period of civil war and/or a coup d'état, the primary focus of the dictatorship is to achieve strict order through the application of military force. Military dictatorships are often installed with the promise of an eventual return to civilian and/or democratic control once the nation has regained stability. In the case of North Korea, one-party communist rule turned into a communist military dictatorship as its leader, Kim Il-Sung, assumed control of the military and brought its leadership into the government.

In the late twentieth and early twenty-first centuries, dictatorships and military dictatorships are most commonly found in developing nations, where poverty rates are high and regional stability is tenuous at best. Many are former European colonies, where charismatic leaders who boast of their national heritage have stepped in to replace colonial governments. National resources are typically directed toward military and security organizations in an attempt to ensure security and internal stability, keeping the regime in power and containing rivals. Human rights records in such political systems are typically heavily criticized by the international community.

Role of the Citizen

Dictatorships and military dictatorships are frequently installed because of the absence of viable democratic governments. There is often a disconnect, therefore, between the people and their leaders in a dictatorship. Of course, many dictatorships are identified as such by external entities and not by their own people. For example, the government of Zimbabwe is technically identified as a parliamentary democracy, with Robert Mugabe—who has been the elected leader of the country since 1980—as its president. However, the international community has long complained that Mugabe "won" his positions through political corruption, including alleged ballot stuffing. In 2008, Mugabe lost his first reelection campaign, but demanded a recount. While the recount continued, his supporters attacked opposition voters, utilizing violence and intimidation until his opponent, Morgan Tsvangirai, withdrew his candidacy, and Mugabe was restored as president.

By definition, citizens do not have a role in changing the course of a dictatorship's agenda. The people are usually called upon to join the military in support of the regime, or cast their vote consistently in favor of the ruling regime. Freedom of speech, the press, and assembly are virtually nonexistent, as those who speak out against the ruling regime are commonly jailed, tortured, or killed.

Michael Auerbach
Marblehead, Massachusetts

Examples

Belarus (dictatorship)
Fiji (military dictatorship)
North Korea (military dictatorship)
Zimbabwe (dictatorship)

Bibliography

Clayton, Jonathan. "China Aims to Bring Peace through Deals with Dictators and Warlords." *Times* [London]. Times Newspapers, 31 Jan. 2007. Web. 6 Feb. 2013.
"Robert Mugabe—Biography." *Biography.com.* A+E Television Networks, 2013. Web. 6 Feb. 2013.

Ecclesiastical

Guiding Premise

An ecclesiastical government is one in which the laws of the state are guided by and derived from religious law. Ecclesiastical governments can take a variety of forms and can be based on many different types of religious traditions. In some traditions, a deity or group of deities are considered to take a direct role in the formation of government, while other traditions utilize religious laws or principles indirectly to craft laws used to manage the state.

In many cultures, religious laws and tenets play a major role in determining the formation of national laws. Historically, the moral and ethical principles derived from Judeo-Christian tradition inspired many laws in Europe and North America. Few modern governments operate according to an ecclesiastical system, but Vatican City, which is commonly classified as a city-state, utilizes a modernized version of the ecclesiastical government model. All states utilizing an ecclesiastical or semi-ecclesiastical system have adopted a single state religion that is officially recognized by the government.

In some predominantly Islamic nations, including the Sudan, Oman, Iran, and Nigeria, Islamic law, known as sharia, is the basis for most national laws, and government leaders often must obtain approval by the leaders of the religious community before being allowed to serve in office. Most modern ecclesiastical or semi-ecclesiastical governments have adopted a mixed theocratic republic system in which individuals approved by religious authorities are elected by citizens to hold public office.

Typical Structure

In an ecclesiastical government, the church or recognized religious authority is the source of all state law. In a theocracy, which is one of the most common types of ecclesiastical governments, a deity or group of deities occupies a symbolic position as head of state, while representatives are chosen to lead the government based on their approval by the prevailing religious authority. In other types of ecclesiastical governments, the chief of state may be the leading figure in the church, such as in Vatican City, where the Catholic Pope is also considered the chief of state.

There are no modern nations that operate on a purely ecclesiastical system, though some Islamic countries, like Iran, have adopted a semi-ecclesiastical form of republican government. In Iran, the popularly elected Assembly of Experts—comprised of Islamic scholars called mujtahids—appoints an individual to serve as supreme leader of the nation for life, and this individual has veto power over all other governmental offices. Iranian religious leaders also approve other individuals to run as candidates for positions in the state legislature. In many cases, the citizens will elect an individual to serve as head of government, though this individual must conform to religious laws.

In an ecclesiastical government, those eligible to serve in the state legislature are generally members of the church hierarchy or have been approved for office by church leaders. In Tibet, which functioned as an ecclesiastical government until the Chinese takeover of 1951, executive and legislative duties were consolidated under a few religious leaders, called lamas, and influential citizens who maintained the country under a theocratic system. Most modern nations separate governmental functions between distinct but interrelated executive, legislative, and judicial branches.

Many modern semi-ecclesiastical nations have adopted a set of state principles in the form of a constitution to guide the operation of government and the establishment of laws. In mixed constitutional/theocratic systems, the constitution may be used to legitimize religious authority by codifying a set of laws and procedures that have been developed from religious scripture.

In addition, the existence of a constitution facilitates the process of altering laws and governmental procedures as religious authorities reinterpret religious scriptures and texts.

Role of the Citizen

Citizens in modern ecclesiastical and semi-ecclesiastical governments play a role in formulating the government though national and local elections. In some cases, religious authorities may approve more than one candidate for a certain position and citizens are then able to exercise legitimate choice in the electoral process. In other cases, popular support for one or more candidates may influence religious authorities when it comes time to nominate or appoint an individual to office.

In ecclesiastical governments, the freedoms and rights afforded to citizens may depend on their religious affiliation. Christians living in a Christian ecclesiastical government, for instance, may be allowed to run for and hold government office, while representatives of other religions may be denied this right. In addition, ecclesiastical governments may not recognize religious rights and rituals of other traditions and may not offer protection for those practicing religions other than the official state religion.

Though religious authority dominates politics and legislative development, popular influence is still an important part of the ecclesiastical system. Popular support for or against certain laws may convince the government to alter official policies. In addition, the populace may join local and regional religious bodies that can significantly affect national political developments. As local and regional religious groups grow in numbers and influence, they may promote candidates to political office, thereby helping to influence the evolution of government.

Micah Issitt
Philadelphia, Pennsylvania

Examples

Afghanistan
Iran
Nigeria
Oman
Vatican City

Bibliography

Barrington, Lowell. *Comparative Politics: Structures and Choices*. Boston: Wadsworth, 2012. Print.
Hallaq, Wael B. *An Introduction to Islamic Law*. New York: Cambridge UP, 2009. Print.
Hirschl, Ran. *Constitutional Theocracy*. Cambridge, MA: Harvard UP, 2010. Print.

Failed State

Guiding Premise

A failed state is a political unit that at one point had a stable government that provided basic services and security to its citizens, but then entered a period marked by devastating conflict, extreme poverty, overwhelming political corruption, and/or unlivable environmental conditions. Often, a group takes hold of a failed state's government through military means, staving off rivals to fill in a power vacuum. The nominal leadership of a failed state frequently uses its power to combat rival factions, implement extreme religious law, or protect and advance illicit activities (such as drug production or piracy). Failed states frequently retain their external borders, but within those borders are regions that may be dominated by a particular faction, effectively carving the state into disparate subunits, with some areas even attaining relative stability and security—a kind of de facto independence.

Typical Structure

Failed states vary in appearance based on a number of factors. One such factor is the type of government that existed prior to the state's collapse. For example, a failed state might have originally existed as a parliamentary democracy, with an active legislature and executive system that developed a functioning legal code and administered to the needs of the people. However, that state may not have adequately addressed the needs of certain groups, fostering a violent backlash and hastening the country's destabilization. An ineffectual legislature might have been dissolved by the executive (a prime minister or president), and in the absence of leadership, the government as a whole ceased to operate effectively.

Another major factor is demographics. Many states are comprised of two or more distinct ethnic, social, or religious groups. When the ruling party fails to effectively govern and/or serve the interests of a certain segment of the population, it may be ousted or simply ignored by the marginalized faction within the state. If the government falls, it creates a power vacuum that rival groups compete to fill. If one faction gains power, it must remain in a constant state of vigilance against its rivals, focusing more on keeping enemies in check than on rebuilding crippled government infrastructure. Some also seek to create theocracies based on extreme interpretations of a particular religious doctrine. Frequently, these regimes are themselves ousted by rivals within a few years, leaving no lasting government and keeping the state in chaos.

Failed states are also characterized by extreme poverty and a lack of modern technology. Potable water, electricity, food, and medicine are scarce among average citizens. In some cases, these conditions are worsened by natural events. Haiti, for example, was a failed state for many years before the devastating 2010 earthquake that razed the capitol city of Port au Prince, deepening the country's poverty and instability. Afghanistan and Ethiopia—with their harsh, arid climates—are also examples of failed states whose physical environments and lack of resources exacerbated an already extreme state of impoverishment.

Most failed states' conditions are also worsened by the presence of foreigners. Because their governments are either unable or unwilling to repel terrorists, for example, failed states frequently become havens for international terrorism. Somalia, Afghanistan, and Iraq are all examples of states that failed, enabling terrorist organizations to set up camp within their borders. As such groups pose a threat to other nations, those nations often send troops and weapons into the failed states to engage the terrorists. In recent years, NATO, the United Nations, and the African Union have all entered failed states to both combat terrorists and help rebuild government.

Role of the Citizen

Citizens of a failed state have very little say in the direction of their country. In most cases, when a faction assumes control over the government, it installs strict controls that limit the rights of citizens, particularly such rights as freedom of speech, freedom of assembly, and freedom of religion. Some regimes allow for "democratic" elections, but a continued lack of infrastructure and widespread corruption often negates the legitimacy of these elections.

Citizens of failed states are often called upon by the ruling regime (or a regional faction) to serve in its militia, helping it combat other factions within the state. In fact, many militias within failed states are comprised of people who were forced to join (under penalty of death) at a young age. Those who do not join militias are often drawn into criminal activity such as piracy and the drug trade.

Some citizens are able to make a difference by joining interest groups. Many citizens are able to achieve a limited amount of success sharing information about women's rights, HIV/AIDS and other issues. In some situations, these groups are able to gain international assistance from organizations that were unable to work with the failed government.

Michael Auerbach
Marblehead, Massachusetts

Examples

Chad
Democratic Republic of the Congo
Somalia
Sudan
Zimbabwe

Bibliography

"Failed States: Fixing a Broken World." *Economist*, 29 Jan. 2009. Web. 6 Feb. 2012.
"Failed States." Global Policy Forum, 2013. Web. 6 Feb. 2012.
"Somalia Tops Failed States Index for Fifth Year." *CNN.com*. Turner Broadcasting System, 18 June 2012. Web. 6 Feb. 2012.
Thürer, Daniel. (1999). "The 'Failed State' and International Law." *International Review of the Red Cross*. International Committee of the Red Cross, 31 Dec. 1999. Web. 6 Feb. 2012.

Federal Republic

Guiding Premise

A federal republic is a political system that features a central government as well as a set of regional subunits such as states or provinces. Federal republics are designed to limit the power of the central government, paring its focus to only matters of national interest. Typically, a greater degree of power is granted to the regional governments, which retain the ability to create their own laws of local relevance. The degree to which the federal and regional governments each enjoy authority varies from nation to nation, based on the country's interpretation of this republican form of government. By distributing authority to these separate but connected government institutions, federal republics give the greatest power to the people themselves, who typically vote directly for both their regional and national political representation.

Typical Structure

A federal republic's structure varies from nation to nation. However, most federal republics feature two distinct governing entities. The first is a central, federal government, usually based in the nation's capital city. The federal government's task is to address issues of national importance. These issues include defense and foreign relations, but also encompass matters of domestic interest that must be addressed in uniform fashion, such as social assistance programs, infrastructure, and certain taxes.

A federal republic is comprised of executive, legislative, and judicial branches. The executive is typically a president or prime minister—the former selected by popular vote, the latter selected by members of the legislature—and is charged with the administration of the federal government's programs and regulations. The legislature—such as the US Congress, the Austrian Parliament, or the German Bundestag—is charged with developing laws and managing government spending. The judiciary is charged

with ensuring that federal and state laws are enforced and that they are consistent with the country's constitution.

The federal government is limited in terms of its ability to assert authority over the regions. Instead, federal republics grant a degree of sovereignty to the different states, provinces, or regions that comprise the entire nation. These regions have their own governments, similar in structure and procedure to those of the federal government. They too have executives, legislatures, and judiciaries whose foci are limited to the regional government's respective jurisdictions.

The federal and regional segments of a republic are not completely independent of one another, however. Although the systems are intended to distribute power evenly, federal and regional governments are closely linked. This connectivity ensures the efficient collection of taxes, the regional distribution of federal funds, and a rapid response to issues of national importance. A federal republic's greatest strength, therefore, is the series of connections it maintains between the federal, regional, and local governments it contains.

Role of the Citizen

A federal republic is distinguished by the limitations of power it places on the national government. The primary goal of such a design was to place the power of government in the hands of the people. One of the ways the citizens' power is demonstrated is by participating in the electoral process. In a federal republic, the people elect their legislators. In some republics, the legislators in turn elect a prime minister, while in others, the people directly elect a president. The electoral process is an important way for citizens to influence the course of their government, both at the regional and federal levels. They do so by placing people who truly represent their diverse interests in the federal government.

The citizen is also empowered by participating in government as opposed to being subjected to it. In addition to taking part in the electoral process, the people are free to join and become active in a political party. A political party serves as a proxy for its members, representing their viewpoint and interests on a local and national level. In federal republics like Germany, a wide range of political parties are active in the legislature, advancing the political agendas of those they represent.

Michael Auerbach
Marblehead, Massachusetts

Examples
Austria
Brazil
Germany
India
Mexico
Nigeria
United States

Bibliography

"The Federal Principle." *Republik Österreich Parlament.* Republik Österreich Parlament, 8 Oct. 2010. Web. 6 Feb. 2013.

"The Federal Republic of Germany." *Deutscher Bundestag.* German Bundestag, 2013. Web. 6 Feb. 2013.

Collin, Nicholas. "An Essay on the Means of Promoting Federal Sentiments in the United States." *Friends of the Constitution: Writings of the "Other" Federalists, 1787–1788.* Ed. Colleen A. Sheehan and Gary L. McDowell. Online Library of Liberty, 2013. Web. 6 Feb. 2013.

Federation

Guiding Premise

A federation is a nation formed from the unification of smaller political entities. Federations feature federal governments that oversee nationwide issues. However, they also grant a degree of autonomy to the regional, state, or other local governments within the system. Federations are often formed because a collective of diverse regions find a common interest in unification. While the federal government is installed to address those needs, regions with their own distinct ethnic, socioeconomic, or political characteristics remain intact. This "separate but united" structure allows federations to avoid conflict and instability among their regions.

Typical Structure

The primary goal of a federation is to unify a country's political subunits within a national framework. The federal government, therefore, features institutions comprised of representatives from the states or regions. The representatives are typically elected by the residents of these regions, and some federal systems give the power to elect certain national leaders to these representatives. The regions themselves can vary considerably in size. The Russian Federation, for example, includes forty-six geographically large provinces as well as two more-concentrated cities as part of its eighty-three constituent federation members.

There are two institutions in which individuals from the constituent parts of a federation serve. The first institution is the legislature. Legislatures vary in appearance from nation to nation. For example, the US Congress is comprised of two chambers—the House of Representatives and the Senate—whose directly elected members act on behalf of their respective states. The German Parliament, on the other hand, consists of the directly elected Bundestag—which is tasked with electing the German federal chancellor, among other things—and the

state-appointed Bundesrat, which works on behalf of the country's sixteen states.

The second institution is the executive. Here, the affairs of the nation are administered by a president or similar leader. Again, the structure and powers of a federal government's executive institutions varies from nation to nation according to their constitutional framework. Federal executive institutions are charged with management of state affairs, including oversight of the military, foreign relations, health care, and education. Similarly diverse is the power of the executive in relation to the legislative branch. Some prime ministers, for example, enjoy considerably greater power than the president. In fact, some presidents share power with other leaders, or councils thereof within the executive branch, serving as the diplomatic face of the nation but not playing a major role in lawmaking. In India, for example, the president is the chief executive of the federal government, but shares power with the prime minister and the Council of Ministers, headed by the prime minister.

In order to promote continuity between the federal government and the states, regions, or other political subunits in the federation, those subunits typically feature governments that largely mirror that of the central government. Some of these regional governments are modified according to their respective constitutions. For example, whereas the bicameral US Congress consists of the Senate and House of Representatives, Nebraska's state legislature only has one chamber. Such distinctive characteristics of state/regional governments reflect the geographic and cultural interests of the region in question. It also underscores the degree of autonomy given to such states under a federation government system.

Role of the Citizen

Federations vary in terms of both structure and distribution of power within government institutions. However, federal systems are typically democratic in nature, relying heavily on the participation of the electorate for installing representatives in those institutions. At the regional level, the people vote for their respective legislators and executives either directly or through political parties. The executive in turn appoints cabinet officials, while the legislators select a chamber leader. In US state governments, for example, such a leader might be a Senate president or speaker of the House of Representatives.

The people also play an important role in federal government. As residents of a given state or region, registered voters—again, through either a direct vote or through political parties—choose their legislators and national executives. In federations that utilize a parliamentary system, however, prime ministers are typically selected by the legislators and/or their political parties and not through a direct, national vote. Many constitutions limit the length of political leaders' respective terms of service and/or the number of times

they may seek reelection, fostering an environment in which the democratic voting process is a frequent occurrence.

Michael Auerbach
Marblehead, Massachusetts

Examples
Australia
Germany
India
Mexico
Russia
United States

Bibliography
"Federal System of India." *Maps of India*. MapsOfIndia. com, 22 Sep. 2011. Web. 7 Feb. 2013.
"Political System." *Facts about Germany*. Frankfurter Societäts-Medien, 2011. Web. 7 Feb. 2013.
"Russia." *CIA World Factbook*. Central Intelligence Agency, 5 Feb. 2013. Web. 7 Feb. 2013.

Monarchy

Guiding Premise

A monarchy is a political system based on the sovereignty of a single individual who holds actual or symbolic authority over all governmental functions. The monarchy is one of the oldest forms of government in human history and was the most common type of government until the nineteenth century. In a monarchy, authority is inherited, usually through primogeniture, or inheritance by the eldest son.

In an absolute monarchy, the monarch holds authority over the government and functions as both head of state and head of government. In a constitutional monarchy, the role of the monarch is codified in the state constitution, and the powers afforded to the monarch are limited by constitutional law. Constitutional monarchies generally blend the inherited authority of the monarchy with popular control in the form of democratic elections. The monarch may continue to hold significant power over some aspects of government or may be relegated to a largely ceremonial or symbolic role.

In most ancient monarchies, the monarch was generally believed to have been chosen for his or her role by divine authority, and many monarchs in history have claimed to represent the will of a god or gods in their ascendancy to the position. In constitutional monarchies, the monarch may be seen as representing spiritual authority or may represent a link to the country's national heritage.

Typical Structure

In an absolute monarchy, a single monarch is empowered to head the government, including the formulation of all laws and leadership of the nation's armed forces. Oman is one example of a type of absolute monarchy called a sultanate, in which a family of leaders, called "sultans," inherits authority and leads the nation under an authoritarian system. Power in the Omani sultanate remains within the royal family. In the event of the sultan's death or incapacitation, the Royal Family Council selects a successor by consensus from within the family line. Beneath the sultan is a council of ministers, appointed by the sultan, to create and disseminate official government policy. The sultan's council serves alongside an elected body of leaders who enforce and represent Islamic law and work with the sultan's ministers to create national laws.

In Japan, which is a constitutional monarchy, the Japanese emperor serves as the chief of state and symbolic representative of Japan's culture and history. The emperor officiates national ceremonies, meets with world leaders for diplomatic purposes, and symbolically appoints leaders to certain governmental posts. Governmental authority in Japan rests with the Diet, a legislative body of elected officials who serve limited terms of office and are elected through popular vote. A prime minister is also chosen to lead the Diet, and the prime minister is considered the official head of government.

The Kingdom of Norway is another example of a constitutional monarchy wherein the monarch serves a role that has been codified in the state constitution. The king of Norway is designated as the country's chief of state, serving as head of the nation's executive branch. Unlike Japan, where the monarch's role is largely symbolic, the monarch of Norway has considerable authority under the constitution, including the ability to veto and approve all laws and the power to declare war. Norway utilizes a parliamentary system, with a prime minister, chosen from individuals elected to the state parliament, serving as head of government. Though the monarch has authority over the executive functions of government, the legislature and prime minister are permitted the ability to override monarchical decisions with sufficient support, thereby providing a system of control to prevent the monarch from exerting a dominant influence over the government.

Role of the Citizen

The role of the citizen in a monarchy varies depending on whether the government is a constitutional or absolute monarchy. In an absolute monarchy, citizens have only those rights given to them by the monarch, and the monarch has the power to extend and retract freedoms and rights at will. In ancient monarchies, citizens accepted the authoritarian role of the monarch, because it was widely believed that the monarch's powers were derived from divine authority. In addition, in many absolute monarchies, the monarch has the power to arrest, detain, and imprison individuals without due process, thereby providing a strong disincentive for citizens to oppose the monarchy.

In a constitutional monarchy, citizens are generally given greater freedom to participate in the development of governmental policies. In Japan, Belgium, and Spain, for instance, citizens elect governmental leaders, and the elected legislature largely controls the creation and enforcement of laws. In some countries, like the Kingdom of Norway, the monarch may exert significant authority, but this authority is balanced by that of the legislature, which represents the sovereignty of the citizens and is chosen to promote and protect the interests of the public.

The absolute monarchies of medieval Europe, Asia, and Africa held power for centuries, but many eventually collapsed due to popular uprisings as citizens demanded representation within the government. The development of constitutional monarchies may be seen as a balanced system in which the citizens retain significant control over the development of their government while the history and traditions of the nation are represented by the continuation of the monarch's lineage. In the United Kingdom, the governments of Great Britain and Northern Ireland are entirely controlled by elected individuals, but the continuation of the monarchy is seen by many as an important link to the nation's historic identity.

Micah Issitt
Philadelphia, Pennsylvania

Examples

Belgium
Bhutan
Japan
Norway
Oman
United Kingdom

Bibliography

Barrington, Lowell. *Comparative Politics: Structures and Choices*. Boston: Wadsworth, 2012. Print.

Dresch, Paul, and James Piscatori, eds. *Monarchies and Nations: Globalisation and Identity in the Arab States of the Gulf*. London: Tauris, 2005. Print.

Kesselman, Mark, et al. *European Politics in Transition*. New York: Houghton, 2009. Print.

Parliamentary Monarchy

Guiding Premise

A parliamentary monarchy is a political system in which leadership of the government is shared between a monarchy, such as a king or queen, and the members of a democratically elected legislative body. In such governments, the monarch's role as head of state is limited by the country's constitution or other founding document, preventing the monarch from assuming too much control over the nation. As head of state, the monarch may provide input during the lawmaking process and other operations of government. Furthermore, the monarch, whose role is generally lifelong, acts as a stabilizing element for the government, while the legislative body is subject to the periodic changes that occur with each election cycle.

Typical Structure

Parliamentary monarchies vary in structure and distribution of power from nation to nation, based on the parameters established by each respective country's constitution or other founding document. In general, however, parliamentary monarchies feature a king, queen, or other sovereign who acts as head of state. In that capacity, the monarch's responsibilities may be little more than ceremonial in nature, allowing him or her to offer input during the lawmaking process, to approve the installation of government officials, and to act as the country's international representative. However, these responsibilities may be subject to the approval of the country's legislative body. For example, the king of Spain approves laws and regulations that have already been passed by the legislative branch; formally appoints the prime minister; and approves other ministers appointed by the prime minister. Yet, the king's responsibilities in those capacities are subject to the approval of the Cortes Generales, Spain's parliament.

In general, parliamentary monarchies help a country preserve its cultural heritage through their respective royal families, but grant the majority of government management and lawmaking responsibilities to the country's legislative branch and its various administrative ministries, such as education and defense. In most parliamentary monarchies, the ministers of government are appointed by the legislative body and usually by the prime minister. Although government ministries have the authority to carry out the country's laws and programs, they are also subject to criticism and removal by the legislative body if they fail to perform to expectations.

The legislative body itself consists of members elected through a democratic, constitutionally defined process. Term length, term limit, and the manner by which legislators may be elected are usually outlined in the country's founding documents. For example, in the Dutch parliament, members of the House of Representatives are elected every four years through a direct vote, while the members of the Senate are elected by provincial government councils every four years. By contrast, three-quarters of the members of Thailand's House of Representatives are elected in single-seat constituencies (smaller districts), while the remaining members are elected in larger, proportional representation districts; all members of the House are elected for four-year terms. A bare majority of Thailand's senators are elected by direct vote, with the remainder appointed by other members of the government.

Role of the Citizen

While the kings and queens of parliamentary monarchies are the nominal heads of state, these political systems are designed to be democratic governments. As such, they rely heavily on the input and involvement of the citizens. Participating in legislative elections is one of the most direct ways in which the citizen is empowered. Because the governments of such systems are subject to legislative oversight, the people—through their respective votes for members of parliament—have influence over their government.

Political parties and organizations such as local and municipal councils also play an important role in parliamentary monarchies. Citizens' participation in those organizations can help shape parliamentary agendas and build links between government and the public. In Norway, for example, nearly 70 percent of citizens are involved in at least one such organization, and consequently Norway's Storting (parliament) has a number of committees that are tied to those organizations at the regional and local levels. Thus, through voting and active political involvement at the local level, the citizens of a parliamentary monarchy help direct the political course of their nation.

Michael Auerbach
Marblehead, Massachusetts

Examples
Netherlands
Norway
Spain
Sweden
Thailand
United Kingdom

Bibliography
"Form of Government." *Norway.org*. Norway–The Official Site in the United States, n.d. Web. 17 Jan. 2013.

"Issues: Parliament." *Governmentl.nl*. Government of the Netherlands, n.d. Web. 17 Jan. 2013.

"King, Prime Minister, and Council of Ministers." *Country Studies: Spain*. Lib. of Congress, 2012. Web. 17 Jan. 2013.

"Thailand." *International Foundation for Electoral Systems*. IFES, 2013. Web. 17 Jan. 2013.

Parliamentary Republic

Guiding Premise

A parliamentary republic is a system wherein both executive and legislative powers are centralized in the legislature. In such a system, voters elect their national representatives to the parliamentary body, which in turn appoints the executive. In such an environment, legislation is passed more quickly than in a presidential system, which requires a consensus between the executive and legislature. It also enables the legislature to remove the executive in the event the latter does not perform to the satisfaction of the people. Parliamentary republics can also prevent the consolidation of power in a single leader, as even a prime minister must defer some authority to fellow legislative leaders.

Typical Structure

Parliamentary republics vary in structure from nation to nation, according to the respective country's constitution or other governing document. In general, such a system entails the merger of the legislature and head of state such as a president or other executive. The state may retain the executive, however. However, the executive's role may be largely ceremonial, as is the case in Greece, where the president has very little political authority. This "outsider" status has in fact enabled the Greek president to act as a diplomatic intermediary among sparring parliamentary leaders.

While many countries with such a system operate with an executive—who may or may not be directly elected, and who typically has limited powers—the bulk of a parliamentary republic's political authority rests with the legislature. The national government is comprised of democratically elected legislators and their appointees. The length of these representatives' respective terms, as well as the manner by which the legislators are elected, depend on the frameworks established by each individual nation. Some parliamentary republics utilize a constitution for this

purpose, while others use a set of common laws or other legal precepts. In South Africa, members of the parliament's two chambers, the National Assembly and the National Council of Provinces, are elected differently. The former's members are elected directly by the citizens in each province, while the latter's members are installed by the provincial legislatures.

Once elected to parliament, legislators are often charged with more than just lawmaking. In many cases, members of parliament oversee the administration of state affairs as well. Legislative bodies in parliamentary republics are responsible for nominating an executive—typically a prime minister—to manage the government's various administrative responsibilities. Should the executive not adequately perform its duties, parliament has the power to remove the executive from office. In Ireland, for example, the Dail Eireann (the House of Representatives) is charged with forming the country's executive branch by nominating the Taoiseach (prime minister) and approving the prime minister's cabinet selections.

Role of the Citizen

A parliamentary republic is a democratic political system that relies on the involvement of an active electorate. This civic engagement includes a direct or indirect vote for representatives to parliament. While the people do not vote for an executive as well, by way of their vote for parliament, the citizenry indirectly influences the selection of the chief executive and the policies he or she follows. In many countries, the people also indirectly influence the national government by their votes in provincial government. As noted earlier, some countries' parliaments include chambers whose members are appointed by provincial leaders.

Citizens may also influence the political system through involvement in political parties. Such organizations help shape the platforms of parliamentary majorities as well as selecting candidates for prime minister and other government positions. The significance of political parties varies from nation to nation, but such organizations require the input and involvement of citizens.

Michael Auerbach
Marblehead, Massachusetts

Examples
Austria
Greece

Iceland
Ireland
Poland
South Africa

Bibliography
"About the Oireachtas." *Oireachtas.ie.* Houses of the Oireachtas, n.d. Web. 7 Feb. 2013.
"Our Parliament." *Parliament.gov.* Parliament of the Republic of South Africa, n.d. Web. 7 Feb. 2013.
Tagaris, Karolina, and Ingrid Melander. "Greek President Makes Last Push to Avert Elections." *Reuters.* Thomson Reuters, 12 May 2012. Web. 7 Feb. 2013.

Presidential

Guiding Premise

A presidential system is a type of democratic government in which the populace elects a single leader—a president—to serve as both head of state and the head of government. The presidential system developed from the monarchic governments of medieval and early modern Europe, in which a royal monarch, holder of an inherited office, served as both head of state and government. In the presidential system, the president does not inherit the office, but is chosen by either direct or indirect popular vote.

Presidential systems differ from parliamentary systems in that the president is both the chief executive and head of state, whereas in a parliamentary system another individual, usually called the "prime minister," serves as head of government and leader of the legislature. The presidential system evolved out of an effort to create an executive office that balances the influence of the legislature and the judiciary. The United States is the most prominent example of a democratic presidential system.

Some governments have adopted a semi-presidential system, which blends elements of the presidential system with the parliamentary system, and generally features a president who serves only as head of state. In constitutional governments, like the United States, Mexico, and Honduras, the role of the president is described in the nation's constitution, which also provides for the president's powers in relation to the other branches of government.

Typical Structure

In most modern presidential governments, power to create and enforce laws and international agreements is divided among three branches: the executive, legislative, and judicial. The executive office consists of the president and a number of presidential advisers—often called the cabinet—who typically serve at the president's discretion and are not elected to office. The terms of office for the president are codified in the state constitution and, in most cases, the president may serve a limited number of terms before he or she becomes ineligible for reelection.

The president serves as head of state and is therefore charged with negotiating and administering international treaties and agreements. In addition, the president serves as head of government and is therefore charged with overseeing the function of the government as a whole. The president is also empowered, in most presidential governments, with the ability to deploy the nation's armed forces. In some governments, including the United States, the approval of the legislature is needed for the country to officially declare war.

The legislative branch of the government proposes new laws, in the form of bills, but must cooperate with the executive office to pass these bills into law. The legislature and the executive branch also cooperate in determining the government budget. Unlike prime ministers under the parliamentary system, the president is not considered a member of the legislature and therefore acts independently as the chief executive, though a variety of governmental functions require action from both branches of government. A unique feature of the presidential system is that the election of the president is separate from the election of the legislature.

In presidential systems, members of the legislature are often less likely to vote according to the goals of their political party and may support legislation that is not supported by their chosen political party. In parliamentary systems, like the government of Great Britain, legislators are more likely to vote according to party policy. Presidential systems are also often marked by a relatively small number of political parties, which often allows one party to achieve a majority in the legislature. If this majority coincides with the election of a president from the same party, that party's platform or agenda becomes dominant until the next election cycle.

The judicial branch in a presidential system serves to enforce the laws among the populace. In most modern presidential democracies, the president appoints judges to federal posts, though in some governments, the legislature appoints judges. In some cases, the president may need the approval of the legislature to make judicial appointments.

Role of the Citizen

In a democratic presidential system, citizens are empowered with the ability to vote for president and therefore have ultimate control over who serves as head of government and head of state. Some presidential governments elect individuals to the presidency based on the result of a popular vote, while other governments use an indirect system, in which citizens vote for a party or for individuals who then serve as their representatives in electing the president. The United States utilizes an indirect system called the Electoral College.

Citizens in presidential systems are also typically allowed, though not required, to join political parties in an effort to promote a political agenda. Some governmental systems that are modeled on the presidential system allow the president to exert a dominant influence over the legislature and other branches of the government. In some cases, this can lead to a presidential dictatorship, in which the president may curtail the political rights of citizens. In most presidential systems, however, the roles and powers of the legislative and executive branches are balanced to protect the rights of the people to influence their government.

In a presidential system, citizens are permitted to vote for a president representing one political party, while simultaneously voting for legislators from other political parties. In this way, the presidential system allows citizens to determine the degree to which any single political party is permitted to have influence on political development.

Micah Issitt
Philadelphia, Pennsylvania

Examples

Benin
Costa Rica
Dominican Republic
Guatemala
Honduras
Mexico
United States
Venezuela

Bibliography

Barington, Lowell. *Comparative Politics*: *Structures and Choices*. Boston: Wadsworth, 2012. Print.
Caramani, Daniele. *Comparative Politics*. New York: Oxford UP, 2008. Print.
Garner, Robert, Peter Ferdinand, and Stephanie Lawson. *Introduction to Politics*. 2nd ed. Oxford: Oxford UP, 2009. Print.

Republic

Guiding Premise

A republic is a type of government based on the idea of popular or public sovereignty. The word "republic" is derived from Latin terms meaning "matters" and "the public." In essence, a republic is a government in which leaders are chosen by the public rather than by inheritance or by force. The republic or republican governmental system emerged in response to absolute monarchy, in which hereditary leaders retained all the power. In contrast, the republican system is intended to create a government that is responsive to the people's will.

Most modern republics operate based on a democratic system in which citizens elect leaders by popular vote. The United States and Mexico are examples of countries that use a democratic republican system to appoint leaders to office. However, universal suffrage (voting for all) is not required for a government to qualify as a republic, and it is possible for a country to have a republican government in which only certain categories of citizens, such as the wealthy, are allowed to vote in elections.

In addition to popular vote, most modern republics are further classified as constitutional republics, because the laws and rules for appointing leaders have been codified in a set of principles and guidelines known as a "constitution." When combined with universal suffrage and constitutional law, the republican system is intended to form a government that is based on the will of the majority while protecting the rights of minority groups.

Typical Structure

Republican governments are typically led by an elected head of state, generally a president. In cases where the president also serves as the head of government, the government is called a "presidential republic." In some republics, the head of state serves alongside an appointed or elected head of government, usually a prime minister.

This mixed form of government blends elements of the republic system with the parliamentary system found in countries such as the United Kingdom or India.

The president is part of the executive branch of government, which represents the country internationally and heads efforts to make and amend international agreements and treaties. The laws of a nation are typically created by the legislative branch, which may also be composed of elected leaders. Typically, the legislative and executive branches must cooperate on key initiatives, such as determining the national budget.

In addition to legislative and executive functions, most republics have a judiciary charged with enforcing and interpreting laws. The judicial branch may be composed of elected leaders, but in many cases, judicial officers are appointed by the president and/or the legislature. In the United States (a federal republic), the president, who leads the executive branch, appoints members to the federal judiciary, but these choices must be approved by the legislature before they take effect.

The duties and powers allotted to each branch of the republican government are interconnected with those of the other branches in a system of checks and balances. For instance, in Mexico (a federal republic), the legislature is empowered to create new tax guidelines for the public, but before legislative tax bills become law, they must first achieve majority support within the two branches of the Mexican legislature and receive the approval of the president. By creating a system of separate but balanced powers, the republican system seeks to prevent any one branch from exerting a dominant influence over the government.

Role of the Citizen

The role of the citizen in a republic depends largely on the type of republican system that the country has adopted. In democratic republics, popular elections and constitutional law give the public significant influence over governmental development and establish the people as the primary source of political power. Citizens in democratic republics are empowered to join political groups and to influence the development of laws and policies through the election of public leaders.

In many republican nations, a powerful political party or other political group can dominate the government, preventing competition from opposing political groups and curtailing the public's role in selecting and approving leaders. For instance, in the late twentieth century, a dominant political party maintained control of the Gambian presidency and legislature for more than thirty years, thereby significantly limiting the role of the citizenry in influencing the development of government policy.

In general, the republican system was intended to reverse the power structure typical of the monarchy system, in which inherited leaders possess all of the political power. In the republican system, leaders are chosen to represent the people's interests with terms of office created in such a way that new leaders must be chosen at regular intervals, thereby preventing a single leader or political entity from dominating the populace. In practice, popular power in a republic depends on preventing a political monopoly from becoming powerful enough to alter the laws of the country to suit the needs of a certain group rather than the whole.

Micah Issitt
Philadelphia, Pennsylvania

Examples
Algeria
Argentina
Armenia
France
Gambia
Mexico
San Marino
South Sudan
Tanzania
United States

Bibliography
Caramani, Daniele. *Comparative Politics*. New York: Oxford UP, 2008. Print.
Przeworski, Adam. *Democracy and the Limits of Self-Government*. New York: Cambridge UP, 2010. Print.

Socialist

Guiding Premise

Socialism is a political and economic system that seeks to elevate the common good of the citizenry by allowing the government to own all property and means of production. In the most basic model, citizens cooperatively elect members to government, and the government then acts on behalf of the people to manage the state's property, industry, production, and services.

In a socialist system, communal or government ownership of property and industry is intended to eliminate the formation of economic classes and to ensure an even distribution of wealth. Most modern socialists also believe that basic services, including medical and legal care, should be provided at the same level to all citizens and not depend on the individual citizen's ability to pay for better services. The origins of socialism can be traced to theorists such as Thomas More (1478–1535), who believed that private wealth and ownership led to the formation of a wealthy elite class that protected its own wealth while oppressing members of lower classes.

There are many different forms of socialist philosophy, some of which focus on economic systems, while others extend socialist ideas to other aspects of society. Communism may be considered a form of socialism, based on the idea that a working-class revolution is needed to initiate the ideal socialist society.

Typical Structure

Socialism exists in many forms around the world, and many governments use a socialist model for the distribution of key services, most often medical and legal aid. A socialist state is a government whose constitution explicitly gives the government powers to facilitate the creation of a socialist society.

The idealized model of the socialist state is one in which the populace elects leaders to head the government, and the government then oversees the distribution of wealth and goods among the populace, enforces the laws, and provides for the well-being of citizens. Many modern socialist governments follow a communist model, in which a national communist political party has ultimate control over governmental legislation and appointments.

There are many different models of socialist states, integrating elements of democratic or parliamentary systems. In these cases, democratic elections may be held to elect the head of state and the body of legislators. The primary difference between a socialist democracy and a capitalist democracy can be found in the state's role in the ownership of key industries. Most modern noncommunist socialist states provide state regulation and control over key industries but allow some free-market competition as well.

In a socialist system, government officials appoint leaders to oversee various industries and to regulate prices based on public welfare. For instance, if the government retains sole ownership over agricultural production, the government must appoint individuals to manage and oversee that industry, organize agricultural labor, and oversee the distribution of food products among the populace. Some countries, such as Sweden, have adopted a mixed model in which socialist industry management is blended with free-market competition.

Role of the Citizen

All citizens in a socialist system are considered workers, and thus all exist in the same economic class. While some citizens may receive higher pay than others—those who work in supervisory roles, for instance—limited ownership of private property and standardized access to services places all individuals on a level field with regard to basic welfare and economic prosperity.

The degree to which personal liberties are curtailed within a socialist system depends upon the type of socialist philosophy adopted and the degree to which corruption and authoritarianism play a role in government. In most modern communist governments, for instance, individuals are often prohibited from engaging in any activity seen as contrary to the overall goals of the state or to the policies of the dominant political party. While regulations of this kind are common in communist societies, social control over citizens is not necessary for a government to follow a socialist model.

Under democratic socialism, individuals are also expected to play a role in the formation of their government by electing leaders to serve in key positions. In Sri Lanka, for instance, citizens elect members to serve in the parliament and a president to serve as head of the executive branch. In Portugal, citizens vote in multi-party elections to elect a president who serves as head of state, and the president appoints a prime minister to serve as head of government. In both Portugal and Sri Lanka, the government is constitutionally bound to promote a socialist society, though both governments allow private ownership and control of certain industries.

Citizens in a socialist society are also expected to provide for one another by contributing to labor and by forfeiting some ownership rights to provide for the greater good. In the Kingdom of Sweden, a mixed parliamentary system, all citizens pay a higher tax rate to contribute to funds that provide for national health care, child care, education, and worker support systems. Citizens who have no children and require only minimal health care benefits pay the same tax rate as those who have greater need for the nation's socialized benefits.

Micah Issitt
Philadelphia, Pennsylvania

Examples

China
Cuba
Portugal
Sri Lanka
Venezuela
Zambia

Bibliography

Caramani, Daniele. *Comparative Politics*. New York: Oxford UP, 2008. Print.

Heilbroner, Robert. "Socialism." *Library of Economics and Liberty*. Liberty Fund, 2008. Web. 17 Jan. 2013.

Howard, Michael Wayne. *Socialism*. Amherst, NY: Humanity, 2001. Print.

Sultanate/Emirate

Guiding Premise

A sultanate or emirate form of government is a political system in which a hereditary ruler— a monarch, chieftain, or military leader—acts as the head of state. Emirates and sultanates are most commonly found in Islamic nations in the Middle East, although others are found in Southeast Asia as well. Sultans and emirs frequently assume titles such as president or prime minister in addition to their royal designations, meshing the traditional ideal of a monarch with the administrative capacities of a constitutional political system.

Typical Structure

A sultanate or emirate combines the administrative duties of the executive with the powers of a monarch. The emir or sultan acts as the head of government, appointing all cabinet ministers and officials. In Brunei, a sultanate, the government was established according to the constitution (set up after the country declared autonomy from Britain in 1959). The sultan did assemble a legislative council in order to facilitate the lawmaking process, but this council has consistently remained subject to the authority of the sultan and not to a democratic process. In 2004, there was some movement toward the election of at least some of the members of this council. In the meantime, the sultan maintains a ministerial system by appointment and also serves as the nation's chief religious leader.

In some cases, an emirate or sultanate appears similar to a federal system. In the United Arab Emirates (UAE), for example, the nation consists of not one but seven emirates. This system came into being after the seven small regions achieved independence from Great Britain. Each emirate developed its own government system under the leadership of an emir. However, in 1971, the individual emirates agreed to join as a federation, drafting a constitution that identified the areas of common interest to the entire

group of emirates. Like Brunei, the UAE's initial government structure focused on the authority of the emirs and the various councils and ministries formed at the UAE's capital of Abu Dhabi. However, beginning in the early twenty-first century, the UAE's legislative body, the Federal National Council, has been elected by electoral colleges from the seven emirates, thus further engaging various local areas and reflecting their interests.

Sultanates and emirates are at times part of a larger nation, with the sultans or emirs answering to the authority of another government. This is the case in Malaysia, where the country is governed by a constitutional monarchy. However, most of Malaysia's western political units are governed by sultans, who act as regional governors and, in many cases, religious leaders, but remain subject to the king's authority in Malaysia's capital of Kuala Lumpur.

Role of the Citizen

Sultanates and emirates are traditionally nondemocratic governments. Like those of other monarchs, the seats of emirs and sultans are hereditary. Any votes for these leaders to serve as prime minister or other head of government are cast by ministers selected by the emirs and sultans. Political parties may exist in these countries as well, but these parties are strictly managed by the sultan or emir; opposition parties are virtually nonexistent in such systems, and some emirates have no political parties at all.

As shown in the UAE and Malaysia, however, there are signs that the traditional sultanate or emirate is increasingly willing to engage their respective citizens. For example, the UAE, between 2006 and 2013, launched a series of reforms designed to strengthen the role of local governments and relations with the people they serve. Malaysia may allow sultans to continue their regional controls, but at the same time, the country continues to evolve its federal system, facilitating multiparty democratic elections for its national legislature.

Michael Auerbach
Marblehead, Massachusetts

Examples

Brunei
Kuwait
Malaysia
Qatar
United Arab Emirates

Bibliography

"Brunei." *The World Factbook*. Central Intelligence Agency, 2 Jan. 2013. Web. 17 Jan. 2013.

"Malaysia." *The World Factbook*. Central Intelligence Agency, 7 Jan. 2013. Web. 17 Jan. 2013.

"Political System." *UAE Interact*. UAE National Media Council, n.d. Web. 17 Jan. 2013.

Prime Minister's Office, Brunei Darussalam. Prime Minister's Office, Brunei Darussalam, 2013. Web. 17 Jan. 2013.

Theocratic Republic

Guiding Premise

A theocratic republic is a type of government blending popular and religious influence to determine the laws and governmental principles. A republic is a governmental system based on the concept of popular rule and takes its name from the Latin words for "public matter." The defining characteristic of a republic is that civic leaders hold elected, rather than inherited, offices. A theocracy is a governmental system in which a supreme deity is considered the ultimate authority guiding civil matters.

No modern nations can be classified as pure theocratic republics, but some nations, such as Iran, maintain a political system largely dominated by religious law. The Buddhist nation of Tibet operated under a theocratic system until it was taken over by Communist China in the early 1950s.

In general, a theocratic republic forms in a nation or other governmental system dominated by a single religious group. The laws of the government are formed in reference to a set of religious laws, either taken directly from sacred texts or formulated by religious scholars and authority figures. Most theocratic governments depend on a body of religious scholars who interpret religious scripture, advise all branches of government, and oversee the electoral process.

Typical Structure

In a typical republic, the government is divided into executive, legislative, and judicial branches, and citizens vote to elect leaders to one or more of the branches of government. In most modern republics, voters elect a head of state, usually a president, to lead the executive branch. In many republics, voters also elect individuals to serve as legislators. Members of the judiciary may be elected by voters or may be appointed to office by other elected leaders. In nontheocratic republics, the citizens are considered the ultimate source of authority in the government.

In a theocratic republic, however, one or more deities are considered to represent the ultimate governmental authority. In some cases, the government may designate a deity as the ultimate head of state. Typically, any individual serving as the functional head of state is believed to have been chosen by that deity, and candidates for the position must be approved by the prevailing religious authority.

In some cases, the religious authority supports popular elections to fill certain governmental posts. In Iran, for instance, citizens vote to elect members to the national parliament and a single individual to serve as president. The Iranian government is ultimately led by a supreme leader, who is appointed to office by the Assembly of Experts, the leaders of the country's Islamic community. Though the populace chooses the president and leaders to serve in the legislature, the supreme leader of Iran can overrule decisions made in any other branch of the government.

In a theocratic republic, the power to propose new laws may be given to the legislature, which works on legislation in conjunction with the executive branch. However, all laws must conform to religious law, and any legislation produced within the government is likely to be abolished if it is deemed by the religious authorities to violate religious principles. In addition, religious leaders typically decide which candidates are qualified to run for specific offices, thereby ensuring that the citizens will not elect individuals who are likely to oppose religious doctrine.

In addition, many modern nations that operate on a partially theocratic system may adopt a set of governmental principles in the form of a constitution, blended with religious law. This mixed constitutional theocratic system has been adopted by an increasing number of Islamic nations, including Iraq, Afghanistan, Mauritania, and some parts of Nigeria.

Role of the Citizen

Citizens in a theocratic republic are expected to play a role in forming the government through elections, but they are constrained in their choices by the prevailing religious authority. Citizens are also guaranteed certain freedoms, typically codified in a constitution, that have been formulated with reference to religious law. All citizens must adhere to religious laws, regardless of their personal religious beliefs or membership within any existing religious group.

In many Middle Eastern and African nations that operate on the basis of an Islamic theocracy, citizens elect leaders from groups of candidates chosen by the prevailing religious authority. While the choices presented to the citizens are more limited than in a democratic, multiparty republic, the citizens nevertheless play a role in determining the evolution of the government through their voting choices.

The freedoms and rights afforded to citizens in a theocratic republic may depend, in part, on the individual's religious affiliation. For instance, Muslims living in Islamic theocracies may be permitted to hold political office or to aspire to other influential political positions, while members of minority religious groups may find their rights and freedoms limited. Religious minorities living in Islamic republics may not be permitted to run for certain offices, such as president, and must follow laws that adhere to Islamic principles but may violate their own religious principles. Depending on the country and the adherents' religion, the practice of their faith may itself be considered criminal.

Micah Issitt
Philadelphia, Pennsylvania

Examples

Afghanistan

Iran

Iraq

Pakistan

Mauritania

Nigeria

Bibliography

Cooper, William W., and Piyu Yue. *Challenges of the Muslim World: Present, Future and Past.* Boston: Elsevier, 2008. Print.

Hirschl, Ran. *Constitutional Theocracy.* Cambridge: Harvard UP, 2010. Print.

Totalitarian

Guiding Premise

A totalitarian government is one in which a single political party maintains absolute control over the state and is responsible for creating all legislation without popular referendum. In general, totalitarianism is considered a type of authoritarian government where the laws and principles used to govern the country are based on the authority of the leading political group or dictator. Citizens under totalitarian regimes have limited freedoms and are subject to social controls dictated by the state.

The concept of totalitarianism evolved in fascist Italy in the 1920s, and was first used to describe the Italian government under dictator Benito Mussolini. The term became popular among critics of the authoritarian governments of Fascist Italy and Nazi Germany in the 1930s. Supporters of the totalitarian philosophy believed that a strong central government, with absolute control over all aspects of society, could achieve progress by avoiding political debate and power struggles between interest groups.

In theory, totalitarian regimes—like that of Nazi Germany and modern North Korea—can more effectively mobilize resources and direct a nation toward a set of overarching goals. Adolf Hitler was able to achieve vast increases in military power during a short period of time by controlling all procedural steps involved in promoting military development. In practice, however, pure totalitarianism has never been achieved, as citizens and political groups generally find ways to subvert complete government control.

Totalitarianism differs from authoritarianism in that a totalitarian government is based on the idea that the highest leader takes total control in order to create a flourishing society for the benefit of the people. By contrast, authoritarian regimes are based on the authority of a single, charismatic individual who develops policies designed to maintain personal power, rather than promote public interest.

Typical Structure

In a fully realized totalitarian system, a single leader or group of leaders controls all governmental functions, appointing individuals to serve in various posts to facilitate the development of legislation and oversee the enforcement of laws. In Nazi Germany, for instance, Adolf Hitler created a small group of executives to oversee the operation of the government. Governmental authority was then further disseminated through a complex network of departments, called ministries, with leaders appointed directly by Hitler.

Some totalitarian nations may adopt a state constitution in an effort to create the appearance of democratic popular control. In North Korea, the country officially operates under a multiparty democratic system, with citizens guaranteed the right to elect leaders to both the executive and legislative branches of government. In practice, the Workers' Party of North Korea is the only viable political party, as it actively controls competing parties and suppresses any attempt to mount political opposition. Under Supreme Leader Kim Il-sung, the Workers' Party amended the constitution to allow Kim to serve as the sole executive leader for life, without the possibility of being removed from office by any governmental action.

In some cases, totalitarian regimes may favor a presidential system, with the dictator serving officially as president, while other totalitarian governments may adopt a parliamentary system, with a prime minister as head of government. Though a single dictator generally heads the nation with widespread powers over a variety of governmental functions, a cabinet or group of high-ranking ministers may also play a prominent role in disseminating power throughout the various branches of government.

Role of the Citizen

Citizens in totalitarian regimes are often subject to strict social controls exerted by the leading political party. In many cases, totalitarian governments restrict the freedom of the press, expression, and speech in an effort to limit opposition to the government. In addition, totalitarian governments may use the threat of police or military action to prevent protest movements against the leading party. Totalitarian governments maintain absolute control over the courts and any security agency, and the legal/judicial system therefore exists only as an extension of the leading political party.

Totalitarian governments like North Korea also attempt to restrict citizens' access to information considered subversive. For instance, North Korean citizens are not allowed to freely utilize the Internet or any other informational source, but are instead only allowed access to government-approved websites and publications. In many cases, the attempt to control access to information creates a black market for publications and other forms of information banned by government policy.

In some cases, government propaganda and restricted access to information creates a situation in which citizens actively support the ruling regime. Citizens may honestly believe that the social and political restrictions imposed by the ruling party are necessary for the advancement of society. In other cases, citizens may accept governmental control to avoid reprisal from the military and police forces. Most totalitarian regimes have established severe penalties, including imprisonment, corporal punishment, and death, for criticizing the government or refusing to adhere to government policy.

Micah Issitt
Philadelphia, Pennsylvania

Examples

Fascist Italy (1922–1943)
Nazi Germany (1933–1945)
North Korea
Stalinist Russia (1924–1953)

Bibliography

Barrington, Lowell. *Comparative Politics: Structures and Choices.* Boston: Wadsworth, 2012. Print.

Gleason, Abbot. *Totalitarianism: The Inner History of the Cold War.* New York: Oxford UP, 1995. Print.

McEachern, Patrick. *Inside the Red Box: North Korea's Post-Totalitarian Regime.* New York: Columbia UP, 2010. Print.

Treaty System

Guiding Premise

A treaty system is a framework within which participating governments agree to collect and share scientific information gathered in a certain geographic region, or otherwise establish mutually agreeable standards for the use of that region. The participants establish rules and parameters by which researchers may establish research facilities and travel throughout the region, ensuring that there are no conflicts, that the environment is protected, and that the region is not used for illicit purposes. This system is particularly useful when the region in question is undeveloped and unpopulated, but could serve a number of strategic and scientific purposes.

Typical Structure

A treaty system of government is an agreement between certain governments that share a common interest in the use of a certain region to which no state or country has yet laid internationally recognized claim. Participating parties negotiate treaty systems that, upon agreement, form a framework by which the system will operate. Should the involved parties be United Nations member states, the treaty is then submitted to the UN Secretariat for registration and publication.

The agreement's founding ideals generally characterize the framework of a treaty. For example, the most prominent treaty system in operation today is the Antarctic Treaty System, which currently includes fifty nations whose scientists are studying Antarctica. This system, which entered into force in 1961, focuses on several topics, including environmental protection, tourism, scientific operations, and the peaceful use of that region. Within these topics, the treaty system enables participants to meet, cooperate, and share data on a wide range of subjects. Such cooperative activities include regional meetings, seminars, and large-scale conferences.

A treaty system is not a political institution in the same manner as state governments. Rather, it is an agreement administered by delegates from the involved entities. Scientists seeking to perform their research in Antarctica, for example, must apply through the scientific and/or government institutions of their respective nations. In the case of the United States, scientists may apply for grants from the National Science Foundation. These institutions then examine the study in question for its relevance to the treaty's ideals.

Central to the treaty system is the organization's governing body. In the case of the Antarctic Treaty, that body is the Antarctic Treaty Secretariat, which is based in Buenos Aires, Argentina. The Secretariat oversees all activities taking place under the treaty, welcomes new members, and addresses any conflicts or issues between participants. It also reviews any activities to ensure that they are in line with the parameters of the treaty. A treaty system is not a sovereign organization, however. Each participating government retains autonomy, facilitating its own scientific expeditions, sending delegates to the treaty system's main governing body, and reviewing the treaty to ensure that it coincides with its national interests.

Role of the Citizen

Although treaty systems are not sovereign government institutions, private citizens can and frequently do play an important role in their function and success. For example, the Antarctic Treaty System frequently conducts large-scale planning conferences, to which each participating government sends delegates. These teams are comprised of qualified scientists who are nominated and supported by their peers during the government's review process. In the United States, for example, the State Department oversees American participation in the Antarctic

Treaty System's events and programs, including delegate appointments.

Another area in which citizens are involved in a treaty system is in the ratification process. Every nation's government—usually through its legislative branch—must formally approve any treaty before the country can honor the agreement. This ratification is necessary for new treaties as well as treaties that must be reapproved every few years. Citizens, through their elected officials, may voice their support or disapproval of a new or updated treaty.

While participating governments administer treaty systems and their secretariats, those who conduct research or otherwise take part in activities in the region in question are not usually government employees. In Antarctica, for example, university professors, engineers, and other private professionals—supported by a combination of private and government funding—operate research stations.

Michael Auerbach
Marblehead, Massachusetts

Example
Antarctic Treaty System

Bibliography
"Antarctic." *Ocean and Polar Affairs.* US Department of State, 22 Mar. 2007. Web. 8 Feb. 2013.
"About Us." *Antarctic Treaty System.* Secretariat of the Antarctic Treaty, n.d. Web. 8 Feb. 2013.
"United Nations Treaty Series." *United Nations Treaty Collection.* United Nations, 2013. Web. 8 Feb. 2013.
"Educational Opportunities and Resources." *United States Antarctic Program.* National Science Foundation, 2013. Web. 8 Feb. 2013.

Appendix Two:
World Religions

African Religious Traditions

General Description

The religious traditions of Africa can be studied both religiously and ethnographically. Animism, or the belief that everything has a soul, is practiced in most tribal societies, including the Dogon (people of the cliffs), an ethnic group living primarily in Mali's central plateau region and in Burkina Faso. Many traditional faiths have extensive mythologies, rites, and histories, such as the Yoruba religion practiced by the Yoruba, an ethnic group of West Africa. In South Africa, the traditional religion of the Zulu people is based on a creator god, ancestor worship, and the existence of sorcerers and witches. Lastly, the Ethiopian or Abyssinian Church (formally the Ethiopian Orthodox Union Church) is a branch of Christianity unique to the east African nations of Ethiopia and Eritrea.

Number of Adherents Worldwide

Some 63 million Africans adhere to traditional religions such as animism. One of the largest groups practicing animism is the Dogon, who number about six hundred thousand. However, it is impossible to know how many practice traditional religion. In fact, many people practice animism alongside other religions, particularly Islam. Other religions have spread their adherence and influence through the African diaspora. In Africa, the Yoruba number between thirty-five and forty million and are located primarily in Benin, Togo and southwest Nigeria. The Zulu, the largest ethnic group in South Africa, total over eleven million. Like Islam, Christianity has affected the number of people who still hold traditional beliefs, making accurate predictions virtually impossible. The Ethiopian or Abyssinian Church has over thirty-nine million adherents in Ethiopia alone.

Basic Tenets

Animism holds that many spiritual beings have the power to help or hurt humans. The traditional faith is thus more concerned with appropriate rituals rather than worship of a deity, and focuses on day-to-day practicalities such as food, water supplies, and disease. Ancestors, particularly those most recently dead, are invoked for their aid. Those who practice animism believe in life after death; some adherents may attempt to contact the spirits of the dead. Animists acknowledge the existence of tribal gods. (However, African people traditionally do not make images of God, who is thought of as Spirit.)

The Dogon divide into two caste-like groups: the inneomo (pure) and innepuru (impure). The hogon leads the inneomo, who may not sacrifice animals and whose leaders are forbidden to hunt. The inneomo also cannot prepare or bury the dead. While the innepuru can do all of the above tasks, they cannot take part in the rituals for agricultural fertility. Selected young males called the olubaru lead the innepuru. The status of "pure" or "impure" is inherited. The Dogon have many gods. The chief god is called Amma, a creator god who is responsible for creating other gods and the earth.

The Dogon have a three-part concept of death. First the soul is sent to the realm of the dead to join the ancestors. Rites are then performed to remove any ritual polluting. Finally, when several members of the village have died, a rite known as dama occurs. In the ritual, a sacrifice is made to the Great Mask (which depicts a large wooden serpent and which is never actually worn) and dancers perform on the housetops where someone has died to scare off any lingering souls. Often, figures of Nommo (a worshipped ancestral spirit) are put near funeral pottery on the family shrine.

The Yoruba believe in predestination. Before birth, the ori (soul) kneels before Olorun, the wisest and most powerful deity, and selects a destiny. Rituals may assist the person in achieving his or her destiny, but it cannot be altered. The Yoruba, therefore, acknowledge a need for ritual and sacrifice, properly done according to the oracles.

Among the Yoruba, the shaman is known as the babalawo. He or she is able to communicate with ancestors, spirits and deities. Training for this work, which may include responsibility as a doctor, often requires three years. The shaman is consulted before major life decisions. During these consultations, the shaman dictates the right rituals and sacrifices, and to which gods they are to be offered for maximum benefit. In addition, the Yoruba poetry covers right conduct. Good character is at the heart of Yoruba ethics.

The Yoruba are polytheistic. The major god is Olorun, the sky god, considered all-powerful and holy, and a father to 401 children, also gods. He gave the task of creating human beings to the deity Obatala (though Olorun breathed life into them). Olorun also determines the destiny of each person. Onlie, the Great Mother Goddess, is in some ways the opposite of Olorun. Olorun is the one who judges a soul following death. For example, if the soul is accounted worthy, it will be reincarnated, while the unworthy go to the place of punishment. Ogun, the god of hunters, iron, and war, is another important god. He is also the patron of blacksmiths. The Yoruba have some 1,700 gods, collectively known as the Orisa.

The Yoruba believe in an afterlife. There are two heavens: one is a hot, dry place with potsherds, reserved for those who have done evil, while the other is a pleasant heaven for persons who have led a good life. There the ori (soul) may choose to "turn to be a child" on the earth once more.

In the Zulu tradition, the king was responsible for rainmaking and magic for the benefit of the nation. Rainmakers were also known as "shepherds of heaven." They performed rites during times of famine, drought or war, as well as during planting season, invoking royal ancestors for aid. Storms were considered a manifestation of God.

The Zulu are also polytheistic. They refer to a wise creator god who lives in heaven. This Supreme Being has complete control of everything in the universe, and is known as Unkulunkulu, the Great Oldest One. The Queen of heaven is a virgin who taught women useful arts; light surrounds her, and her glory is seen in rain, mist, and rainbows.

The Ethiopian Church incorporates not only Orthodox Christian beliefs, but also aspects of Judaism. The adherents distinguish between clean and unclean meats, practice circumcision, and observe the seventh-day Sabbath. The Ethiopian (or Abyssinian) Church is monotheistic and believes in the Christian God.

Sacred Text

Traditional religions such as animism generally have no written sacred texts. Instead, creation stories and other tales are passed down orally. The Yoruba do have some sacred poetry, in 256 chapters, known as odus. The text covers both right action in worship and ethical conduct. The Ethiopian Church has scriptures written in the ancient Ge'ez language, which is no longer used, except in church liturgy.

Major Figures

A spiritual leader, or hogon, oversees each district among the Dogon. There is a supreme hogon for the entire country. Among the Yoruba, the king, or oba, rules each town. He is also considered sacred and is responsible for performing rituals. Isaiah Shembe is a prophet or messiah among the Zulu. He founded the Nazareth Baptist Church (also called the amaNazaretha Church or Shembe Church), an independent Zulu Christian denomination. His son, Johannes Shembe, took the title Shembe II. In the Ethiopian Church, now fully independent, the head of the church is the Patriarch. Saint Frumentius, the first bishop of Axum in northern Ethiopia, is credited with beginning the Christian tradition during the fourth century. King Lalibela, noted for authorizing construction of monolithic churches carved underground, was a major figure in the twelfth century.

Major Holy Sites

Every spot in nature is sacred in animistic thinking. There is no division between sacred and profane—all of life is sacred, and Earth is Mother. Sky and mountains are often regarded as sacred space.

For the Yoruba of West Africa, Osogbo in Nigeria is a forest shrine. The main goddess is Oshun, goddess of the river. Until she arrived, the work done by male gods was not succeeding. People seeking to be protected from illness and women wishing to become pregnant seek Osun's help. Ilé-Ifè, an ancient Yoruba city in Nigeria, is another important site, and considered the spiritual hub of the Yoruba. According to the Yoruba creation myth, Olorun, god of the sky, set down Odudua, the founder of the Yoruba, in Ilé-Ifè. Shrines within the city include one to Ogun. The shrine is made of stones and wooden stumps.

Mount Nhlangakazi (Holy Mountain) is considered sacred to the Zulu Nazareth Baptist Church (amaNazaretha). There Isaiah Shembe built a High Place to serve as his headquarters. It is a twice-yearly site of pilgrimage for amaNazarites.

Sacred sites of the Ethiopian Church include the Church of St. Mary of Zion in Axum, considered the most sacred Ethiopian shrine. According to legend, the church stands adjacent to a guarded chapel which purportedly houses the Ark of the Covenant, a powerful biblical relic. The Ethiopian Church also considers sacred the eleven monolithic (rock-hewn) churches, still places of pilgrimage and devotion, that were recognized as a collective World Heritage Site by the United Nations Educational, Scientific and Cultural Organization.

Major Rites & Celebrations

Most African religions involve some sacrifice to appease or please the gods. Among the Yoruba, for example, dogs, which are helpful in both hunting and war, are sacrificed to Ogun. In many tribes, including the Yoruba, rites of passage for youth exist. The typical pattern is three-fold: removal from the tribe, instruction, and return to the tribe ready to assume adult responsibilities. In this initiation, the person may be marked bodily through scarification or circumcision. The Yoruba also have a yearly festival re-enacting

the story of Obatala and Oduduwa (generally perceived as the ancestor of the Yorubas). A second festival, which resembles a passion play, re-enacts the conflict between the grandsons of these two legendary figures. A third festival celebrates the heroine Moremi, who led the Yoruba to victory over the enemy Igbo, an ethnicity from southeastern Nigeria, and who ultimately reconciled the two tribes.

Yoruba death rites include a masked dancer who comes to the family following a death, assuring them of the ancestor's ongoing care for the family. If the person was important in the village, a mask will be carved and named for them. In yearly festivals, the deceased individual will then appear with other ancestors.

Masks are also used in a Dogon funeral ritual, the dama ceremony, which is led by the Awa, a secret society comprised of all adult Dogon males of the innepuru group. During ceremonial times, the hogon relinquishes control and the Awa control the community. At the end of the mourning period the dama ceremony begins when the Awa leave the village and return with both the front and back of their heads masked. Through rituals and dances, they lead the spirit of the deceased to the next world. Control of the village reverts to the hogon at that point. The Wagem rites govern contact with the ancestors. Following the dama ceremony, the eldest male descendant, called the ginna bana, adds a vessel to the family shrine in the name of the deceased. The spirit of the ancestor is persuaded to return to the descendents through magic and sacrificial offerings, creating a link from the living to the first ancestors.

Ethiopian Christians observe and mark most typical Christian rites, though some occur on different dates because of the difference in the Ethiopian and Western calendars. For example, Christmas in Ethiopia is celebrated on January 7.

ORIGINS

History & Geography

The Dogon live along the Bandiagara Cliffs, a rocky and mountainous region. (The Cliffs of Bandiagara, also called the Bandiagara Escarpment, were recognized as a UNESCO World Heritage Site due to the cultural landscape, including the ancient traditions of the Dogon and their architecture.) This area is south of the Sahara in a region called the Sahel, another region prone to drought (though not a desert). The population of the villages in the region is typically a thousand people or less. The cliffs of the Bandiagara have kept the Dogon separate from other people.

Myths of origin regarding the Dogon differ. One suggestion is that the Dogon came from Egypt, and then lived in Libya before entering the the region of what is now Burkina Faso, Mauritania, or Guinea. Near the close of the fifteenth century, they arrived in Mali.

Among the Yoruba, multiple myths regarding their origin exist. One traces their beginnings to Uruk in Mesopotamia or to Babylon, the site of present-day Iraq. Another story has the Yoruba in West Africa by 10,000 BCE.

After the death of the Zulu messiah Isaiah Shembe in 1935, his son Johannes became the leader of the Nazareth Baptist Church. He lacked the charisma of his father, but did hold the church together. His brother, Amos, became regent in 1976 when Johannes died. Johannes's son Londa split the church in 1979 when Amos refused to give up power. Tangled in South African politics, Londa was killed in 1989.

The Ethiopian Orthodox Church is the nation's official church. A legend states that Menelik, supposed to have been the son of the Queen of Sheba and King Solomon, founded the royal line. When Jesuits arrived in the seventeenth century, they failed to change the church, and the nation closed to missionary efforts for several hundred years. By retaining independence theologically and not being conquered politically, Ethiopia is sometimes considered a model for the new religious movements in Africa.

Founder or Major Prophet

The origins of most African traditional religions or faiths are accounted for through the actions of deities in creation stories rather than a particular founder. One exception, however, is Isaiah Shembe, who founded the Nazareth Baptist Church, also known as the Shembe Church or amaNazarite Church, in 1910 after receiving a number of revelations during a thunderstorm. Shembe was an itinerant Zulu preacher and healer. Through his influence and leadership, amaNazarites follow more Old Testament regulations than most Christians, including celebrating the Sabbath on Saturday rather than Sunday. They also refer to God as Jehovah, the Hebrew name for God. Shembe was regarded as the new Jesus Christ for his people, adapting Christianity to Zulu practice. He adopted the title Nkosi, which means king or chief.

The Ethiopian Orthodox church was founded, according to legend, by preaching from one of two New Testament figures—the disciple Matthew or the unnamed eunuch mentioned in Acts 8. According to historical evidence, the church began when Frumentius arrived at the royal court. Athanasius of Alexandria later consecrated Frumentius as patriarch of the church, linking it to the Christian church in Egypt.

Creation Stories

The Dogon believe that Amma, the sky god, was also the creator of the universe. Amma created two sets of twins, male and female. One of the males rebelled. To restore order, Amma sacrificed the other male, Nommo, strangling and scattering him to the four directions, then restoring him to life after five days. Nommo then became ruler of the universe and the children of his spirits became the Dogon. Thus the world continually moves between chaos and order, and the task of the Dogon is to keep the world in balance through rituals. In a five-year cycle, the aspects of this creation myth are re-enacted at altars throughout the Dogon land.

According to the Yoruba, after one botched attempt at creating the world, Olorun sent his son Obatala to create earth upon the waters. Obatala tossed some soil on the water and released a five-toed hen to spread it out. Next, Olorun told Obatala to make people from clay. Obatala grew bored with the work and drank too much wine. Thereafter, the people he made were misshapen or defective (handicapped). In anger, Olorun relieved him of the job and gave it to Odudua to complete. It was Odudua who made the Yoruba and founded a kingdom at Ilé-Ifè.

The word *Zulu* means "heaven or sky." The Zulu people believe they originated in heaven. They also believe in phansi, the place where spirits live and which is below the earth's surface.

Holy Places

Osun-Osogbo is a forest shrine in Nigeria dedicated to the Yoruba river goddess, Osun. It may be the last such sacred grove remaining among the Yoruba. Shrines, art, sculpture, and sanctuaries are part of the grove, which became a UNESCO World Heritage site in 2005.

Ilé-Ifè, regarded as the equivalent of Eden, is thought to be the site where the first Yoruba was placed. It was probably named for Ifa, the god associated with divination. The palace (Afin) of the spiritual head of the Yoruba, the oni, is located there. The oni has the responsibility to care for the staff of Oranmiyan, a Benin king. The staff, which is eighteen feet tall, is made of granite and shaped like an elephant's tusk.

Axum, the seat of the Ethiopian Christian Church, is a sacred site. The eleven rock-hewn churches of King Lalibela, especially that of Saint George, are a pilgrimage site. According to tradition, angels helped to carve the churches. More than 50,000 pilgrims come to the town of Lalibela at Christmas. After the Muslims captured Jerusalem in 1187, King Lalibela proclaimed his city the "New Jerusalem" because Christians could no longer go on pilgrimage to the Holy Land.

AFRICAN RELIGIONS IN DEPTH

Sacred Symbols

Because all of life is infused with religious meaning, any object or location may be considered or become sacred in traditional African religions. Masks, in particular, have special meaning and

may be worn during ceremonies. The mask often represents a god, whose power is passed to the one wearing the mask.

Sacred Practices & Gestures

The Yoruba practice divination in a form that is originally Arabic. There are sixteen basic figures—combined, they deliver a prophecy that the diviner is not to interpret. Instead, he or she recites verses from a classic source. Images may be made to prevent or cure illness. For example, the Yoruba have a smallpox spirit god that can be prayed to for healing. Daily prayer, both morning and evening, is part of life for most Yoruba.

In the amaNazarite Church, which Zulu Isaiah Shembe founded, singing is a key part of the faith. Shembe himself was a gifted composer of hymns. This sacred music was combined with dancing, during which the Zulu wear their traditional dress.

Rites, Celebrations & Services

The Dogon have three major cults. The Awa are associated with dances, featuring ornately carved masks, at funerals and on the anniversaries of deaths. The cult of the Earth god, Lebe, concerns itself with the agricultural cycles and fertility of the land; the hogon of the village guards the soil's purity and presides at ceremonies related to farming. The third cult, the Binu, is involved with communication with spirits, ancestor worship, and sacrifices. Binu shrines are in many locations. The Binu priest makes sacrifices of porridge made from millet and blood at planting time and also when the help of an ancestor is needed. Each clan within the Dogon community has a totem animal spirit—an ancestor spirit wishing to communicate with descendents may do so by taking the form of the animal.

The Dogon also have a celebration every fifty years at the appearing of the star Sirius B between two mountains. (Sirius is often the brightest star in the nighttime sky.) Young males leaving for three months prior to the sigui, as it is called, for a time of seclusion and speaking in private language. This celebration is rooted in the Dogon belief that amphibious creatures, the Nommo, visited their land about three thousand years ago.

The Yoruba offer Esu, the trickster god, palm wine and animal sacrifices. Because he is a trickster, he is considered a cheater, and being on his good side is important. The priests in Yoruba traditional religion are responsible for installing tribal chiefs and kings.

Among the Zulu, families determine the lobola, or bride price. They believe that a groom will respect his wife more if he must pay for her. Further gifts are then exchanged, and the bride's family traditionally gives the groom a goat or sheep to signify their acceptance of him. The groom's family provides meat for the wedding feast, slaughtering a cow on the morning of the wedding. The families assemble in a circle and the men, in costume, dance. The bride gives presents, usually mats or blankets, to members of her new family, who dance or sing their thanks. The final gift, to the groom, is a blanket, which is tossed over his head. Friends of the bride playfully beat him, demonstrating how they will respond if he mistreats his new wife. After the two families eat together, the couple is considered one.

In the traditional Zulu religion, ancestors three generations back are regarded as not yet settled in the afterlife. To help them settle, offerings of goats or other animals are made and rituals to help them settle into the community of ancestors are performed.

Christmas is a major celebration in Ethiopian Christianity. Priests rattle an instrument derived from biblical times, called the sistra, and chant to begin the mass. The festivities include drumming and a dance known as King David's dance.

Judy A. Johnson, MTS

Bibliography

A, Oladosu Olusegun. "Ethics and Judgement: A Panacea for Human Transformation in Yoruba Multireligious Society." *Asia Journal of Theology* 26.1 (2012): 88–104. Print.

Barnes, Trevor. *The Kingfisher Book of Religions*. New York: Kingfisher, 1999. Print.

Dawson, Allan Charles, ed. *Shrines in Africa: history, politics, and society*. Calgary: U of Calgary P, 2009. Print.

Doumbia, Adama, and Naomi Doumbia. *The Way of the Elders: West African Spirituality*. St. Paul: Llewellyn, 2004. Print.

Douny, Laurence. "The Role of Earth Shrines in the Socio-Symbolic Construction of the Dogon Territory: Towards a Philosophy of Containment." *Anthropology & Medicine* 18.2 (2011): 167–79. Print.

Friedenthal, Lora, and Dorothy Kavanaugh. *Religions of Africa*. Philadelphia: Mason Crest, 2007. Print.

Hayes, Stephen. "Orthodox Ecclesiology in Africa: A Study of the 'Ethiopian' Churches of South Africa." *International Journal for the Study of the Christian Church* 8.4 (2008). 337–54. Print.

Lugira, Aloysius M. *African Religion*. New York: Facts on File, 2004. Print.

Mbiti, John S. *African Religions and Philosophy*. 2nd ed. Oxford: Heinemann, 1991. Print.

Monteiro-Ferreira, Ana Maria. "Reevaluating Zulu Religion." *Journal of Black Studies* 35.3 (2005): 347–63. Print.

Peel, J. D. Y. "Yoruba Religion as a Global Phenomenon." *Journal of African History* 5.1 (2010): 107–8. Print.

Ray, Benjamin C. *African Religions*. 2nd ed. Upper Saddle River: Prentice, 2000. Print.

Thomas, Douglas E. *African Traditional Religion in the Modern World*. Jefferson: McFarland, 2005. Print.

Bahá'í Faith

General Description

The Bahá'í faith is the youngest of the world's religions. It began in the mid-nineteenth century, offering scholars the opportunity to observe a religion in the making. While some of the acts of religious founders such as Buddha or Jesus cannot be substantiated, the modern founders of Bahá'í were more contemporary figures.

Number of Adherents Worldwide

An estimated 5 to 7 million people follow the Bahá'í faith. Although strong in Middle Eastern nations such as Iran, where the faith originated, Bahá'í has reached people in many countries, particularly the United States and Canada.

Basic Tenets

The Bahá'í faith has three major doctrines. The first doctrine is that there is one transcendent God, and all religions worship that God, regardless of the name given to the deity. Adherents believe that religious figures such as Jesus Christ, the Buddha, and the Prophet Muhammad were different revelations of God unique to their time and place. The second doctrine is that there is only one religion, though each world faith is valid and was founded by a ""manifestation of God" who is part of a divine plan for educating humanity. The third doctrine is a belief in the unity of all humankind. In light of this underlying unity, those of the Bahá'í faith work for social justice. They believe that seeking consensus among various groups diffuses typical power struggles and to this end, they employ a method called consultation, which is a nonadversarial decision-making process.

The Bahá'í believe that the human soul is immortal, and that after death the soul moves nearer or farther away from God. The idea of an afterlife comprised of a literal "heaven" or "hell" is not part of the faith.

Sacred Text

The Most Holy Book, or the Tablets, written by Baha'u'llah, form the basis of Bahá'í teachings. Though not considered binding, scriptures from other faiths are regarded as "Divine Revelation."

Major Figures

The Bab (The Gate of God) Siyyad 'Ali Mohammad (1819–50), founder of the Bábí movement that broke from Islam, spoke of a coming new messenger of God. Mirza Hoseyn 'Ali Nuri (1817–92), who realized that he was that prophet, was given the title Baha'u'llah (Glory of God). From a member of Persia's landed gentry, he was part of the ruling class, and is considered the founder of the Bahá'í faith. His son, 'Abdu'l-Bahá (Servant of the Glory of God), who lived from 1844 until 1921, became the leader of the group after his father's death in 1892. The oldest son of his eldest daughter, Shogi Effendi Rabbani (1899–1957), oversaw a rapid expansion, visiting Egypt, America, and nations in Europe. Tahirih (the Pure One) was a woman poet who challenged stereotypes by appearing unveiled at meetings.

Major Holy Sites

The Bahá'í World Center is located near Haifa, Israel. The burial shrine of the Bab, a pilgrimage site, is there. The Shrine of Baha'u'llah near Acre, Israel, is another pilgrimage site. The American headquarters are in Wilmette, Illinois. Carmel in Israel is regarded as the world center of the faith.

Major Rites & Celebrations

Each year, the Bahá'í celebrate Ridvan Festival, a twelve-day feast from sunset on April 20 to sunset on May 2. The festival marks Baha'u'llah's declaration of prophethood, as prophesized by the Bab, at a Baghdad garden. (Ridvan means Paradise.) The holy days within that feast are the first (Baha'u'llah's garden arrival), ninth (the arrival of his family), and twelfth (his departure from Ridvan Garden)—on these days, the Bahá'í do not work. During this feast, people attend social events and meet for devotions. Baha'u'llah referred to it as the King of Festivals and Most Great Festival. The Bahá'í celebrate several other events, including World Religion Day and Race Unity Day, both founded by Bahá'í, as well as days connected with significant events in the life of the founder. Elections to the Spiritual Assemblies, and the national and local administrations; international elections are held every five years.

ORIGINS

History & Geography

Siyyad 'Ali Muhammad was born into a merchant family of Shiraz in 1819. Both his parents were descendents of the Prophet Muhammad, Islam's central figure. Like the Prophet, the man who became the Bab lost his father at an early age and was raised by an uncle. A devout child, he entered his uncle's business by age fifteen. After visiting Muslim holy cities, he returned to Shiraz, where he married a distant relative named Khadijih.

While on pilgrimage in 1844 to the black stone of Ka'bah, a sacred site in Islam, the Bab stood with his hand on that holy object and declared that he was the prophet for whom they had been waiting. The Sunni did not give credence to these claims. The Bab went to Persia, where the Shia sect was the majority. However, because Muhammad had been regarded as the "Seal of the Prophets," and the one who spoke the final revelation, Shia clergy viewed his claims as threatening, As such, nothing further would be revealed until the Day of Judgment. The authority of the clergy was in danger from this new movement.

The Bab was placed under house arrest, and then confined to a fortress on the Russian frontier. That move to a more remote area only increased the number of converts, as did a subsequent move to another Kurdish fortress. He was eventually taken to Tabriz in Iran and tried before the Muslim clergy in 1848. Condemned, he was caned on the soles of his feet and treated by a British doctor who was impressed by him.

Despite his treatment and the persecution of his followers—many of the Bab's eighteen disciples, termed the "Letters of the Living," were persistently tortured and executed—the Bab refused to articulate a doctrine of jihad. The Babis could defend themselves, but were forbidden to use holy war as a means of religious conquest. In three major confrontations sparked by the Shia clergy, Babis were defeated. The Bab was sentenced as a heretic and shot by a firing squad in 1850. Lacking leadership and grief-stricken, in 1852 two young Babis fired on the shah in 1852, unleashing greater persecutions and cruelty against those of the Bahá'í faith.

A follower of the Bab, Mirza Hoseyn 'Ali Nuri, announced in 1863 that he was the one who was to come (the twelfth imam of Islam), the "Glory of God," or Baha'u'llah. Considered the founder of the Bahá'í Faith, he was a tireless writer who anointed his son, 'Abdu'l-Bahá, as the next leader. Despite deprivations and imprisonments, Baha'u'llah lived to be seventy-five years old, relinquishing control of the organization to 'Abdu'l-Bahá before the time of his death.

'Abdu'l-Bahá, whom his father had called "the Master," expanded the faith to the nations of Europe and North America. In 1893, at the Parliament of Religions at the Chicago World's Fair, the faith was first mentioned in the United States. Within a few years, communities of faith were established in Chicago and Wisconsin. In 1911, 'Abdu'l-Bahá began a twenty-eight month tour of Europe and North America to promote the Bahá'í faith. Administratively, he established the spiritual assemblies that were the forerunner of the Houses of Justice that his father had envisioned.

During World War I, 'Abdu'l-Bahá engaged in humanitarian work among the Palestinians in the Holy Land, where he lived. In recognition of his efforts, he was granted knighthood by the British government. Thousands of people, including many political and religious dignitaries, attended his funeral in 1921.

'Abdu'l-Bahá conferred the role of Guardian, or sole interpreter of Bahá'í teaching, to his eldest grandson, Shoghi Effendi Rabbani. To him, all questions regarding the faith were to be addressed. Shoghi Effendi Rabbani was a descendent of Baha'u'llah through both parents. He headed the Bahá'í faith from 1921 to 1963, achieving four major projects: he oversaw the physical development of the World Centre and expanded the administrative order; he carried out the plan his father had set in motion; and he provided for the translating and interpreting of Bahá'í teachings, as the writings of both the Bab and those of Baha'u'llah and 'Abdu'l-Bahá have been translated and published in more than eight hundred languages.

Beginning in 1937, Shoghi Effendi Rabbani began a series of specific plans with goals tied to deadlines. In 1953, during the second seven-year plan, the house of worship in Wilmette, Illinois, was completed and dedicated.

Although the beliefs originated in Shi'ite Islam, the Bahá'í Faith has been declared a new religion without connections to Islam. To followers of Islam, it is a heretical sect. During the reign of the Ayatollah Khomeini, a time when Iran was especially noted as intolerant of diverse views, the Bahá'í faced widespread persecution.

Founder or Major Prophet

Mirza Husayn Ali Nuri, known as Baha'u'llah, was born into privilege in 1817 in what was then Persia, now present-day Iran. At twenty-two, he declined a government post offered at his father's death. Although a member of a politically prestigious family, he did not follow the career path of several generations of his ancestors. Instead, he managed the family estates and devoted himself to charities, earning the title "Father of the Poor."

At twenty-seven, he followed the Babis's movement within Shia Islam, corresponding with the Bab and traveling to further the faith. He also provided financial support. In 1848, he organized and helped to direct a conference that explained the Bab's teaching. At the conference, he gave symbolic names to the eighty-one followers who had attended, based on the spiritual qualities he had observed.

Although he managed to escape death during the persecutions before and after the Bab's death, a fact largely attributed to his upbringing, Baha'u'llah was imprisoned several times. During a four-month stay in an underground dungeon in Tehran, he realized from a dream that he was the one of whom the Bab had prophesied. After being released, he was banished from Persia and had his property confiscated by the shah. He went to Baghdad, refusing the offer of refuge that had come from Russia. Over the following three years a small band of followers joined him, including members of his family. When his younger brother attempted to take over the leadership of the Babis, Baha'u'llah spent two years in a self-imposed exile in the Kurdistan wilderness. In 1856, with the community near anarchy as a result of his brother's failure of leadership, Baha'u'llah returned to the community and restored its position over the next seven years.

Concerned by the growing popularity of the new faith, the shah demanded that the Babis move further away from Persia. They went to Constantinople where, in 1863, Baha'u'llah revealed to the whole group that he was "He Whom God Will Make Manifest." From there the Bahá'í were sent to Adrianople in Turkey, and at last, in 1868, to the town of Acre in the Holy Land. Baha'u'llah was imprisoned in Acre and survived severe prison conditions. In 1877, he moved from prison to a country estate, then to a mansion. He died in 1892 after a fever.

Philosophical Basis

The thinking of Shia Muslims contributed to the development of Bahá'í. The writings incorporate language and concepts from the Qur'an (Islam's holy book). Like Muslims, the Bahá'í believe that God is one. God sends messengers, the Manifestations of God, to instruct people and benefit society. These have included Jesus Christ, the Buddha, the Prophet Muhammad, Krishna, and the Bab. Bahá'í also goes further than Islam in accepting all religions—not just Judaism, Christianity, and Islam—as being part of a divinely inspired plan.

Shia Muslims believe that Muhammad's descendents should lead the faithful community. The leaders, known as imams, were considered infallible. The Sunni Muslims believed that following the way (sunna) of Muhammad was sufficient qualification for leadership. Sunni dynasties regarded the imams as a threat and executed them, starting with two of Muhammad's grandsons, who became Shia martyrs.

In Persia, a state with a long tradition of divinely appointed rulers, the Shia sect was strong. When the Safavids, a Shia dynasty, came to power in the sixteenth century, the custom of the imamate was victorious. One tradition states that in 873, the last appointed imam, who was still a child, went into hiding to avoid being killed. For the following sixty-nine years, this twelfth imam communicated through his deputies to the faithful. Each of the deputies was called bab, or gate, because they led to the "Hidden Imam." Four babs existed through 941, and the last one died without naming the next bab. The Hidden Imam is thought to emerge at the end of time to bring in a worldwide reign of justice. From this tradition came the expectation of a Mahdi (Guided One) to lead the people.

During the early nineteenth century, many followers of both the Christian and Islamic faiths expected their respective messiahs to return. Shia teachers believed that the return of the Mahdi imam was near. In 1843, one teacher, Siyyid Kázim, noted that the Hidden Imam had disappeared one thousand lunar years earlier. He urged the faithful to look for the Mahdi imam.

The following year in Shiraz, Siyyad 'Ali Mohammad announced that he was the Mahdi. (*Siyyad* is a term meaning descended from Muhammad.) He referred to himself as the Bab, though he expanded the term's meaning. Eighteen men, impressed with his ability to expound the Qur'an, believed him. They became the Letters of the Living, and were sent throughout Persia (present-day Iran) to announce the dawning of the Day of God.

In 1853, Mirza Husayn Ali Nuri experienced a revelation that he was "He Whom God Shall Make Manifest," the one of whom the Bab prophesied. Accepted as such, he began writing the words that became the Bahá'í scriptures. Much of what is known of the early days of the faith comes from a Cambridge academic, Edward Granville Browne, who first visited Baha'u'llah in the 1890. Browne wrote of his meeting, introducing this faith to the West.

The emphasis of the Bahá'í faith is on personal development and the breaking down of barriers between people. Service to humanity is important and encouraged. Marriage, with a belief in the equality of both men and women, is also encouraged. Consent of both sets of parents is required prior to marrying.

Holy Places

The shrine of the Bab near Haifa and that of Baha'u'llah near Acre, in Israel, are the two most revered sites for those of the Bahá'í faith. In 2008, the United Nations Educational, Scientific, and Cultural Organization (UNESCO) recognized both as World Heritage Sites. They are the first such sites from a modern religious tradition to be added to the list of sites. Both sites are appreciated for the formal gardens surrounding them that blend design elements from different cultures. For the Bahá'í, Baha'u'llah's shrine is the focus of prayer, comparable to the significance given to the Ka'bah in Mecca for Muslims or to the Western Wall for Jews.

As of 2013, there are seven Bahá'í temples in the world; an eighth temple is under construction in Chile. All temples are built with a center dome and nine sides, symbolizing both diversity and world unity. The North American temple is located in Wilmette, Illinois. There, daily prayer services take place as well as a Sunday service.

THE BAHÁ'Í FAITH IN DEPTH

Governance

Elected members of lay councils at international, national, and local levels administer the work of the faith. The Universal House of Justice in Haifa, Israel, is the location of the international nine-member body. Elections for all of these lay councils are by secret ballot, and do not include nominating, candidates, or campaigns. Those twenty-one and older are permitted to vote. The councils make decisions according to a process of collective decision-making called consultation. They strive to serve as a model for governing a united global society.

Personal Conduct

In addition to private prayer and acts of social justice, those of the Bahá'í faith are encouraged to have a profession, craft, or trade. They are also asked to shun and refrain from slander and partisan politics. Homosexuality and sexual activity outside marriage are forbidden, as is gambling.

The Bahá'í faith does not have professional clergy, nor does it engage in missionary work. However, Bahá'í may share their faith with others and may move to another country as a "pioneer." Pioneers are unlike traditional missionaries, and are expected to support themselves through a career and as a member of the community.

Avenues of Service

Those of the Bahá'í Faith place a high value on service to humanity, considering it an act of worship. This can be done through caring for one's own family or through one's choice of vocation. Within the local community, people may teach classes for children, mentor youth groups, host devotional programs, or teach adult study circles. Many are engaged in economic or social development programs as well. Although not mandated, a year or two of service is often undertaken following high school or during college.

United Nations Involvement

Beginning in 1947, just one year after the United Nations (UN) first met, the Bahá'í Faith was represented at that body. In 1948, the Bahá'í International Community was accredited by the UN as an international nongovernmental organization (NGO). In 1970, the faith received special consultative status with the UN Economic and Social Council (ECOSOC). Following World War I, a Bahá'í office opened in Geneva, Switzerland, where the League of Nations was headquartered. Thus the Bahá'í Faith has a long tradition of supporting global institutions.

Money Matters

The International Bahá'í Fund exists to develop and support the growth of the faith, and the Universal House of Justice oversees the distribution of the money. Contributions are also used to maintain the Bahá'í World Center. No money is accepted from non-Bahá'í sources. National and local funds, administered by National or Local Spiritual Assemblies, are used in supporting service projects, publishing endeavors, schools, and Bahá'í centers. For the Bahá'í, the size of the donation is less important than regular contributions and the spirit of sacrifice behind them.

Food Restrictions

Bahá'í between fifteen and seventy years of age **fast** nineteen days a year, abstaining from food and drink from sunrise to sunset. Fasting occurs the first day of each month of the Bahá'í calendar, which divides the year into nineteen months of nineteen days each. The Bahá'í faithful do not drink alcohol or use narcotics, because these will deaden the mind with repeated use.

Rites, Celebrations & Services

Daily prayer and meditation is recommended in the Bahá'í faith. During services there are mediations and prayers, along with the reading of Bahá'í scriptures and other world faith traditions. There is no set ritual, no offerings, and no sermons. Unaccompanied by musical instruments, choirs also sing. Light refreshments may be served afterwards.

Bahá'í place great stress on marriage, the only state in which sex is permitted. Referred to as "a fortress for well-being and salvation," a monogamous, heterosexual marriage is the ideal. To express the oneness of humanity, interracial marriages are encouraged. After obtaining the consent of their parents, the couple takes the following vow: "We will all, verily, abide by the will of God." The remainder of the service may be individually crafted and may also include dance, music, feasting, and ceremony. Should a couple choose to end a marriage, they must first complete a year of living apart while trying to reconcile differences. Divorce is discouraged, but permitted after that initial year.

Judy A. Johnson, MTS

Bibliography

Albertson, Lorelei. *All about Bahá'í Faith*. University Pub., 2012. E-book.

Bowers, Kenneth E. *God Speaks Again: an Introduction to the Bahá'í Faith*. Wilmette: Bahá'í, 2004. Print.

Buck, Christopher. "The Interracial 'Bahá'í Movement' and the Black Intelligentsia: The Case of W. E. B. Du Bois." *Journal of Religious History* 36.4 (2012): 542–62. Print.

Cederquist, Druzelle. *The Story of Baha'u'llah*. Wilmette: Bahá'í, 2005. Print.

Echevarria, L. *Life Stories of Bahá'í Women in Canada: Constructing Religious Identity in the Twentieth Century*. Lang, 2011. E-book.

Garlington, William. *The Bahá'í Faith in America*. Lanham: Rowman, 2008. Print.

Hartz, Paula R. *Bahá'í Faith*. New York: Facts on File, 2006. Print.

Hatcher, William S. and J. Douglas Martin. *The Bahá'í Faith: The Emerging Global Religion*. Wilmette: Bahá'í, 2002. Print.

Karlberg, Michael. "Constructive Resilience: The Bahá'í Response to Oppression." *Peace & Change* 35.2 (2010): 222–57. Print.

Lee, Anthony A. *The Bahá'í Faith in Africa: Establishing a New Religious Movement, 1952–1962*. Brill NV, E-book.

Momen, Moojan. "Bahá'í Religious History." *Journal of Religious History* 36.4 (2012): 463–70. Print.

Momen, Moojan. *The Bahá'í Faith: A Beginner's Guide*. Oxford: Oneworld, 2007. Print.

Smith, Peter. *The Bahá'í Faith*. Cambridge: Cambridge UP, 2008. Print.

Wilkinson, Philip. *Religions*. New York: DK, 2008. Print.

Buddhism

General Description

Buddhism has three main branches: Theravada (Way of the Elders), also referred to as Hinayana (Lesser Vehicle); Mahayana (Greater Vehicle); and Vajrayana (Diamond Vehicle), also referred to as Tantric Buddhism. Vajrayana is sometimes thought of as an extension of Mahayana Buddhism. These can be further divided into many sects and schools, many of which are geographically based. In Buddhism, these different divisions or schools are regarded as alternative paths to enlightenment (Wilkinson 2008).

Number of Adherents Worldwide

An estimated 474 million people around the world are Buddhists. Of the major sects, Theravada Buddhism is the oldest, developed in the sixth century BCE. Its adherents include those of the Theravada Forest Tradition. From Mahayana Buddhism, which developed in the third to second centuries BCE, came several offshoots based on location. In what is now China, Pure Land Buddhism and Tibetan Buddhism developed in the seventh century. In Japan, Zen Buddhism developed in the twelfth century, Nichiren Buddhism developed a century later, and Soka Gakkai was founded in 1937. In California during the 1970s, the Serene Reflection Meditation began as a subset of Sōtō Zen. In Buddhism, these different divisions or schools are regarded as alternative paths to enlightenment.

Basic Tenets

Buddhists hold to the Three Universal Truths: impermanence, the lack of self, and suffering. These truths encompass the ideas that everything is impermanent and changing and that life is not satisfying because of its impermanence and the temporary nature of all things, including contentment. Buddhism also teaches the Four Noble Truths: All life is suffering (Dukkha). Desire and attachment cause suffering (Samudaya). Ceasing to desire or crave conceptual attachment

ends suffering and leads to release (Nirodha). This release comes through following the Noble Eightfold Path—right understanding (or view), right intention, right speech, right conduct, right occupation, right effort, right mindfulness, and right concentration (Magga).

Although Buddhists do not believe in an afterlife as such, the soul undergoes a cycle of death and rebirth. Following the Noble Eightfold Path leads to the accumulation of good karma, allowing one to be reborn at a higher level. Karma is the Buddhist belief in cause-effect relationships; actions taken in one life have consequences in the next. Ultimately, many refer to the cessation or elimination of suffering as the primary goal of Buddhism.

Buddhists do not believe in gods. Salvation is to be found in following the teachings of Buddha, which are called the Dharma (law or truth). Buddhism does have saint-like bodhisattvas (enlightened beings) who reject ultimate enlightenment (Nirvana) for themselves to aid others.

Sacred Text

Buddhism has nothing comparable to the Qur'an (Islam's holy book) or the Bible. For Theravada Buddhists, an important text is the Pāli Canon, the collection of Buddha's teachings. Mahayana Buddhists recorded their version of these as sutras, many of them in verse. The Lotus Sutra is among the most important. The Buddhist scriptures are written in two languages of ancient India, Pali and Sanskrit, depending on the tradition in which they were developed. Some of these words, such as karma, have been transliterated into English and gained common usage.

Major Figures

Siddhartha Gautama (ca. 563 to 483 BCE) is the founder of Buddhism and regarded as the Buddha or Supreme Buddha. He is the most highly regarded historical figure in Buddhism.

He had two principle disciples: Sariputta and Mahamoggallana (or Maudgalyayana). In contemporary Buddhism, the fourteenth Dalai Lama, Tenzin Gyatso, is a significant person. Both he and Aung San Suu Kyi, a Buddhist of Myanmar who was held as a political prisoner for her stand against the oppressive regime of that nation, have been awarded the Nobel Peace Prize.

Major Holy Sites

Buddhist holy sites are located in several places in Asia. All of those directly related to the life of Siddhartha Gautama are located in the northern part of India near Nepal. Lumbini Grove is noted as the birthplace of the Buddha. He received enlightenment at Bodh Gaya and first began to teach in Sarnath. Kusinara is the city where he died.

In other Asian nations, some holy sites were once dedicated to other religions. Angkor Wat in Cambodia, for example, was constructed for the Hindu god Vishnu in the twelfth century CE. It became a Buddhist temple three hundred years later. It was once the largest religious monument in the world and still attracts visitors. In Java's central highlands sits Borobudur, the world's largest Buddhist shrine. The name means "Temple of Countless Buddhas." Its five terraces represent what must be overcome to reach enlightenment: worldly desires, evil intent, malicious joy, laziness, and doubt. It was built in the eighth and ninth centuries CE, only to fall into neglect at about the turn of the millennium; it was rediscovered in 1815. The complex has three miles of carvings illustrating the life and teachings of the Buddha. In Sri Lanka, the Temple of the Tooth, which houses what is believed to be one of the Buddha's teeth, is a popular pilgrimage site.

Some of the holy sites incorporate gifts of nature. China has four sacred Buddhist mountains, symbolizing the four corners of the universe. These mountains—Wŭtái Shān, Émái Shān, Jiŭhuá Shān, and Pŭtuó Shān—are believed to be the homes of bodhisattvas. In central India outside Fardapur, there are twenty-nine caves carved into the granite, most of them with frescoes based on the Buddha's life. Ajanta, as

the site is known, was created between 200 BCE and the fifth century CE. Five of the caves house temples.

The Buddha's birthday, his day of death, and the day of his enlightenment are all celebrated, either as one day or several. Different traditions and countries have their own additional celebrations, including Sri Lanka's Festival of the Tooth. Buddhists have a lunar calendar, and four days of each month are regarded as holy days.

ORIGINS

History & Geography

Buddhism began in what is now southern Nepal and northern India with the enlightenment of the Buddha. Following his death, members of the sangha, or community, spread the teachings across northern India. The First Buddhist Council took place in 486 BCE at Rajagaha. This council settled the Buddhist canon, the Tipitaka. In 386 BCE, a little more than a century after the Buddha died, a second Buddhist Council was held at Vesali. It was at this meeting that the two major schools of Buddhist thought—Theravada and Mahayana—began to differ.

Emperor Asoka, who ruled most of the Indian subcontinent from around 268 to 232 BCE, converted to Buddhism. He sent missionaries across India and into central parts of Asia. He also set up pillars with Buddhist messages in his own efforts to establish "true dharma" in the kingdom, although he did not create a state church. His desire for his subjects to live contently in this life led to promoting trade, maintaining canals and reservoirs, and the founding a system of medical care for both humans and animals. Asoka's son Mahinda went to southern Indian and to Sri Lanka with the message of Buddhism.

Asoka's empire fell shortly after his death. Under the following dynasties, evidence suggests Buddhists in India experienced persecution. The religion continued to grow, however, and during the first centuries CE, monasteries and monuments were constructed with support from local rulers. Some additional support came from women within the royal courts. Monastic centers also grew in number. By the fourth century CE, Buddhism had become one of the chief religious traditions in India.

During the Gupta dynasty, which lasted from about 320 to 600 CE, Buddhists and Hindus began enriching each other's traditions. Some Hindus felt that the Buddha was an incarnation of Vishnu, a Hindu god. Some Buddhists showed respect for Hindu deities.

Also during this era, Mahavihara, the concept of the "Great Monastery," came to be. These institutions served as universities for the study and development of Buddhist thinking. Some of them also included cultural and scientific study in the curriculum.

Traders and missionaries took the ideas of Buddhism to China. By the first century CE, Buddhism was established in that country. The religion died out or was absorbed into Hinduism in India. By the seventh century, a visiting Chinese monk found that Huns had invaded India from Central Asia and destroyed many Buddhist monasteries. The religion revived and flourished in the northeast part of India for several centuries.

Muslim invaders reached India in the twelfth and thirteenth centuries. They sacked the monasteries, some of which had grown very wealthy. Some even paid workers to care for both the land they owned and the monks, while some had indentured slaves. Because Buddhism had become monastic rather than a religion of the laity, there was no groundswell for renewal following the Muslim invasion.

Prominent in eastern and Southeast Asia, Buddhism is the national religion in some countries. For example, in Thailand, everyone learns about Buddhism in school. Buddhism did not begin to reach Western culture until the nineteenth century, when the Lotus Sutra was translated into German. The first Buddhist temple in the United States was built in 1853 in San Francisco's Chinatown.

Chinese Communists took control of Tibet in 1950. Nine years later, the fourteenth Dalai Lama left for India, fearing persecution. The Dalai Lama is considered a living teacher (lama) who is to instruct others. (The term *dalai* means "great as the ocean.") In 1989, he received the Nobel Peace Prize.

Buddhism experienced a revival in India during the twentieth century. Although some of this new beginning was due in part to Tibetan immigrants seeking safety, a mass conversion in 1956 was the major factor. The year was chosen to honor the 2,500th anniversary of the Buddha's death year. Buddhism was chosen as an alternative to the strict caste structure of Hinduism, and hundreds of thousands of people of the Dalit caste, once known as untouchables, converted in a ceremony held in Nagpur.

Founder or Major Prophet

Siddhartha Gautama, who became known as the "Enlightened One," or Buddha, was a prince in what is now southern Nepal, but was then northern India during the sixth century BCE. The name Siddhartha means "he who achieves his aim." He was a member of the Sakya tribe of Nepal, belonging to the warrior caste. Many legends have grown around his birth and early childhood. One states that he was born in a grove in the woods, emerging from his mother's side able to walk and completely clean.

During Siddhartha's childhood, a Brahmin, or wise man, prophesied that he would grow to be a prince or a religious teacher who would help others overcome suffering. Because the life of a sage involved itinerant begging, the king did not want this life for his child. He kept Siddhartha in the palace and provided him with all the luxuries of his position, including a wife, Yashodhara. They had a son, Rahula.

Escaping from the palace at about the age of thirty, Gautama first encountered suffering in the form of an old man with a walking stick. The following day, he saw a man who was ill. On the third day, he witnessed a funeral procession. Finally he met a monk, who had nothing, but who radiated happiness. He determined to leave his privileged life, an act called the Great Renunciation. Because hair was a sign of vanity in his time, he shaved his head. He looked for enlightenment via an ascetic life of little food or sleep. He followed this path for six years, nearly starving to death. Eventually, he determined on a Middle Way, a path neither luxurious as he had known in the palace, nor ascetic as he had attempted.

After three days and nights of meditating under a tree at Bodh Gaya, Siddhartha achieved his goal of enlightenment, or Nirvana. He escaped fear of suffering and death.

The Buddha began his preaching career, which spanned some forty years, following his enlightenment. He gave his first sermon in northeast India at Sarnath in a deer park. The first five followers became the first community, or sangha. Buddha died around age eighty, in 483 BCE after he had eaten poisoned food. After warning his followers not to eat the food, he meditated until he died.

Buddhists believe in many enlightened ones. Siddhartha is in one tradition regarded as the fourth buddha, while other traditions hold him to have been the seventh or twenty-fifth buddha.

His disciples, who took the ideas throughout India, repeated his teachings. When the later Buddhists determined to write down the teachings of the Buddha, they met to discuss the ideas and agreed that a second meeting should occur in a century. At the third council, which was held at Pataliputta, divisions occurred. The two major divisions—Theravada and Mahayana—differ over the texts to be used and the interpretation of the teachings. Theravada can be translated as "the Teachings of the Elders," while Mahayana means "Great Vehicle."

Theravada Buddhists believe that only monks can achieve enlightenment through the teachings of another buddha, or enlightened being. Thus they try to spend some part of their lives in a monastery. Buddhists in the Mahayana tradition, on the other hand, feel that all people can achieve enlightenment, without being in a monastery. Mahayanans also regard some as bodhisattvas, people who have achieved the enlightened state but renounce Nirvana to help others achieve it.

Philosophical Basis

During Siddhartha's lifetime, Hinduism was the predominant religion in India. Many people, especially in northern India, were dissatisfied with the rituals and sacrifices of that religion. In addition, as many small kingdoms expanded and the unity of the tribes began to break down, many people were in religious turmoil and doubt. A number of sects within Hinduism developed.

The Hindu belief in the cycle of death and rebirth led some people to despair because they could not escape from suffering in their lives. Siddhartha was trying to resolve the suffering he saw in the world, but many of his ideas came from the Brahmin sect of Hinduism, although he reinterpreted them. Reincarnation, dharma, and reverence for cows are three of the ideas that carried over into Buddhism.

In northeast India at Bodh Gaya, he rested under a bodhi tree, sometimes called a bo tree. He meditated there until he achieved Nirvana, or complete enlightenment, derived from the freedom of fear that attached to suffering and death. As a result of his being enlightened, he was known as Buddha, a Sanskrit word meaning "awakened one." Wanting to help others, he began teaching his Four Noble Truths, along with the Noble Eightfold Path that would lead people to freedom from desire and suffering. He encouraged his followers to take Triple Refuge in the Three Precious Jewels: the Buddha, the teachings, and the sangha, or monastic community. Although at first Buddha was uncertain about including women in a sangha, his mother-in-law begged for the privilege.

Greed, hatred, and ignorance were three traits that Buddha felt people needed to conquer. All three create craving, the root of suffering. Greed and ignorance lead to a desire for things that are not needed, while hatred leads to a craving to destroy the hated object or person.

To the Four Noble Truths and Eightfold Path, early devotees of Buddhism added the Five Moral Precepts. These are to avoid taking drugs and alcohol, engaging in sexual misconduct, harming others, stealing, and lying.

The precepts of the Buddha were not written down for centuries. The first text did not appear for more than 350 years after the precepts were first spoken. One collection from Sri Lanka written in Pāli during the first century BCE is known as Three Baskets, or Tipitaka. The three baskets include Buddha's teaching (the Basket of Discourse), commentary on the sayings (the Basket of Special Doctrine), and the rules for monks to follow (the Basket of Discipline). The name Three Baskets refers to the fact that the sayings were first written on leaves from a palm tree that were then collected in baskets.

Holy Places

Buddhists make pilgrimages to places that relate to important events in Siddhartha's life. While Lumbini Grove, the place of Siddhartha's birth, is a prominent pilgrimage site, the primary site for pilgrimage is Bodh Gaya, the location where Buddha received enlightenment. Other pilgrimage sites include Sarnath, the deer park located in what is now Varanasi (Benares) where the Buddha first began to teach, and Kusinara, the city where he died. All of these are in the northern part of India near Nepal.

Other sites in Asia that honor various bodhisattvas have also become pilgrimage destinations. Mountains are often chosen; there are four in China, each with monasteries and temples built on them. In Japan, the Shikoku pilgrimage covers more than 700 miles and involves visits to eighty-eight temples along the route.

BUDDHISM IN DEPTH

Sacred Symbols

Many stylized statue poses of the Buddha exist, each with a different significance. One, in which the Buddha has both hands raised, palms facing outward, commemorates the calming of an elephant about to attack the Buddha. If only the right hand is raised, the hand symbolizes friendship and being unafraid. The teaching gesture is that of a hand with the thumb and first finger touching.

In Tibetan Buddhism, the teachings of Buddha regarding the cycle of rebirth are symbolized in the six-spoke wheel of life. One may be reborn into any of the six realms of life: hell, hungry spirits, warlike demons called Asuras, animals, humans, or gods. Another version of the wheel has eight spokes rather than six, to represent the Noble Eightfold Path. Still another wheel has twelve spokes, signifying both the Four Noble Truths and the Noble Eightfold Path.

Tibetan Buddhists have prayer beads similar to a rosary, with 108 beads representing the number of desires to be overcome prior to reaching enlightenment. The worshipper repeats the Triple Refuge—Buddha, dharma, and sangha—or a mantra.

The prayer wheel is another device that Tibetan Buddhists use. Inside the wheel is a roll of paper on which the sacred mantra—Hail to the jewel in the lotus—is written many times. The lotus is a symbol of growing spiritually; it grows in muddied waters, but with the stems and flowers, it reaches toward the sun. By turning the wheel and spinning the mantra, the practitioner spreads blessings. Bells may be rung to wake the hearer out of ignorance.

In Tantric Buddhism, the mandala, or circle, serves as a map of the entire cosmos. Mandalas may be made of colored grains of sand, carved or painted. They are used to help in meditation and are thought to have a spiritual energy.

Buddhism recognizes Eight Auspicious Symbols, including the banner, conch shell, fish, knot, lotus, treasure vase, umbrella, and wheel. Each has a particular significance. A conch shell, for example, is often blown to call worshippers to meetings. Because its sound travels far, it signifies the voice of Buddha traveling throughout the world. Fish are fertility symbols because they have thousands of offspring. In Buddhist imagery, they are often in facing pairs and fashioned of gold. The lotus represents spiritual growth, rooted in muddy water but flowering toward the sun. The umbrella symbolizes protection, because servants once used them to protect royalty from both sun and rain.

Sacred Practices & Gestures

Two major practices characterize Buddhism: gift-giving and showing respect to images and relics of the Buddha. The first is the transaction between laity and monks in which laypersons present sacrificial offerings to the monks, who in return share their higher state of spiritual being with the laity. Although Buddhist monks are permitted to own very little, they each have a begging bowl, which is often filled with rice.

Buddhists venerate statues of the Buddha, bodhisattvas, and saints; they also show respect to his relics, housed in stupas. When in the presence of a statue of the Buddha, worshippers have a series of movements they repeat three times, thus dedicating their movements to the Triple Refuge. It begins with a dedicated body: placing hands together with the palms cupped slightly and fingers touching, the devotee raises the hands to the forehead. The second step symbolizes right speech by lowering the hands to just below the mouth. In the third movement, the hands are lowered to the front of the chest, indicating that heart—and by extension, mind—are also dedicated to the Triple Refuge. The final movement is prostration. The devotee first gets on all fours, then lowers either the entire body to the floor or lowers the head, so that there are five points of contact with the floor.

Statues of the Buddha give a clue to the gestures held important to his followers. The gesture of turning the hand towards the ground indicates that one is observing Earth. Devotees assume a lotus position, with legs crossed, when in meditation.

Allowing the left hand to rest in the lap and the right hand to point down to Earth is a gesture used in meditation. Another common gesture is to touch thumb and fingertips together while the palms of both hands face up, thus forming a flat triangular shape. The triangle signifies the Three Jewels of Buddhism.

Food Restrictions

Buddhism does not require one to be a vegetarian. Many followers do not eat meat, however, because to do so involves killing other creatures. Both monks and laypersons may choose not to eat after noontime during the holy days of each month.

Rites, Celebrations, & Services

Ancient Buddhism recognized four holy days each month, known as *uposatha*. These days included the full moon and new moon days of each lunar month, as well as the eighth day after each of these moons appeared. Both monks and members of the laity have special religious duties during these four days. A special service takes place in which flowers are offered to images of the Buddha, precepts are repeated, and a sermon is preached. On these four days, an additional three precepts may be undertaken along with the five regularly observed. The three extra duties are to refrain from sleeping on a luxurious bed, eating any food after noon, and adorning the body or going to entertainments.

In Theravada nations, three major life events of the Buddha—birth, enlightenment, and entering nirvana—are celebrated on Vesak, or Buddha Day. In temples, statues of Buddha as a child are ceremonially cleaned. Worshippers may offer incense and flowers. To symbolize the Buddha's enlightenment, lights may be illuminated in trees and temples. Because it is a day of special kindness, some people in Thailand refrain from farm work that could harm living creatures. They may also seek special merit by freeing captive animals.

Other Buddhist nations that follow Mahayana Buddhism commemorate these events on three different days. In Japan, Hana Matsuri is the celebration of Buddha's birth. On that day, people create paper flower gardens to recall the gardens of Lumbini, Siddhartha's birthplace. Worshippers also pour perfumed tea over statues of Buddha; this is because, according to tradition, the gods provided scented water for Siddhartha's first bath.

Poson is celebrated in Sri Lanka to honor the coming of Buddhism during the reign of Emperor Asoka. Other holy persons are also celebrated in the countries where they had the greatest influence. In Tibet, for instance, the arrival of

Padmasambhava, who brought Buddhism to that nation, is observed.

Buddhists also integrate their own special celebrations into regular harvest festivals and New Year activities. These festivities may include a performance of an event in the life of any buddha or bodhisattva. For example, troupes of actors in Tibet specialize in enacting Buddhist legends. The festival of the Sacred Tooth is held in Kandy, Sri Lanka. According to one legend, a tooth of Buddha has been recovered, and it is paraded through the streets on this day. The tooth has been placed in a miniature stupa, or sealed mound, which is carried on an elephant's back.

Protection rituals have been common in Buddhism from earliest days. They may be public rituals meant to avoid a collective danger, such as those held in Sri Lanka and other Southeast Asia nations. Or they may be designed for private use. The role of these rituals is greater in Mahayana tradition, especially in Tibet. Mantras are chanted for this reason.

Customs surrounding death and burial differ between traditions and nations. A common factor, however, is the belief that the thoughts of a person at death are significant. This period may be extended for three days following death, due to a belief in consciousness for that amount of time after death. To prepare the mind of the dying, another person may read sacred texts aloud.

Judy A. Johnson, MTS

Bibliography

Armstrong, Karen. *Buddha*. New York: Penguin, 2001. Print.

Barnes, Trevor. *The Kingfisher Book of Religions*. New York: Kingfisher, 1999. Print.

Chodron, Thubten. *Buddhism for Beginners*. Ithaca: Snow Lion, 2001. Print.

Eckel, Malcolm David. *Buddhism*. Oxford: Oxford UP, 2002. Print.

Epstein, Ron. "Application of Buddhist Teachings in Modern Life." *Religion East & West* Oct. 2012: 52–61. Print.

Harding, John S. *Studying Buddhism in Practice*. Routledge, 2012. E-book. Studying Religions in Practice.

Harvey, Peter. *An Introduction to Buddhism: Teachings, History and Practices*. 2nd ed. Cambridge UP, 2013. E-book.

Heirman, Ann. "Buddhist Nuns: Between Past and Present." *International Review for the History of Religions* 58.5/6 (2011): 603–31. Print.

Langley, Myrtle. *Religion*. New York: Knopf, 1996. Print.

Low, Kim Cheng Patrick. "Three Treasures of Buddhism & Leadership Insights." *Culture & Religion Review Journal* 2012.3 (2012): 66–72. Print.

Low, Patrick Kim Cheng. "Leading Change, the Buddhist Perspective." *Culture & Religion Review Journal* 2012.1 (2012): 127–45. Print.

McMahan, David L. *Buddhism in the Modern World*. Routledge, 2012. E-book.

Meredith, Susan. *The Usborne Book of World Religions*. London: Usborne, 1995. Print.

Morgan, Diane. *Essential Buddhism: A Comprehensive Guide to Belief and Practice*. Praeger, 2010. E-book.

Wilkinson, Philip. *Buddhism*. New York: DK, 2003.Print.

Wilkinson, Philip. *Religions*. New York: DK, 2008. Print.

Christianity

General Description

Christianity is one of the world's major religions. It is based on the life and teachings of Jesus of Nazareth, called the Christ, or anointed one. It is believed that there are over thirty thousand denominations or sects of Christianity worldwide. Generally, most of these sects fall under the denominational families of Catholicism, Protestant, and Orthodox. (Anglican and Oriental Orthodox are sometimes added as separate branches.) Most denominations have developed since the seventeenth-century Protestant Reformation.

Number of Adherents Worldwide

Over 2.3 billion people around the world claim allegiance to Christianity in one of its many forms. The three major divisions are Roman Catholicism, Eastern Orthodox, and Protestant. Within each group are multiple denominations. Roman Catholics number more than 1.1 billion followers, while the Eastern Orthodox Church has between 260 and 278 million adherents. An estimated 800 million adherents follow one of the various Protestant denominations, including Anglican, Baptist, Lutheran, Presbyterian, and Methodist. Approximately 1 percent of Christians, or 28 million adherents, do not belong to one of the three major divisions

There are a number of other groups, such as the Amish, with an estimated 249,000 members, and the Quakers, numbering approximately 377,000. Both of these churches—along with Mennonites, who number 1.7 million—are in the peace tradition (their members are conscientious objectors). Pentecostals have 600 million adherents worldwide. Other groups that are not always considered Christian by more conservative groups include Jehovah's Witnesses (7.6 million) and Mormons (13 million) (Wilkinson, p. 104-121).

Basic Tenets

The summaries of the Christian faith are found in the Apostles Creed and Nicene Creed.

In addition, some churches have developed their own confessions of faith, such as Lutheranism's Augsburg Confession. Christianity is a monotheistic tradition, although most Christians believe in the Trinity, defined as one God in three separate but equal persons—Father, Son, and Holy Spirit. More modern, gender-neutral versions of the Trinitarian formula may refer to Creator, Redeemer, and Sanctifier. Many believe in the doctrine of original sin, which means that the disobedience of Adam and Eve in the Garden of Eden has been passed down through all people; because of this sin, humankind is in need of redemption. Jesus Christ was born, lived a sinless life, and then was crucified and resurrected as a substitute for humankind. Those who accept this sacrifice for sin will receive eternal life in a place of bliss after death. Many Christians believe that a Second Coming of Jesus will inaugurate a millennial kingdom and a final judgment (in which people will be judged according to their deeds and their eternal souls consigned to heaven or hell), as well as a resurrected physical body.

Sacred Text

The Bible is the sacred text of Christianity, which places more stress on the New Testament. The canon of the twenty-six books of the New Testament was finally determined in the latter half of the fourth century CE.

Major Figures

Christianity is based on the life and teachings of Jesus of Nazareth. His mother, Mary, is especially revered in Roman Catholicism and the Eastern Orthodox tradition, where she is known as Theotokos (God-bearer). Jesus spread his teachings through the twelve apostles, or disciples, who he himself chose and named. Paul (Saint Paul or Paul the Apostle), who became the first missionary to the Gentiles—and whose writings comprise a bulk of the New Testament—is a key figure for the theological treatises embedded in his letters to early churches. His conversion occurred after Jesus' crucifixion. All of these figures are biblically represented.

Under the Emperor Constantine, Christianity went from a persecuted religion to the state religion. Constantine also convened the Council of Nicea in 325 CE, which expressed the formula defining Jesus as fully God and fully human. Saint Augustine (354–430) was a key thinker of the early church who became the Bishop of Hippo in North Africa. He outlined the principles of just war and expressed the ideas of original sin. He also suggested what later became the Catholic doctrine of purgatory.

In the sixth century, Saint Benedict inscribed a rule for monks that became a basis for monastic life. Martin Luther, the monk who stood against the excesses of the Roman Catholic Church, ignited the seventeenth-century Protestant Reformation. He proclaimed that salvation came by grace alone, not through works. In the twentieth century, Pope John XXIII convened the Vatican II Council, or Second Vatican Council, which made sweeping changes to the liturgy and daily practice for Roman Catholics.

Major Holy Sites

The key events in the life of Jesus Christ occurred in the region of Palestine. Bethlehem is honored as the site of Jesus's birth; Jerusalem is especially revered as the site of Jesus's crucifixion. The capital of the empire, Rome, also became the center of Christianity until the Emperor Constantine shifted the focus to Constantinople. Rome today is the seat of the Vatican, an independent city-state that houses the government of the Roman Catholic Church. Canterbury, the site of the martyrdom of Saint Thomas Becket and seat of the archbishop of the Anglican Communion, is a pilgrimage site for Anglicans. There are also many pilgrimage sites, such as Compostela and Lourdes, for other branches of Christianity. In Ethiopia, Lalibela is the site of eleven churches carved from stone during the twelfth century. The site serves as a profound testimony to the vibrancy of the Christian faith in Africa.

Major Rites & Celebrations

The first rite of the church is baptism, a water-related ritual that is traditionally administered to infants or adults alike through some variant of sprinkling or immersion. Marriage is another rite of the church. Confession is a major part of life for Roman Catholics, although the idea is also present in other branches of Christianity.

The celebration of the Eucharist, or Holy Communion, is a key part of weekly worship for the liturgical churches such as those in the Roman Catholic or Anglican traditions. Nearly all Christians worship weekly on Sunday; services include readings of scripture, a sermon, singing of hymns, and may include Eucharist. Christians honor the birth of Jesus at Christmas and his death and resurrection at Easter. Easter is often considered the most significant liturgical feast, particularly in Orthodox branches.

Many Christians follow a calendar of liturgical seasons. Of these seasons, perhaps the best known is Lent, which is immediately preceded by Shrove Tuesday, also known as Mardi Gras. Lent is traditionally a time of fasting and self-examination in preparation for the Easter feast. Historically, Christians gave up rich foods. The day before Lent was a time for pancakes—to use up the butter and eggs—from which the term Mardi Gras (Fat Tuesday) derives. Lent begins with Ash Wednesday, when Christians are marked with the sign of the cross on their foreheads using ashes, a reminder that they are dust and will return to dust.

ORIGINS

History & Geography

Christianity was shaped in the desert and mountainous landscapes of Palestine, known as the Holy Land. Jesus was driven into the wilderness following his baptism, where he remained for forty days of fasting and temptation. The Gospels record that he often went to the mountains for solitude and prayer. The geography of the deserts and mountains also shaped early Christian spirituality, as men and women went into solitude to pray, eventually founding small communities of the so-called desert fathers and mothers.

Christianity at first was regarded as a sect within Judaism, though it differentiated itself early in the first century CE by breaking with the code of laws that defined Judaism, including the need for circumcision and ritual purity. Early Christianity then grew through the missionary work of the apostles, particularly Paul the Apostle, who traveled throughout the Mediterranean world and beyond the Roman Empire to preach the gospel (good news) of Jesus. (This is often called the Apostolic Age.)

Persecution under various Roman emperors only served to strengthen the emerging religion. In the early fourth century, the Emperor Constantine (ca. 272-337) made Christianity the official religion of the Roman Empire. He also convened the Council of Nicea in 325 CE to quell the religious controversies threatening the Pax Romana (Roman Peace), a time of stability and peace throughout the empire in the first and second centuries.

In 1054 the Great Schism, which involved differences over theology and practice, split the church into Eastern Orthodox and Roman Catholic branches. As Islam grew stronger, the Roman Catholic nations of Europe entered a period of Crusades—there were six Crusades in approximately 175 years, from 1095-1271—that attempted to take the Holy Land out of Muslim control.

A number of theologians became unhappy with the excesses of the Roman church and papal authority during the fifteenth and sixteenth centuries. The Protestant Reformation, originally an attempt to purify the church, was led by several men, most notably Martin Luther (1483-1546), whose ninety-five theses against the Catholic Church sparked the Reformation movement. Other leaders of the Protestant Reformation include John Knox (ca. 1510-1572), attributed as the founder of the Presbyterian denomination, John Calvin (1509-1564), a principle early developer of Calvinism, and Ulrich Zwingli (1484-1531), who initially spurred the Reformation in Switzerland. This period of turmoil resulted in the founding of a number of church denominations: Lutherans, Presbyterians, and Anglicans. These groups were later joined by the Methodists and the Religious Society of Friends (Quakers).

During the sixteenth and seventeenth centuries, the Roman Catholic Church attempted to stem this wave of protest and schism with the Counter-Reformation. Concurrently, the Inquisition, an effort to root out heresy and control the rebellion, took place. There were various inquisitions, including the Spanish Inquisition, which was led by Ferdinand II of Aragon and Isabella I of Castile in mid-fifteenth century and sought to "guard" the orthodoxy of Catholicism in Spain. There was also the Portuguese Inquisition, which began in 1536 in Portugal under King John III, and the Roman Inquisition, which took place in the late fifteenth century in Rome under the Holy See.

During the modern age, some groups became concerned with the perceived conflicts between history (revealed through recent archaeological findings) and the sciences (as described by Charles Darwin and Sigmund Freud) and the literal interpretation of some biblical texts. Fundamentalist Christianity began at an 1895 meeting in Niagara Falls, New York, with an attempt to define the basics (fundamentals) of Christianity. These were given as the inerrant nature of the Bible, the divine nature of Jesus, his literal virgin birth, his substitutionary death and literal physical resurrection, and his soon return. Liberal Christians, on the other hand, focused more on what became known as the Social Gospel, an attempt to relieve human misery.

Controversies in the twenty-first century throughout Christendom focused on issues such as abortion, homosexuality, the ordination of women and gays, and the authority of the scriptures. An additional feature is the growth of Christianity in the Southern Hemisphere. In Africa, for example, the number of Christians grew from 10 million in 1900 to over 506 million a century later. Initially the result of empire-building and colonialism, the conversions in these nations have resulted in a unique blend of native religions and Christianity. Latin America has won renown for its liberation theology, which was first articulated in 1968 as God's call for justice and God's preference for the poor, demonstrated in the ministry and teachings of Jesus Christ. Africa, Asia, and South America are regions that are considered more morally and theologically conservative. Some suggest that by 2050, non-Latino white persons will comprise only 20 percent of Christians.

Founder or Major Prophet

Jesus of Nazareth was born into a peasant family. The date of his birth, determined by accounts in the Gospels of Matthew and Luke, could be as early as 4 or 5 BCE or as late as 6 CE. Mary, his mother, was regarded as a virgin; thus, Jesus' birth was a miracle, engendered by the Holy Spirit. His earthly father, Joseph, was a carpenter.

At about age thirty, Jesus began an itinerant ministry of preaching and healing following his baptism in the Jordan River by his cousin, John the Baptist. He selected twelve followers, known as apostles (sent-ones), and a larger circle of disciples (followers). Within a short time, Jesus' ministry and popularity attracted the negative attention of both the Jewish and Roman rulers. He offended the Jewish leaders with his emphasis on personal relationship with God rather than obedience to rules, as well as his claim to be coequal with God the Father.

For a period of one to three years (Gospel accounts vary in the chronology), Jesus taught and worked miracles, as recorded in the first four books of the New Testament, the Gospels of Matthew, Mark, Luke, and John. On what has become known as Palm Sunday, he rode triumphantly into Jerusalem on the back of a donkey while crowds threw palm branches at his feet. Knowing that his end was near, at a final meal with his disciples, known now to Christians as the Last Supper, Jesus gave final instructions to his followers.

He was subsequently captured, having been betrayed by Judas Iscariot, one of his own twelve apostles. A trial before the Jewish legislative body, the Sanhedrin, led to his being condemned for blasphemy. However, under Roman law, the Jews did not have the power to put anyone to death. A later trial under the Roman governor, Pontius Pilate, resulted in Jesus being crucified, although Pilate tried to prevent this action, declaring Jesus innocent.

According to Christian doctrine, following the crucifixion, Jesus rose from the dead three days later. He appeared before many over a span of forty days and instructed the remaining eleven apostles to continue spreading his teachings. He then ascended into heaven. Ultimately, his followers believed that he was the Messiah, the savior who was to come to the Jewish people and deliver them. Rather than offering political salvation, however, Jesus offered spiritual liberty.

Philosophical Basis

Jesus was a Jew who observed the rituals and festivals of his religion. The Gospels reveal that he attended synagogue worship and went to Jerusalem for celebrations such as Passover. His teachings both grew out of and challenged the religion of his birth.

The Jews of Jesus' time, ruled by the Roman Empire, hoped for a return to political power. This power would be concentrated in a Messiah, whose coming had been prophesied centuries before. There were frequent insurrections in Judea, led in Jesus' time by a group called the Zealots. Indeed, it is believed that one of the twelve apostles was part of this movement. Jesus, with his message of a kingdom of heaven, was viewed as perhaps the one who would usher in a return to political ascendancy.

When challenged to name the greatest commandment, Jesus answered that it was to love God with all the heart, soul, mind, and strength. He added that the second was to love one's neighbor as one's self, saying that these two commands summarized all the laws that the Jewish religion outlined.

Jewish society was concerned with ritual purity and with following the law. Jesus repeatedly flouted those laws by eating with prostitutes and tax collectors, by touching those deemed unclean, such as lepers, and by including

Gentiles in his mission. Women were part of his ministry, with some of them providing for him and his disciples from their own purses, others offering him a home and a meal, and still others among those listening to him teach.

Jesus's most famous sermon is called the Sermon on the Mount. In it, he offers blessings on those on the outskirts of power, such as the poor, the meek, and those who hunger and thirst for righteousness. While not abolishing the law that the Jews followed, he pointed out its inadequacies and the folly of parading one's faith publicly. Embedded in the sermon is what has become known as the Lord's Prayer, the repetition of which is often part of regular Sunday worship. Much of Jesus' teaching was offered in the form of parables, or short stories involving vignettes of everyday life: a woman adding yeast to dough or a farmer planting seeds. Many of these parables were attempts to explain the kingdom of heaven, a quality of life that was both present and to come.

Holy Places

The Christian church has many pilgrimage sites, some of them dating back to the Middle Ages. Saint James is thought to have been buried in Compostela, Spain, which was a destination for those who could not make the trip to the Holy Land. Lourdes, France, is one of the spots associated with healing miracles. Celtic Christians revere places such as the small Scottish isle of Iona, an early Christian mission. Assisi, Italy, is a destination for those who are attracted to Saint Francis (1181-1226), founder of the Franciscans. The Chartres Cathedral in France is another pilgrimage destination from the medieval period.

Jerusalem, Rome, and Canterbury are considered holy for their associations with the early church and Catholicism, as well as with Anglicanism. Within the Old City of Jerusalem is the Church of the Holy Sepulchre, an important pilgrimage site believed to house the burial place of Jesus. Another important pilgrimage site is the Church of the Nativity in Bethlehem. It is built on a cave believed to be the birthplace of Jesus, and is one of the oldest operating churches in existence.

CHRISTIANITY IN DEPTH

Sacred Symbols

The central symbol of Christianity is the cross, of which there are many variant designs. Some of them, such as Celtic crosses, are related to regions of the world. Others, such as the Crusader's cross, honor historic events. The dove is the symbol for the Holy Spirit, which descended in that shape on the gathered disciples at Pentecost after Jesus's ascension.

Various symbols represent Jesus. Candles allude to his reference to himself as the Light of the World, while the lamb stands for his being the perfect sacrifice, the Lamb of God. The fish symbol that is associated with Christianity has a number of meanings, both historic and symbolic. A fish shape stands for the Greek letters beginning the words Jesus Christ, Son of God, Savior; these letters form the word *ichthus*, the Greek word for "fish." Fish also featured prominently in the scriptures, and the early apostles were known as "fishers of man." The crucifixion symbol is also a popular Catholic Christian symbol.

All of these symbols may be expressed in stained glass. Used in medieval times, stained glass often depicted stories from the Bible as an aid to those who were illiterate.

Sacred Practices & Gestures

Roman Catholics honor seven sacraments, defined as outward signs of inward grace. These include the Eucharist, baptism, confirmation, marriage, ordination of priests, anointing the sick or dying with oil, and penance. The Eastern Orthodox Church refers to these seven as mysteries rather than sacraments.

Priests in the Roman Catholic Church must remain unmarried. In the Eastern Orthodox, Anglican, and Protestant denominations, they may marry. Both Roman Catholic and Eastern Orthodox refuse to ordain women to the priesthood.

The Orthodox Church practices a rite known as chrismation, anointing a child with oil following its baptism. The "oil of gladness," as it is known, is placed on the infant's head, eyes, ears, and mouth. This is similar to the practice of confirmation in some other denominations. Many Christian denominations practice anointing the sick or dying with oil, as well as using the oil to seal those who have been baptized.

Many Christians, especially Roman Catholics, use a rosary, or prayer beads, when praying. Orthodox believers may have icons, such as small paintings of God, saints or biblical events, as part of their worship. There may be a font of water that has been blessed as one enters some churches, which the worshippers use to make the sign of the cross, touching fingers to their forehead, heart, right chest, and left chest. Some Christians make the sign of the cross on the forehead, mouth, and heart to signify their desire for God to be in their minds, on their lips, and in their hearts.

Christians may genuflect, or kneel, as they enter or leave a pew in church. In some churches, particularly the Catholic and Orthodox, incense is burned during the service as a sweet smell to God.

In some traditions, praying to or for the dead is encouraged. The rationale for this is known as the communion of saints—the recognition that those who are gone are still a part of the community of faith.

Catholic, Orthodox, and some branches of other churches have monastic orders for both men and women. Monks and nuns may live in a cloister or be engaged in work in the wider world. They generally commit to a rule of life and to the work of prayer. Even those Christians who are not part of religious orders sometimes go on retreats, seeking quiet and perhaps some spiritual guidance from those associated with the monastery or convent.

Food Restrictions
Historically, Christians fasted during Lent as preparation for the Easter celebration. Prior to the Second Vatican Council in 1962,

Roman Catholics did not eat meat on Fridays. Conservative Christians in the Evangelical tradition tend to eliminate the use of alcohol, tobacco, and drugs.

Rites, Celebrations & Services
For churches in the liturgical tradition, the weekly celebration of the Eucharist is paramount. While many churches celebrate this ritual feast with wine and a wafer, many Protestant churches prefer to use grape juice and crackers or bread.

Church services vary widely. Quakers sit silently waiting for a word from God, while in many African American churches, hymns are sung for perhaps an hour before the lengthy sermon is delivered. Some churches have a prescribed order of worship that varies little from week to week. Most services, however, include prayer, a sermon, and singing, with or without musical accompaniment.

A church's architecture often gives clues as to the type of worship one will experience. A church with the pulpit in the center at the front generally is a Protestant church with an emphasis on the Word of God being preached. If the center of the front area is an altar, the worship's focus will be on the Eucharist.

Christmas and Easter are the two major Christian celebrations. In liturgical churches, Christmas is preceded by Advent, a time of preparation and quiet to ready the heart for the coming of Christ. Christmas has twelve days, from the birth date of December 25 to the Epiphany on January 6. Epiphany (to show) is the celebration of the arrival of the Magi (wise men) from the East who came to worship the young Jesus after having seen his star. Their arrival is believed to have been foretold by the Old Testament prophet Isaiah, who said "And the Gentiles shall come to thy light, and kings to the brightness of thy rising" (Isaiah 60:3). Epiphany is the revealing of the Messiah to the Gentiles.

In the early church, Easter was preceded by a solemn period of fasting and examination, especially for candidates for baptism and penitent sinners wishing to be reconciled. In Western churches, Lent begins with Ash Wednesday, which is six and half weeks prior to Easter. By excluding Sundays from the fast, Lent thus gives a forty-day fast, imitating that of Jesus in the wilderness. Historically forbidden foods during the fast included eggs, butter, meat, and fish. In the Eastern Church, dairy products, oil, and wine are also forbidden.

The week before Easter is known as Holy Week. It may include extra services such as Maundy Thursday, a time to remember Jesus's new commandment (*maundy* is etymologically related to *mandate*) to love one another. In some Catholic areas, the crucifixion is reenacted in a Passion play (depicting the passion—trial, suffering, and death—of Christ). Some churches will have an Easter vigil the Saturday night before or a sunrise service on Easter morning.

Judy A. Johnson, MTS

Bibliography

Bakker, Janel Kragt. "The Sister Church Phenomenon: A Case Study of the Restructuring of American Christianity against the Backdrop of Globalization." *International Bulletin of Missionary Research* 36.3 (2012): 129–34. Print.

Bandak, Andreas and Jonas Adelin Jørgensen. "Foregrounds and Backgrounds—Ventures in the Anthropology of Christianity." *Ethos: Journal of Anthropology* 77.4 (2012): 447–58. Print.

Barnes, Trevor. *The Kingfisher Book of Religions*. New York: Kingfisher, 1999. Print.

Chandler, Daniel Ross. "Christianity in Cross-Cultural Perspective: A Review of Recent Literature." *Asia Journal of Theology* 26.2 (2012): 44–57. Print.

Daughrity, Dyron B. "Christianity Is Moving from North to South—So What about the East?" *International Bulletin of Missionary Research* 35.1 (2011): 18–22. Print.

Kaatz, Kevin. *Voices of Early Christianity: Documents from the Origins of Christianity*. Santa Barbara: Greenwood, 2013. E-book.

Langley, Myrtle. *Religion*. New York: Alfred A. Knopf, 1996.

Lewis, Clive Staples. *Mere Christianity*. New York: Harper, 2001. Print.

McGrath, Alistair. *Christianity: An Introduction*. Hoboken, New Jersey: Wiley, 2006. Print.

Meredith, Susan. *The Usborne Book of World Religions*. London: Usborne, 1995. Print.

Ripley, Jennifer S. "Integration of Psychology and Christianity: 2022." *Journal of Psychology & Theology* 40.2 (2012): 150–54. Print.

Stefon, Matt. *Christianity: History, Belief, and Practice*. New York: Britannica Educational, 2012. E-book.

Wilkinson, Philip. *Christianity*. New York: DK, 2003. Print.

Wilkinson, Philip. *Religions*. New York: DK, 2008. Print.

Zoba, Wendy Murray. *The Beliefnet Guide to Evangelical Christianity*. New York: Three Leaves, 2005. Print.

East Asian Religions

General Description

East Asian religious and philosophical traditions include, among others, Confucianism, Taoism, and Shintoism. Confucianism is a philosophy introduced by the Chinese philosopher Confucius (Kongzi; 551–479 BCE) in the sixth century BCE, during the Zhou dynasty. Taoism, which centers on Tao, or "the way," is a religious and philosophical tradition that originated in China about two thousand years ago. Shinto, "the way of the spirits," is a Japanese tradition of devotion to spirits and rituals.

Number of Adherents Worldwide

Between 5 and 6 million people, the majority of them in China, practice Confucianism, once the state religion of China. About 20 million people identify as Taoists. Most of the Taoist practitioners are in China as well. In Japan, approximately 107 million people practice Shintoism, though many practitioners also practice Buddhism. Sects of Shinto include Tenrikyo (heavenly truth), founded in 1838, with nearly 2 million devotees. Shukyo Mahikari (divine light) is another, smaller sect founded in the 1960s. Like other sects, it is a blend of different religious traditions (Wilkinson 332–34).

Basic Tenets

Confucianism is a philosophy of life and does concerns itself not with theology but with life conduct. Chief among the aspects of life that must be tended are five key relationships, with particular focus on honoring ancestors and showing filial piety. Confucianism does not take a stand on the existence of God, though the founder, Confucius, referred to "heaven." Except for this reference, Confucianism does not address the question of life after death.

Taoists believe that Tao (the way or the flow) is in everything. Taoism teaches that qi, or life energy, needs to be balanced between yin and yang, which are the female and male principles

of life, respectively. With its doctrine of the evil of violence, Taoism borders on pacifism, and it also preaches simplicity and naturalness. Taoists believe in five elements—wood, earth, air, fire and water—that need to be in harmony. The five elements lie at the heart of Chinese medicine, particularly acupuncture. In Taoism, it is believed that the soul returns to a state of nonbeing after death.

Shinto emphasizes nature and harmony, with a focus on lived experience rather than doctrine. Shinto, which means "the way of the gods," is a polytheistic religion; Amaterasu, the sun goddess, is the chief god. At one point in Japan's history, the emperor was believed to be a descendant of Amaterasu and therefore divine. In Tenrikyo Shinto, God is manifested most often as Oyakami, meaning "God the parent."

Shinto teaches that some souls can become kami, a spirit, following death. Each traditional home has a god-shelf, which honors family members believed to have become kami. An older family member tends to the god-shelf, placing a bit of food and some sake (rice wine) on the shelf. To do their work, kami must be nourished. The Tenrikyo sect includes concepts from Pure Land Buddhism, such as an afterlife and the idea of salvation.

Sacred Texts

Five classic texts are sacred to the Confucians. These include the I Ching, or Book of Changes; the Book of Odes; the Book of History; the Book of Rites; and the Annals of Spring and Autumn. The Analects, a collection of Confucius's sayings, is another revered classic. The Tao Te Ching (The Way of Power) is the most sacred book of the Taoists. Those who practice Shinto hold sacred two works: the Kojiki (Record of Ancient Matters) and the Nihon-gi (Chronicles of Japan). Both texts, which contain legends and creation myths, were written during the eighth century.

Major Figures

Confucius, who lived during the sixth century, was the first great philosopher of China. Mengzi (Meng-tzu; 371–289 BCE), known in the West as Mencius, developed Confucius's teachings about the higher power guiding human life. Another ancient Chinese philosopher, Laozi(or Lao-tzu), is the founder of Taoism. He is believed to have been a contemporary of Confucius's in the central region of China. Modern scholars are not certain he ever existed, though one account includes the story of Confucius visiting Laozi. Chuang Tzu wrote of Laozi and his ideas during the fourth and third centuries BCE. Shinto's major figures include Ō no Yasumaro (d. 723), the compiler of the Kokiji who acted under the orders of Empress Gemmei and consulted a bard known to have an infallible memory; the scholar Motoori Norinaga (1730–1800), whose work led to a revived interest in ancient Shinto texts; and Nakayama Miki (1798–1887), the farmer's wife who founded Tenrikyo.

Major Holy Sites

Most Confucian sacred places are located within private homes, where an ancestral shrine and an altar to gods and spirits are maintained. In China's Shandong Province is Qufu, the site of Confucius's family mansion, temple, and cemetery. The temple was built in 478 BCE, only a year after Confucius's death, and has been maintained and enlarged. In addition to its status as a holy site, the United Nations Educational, Scientific, and Cultural Organization (UNESCO) has placed it on their World Heritage List.

Taoists regard mountains as a way to communicate with Earth's primeval powers and with those who are immortal. Five of the nine sacred mountains in China are associated with Taoism: Hengshan in both the north and the south, Songshan in the south, Taishan in the east, and Huashan in the west. The holiest of the five is Taishan, which symbolizes stability, prevents natural disasters, and ensures fertility.

Shintoism has a high regard for natural beauty. As such, Shinto shrines are everywhere, particularly in mountains or near waterfalls.

Mountains in particular are regarded as homes of the gods. Mount Fuji is the holiest Shinto mountain, and climbing it to reach the shrine on its peak is an act of worship. More than forty thousand shrines are dedicated to Inari, the rice god.

Shinto was formalized during the Yamato period (the name for ancient Japan), and because the emperor of the imperial dynasty was from the Yamato area and was considered divine, the whole region is revered. At Ise, located near the coast in Mie Prefecture, southeast of Nara, the shrine has been rebuilt every twenty years for at least fourteen centuries. This rebuilding ensures that Toyouke-Ōmikami (the harvest goddess) and Amaterasu (the sun goddess) are renewed in vigor, which in turn invigorates both the rice crop and the imperial line. Those who have died in war are revered as kami in Japan. In Tokyo, a shrine called Yasukuni is dedicated to them. However, there is controversy surrounding the place because of its association with Japan's extreme nationalism prior to World War II.

Sacred Texts

Five classic texts are sacred to the Confucians. These include the I Ching, or Book of Changes; the Book of Odes; the Book of History; the Book of Rites; and the Annals of Spring and Autumn. The Analects, a collection of Confucius's sayings, is another revered classic. The Tao te Ching (The Way of Power) is the most sacred book of the Taoists. Those who practice Shinto hold sacred two works: the Kojiki (Record of Ancient Matters) and the Nihon-gi (Chronicles of Japan). Both texts, which contain legends and creation myths, were written during the eighth century.

Major Figures

Confucius, who lived during the sixth century, was the first great philosopher of China. Mengzi (Meng-tzu; 371–289 BCE), known in the West as Mencius, developed Confucius's teachings about the higher power guiding human life. Another ancient Chinese philosopher, Laozi,(or Lao-tzu) is the founder of Taoism. He is believed to have been a contemporary of Confucius in the central region of China. Modern scholars are not certain he ever existed, though one account includes the story of Confucius visiting Laozi. Chuang Tzu wrote of Laozi and his ideas during the fourth and third centuries BCE. Shinto's major figures include Ō no Yasumaro, the compiler of the Kokiji who acted under the orders of Empress Gemmei and consulted a bard known to have an infallible memory; the scholar Motoori Norinaga (1730–1800), whose work led to a revived interest in ancient Shinto texts; and Nakayama Miki (1798–1887), the farmer's wife who founded Tenrikyo.

Major Holy Sites

Most Confucian sacred places are located within private homes, where an ancestral shrine and an altar to gods and spirits are maintained. In China's Shandong Province is Qufu, the site of Confucius's family mansion, temple and cemetery. The temple was built in 478 BCE, only a year after Confucius's death, and has been maintained and enlarged. In addition to being a holy site, the United Nations Educational, Scientific, and Cultural Organization (UNESCO) has placed it on their World Heritage List.

Taoists consider mountains as a way to communicate with Earth's primeval powers and with those who are immortal. Five of the nine sacred mountains in China are associated with Taoism. They are Hengshan in both the north and south, Songshan in the south, Taishan in the east, and Huashan in the west. The holiest of the five is Taishan, which symbolizes stability, prevents natural disasters, and ensures fertility.

Shintoism has a high regard for natural beauty. As such, Shinto shrines are everywhere, particularly in mountains or near waterfalls. Mountains in particular are regarded as homes of the gods. Mount Fuji is the holiest Shinto mountain, and climbing it to reach the shrine on its peak is an act of worship. More than forty thousand shrines are dedicated to Inari, the rice god.

Shinto was formalized during the Yamato period (the name for ancient Japan), and because the emperor of the imperial dynasty is from the Yamato area, and was considered divine, the whole region is revered. At Ise, located near the coast in the Mie prefecture southeast of Nara, the shrine has been rebuilt every twenty years for at least fourteen centuries. This rebuilding ensures that Toyouke-Ōmikami (the harvest goddess) and Amaterasu (the sun goddess) are renewed in vigor, which in turn invigorates both the rice crop and the imperial line. Those who have died in war are revered as kami in Japan. In Tokyo, a shrine called Yasukuni is dedicated to them. However, there is controversy surrounding the place because of its association with Japan's extreme nationalism prior to World War II.

Major Rites & Celebrations

Confucian celebrations have to do with honoring people rather than gods. At Confucian temples, the philosopher's birthday is celebrated each September. In Taiwan, this day is called "Teacher's Day." Sacrifices, music and dance are part of the event.

Taoism has a jiao (offering) festival near the winter solstice. It celebrates the renewal of the yang force at this turning of the year. During the festival priests, who have been ritually purified, wear lavish clothing. The festival includes music and dancing, along with large effigies of the gods which are designed to frighten away the evil spirits. Yang's renewal is also the focus of New Year celebrations, which is a time for settling debts and cleaning house. Decorations in the yang warm colors of gold, orange and red abound.

Many of the Shinto festivals overlap with Buddhist ones. There are many local festivals and rituals, and each community has an annual festival at the shrine dedicated to the kami of the region. Japanese New Year, which is celebrated for three days, is a major feast. Since the sixteenth century, the Gion Festival has taken place in Kyoto, Japan. Decorated floats are part of the celebration of the shrine.

ORIGINS

History & Geography
During the Zhou dynasty (1050–256 BCE) in China, the idea of heaven as a force that controlled

events came to the fore. Zhou rulers believed that they ruled as a result of the "Mandate of Heaven," viewing themselves as morally superior to those of the previous dynasty, the Shang dynasty (1600-1046 BCE). They linked virtue and power as the root of the state.

By the sixth century the Zhou rulers had lost much of their authority. Many schools of thought developed to restore harmony, and were collectively known as the "Hundred Schools." Confucius set forth his ideas within this historical context. He traveled China for thirteen years, urging rulers to put his ideas into practice and failing to achieve his goals. He returned home to teach for the rest of his life and his ideas were not adopted until the Han dynasty (206 BCE–220 CE). During the Han period, a university for the nation was established, as well as the bureaucratic civil service that continued until the twentieth century. When the Chinese Empire fell in 1911, the Confucian way became less important.

Confucianism had influenced not only early Chinese culture, but also the cultures of Japan, Korea, and Vietnam. The latter two nations also adopted the bureaucratic system. In Japan, Confucianism reached its height during the Tokugawa age (1600–1868 CE). Confucian scholars continue to interpret the philosophy for the modern period. Some regard the ideas of Confucius as key to the recent economic booms in the so-called "tiger" economies of East Asia (Hong Kong, Singapore, South Korea, Taiwan, and Thailand). Confucianism continues to be a major influence on East Asian nations and culture.

Taoism's power (te) manifests itself as a philosophy, a way of life, and a religion. Philosophically, Taoism is a sort of self-help regimen, concerned with expending power efficiently by avoiding conflicts and friction, rather than fighting against the flow of life. In China, it is known as School Taoism. As a way of life, Taoism is concerned with increasing the amount of qi available through what is eaten and through meditation, yoga, and tai chi (an ancient Chinese martial art form). Acupuncture and the use of medicinal herbs are outgrowths of this way of life. Church Taoism, influenced by Buddhism and Tao Chiao (religious Taoism), developed during the second century. This church looked for ways to use power for societal and individual benefit.

By the time of the Han dynasty (206–220 CE), Laozi had been elevated to the status of divine. Taoism found favor at court during the Tang dynasty (618–917 CE), during which the state underwrote temples. By adapting and encouraging people to study the writings of all three major faiths in China, Taoism remained relevant into the early twentieth century. During the 1960s and 1970s, Taoist books were burned and their temples were destroyed in the name of the Cultural Revolution (the Great Proletarian Cultural Revolution). Taoism remains popular and vital in Taiwan.

Shinto is an ancient religion, and some of its characteristics appeared during the Yayoi culture (ca. 300 BCE–300 CE). The focus was on local geographic features and the ancestry of local clan leaders. At first, women were permitted to be priests, but that equality was lost due to the influence of Confucian paternalism. The religion declined, but was revived in 1871 following the Meiji Restoration of the emperor. Shoguns (warlords) had ruled Japan for more than 250 years, and Shinto was the state religion until 1945. It was associated with the emperor cult and contributed to Japan's militarism. After the nation's defeat in World War II, the 1947 constitution forbade government involvement in any religion. In contemporary Shinto, women are permitted to become priests and girls, in some places, are allowed to carry the portable shrines during festivals.

Founder or Major Prophet

Confucius, or Kongzi ("Master Kong"), was a teacher whose early life may have included service in the government. He began traveling throughout the country around age fifty, attempting and failing to interest rulers in his ideas for creating a harmonious state. He returned to his home state after thirteen years, teaching a group of disciples who spread his ideas posthumously.

According to legend, Taoism's founder, Laozi, lived during the sixth century. Laozi may be translated as "Grand Old Master," and may be simply a term of endearment. He maintained the archives and lived simply in a western state of China. Weary of people who were uninterested in natural goodness and perhaps wanting greater solitude in his advanced years, he determined to leave China, heading for Tibet on a water buffalo. At the border, a gatekeeper wanted to persuade him to stay, but could not do so. He asked Laozi to leave behind his teachings. For three days Laozi transcribed his teachings, producing the five-thousand-word Tao Te Ching. He then rode off and was never heard of again. Unlike most founders of religions, he neither preached nor promoted his beliefs. Still, he was held with such regard that some emperors claimed descent from him.

No one is certain of the origin of Shinto, which did not have a founder or major prophet. Shinto—derived from two Chinese words, *shen* (spirit) and *dao* (way)—has been influenced by other religions, notably Confucianism and Buddhism.

Philosophical Basis

Confucianism sought to bring harmony to the state and society as a whole. This harmony was to be rooted in the Five Constant Relationships: between parents and children; husbands and wives; older and younger siblings; older and younger friends; and rulers and subjects. Each of these societal relationships existed to demonstrate mutual respect, service, honor, and love, resulting in a healthy society. The fact that three of the five relationships exist within the family highlights the importance of honoring family. Ritual maintains the li, or rightness, of everything, and is a way to guarantee that a person performed the correct action in any situation in life.

Taoism teaches that two basic components—yin and yang—are in all things, including health, the state, and relationships. Yin is the feminine principle, associated with soft, cold, dark, and moist things. Yang is the masculine principle,

and is associated with hard, warm, light, and dry things. By keeping these two aspects of life balanced, harmony will be achieved. Another concept is that of wu-wei, action that is in harmony with nature, while qi is the life force in all beings. The Tao is always in harmony with the universe. Conflict is to be avoided, and soldiers are to go as if attending a funeral, solemnly and with compassion. Taoism also teaches the virtues of humility and selflessness.

Shinto is rooted in reverence for ancestors and for the spirits known as kami, which may be good or evil. By correctly worshipping the kami, Shintoists believe that they are assisting in purifying the world and aiding in its functioning.

Holy Places

Confucianism does not always distinguish between sacred and profane space. So much of nature is considered a holy place, as is each home's private shrine. In addition, some Confucian temples have decayed while others have been restored. Temples do not have statues or images. Instead, the names of Confucius and his noted followers are written on tablets. Like the emperor's palace, temples have the most important halls placed on the north-south axis of the building. Temples are also internally symmetrical, as might be expected of a system that honors order. In Beijing, the Temple of Heaven, just south of the emperor's palace, was one of the holiest places in imperial China.

Taoism's holy places are often in nature, particularly mountains. The holiest of the five sacred mountains in China is Taishan, located in the east. Taoism also reveres grottoes, which are caves thought to be illuminated by the light of heaven.

In the Shinto religion, nature is often the focus of holy sites. Mount Fuji is the most sacred mountain. Near Kyoto the largest shrine of Inari, the rice god, is located. The Grand Shrines at Ise are dedicated to two divinities, and for more than one thousand years, pilgrims have come to it. The Inner Shrine (Naiku) is dedicated to Amaterasu, the sun goddess, and is Shinto's most holy location. The Outer Shrine (Geku) is dedicated to

Toyouke, the goddess of the harvest. Every twenty years, Ise is torn down and rebuilt, thus renewing the gods. Shinto shrines all have torii, the sacred gateway. The most famous of these is built in the sea near the island of Miyajima. Those going to the shrine on this island go by boat through the torii.

EAST ASIAN RELIGIONS IN DEPTH

Sacred Symbols

Water is regarded as the source of life in Confucianism. The water symbol has thus become an unofficial symbol of Confucianism, represented by the Japanese ideogram or character for water, the Mizu, which somewhat resembles a stick figure with an extra leg. Other sacred symbols include the ancestor tablets in shrines of private homes, which are symbolic of the presence of the ancestor to whom offerings are made in hopes of aid.

While not a sacred symbol as the term is generally used, the black and white symbol of yin and yang is a common Taoist emblem. Peaches are also of a symbolic nature in Taoism, and often appear in Asian art. They are based on the four peaches that grew every three thousand years and which the mother of the fairies gave to the Han emperor Wu Ti (140–87 BCE). They are often symbolic of the Immortals.

The Shinto stylized sun, which appears on the Japanese flag, is associated with Amaterasu, the sun goddess. The torii, the gateway forming an entrance to sacred space, is another symbol associated with Shinto.

Sacred Practices & Gestures

Confucian rulers traditionally offered sacrifices honoring Confucius at the spring and autumnal equinoxes. Most of the Confucian practices take place at home shrines honoring the ancestors.

Taoists believe that one can reach Tao (the way) through physical movements, chanting, or meditation. Because mountains, caves, and springs are often regarded as sacred sites, pilgrimages are important to Taoists. At a Taoist

funeral, a paper fairy crane is part of the procession. After the funeral, the crane, which symbolizes a heavenly messenger, is burned. The soul of the deceased person is then thought to ride to heaven on the back of the crane.

Many Shinto shrines exist throughout Japan. Most of them have a sacred arch, known as a torii. At the shrine's entrance, worshippers rinse their mouths and wash their hands to be purified before entering the prayer hall. Before praying, a worshipper will clap twice and ring a bell to let the kami know they are there. Only priests may enter the inner hall, which is where the kami live. During a festival, however, the image of the kami is placed in a portable shrine and carried in a procession through town, so that all may receive a blessing.

Rites, Celebrations & Services

Early Confucianism had no priests, and bureaucrats performed any rituals that were necessary. When the Chinese Empire fell in 1911, imperial ceremonies ended as well. Rituals have become less important in modern times. In contemporary times the most important rite is marriage, the beginning of a new family for creating harmony. There is a correct protocol for each aspect of marriage, from the proposal and engagement to exchanging vows. During the ceremony, the groom takes the bride to his family's ancestor tablets to "introduce" her to them and receive a blessing. The couple bows to the ancestors during the ceremony.

After a death occurs, mourners wear coarse material and bring gifts of incense and money to help defray the costs. Added to the coffin holding are food offerings and significant possessions. A willow branch symbolizing the deceased's soul is carried with the coffin to the place of burial. After the burial, family members take the willow branch to their home altar and perform a ritual to add the deceased to the souls at the family's shrine.

Confucians and Taoists celebrate many of the same Chinese festivals, some of which originated before either Confucianism or Taoism began and reflect aspects of both traditions. While some festivals are not necessarily Taoist, they may be led by Taoist priests. During the Lantern Festival, which occurs on the first full moon of the New Year, offerings are made to the gods. Many of the festivals are tied to calendar events. Qingming (Clear and Bright) celebrates the coming of spring and is a time to remember the dead. During this time, families often go to the family gravesite for a picnic. The Double Fifth is the midsummer festival that occurs on the fifth day of the fifth month, and coincides with the peak of yang power. To protect themselves from too much of the male force, people don garments of the five colors—black, blue, red, white, and yellow—and with the five "poisons"—centipede, lizard, scorpion, snake, and toad—in the pattern of their clothes and on amulets. The gates of hell open at the Feast of the Hungry Ghosts. Priests have ceremonies that encourage the escaped evil spirits to repent or return to hell.

Marriage is an important rite in China, and thus in Taoism as well. Astrologers look at horoscopes to ensure that the bride and groom are well matched and to find the best day for the ceremony. The groom's family is always placed at the east (yang) and the bride's family to the west (yin) to bring harmony. When a person dies, the mourners again sit in the correct locations, while the head of the deceased points south. White is the color of mourning and of yin. At the home of the deceased, white cloths cover the family altar. Mourners may ease the soul's journey with symbolic artifacts or money. They may also go after the funeral to underground chambers beneath the temples to offer a sacrifice on behalf of the dead.

In the Shinto religion, rites exist for many life events. For example, pregnant women ask at a shrine for their children to be born safely, and the mother or grandmother brings a child who is thirty-two or thirty-three-days-old to a shrine for the first visit and blessing. A special festival also exists for children aged three, five or seven, who go to the shrine for purifying. In addition, a bride and groom are purified before the wedding, usually conducted by Shinto priests. Shinto priests may also offer blessings for a new car or building. The New Year and the Spring Festival are among the most important festivals, and shrine virgins, known as miko girls, may dance to celebrate life's renewal. Other festivals include the Feast of the Puppets, Boys' Day, the Water Kami Festival, the Star Feast, the Festival of the Dead, and the autumnal equinox.

Judy A. Johnson, MTS

Bibliography

Barnes, Trevor. *The Kingfisher Book of Religions*. New York: Kingfisher, 1999. Print.

Bell, Daniel A. "Reconciling Socialism and Confucianism? Reviving Tradition in China." *Dissent* 57.1 (2010): 91–99. Print.

Chang, Chung-yuan. *Creativity and Taoism: A Study of Chinese Philosophy, Art and Poetry*. London: Kingsley, 2011. E-book.

Coogan, Michael D., ed. *Eastern Religions*. New York: Oxford UP, 2005. Print.

Eliade, Mircea, and Ioan P. Couliano. *The Eliade Guide to World Religions*. New York: Harper, 1991. Print.

Lao Tzu. *Tao Te Ching*. Trans. Stephen Mitchell. New York: Harper, 1999. Print.

Li, Yingzhang. *Lao-tzu's Treatise on the Response of the Tao*. Trans. Eva Wong. New Haven: Yale UP, 2011. Print.

Littlejohn, Ronnie. *Confucianism: An Introduction*. New York: Tauris, 2011. E-book.

Littleton, C. Scott. *Shinto*. Oxford: Oxford UP, 2002. Print.

Mcvay, Kera. *All about Shinto*. Delhi: University, 2012. Ebook.

Merton, Thomas. *The Way of Chuang Tzu*. New York: New Directions, 1965. Print.

Oldstone-Moore, Jennifer. *Confucianism*. Oxford: Oxford UP, 2002. Print.

Poceski, Mario. *Chinese Religions: The EBook*. Providence, UT: Journal of Buddhist Ethics Online Books, 2009. E-book.

Van Norden, Bryan W. *Introduction to Classical Chinese Philosophy*. Indianapolis: Hackett, 2011. Print.

Wilkinson, Philip. *Religions*. New York: DK, 2008. Print.

Hinduism

General Description

Hinduism; modern Hinduism is comprised of the devotional sects of Vaishnavism, Shaivism, and Shaktism (though Smartism is sometimes listed as the fourth division). Hinduism is often used as umbrella term, since many point to Hinduism as a family of different religions.

Number of Adherents Worldwide

Between 13.8 and 15 percent of the world's population, or about one billion people, are adherents of Hinduism, making it the world's third largest religion after Christianity and Islam. The predominant sect is the Vaishnavite sect (Wilkinson, p. 333).

Basic Tenets

Hinduism is a way of life rather than a body of beliefs. Hindus believe in karma, the cosmic law of cause and effect that determines one's state in the next life. Additional beliefs include dharma, one's religious duty.

Hinduism has no true belief in an afterlife. Rather, it teaches a belief in reincarnation, known as samsara, and in moksha, the end of the cycle of rebirths. Different sects have different paths to moksha.

Hinduism is considered a polytheist religion. However, it is also accurate to say that Hinduism professes a belief in one God or Supreme Truth that is beyond comprehension (an absolute reality, called Brahman) and which manifests itself in many forms and names. These include Brahma, the creator; Vishnu, the protector; and Shiva, the re-creator or destroyer. Many sects are defined by their belief in multiple gods, but also by their worship of one ultimate manifestation. For example, Shaivism and Vaishnavism are based upon the recognition of Shiva and Vishnu, respectively, as the manifestation. In comparison, Shaktism recognizes the Divine Mother (Shakti) as the Supreme Being, while followers of Smartism worship a particular deity of their own choosing.

Major Deities

The Hindu trinity (Trimurti) is comprised of Brahma, the impersonal and absolute creator; Vishnu, the great preserver; and Shiva, the destroyer and re-creator. The goddesses corresponding to each god are Sarasvati, Lakshimi, and Parvati. Thousands of other gods (devas) and goddesses (devis) are worshipped, including Ganesha, Surya, and Kali. Each is believed to represent another aspect of the Supreme Being.

Sacred Texts

Hindus revere ancient texts such as the four Vedas, the 108 Upanishads, and others. No single text has the binding authority of the Qur'an (Islam's holy book) or Bible. Hindu literature is also defined by Sruti (revealed truth), which is heard, and Smriti (realized truth), which is remembered. The former is canonical, while the latter can be changing. For example, the Vedas and the Upanishads constitute Sruti texts, while epics, history, and law books constitute the latter. The Bhagavad Gita (The Song of God) is also considered a sacred scripture of Hinduism, and consists of a philosophical dialogue.

Major Figures

Major figures include: Shankara (788–820 CE), who defined the unity of the soul (atman) and absolute reality (Brahman); Ramanuja (1077–1157 CE), who emphasized bhakti, or love of God; Madhva (1199–1278 CE), scholar and writer, a proponent of dualism; Ramprahsad Sen (1718–1775 CE), composer of Hindu songs of devotion, poet, and mystic who influenced goddess worship in the; Raja Rammohun Roy (1772–1833 CE), abolished the custom of suttee, in which widows were burned on the funeral pyres of their dead husbands, and decried polygamy, rigid caste systems, and dowries; Rabindranath Tagore (1861–1941 CE), first Asian to win the Nobel Prize in Literature; Dr. Babasaheb R. Ambedkar (1891–1956 CE), writer of India's constitution and leader of a mass conversion to Buddhism; Mohandas K. Gandhi (1869–1948 CE), the "great soul" who left a legacy of effective use of nonviolence.

Major Holy Sites

The major holy sites of Hinduism are located within India. They include the Ganges River, in whose waters pilgrims come to bathe away their sins, as well as thousands of tirthas (places of pilgrimage), many of which are associated with particular deities. For example, the Char Dham pilgrimage centers, of which there are four—Badrinath (north), Puri (east), Dwarka (west) and Rameshwaram (south)—are considered the holy abodes or sacred temples of Vishnu. There are also seven ancient holy cities in India, including Ayodhya, believed to be the birthplace of Rama; Varanasi (Benares), known as the City of Light; Dwarka; Ujjian; Kanchipuram; Mathura; and Hardwar.

Major Rites & Celebrations

Diwali, the Festival of Lights, is a five-day festival that is considered a national holiday in India. Holi, the Festival of Colors, is the spring festival. Krishna Janmashtmi is Krishna's birthday. Shivaratri is Shiva's main festival. Navaratri, also known as the Durga festival or Dasserah, celebrates one of the stories of the gods and the victory of good over evil. Ganesh Chaturthi is the elephant-headed god Ganesha's birthday. Rathayatra, celebrated at Puri, India, is a festival for Jagannath, another word for Vishnu.

ORIGINS

History & Geography

Hinduism, which many people consider to be the oldest world religion, is unique in that it has no recorded origin or founder. Generally, it developed in the Indus Valley civilization several thousand years before the Common Era. The faith blends the Vedic traditions of the Indus Valley civilization and the invading nomadic tribes of the Aryans (prehistoric Indo-Europeans). Most of what is known of the Indus Valley

civilization comes from archaeological excavations at Mohenjo-Daro (Mound of the Dead) and Harappa. (Because Harappa was a chief city of the period, the Indus Valley civilization is also referred to as the Harappan civilization.) The Vedas, a collection of ancient hymns, provides information about the Aryan culture.

The ancient Persian word *hind* means Indian, and for centuries, to be Indian was to be Hindu. Even now, about 80 percent of India's people consider themselves Hindu. The root word alludes to flowing, as a river flows. It is also etymologically related to the Indus River. At first, the term Hindu was used as an ethnic or cultural term, and travelers from Persia and Greece in the sixteenth century referred to those in the Indus Valley by that name. British writers coined the term *Hinduism* during the early part of the nineteenth century to describe the culture of India. The Hindus themselves often use the term Sanatana Dharma, meaning eternal law.

The Rigveda, a collection of hymns to various gods and goddesses written around 1500 BCE, is the first literary source for understanding Hinduism's history. The Vedas were chanted aloud for centuries before being written down around 1400 CE. The Rigveda is one of four major collections of Vedas, or wisdom: Rigveda, Yajurveda, Samaveda, and Atharvaveda. Together these four are called Samhitas.

Additionally, Hinduism relies on three other Vedic works: the Aranyakas, the Brahamans, and the Upanishads. The Upanishads is a philosophical work, possibly written down between 800 and 450 BCE, that attempts to answer life's big questions. Written in the form of a dialogue between a teacher (guru) and student (chela), the text's name means "to sit near," which describes the relationship between the two. Along with the Samhitas, these four are called Sruti (heard), a reference to their nature as revealed truth. The words in these texts cannot be altered.

Remaining works are called Smriti, meaning "remembered," to indicate that they were composed by human writers. The longer of the Smriti epics is the Mahabharata, the Great Story of the Bharatas. Written between 300 and 100 BCE, the epic is a classic tale of two rival, related families, including teaching as well as story. It is considered the longest single poem in existence, with about 200,000 lines. (A film made of it lasts for twelve hours.)

The Bhagavad Gita, or Song of the Lord, is the sixth section of the Mahabharata, but is often read as a stand-alone narrative of battle and acceptance of one's dharma. The Ramayana is the second, shorter epic of the Mahabharata, with about fifty thousand lines. Rama was the seventh incarnation, or avatar, of Vishnu. The narrative relates the abduction of his wife, Sita, and her rescue, accomplished with the help of the monkey god, Hanuman. Some have regarded the Mahabharata as an encyclopedia, and the Bhagavad Gita as the Bible within it.

Although many of the practices in the Vedas have been modified or discontinued, sections of it are memorized and repeated. Some of the hymns are recited at traditional ceremonies for the dead and at weddings.

Hinduism has affected American life and culture for many years. For example, the nineteenth-century transcendental writers Margaret Fuller and Ralph Waldo Emerson were both influenced by Hindu and Buddhist literature, while musician George Harrison, a member of the Beatles, adopted Hinduism and explored his new faith through his music, both with and without the Beatles. In 1965, the International Society for Krishna Consciousness (ISKCON), or the Hare Krishna movement, came to the Western world. In addition, many people have been drawn to yoga, which is associated with Hinduism's meditative practices.

Founder or Major Prophet

Hinduism has no founder or major prophet. It is a religion that has developed over many centuries and from many sources, many of which are unknown in their origins.

Philosophical Basis

Hinduism recognizes multiple ways to achieve salvation and escape the endless cycle of rebirth. The way of devotion is the most popular. Through worship of a single deity, the worshipper hopes to attain union with the divine. A second path is the way of knowledge, involving the use of meditation and reason. The third way is via action, or correctly performing religious observances in hope of receiving a blessing from the gods by accomplishing these duties.

Hinduism is considered the world's oldest religion, but Hindus maintain that it is also a way of living, not just a religion. There is great diversity as well as great tolerance in Hinduism. While Hinduism does not have a set of dogmatic formulations, it does blend the elements of devotion, doctrine, practice, society, and story as separate strands in a braid.

During the second century BCE, a sage named Patanjali outlined four life stages, and the fulfilled responsibilities inherent in each one placed one in harmony with dharma, or right conduct. Although these life stages are no longer observed strictly, their ideas still carry weight. Traditionally, these codes applied to men, and only to those in the Brahman caste; members of the warrior and merchant classes could follow them, but were not obligated. The Shudra and Dalit castes, along with women, were not part of the system. Historically, women were thought of as protected by fathers in their childhood, by husbands in their youth and adulthood, and by sons in old age. Only recently have women in India been educated beyond the skills of domestic responsibility and child rearing.

The earliest life stage is the student stage, or brahmacharya, a word that means "to conduct oneself in accord with Brahman." From ages twelve to twenty-four, young men were expected to undertake learning with a guru, or guide. During these twelve years of studying the Veda they were also expected to remain celibate.

The second stage, grihastha, is that of householder. A Hindu man married the bride that his parents had chosen, sired children, and created a livelihood on which the other three stages depended.

Vanaprastha is the third stage, involving retirement to solitude. Historically, this involved leaving the house and entering a forest dwelling.

A man's wife had the option to go with him or to remain. This stage also involved giving counsel to others and further study.

At the final stage of life, sannyasis, the Hindu renounces material goods, including a home of any sort. He may live in a forest or join an ashram, or community. He renounces even making a fire, and lives on fruit and roots that can be foraged. Many contemporary Hindus do not move to this stage, but remain at vanaprastha.

Yoga is another Hindu practice, more than three millennia old, which Patanjali codified. The four forms of yoga corresponded to the Hindu avenues of salvation. Hatha yoga is the posture yoga seeking union with god through action. Jnana yoga is the path to god through knowledge. Bhakti yoga is the way of love to god. Karma yoga is the method of finding god through work. By uniting the self, the practitioner unites with God. Yoga is related etymologically to the English word *yoke*—it attempts to yoke the individual with Brahman. All forms of yoga include meditation and the acceptance of other moral disciplines, such as self-discipline, truthfulness, nonviolence, and contentment.

Aryan society was stratified, and at the top of the social scale were the priests. This system was the basis for the caste system that had long dominated Hinduism. Caste, which was determined by birth, affected a person's occupation, diet, neighborhood, and marriage partner. Vedic hymns allude to four varnas, or occupations: Brahmins (priests), Kshatriyas (warriors), Vaishyas (merchants and common people), and Shudras (servants). A fifth class, the Untouchables, later known as Dalit (oppressed), referred to those who were regarded as a polluting force because they handled waste and dead bodies. The belief was that society would function properly if each group carried out its duties. These varnas later became wrongly blended with castes, or jatis, which were smaller groups also concerned with a person's place in society.

The practice of Hinduism concerns itself with ritual purity; even household chores can be done in a ritualistic way. Some traditions demand ritual purity before one can worship. Brahmin priests, for example, may not accept water or food from non-Brahmins. Refusal to do so is not viewed as classism, but an attempt to please the gods in maintaining ritual purity.

Mohandas Gandhi was one of those who refused to use the term *Untouchable*, using the term *harijan*(children of God), instead. Dr. Babasaheb R. Ambedkar, who wrote India's constitution, was a member of this class. Ambedkar and many of his supporters became Buddhists in an attempt to dispel the power of caste. In 1947, following India's independence from Britain, the caste system was officially banned, though it has continued to influence Indian society.

Ahimsa, or dynamic harmlessness, is another deeply rooted principle of Hinduism. It involves six pillars: refraining from eating all animal products; revering all of life; having integrity in thoughts, words, and deeds; exercising self-control; serving creation, nature, and humanity; and advancing truth and understanding.

Holy Places

In Hinduism, all water is considered holy, symbolizing the flow of life. For a Hindu, the Ganges River is perhaps the most holy of all bodies of water. It was named for the goddess of purification, Ganga. The waters of the Ganges are said to flow through Shiva's hair and have the ability to cleanse sin. Devout Hindus make pilgrimages to bathe in the Ganges. They may also visit fords in the rivers to symbolize the journey from one life to another.

Pilgrimages are also made to sites associated with the life of a god. For example, Lord Rama was said to have been born in Ayodhya, one of the seven holy cities in India. Other holy sites are Dwarka, Ujjian, Kanchipuram, Mathura, Hardwar, and Varanasi, the City of Light.

After leaving his mountain home, Lord Shiva was thought to have lived in Varanasi, or Benares, considered the holiest city. Before the sixth century, it became a center of education for Hindus. It has four miles of palaces and temples along the river. One of the many pilgrimage circuits covers thirty-five miles, lasts for five days, and includes prayer at 108 different shrines. Because of the river's sacred nature, Hindus come to bathe from its many stone steps, called ghats, and to drink the water. It is also the place where Hindus desire to be at their death or to have their ashes scattered. Because Varanasi is regarded as a place of crossing between earth and heaven, dying there is thought to free one from the cycle of rebirth.

The thirty-four Ellora Caves at Maharashtra, India, are known for their sculptures. Built between 600 and 1000 CE, they were cut into a tufa rock hillside on a curve shaped like a horseshoe, so that the caves go deeply into the rock face. Although the one-mile site includes temples for Buddhist, Jain, and Hindu faiths, the major figure of the caves is Shiva, and the largest temple is dedicated to Shiva.

Lastly, Hindu temples, or mandirs, are regarded as the gods' earthly homes. The buildings themselves are therefore holy, and Hindus remove their shoes before entering.

HINDUISM IN DEPTH

Sacred Symbols

The wheel of life represents samsara, the cycle of life, death and rebirth. Karma is what keeps the wheel spinning. Another circle is the hoop of flames in which Shiva, also known as the Lord of the Dance, or Natraja, is shown dancing creation into being. The flames signify the universe's energy and Shiva's power of both destruction and creation. Shiva balances on his right foot, which rests on a defeated demon that stands for ignorance.

The lotus is the symbol of creation, fertility, and purity. This flower is associated with Vishnu because as he slept, a lotus flower bloomed from his navel. From this lotus Brahma came forth to create the world. Yoga practitioners commonly assume the lotus position for meditation.

Murtis are the statues of gods that are found in both temples and private homes. They are often washed with milk and water, anointed with oil, dressed, and offered gifts of food or flowers. Incense may also be burned to make the air around the murti sweet and pure.

One of Krishna's symbols is the conch shell, a symbol of a demon he defeated. A conch shell is blown at temples to announce the beginning of the worship service. It is a visual reminder for followers of Krishna to overcome ignorance and evil in their lives.

For many years, the Hindus used the swastika as a holy symbol. (*Swastika* is a Sanskrit word for good fortune and well-being.) The four arms meet at a central point, demonstrating that the universe comes from one source. Each arm of the symbol represents a path to God and is bent to show that all paths are difficult. It is used at a time of new beginnings, such as at a wedding, where it is traditionally painted on a coconut using a red paste called kum kum. The symbol appears as a vertical gash across the horizontal layers on the southern face of Mount Kailas, one of the Himalayas's highest peaks, thought to have been the home of Shiva. The mountain is also near the source of the Ganges and the Indus Rivers. The use of the swastika as a symbol for Nazi Germany is abhorrent to Hindus.

Some Hindus use a mala, or rosary, of 108 wooden beads when they pray. As they worship, they repeat the names of God.

Sacred Practices & Gestures

Many homes have private altars or shrines to favorite gods. Statues or pictures of these deities are offered incense, flowers and food, as well as prayers. This daily devotion, known as puja, is generally the responsibility of women, many of whom are devoted to goddesses such as Kali or Sita. A rich family may devote an entire room of their house to the shrine.

Om, or Aum, a sacred syllable recorded first in the Upanishads, is made up of three Sanskrit letters. Writing the letter involves a symbol resembling the Arabic number three. Thus, it is a visual reminder of the Trimurti, the three major Hindu gods. The word is repeated at the beginning of all mantras or prayers.

Each day the Gayatri, which is perhaps the world's oldest recorded prayer, is chanted during the fire ritual. The prayer expresses gratitude to the sun for its shining and invokes blessings of prosperity on all. The ritual, typically done at large consecrated fire pits, may be done using burning candles instead.

Holy Hindu men are known as sadhus. They lead ascetic lives, wandering, begging, and living in caves in the mountains. Regarded as having greater spiritual power and wisdom, they are often consulted for advice.

Food Restrictions

Many Hindus are vegetarians because they embrace ahimsa (reverence for and protection of all life) and oppose killing. In fact, Hindus comprise about 70 percent of the world's vegetarians. They are generally lacto-vegetarians, meaning that they include dairy products in their diets. However, Hindus residing in the cold climate of Nepal and Tibet consume meat to increase their caloric intake.

Whether a culture practices vegetarianism or not, cows are thought to be sacred because Krishna acted as a cowherd as a young god. Thus cows are never eaten. Pigs are also forbidden, as are red foods, such as tomatoes or red lentils. In addition, garlic and onions are also not permitted. Alcohol is strictly forbidden.

Purity rituals before eating include cleaning the area where the food is to be eaten and reciting mantras or praying while sprinkling water around the food. Other rituals include Annaprasana, which celebrates a child's eating of solid food—traditionally rice—for the first time. In addition, at funerals departed souls are offered food, which Hindus believe will strengthen the soul for the journey to the ancestors' world.

Serving food to those in need also generates good karma. Food is offered during religious ceremonies and may later be shared with visiting devotees of the god.

To show their devotion to Shiva, many Hindus fast on Mondays. There is also a regular fast, known as agiaras, which occurs on the eleventh day of each two-week period. On that day, only one meal is eaten. During the month of Shravan, which many consider a holy month, people may eat only one meal, generally following sunset.

Rites, Celebrations & Services

Many Hindu celebrations are connected to the annual cycle of nature and can last for many days. In addition, celebrations that honor the gods are common. Shiva, one of the three major gods, is honored at Shivaratri in February or March. In August or September, Lord Krishna is honored at Krishnajanmashtmi. Prayer and fasting are part of this holiday.

During the spring equinox and just prior to the Hindu New Year, Holi is celebrated. It is a time to resolve disputes and forgive or pay debts. During this festival, people often have bonfires and throw objects that represent past impurity or disease into the fire.

Another festival occurs in July or August, marking the beginning of the agricultural year in northern India. Raksha Bandhan (the bond of protection) is a festival which celebrates sibling relationships. During the festivities, Hindus bind a bauble with silk thread to the wrists of family members and friends.

To reenact Rama's defeat of the demon Ravana, as narrated in the Ramayana, people make and burn effigies. This festival is called Navaratri in western India, also known as the Durgapuja in Bengal, and Dasserah in northern India. It occurs in September or October each year as a festival celebrating the victory of good over evil. September is also time to celebrate the elephant-headed god Ganesha's birthday at the festival of Ganesh Chaturthi.

Diwali, a five-day festival honoring Lakshmi (the goddess of good fortune and wealth), occurs in October or November. This Festival of Lights is the time when people light oil lamps and set off fireworks to help Rama find his way home after exile. Homes are cleaned in hopes that Lakshmi will come in the night to bless it. People may use colored rice flour to make patterns on their doorstep. Competitions for designs of these patterns, which are meant to welcome God to the house, frequently take place.

Jagannath, or Vishnu, is celebrated during the festival Rathayatra. A large image of Jagannath rides in a chariot pulled through the city of Puri.

The temple for Hindus is the home of the god. Only Brahmin priests may supervise worship there. The inner sanctuary of the building is called the garbhagriha, or womb-house; there the god resides. Worshippers must be ritually pure before the worship starts. The priest recites the mantras and reads sacred texts. Small lamps are lit, and everyone shares specially prepared and blessed food after the service ends.

Judy A. Johnson, MTS

Bibliography

Barnes, Trevor. *The Kingfisher Book of Religions*. New York: Kingfisher, 1999. Print.

Harley, Gail M. *Hindu and Sikh Faiths in America*. New York: Facts on File, 2003. Print.

Iyengar, B. K. S. and Noelle Perez-Christiaens. *Sparks of Divinity: The Teachings of B. K. S. Iyengar from 1959 to 1975*. Berkeley: Rodmell, 2012. E-book.

"The Joys of Hinduism." *Hinduism Today* Oct./Dec. 2006. 40–53. Print.

Langley, Myrtle. *Religion*. New York: Knopf, 1996. Print.

Meredith, Susan. *The Usborne Book of World Religions*. London: Usborne, 1995. Print.

Rajan, Rajewswari. "The Politics of Hindu 'Tolerance.'" *Boundary 2* 38.3 (2011): 67–86. Print.

Raman, Varadaraja V. "Hinduism and Science: Some Reflections." *Journal of Religion & Science* 47.3 (2012): 549–74. Print.

Renard, John. *Responses to 101 Questions on Hinduism*. Mahwah: Paulist, 1999. Print.

Siddhartha. "Open-Source Hinduism." *Religion & the Arts* 12.1–3 (2008): 34–41. Print.

Shouler, Kenneth and Susai Anthony. *The Everything Hinduism Book*. Avon: Adams, 2009. Print.

Soherwordi, Syed Hussain Shaheed. "'Hinduism'—A Western Construction or an Influence?" *South Asian Studies* 26.1 (2011): 203–14. Print.

Theodor, Ithamar. *Exploring the Bhagavad Gita: Philosophy, Structure, and Meaning*. Farnham and Burlington: Ashgate, 2010. E-book.

Whaling, Frank. *Understanding Hinduism*. Edinburgh: Dunedin, 2010. E-book.

Wilkinson, Philip. *Religions*. New York: DK, 2008. Print.

Islam

General Description

The word *Islam* derives from a word meaning "submission," particularly submission to the will of Allah. Muslims, those who practice Islam, fall into two major groups, Sunni and Shia (or Shi'i,) based on political rather than theological differences. Sunni Muslims follow the four Rightly Guided Caliphs, or Rashidun and believe that caliphs should be elected. Shia Muslims believe that the Prophet's nearest male relative, Ali ibn Abi Talib, should have ruled following Muhammad's death, and venerate the imams (prayer leaders) who are directly descended from Ali and the Prophet's daughter Fatima.

Number of Adherents Worldwide

Approximately 1.6 billion people, or 23 percent of the world's population, are Muslims. Of that total, between 87 and 90 percent of all Muslims are Sunni Muslims and between 10 and 13 percent of all Muslims are Shia. Followers of the Sufi sect, noted for its experiential, ecstatic focus, may be either Sunni or Shia.

Basic Tenets

Islam is a monotheistic faith; Muslims worship only one God, Allah. They also believe in an afterlife and that people are consigned to heaven or hell following the last judgment.

The Islamic faith rests on Five Pillars. The first pillar, Shahadah is the declaration of faith in the original Arabic, translated as: "I bear witness that there is no god but God and Muhammad is his Messenger." The second pillar, Salah, are prayers adherents say while facing Mecca five times daily at regular hours and also at the main service held each Friday at a mosque. Zakat, "the giving of a tax," is the third pillar and entails giving an income-based percentage of one's wealth to help the poor without attracting notice. The fourth pillar is fasting, or Sawm, during Ramadan, the ninth month of the Islamic calendar. Certain groups of people are excused from the fast, however. The final pillar is the Hajj, the pilgrimage to Mecca required of every able-bodied Muslim at least once in his or her lifetime.

Sacred Text

The Qur'an (Koran), meaning "recitation," is the holy book of Islam.

Major Figures

Muhammad, regarded as the Prophet to the Arabs—as Moses was to the Jews—is considered the exemplar of what it means to be a Muslim. His successors—Abu Bakr, Umar, Uthman, and Ali—were known as the four Rightly Guided Caliphs.

Major Holy Sites

Islam recognizes three major holy sites: Mecca, home of the Prophet; Medina, the city to which Muslims relocated when forced from Mecca due to persecution; and the Dome of the Rock in Jerusalem, believed to be the oldest Islamic building in existence. Muslims believe that in 621 CE Muhammad ascended to heaven (called the Night Journey) from a sacred stone upon which the Dome was constructed. Once in heaven, God instructed Muhammad concerning the need to pray at regular times daily...

There are also several mosques which are considered primary holy sites. These include the al-Aqsa Mosque in the Old City of Jerusalem, believed by many to be the third holiest site in Islam. The mosque, along with the Dome of the Rock, is located on Judaism's holiest site, the Temple Mount, where the Temple of Jerusalem is believed to have stood. Muslims also revere the Mosque of the Prophet (Al-Masjid al-Nabawi) in Medina, considered the resting place of the Prophet Muhammad and the second largest mosque in the world; and the Mosque of the Haram (Masjid al-Haram or the Sacred or Grand Mosque) in Mecca, thought to be the largest mosque in the world and site of the Ka'bah, "the sacred house," also known as "the Noble Cube," Islam's holiest structure.

Major Rites & Celebrations

Two major celebrations mark the Islamic calendar. 'Id al-Adha, the feast of sacrifice—including animal sacrifice—held communally at the close of the Hajj (annual pilgrimage), commemorates the account of God providing a ram instead of the son Abraham had been asked to sacrifice. The second festival, 'Id al-Fitr, denotes the end of Ramadan and is a time of feasting and gift giving.

ORIGINS

History & Geography

In 610 CE, a forty-year-old businessman from Mecca named Muhammad ibn Abdullah, from the powerful Arab tribe Quraysh, went to Mount Hira to meditate, as he regularly did for the month of Ramadan. During that month, an entire group of men, the hanif, retreated to caves. The pagan worship practiced in the region, as well as the cruelty and lack of care for the poor, distressed Muhammad. As the tribe to which he belonged had become wealthy through trade, it had begun disregarding traditions prescribed by the nomadic code.

The archangel Jibra'il (Gabriel) appeared in Muhammad's cave and commanded him to read the words of God contained in the scroll that the angel showed him. Like most people of his time, Muhammad was illiterate, but repeated the words Jibra'il said. Some followers of Islam believe that this cave at Jebel Nur, in what is now Saudi Arabia, is where Adam, the first human Allah created, lived.

A frightened Muhammad told only his wife, Khadija, about his experience. For two years, Muhammad received further revelations, sharing them only with family and close friends. Like other prophets, he was reluctant about his calling, fearing that he was—or would be accused of being—possessed by evil spirits or insane. At one point, he tried to commit suicide, but was stopped by the voice of Jibra'il affirming his status as God's messenger.

Muhammad recalled the words spoken to him, which were eventually written down. The Qur'an is noted for being a book of beautiful language, and Muhammad's message reached many. The Prophet thus broke the old pattern of allegiance to tribe and forged a new community based on shared practice.

Muhammad considered himself one who was to warn the others of a coming judgment. His call for social justice and denunciation of the wealthy disturbed the powerful Arab tribe members in Mecca. These men stood to lose the status and income derived from the annual festival to the Ka'bah. The Prophet and his followers were persecuted and were the subject of boycotts and death threats. In 622 CE, Muslim families began a migration (hijrah) to Yathrib, later known as Medina. Two years earlier, the city had sent envoys seeking Muhammad's leadership for their own troubled society. The hijrah marks the beginning of the Islamic calendar.

The persecutions eventually led to outright tribal warfare, linking Islam with political prowess through the victories of the faithful. The Muslims moved from being an oppressed minority to being a political force. In 630 CE, Muhammad and ten thousand of his followers marched to Mecca, taking the city without bloodshed. He destroyed the pagan idols that were housed and worshipped at the Ka'bah, instead associating the hajj with the story of Abraham sending his concubine Hagar and their son Ishmael (Ismail in Arabic) out into the wilderness. With this victory, Muhammad ended centuries of intertribal warfare.

Muhammad died in 632, without designating a successor. Some of the Muslims believed that his nearest male relative should rule, following the custom of the tribes. Ali ibn Abi Talib, although a pious Muslim, was still young. Therefore, Abu Bakr, the Prophet's father-in-law, took the title khalifah, or caliph, which means successor or deputy. Within two years Abu Bakr had stabilized Islam. He was followed by three additional men whom Muhammad had known. Collectively, the four are known as the Four Rightly Guided Caliphs, or the Rashidun. Their rule extended from 632 until 661. Each of the final three met a violent death.

Umar, the second caliph, increased the number of raids on adjacent lands during his ten-year rule, which began in 634. This not only increased wealth, but also gave Umar the authority he needed, since Arabs objected to the idea of a monarchy. Umar was known as the commander of the faithful. Under his leadership, the Islamic community marched into present-day Iraq, Syria, and Egypt and achieved victory over the Persians in 637.

Muslims elected Uthman ibn Affan as the third caliph after Umar was stabbed by a Persian prisoner of war. He extended Muslim conquests into North Africa as well as into Iran, Afghanistan, and parts of India. A group of soldiers mutinied in 656, assassinating Uthman.

Ali, Muhammad's son-in-law, was elected caliph of a greatly enlarged empire. Conflict developed between Ali and the ruler in Damascus whom Uthman had appointed governor of Syria. The fact that the governor came from a rival tribe led to further tensions. Increasingly, Damascus rather than Medina was viewed as the key Muslim locale. Ali was murdered in 661 during the internal struggles.

Within a century after Muhammad's death, Muslims had created an empire that stretched from Spain across Asia to India and facilitated the spread of Islam. The conquerors followed a policy of relative, though not perfect, tolerance toward adherents of other religions. Christians and Jews received special status as fellow "People of the Book," though they were still required to pay a special poll tax in exchange for military protection. Pagans, however, were required to convert to Islam or face death. Later, Hindus, Zoroastrians, and other peoples were also permitted to pay the tax rather than submit to conversion. Following the twelfth century, Sufi mystics made further converts in Central Asia, India, sub-Saharan Africa, and Turkey. Muslim traders also were responsible for the growth of Islam, particularly in China, Indonesia, and Malaya.

The Muslim empire continued to grow until it weakened in the fourteenth century, when it was replaced as a major world power by European states. The age of Muslim domination ended with the 1683 failure of the Ottoman Empire to capture Vienna, Austria.

Although lacking in political power until recent years, a majority of nations in Indonesia, the Middle East, and East and North Africa are predominately Islamic. The rise of Islamic fundamentalists who interpret the Qur'an literally and seek victory through acts of terrorism began in the late twentieth century. Such extremists do not represent the majority of the Muslim community, however.

Like Judaism and Christianity, Islam has been influenced by its development in a desert climate. Arabia, a region three times the size of France, is a land of steppe and desert whose unwelcoming climate kept it from being mapped with any precision until the 1950s. Because Yemen received monsoon rains, it could sustain agriculture and became a center for civilization as early as the second millennium BCE. In the seventh century CE, nomads roamed the area, guarding precious wells and oases. Raiding caravans and other tribes were common ways to obtain necessities.

Mecca was a pagan center of worship, but it was located not far from a Christian kingdom, Ethiopia, across the Red Sea. Further north, followers of both Judaism and Christianity had influenced members of Arab tribes. Jewish tribes inhabited Yathrib, the city later known as Medina. Neither Judaism nor Christianity was especially kind to those they considered pagans. According to an Arabian tradition, in 570 the Ethiopians attacked Yemen and attempted an attack on Mecca. Mecca was caught between two enemy empires—Christian Byzantine and Zoroastrian Persia—that fought a lengthy war during Muhammad's lifetime.

The contemporary clashes between Jews and Muslims are in part a result of the dispersion of Muslims who had lived in Palestine for centuries. More Jews began moving into the area under the British Mandate; in 1948, the state of Israel was proclaimed. Historically, Jews had been respected as a People of the Book.

Founder or Major Prophet

Muslims hold Allah to be the founder of their religion and Abraham to have been the first Muslim. Muhammad is God's prophet to the Arabs. The instructions that God gave Muhammad through the archangel Jibra'il and through direct revelation are the basis for the Islamic religion. These revelations were given over a period of twenty-one years. Because Muhammad and most of the Muslims were illiterate, the teachings were read publicly in chapters, or suras.

Muhammad did not believe he was founding a new religion. Rather, he was considered God's final Prophet, as Moses and Jesus had been prophets. His task was to call people to repent and to return to the straight path of God's law, called Sharia. God finally was sending a direct revelation to the Arab peoples, who had sometimes been taunted by the other civilizations as being left out of God's plan.

Muhammad, who had been orphaned by age six, was raised by an uncle. He became a successful businessman of an important tribe and married Khadija, for whom he worked. His integrity was such that he was known as al-Amin, the trusted one. He and Khadija had six children, four daughters survived. After Khadija's death, Muhammad married several women, as was the custom for a great chief. Several of the marriages were political in nature.

Muhammad is regarded as the living Qur'an. He is sometimes referred to as the perfect man, one who is an example of how a Muslim should live. He was ahead of his time in his attitudes toward women, listening to their counsel and granting them rights not enjoyed by women in other societies, including the right to inherit property and to divorce. (It should be noted that the Qur'an does not require the seclusion or veiling of all women.)

Islam has no religious leaders, especially those comparable to other religions. Each mosque has an imam to preach and preside over prayer at the Friday services. Although granted a moral authority, the imam is not a religious leader with a role comparable to that of rabbis or priests.

Philosophical Basis

Prior to Muhammad's receiving the Qur'an, the polytheistic tribes believed in Allah, "the god." Allah was far away and not part of worship rituals, although he had created the world and sustained it. He had three daughters who were goddesses.

Islam began pragmatically—the old tribal ways were not working—as a call for social justice, rooted in Muhammad's dissatisfaction with the increasing emphasis on accumulating wealth and an accompanying neglect of those in need. The struggle (jihad) to live according to God's desire for humans was to take place within the community, or the ummah. This effort was more important than dogmatic statements or beliefs about God. When the community prospered, this was a sign of God's blessing.

In addition, the revelation of the Qur'an gave Arab nations an official religion. The Persians around them had Zoroastrianism, the Romans and Byzantines had Christianity, and the Jews of the Diaspora had Judaism. With the establishment of Islam, Arabs finally could believe that they were part of God's plan for the world.

Four principles direct Islam's practice and doctrine. These include the Qur'an; the traditions, or sunnah; consensus, or ijma'; and individual thought, or ijtihad. The term sunnah, "well-trodden path," had been used by Arabs before Islam to refer to their tribal law.

A fifth important source for Islam is the Hadith, or report, a collection of the Prophet's words and actions, intended to serve as an example. Sunni Muslims refer to six collections made in the ninth century, while Shia Muslims have a separate Hadith of four collections.

Holy Places

Mecca was located just west of the Incense Road, a major trade route from southern Arabia to Palestine and Syria. Mecca was the Prophet's home and the site where he received his revelations. It is also the city where Islam's holiest structure, the Ka'bah, "the sacred house," was located. The Ka'bah was regarded as having been built by Abraham and his son Ishmael. This forty-three-foot gray stone cube was a center for pagan idols in the time of Muhammad. In 628 the Prophet removed 360 pagan idols—one for each day of the Arabic lunar year—from inside the Ka'bah.

When the followers of Muhammad experienced persecution for their beliefs, they fled to the city of Medina, formerly called Yathrib. When his uncle Abu Talib died, Muhammad lost the protection from persecution that his uncle had provided. He left for Ta'if in the mountains, but it was also a center for pagan cults, and he was driven out. After a group of men from Yathrib promised him protection, Muhammad sent seventy of his followers to the city, built around an oasis about 215 miles north. This migration, called the hijra, occurred in 622, the first year of the Muslim calendar. From this point on, Islam became an organized religion rather than a persecuted and minority cult. The Prophet was buried in Medina in 632, and his mosque in that city is deeply revered.

Islam's third holiest site is the Dome of the Rock in Jerusalem. Muslims believe that the Prophet Muhammad ascended to heaven in 621 from the rock located at the center of this mosque. During this so-called night journey, Allah gave him instructions about prayer. In the shrine at the Dome of the Rock is a strand of hair that Muslims believe was Muhammad's.

Shia Muslims also revere the place in present-day Iraq where Ali's son, Husayn, was martyred. They regard the burial place of Imam Ali ar-Rida in Meshed, Iran, as a site of pilgrimage as well.

ISLAM IN DEPTH

Sacred Symbols
Muslims revere the Black Stone, a possible meteorite that is considered a link to heaven. It is set inside the Ka'bah shrine's eastern corner. The Ka'bah is kept covered by the kiswa, a black velvet cloth decorated with embroidered calligraphy in gold. At the hajj, Muslims walk around it counterclockwise seven times as they recite prayers to Allah.

Muslim nations have long used the crescent moon and a star on their flags. The crescent moon, which the Ottomans first adopted as a symbol during the fifteenth century, is often placed on the dome of a mosque, pointing toward Mecca. For Muhammad, the waxing and waning of the moon signified the unchanging and eternal purpose of God. Upon seeing a new moon, the Prophet confessed his faith in God. Muslims rely on a lunar calendar and the Qur'an states that God created the stars to guide people to their destinations.

Islam forbids the making of graven images of animals or people, although not all Islamic cultures follow this rule strictly. The decorative arts of Islam have placed great emphasis on architecture and calligraphy to beautify mosques and other buildings. In addition, calligraphy, floral motifs, and geometric forms decorate some editions of the Qur'an's pages, much as Christian monks once decorated hand-copied scrolls of the Bible. These elaborate designs can also be seen on some prayer rugs, and are characteristic of Islamic art in general.

Sacred Practices & Gestures
When Muslims pray, they must do so facing Mecca, a decision Muhammad made in January 624 CE. Prior to that time, Jerusalem—a holy city for both Jews and Christians—had been the geographic focus. Prayer involves a series of movements that embody submission to Allah.

Muslims sometimes use a strand of prayer beads, known as subhah, to pray the names of God. The beads can be made of bone, precious stones, or wood. Strings may have twenty-five, thirty-three or 100 beads.

Food Restrictions
Those who are physically able to do so fast from both food and drink during the daylight hours of the month Ramadan. Although fasting is not required of the sick, the aged, menstruating or pregnant women, or children, some children attempt to fast, imitating their parents' devotion. Those who cannot fast are encouraged to do so

the following Ramadan. This fast is intended to concentrate the mind on Allah. Muslims recite from the Qur'an during the month.

All meat must be prepared in a particular way so that it is halal, or permitted. While slaughtering the animal, the person must mention the name of Allah. Blood, considered unclean, must be allowed to drain. Because pigs were fed garbage, their meat was considered unclean. Thus Muslims eat no pork, even though in modern times, pigs are often raised on grain.

In three different revelations, Muslims are also forbidden to consume fermented beverages. Losing self-control because of drunkenness violates the Islamic desire for self-mastery.

Rites, Celebrations, and Services

The **mosque** is the spiritual center of the Muslim community. From the minaret (a tower outside the mosque), the call to worship occurs five times daily—at dawn, just past noon, at midafternoon, at sunset, and in the evening. In earliest times, a muezzin, the official responsible for this duty, gave the cry. In many modern countries, the call now comes over a speaker system. Also located outside are fountains to provide the necessary water for ritual washing before prayer. Muslims wash their face, hands, forearms, and feet, as well as remove their shoes before beginning their prayers. In the absence of water, ritual cleansing may occur using sand or a stone.

Praying involves a series of movements known as rak'ah. From a standing position, the worshipper recites the opening sura of the Qur'an, as well as a second sura. After bowing to demonstrate respect, the person again stands, then prostrates himself or herself to signal humility. Next, the person assumes a sitting posture in silent prayer before again prostrating. The last movement is a greeting of "Peace be with you and the mercy of Allah." The worshipper looks both left and right before saying these words, which are intended for all persons, present and not.

Although Muslims stop to pray during each day when the call is given, Friday is the time for communal prayer and worship at the mosque. The prayer hall is the largest space within the mosque. At one end is a niche known as the mihrab, indicating the direction of Mecca, toward which Muslims face when they pray. At first, Muhammad instructed his followers to pray facing Jerusalem, as the Jewish people did. This early orientation was also a way to renounce the pagan associations of Mecca. Some mosques serve as community centers, with additional rooms for study.

The hajj, an important annual celebration, was a custom before the founding of Islam. Pagan worship centered in Mecca at the Ka'bah, where devotees circled the cube and kissed the Black Stone that was embedded in it. All warfare was forbidden during the hajj, as was argument, speaking crossly, or killing even an insect.

Muslims celebrate the lives of saints and their death anniversaries, a time when the saints are thought to reach the height of their spiritual life. Mawlid an-Nabi refers to "the birth of the Prophet." Although it is cultural and not rooted in the Qur'an, in some Muslim countries this is a public holiday on which people recite the Burdah, a poem that praises Muhammad. Muslims also celebrate the night that the Prophet ascended to heaven, Lailat ul-Miraj. The Night of Power is held to be the night on which Allah decides the destiny of people individually and the world at large.

Like Jews, Muslims practice circumcision, a ceremony known as khitan. Unlike Jews, however, Muslims do not remove the foreskin when the male is a baby. This is often done when a boy is about seven, and must be done before the boy reaches the age of twelve.

Healthy adult Muslims fast between sunrise and sunset during the month of Ramadan. This commemorates the first of Muhammad's revelations. In some Muslim countries, cannons are fired before the beginning of the month, as well as at the beginning and end of each day of the month. Some Muslims read a portion of the Qur'an each day during the month.

Judy A. Johnson, MTS

Bibliography

Al-Saud, Laith, Scott W. Hibbard, and Aminah Beverly. *An Introduction to Islam in the 21st Century*. Wiley, 2013. E-book.

Armstrong, Lyall. "The Rise of Islam: Traditional and Revisionist Theories." *Theological Review* 33.2 (2012): 87–106. Print.

Armstrong, Karen. *Islam: A Short History*. New York: Mod. Lib., 2000. Print.

Aslan, Reza. *No god but God: The Origins, Evolution, and Future of Islam*. New York: Random, 2005. Print.

Badawi, Emran El-. "'For All Times and Places': A Humanistic Reception of the Qur'an." *English Language Notes* 50.2 (2012): 99–112. Print.

Barnes, Trevor. *The Kingfisher Book of Religions*. New York: Kingfisher, 1999. Print.

Ben Jelloun, Tahar. *Islam Explained*. Trans. Franklin Philip. New York: New, 2002. Print.

Esposito, John L. *Islam: the Straight Path*. New York: Oxford UP, 1988. Print.

Glady, Pearl. *Criticism of Islam*.Library, 2012. E-book.

Holland, Tom. "Where Mystery Meets History." *History Today* 62.5 (2012): 19–24. Print.

Langley, Myrtle. *Religion*. New York: Knopf, 1996. Print.

Lunde, Paul. *Islam: Faith, Culture, History*. London: DK, 2002. Print.

Nasr, Seyyed Hossein. *Islam: Religion, History, and Civilization*. New York: Harper, 2002. Print.

Pasha, Mustapha Kamal. "Islam and the Postsecular." *Review of International Studies* 38.5 (2012): 1041–56. Print.

Sayers, Destini and Simone Peebles. *Essence of Islam and Sufism*. College, 2012. E-book.

Schirmacher, Christine. "They Are Not All Martyrs: Islam on the Topics of Dying, Death, and Salvation in the Afterlife." *Evangelical Review of Theology* 36.3 (2012): 250–65. Print.

Wilkinson, Philip. *Islam*. New York: DK, 2002. Print.

Wilkinson, Philip. *Religions*. New York: DK, 2008. Print.

Jainism

General Description

Jainism is one of the major religions of India. The name of the religion itself is believed to be based on the Sanskrit word *ji*, which means "to conquer or triumph," or *jina*, which means "victor or conqueror." The earliest name of the group was Nirgrantha, meaning bondless, but it applied to monks and nuns only. There are two sects: the Svetambaras (the white clad), which are the more numerous and wear white clothing, and the Digambaras (the sky clad), the most stringent group; their holy men or monks do not wear clothing at all.

Number of Adherents Worldwide

Jainism has about five million adherents, most of them in India (in some estimates, the religion represents approximately 1 percent of India's population). Because the religion is demanding in nature, few beyond the Indian subcontinent have embraced it. Jainism has spread to Africa, the United States, and nations in the Commonwealth (nations once under British rule) by virtue of Indian migration to these countries.

Basic Tenets

The principle of nonviolence (ahimsa) is a defining feature of Jainism. This results in a pacifist religion that influenced Mohandas Gandhi's ideas on nonviolent resistance. Jains believe that because all living creatures have souls, harming any of those creatures is wrong. They therefore follow a strict vegetarian diet, and often wear masks so as to not inhale living organisms. The most important aspect of Jainism is perhaps the five abstinences: ahimsa, satya (truthfulness), asteya (refrain from stealing), brahmacarya (chaste living), and aparigraha (refrain from greed).

A religion without priests, Jainism emphasizes the importance of the adherents' actions. Like Buddhists and Hindus, Jainists believe in karma and reincarnation. Unlike the Buddhist and Hindu idea of karma, Jainists regard karma as tiny particles that cling to the soul as mud clings to shoes, gradually weighing down the soul. Good deeds wash away these particles. Jainists also believe in moksha, the possibility of being freed from the cycle of death and rebirth. Like many Indian religions, Jainism does not believe in an afterlife, but in a cycle of death and rebirth. Once freed from this cycle, the soul will remain in infinite bliss.

While Jains do not necessarily believe in and worship God or gods, they believe in divine beings. Those who have achieved moksha are often regarded by Jains in the same manner in which other religions regard deities. These include the twenty-four Tirthankaras (ford makers) or jinas (victors), those who have escaped the cycle of death and rebirth, and the Siddhas, the liberated souls without physical form. The idea of a judging, ruling, or creator God is not present in Jainism.

Jainists believe that happiness is not found in material possessions and seek to have few of them. They also stress the importance of environmentalism. Jainists follow the Three Jewels: Right Belief, Right Knowledge, and Right Conduct. To be completely achieved, these three must be practiced together. Jainists also agree to six daily obligations (avashyaka), which include confession, praising the twenty-four Tirthankaras (the spiritual leaders), and calm meditation.

Sacred Text

The words of Mahavira were passed down orally, but lost over a few centuries. During a famine in the mid-fourth century BCE, many monks died. The texts were finally written down, although the Jain sects do not agree as to whether they are Mahavira's actual words. There are forty-five sacred texts (Agamas), which make up the Agam Sutras, Jainism's canonical literature. They were probably written down no earlier than 300 BCE. Two of the primary texts are the Akaranga

Sutra, which outlines the rule of conduct for Jain monks, and the Kalpa Sutra, which contains biographies of the last two Tirthankara. The Digambaras, who believe that the Agamas were lost around 350 BCE, have two main texts and four compendia written between 100 and 800 CE by various scholars.

Major Figures

Jainism has no single founder. However, Mahavira (Great Hero) is one of the Tirthankaras or jinas (pathfinders). He is considered the most recent spiritual teacher in a line of twenty-four. Modern-day Jainism derives from Mahavira, and his words are the foundation of Jain scriptures. He was a contemporary of Siddhartha Gautama, who was revered as the Buddha. Both Mahavira and Rishabha (or Adinatha), the first of the twenty-four Tirthankaras, are attributed as the founder of Jainism, though each Tirthankara maintains founding attributes.

Major Holy Sites

The Jain temple at Ranakpur is located in the village of Rajasthan. Carved from amber stone with marble interiors, the temple was constructed in the fifteenth century CE. It is dedicated to the first Tirthankara. The temple has twenty-nine large halls and each of the temple's 1,444 columns has a unique design with carvings.

Sravanabegola in Karnataka state is the site of Gomateshwara, Lord Bahubali's fifty-seven-foot statue. It was constructed in 981 CE from a single chunk of gneiss. Bahubali is considered the son of the first Tirthankara. The Digambara sect believes him to have been the first human to be free from the world.

Other pilgrimage sites include the Palitana temples in Gujarat and the Dilwara temples in Rajasthan. Sometimes regarded as the most sacred of the many Jain temples, the Palitana temples include 863 marble-engraved temples. The Jain temples at Dilwara were constructed of marble during the eleventh and thirteenth centuries CE. These five temples are often considered the most beautiful Jain temples in existence.

Major Rites & Celebrations

Every twelve years, the festival of Mahamastakabhisheka (anointing of the head) occurs at a statue of one of Jain's holy men, Bahubali, the second son of the first Tirthankara. The statue is anointed with milk, curd, and ghee, a clarified butter. Nearly a million people attend this rite. Jainists also observe Diwali, the Hindu festival of lights, as it symbolizes Mahavira's enlightenment.

The solemn festival of Paryusana marks the end of the Jain year for the Svetambaras (also spelled Shvetambaras). During this eight-day festival, all Jains are asked to live as an ascetic (monk or nun) would for one day. Das Laxana, a ten-day festival similar to that of Paryusana, immediately follows for the Digambara sect. During these special religious holidays, worshippers are involved in praying, meditating, fasting, forgiveness, and acts of penance. These holy days are celebrated during August and September, which is monsoon season in India. During the monsoons, monks prefer to remain in one place so as to avoid killing the smallest insects that appear during the rainy season. The Kalpa Sutra, one of the Jain scriptures, is read in the morning during Paryusana.

The feast of Kartaki Purnima follows the four months of the rainy season. It is held in the first month (Kartik) according to one calendar, and marked by a pilgrimage to the Palitana temples. Doing so with a pure heart is said to remove all sins of both the present and past life. Those who do so are thought to receive the final salvation in the third or fifth birth.

ORIGINS

History & Geography

In the eastern basin of the Ganges River during the seventh century BCE, a teacher named Parshvanatha (or Parshva) gathered a community founded on abandoning earthly concerns. He is considered to be the twenty-third Tirthankara (ford-maker), the one who makes a path for salvation. During the following century, Vardhamana, called Mahavira (Great Hero), who was considered the twenty-fourth and final spiritual teacher of the age, formulated most Jain doctrine and practice. By the time of Mahavira's death, Jains numbered around 36,000 nuns and 14,000 monks.

A division occurred within Jainism during the fourth century CE. The most extreme ascetics, the Digambaras (the sky-clad), argued that even clothing showed too great an attachment to the world, and that laundering them in the river risked harming creatures. This argument applied only to men, as the Digambaras denied that a soul could be freed from a woman's body. The other group, the Svetambaras (the white clad), believed that purity resided in the mind.

In 453 or 456 CE, a council of the Svetambara sect at Saurashtra in western India codified the canon still used. The split between the Digambaras, who did not take part in the meeting, and Svetambaras thus became permanent. Despite the split, Jainism's greatest flowering occurred during the early medieval age. After that time, Hindu sects devoted to the Hindu gods of Vishnu and Shiva flourished under the Gupta Empire (often referred to as India's golden age), slowing the spread of Jainism. Followers migrated to western and central India and the community became stronger.

The Digambaras were involved in politics through several medieval dynasties, and some Jain monks served as spiritual advisers. Royalty and high-ranking officials contributed to the building and maintenance of temples. Both branches of Jainism contributed a substantial literature. In the late medieval age, Jain monks ceased to live as ascetic wanders. They chose instead to don orange robes and to live at temples and other holy places.

The Muslims invaded India in the twelfth century. The Jains lost power and fractured over the next centuries into subgroups, some of which repudiated the worship of images. The poet and Digambara layman Banarsidas (1586-1643) played a significant role in a reform movement during the early 1600s. These reforms focused on the mystical side of Jainism, such as spiritual exploration of the inner self (meditation),

and denounced the formalized temple ritual. The movement, known as the Adhyatma movement, resulted in the Digambara Terapanth, a small Digambara sect.

The Jainists were well positioned in society following the departure of the British from India. Having long been associated with the artisan and merchant classes, they found new opportunities. As traditional Indian studies grew, spurred by Western interest, proponents of Jainism began to found publications and places of study (In fact, Jain libraries are believed to be the oldest in India.) The first Jain temple outside India was consecrated in Britain during the 1960s after Jains had gone there in the wake of political turmoil.

The Jains follow their typical profession as merchants. They publish English-language periodicals to spread their ideas on vegetarianism, environmentalism, and nonviolence (ahimsa). The ideas of ahimsa were formative for Mohandas Gandhi, born a Hindu. Gandhi used nonviolence as a wedge against the British Empire in India. Eventually, the British granted independence to India in 1947.

Virchand Gandhi (1864–1901) is believed to be the first Jain to arrive in America when he came over in 1893. He attended the first Parliament of World Religions, held in Chicago. Today North America has more than ninety Jain temples and centers. Jains in the West often follow professions such as banking and business to avoid destroying animal or plant life.

Founder or Major Prophet

Mahavira was born in India's Ganges Basin region. By tradition, he was born around 599 BCE, although some scholars think he may have lived a century later. His story bears a resemblance to that of the Buddha, with whom he was believed to have been a contemporary. His family was also of the Kshatriya (warrior) caste, and his father was a ruler of his clan. One tradition states that Mahavira's mother was of the Brahman (priestly) caste, although another places her in the Kshatriya.

Because he was not the eldest son, Mahavira was not in line for leadership of the clan.

He married a woman of his own caste and they had a daughter. Mahavira chose the life of a monk, with one garment. Later, he gave up wearing even that. He became a wandering ascetic around age thirty, with some legends stating that he tore out his hair before leaving home. He sought shelter in burial grounds and cremation sites, as well as at the base of trees. During the rainy season, however, he lived in towns and villages.

He followed a path of preaching and self-denial, after which he was enlightened (kevala). He spent the next thirty years teaching. Eleven disciples, all of whom were of the Brahman caste, gathered around him. At the end of his life, Mahavira committed Santhara, or ritual suicide through fasting.

Philosophical Basis

Like Buddhists and the Brahmin priests, the Jains believe in human incarnations of God, known as avatars. These avatars appear at the end of a time of decline to reinstate proper thinking and acting. Such a person was Mahavira. At the time of Mahavira's birth, India was experiencing great societal upheaval. Members of the warrior caste opposed the priestly caste, which exercised authority based on its supposed greater moral purity. Many people also opposed the slaughter of animals for the Vedic sacrifices.

Jainists share some beliefs with both Hinduism and Buddhism. The Hindu hero Rama, for example, is co-opted as a nonviolent Jain, while the deity Krishna is considered a cousin of Arishtanemi, the twenty-second Tirthankara. Like Buddhism, Jainism uses a wheel with twelve spokes; however, Jainism uses the wheel to explain time. The first half of the circle is the ascending stage, in which human happiness, prosperity, and life span increase. The latter half of the circle is the descending stage, involving a decrease of life span, prosperity, and happiness. The wheel of time is always in motion.

For Jainists, the universe is without beginning or ending, and contains layers of both heaven and hell. These layers include space beyond, which is without time, matter, or soul. The cosmos is depicted in art as a large human. The cloud layers surrounding the upper world are called universe space. Above them is the base, Nigoda, where lowest life forms live. The netherworld contains seven hells, each with a different stage of punishment and misery. The middle world contains the earth and remainder of the universe—mankind is located near the waist. There are thirty heavens in the upper world, where heavenly beings reside. In the supreme abode at the apex of the universe, liberated souls (siddha) live.

Jainism teaches that there are six universal entities. Only consciousness or soul is a living substance, while the remaining five are non-living. They include matter, medium of rest, medium of motion, time, and space. Jainism also does not believe in a God who can create, destroy, or protect. Worshipping goddesses and gods to achieve personal gain or material benefit is deemed useless.

Mahavira outlined five basic principles (often referred to as abstinences) for Jainist life, based on the teachings of the previous Tirthankara. They are detachment (aparigraha); the conduct of soul, primarily in sexual morality (brahmacharya); abstinence from stealing (asteya); abstinence from lying (satya); and nonviolence in every realm of the person (ahimsa).

Like other Indian religions, Jainism perceives life as four stages. The life of a student is brahmacharya-ashrama; the stage of family life is gruhasth-ashrama; in vanaprasth-ashrama, the Jainist concentrates on both family and aiding others through social services; and the final stage is sanyast-ashrama, a time of renouncing the world and becoming a monk.

Like many religions, Jainism has a bias toward males and toward the rigorous life of monks and nuns. A layperson cannot work off bad karma, but merely keeps new bad karma from accruing. By following a path of asceticism, however, monks and nuns can destroy karma. Even members of the laity follow eight rules of behavior and take twelve vows. Physical austerity is a key concept in Jainism, as a saint's highest ideal is to starve to death.

Holy Places

There are four major Jain pilgrimage sites: the Dilwara temples near Rajasthan; the Palitana temples; the Ranakpur temple; and Shravan Begola, the site of the statue of Lord Bahubali. In addition, Jains may make pilgrimages to the caves of Khandagiri and Udayagiri, which were cells for Jain monks carved from rock. The spaces carved are too short for a man to stand upright. They were essentially designed for prayer and meditation. Udayagiri has eighteen caves and Khandagiri has fifteen. The caves are decorated with elaborate carvings.

JAINISM IN DEPTH

Sacred Symbols

The open palm (Jain Hand) with a centered wheel, sometimes with the word *ahimsa* written on it, is a prominent Jain symbol. Seen as an icon of peace, the open palm symbol can be interpreted as a call to stop violence, and also means "assurance." It appears on the walls of Jain temples and in their publications. Jainism also employs a simple swastika symbol, considered to be the holiest symbol. It represents the four forms of worldly existence, and three dots above the swastika represent the Three Jewels. The Jain emblem, adopted in 1975, features both the Jain Hand (the open palm symbol with an inset wheel) and a swastika. This year was regarded as the 2,500th anniversary of Mahavira being enlightened.

Sacred Practices & Gestures

Jains may worship daily in their homes at private shrines. The Five Supreme Beings stand for stages in the path to enlightenment. Rising before daybreak, worshippers invoke these five. In addition, devout Jainists set aside forty-eight minutes daily to meditate.

To demonstrate faithfulness to the five vows that Jains undertake, there are four virtuous qualities that must be cultivated. They are compassion (karuna), respect and joy (pramoda), love and friendship (maitri), and indifference toward and noninvolvement with those who are arrogant (madhyastha). Mahavira stressed that Jains must be friends to all living beings. Compassion goes beyond mere feeling; it involves offering both material and spiritual aid. Pramoda carries with it the idea of rejoicing enthusiastically over the virtues of others. There are contemplations associated with these virtues, and daily practice is suggested to attain mastery.

Some Jainists, both men and women, wear a dot on the forehead. This practice comes from Hinduism. During festivals, Jains may pray, chant, fast, or keep silent. These actions are seen as removing bad karma from the soul and moving the person toward ultimate happiness.

Food Restrictions

Jainists practice a strict vegetarian way of life (called Jain vegetarianism) to avoid harming any creature. They refuse to eat root vegetables, because by uprooting them, the entire plant dies. They prefer to wait for fruit to drop from trees rather than taking it from the branches. Starving to death, when ready, is seen as an ideal.

Rites, Celebrations & Services

Some festivals are held annually and their observances are based on a lunar calendar. Mahavir Jayanti is an example, as it celebrates Mahavira's birthday.

Jains may worship, bathe, and make offerings to images of the Tirthankaras in their home or in a temple. Svetambaras Jains also clothe and decorate the images. Because the Tirthankaras have been liberated, they cannot respond as a deity granting favors might. Although Jainism rejects belief in gods in favor of worshipping Tirthankaras, in actual practice, some Jainists pray to Hindu gods.

When Svetambara monks are initiated, they are given three pieces of clothing, including a small piece of white cloth to place over the mouth. The cloth, called a mukhavastrika, is designed to prevent the monk from accidentally eating insects.

Monks take great vows (mahavratas) at initiation. These include abstaining from lying, stealing, sexual activity, injury to any living thing, and personal possessions. Monks own a broom to sweep in front of where they are going to walk so that no small creatures are injured, along with an alms bowl and a robe. The Digambara monks practice a more stringent lifestyle, eating one meal a day, for which they beg.

Nuns in the Svetambaras are three times more common than are monks, even though they receive less honor, and are required to defer to the monks. In Digambara Jainism, the nuns wear robes and accept that they must be reborn as men before progressing upward.

The observance of Santhara, which is religious fasting until death, is a voluntary fasting undertaken with full knowledge. The ritual is also known as Sallekhana, and is not perceived as suicide by Jains, particularly as the prolonged nature of the ritual provides ample time for reflection. It is believed that at least one hundred people die every year from observing Santhara.

Judy A. Johnson, MTS

Bibliography

Aristarkhova, Irina. "Thou Shall Not Harm All Living Beings: Feminism, Jainism, and Animals." *Hypatia* 27.3 (2012): 636–50. Print.

Aukland, Knut. "Understanding Possession in Jainism: A Study of Oracular Possession in Nakoda." *Modern Asian Studies* 47.1 (2013): 103–34. Print.

Barnes, Trevor. *The Kingfisher Book of Religions*. New York: Kingfisher, 1999. Print.

Langley, Myrtle. *Religion*. New York: Knopf, 1996. Print.

Long, Jeffery. *Jainism: An Introduction*. London: I. B. Tauris, 2009. Print.

Long, Jeffrey. "Jainism: Key Themes." *Religion Compass* 5.9 (2011): 501–10. Print.

Rankin, Aidan. *The Jain Path*. Berkeley: O Books, 2006. Print.

Shah, Bharat S. *An Introduction to Jainism*. Great Neck: Setubandh, 2002. Print.

Titze, Kurt. *Jainism: A Pictorial Guide to the Religion of Non-Violence*. Delhi: Motilal Banarsidass, 2001. Print.

Tobias, Michael. *Life Force: the World of Jainism*. Berkeley: Asian Humanities, 1991. E-book, print.

Wiley, Kristi L. *The A to Z of Jainism*. Lanham: Scarecrow, 2009. Print.

Wiley, Kristi L. *Historical Dictionary of Jainism*. Lanham: Scarecrow, 2004. Print.

Wilkinson, Philip. *Religions*. New York: DK, 2008. Print.

Judaism

General Description

In modern Judaism, the main denominations (referred to as movements) are Orthodox Judaism (including Haredi and Hasidic Judaism); Conservative Judaism; Reform (Liberal) Judaism; Reconstructionist Judaism; and to a lesser extent, Humanistic Judaism. In addition, the Jewry of Ethiopia and Yemen are known for having distinct or alternative traditions. Classical Judaism is often organized by two branches: Ashkenazic (Northern Europe) and Sephardic Jews (Spain, Portugal, and North Africa).

Number of Adherents Worldwide

Judaism has an estimated 15 million adherents worldwide, with roughly 41 percent living in Israel and about 41 percent living in the United States. Ashkenazi Jews represent roughly 75 percent, while Sephardic Jews represent roughly 25 percent, with the remaining 5 percent split among alternative communities. Within the United States, a 2000-01 survey stated that 10 percent of American Jews identified as Orthodox (with that number increasing), 35 percent as Reform, 26 percent as Conservative, leaving the remainder with an alternative or no affiliation. [Source: Wilkinson, 2008]

Orthodox Judaism, which was founded around the thirteenth century BCE, has 3 million followers. Members of Reform Judaism, with roots in nineteenth-century Germany, wanted to live peacefully with non-Jews. Therefore, they left the laws that prevented this vision of peace and downplayed the idea of a Jewish state. Reform Judaism, also known as Progressive or Liberal Judaism, allows women rabbis and does not require its adherents to keep kosher. About 1.1 million Jews are Reform; they live primarily in the United States. When nonkosher food was served at the first graduation ceremony for Hebrew Union College, some felt that the Reform movement had gone too far. Thus the Conservative movement began in 1887. A group

of rabbis founded the Jewish Theological Seminary in New York City, wanting to emphasize biblical authority above moral choice, as the Reform tradition stressed. Currently about 900,000 Jews practice this type of Judaism, which is theologically midway between Orthodox and Reform. The Hasidim, an ultra-conservative group, began in present-day Ukraine around 1740. There are 4.5 million Hasidic Jews.

Basic Tenets

Though there is no formal creed (statement of faith or belief), Jews value all life, social justice, education, generous giving, and the importance of living based on the principles and values espoused in the Torah (Jewish holy book). They believe in one all-powerful and creator God, Jehovah or Yaweh, a word derived from the Hebrew letters "YHWH," the unpronounceable name of God. The word is held to be sacred; copyists were required to bathe both before and after writing the word. Jews also believe in a coming Messiah who will initiate a Kingdom of Righteousness. They follow a complex law, composed of 613 commandments or mitzvot. Jews believe that they are God's Chosen People with a unique covenant relationship. They have a responsibility to practice hospitality and to improve the world.

The belief in the afterlife is a part of the Jewish faith. Similar to Christianity, this spiritual world is granted to those who abide by the Jewish faith and live a good life. Righteous Jews are rewarded in the afterlife by being able to discuss the Torah with Moses, who first received the law from God. Furthermore, certain Orthodox sects believe that wicked souls are destroyed or tormented after death.

Sacred Text

The complete Hebrew Bible is called the Tanakh. It includes the prophetic texts, called the Navi'im, the poetic writings, the Ketubim, and the Torah, meaning teaching, law, or guidance. Torah may refer to the entire body of Jewish law or to the first five books of the Hebrew Bible, known as the Pentateuch (it is the Old Testament in the Christian Bible). Also esteemed is the Talmud, made up of the Mishnah, a written collection of oral traditions, and Gemara, a commentary on the Mishnah. The Talmud covers many different subjects, such as law, stories and legends, medicine, and rituals.

Major Figures

The patriarchs are held to be the fathers of the faith. Abraham, the first patriarch, was called to leave his home in the Fertile Crescent for a land God would give him, and promised descendents as numerous as the stars. His son Isaac was followed by Jacob, whom God renamed Israel, and whose twelve sons became the heads of the twelve tribes of Israel. Moses was the man who, along with his brother Aaron, the founder of a priestly line, and their sister Miriam led the chosen people out of slavery in Egypt, where they had gone to escape famine. The Hebrew Bible also details the careers of a group of men and women known as judges, who were really tribal rulers, as well as of the prophets, who called the people to holy lives. Chief among the prophets was Elijah, who confronted wicked kings and performed many miracles. Several kings were key to the biblical narrative, among them David, who killed the giant Goliath, and Solomon, known for his wisdom and for the construction of a beautiful temple.

Major Holy Sites

Most of Judaism's holy sites are within Israel, the Holy Land, including Jerusalem, which was the capital of the United Kingdom of Israel under kings David and Solomon; David captured it from a Canaanite tribe around 1000 BCE. Within the Old City of Jerusalem is the Temple Mount (where the Temple of Jerusalem was built), often considered the religion's holiest site, the Foundation Stone (from which Judaism claims the world was created), and the Western (or Wailing) Wall. Other sites include Mount Sinai in Egypt, the mountain upon which God gave Moses his laws.

Major Rites & Celebrations

The Jewish calendar recognizes several important holidays. Rosh Hashanah, literally "first of the year," is known as the Jewish New Year and inaugurates a season of self-examination and repentance that culminates in Yom Kippur, the Day of Atonement. Each spring, Passover commemorates the deliverance of the Hebrew people from Egypt. Shavuot celebrates the giving of the Torah to Moses, while Sukkot is the harvest festival. Festivals celebrating deliverance from enemies include Purim and Hanukkah. Young adolescents become members of the community at a bar or bat mitzvah, held near the twelfth or thirteenth birthday. The Sabbath, a cessation from work from Friday at sundown until Saturday when the first star appears, gives each week a rhythm.

ORIGINS

History & Geography

Called by God perhaps four thousand years ago, Abraham left from Ur of the Chaldees, or the Fertile Crescent in Mesopotamia in present-day Iraq, to go the eastern Mediterranean, the land of Canaan. Several generations later, the tribe went to Egypt to escape famine. They were later enslaved by a pharaoh, sometimes believed to have been Ramses II (ca. 1279–1213 BCE), who was noted for his many building projects. The Israelites returned to Canaan under Moses several hundred years after their arrival in Egypt. He was given the law, the Ten Commandments, plus the rest of the laws governing all aspects of life, on Mount Sinai about the thirteenth century BCE. This marked the beginning of a special covenant relationship between the new nation, known as Israel, and God.

Following a period of rule by judges, kings governed the nation. Major kings included David, son-in-law to the first king, Saul, and David's son, Solomon. The kingdom split at the beginning of the reign of Solomon's son

Rehoboam, who began ruling about 930 BCE. Rehoboam retained the ten northern tribes, while the two southern tribes followed a military commander rather than the Davidic line.

Rehoboam's kingdom was known as Israel, after the name Jehovah gave to Jacob. Judah was the name of the southern kingdom—one of Jacob's sons was named Judah. Prophets to both nations warned of coming judgment unless the people repented of mistreating the poor and other sins, such as idolatry. Unheeding, Israel was taken into captivity by the Assyrians in 722 BCE. and the Israelites assimilated into the nations around them.

The Babylonians captured Judah in 586 BCE. After Babylon had been captured in turn by Persians, the Jewish people were allowed to return to the land in 538 BCE. There they began reconstructing the temple and the walls of the city. In the second century BCE, Judas Maccabeus led a rebellion against the heavy taxes and oppression of the Greek conquerors, after they had levied high taxes and appointed priests who were not Jewish. Judas Maccabeus founded a new ruling dynasty, the Hasmoneans, which existed briefly before the region came under the control of Rome.

The Jewish people revolted against Roman rule in 70 CE, leading to the destruction of the second temple. The final destruction of Jerusalem occurred in 135 under the Roman Emperor Hadrian. He changed the city's name to Aelia Capitolina and the name of the country to Palaestina. With the cultic center of their religion gone, the religious leaders developed new methods of worship that centered in religious academies and in synagogues.

After Christianity became the official state religion of the Roman Empire in the early fourth century, Jews experienced persecution. They became known for their scholarship, trade, and banking over the next centuries, with periods of brutal persecution in Europe. Christians held Jews responsible for the death of Jesus, based on a passage in the New Testament. The Blood Libel, begun in England in 1144, falsely accused Jews of killing a Christian child to bake unleavened bread for Passover. This rumor persisted for centuries, and was repeated by Martin Luther during the Protestant Reformation. England expelled all Jews in 1290; they were not readmitted until 1656 under Oliver Cromwell, and not given citizenship until 1829. Jews were also held responsible for other catastrophes—namely poisoning wells and rivers to cause the Black Death in 1348—and were often made to wear special clothing, such as pointed hats, or badges with the Star of David or stone tablets on them.

The relationship between Muslims and Jews was more harmonious. During the Muslim Arab dominance, there was a "golden age" in Spain due to the contributions of Jews and Muslims, known as Moors in Spain. This ideal and harmonious period ended in 1492, when both Moors and Jews were expelled from Spain or forced to convert to Christianity.

Jews in Russia suffered as well. An estimated two million Jews fled the country to escape the pogroms (a Russian word meaning devastation) between 1881 and 1917. The twentieth-century Holocaust, in which an estimated six million Jews perished at the hands of Nazi Germany, was but the culmination of these centuries of persecution. The Nazis also destroyed more than six hundred synagogues.

The Holocaust gave impetus to the creation of the independent state of Israel. The Zionist movement, which called for the founding or reestablishment of a Jewish homeland, was started by Austrian Jew Theodor Herzl in the late nineteenth century, and succeeded in 1948. The British government, which had ruled the region under a mandate, left the area, and Israel was thus established. This ended the Diaspora, or dispersion, of the Jewish people that had begun nearly two millennia before when the Romans forced the Jews to leave their homeland.

Arab neighbors, some of whom had been removed forcibly from the land to create the nation of Israel, were displeased with the new political reality. Several wars have been fought, including the War of Independence in 1948, the Six-Day War in 1967, and the Yom Kippur War in 1973. In addition, tension between Israel and its neighboring Arab states is almost constant.

When the Jewish people were dispersed from Israel, two traditions began. The Ashkenazi Jews settled in Germany and central Europe. They spoke a mixture of the Hebrew dialect and German called Yiddish. Sephardic Jews lived in the Mediterranean countries, including Spain; their language, Ladino, mixed Hebrew and old Spanish.

Founder or Major Prophet

Judaism refers to three major patriarchs: Abraham, his son Isaac, and Isaac's son Jacob. Abraham is considered the first Jew and worshipper in Judaism, as the religion began through his covenant with God. As the forefather of the religion, he is often associated as the founder, though the founder technically is God, or Yahweh (YHWH). Additionally, the twelve sons of Jacob, who was also named Israel, became the founders of the twelve tribes of Israel.

Moses is regarded as a major prophet and as the Lawgiver. God revealed to Moses the complete law during the forty days that the Jewish leader spent on Mount Sinai during the wilderness journey from Egypt to Canaan. Thus, many attribute Moses as the founder of Judaism as a religion.

Philosophical Basis

Judaism began with Abraham's dissatisfaction with the polytheistic worship of his culture. Hearing the command of God to go to a land that would be shown to him, Abraham and his household obeyed. Abraham practiced circumcision and hospitality, cornerstones of the Jewish faith to this day. He and his descendents practiced a nomadic life, much like that of contemporary Bedouins. They migrated from one oasis or well to another, seeking pasture and water for the sheep and goats they herded.

The further development of Judaism came under the leadership of Moses. A Jewish child adopted by Pharaoh's daughter, he was raised and educated in the palace. As a man, he identified with the Jewish people, killing one of the Egyptians who was oppressing a Jew. He subsequently fled for his life, becoming a shepherd in the wilderness, where he remained for forty years. Called by God from a bush that burned but was not destroyed, he was commissioned to lead the people out of slavery in Egypt back to the Promised Land. That forty-year pilgrimage in the wilderness and desert of Arabia shaped the new nation.

Holy Places

The city of Jerusalem was first known as Salem. When King David overcame the Jebusites who lived there, the city, already some two thousand years old, became the capital of Israel. It is built on Mount Zion, which is still considered a sacred place. David's son Solomon built the First Temple in Jerusalem, centering the nation's spiritual as well as political life in the city. The Babylonians captured the city in 597 BCE and destroyed the Temple. For the next sixty years, the Jews remained in exile, until Cyrus the Persian conqueror of Babylon allowed them to return. They rebuilt the temple, but it was desecrated by Antiochus IV of Syria in 167 BCE. In 18 BCE, during a period of Roman occupation, Herod the Great began rebuilding and expanding the Temple. The Romans under the general Titus destroyed the Temple in 70 CE, just seven years after its completion.

The city eventually came under the rule of Persia, the Muslim Empire, and the Crusaders before coming under control of Britain. In 1948 an independent state of Israel was created. The following year, Jerusalem was divided between Israel, which made the western part the national capital, and Jordan, which ruled the eastern part of the city. The Western or Wailing Wall, a retaining wall built during Herod's time, is all that remains of the Second Temple. Devout Jews still come to the Wailing Wall to pray, sometimes placing their petitions on paper and folding the paper into the Wall's crevices. The Wall is known as a place where prayers are answered and a reminder of the perseverance of the Jewish people and faith. According to tradition, the Temple will be rebuilt when Messiah comes to inaugurate God's Kingdom.

The Temple Mount, located just outside Jerusalem on a natural acropolis, includes the Dome of the Rock. This shrine houses a rock held sacred by both Judaism and Islam. Jewish tradition states that it is the spot from which the world was created and the spot on which Abraham was asked to sacrifice his son Isaac. Muslims believe that from this rock Muhammad ascended for his night journey to heaven. Much of Jerusalem, including this holy site, has been and continues to be fought over by people of three faiths: Judaism, Islam, and Christianity.

Moses received the law from God on Mount Sinai. It is still regarded as a holy place.

JUDAISM IN DEPTH

Sacred Symbols

Observant Jewish men pray three times daily at home or in a synagogue, a center of worship, from the word meaning "meeting place." They wear a tallis, or a prayer shawl with tassles, during their morning prayer and on Yom Kippur, the Day of Atonement. They may also cover their heads as a sign of respect during prayer, wearing a skullcap known as a kippah or yarmulka. They find their prayers and blessings in a siddur, which literally means "order," because the prayers appear in the order in which they are recited for services. Jewish daily life also includes blessings for many things, including food.

Tefillin or phylacteries are the small black boxes made of leather from kosher animals that Jewish men wear on their foreheads and their left upper arms during prayer. They contain passages from the Torah. Placing the tefillin on the head reminds them to think about the Torah, while placing the box on the arm puts the Torah close to the heart.

The Law of Moses commands the people to remember the words of the law and to teach them to the children. A mezuzah helps to fulfill that command. A small box with some of the words of the law written on a scroll inside, a mezuzah is hung on the doorframes of every door in the house. Most often, the words of the Shema,

the Jewish recitation of faith, are written on the scroll. The Shema is repeated daily. "Hear, O Israel: the Lord your God, the Lord is one. . . . Love the Lord your God with all your heart, and with all your soul, and with all your might."

Jews adopted the Star of David, composed of two intersecting triangles, during the eighteenth century. There are several interpretations of the design. One is that it is the shape of King David's shield. Another idea is that it stands for daleth, the first letter of David's name. A third interpretation is that the six points refer to the days of the work week, and the inner, larger space represented the day of rest, the Sabbath, or Shabot. The Star of David appears on the flag of Israel. The flag itself is white, symbolizing peace and purity, and blue, symbolizing heaven and reminding all of God's activity.

The menorah is a seven-branch candlestick representing the light of the Torah. For Hanukkah, however, an eight-branched menorah is used. The extra candle is the servant candle, and is the one from which all others are lit.

Because the Torah is the crowning glory of life for Jewish people, a crown is sometimes used on coverings for the Torah. The scrolls of Torah are stored in a container, called an ark, which generally is covered with an ornate cloth called a mantle. The ark and mantle are often elaborately decorated with symbols, such as the lion of Judah. Because the Torah scroll, made of parchment from a kosher animal, is sacred and its pages are not to be touched, readers use a pointed stick called a yad. Even today, Torahs are written by hand in specially prepared ink and using a quill from a kosher bird. Scribes are trained for seven years.

A shofar is a ram's horn, blown as a call to repentance on Rosh Hashanah, the Jewish New Year. This holiday is the beginning of a ten-day preparation for the Day of Atonement, which is the most holy day in the Jewish calendar and a time of both fasting and repentance.

Sacred Practices & Gestures

Sacred practices can apply daily, weekly, annually, or over a lifetime's events. Reciting the Shema, the monotheistic creed taken from the

Torah, is a daily event. Keeping the Sabbath occurs weekly. Each year the festivals described above take place. Circumcision and bar or bat mitzvah are once-in-a-lifetime events. Each time someone dies, the mourners recite the Kaddish for seven days following death, and grieve for a year.

Food Restrictions

Kosher foods are those that can be eaten based on Jewish law. Animals that chew the cud and have cloven hooves, such as cows and lamb, and domestic poultry are considered kosher. Shellfish, pork, and birds of prey are forbidden. Keeping kosher also includes the method of preparing and storing the food. This includes animals which are slaughtered in a way to bring the least amount of pain and from which all blood is drained. In addition, dairy and meat products are to be kept separate, requiring separate refrigerators in the homes of the Orthodox.

Rites, Celebrations & Services

Sabbath is the weekly celebration honoring one of the Ten Commandments, which commands the people to honor the Sabbath by doing no work that day. The practice is rooted in the Genesis account that God rested on the seventh day after creating the world in six days. Because the Jewish day begins at sundown, the Sabbath lasts from Friday night to Saturday night. Special candles are lit and special food—included the braided egg bread called challah—for the evening meal is served. This day is filled with feasting, visiting, and worship.

Boys are circumcised at eight days of age. This rite, B'rit Milah, meaning "seal of the covenant," was first given to Abraham as a sign of the covenant. A trained circumciser, or mohel, may be a doctor or rabbi. The boy's name is officially announced at the ceremony. A girl's name is given at a special baby-naming ceremony or in the synagogue on the first Sabbath after she is born.

A boy becomes a "son of the commandment," or bar mitzvah, at age thirteen. At a special ceremony, the young man reads a portion of

Torah that he has prepared ahead of time. Most boys also give a speech at the service. Girls become bat mitzvah at age twelve. This ceremony developed in the twentieth century. Not all Orthodox communities will allow this rite. Girls may also read from the Torah and give a sermon in the synagogue, just as boys do.

When a Jewish person dies, mourners begin shiva, a seven-day mourning period. People usually gather at the home of the deceased, where mirrors are covered. In the home, the Kaddish, a collection of prayers that praise God and celebrate life, is recited. Traditionally, family members mourn for a full year, avoiding parties and festive occasions.

The Jewish calendar offers a series of feasts and festivals, beginning with Rosh Hashanah, the Jewish New Year. At this time, Jews recall the creation. They may also eat apples that have been dipped into honey and offer each other wishes for a sweet New Year. The next ten days are a time of reflection on the past year, preparing for Yom Kippur.

This Day of Atonement once included animal sacrifice at the Temple. Now it includes an all-day service at the synagogue and a twenty-five-hour fast. A ram's horn, called a shofar, is blown as a call to awaken to lead a holier life. The shofar reminds Jewish people of the ram that Abraham sacrificed in the place of his son, Isaac.

Passover, or Pesach, is the spring remembrance of God's deliverance of the people from slavery in Egypt. In the night that the Jewish people left Egypt, they were commanded to sacrifice a lamb for each household and sprinkle the blood on the lintels and doorposts. A destroying angel from God would "pass over" the homes with blood sprinkled. During the first two nights of Passover, a special meal is served known as a Seder, meaning order. The foods symbolize different aspects of the story of deliverance, which is told during the meal by the head of the family.

Shavuot has its origins as a harvest festival. This celebration of Moses receiving the Torah on Mount Sinai occurs fifty days after the second day of Passover. To welcome the first fruits of the season, the synagogue may be decorated with fruit and flowers. Traditionally, the Ten Commandments are read aloud in the synagogue.

Purim, which occurs in February or March, celebrates the deliverance of the Jews during their captivity in Persia in the fifth century BCE. The events of that experience are recorded in the Book of Esther in the Hebrew Bible (Tanakh). The book is read aloud during Purim.

Sukkot, the feast celebrating the end of the harvest, occurs in September or October. Jews recall God's provision for them in the wilderness when they left Egypt to return to Canaan. Traditionally, huts are made and decorated with flowers and fruits. The conclusion of Sukkot is marked by a synagogue service known as Simchat Torah, or Rejoicing in the Law. People sing and dance as the Torah scrolls are carried and passed from person to person.

Hanukkah, known as the Festival of Lights, takes place over eight days in December. It celebrates the rededicating of the Temple under the leader Judas Maccabeus, who led the people in recapturing the structure from Syria in 164 BCE. According to the story, the Jews had only enough oil in the Temple lamp to last one day, but the oil miraculously lasted for eight days, after which Judas Maccabeus re-dedicated the Temple. On each day of Hanukkah, one of the eight candles is lit until all are burning. The gift-giving custom associated with Hanukkah is relatively new, and may derive from traditional small gifts of candy or money. The practice may also have been encouraged among those integrated with communities that exchange gifts during the Christmas season.

Judy A. Johnson, MTS

Bibliography

Barnes, Trevor. *The Kingfisher Book of Religions.* New York: Kingfisher, 1999. Print.

"A Buffet to Suit All Tastes." *Economist* 28 Jul. 2012: Spec. section 4–6. Print.

Charing, Douglas. *Judaism.* London: DK, 2003. Print.

Coenen Snyder, Saskia. *Building a Public Judaism: Synagogues and Jewish Identity in Nineteenth-Century Europe.* Cambridge: Harvard UP, 2013. E-book.

Diamant, Anita. *Living a Jewish Life.* New York: Collins, 1996. Print.

Exler, Lisa and Rabbi Jill Jacobs. "A Judaism That Matters." *Journal of Jewish Communal Service* 87.1/2 (2012): 66–76. Print.

Gelernter, David Hillel. *Judaism: A Way of Being.* New Haven: Yale UP, 2009. E-book.

Kessler, Edward. *What Do Jews Believe?* New York: Walker, 2007. Print.

Krieger, Aliza Y. "The Role of Judaism in Family Relationships." *Journal of Multicultural Counseling & Development* 38.3 (2010): 154–65. Print.

Langley, Myrtle. *Religion.* New York: Knopf, 1996. Print.

Madsen, Catherine. "A Heart of Flesh: Beyond 'Creative Liturgy.'" *Cross Currents* 62.1 (2012): 11–20. Print.

Meredith, Susan. *The Usborne Book of World Religions.* London: Usborne, 1995. Print.

Schoen, Robert. *What I Wish My Christian Friends Knew About Judaism.* Chicago: Loyola, 2004. Print.

Stefnon, Matt. *Judaism: History, Belief, and Practice.* New York: Britannica Educational, 2012. E-book.

Wertheimer, Jack. "The Perplexities of Conservative Judaism." *Commentary* Sept. 2007: 38–44. Print.

Wilkinson, Philip. *Religions.* New York: DK, 2008. Print.

Sikhism

General Description

The youngest of the world religions, Sikhism has existed for only about five hundred years. Sikhism derives from the Sanskrit word *sishyas*, which means "disciple"; in the Punjabi language, it also means "disciple."

Number of Adherents Worldwide

An estimated 24.5 million people follow the Sikh religion. Most of the devotees live in Asia, particularly in the Punjab region of India (Wilkinson, p. 335).

Basic Tenets

Sikhism is a monotheistic religion. The deity is God, known as Nam, or Name. Other synonyms include the Divine, Ultimate, Ultimate Reality, Infinity, the Formless, Truth, and other attributes of God.

Sikhs adhere to three basic principles. These are hard work (kirt kao), worshipping the Divine Name (nam japo), and sharing what one has (vand cauko). Meditating on the Divine Name is seen as a method of moving toward a life totally devoted to God. In addition, Sikhs believe in karma, or moral cause and effect. They value hospitality to all, regardless of religion, and oppose caste distinctions. Sikhs delineate a series of five stages that move upward to gurmukh, total devotion to God. This service is called Seva. Sahaj, or tranquility, is practiced as a means of being united with God as well as of generating external good will. Sikhs are not in favor of external routines of religion; they may stop in their temple whenever it is convenient during the day.

Sikhism does not include a belief in the afterlife. Instead, the soul is believed to be reincarnated in successive lives and deaths, a belief borrowed from Hinduism. The goal is then to break this karmic cycle, and to merge the human spirit with that of God.

Sacred Text

The Guru Granth Sahib (also referred to as the Aad Guru Granth Sahib, or AGGS), composed of Adi Granth, meaning First Book, is the holy scripture of Sikhism. It is a collection of religious poetry that is meant to be sung. Called shabads, they were composed by the first five gurus, the ninth guru, and thirty-six additional holy men of northern India. Sikhs always show honor to the Guru Granth Sahib by carrying it above the head when in a procession.

A second major text is the Dasam Granth, or Tenth Book, created by followers of Guru Gobind Singh, the tenth guru. Much of it is devoted to retelling the Hindu stories of Krishna and Rama. Those who are allowed to read and care for the Granth Sahib are known as granthi. Granthi may also look after the gurdwara, or temple. In the gurdwara, the book rests on a throne with a wooden base and cushions covered in cloths placed in a prescribed order. If the book is not in use, it is covered with a cloth known as a rumala. When the book is read, a fan called a chauri is fanned over it as a sign of respect, just as followers of the gurus fanned them with chauris. At Amritsar, a city in northwestern India that houses the Golden Temple, the Guru Granth Sahib is carried on a palanquin (a covered, carried bed). If it is carried in the city, a kettle drum is struck and people welcome it by tossing rose petals.

Major Figures

Guru Nanak (1469–1539) is the founder of Sikhism. He was followed by nine other teachers, and collectively they are known as the Ten Gurus. Each of them was chosen by his predecessor and was thought to share the same spirit of that previous guru. Guru Arjan (1581–1606), the fifth guru, oversaw completion of the Golden Temple in Amritsar, India. Guru Gobind Singh (1675–1708) was the tenth and last human guru. He decreed that the True Guru henceforth would be the Granth Sahib, the scripture of the Sikhs. He also founded the Khalsa, originally a military order of male Sikhs willing to die for the faith; the term is now used to refer to all baptized Sikhs.

Major Holy Sites

Amritsar, India, is the holy city of Sikhism. Construction of the city began under Guru Ram Das (1574–1581), the fourth guru, during the 1570s. One legend says that the Muslim ruler, Emperor Akbar, gave the land to the third guru, Guru Amar Das (1552–74). Whether or not that is true, Amar Das did establish the location of Amritsar. He chose a site near a pool believed to hold healing water.

When construction of the Golden Temple began, only a small town existed. One legend says that a Muslim saint from Lahore, India, named Mian Mir laid the foundation stone of the first temple. It has been demolished and rebuilt three times. Although pilgrimage is not required of Sikhs, many come to see the shrines and the Golden Temple. They call it Harmandir Sahib, God's Temple, or Darbar Sahib, the Lord's Court. When the temple was completed during the tenure of the fifth guru, Arjan, he placed the first copy of the Guru Granth Sahib inside.

Every Sikh temple has a free kitchen attached to it, called a langar. After services, all people, regardless of caste or standing within the community, sit on the floor in a straight line and eat a simple vegetarian meal together. As a pilgrimage site, the langar serves 30,000–40,000 people daily, with more coming on Sundays and festival days. About forty volunteers work in the kitchen each day.

Major Rites & Celebrations

In addition to the community feasts at temple langars, Sikhs honor four rites of passage in a person's life: naming, marriage, initiation in Khalsa (pure) through the Amrit ceremony, and death.

There are eight major celebrations and several other minor ones in Sikhism. Half of them commemorate events in the lives of the ten gurus.

The others are Baisakhi, the new year festival; Diwali, the festival of light, which Hindus also celebrate; Hola Mahalla, which Gobind Singh created as an alternative to the Hindu festival of Holi, and which involves military parades; and the installing of the Guru Granth Sahib.

ORIGINS

History & Geography

The founder of Sikhism, Nanak, was born in 1469 CE in the Punjab region of northeast India, where both Hinduism and Islam were practiced. Both of these religions wanted control of the region. Nanak wanted the fighting between followers of these two traditions to end and looked for solutions to the violence.

Nanak blended elements of both religions and also combined the traditional apparel of both faiths to construct his clothing style. The Guru Granth Sahib further explains the division between Sikhs and the Islamic and Muslim faiths:

Nanak would become the first guru of the Sikh religion, known as Guru Nanak Dev. A Muslim musician named Dhai Mardana, considered the first follower, accompanied Nanak in his travels around India and Asia. Guru Nanak often sang, and singing remains an important part of worship for Sikhs. Before his death, Nanak renamed one of his disciples Angad, a word meaning "a part of his own self." He became Guru Angad Dev, the second guru, thus beginning the tradition of designating a successor and passing on the light to that person.

Guru Baba Ram Das, the fourth guru, who lived in the sixteenth century, began constructing Amritsar's Golden Temple. The structure was completed by his successor, Guru Arjan Dev, who also collected poems and songs written by the first four gurus and added his own. He included the work of Kabir and other Hindu and Muslim holy men as well. This became the Adi Granth, which he placed in the Golden Temple.

Guru Arjan was martyred in 1606 by Jehangir, the Muslim emperor. His son Hargobind became the sixth guru and introduced several important practices and changes. He wore two swords, representing both spiritual and worldly authority. Near the Golden Temple he had a building known as Akal Takht, or Throne of the Almighty, erected. In it was a court of justice as well as a group of administrators. Even today, orders and decisions enter the community from Akal Takht. Guru Hargobind was the last of the gurus with a direct link to Amritsar. Because of conflict with the Muslim rulers, he and all subsequent gurus moved from the city.

The tenth guru, Gobind Singh, created the Khalsa, the Community of the Pure, in 1699. The members of the Khalsa were to be known by five distinctive elements, all beginning with the letter *k*. These include kes, the refusal to cut the hair or trim the beard; kangha, the comb used to keep the long hair neatly combed in contrast to the Hindu ascetics who had matted hair; kaccha, shorts that would allow soldiers quick movement; kara, a thin steel bracelet worn to symbolize restraint; and kirpan, a short sword not to be used except in self-defense. Among other duties, members of this elite group were to defend the faith. Until the middle of the nineteenth century, when the British created an empire in India, the Khalsa remained largely undefeated.

In 1708, Guru Gobind Singh announced that he would be the final human guru. All subsequent leadership would come from the Guru Granth Sahib, now considered a living guru, the holy text Arjan had begun compiling more than a century earlier.

Muslim persecution under the Mughals led to the defeat of the Sikhs in 1716. The remaining Sikhs headed for the hills, re-emerging after decline of Mughal power. They were united under Ranjit Singh's kingdom from 1820 to 1839. They then came under the control of the British.

The British annexed the Punjab region, making it part of their Indian empire in 1849, and recruited Sikhs to serve in the army. The Sikhs remained loyal to the British during the Indian Mutiny of 1857–1858. As a result, they were given many privileges and land grants, and with peace and prosperity, the first Singh Sabha was founded in 1873. This was an educational and religious reform movement.

During the early twentieth century, Sikhism was shaped in its more modern form. A group known as the Tat Khalsa, which was more progressive, became the dominant way of understanding the faith.

In 1897, a group of Sikh musicians within the British Army was invited to attend the Diamond Jubilee of Queen Victoria in England. They also traveled to Canada and were attracted by the nation's prairies, which were perfect for farming. The first group of Sikhs came to Canada soon after. By 1904, more than two hundred Sikhs had settled in British Columbia. Some of them later headed south to Washington, Oregon, and California in the United States. The first Sikh gurdwara in the United States was constructed in Stockton, California, in 1912. Sikhs became farmers, worked in lumber mills, and helped to construct the Western Pacific railroad. Yuba City, California, has one of the world's largest Sikh temples, built in 1968.

Sikh troops fought for Britain in World War I, achieving distinction. Following the war, in 1919, however, the British denied the Sikhs the right to gather for their New Year festival. When the Sikhs disobeyed, the British troops fired without warning on 10,000 Sikhs, 400 of whom were killed. This became known as the first Amritsar Massacre.

The British government in 1925 did give the Sikhs the right to help manage their own shrines. A fragile peace ensued between the British and the Sikhs, who again fought for the British Empire during World War II.

After the war ended, the Sikh hope for an independent state was dashed by the partition of India and Pakistan in 1947. Pakistan was in the Punjab region; thus, 2.5 million Sikhs lived in a Muslim country where they were not welcome. Many of them became part of the mass internal migration that followed Indian independence.

In 1966, a state with a Sikh majority came into existence after Punjab boundaries were redrawn. Strife continued throughout second half of twentieth century, however, as a result of continuing demands for Punjab autonomy. A second massacre at Amritsar occurred in 1984, resulting in the death of 450 Sikhs (though some estimates of the death toll are higher). Indian troops, under orders from Indian Prime Minister Indira Gandhi, fired on militant leaders of Sikhs, who had gone to the Golden Temple for refuge. This attack was considered a desecration of a sacred place, and the prime minister was later assassinated by her Sikh bodyguards in response. Restoration of the Akal Takht, the administrative headquarters, took fifteen years. The Sikh library was also burned, consuming ancient manuscripts.

In 1999, Sikhs celebrated the three-hundredth anniversary of the founding of Khalsa. There has been relative peace in India since that event. In the United States, however, Sikhs became the object of slander and physical attack following the acts of terrorism on September 11, 2001, as some Americans could not differentiate between Arab head coverings and Sikh turbans.

Founder or Major Prophet

Guru Nanak Dev was born into a Hindu family on April 15, 1469. His family belonged to the merchant caste, Khatri. His father worked as an accountant for a Muslim, who was also a local landlord. Nanak was educated in both the Hindu and Islamic traditions. According to legends, his teachers soon realized they had nothing further to teach him. After a direct revelation from Ultimate Reality that he received as a young man, Nanak proclaimed that there was neither Muslim nor Hindu. God had told Nanak "Rejoice in my Name," which became a central doctrine of Sikhism.

Nanak began to preach, leaving his wife and two sons behind. According to tradition, he traveled not only throughout India, but also eventually to Iraq, Saudi Arabia, and Mecca. This tradition and others were collected in a volume known as Janamsakhis. A Muslim servant of the family, Mardana, who also played a three-stringed musical instrument called the rebec, accompanied him, as did a Hindu poet, Bala Sandhu, who had been a friend from childhood

(though the extent of his importance or existence is often considered controversial).

Nanak traveled as an itinerant preacher for a quarter century and then founded a village, Kartarpur, on the bank of Punjab's Ravi River. Before his death he chose his successor, beginning a tradition that was followed until the tenth and final human guru.

Philosophical Basis

When Guru Nanak Dev, the first guru, began preaching in 1499 at about age thirty, he incorporated aspects of both Hinduism and Islam. From Hinduism, he took the ideas of karma and reincarnation. From Islam, he borrowed the Ultimate as the name of God. Some scholars see the influence of the religious reformer and poet Kabir, who lived from 1440 until 1518. Kabir merged the Bhakti (devotional) side of Hinduism with the Islamic Sufis, who were mystics.

Within the Hindu tradition in northern India was a branch called the Sants. The Sants believed that God was both with form and without form, unable to be represented concretely. Most of the Sants were illiterate and poor, but created poems that spoke of the divine being experienced in all things. This idea also rooted itself in Sikhism.

Guru Nanak Dev, who was raised as a Hindu, rejected the caste system in favor of equality of all persons. He also upheld the value of women, rejecting the burning of widows and female infanticide. When eating a communal meal, first begun as a protest against caste, everyone sits in a straight line and shares karah prasad (a pudding), which is provided by those of all castes. However, Sikhs are expected to marry within their caste. In some cases, especially in the United Kingdom, gurdwaras (places of worship) for a particular caste exist.

Holy Places

Amritsar, especially the Golden Temple, which was built in the sixteenth century under the supervision of the fifth guru, Guru Arjan, is the most sacred city.

Ram Das, the fourth guru, first began constructing a pool on the site in 1577. He called it

Amritsar, the pool of nectar. This sacred reflecting pool is a pilgrimage destination. Steps on the southern side of the pool allow visitors to gather water in bottles, to drink it, to bathe in it, or to sprinkle it on themselves.

SIKHISM IN DEPTH

Sacred Symbols

The khanda is the major symbol of Sikhism. It features a two-edged sword, representing justice and freedom, in the center. It is surrounded by a circle, a symbol of both balance and of the unity of God and humankind. A pair of curved swords (kirpans) surrounds the circle. One sword stands for religious concerns, the other for secular concerns. The khanda appears on Sikh flags, which are flown over every temple.

Members of the Khalsa have five symbols. They do not cut their hair, and men do not trim their beards. This symbol, kes, is to indicate a harmony with the ways of nature. To keep the long hair neat, a comb called a kangha is used. The third symbol is the kara, a bracelet usually made of steel to represent continuity and strength. When the Khalsa was first formed, soldiers wore loose-fitting shorts called kaccha. They were worn to symbolize moral restraint and purity. The final symbol is a short sword known as a kirpan, to be used only in self-defense. When bathing in sacred waters, the kirpan is tucked into the turban, which is worn to cover the long hair. The turban, which may be one of many colors, is wound from nearly five yards of cloth.

Sacred Practices & Gestures

Sikhs use Sat Sri Akal (truth is timeless) as a greeting, putting hands together and bowing toward the other person. To show respect, Sikhs keep their heads covered with a turban or veil. Before entering a temple, they remove their shoes. Some Sikhs may choose to wear a bindhi, the dot on the forehead usually associated with Hinduism.

When Guru Gobind Singh initiated the first men into the Khalsa, he put water in a steel bowl and added sugar, stirring the mixture with his sword and reciting verses from the Guru Granth as he did so. He thus created amrit (immortal), a holy water also used in baptism, or the Amrit ceremony. The water represents mental clarity, while sugar stands for sweetness. The sword invokes military courage, and the chanting of verses brings a poetic spirituality.

The Sikh ideal of bringing Ultimate Reality into every aspect of the day is expressed in prayers throughout the day. Daily morning prayer (Bani) consists of five different verses, most of them the work of one of the ten gurus; there are also two sets of evening prayers. Throughout the day, Sikhs repeat the Mul Mantra, "Ikk Oan Kar" (There is one Being). This is the first line of a brief creedal statement about Ultimate Reality.

Food Restrictions

Sikhs are not to eat halal meat, which is the Muslim equivalent of kosher. Both tobacco and alcohol are forbidden. Many Sikhs are vegetarians, although this is not commanded. Members of the Khalsa are not permitted to eat meat slaughtered according to Islamic or Hindu methods, because they believe these means cause pain to the animal.

Rites, Celebrations, & Services

The Sikhs observe four rite of passage rituals, with each emphasizing their distinction from the Hindu traditions. After a new mother is able to get up and bathe, the new baby is given a birth and naming ceremony in the gurdwara. The child is given a name based on the first letter of hymn from the Guru Granth Sahib at random. All males are additionally given the name Singh (lion); all females also receive the name Kaur (princess).

The marriage ceremony (anand karaj) is the second rite of passage. Rather than circle a sacred fire as the Hindus do, the Sikh couple walks four times around a copy of the Guru Granth Sahib, accompanied by singing. The bride often wears red, a traditional color for the Punjabi.

The amrit initiation into the Khalsa is considered the most important rite. It need not take place in a temple, but does require that five

Sikhs who are already Khalsa members conduct the ceremony. Amrit initiation may occur any time after a child is old enough to read the Guru Granth and understand the tenets of the faith. Some people, however, wait until their own children are grown before accepting this rite.

The funeral rite is the fourth and final rite of passage. A section of the Guru Granth is read. The body, dressed in the Five "K's," is cremated soon after death.

Initiation into the Khalsa is now open to both men and women. The earliest gurus opposed the Hindu custom of sati, which required a widow to be burned on her husband's funeral pyre. They were also against the Islamic custom of purdah, which required women to be veiled and covered in public. Women who are menstruating are not excluded from worship, as they are in some religions. Women as well as men can be leaders of the congregation and are permitted to read from the Guru Granth and recite sacred hymns.

The Sikh houses of worship are known as gurdwaras and include a langar, the communal dining area. People remove their shoes and cover their heads before entering. They touch their foreheads to the floor in front of the scripture to show respect. The service itself is in three parts. The first segment is Kirtan, singing hymns (kirtans) accompanied by musical instruments, which can last for several hours. It is followed by a set prayer called the Ardas, which has three parts. The first and final sections cannot be altered. In the first, the virtues of the gurus are extolled. In the last, the divine name is honored. In the center of the Ardas is a list of the Khalsa's troubles and victories, which a prayer leader recites in segments and to which the congregation responds with Vahiguru, considered a word for God. At the end of the service, members eat karah prasad, sacred food made of raw sugar, clarified butter, and coarse wheat flour. They then adjourn for a communal meal, Langar, the third section of worship.

Sikhism does not have a set day for worship similar to the Jewish Sabbath or Christian Sunday worship. However, the first day of the month on the Indian lunar calendar, sangrand,

and the darkest night of the month, masia, are considered special days. Sangrand is a time for praying for the entire month. Masia is often considered an auspicious time for bathing in the holy pool at the temple.

Four of the major festivals that Sikhs observe surround important events in the lives of the gurus. These are known as gurpurabs, or anniversaries. Guru Nanak's birthday, Guru Gobind Singh's birthday, and the martyrdoms of the Gurus Arjan and Tegh Bahadur comprise the four main gurpurabs. Sikhs congregate in the gurudwaras to hear readings of the Guru Granth and lectures by Sikh scholars.

Baisakhi is the Indian New Year, the final day before the harvest begins. On this day in 1699, Guru Gobind Singh formed the first Khalsa, adding even more importance to the day for Sikhs. Each year, a new Sikh flag is placed at all temples.

Diwali, based on a word meaning string of lights, is a Hindu festival. For Sikhs, it is a time to remember the return of the sixth guru, Hargobind, to Amritsar after the emperor had imprisoned him. It is celebrated for three days at the Golden Temple. Sikhs paint and whitewash their houses and decorate them with candles and earthenware lamps.

Hola Mohalla, meaning attack and place of attack, is the Sikh spring festival, which corresponds to the Hindu festival Holi. It is also a three-day celebration and a time for training Sikhs as soldiers. Originally, it involved military exercises and mock battles, as well as competitions in archery, horsemanship, and wrestling. In contemporary times, the festival includes athletic contests, discussion, and singing.

Judy A. Johnson, MTS

Bibliography

Barnes, Trevor. *The Kingfisher Book of Religions*. New York: Kingfisher, 1999. Print.

Dhanjal, Beryl. *Amritsar*. New York: Dillon, 1993. Print.

Dhavan, Purnima. *When Sparrows Became Hawks: The Making of the Sikh Warrior Tradition, 1699–1799*. Oxford: Oxford UP, 2011. Print.

Eraly, Abraham, et. al. *India*. New York: DK, 2008. Print.

Harley, Gail M. *Hindu and Sikh Faiths in America*. New York: Facts on File, 2003. Print.

Jakobsh, Doris R. *Sikhism and Women: History, Texts, and Experience*. Oxford, New York: Oxford UP, 2010. Print.

Jhutti-Johal, Jagbir. *Sikhism Today*. London, New York: Continuum, 2011. Print.

Langley, Myrtle. *Religion*. New York: Knopf, 1996. Print.

Mann, Gurinder Singh. *Sikhism*. Upper Saddle River: Prentice, 2004. Print.

Meredith, Susan. *The Usborne Book of World Religions*. London: Usborne, 1995. Print.

Sidhu, Dawinder S. and Neha Singh Gohil. *Civil Rights in Wartime: The Post-9/11 Sikh Experience*. Ashgate, 2009. E-book.

Singh, Nikky-Guninder Kaur. *Sikhism*. New York: Facts on File, 1993. Print.

Singh, Nikky-Guninder Kaur. *Sikhism: An Introduction*. Tauris, 2011. E-book.

Singh, Surinder. *Introduction to Sikhism and Great Sikhs of the World*. Gurgaon: Shubhi, 2012. Print.

Wilkinson, Philip. *Religions*. New York: DK, 2008. Print.

Index